CHOICE OF VENUE IN INTERNATIONAL ARBITRATION

CHOICE OF VENUE IN INTERNATIONAL ARBITRATION

Edited by

MICHAEL OSTROVE

Partner, DLA Piper UK LLP, Paris

CLAUDIA T SALOMON

Partner, Latham & Watkins, New York

BETTE SHIFMAN

Vice President, CPR International Institute for Conflict Prevention and Resolution, New York

OXFORD
UNIVERSITY PRESS

OXFORD
UNIVERSITY PRESS

Great Clarendon Street, Oxford, OX2 6DP,
United Kingdom

Oxford University Press is a department of the University of Oxford.
It furthers the University's objective of excellence in research, scholarship,
and education by publishing worldwide. Oxford is a registered trade mark of
Oxford University Press in the UK and in certain other countries

First Edition published in 2014

Impression: 1

Published in the United States of America by Oxford University Press
198 Madison Avenue, New York, NY 10016, United States of America

British Library Cataloguing in Publication Data
Data available

Library of Congress Control Number: 2013946098

ISBN 978–0–19–965571–7

Printed in Great Britain by
CPI Group (UK) Ltd, Croydon, CR0 4YY

FOREWORD

'Location, location, location'[1] is the catch-phrase used to describe the most important factors in the real estate property development business. Although there is no correlation between the property world's focus on growth of asset value, profits, and income, and the focus of international arbitration on providing a fair, just, and effective final determination of disputes (rather than profits), the triple recommendation of 'location, location, location' can also be applied to the selection of the form and venue of arbitration.

When choosing arbitration as the dispute resolution mechanism, key questions are the form and venue. Form is either institutional (and then which institution?) or ad hoc. Venue is the location of the arbitration. These are separate questions but will invariably be considered together, particularly because the venue of the arbitration takes on even greater importance when the form of the arbitration is ad hoc. There are many practical, legal, commercial, and political questions to be taken into account when choosing form and venue. This book aims to assist in answering these questions with respect to the various jurisdictions it covers.

The venue of arbitration is the place where the arbitration has its seat. It is also called the place of arbitration or the *siège de l'arbitrage*.[2] This reflects the place where the arbitration belongs and where its character may be determined or at least influenced.

The venue of an international arbitration is generally determined by agreement, and will be recorded in the arbitration agreement. It may also be fixed in a submission agreement after the dispute has arisen, or at the same time as the tribunal is being established. If not fixed by agreement, the selection may fall to the relevant arbitration institution,[3] or to the arbitral tribunal.[4] Where no choice is made by the parties, the venue remains uncertain and becomes an additional area for dispute, which adds an undesirable layer of litigation in national courts or before arbitrators. As a general rule it is always preferable for the parties to agree the venue rather than leave it to the institution or third party to select.

Unfortunately, the venue of arbitration is often forgotten or not fully considered when parties are discussing the dispute resolution mechanism to include in an international commercial contract. Often, parties will incorporate standard form arbitration clauses, adopt a multi-tier dispute resolution arrangement, and provide for applicable law, but not provide for where the arbitration is to have its seat. Furthermore, even when fixing the venue of arbitration it may be without adequate consideration and understanding of the legal and procedural implications of that venue.

The choices of form and place of arbitration are many and increasing. New national and international arbitration institutions around the world are being established, all seeking to

[1] This quotation is generally attributed to Lord Harold Samuel, an English real estate businessman. See William Safire's 'On Language' column, *New York Times*, 26 June 2009.

[2] The *siège de l'arbitrage* was considered in the resolutions of the Institut de Droit International in 1957 and 1959 to govern and control all aspects of an arbitration, including the procedure to be followed and the conflict of laws rules to be applied.

[3] See eg ICC Rules, Art 18; LCIA Rules, Art 16.1; SCC Rules, Art 20; WIPO Arbitration Rules, Art 39.

[4] UNCITRAL Arbitration Rules, Art 18.

provide an independent arbitration system. Some arbitration institutions administer arbitrations in countries other than where they are based. Several institutions have offices or affiliated institutions to promote their activities in countries other than where they are based. As an incentive to the choice of venue, arbitration hearing centres have been established in several countries to provide an efficient and convenient place to hold hearings.

The location of the venue or seat is a crucial decision in every arbitration for three principal reasons.

First, it is the place where the arbitration has its legal base and according to which law it will be managed and supervised. This is important because although in most cases arbitrations are conducted in accordance with the agreement of the parties and the tribunal's discretion, an arbitration must comply with the mandatory law of the place where it has its seat.

Furthermore, the courts of the seat of arbitration have supervisory responsibility for the conduct and effectiveness of the arbitration. This might include providing support for the process, for example, enforcing an order for production of documents or the preservation of property, enforcing a tribunal's orders for interim measures, assisting with the collection of evidence, removing and replacing arbitrators, and ultimately setting aside or upholding and enforcing the award. Parties may want to avoid countries where the courts are overly interventionist and willing to review, second-guess, and control the decisions of arbitrators.

For this reason parties and lawyers should look to see that the proposed venue has a modern and supportive arbitration law. This may be in one of the traditional arbitration centres. However, increasingly one can expect that there will be confidence in choosing a venue in a country which has adopted the UNCITRAL Model Law on International Commercial Arbitration (adopted in full or in part in 66 jurisdictions as at 30 June 2013). This is because parties may come from a country that has also adopted the UNCITRAL Model Law so there will be an understanding of how it works and is likely to be interpreted and applied. Although the national laws may differ in their approach to arbitration, it is to be expected that over time a commonality will develop in how the Model Law applies and should be implemented in given situations.

Second, the venue is important for the ultimate enforcement of the final award. The ability to give practical effect to a tribunal's conclusion is the very *raison d'être* of international arbitration. An award that is unenforceable defeats the whole object of the arbitral exercise. The United Nations Convention on the Recognition and Enforcement of Foreign Arbitral Awards 1958 (New York Convention) was adopted to facilitate the enforcement in countries where the losing party resides or has assets of awards rendered by tribunals in a different country. As of June 2013, 149 countries are party to the New York Convention. Under Article 1(3), states may declare that they will enforce only those awards made in the New York Convention countries. For this reason parties should always be careful to ensure that the country in which the arbitration is to take place is a party to the New York Convention.

Third, on a practical level, the venue is generally also the place where the arbitration will physically take place. It should have easy access both physically (ie by air, sea, or train) and legally (ie parties, lawyers, and witnesses should be able to obtain visas to attend hearings). The arbitration should be able to continue without interference or any breach of the private and (where applicable) confidential nature of the proceedings. The venue should also have other support facilities, including good hotels, hearing rooms, translation and transcription services, and experts if needed to support the work of the parties and the tribunal.

It is nevertheless important to distinguish between the seat or venue of arbitration and the place where hearings are held. The former is a legal fact with legal consequences. The latter has practical implications because there may be circumstances or reasons which preclude meeting at the seat or where it makes more sense for a tribunal to meet other than at the seat (eg where a witness is too ill to travel, or unwilling to come, to the country of the seat, or where most of the participants in the arbitration are not at the seat and for time and expense reasons it is considered appropriate that they meet elsewhere). It is important to check that this is allowed under the law of the seat.

When selecting the venue of arbitration there are many legal issues that the parties will wish to understand and review before making a choice. This information will also be important when any arbitration is commenced both with respect to how the arbitration is conducted, any relevant mandatory laws, and the extent to which the courts of the country are supportive of or have an interventionist attitude to the arbitral process.

This book is to be commended. It provides the parties and their lawyers, and others involved with international arbitration, with an informative tool to aid their understanding of the legal systems and arbitration regimes in 20 different countries. It is essential that parties and lawyers understand the effect of the selection of a country as the venue and seat for their arbitration. This book will be a very useful aid to all those making decisions concerning, and involved as lawyers or arbitrators in, international arbitration.

Julian Lew
London
June 2013

ACKNOWLEDGEMENTS

The editors wish to thank each of the contributors for their diligence, patience, and cooperation in putting this book together, and all of the law firms—especially the editors' own—for making time and resources available to support the process. Special thanks go to Andrea Lapunzina at DLA Piper and Lilia Vazova at Latham & Watkins for their contributions to the Introduction, as well as to our teams of hard-working, conscientious paralegals, who so ably assisted with style and cite-checking: at DLA Piper, Margaret Austin, Ivy Hamlin, Donna Look, Gabriel Mikulich, and Sara Tumey, coordinated by New York-based Paralegal Manager, Christine Farrelly; and at Latham and Watkins, Amy Chambers.

The editors thank the editorial team at Oxford University Press, particularly Vicky Pittman, Rachel Holt, and Zoe Organ, for their patience and support for a book that presented the challenge of coordinating work by multiple authors around the world who are each primarily engaged in busy arbitration practices. The editors also thank the International Law Section of the American Bar Association for its recognition of the importance of this topic during the Section's 2010 Fall Meeting in Paris, where a lively debate on this topic involving many of the editors and contributors planted the seed for this book.

Finally, a special thanks to our spouses, Ariela Katz, Jorn Ake, and David Burfoot, for their patience and support throughout the process of completing this book.

Michael Ostrove, Claudia Salomon, and Bette Shifman
Paris and New York
June 2013

CONTENTS

TABLE OF CASES

INTERNATIONAL CASES

NATIONAL CASES

Australia

Austria

Belgium

Brazil

Canada

China

Dubai

Egypt

France

Germany

Hong Kong

India

Ireland

Russia

Singapore

Sweden

Switzerland

United Kingdom

United States

TABLE OF LEGISLATION

INTERNATIONAL LEGISLATION

Conventions, Treaties, Agreements, Rules and Model Laws

European Union

NATIONAL LEGISLATION

Argentina

Australia

Austria

Bahrain

Brazil

China

Dubai

Egypt

India

Ireland

Mexico

Switzerland

United Arab Emirates

United Kingdom

United States

EDITORS AND CONTRIBUTORS

Editors

Michael Ostrove, Head of Litigation & Regulatory Paris, DLA Piper, Paris, France A member of both the Paris and New York bars, Mr Ostrove heads DLA Piper's French Litigation and Regulatory group and leads its international arbitration practice in Paris, where he has practiced since 1998. With 20 years' experience handling international commercial, investment, and public international law disputes, Mr Ostrove has represented clients in scores of arbitrations in both English and French, administered by the ICC, LCIA, PCA, ICSID, and Swiss Chambers, as well as ad hoc arbitrations pursuant to the UNCITRAL Rules. Mr Ostrove's litigation experience includes a wide range of matters before the US, French, and other national courts, as well as before the International Court of Justice. Mr Ostrove began his professional career as a law clerk to the Hon Eugene H Nickerson of the US District Court for the Eastern District of New York. Mr Ostrove is a frequent speaker on international arbitration and has regularly been named as a leading arbitration practitioner by the specialized press.

Claudia T Salomon, Global Co-Chair, International Arbitration Practice, Latham & Watkins LLP, New York, NY, USA A partner in the New York office of Latham & Watkins, Claudia Salomon's practice focuses on complex international disputes. She is a leading practitioner in significant investor treaty arbitration and international commercial arbitration cases under the major arbitral rules around the world, under a wide variety of governing laws. Ms Salomon is also experienced in handling litigation connected to arbitration, including enforcing arbitral awards worldwide and obtaining emergency relief. Ms Salomon is widely recognized as a leader in the field of international arbitration, recommended by Chambers Global, Chambers USA, The Legal 500 Latin America, Super Lawyers, and The Best Lawyers in America. The Global Arbitration Review named Ms Salomon one of the world's top 30 women in international arbitration and one of its '45 Under 45'. Ms Salomon serves on the ICC Commission on Arbitration.

Bette Shifman, Vice President, CPR International Institute for Conflict Prevention and Resolution, New York, NY, USA Bette Shifman is Special Counsel and Director of Publications at CPR, where her responsibilities include the editorship of the award-winning newsletter *Alternatives*. Prior to joining CPR, she served as Practice Group Manager for the global International Arbitration practice group at DLA Piper in New York, where she was Of Counsel. Ms Shifman has extensive experience in international law and dispute resolution, including positions at the International Court of Justice, and at the Permanent Court of Arbitration (PCA), in The Hague, where she served as registrar to state-state and investor-state international arbitration tribunals. Ms Shifman is a former general editor of the *Journal of International Arbitration* and *World Trade and Arbitration Materials*, and has served as special consultant to Kluwer Law International's international arbitration database and web portal. Ms Shifman is an accredited mediator (CEDR), and holds a recent master's degree in information science with a focus on the digital information lifecycle. Ms Shifman was also Executive Director of ADR Chambers in Toronto, where she also headed the ADR Chambers Banking Ombuds Office. Other previous legal experience includes positions in New York, Amsterdam, Brussels, and Kinshasa.

Contributors

Essam Al Tamimi, Senior Partner, Al Tamimi & Co, Dubai, UAE The founder and senior partner of Al Tamimi & Co, the largest law firm in the Middle East, Essam Al Tamimi has over 24 years' experience in litigation and dispute resolution in the UAE and other GCC countries. He is a strong advocate for arbitration and ADR processes as a means of resolving disputes efficiently and effectively for clients. He was a Council member involved in the production of the ICC and LCIA Rules and the author and editor of several books including *The Practitioners Guide to Arbitration in the Middle East and Northern Africa* (Juris, 2009).

Fredrik Andersson, Partner, Mannheimer Swartling, Sweden With an LLM from the University of Gothenburg, Fredrik Andersson served as a junior judge at the District Court of Gothenburg from 1998 to 2000. He joined Mannheimer Swartling in 2000 and was made partner in 2008. Fredrik specializes in commercial litigation and arbitration and has acted as counsel in a large number of Swedish and international proceedings. He also sits as an arbitrator. He regularly lectures and has authored several publications on dispute resolution.

Antonio Marzagão Barbuto Neto, Partner, TozziniFreire Advogados, São Paulo, Brazil A partner in the Dispute Resolution Department of TozziniFreire Advogados, Tony Barbuto has an LLM degree from New York University School of Law and is also admitted to practice law in the state of New York, where he spent one year as foreign associate at an international law firm. He has participated in several domestic and international arbitration proceedings and also takes advantage of his overseas experience to represent foreign companies in lawsuits before the Brazilian courts.

Dominique Brown-Berset, Partner, Brown & Page, Geneva, Switzerland A founding partner of Brown & Page, a law firm specializing in dispute resolution, contract and commercial law, and public international law, Dominique Brown-Berset practices mainly in the field of international arbitration and business transactions. She holds law degrees from Lausanne University Law School, Paris I Panthéon-Sorbonne, and Harvard Law School. She is a member of the management board and of the supervisory council of the Swiss Institute of Comparative Law and of the Board of the Swiss Society of Jurists. She is a former co-chair of the Arbitration Committee of the International Bar Association (IBA), and former International Vice-President of the Chartered Institute of Arbitrators. Dominique is also the current President of Arbitral Women. She has acted as counsel, co-counsel, and arbitrator in 180 cases, covering a broad range of commercial disputes, in particular in ad hoc cases involving states and international organizations at both the private and governmental level.

Christian Camboulive, Partner, Gide Loyrette Nouel, Paris, France Holding a diploma from the Bordeaux *Institut d'Etudes Politiques* and a post-graduate degree in law from the University of Paris, Christian Camboulive qualified as an *Avocat à la Cour* in 1987. He is a partner of Gide Loyrette Nouel, which he joined in 1988. He has acted as counsel to parties in numerous international arbitration cases, conducted under all major international arbitration rules, in cases related primarily to construction/turnkey contracts, investments, shareholder and joint-venture partner disputes, international sales, distribution, and licensing, all covering a wide range of sectors. Christian Camboulive also sits as an arbitrator. A former vice-Chair of the IBA Arbitration Committee, he is a member of the Executive Committee of FIAA and a member of several arbitration-related associations.

John Choong, Freshfields Bruckhaus Deringer, Hong Kong John Choong is with the Asia Dispute Resolution group, focusing on international arbitration, cross-border disputes, and investigations throughout Asia. He has practised in the region for over ten years and represented clients in a wide range of international commercial and investment arbitrations under various rules and involving the laws of all major jurisdictions in Asia. John is admitted in Hong Kong, England and Wales, and Singapore, and is a Fellow of the Chartered Institute of Arbitrators. He has lectured and written regularly on arbitration, and is co-Editor of the *Asia Arbitration Handbook* (OUP, 2011), the *Hong Kong Arbitration Ordinance: Commentary and Annotations* (Sweet & Maxwell, 2011), and a Contributing Arbitration Editor of the *Hong Kong White Book* (Sweet & Maxwell, 2013).

Maarten Draye, Senior Associate, Hanotiau & van den Berg, Brussels, Belgium Focusing on international commercial arbitration and commercial litigation across various industry sectors, Maarten Draye has acted as arbitrator, counsel, and secretary to the tribunal under various arbitration rules as well as in ad hoc proceedings. Mr Draye holds a Master of Laws degree (Lic Jur) (2004) and Master in Economic Policy (2005) from Katholieke Universiteit Leuven (Belgium). In 2006, he obtained an LLM in International Business Law from Queen Mary, University of London. He was admitted to the Brussels bar in 2007.

Hagit Elul, Hughes Hubbard & Reed LLP, New York, NY, USA A partner in the New York office of Hughes Hubbard & Reed LLP, focusing on international arbitration and litigation, Hagit Elul received a BA with honours from University of California, Berkeley and a JD from Columbia Law School, where she was named a Harlan Fiske Stone Scholar. Ms Elul has served as counsel in arbitrations under all major institutional rules and involving a wide array of sectors, including financial services, energy, pharmaceutical, construction, telecommunications, and professional services. She has also advised on investment and bilateral treaty disputes. Ms Elul has served as an expert witness on New York law in proceedings in other countries. She writes and speaks widely on the subject of arbitration. She has been recognized as a Rising Star in the 2013 Commercial Arbitration Expert Guide and as a name to know by *Global Arbitration Review*.

John Fellas, Hughes Hubbard & Reed LLP, New York, NY, USA A partner and co-chair of the Arbitration Practice and co-chair of the International Practice of Hughes Hubbard & Reed LLP, John Fellas is based in the New York office. He received a BA (Hons) from the University of Durham, England, and both an LLM and an SJD from the Harvard Law School, and has practiced in both the United States and England. He has been recognized for his practice in international arbitration by: *Who's Who Legal—The International Who's Who Of Business Lawyers*; *Chambers USA—Guide to America's Leading Business Lawyers*; *Chambers Global*; *The Best Lawyers In America; Euromoney Expert Guides—Best of the Best USA*. The most recent editions of Chambers Global and Chambers USA noted that he is 'a wonderful lawyer with very thorough legal knowledge', and is 'one of the best—his reputation is phenomenal and deserved'. He is co-editor of *International Commercial Arbitration in New York* (OUP, 2010).

Michael A Fernández, Stroock & Stroock & Lavan LLP, New York, NY, USA Mr Fernández has a BA in Spanish and Political Science from Yale University and an MA in Law and Diplomacy from The Fletcher School. He earned his juris doctor from Columbia Law School, where he was named a Harlan Fiske Stone Scholar and awarded a Parker School Recognition of Achievement in International and Comparative Law. Prior to Stroock, he interned for the Hon Rolando T Acosta of the New York Appellate Division, First Judicial Department, as well as the Hon Barbara Lagoa of the Florida Third District Court of Appeal. He also worked as a staff associate for Professors Alejandro M Garro and Kent Greenawalt. Mr Fernández is currently an associate in the litigation department of Stroock & Stroock & Lavan LLP.

Alejandro M Garro, Professor of Law, Columbia University, New York, NY, USA Professor Garro earned his JD degree (*abogado*) at the National University of La Plata, a Master's degree in law (LLM) at the Louisiana State University, and his doctoral degree in law (JSD) at Columbia University School of Law, where he teaches in the fields of comparative law, Latin American law, international business transactions (including sales and secured transactions), and international commercial and investment arbitration. He served as a staff attorney of the Louisiana State Law Institute (1979–81) and a scientific researcher (*collaborateur scientifique*) at the Swiss Institute of Comparative Law (1982–85). He has been a member of UNCITRAL's working groups on dispute resolution (WG II) and secured transactions (WP VI), serving as a special adviser to the Argentine delegation in both groups. Professor Garro also contributed to the preparation of the UNIDROIT Principles on International Commercial Contracts (1994–2010). He has published numerous books, articles, reports, and contributions to books on such subjects as international commercial arbitration, international sales law, secured transactions, and comparative law.

Diane Grisel, Brown & Page, Geneva, Switzerland An associate at Brown & Page, a law firm specializing in dispute resolution, contract and commercial law, and public international law, Diane Grisel holds a master of law degree with highest honours from Neuchâtel University, an LLM (master in European legal studies) from the College of Europe (Brugge), and the Diploma of the Academy of European law from the European University Institute. She is a PhD candidate at the University of Geneva and has spent one year at King's College, London, as a visiting researcher. She is a qualified Swiss lawyer and a member of the Swiss Arbitration Association Below 40.

Karim Hafez, Senior Partner, HAFEZ, Cairo, Egypt A full-time international arbitration lawyer, Karim read law at Cairo, Cambridge, and Harvard. His PhD, from Cambridge University (2004), is for a dissertation entitled 'Complex Arbitration'. He is qualified to practice law in Egypt, and is fluent in Arabic, English, and French. Karim regularly acts as chairman, sole, and party-appointed arbitrator, and as counsel in disputes spanning the economic spectrum. He has prosecuted, defended, and advised on scores of high-value complex arbitrations in most industries, with an emphasis on telecommunications, investment, construction, project finance, power generation, oil and gas, and corporate disputes.

Dr Richard Happ, Partner, Luther Law Firm, Hamburg, Germany Having studied law at the Universities of Kiel (Germany) and Surrey (UK), Dr Happ received his doctoral degree in 2000 and completed his legal clerkship in Kiel, Hamburg, Brussels, and Speyer. He joined Luther's Hamburg office in 2001, was made partner in 2009, and is co-head of the firm's arbitration practice. He advises clients in complex litigation and arbitration proceedings and specializes in arbitration proceedings in the energy sector. He also frequently sits as an arbitrator. Dr Happ is ranked/listed in *Chambers Europe*, *The Legal 500*, and the *International Who's Who of Commercial Arbitration*.

Pascal Hollander, Partner, Hanotiau & van den Berg, Brussels, Belgium Representing clients in complex arbitration and litigation proceedings and also regularly acting in international and domestic arbitration as chairman of tribunals, sole arbitrator, or co-arbitrator, Pascal Hollander's practice focuses on areas such as commercial distribution, corporate disputes, intellectual property, or disputes pertaining to large industrial projects. Mr Hollander regularly speaks and publishes on these topics and teaches arbitration law at the Professional School of the Brussels Bar. He holds a JD degree (magna cum laude), from the *Université Libre de Bruxelles* (1984) and an LLM from the University of Pennsylvania Law School (1986). Mr Hollander has been a member of the Brussels Bar since 1984.

Mikhail Ivanov, Partner, legacy Head of the Russian Litigation/Arbitration Practice, Dentons, St Petersburg, Russia A Partner in and legacy Head of the Russian Litigation/Arbitration practice of Dentons, Mikhail Ivanov specializes in litigation, arbitration, corporate law, securities law, and mergers and acquisitions, particularly in emerging markets in the CIS and in Central and Eastern Europe. Mr Ivanov is also part of the firm's German practice. Mikhail advises clients on a broad range of legal matters involving investment in the Russian Federation, specializing in dispute resolution between foreign investors and major Russian companies, in particular before Russian commercial and general courts. He also participates in international commercial arbitration and is ranked among the best lawyers in Dispute Resolution in Russian (2012—winner of Lawyer of the Year award) in Best Lawyers 2010–2012.

Stephen Jagusch, Partner and Global Chair of International Arbitration, Quinn Emanuel, London, UK As a Partner in and Global Chair of Quinn Emanuel's International Arbitration Practice, Stephen Jagusch specializes in international commercial and investment treaty arbitration, having acted as adviser and advocate in dozens of ad hoc and institutional international arbitrations, conducted in many countries, and subject to a wide variety of governing substantive and procedural laws. He is recognized as a leading expert in the field of ICSID arbitration and disputes arising under bilateral or multilateral investment treaties. He regularly sits as an arbitrator.

Stephen is highly ranked by all international and domestic legal publications in international arbitration and public international law. He routinely speaks at leading conferences and seminars, and is widely published on the subject of international arbitration. He has won the inaugural (and subsequent) Client Choice Award for Best Arbitration Lawyer in the UK, according to surveys conducted by the International Law Office. Prior to joining Quinn Emanuel, Stephen was Chair of the Global International Arbitration Practice of Allen & Overy LLP.

Doug Jones, Partner, Clayton Utz, Sydney, Australia An international infrastructure and dispute resolution lawyer, and a Sydney-based partner in the Australian law firm of Clayton Utz, where he heads the International Arbitration Group, Doug Jones AO is a chartered arbitrator and door tenant at Atkin Chambers, London. Doug is a professorial fellow at Melbourne University and an adjunct professor at Murdoch University, Australia. He is president of the Australian Centre for International Commercial Arbitration and past president of the Chartered Institute of Arbitrators, London (2011). He was made an Officer of the Order of Australia in 2012 for distinguished service to the law as a leader in the areas of arbitration and alternative dispute resolution.

Robert Karrar-Lewsley, Senior Associate, Al Tamimi & Co, Dubai, UAE An English barrister and a senior associate in the arbitration department of Al Tamimi & Co (DIFC office), Robert Karrar-Lewsley regularly advises and represents clients in high-value arbitrations relating to commercial, construction, and property disputes under the auspices of various Institutions, including the ICC, LCIA, and DIAC. His clients include government entities, multinational companies, and large real estate developers.

Julian DM Lew, Professor and Head, School of International Arbitration, Queen Mary University, London, UK Professor Julian Lew has been involved with international arbitration for more than three decades, as counsel and arbitrator. He has been involved in cases arising out of all types of international commercial and investments contracts. He has been appointed as an arbitrator under all the major arbitration rules, including: ICC, ICSID, LCIA, SCC, SIAC, WIPO, Cairo Regional Centre for International Commercial Arbitration, Arbitration Court attached to the Economic Chamber of the Czech Republic, and ad hoc arbitrations under UNCITRAL Arbitration Rules and the Swiss Arbitration Rules. He has written extensively on all aspects of international arbitration.

Kristoffer Löf, Partner, Mannheimer Swartling, Sweden With an LLM from Uppsala University, Kristoffer Löf specializes in commercial arbitration, with an emphasis on energy (oil and gas) and construction disputes. He has acted as counsel in international arbitrations under a wide range of rules, including the SCC, ICC, UNCITRAL, and ICDR Rules. He is a member of the board of Young Arbitrators Sweden (YAS) and of the Global Advisory Board of ICDR Young & International.

Carole Malinvaud, Partner, Gide Loyrette Nouel, Paris, France A partner of Gide Loyrette Nouel, where she has practiced international arbitration since 1990 as counsel and as arbitrator in ad hoc and institutional arbitrations, Carole Malinvaud is a member of the Paris and the New York bars and holds a postgraduate degree from the University of Paris-II and an LLM from Harvard Law School. Carole, who is a former officer of the IBA Arbitration Committee, was elected chair of the French Committee on Arbitration (CFA) in January 2013 and has chaired the French international arbitration commission (ICC France) of the International Chamber of Commerce since May 2012.She regularly appears at conferences and recently co-chaired the session on 'Deliberations: an opaque and disorganized process?' at the 16th International Bar Association (IBA) Arbitration Day in February 2013 in Bogota, Columbia.

Inna Manassyan, Associate, Dentons, Paris, France An associate with the International Arbitration Group, of Dentons, Paris, Inna Manassyan holds a law degree magna cum laude from the Moscow State University, and a master of law degree in international commercial arbitration from Stockholm University. Ms Manassyan focuses her practice on international arbitration, representing multinational companies in international business disputes. She has participated in international arbitrations involving both complex commercial disputes and issues of enforcement of arbitral awards in the Russian Federation.

Michael J Moser, 20 Essex Street Chambers, London and Hong Kong An international arbitrator and lawyer with long experience in Asia, Michael J Moser is honorary chairman of the Hong Kong International Arbitration Centre, a court member of the LCIA, and a board member of the Arbitration Institute of the Stockholm Chamber of Commerce (SCC) and the Vienna International Arbitral Centre (VIAC). He is also a commission member of CIETAC and was the first foreigner to be appointed as an arbitrator in China. Mr Moser received his law degree from the Harvard Law School and holds a PhD (with distinction) from Columbia University. He is the author of many books and articles and is the general editor of the *Journal of International Arbitration*. Mr Moser was formerly China managing partner of Freshfields Bruckhaus Deringer. He now practices as an independent arbitrator with 20 Essex Street Chambers in London and maintains offices in Hong Kong and Singapore.

Ciccu Mukhopadhaya, Senior Advocate, New Delhi, India Mr Mukhopadhaya has a Master's Degree in Law (Temple University, Philadelphia, USA). He was designated as a Senior Counsel in December 2011. Prior to his designation as Senior Counsel, Mr Mukhopadhaya was a Senior Partner in India's premier law firm, Amarchand & Mangaldas & Suresh A Shroff & Co. His practice of over 25 years has been wide-ranging, covering commercial and investment treaty arbitrations, constitutional law, environmental law, mining law, etc. His expertise in the field of international arbitration is well known. He has been actively involved in a large number of domestic and international commercial arbitrations, both ad hoc and institutional, including arbitrations under the ICC, LCIA, UNCITRAL, SIAC, GAFTA, and FOSFA Rules. He is also involved in arbitration-related court proceedings for reference to arbitrations, grant of interim measures of protection, post-award challenges, and enforcement of foreign arbitral awards. His non-litigation experience includes mergers and acquisitions, international commercial contracts, contracts for the transfer of technology, financing transactions, major supply agreements, construction contracts including EPC contracts in infrastructure projects, distributorship and agency agreements, BOOT and BOLT Contracts, software licensing agreements, and shareholders' agreements. He has appeared as counsel or co-counsel in international arbitrations at various venues and domestic arbitrations in India. He has also acted as an arbitrator in both domestic and international arbitrations. He is currently one of the 15 vice-presidents of the International Chamber of Commerce (ICC) Court of International Arbitration in Paris. He is also on the panel of arbitrators of SIAC and KLIAC, as well as other institutions.

Minn Naing Oo, Partner, Allen & Gledhill LLP, Singapore Minn leads the firm's Myanmar practice. He was previously the Chief Executive Officer and Registrar of the Singapore International Arbitration Centre, and before that a Director at the Ministry of Trade and Industry Singapore, with oversight for Singapore's trade agreements and World Trade Organisation-related matters including policy review, formulation, and negotiations. He has presented papers and spoken at numerous conferences and seminars on international arbitration and international trade. Minn graduated from the National University of Singapore with an LLB. After he was called to the Singapore Bar in 1997, Minn was in legal practice before he obtained an LLM in 2001 from Columbia University as a Harlan Fiske Stone Scholar. Minn has been a panellist in WTO disputes. He is also a fellow of the Chartered Institute of Arbitrators and the Singapore Institute of Arbitrators.

Nikolaus Pitkowitz, Partner and Head of Dispute Resolution, Graf & Pitkowitz, Vienna, Austria Founding partner and head of dispute resolution at Graf & Pitkowitz, Vienna, Nikolaus Pitkowitz holds law degrees from the University of Vienna (JD and PhD) and the University of Sankt Gallen, Switzerland (MBL), and is also qualified and certified as a mediator. Dr Pitkowitz has been practising law since 1985 and is considered one of the pre-eminent Austrian dispute resolution practitioners. He has acted as counsel and arbitrator in a multitude of international arbitrations, including several high profile disputes, including the largest ever pending Austrian arbitration (a multibillion telecommunications dispute). Dr Pitkowitz is vice-president of VIAC (Vienna International Arbitral Centre). He is an arbitrator and panel member of several arbitral institutions, including ICC, SIAC, CIETAC, and ICDR; FCIArb; vice-chair of the International Arbitration Committee of the Section of International law of the American Bar Association (ABA), and past Co-chair of the Mediation Techniques Committee of the International Bar Association (IBA). Nikolaus Pitkowitz frequently speaks at seminars and is author of numerous publications, including the leading treatise on setting aside arbitral awards under Austrian law. Dr Pitkowitz is a co-editor of the *Austrian Yearbook on International Arbitration* (CH Beck/Stämpfli/Manz, 2013) and co-organizer of the Vienna Arbitration Days.

Klaus Reichert, Barrister, London, England, and Dublin, Ireland Klaus Reichert SC specializes in international arbitration and has undertaken, both as lead counsel and as arbitrator (frequently as chair), in excess of 120 such cases across a broad spectrum of complex subject matters, industries, and governing laws, involving parties from all over the world (ICSID, DIAC, ICC, LCIA, ICDR, CAS, DIFC-LCIA, and UNCITRAL; in Paris, Helsinki, New York, London, Munich, Seoul, Geneva, Dublin, Dubai, Stockholm, Zurich, and elsewhere). He is a member of the International Basketball Federation (BAT) panel of arbitrators, a member of the Court of Arbitration for Sport, the SIAC, WIPO, ICDR, and DIAC Panels. He was counsel for Dallah in the landmark New York Convention case in the English courts against the Government of Pakistan. In 2012 he was honoured by his election to the Governing Board of the International Council for Commercial Arbitration (ICCA), the world's leading NGO in the field of international arbitration. He is a silk (Senior Counsel) at the Bar of Ireland and has been involved as counsel in a large number of leading cases in the field of private international law.

Fernando Eduardo Serec, Partner, TozziniFreire Advogados, São Paulo, Brazil Head partner in the Dispute Resolution Department of TozziniFreire Advogados, Fernando Eduardo Serec has practiced in international arbitrations conducted under the rules of the ICC, ICDR, LCA, and in a large number of local arbitration proceedings carried out under the rules of the CCBC, CMA (CIESP), CAMARB, and FGV-RJ. He also acts as attorney in ad hoc arbitrations, court cases, and widely-known arbitration proceedings. He is constantly recognized and recommended as leader in the most important international legal publications, such as *Chambers Global, Chambers Latin America, Latin Lawyer 250, PLC Which Lawyer?, International Financial Law Review 1000, Expert Guides, The International Who's Who Legal, Global Arbitration Review*, and *Análise Advocacia 500.*

Jingzhou Tao, Managing Partner, Dechert LLP Beijing, People's Republic of China A partner at Dechert LLP, and adjunct professor at Peking University Law School and East-China University of Political Science and Law, Mr Jingzhou Tao has advised on China-related matters since 1985 and has maintained an active practice in China for over 20 years, acting as counsel, chief arbitrator, and party-nominated arbitrator in a significant number of international arbitrations. He also counsels numerous Chinese companies on their arbitration activities in foreign countries. Mr Tao is an *avocat à la Cour de Paris* and also qualified in China. He has been a member of the ICC International Court of Arbitration from 1999 to the present and sits on the board of the London Court of International Arbitration (LCIA). He is also a member of the advisory committee of CIETAC, co-chair of China International Arbitration Club, and Chair of the Commission on International Commercial Arbitration of ICC China.

Epaminontas Triantafilou, Of Counsel, Quinn Emanuel, London, UK Mr Triantafilou is Of Counsel in Quinn Emanuel's International Arbitration Practice, where he represents private corporations and sovereign states in commercial and investment arbitrations. His experience includes disputes in Europe, Africa, Central Asia, Southeast Asia, and Latin America. He has served as Legal Counsel at the Permanent Court of Arbitration in The Hague, the Netherlands, and as Legal Assistant to the Hon Charles N Brower. He also practiced international arbitration for several years with a major international law firm in Washington, DC. Epaminontas has published and delivered lectures and presentations on various topics in international law and arbitration. He serves as Co-Managing Editor of the *World Arbitration and Mediation Review*, the premier journal of the Institute for Transnational Arbitration in Dallas, Texas.

Claus von Wobeser, Partner, Von Wobeser y Sierra, Mexico City, Mexico As managing partner of Von Wobeser y Sierra advising both multinational Fortune 500 clients as well as governments, Mr Von Wobeser has experience acting as counsel and arbitrator appointed by international companies and governments involved in international investor-state or commercial disputes. Mr von Wobeser has been involved in more than a hundred arbitral proceedings globally, including in the Latin America region, North America, Europe, Africa, and Asia. He has represented foreign and Mexican companies in international arbitrations conducted under the rules of the ICC, AAA, ICDR, UNCITRAL Arbitration Rules, ICSID, NAFTA, Inter-American Commercial Arbitration Commission, Hong Kong International Arbitration Centre, and the LCIA. He has also served as an arbitrator in more than 15 investor-state arbitration cases under UNCITRAL Arbitration Rules, ICSID, and the ICSID Additional Facility Mechanism. Additionally, he has acted as an arbitrator in ad hoc arbitrations as well as a judge ad hoc in the Inter-American Court of Human Rights. Mr von Wobeser has acted as an expert witness on Mexican and international law in several international arbitrations, as well as before US and English Courts.

INTRODUCTION

The choice of venue of an arbitration is often the last decision made during the drafting of a dispute resolution clause—itself often the last clause agreed in a complex contract negotiation. Contracting parties all too often neglect to select a venue, either for lack of care or because the topic is considered to be a matter of personal preference too contentious to address when a deal is ready to close. The venue is, however, much more than a matter of personal preference or party convenience. It plays a critical role in setting the legal foundation for any resulting arbitration.

While most people familiar with arbitration are at least generally aware of the role the venue plays in determining both the substance of and procedure for challenges to arbitration awards after they are rendered, the law of the venue has an impact on every stage of the arbitral procedure. The law of arbitration and the judicial attitude towards arbitration at the place the parties have chosen (or that has been chosen for them in the absence of agreement) will most critically determine whether the local courts will support or hinder the commencement of arbitration proceedings. It will determine the availability and timing of challenges to arbitral jurisdiction. It will determine the scope of independence and impartiality requirements for the selection of arbitrators and the process for challenges to and replacement of arbitrators. The law of the venue can play a key role in determining access to evidence held by the opposing party or by third parties.

This book reviews the impact of the choice of venue in international arbitration by studying these key legal issues affecting all phases of arbitration proceedings using a thorough and comparative method across the most commonly used arbitral seats in the world. The aim of this review is two-fold. First, both practitioners and users of arbitration will be able to make more informed choices for the venues of their arbitrations. Similarly, when faced with an arbitration in an unfamiliar jurisdiction, they will quickly be able to identify legal issues that may affect their strategy—and their costs. Second, students of arbitration law will have access to parallel, in-depth studies of multiple jurisdictions that go beyond a 'practitioner's handbook'. Comparative legal studies of arbitration venues can find their start here.

No introduction can substitute for the detailed analysis that follows. We nevertheless aim to present an overview of the broad range of topics affected by arbitral venue, while giving insight into some of the key variations that can be found even between the leading centres for arbitration practice.

Other than tangential references, questions of enforcement of arbitration awards are excluded from this overview, and this book. Venue, after all, will take us only through the issuance and subsequent challenge to an international arbitration award. Afterwards, the question of that award's enforceability will in large part be independent of the venue of its origin.

Sources of Law

In any jurisdiction, local arbitration law and international agreements provide the legal framework defining the international arbitration regime. Concerning international arbitration, the 1985 UNCITRAL Model Law on International Commercial Arbitration, as amended in 2006 (the Model Law)[1] is generally considered the paragon of a law conducive to international arbitration. Accordingly, a number of prominent international arbitration venues (Hong Kong, Singapore, Stockholm), as well as jurisdictions on the rise as such venues (Cairo, Dubai, Mexico City), have arbitration laws based entirely or in part on the Model Law. For jurisdictions traditionally perceived as less arbitration-friendly, reluctance to adopt the Model Law generally correlates with greater judicial interference with arbitration, even where this interference is not mandated by the law, and a less effective arbitration regime (Argentina, China, India). On the other hand, the arbitration laws of traditional international arbitration strongholds, such as London, Paris, New York, and Switzerland are not based on the Model Law. This suggests that the Model Law is not necessary for the establishment of a strong foundation for international arbitration, but that for up-and-coming venues, the adoption of the Model Law is an important first step in developing a modern arbitration regime and signals their commitment to developing an arbitration-friendly legal environment.

As far as international sources of law are concerned, the 1958 New York Convention on the Recognition and Enforcement of Foreign Arbitral Awards[2] is without question the principal international instrument governing arbitration. Of the 20 jurisdictions in this book, every single state is a signatory to the Convention, regardless of its perceived stance towards arbitration. The only tangible variable between jurisdictions in this respect relates to their host states' treatment of the principle of reciprocity: while some have committed to enforce foreign arbitral awards under the Convention regardless of where the award was issued (eg Dubai, Brazil (São Paolo), Egypt (Cairo), and Australia (Sydney)), others have ratified the Convention subject to the reciprocity reservation, meaning that they will only enforce

[1] UNCITRAL Model Law on International Commercial Arbitration (the UNCITRAL Model Law) (1985) 24 ILM 1302, with amendments as adopted in 2006.

[2] New York Convention on the Recognition and Enforcement of Foreign Arbitral Awards (the New York Convention) (1968) 330 UNTS 38; 7 ILM 1046.

awards issued in other signatory states (eg China, India, the Russian Federation (Moscow), the United Kingdom (London), and the United States).

Judicial Attitude to Arbitration

Judicial attitudes towards arbitration appear to correlate with how long-standing the practice of arbitration is in the respective jurisdiction. Thus, courts in Hong Kong, London, Paris, Singapore, Stockholm, Switzerland, and the United States tend to exhibit a markedly pro-arbitration attitude. In London and Paris, there are even specialized judicial resources dedicated to arbitration cases, the Commercial Court and the Technology and Construction Court in London, and the bench of the *juges d'appui*, or supporting judges, on the *Tribunal de Grande Instance* in Paris. On the whole, the courts of arbitration venues on the rise also tend to be arbitration-friendly, even though the extent to which this attitude has been internalized varies (eg it is very well developed in Dubai, and only recently adopted in São Paolo). Among the venues examined in this book, only a handful bear the risk of unsupportive or even anti-arbitration courts: Buenos Aires, where some court decisions indicate judicial hostility towards arbitration, which may well be a by-product of the host of investment arbitration cases against Argentina in the past years; India, where courts tend to be interventionist and to set aside arbitration awards with some frequency; and Moscow, where court practice can be unpredictable.

Court Assistance in Commencing the Arbitration

Generally speaking, a dispute subject to arbitration should proceed largely extra-judicially, as long as neither party is attempting to undercut the proceedings. In accordance with this principle, most courts become involved in the commencement of the proceedings only when a party brings judicial proceedings over a dispute that another party considers subject to arbitration. In these circumstances, most courts follow the generally accepted principle that the suit must be dismissed as long as there is a valid and enforceable arbitration agreement in place. The only exception arises in Vienna, where a court does not necessarily need to decline jurisdiction over a dispute covered by a valid arbitration agreement: instead, the court may hear the dispute if the tribunal declines jurisdiction, or fails to rule on its jurisdiction within a reasonable time.

It is largely incumbent upon the parties to object to a court's jurisdiction on the basis that a dispute is subject to arbitration. A party's failure to raise that objection before a certain juncture in the proceedings is usually considered a waiver of the right to arbitrate the dispute. Typically, a party must raise the objection prior to its first submission on the merits (eg in Brussels, Dublin, Hong Kong, India, London, Mexico, Stockholm, and Switzerland), even though some jurisdictions require that an objection be made before the party participates in the proceedings in any way (Buenos Aires, Cairo, Dubai, and Singapore), while others extend the waiver deadline until the first court hearing (China and Germany). In Vienna, on the other hand, a court faced with a dispute potentially subject to arbitration may raise the issue *ex officio*, even where a party fails to avail itself of the right to arbitrate.

In determining whether there is a valid arbitration agreement in place, courts will look to a variety of formal and substantive requirements. Substantive requirements tend to be a question of contract law, covering matters such as the parties' capacity to enter into the agreement (eg in Brussels), or whether the agreement conveys a clear intention to arbitrate (eg in Sydney and Vienna). The most ubiquitous formal requirement is that an arbitration agreement be in writing, even though this is not necessary in every jurisdiction (eg an agreement need not be in writing in Stockholm and Switzerland).

A number of jurisdictions treat the validity of an arbitration agreement separately from the validity of the contract containing that agreement (eg Brussels, Dublin, Mexico City, Paris, Switzerland, the United States, and Vienna). This approach—known as the principle of severability or separability—effectively immunizes the arbitration agreement from the nullity or unenforceability of the overall contract.

Sometimes folded in the analysis of the validity of the arbitration agreement is the question of the arbitrability of the dispute, or whether the dispute is capable of being settled by arbitration. Commercial matters are generally considered arbitrable, with some jurisdiction-specific exceptions: some insurance contracts (eg in Brussels and Sydney), some property rights (eg in Buenos Aires), some consumer contracts (eg in Dubai and Hong Kong), intellectual property matters (eg in London and Sydney), insolvency matters (eg in Sydney), and disputes of a public policy nature (eg in Moscow). Singapore arguably has the most liberal arbitrability regime, deeming any dispute that the parties have agreed to arbitrate to be subject to arbitration, unless proceeding to arbitrate the dispute would be contrary to public policy. Criminal and family matters are not considered arbitrable in most jurisdictions.

Court Assistance in Appointing the Tribunal

Courts may also be called upon to assist in the appointment of arbitrators to the arbitral tribunal in cases of vacancy due to failure of the appointment procedure or the removal of an arbitrator from the tribunal. Courts typically have the power to make such appointments in order to enable the arbitration proceedings to continue. The exceptions to this are China, Russia, and Hong Kong, whose courts do not have the authority to appoint arbitrators.

Jurisdiction of the Tribunal

In cases in which the jurisdiction of the arbitral tribunal is challenged, most states follow the generally accepted principle of *competence-competence*, pursuant to which an arbitral tribunal is empowered to rule on its own jurisdiction. Indeed, in the majority of the jurisdictions covered in this book, the principle of *competence-competence* is explicitly set out in the local arbitration law and followed by the courts. One exception is India, where, even though *competence-competence* is recognized by the law, its application has been undermined by a recent court decision. In 2005, the Supreme Court of India held that where a court had exercised its authority to appoint an arbitrator, questions relating to the jurisdiction of the arbitral tribunal so constituted were to be finally decided by the court; the full implications of this decision on the principle of *competence-competence* are yet to be seen.[3]

[3] *SBP & Co v Patel Engineering Ltd* [2005] 8 SCC 618.

In other instances, the principle of *competence-competence*, while set out in the local arbitration law, may be limited. This is the case where, for example, the law also provides for recourse to the courts on matters relating to the jurisdiction of the arbitral tribunal prior to the commencement of the proceedings (London) or even during the proceedings (Stockholm).

Finally, in some jurisdictions *competence-competence* is not recognized under the local arbitration law and is applied restrictively either because the law directs matters relating to the jurisdiction of the arbitral tribunal to the courts (China, Germany) or arbitration institutions (China), or because of judicial attitudes towards the doctrine (Buenos Aires, the United States).

Even in jurisdictions that recognize and apply *competence-competence*, however, the courts exercise judicial oversight over the tribunal's determination on its jurisdiction. Typically, the tribunal's decision is immediately subject to challenge before the courts, with the exceptions of Brussels and Paris, where the challenge against a tribunal's jurisdiction can be brought only after the conclusion of the proceedings, as grounds for setting aside the award.

Courts' Role in Enjoining Arbitration

Courts may also be seised to use their injunctive powers to preclude arbitration proceedings from commencing or proceeding. However, this is not common. In many of the jurisdictions dealt with in this work, the courts have never been seised with such a request, and, should one be made, the likelihood of its succeeding is low (eg in Brussels, Dubai, Dublin, Hong Kong, and Sydney). Some courts' restrictive powers over arbitration are limited to rulings relating to the validity of the arbitration agreement or the tribunal's jurisdiction, and do not extend to enjoining arbitration proceedings (eg in Germany and Stockholm). At the other extreme are Buenos Aires and India: the Argentinian courts have enjoined arbitrations involving government-owned entities, and the Indian courts frequently take it upon themselves to enjoin arbitration proceedings, including ones seated abroad. Finally, while the courts in some jurisdictions are empowered to enjoin arbitration, anti-arbitration injunctions are not issued at alarming rates, arguably either because of judicial restraint (eg in Moscow and some states in the United States), or because the law limits the circumstances where injunctions are appropriate (eg in Cairo, limiting injunctions to situations in which the tribunal has failed to render a timely award, and London, where the likelihood of an injunction largely depends on the procedural basis for the request).

During the Arbitration

The logical consequence of the initiation of arbitral proceedings should be that courts no longer have to intervene in the dispute or in its resolution. However, courts may intervene either to assist the arbitral process, or to prevent it from continuing. The venue will necessarily have an impact on each of these relationships between the arbitral tribunal and the domestic courts: the law applicable to the arbitral procedure or to different elements of the arbitral procedure (such as the production of evidence or the calling of witnesses) will influence the pursuit of arbitration itself.

Although at first glance this might look like an obstacle to arbitration (why choose arbitration if state court intervention will still be necessary?), overall, a balanced relationship between state jurisdictions and arbitral tribunals seems to exist in the different venues. This is shown by the collaborative and complementary role generally adopted by state courts with regard to arbitral tribunals.

The range of occasions leading to state court intervention is an important issue in choosing a venue—indeed, counsel and parties will have to examine carefully the role given to the state courts and the role these courts understand themselves to have. While some aspects of a law might seem particularly attractive, others might not be—it will be necessary to analyse the overall provisions of the law of the venue that can affect the arbitration. The multiplicity of elements to be taken into consideration makes the choice of a venue in arbitration an algebraic activity with different unknowns to be determined.

Roles of courts in deciding challenges to arbitrators

Challenges are often first dealt with by the arbitral tribunal itself (eg in Argentina, Austria, Germany, and Mexico). They can also be dealt with by the administering institution, when the arbitration is not ad hoc.[4] Courts will rarely have the opportunity—or even be allowed—to intervene during the course of an arbitration when an administrative body exists to oversee challenges. For example, French courts have no jurisdiction to review an institutional decision regarding a challenge, although they may ultimately review the question upon a challenge to an award. In some jurisdictions, the institution's decision may be attacked without waiting (eg the Netherlands).[5] This is unusual and may be criticized as ignoring the parties' intent to submit their arbitration to an administrative institution. So long as the courts act quickly, however, it can be deemed an advantage by providing a final view on the challenge without needing to await a challenge to a final award. In any event, it is clear that courts will be called upon more frequently to intervene in ad hoc arbitrations, where no institution exists to review the challenge in the first instance.

There appears to be uniformity in the conceptual basis for challenging arbitrators—namely issues relating to their impartiality and independence. One exception is the English Arbitration Act 1996, which deliberately omitted the term 'independence', precisely to avoid controversy on the definition of the term. Although the dictionary definition of these terms is seemingly uniform throughout the different jurisdictions, the interpretation of these concepts is quite varied. While often a question of degree, local particularities still appear—in India, for example, a company's employee may sit as arbitrator in a dispute opposing the employer and another private company.

In reaction to the difficulty of setting clear standards for independence and impartiality, an obligation of disclosure has progressively emerged not just as a procedure, but as an obligation in its own right. This obligation has recently been incorporated into different sets of arbitration rules[6] and newly modified legislation (eg in Mexico). This emerging obligation, which can be seen as displacing in some measure the underlying impartiality and independence obligations, has created recent turbulence in various jurisdictions. For example, French

[4] ICC Rules 2012, Art 14.1.

[5] A well-known example involved a challenge to an arbitrator in the courts of The Hague immediately following a decision by the Permanent Court of Arbitration not to accept a challenge within the arbitral proceedings. See J van Haersolte-van Hof, 'United Nations Commmission on International Trade Law (UNCITRAL) Arbitration Rules, 1976' in *Concise International Arbitration* (Kluwer, 2010) 187.

[6] ICC Rules 2012, Art 11(2).

courts are leading the way in considering a failure of disclosure of matters potentially affecting independence or impartiality as itself being a failure to meet the independent and impartial standard. This occurred recently in the highly-publicized *Tecnimont* decision, which annulled an ICC award after an arbitrator failed to disclose matters handled by his firm of which he was in fact unaware.[7] The *Tecnimont* case itself, however, illustrates the difficulty of evaluating compliance with the disclosure obligation and has created significant debate. The question remains whether this decision—if it survives a pending review on *cassation*—will make France more desirable as a venue by requiring the highest level of care on disclosure or less desirable due to the fear that awards that can be years in the making will be subject to attack on the basis of information that did not in fact affect the independence or impartiality of the arbitrator.

The interpretation and application of the concepts of independence, impartiality, and disclosure may affect both the effectiveness of arbitration in general and the award rendered in particular. Overly stringent criteria of impartiality and independence—and the concomitant disclosure requirement—in any given venue may form a hurdle to arbitration, especially in specialized fields in which there are a limited number of qualified arbitrators. Overly permissive criteria, however, may make it difficult to enforce the award in other jurisdictions, because a tribunal deemed acceptable at the venue may be considered improperly constituted at the place of enforcement.

Role of courts in implementing provisional measures/provisional relief

In some venues, arbitral tribunals are allowed to issue orders related to provisional measures (eg in Belgium, Brazil, England and Wales, France, Germany, and Switzerland). Indeed, the ability of arbitral tribunals to issue provisional measures has become an important issue in arbitration—and led to legislative amendments (eg by Mexico).

In some countries, the arbitral tribunal's power to implement provisional measures is complete, in that the existing legislation provides that the arbitral tribunal can impose a fine on the parties until they comply with the measures ordered—as is the case in France and Belgium. This is, however, not automatic: thus, in Germany, although the arbitral tribunal has the power to issue provisional measures, it lacks the power to declare them enforceable—the parties must go to the state courts to demand the enforceability of the measures. This supplementary procedure adds both costs and time to the arbitration and is open to criticism.

State courts can have a role not only in enforcing tribunal-issued provisional measures, but also in issuing such measures themselves, whether aimed at parties or at third parties. The question is whether state courts retain this capacity at all times or whether that power is put aside when arbitral proceedings are initiated. In some venues (eg in France), the courts' competence with respect to provisional measures is generally limited to the period prior to the constitution of the arbitral tribunal,[8] while in others, the courts have authority to order provisional measures during the arbitration (eg in Germany, Mexico, and Switzerland). The

[7] CA Reims 2 November 2011, *SAJ & P Avax v Société Tecnimont SPA* (2012) ASA Bulletin 197, (2012) Rev arb 112 (Regional Court of Appeal).

[8] Code de procédure civile, art 1449. Although not yet tested, the courts in France would still be likely to grant provisional measures after the tribunal is constituted in urgent and essentially uncontested cases or to prevent imminent or manifestly illicit harm. C Jarrosson and J Pellerin, 'Le droit français de l'arbitrage après le décret du 13 janvier 2011' (2011) Rev arb 5, paras 17–18.

courts' competence to intervene in the arbitral proceedings by ordering interim measures may yet be circumscribed by the parties; thus, in England, the *Scott v Avery* clause means that the parties have precluded any judicial remedy by the state courts, whether before or during the arbitration.

Role of courts in compelling testimony and evidence

The question of the ability to ensure the presence of witnesses and the production of essential documents in the arbitral proceedings is of course critical, as the reasoning of the award will be based upon the facts derived from witness testimony and documentary evidence available to the tribunal.

A preliminary issue is determining who can be called upon as witness in front of the arbitral tribunal—in some venues, parties may not be allowed to appear as witnesses (eg in Argentina). This will, of course, pose great difficulties insofar as the interest of arbitration is precisely its flexibility in providing private resolution to (generally commercial) disputes. In French court proceedings, for example, parties and employees of parties may not testify, which is seen as a hurdle in judicial commercial proceedings. In France, this limitation is often circumvented by introducing an arbitration agreement between commercial parties, which will lead to a more flexible procedure, allowing parties and their employees to testify. No such exit door is available in arbitration in Argentina.

A peculiarity of arbitration, of course, is that it is born of a contractual agreement and is thus limited to those parties that have consented to arbitration. One consequence of this is that the arbitral tribunal has no authority over third parties and cannot compel third parties to testify. It may therefore be necessary to rely on state courts for assistance in obtaining evidence. Whether the parties or the arbitral tribunal will be allowed to apply to the state courts for this depends on local legislation. In some venues (eg in France), a filter will be implemented as parties will have to request the arbitral tribunal's authorization before applying to state courts to ask for a third party's testimony. The assistance of courts may go to issuing a subpoena to a potential witness in an arbitration proceeding (eg in Singapore and Sydney). In India, the courts may issue summonses for witnesses to appear in front of an arbitral tribunal, whether at the tribunal's request or at a party's request (following approval of the arbitrators). If the witnesses were not to comply, they could be sanctioned for contempt of court. These systems have their limitations, however, as subpoenas will likely be enforced only in the country of the court issuing the order.

Solutions to this difficulty may come in surprising ways. Thus, in Belgium, the arbitral tribunal may not be able to hear a witness when it refuses to appear before the panel or if it refuses to take an oath when required to do so. The parties can be authorized to request that a state court hear the witness, the arbitral tribunal relying on the testimony thus provided. This may be considered as a good alternative way to obtain the necessary information. However, this also means that the arbitral tribunal will not have direct access to the witness and will not be able to ask questions or assess the witness's demeanour. In Austria, this difficulty is set aside as the arbitral tribunal and the parties will be allowed to assist and participate in the witness hearing in front of the state courts. This may indeed be the high water mark of collaboration between the judiciary and arbitration tribunals.

Although oaths are generally not considered necessary, it is habitual that arbitrators will ask witnesses to acknowledge that they will tell the truth. While criminal prosecutions are rare, witnesses who lie in arbitration proceedings can variously be subject to criminal and/or civil liability.

Some parties may request—sometimes simply for cultural reasons—that a witness be sworn in. Swedish legislation provides that if a party considers an oath to be absolutely necessary for a witness testimony, the examination will have to be realized with the assistance of a district court judge. Careful attention to whether a witness must be sworn in or not in a given venue may be of crucial importance at the moment of evaluating the validity of the award.

Regarding the preservation or the production of evidence, the arbitral tribunal may also need to rely on the assistance of state courts. Parties may apply for the preservation of evidence to the arbitral tribunal (eg in France and Germany), to state courts when the arbitral procedure has not yet been initiated (eg in France), or to the competent arbitral authorities (eg in China). Regarding the production of evidence—in particular evidence held by third parties—the cooperation of state courts becomes crucial. A balanced position seems to have been reached in different venues (eg in France and Sweden), where parties may obtain evidence held by third parties by applying to state courts after being so authorized by the arbitral tribunal. This implies that the arbitral tribunal itself will not be allowed to require the state courts' assistance in obtaining evidence. In Germany, both arbitral tribunals and parties (with the arbitrators' consent) may apply directly to the German courts to have their support in taking evidence. Courts, however, will not have the power to compel document production (by parties or by third parties) and will be allowed to draw adverse inferences only from any refusal.

More expansive assistance by the courts has been implemented in the United States in the wake of the 2004 *Intel* decision of the Supreme Court.[9] In that case, the Supreme Court indicated that arbitral tribunals seated in other venues may be 'foreign or international tribunals' under the terms of section 1782 of Title 28 of the United States Code, which provides for judicial assistance in obtaining evidence for such tribunals. Various federal courts have since granted assistance to arbitral tribunals in the preservation and production of evidence. Both parties and the arbitral tribunal may request the assistance of the federal courts in obtaining evidence for the arbitral proceedings, which may impose penalties for failure to comply with a production order.

In Ireland, a specific provision of the legislation specifies that the High Court may assist foreign-seated arbitral tribunals in taking evidence located in Ireland; this, however, is limited by the requirement that the parties specify that the Irish High Court is allowed to make document discovery orders. The most expansive view regarding foreign-seated arbitral tribunals thus seems to be embodied by the US jurisprudence.

As to the authenticity of documents provided to the arbitral tribunal, the powers granted to the arbitrators differ from venue to venue. Whereas the arbitral tribunal's power to evaluate the authenticity of an element of proof has long been admitted in France,[10] legislation in other venues does not grant arbitrators that right—thus, in Belgium, state courts have the prerogative to evaluate the authenticity of a document. This can be considered to be

[9] *Intel Corp v Advanced Micro Devices, Inc* 542 US 241 (2004).
[10] CPC, art 1470.

an unnecessary burden, causing both supplementary delays and costs to the parties to arbitration.

Restrictions/requirements regarding the ability of foreign practitioners to appear as counsel or arbitrators

There are few, if any, restrictions or requirements regarding the ability of foreign practitioners to appear as counsel or arbitrators. Proper qualifications are generally left to the parties' discretion; an insufficiently qualified arbitrator may be removed under English law on this ground.

The lack of nationality-related criteria is probably due to the fact that, although materially localized, international arbitration is independent of any state procedure or substantive law. Nationality issues are more relevant regarding arbitrators—parties may, as such, prefer that none of the arbitrators sitting on the panel shares the nationality of one of the parties. This would usually have to be expressly mentioned in the arbitration agreement, as this question is generally not dealt with by the applicable legislation (eg in France, Germany, or Mexico). Whether arbitrators may or may not be required to be of a different nationality than the parties is currently being analysed by the European Commission in the *Jivraj* case.[11]

A more recurrent restriction on counsel or arbitrators would seem to be professional qualifications. If having the bar exam is not a condition in Belgium, the qualification as *agent d'affaires* bars the person from acting as counsel in arbitration. *A contrario*, in Mexico, having the bar exam is a mandatory requirement for participation as counsel in arbitration proceedings.

Local requirements for conduct of arbitration hearings (limitations of language, swearing of witnesses, etc)

Hearings are not mandatory in arbitration, although they are held in most proceedings. The local requirements for the conduct of hearings must be determined before choosing the venue, as they are not necessarily known or even expected by the arbitrators or the parties. The respect of these local requirements is crucial to protect the validity and enforceability of an ensuing award. Generally, the basic principles of legal hearings are to be respected—fair and equal treatment of the parties, due process, and assistance by counsel chosen by the parties. These reflect general conceptions of the right of access to justice.[12]

As legislators seem to be aware, imposing too many local particularities might be seen as a hurdle for the development of a venue for international arbitration. As such, few local requirements for the arbitration hearings themselves are to be found. As explained earlier, regarding the swearing in of witnesses, there are usually no provisions in the laws of the different venues described throughout this book. Equally, there are usually no mandatory language provisions, except in some very restrictive cases, for example in Brazil, where public-private partnerships and concession disputes submitted to arbitration must be conducted in Brazil and in Portuguese.

---

[11] Following the decision of the UK Supreme Court's in *Jivraj v Hashwani* [2011] UKSC 40.

[12] See eg the European Convention on Human Rights, Art 6; and the 1966 International Covenant on Civil and Political Rights, Art 14.

The Award

The award is the final result of the arbitral proceedings, granting the parties rights that are to be enforced. The award must respect some basic rules in order to be recognized and enforced.

Mandatory rules as to form

Awards must comply with certain basic formal requirements in order to be effective, and ultimately, to be recognized and enforced. Some elements are basic guarantees of the award's existence and authenticity, for example the names of the parties and of the arbitrators, the signatures of the arbitrators on the award, the date, and the seat of the arbitration. Each of these elements will have bearing on the award—for example the date will determine the moment the award has *res judicata*; the seat of the arbitration will determine the jurisdiction for the annulment procedure. The absence of some of these elements will not necessarily per se lead to a possible setting aside of the award, such as the lack of a date (eg in Austria and France). Some states may require more elements, which must be carefully studied beforehand, as they may seem unusual to the parties and their counsel. One example is the requirement, in India, to have a stamp on the award in accordance with the Indian Stamp Act.

The reasoning of an award is considered to be a formal requirement rather than a substantive requirement. State courts are not allowed to review the arbitral tribunal's reasoning, but only to check whether the arbitral tribunal motivated its decision on a *prima facie* reading of the award (eg in Belgium, France, and Mexico). This obligation to include the reasons may, under Austrian law, be excluded by the parties at any stage, whether expressly or implicitly. Such a decision implies that the parties waive the right to request that the award be set aside for lack of reasoning.

Mandatory rules as to substance

It must be kept in mind that, in most countries, the substance of the award will not be subject to review by courts. As such, although there are some mandatory rules as to substance, these will not be reviewed in depth, but only in a formalist manner.

Thus, for example, the award must answer the claims of the parties in accordance with their chosen law and establish the costs and damages to be attributed to the parties. Some legislation provides for a default, applicable law if the parties have not chosen one, for instance in India when all the parties are Indian.

In some countries, there is determined content as to costs, for example whether the award on costs shall include counsels' fees or not (eg in Germany), or whether the parties can agree in advance that each side will bear its own costs (as is the case in Ireland). There may also be determined content for damages. For example, in some venues punitive damages will not be admitted or enforced (eg in Mexico). In other venues the issue is unresolved, for instance in France, where the courts have recognized a foreign judiciary decision applying punitive damages, when these are forbidden in French law. It remains to be determined whether the same approach can be retained for arbitral awards.

Post-Award

Despite the extent of the venue-related issues reviewed above that may have an impact on an arbitration proceeding until the award is rendered, it is often the case that the venue is of only incidental effect on a smoothly run arbitration until the award is in hand. It is post-award, and in particular if one party seeks to set the award aside in front of the courts, that the choice of venue will show its most important effects.

Local standards for setting aside/annulment

The basic standards for setting aside or annulment of an arbitral award are fairly standard across all venues, and they track the grounds for refusing enforcement set in the New York Convention. Some venues have, however, generated additional grounds for the annulment of an award or interpreted the core standards in ways not generally accepted elsewhere.

In particular, although the United States generally accepts that courts may not review the substance of an international arbitration award, a concept of 'manifest disregard of the law' as a ground for annulment continues to appear. Despite some attempts to justify this concept as procedural, it inevitably implies that the courts will delve into the merits of the case. A similar practice exists in England, although on the basis of clear statutory authority, where it is possible to appeal against an award on a point of law in some instances. However, this cannot be generalized to all common law venues. Substantive review of an award is as such prohibited in Ireland, Hong Kong, and Singapore.[13]

Of the core grounds for annulment existing in all venues, the most undefinable notion is that of a violation of public policy, varying according to each state's interpretation of the concept. For example, Singapore has distinguished between the grounds for breach of public policy and breach of natural justice, whereas in most states (in particular civil law states), a violation of basic principles of natural justice (such as due process) will be encompassed by the notion of public policy.

Public policy can, of course, be highly dependant on political elements. As such, and as underscored by Jingzhou Tao, the concept of public policy in China is malleable because it is highly dependent on political preoccupations and interests. The influence of politics may also be seen in other countries, such as in Argentina, where opportunistic decisions have led to loosely-reasoned conclusions, preventing a clear development of the notion of public policy. However, as highlighted by Alejandro M Garro and Michael Fernandez, these decisions are not necessarily being followed either by lower courts or by the Argentine Supreme Court of Justice.

The approach to public policy may either define the attractiveness of a venue or become one of its worst marketing points. Thus, the French position regarding the verification that the award is not contrary to public policy is generally hailed as a very liberal approach—with only the most egregious violations of international public policy, rather than domestic public

[13] Substantive challenges are possible according to Hong Kong law, but only if parties have opted for this. That is usually not the case in international arbitration.

policy, being considered. However, this approach can be criticized as leading to the absence of any real control of awards for the respect of public policy.[14] *A contrario*, the Indian conception of public policy, including the patent illegality of the award, its unfairness or unreasonableness, has led to criticisms of the Indian system as unreliable. In Singapore, a leading regional centre in international arbitration, the courts consider themselves entitled to correct an arbitral tribunal's decision on the issue of illegality.

The timeframe in which parties may demand the annulment or setting aside of an award for violation of public policy is also significant in evaluating the importance granted to this ground by each venue. Whereas in France this particular ground is not treated differently from the four other grounds allowing the setting aside of an award, other venues have granted longer timeframes or even decided to have no time limits for parties to raise an argument based on the violation of public policy.

Whether deemed to be arising out of public policy or not, it is important to note a new ground for setting aside arbitral awards that has been developing in recent years: an award may be annulled if it has been obtained by fraud in Austria or in Belgium. While under Belgian law there is no limitation to raise this particular objection, in Austrian law, the party must raise its claim in the four weeks after actually learning of the circumstances giving rise to the challenge.

Local procedures for setting aside/annulment

Although time limits may differ according to the grounds underlying the request for the annulment (see the preceding paragraph), the time limits for seeking annulment are generally short. They range from one month (eg in France) to six months (eg China), with most venues keeping the UNCITRAL-defined time limit of three months (eg in Brazil, Germany, and Sweden). In some countries, supplementary recourses are available, through constitutional contestation of the decision of the court regarding the request for setting aside (*amparo*, eg in Mexico).

Parties and counsel must also bear in mind that any action to set aside an award will have to be carried out in the local courts of the venue of arbitration. This can have a number of effects on procedural efficiency, party comfort, and cost. The most obvious example is that local litigation generally leads to local language requirements (in France, proceedings will be in French, while in Belgium, proceedings may be in French or in Dutch). This means not only that pleadings will be in the local language, but also that the award being challenged may need to be translated—although in Germany, the requirement of translation is often waived for English-language documents. Parties will also need to engage local counsel, to the extent the counsel used in the arbitration are not admitted to practice in the courts of the venue.

Finally, the time and cost associated with local annulment actions varies tremendously from venue to venue. In most civil law venues (and notably France and Switzerland, where the courts have extensive experience with such actions), annulment actions are relatively quick, with only very short hearings. Costs are accordingly low. In other civil law venues (eg in

14 P Mayer, 'La sentence contraire a l'ordre public au fond' (1994) Rev arb 615.

Stockholm) and many common law venues, local court procedures can involve lengthy hearings with the accompanying costs.

Each of the issues presented in this overview, and analysed in great detail for each of the covered venues in this book, can individually make the choice of venue a critical moment in the decision to arbitrate disputes. Taken together, the choice of venue in international arbitration should never be taken lightly.

1

BRUSSELS

Pascal Hollander and Maarten Draye

1.1 Background

1.1.1 History and development of arbitration

Because of its central location in Europe, Brussels has played a leading role as an administrative hub throughout its history, a role it still enjoys today. Brussels is not only the capital of Belgium, but also of the European Union, and is home to the European Commission and a number of European administrative agencies and other international organizations, including NATO. Brussels has become a truly international city that attracts professionals from all over the European Union and beyond, and has, moreover, managed to position itself at the forefront of European business centres. **1.01**

At the same time, in line with the evolution of arbitration worldwide, arbitration in Belgium has developed steadily since the second half of the twentieth century. A favourable climate for arbitration was created in 1972, with the implementation of a new legislative framework for arbitration that matched the needs of the business community. Belgian courts have supplemented this with a generally pro-arbitration stance. A complete revision of the arbitration **1.02** law was adopted in June 2013 with the aim of making Belgium a more attractive place in which to arbitrate.

1.03 Particularly interesting from an international perspective is that—compared to arbitration hubs such as London or Paris—arbitrating in Brussels is generally more cost-effective. Moreover, parties without a connection to Belgium may opt out of judicial recourse for setting aside an arbitral award.

1.04 Against this background, Brussels has become an increasingly attractive venue for international arbitration proceedings.

1.1.2 Modern and recent developments

Legislative framework

1.05 The Belgian Law on Arbitration (BLA) is integrated into the Belgian Code of Civil Procedure (*Code Judiciaire/Gerechtelijk Wetboek*, hereinafter 'BCCP') as Chapter VI, entitled 'Arbitration'.

1.06 Modern arbitration legislation was first introduced in Belgium in 1972, with the enactment of the model law annexed to the European Convention on International Commercial Arbitration of 20 January 1966. This law was revised and substantially reformed in 1985 and 1998, in the light of developments in other countries and the introduction of the UNCITRAL Model Law (which was not, however, adopted in full by Belgium).

1.07 In the light of an express policy to make Belgium a more attractive place for arbitratration, in 2013 the entire BLA was replaced by a modern and progressive new law. The new BLA largely adopts the UNCITRAL Model Law (as revised in 2006), but retains a number of provisions from the earlier versions of the BLA[1] and adopts a number of solutions featured in other laws (in particular the French, German, and Swiss arbitration laws). It spans articles 1676 to 1722 of the BCCP.

1.08 Underpinning the BLA are the general principles of equality of the parties and due process, party autonomy, parties' freedom to determine the arbitral procedure, and non-intervention by local courts. Particular efforts have been made to increase the efficiency and celerity of court support to arbitration proceedings.

1.09 The BLA applies to both domestic and international arbitrations with a seat in Belgium, unless—and to the extent that—the parties have, expressly or by reference to arbitration rules, excluded its application.[2] With a few exceptions, the parties may by agreement deviate from the provisions of the BLA.[3]

1.10 Finally, Belgium is a party to the 1958 New York Convention, with the reciprocity reservation of Article I(3) (ie Belgium will only apply the Convention to recognize and enforce awards made in the territory of another contracting state), as well as the European Convention on International Commercial Arbitration of 21 April 1961. Both of these conventions entered

---

[1] One notable attempt in this regard can be found in BCCP, art 1718, pursuant to which parties who have chosen a venue in Belgium as the place of arbitration but who have no further connection with Belgium may exclude any right to apply for an arbitral award to be set aside (see para 1.158).

[2] BCCP, art 1676(7).

[3] BCCP, art 1676(8).

into force in Belgium in 1975. Belgium has also adopted the Washington Convention on the Settlement of Investments Disputes (ICSID Convention), which entered into force in 1970.

Court system

Generally speaking, the Belgian court system provides for a three-tier system of dispute resolution: a first level of 27 courts of first instance, with a possibility of recourse before one of the five courts of appeal, and above that, limited review by a supreme court. In the interest of efficiency and specialization, however, the new BLA derogates from this general rule and has abolished appeals from court decisions related to arbitration proceedings. Moreover, the new BLA centralizes the competence to hear applications concerning arbitration proceedings before the five courts of first instance at the seats of the Courts of Appeal.[4] Finally, for a number of issues, the BLA gives competence to the president of the Court of First Instance, who decides by means of fast-track summary proceedings.[5] As a result, applications concerning arbitration must be brought before the Court of First Instance—or, as the case may be, its president—located at the seat of one of the five Courts of Appeal, whose decision will be final and not susceptible to further appeal.[6] **1.11**

Specific and limited recourse against arbitration-related decisions from the Court of First Instance is available only before the Supreme Court (*Cour de cassation/Hof van Cassatie*).[7] The Supreme Court will, however, review the case on points of law or compliance with fundamental procedural rules only and will not reassess the facts. If the Supreme Court finds that the Court of First Instance has violated provisions of law or fundamental rules of procedure, it will annul the judgment (or parts thereof) and send the case back to another Court of First Instance for full review. **1.12**

Brussels is seat to various courts at first instance level as well as the seat of one of the five Courts of Appeal. The Supreme Court is located in Brussels. Consequently, applications relating to arbitration proceedings with a seat in Brussels should in principle be brought before the Court of First Instance of Brussels (*Tribunal de première instance/Rechtbank van Eerste Aanleg*). **1.13**

Because their competence *ratione loci* in arbitration-related matters corresponds with the Court of Appeal of Brussels, and hence, includes the bilingual (French-Dutch) area of Brussels as well as parts of monolingual Dutch- and French-speaking areas of Belgium, the Court of First Instance of Brussels is unique in that it may hear cases in both French and Dutch. The choice between one language and the other is not, however, left to the parties' discretion. The use of languages in court cases in Belgium is strictly regulated by the Law of 15 June 1935 on the Use of Languages in Court Proceedings (hereinafter 'Law of 1935'), which is part of public policy. With some specific exceptions, the Law of 1935 sets forth a general rule of territoriality, providing that the language of the place where the competent court is situated determines the language of the proceedings. Given the bilingual status of **1.14**

---

4 Belgium has 27 courts of first instance and five Courts of Appeal (Antwerp, Brussels, Ghent, Liège, and Mons). Consequently, only the five courts of first instance at the seats of these Courts of Appeal have the competence to hear claims in relation to arbitration. Their territorial jurisdiction is determined on the basis of the place of arbitration—or, if such place is not determined, by the rules of competence that would have applied if no arbitration agreement existed—in the same manner as the Courts of Appeal.

5 BCCP, art 1680(1)–(4).

6 BCCP, art 1680(4) and (5).

7 BCCP, art 609 °1.

Brussels, however, a special regime applies, whereby the language to be used is determined on the basis of the domicile of the responding party.

1.15 The Law of 1935 does not apply to arbitration proceedings in Belgium, in which the parties are free to choose any language for the proceedings.[8] It does, however, apply to applications in relation to such proceedings before the Belgian courts. As indicated in the preceding commentary, the Court of First Instance of Brussels is competent to hear applications relating to arbitration proceedings with their seat in Brussels. If none of the parties resides or has its seat in Belgium, the parties are free to choose whether they wish to bring such proceedings in French or Dutch. If, however, the respondent resides in Belgium, the Law of 1935 may require that either Dutch or French be used, or may permit the party residing in Belgium to request a change of language (especially when that party is a natural person).

Popularity of and approach to arbitration

1.16 Arbitration is becoming increasingly popular as an alternative to court proceedings in Belgium, especially in international commercial contracts and business relationships. This is typically the case for disputes relating to cooperation and services agreements, transfers of shares, post-acquisition issues, commercial contracts (distribution, agency, franchising), and construction-related disputes.

1.17 The vast majority of domestic commercial disputes are still brought before the courts; however, as arbitration becomes better known among potential users, interest in its advantages is gradually increasing. In certain sectors (eg the travel sector, where an arbitration commission for consumer disputes has been set up by the government) arbitration has become the norm.

1.18 This evolution has been embraced and stimulated by both the government and the legislature, most notably with the unanimous adoption of a new state-of-the-art arbitration law in 2013. In its proposal to the Parliament, the government expressly indicated that: 'By adopting the majority of the Model Law, often with the exact wording, in the BCCP, Belgium wishes to present itself as a country open to arbitration, in particular to international arbitration, and as a country with a progressive law on arbitration.'[9] In addition, the government announced that it would actively promote the new BLA to possible stakeholders.[10]

1.19 While many arbitration proceedings in Belgium are conducted in either Dutch or French, the increase in arbitrations with an international element has led to a steady increase in the use of English as the language of arbitration in Belgium. The permitted use of English also explains why more and more domestic commercial disputes are arbitrated, as this is a neutral language when the parties come from different linguistic areas within Belgium.

1.20 The vast majority of arbitration proceedings with an international element take place in Brussels. The only other notable venue is Antwerp, where the presence of the Port of Antwerp gives rise to some arbitration of maritime and transport disputes. Brussels is also a popular choice for domestic arbitration proceedings, although other Belgian cities are chosen as the seat as well.

1.21 Generally speaking, Belgian courts have adopted a favourable approach to arbitration. As discussed in more detail in the following commentary, courts may act as appointing

[8] BCCP, art 1703(1).

[9] *Travaux préparatoires*, DOC (Ch) 53 2743/001, p 6.

[10] *Travaux préparatoires*, DOC (Ch) 53 2743/003, p 8.

authorities, generally enforce arbitration agreements, and provide support before and during arbitration proceedings when needed. In addition, they usually apply grounds for the annulment of arbitral awards with moderation. It is to be expected that the clear and unequivocal pro-arbitration stance underlying the 2013 revision of the BLA, and the centralization of all arbitration-related disputes before the Courts of First Instance of Antwerp, Brussels, Ghent, Liège, and Mons will increase the efficiency of court support of arbitration proceedings taking place in Belgium.

Finally, an increased interest in arbitration can be also seen at the level of the Brussels bar. In **1.22** 2010, the French-speaking section of the Brussels bar amended its professional and ethical rules to lift the traditional and long-standing ban on preparatory contact with witnesses for both domestic and international arbitration disputes. The Dutch-speaking section of the Brussels bar—which had already lifted this ban for international disputes—has since lifted this ban for domestic arbitration disputes as well. While in practice Belgian attorneys already engaged in preparatory contact with witnesses, this modification was welcome. Not only did it put the professional and ethical rules in line with international arbitration practice, and Belgian attorneys on a level playing field with their opponents from other jurisdictions, it also underlined and raised awareness among practitioners of the wider possibilities of taking oral evidence in arbitration as opposed to court. Indeed, the procedure for presenting oral evidence in Belgian courts is burdensome and inefficient (for instance, witnesses are examined by the judge, not by counsel, and no cross-examination is allowed). Furthermore, oral evidence is not admitted in civil disputes (save for a few exceptions). Hence, the use of oral evidence in civil or commercial court litigation is almost non-existent. Arbitration is therefore seen as an effective alternative, as it allows almost unrestricted use of oral evidence if the parties have not agreed to exclude it.

1.2 Commencing the Arbitration

1.2.1 Disputes brought before local courts despite the existence of an arbitration agreement

Courts are required to assist arbitral proceedings by declining jurisdiction when a party **1.23** commences court proceedings despite the existence of an arbitration agreement. Such proceedings may be initiated in error, for asserted lack of validity of the arbitration agreement, or for purely dilatory or strategic reasons.

Pursuant to article 1682(1) BCCP, a court 'seized of a dispute which is the subject of an arbi- **1.24** tration agreement shall, at the request of a party, declare that it has no jurisdiction, unless, in relation to the dispute, the agreement is not valid or has come to an end. To be admissible, this objection must be raised before any other plea or defense'. In other words, when a party raises a timely challenge to the court's jurisdiction on the basis of a valid arbitration agreement for a dispute falling within the scope of the arbitration agreement, the court must decline jurisdiction and refer the parties to arbitration. This is in line with the provisions of Article II(3) of the 1958 New York Convention.

First, it is important to note that Belgian courts will not raise the issue of the existence of an **1.25** arbitration agreement *ex officio*. It is indeed the party wishing to rely on an arbitration agreement that must take the initiative to contest the jurisdiction of the state court by raising an *exceptio arbitri*.

1.26 Second, article 1682(1) BCCP specifies that the objection to the court's jurisdiction must be raised *in limine litis*, ie at the outset of the proceedings. This requirement is met when the objection is raised during the first submissions and prior to any defence on the merits of the case. A failure to raise a timely objection will be considered a waiver of the arbitration agreement and preclude a party from invoking the *exceptio arbitri* later in the proceedings. In assessing an objection to its jurisdiction, the court will assess the validity of the arbitration agreement, and ensure that the dispute falls within its scope.

1.27 Finally, commencing court proceedings despite the existence of an arbitration agreement will not delay the arbitration proceedings. An application to the state courts does not prevent arbitration proceedings from being initiated or continued and an arbitral award from being rendered.[11] In the case of parallel proceedings, any conflict between a judgment and an award will have to be addressed at the stage of enforcement.

Validity of the arbitration agreement

1.28 Article 1681 BCCP defines an arbitration agreement as 'an agreement by the parties to submit to arbitration all or certain disputes which have arisen or which may arise between them in respect of a defined legal relationship, whether contractual or not'.

1.29 For an arbitration agreement to be valid, the parties must have expressed a clear intention to submit their dispute to arbitration. Furthermore, they must have been capable of concluding an agreement and the subject matter must be arbitrable.

1.30 **Intention to arbitrate** The BLA does not contain any formal validity requirements. For the validity and existence of an arbitration agreement, the BLA requires only that the parties have expressed a clear intention to arbitrate. While a written arbitration agreement is to be recommended from an evidentiary perspective, an oral arbitration agreement is in principle valid. In the event of a dispute, the existence of an oral arbitration agreement may, for example, be proven by witnesses.[12]

1.31 Particular issues may arise when an arbitration clause is contained in a party's general conditions. Generally, Belgian courts tend to enforce such clauses provided that (a) the parties had—or could have had—knowledge of the contents of the general conditions, and (b) they accepted them, even if implicitly by performance of the agreement.[13]

1.32 In addition to the commitment to arbitrate, parties are free to provide for other procedural matters in their arbitration agreement, and to determine the content and modalities thereof as they see fit.

1.33 **Capacity** The parties must have capacity to conclude a valid arbitration agreement (subjective arbitrability). In this regard, article 1676(2) BCCP provides that 'Anyone who has the capacity or power to conclude a settlement agreement may conclude an arbitration agreement'. Article 2045 of the Belgian Civil Code (hereinafter BCC) provides that a person may conclude a settlement agreement, provided that he is competent to dispose of the objects included in the settlement agreement. In practice, any adult (ie natural person above the age of 18) and any validly constituted and represented legal person may conclude an arbitration agreement,

---

[11] BCCP, art 1682(2).

[12] *Travaux préparatoires*, DOC (Ch) 53 2743/001, p 15.

[13] For a discussion of relevant case law on this issue, see H Van Houtte, K Cox, and S Cools, 'Overzicht van Rechtspraak: Arbitrage (1972–2006)' (2007) 2 *Tijdschrift voor Belgisch Handelsrecht* para 39.

unless specific circumstances exist. Notable exceptions are public legal entities.[14] However, pursuant to article 1676(3) BCCP, public legal entities are also authorized to conclude an arbitration agreement, provided that it relates to the settlement of contractual disputes. In this situation, any conditions applicable to the public entity's capacity to enter into the underlying agreement will equally apply to the arbitration agreement. In addition, public legal entities may be authorized by law or royal decree to conclude arbitration agreements relating to matters other than contractual disputes, subject to any applicable conditions.

Arbitrability of subject matter The arbitration agreement must relate to matters that may be submitted to arbitration (objective arbitrability). Pursuant to article 1676(1) BCCP, 'All claims involving an economic interest may be the object of arbitration'.[15] Claims of a non-economic nature that may be resolved by a settlement agreement may also be the object of arbitration.[16] In practice, most commercial disputes are arbitrable, unless specifically excluded by law.[17] As will be discussed in more detail in the following commentary, statutory exceptions may exist for disputes in relation to certain insurance contracts governed by Belgian law, disputes relating to the termination of exclusive distribution agreements when the territory covers (part of) Belgium, and agency agreements when the agent has his principal place of business in Belgium. **1.34**

In a number of recent decisions, the Belgian Supreme Court has interpreted Article II(3) of the New York Convention, which provides that courts must refer to arbitration disputes that are the subject of an arbitration agreement, 'unless it finds that the said agreement is null and void, inoperative or incapable of being performed', and has held that the law to which the court must refer in order to determine whether or not a dispute is arbitrable is the *lex fori*, ie the law of the state before whose courts the arbitrability is challenged.[18] **1.35**

Arbitration agreements regarding labour-related issues may only be concluded after the dispute has arisen. Prior arbitration agreements regarding such issues are null and void *ipso jure*.[19] **1.36**

The issue of objective arbitrability may also arise at the enforcement stage, when an application is made to the local court to enforce or to set aside an award. When seised of an application *ex parte* to grant *exequatur* to an award, Belgian courts will ascertain *ex officio* whether the subject matter in dispute is arbitrable under Belgian law.[20] Lack of arbitrability is also a ground for setting aside an award under article 1717(3)(b)(i) BCCP (see paragraph 1.128). **1.37**

Separability Finally, it is worth noting that the validity of the arbitration clause must be determined separately from the validity of the main agreement, as the arbitration clause is entirely autonomous from the underlying commercial agreement. This principle of separability of the arbitration agreement is set forth in article 1690 BCCP, which provides in **1.38**

[14] BCC, art 2045, third para.
[15] BCCP, art 1676(1).
[16] BCCP, art 1676(2).
[17] BCCP, art 1676(4).
[18] Supreme Court [2004] (2005) *Tijdschrift voor Belgisch Handelsrecht* 488, w note M Traest and note P Hollander; Supreme Court [2006] (2007) *Tijdschrift voor Belgisch Handelsrecht* 889, w note L Mertens; and Supreme Court [2010] (2010–11) *Rechtskundig Weekblad* 1087–91, w note D Mertens; Supreme Court [2012] (2012) 04 *Arresten van het Hof van Cassatie* 886.
[19] BCCP, art 1676(5).
[20] BCCP, art 1721(1)(b)(i).

relevant part that: 'An arbitration clause which forms part of a contract shall be treated as an agreement independent of the other terms of the contract. A decision by the arbitral tribunal that the contract is null and void shall not entail *ipso jure* the invalidity of the arbitration clause.' In other words, unless the arbitration clause itself is void, it remains valid even if the underlying agreement is null and void or has been terminated.

1.39 In practice, Belgian courts tend to refer the parties to arbitration as soon as they are satisfied that the parties intended to submit to arbitration, unless the subject matter of the dispute is not arbitrable under Belgian law.

Scope of the arbitration agreement

1.40 Once the validity of the arbitration agreement has been established, another issue that may arise is whether a specific dispute falls within its scope. This may require interpretation of the arbitration agreement. While older case law suggested that arbitration agreements are to be interpreted restrictively (on the consideration that arbitration was an exceptional form of dispute resolution), it is now generally agreed that the essential question lies not in whether or not a strict or liberal interpretation is required, but rather what the parties intended. This may require an assessment beyond the wording of the arbitration agreement itself, in order to give full effect to the will of the parties.[21]

1.41 In practice, Belgian courts will generally enforce the arbitration agreement and refer the parties to arbitration if the parties' intention to submit their disputes to arbitration is apparent. Consequently, when satisfied that the parties to a contract intended to arbitrate disputes arising out of or in relation to it, courts will, to the extent possible, even give effect to pathological clauses, for example clauses referring to a non-existent arbitration institution or arbitration rules.

1.42 Furthermore, in the interest of legal certainty, courts will be cautious in limiting the scope of the arbitration agreement to certain types of disputes arising out of the agreement, unless the parties have included a clear and unambiguous provision to that effect.[22]

1.2.2 The role of courts in appointing arbitrators

1.43 At the early stages of arbitration proceedings seated in Brussels, the local courts may assist the parties in various ways in the constitution of the arbitral tribunal.

1.44 As indicated here, party autonomy underlies the BLA, and is apparent in the method of selection of an arbitral tribunal. Pursuant to article 1685(2) BCCP, parties may determine the procedure for selecting a sole arbitrator or panel in their arbitration agreement. While they may even name an arbitrator, this is not recommended, as the unavailability of that person might render the arbitration clause inoperable. Parties may designate a third party as appointing authority (often by reference to the rules of an arbitration institution), or agree on this issue once the dispute has arisen. Article 1684(1) BCCP requires only that the arbitral tribunal be composed of an uneven number of arbitrators.[23] If the parties have not

[21] See G Keutgen and G-A Dal, *L'arbitrage en droit belge et international—tome 1* (2nd edn, Brussels, Bruylandt, 2006) 180–1.

[22] See Keutgen and Dal (n 21) 180–1.

[23] Where the parties designated an even number of arbitrators, an additional arbitrator will be added to the arbitral tribunal (BCCP, art 1684(2)). In the absence of an agreement on the number of arbitrators, a three-member tribunal will be appointed (BCCP art 1684(3)).

agreed on any alternative procedure for the selection of arbitrators, each party will appoint an arbitrator, and those arbitrators will subsequently jointly appoint the president.[24]

Although the appointment process is often set out by the parties in the arbitration agreement or by reference to a set of arbitration rules, situations may arise in which the parties require assistance from the courts in the appointment of arbitrators. For these situations, the BLA has attributed specific competences to the president of the Court of First Instance of Brussels.[25] **1.45**

When a party, an appointing authority, or the party-appointed arbitrators fail to appoint the arbitrator(s) in accordance with the procedure agreed upon, either party may file a request to the president of the Court of First Instance to proceed with the appointment.[26] This is also the case when the parties have not agreed on a procedure for the selection of arbitrators and one of the parties fails to appoint an arbitrator within a month following the notice; when the party-appointed arbitrators fail to agree on the appointment of a president of the arbitral tribunal within one month of the appointment of the second arbitrator; or when parties fail to agree on the composition of the arbitral tribunal in a situation with more than three arbitrators.[27] A particular situation in which court intervention may be required involves multi-party disputes: in principle, unless a different mechanism has been agreed between the parties, parties on the 'same side' are to jointly appoint one arbitrator. Failing an agreement among these parties on 'their' arbitrator, and in the event that the parties (or rules to which they have referred) do not cover this situation, either party may apply to the president of the Court of First Instance to proceed with the appointment. **1.46**

A request to appoint an arbitrator is brought before the president of the Court of First Instance by means of a unilateral request. The president will decide as in summary proceedings.[28] When appointing an arbitrator, the president of the Court of First Instance takes into account all capacities required in the light of the facts and circumstances of the case as well as all relevant considerations to ensure the arbitrator's impartiality and independence.[29] The president's decision to appoint an arbitrator is final. However, as a matter of exception, a decision not to appoint an arbitrator is susceptible to appeal before the Court of Appeal.[30] **1.47**

It is important to note that an appointment decision of the president of the Court does not limit the arbitral tribunal in determining its own jurisdiction in application of the *competence-competence* principle.[31] Nor does it prevent the parties from contesting jurisdiction, or from bringing a challenge against a member of the arbitral tribunal in accordance with the applicable arbitration rules or legal provisions. **1.48**

By entrusting decisions regarding the appointment of arbitrators to the president of the Court of First Instance and limiting appeal against such decisions to negative decisions only, the BLA provides an efficient support mechanism for the appointment of the arbitral **1.49**

---

24 BCCP, art 1684(3) with BCCP, art 1685(3)(a).
25 BCCP, art 1680(1).
26 BCCP, art 1685(3) and (4).
27 BCCP, art 1685(3)(a) and (c).
28 BCCP, art 1680(1).
29 BCCP, art 1685(5).
30 BCCP, art 1680(1), third and fourth paras. As indicated in para 1.48, the possibility to appeal arbitration-related court decisions was abolished by the 2013 revision of the BLA.
31 BCCP, art 1690(1).

tribunal. This reduces the potential for parties to stall the proceedings by refusing to appoint an arbitrator, while still allowing parties to raise genuine jurisdictional concerns before the arbitral tribunal. Considering that arbitration rules generally provide for an appointment mechanism and appointing authority, this support mechanism is particularly useful for ad hoc arbitrations. However, it may also turn out to be useful when a third party has been entrusted with making the appointment, but fails to do so within a reasonable timeframe.

1.2.3 Role of courts in resolving jurisdictional questions

1.50 The BLA expressly sets out the *competence-competence* principle. Pursuant to article 1690(1) BCCP: 'The arbitral tribunal may rule on its own jurisdiction, including any objections with respect to the existence or validity of the arbitration agreement'. Any objection against the arbitral tribunal's jurisdiction must be raised *in limine litis*.[32]

1.51 The arbitral tribunal's power to assess its own jurisdiction is subject to judicial control only at the annulment phase. Pursuant to article 1690(4) BCCP: 'The decision by which the arbitral tribunal declares that it has jurisdiction may only be challenged . . . together with the final award and by the same procedure . . . '. The notion of final award should be understood as an award finally disposing of one or more of the issues in dispute. According to article 1717(1) BCCP, a request for setting aside the award 'is admissible only if the award can no longer be contested before the arbitrators'. This may be the case when the arbitral tribunal issues a partial award in which it finally decides on a number of issues, but retains jurisdiction to deal with the remaining issues in later awards. As this partial award may no longer be contested before the arbitrators, it is susceptible to annulment, and a party contesting the arbitral tribunal's decision to assume jurisdiction is allowed to contest this decision from this moment onwards.

1.52 When, on the other hand, the arbitral tribunal bifurcates the arbitration proceedings and deals only with the issue of jurisdiction in a first partial award, the award on jurisdiction may not be contested until a later stage.

1.53 In the event that the arbitral tribunal declares itself without jurisdiction, the arbitration proceedings will be terminated. Either party may, however, apply to the Court of First Instance, which may review the merits of the arbitral tribunal's decision that it lacks jurisdiction.[33] Should the court find that the arbitral tribunal does have jurisdiction, this decision has the authority of *res judicata*, which binds the arbitral tribunal, and the arbitration will resume.[34]

1.54 As discussed previously, Belgian courts will refer a dispute to arbitration at the request of a party, unless the arbitration agreement is either invalid with regard to the dispute or has ceased to exist.[35] In application of the *competence-competence* principle, a finding by the courts that the arbitration agreement is valid does not, however, preclude the arbitral tribunal from ruling on its own jurisdiction, if this is still contested.

1.2.4 Role of courts in enjoining arbitration

1.55 Belgian law does not provide any grounds to apply for measures, such as anti-suit injunctions, prohibiting another party from starting or continuing legal proceedings abroad.

[32] BCCP, art 1690(2).
[33] BCCP, art 1690(4).
[34] See Keutgen and Dal (n 21) 330.
[35] BCCP, art 1682(1).

Furthermore, Belgian courts will generally refuse to uphold anti-suit injunctions ordered by foreign courts. No case law on this issue has been reported, with one notable exception. In 1989, the president of the Court of First Instance of Brussels held that a US issued anti-suit injunction could not be upheld in Belgium, as this would constitute a violation of Belgian public policy.[36]

While there have been no cases published in which Belgian courts have had to decide specifically on applications to enjoin arbitration, the outcome is likely to be the same. Anti-suit injunctions in favour of arbitration are in any case not permitted between EU Member States. In *West Tankers*,[37] the European Court of Justice held that anti-suit injunctions issued by a court of a European Member State on the basis of the existence of an arbitration agreement are incompatible with the Brussels I Regulation,[38] when this would prevent the court of another EU Member State from exercising the jurisdiction conferred on it by the Regulation. **1.56**

1.2.5 Role of courts in joinder, consolidation, and intervention

Parties may be confronted with a situation in which multiple claims that are very closely connected are brought before different instances. Such connection may exist when one claimant wishes to bring multiple claims against a counterparty and/or when multiple parties are involved on either side. As this could potentially lead to conflicting decisions, most procedural laws allow courts to join such parallel proceedings in litigation. The question is to what extent the courts could play a similar role for the joinder of arbitration proceedings. **1.57**

First, joinder is not possible when one proceeding is brought before an arbitral tribunal and the other before a state court, and at least one party to the court proceedings is not a party to the arbitration agreement, unless the parties to the arbitration agreement waive their right to arbitrate and agree to joinder before the court. This is a consequence of the principle that, pursuant to article 1165 BCC, contracts (including arbitration agreements) bind only their signatories and cannot be extended to third parties. Under Belgian law, the extension of an arbitration agreement to non-signatories would be possible only under such mechanisms as consent by conduct, assignment of contract, subrogation, or legal succession of parties. **1.58**

Second, the BLA does not contain any specific provisions regarding the consolidation of related proceedings that are brought before two arbitration tribunals. Some arbitration rules do, however, provide for this situation. The new CEPANI rules that entered into force on 1 January 2013 deal, in articles 10 to 13, with issues relating to multi-party and complex arbitration proceedings. Article 13, entitled 'Consolidation', sets out the conditions under which the Appointments Committee or Chairman of CEPANI may, at the request of either a party or of the arbitral tribunal, order the joinder of different arbitration proceedings when one or more contracts with a CEPANI arbitration clause give rise to separate—yet related or indivisible—arbitration proceedings. Such a request will be granted when all parties agree to consolidation as well as to the manner in which such consolidation shall occur. Failing such agreement, the chairman or the appointments committee will decide on the joinder with **1.59**

36 President of the Court of First Instance Brussels [1989] (1990–91) *Rechtskundig Weekblad* 676.

37 Case C-185/07 *Allianz SpA (formerly Riunione Adriatica di Sicurta SpA) v Generali Assicurazioni Generali SpA/West Tankers Inc* [2009] ECR I-663.

38 Council Regulation (EC) 44/2001 on jurisdiction and the recognition and enforcement of judgments in civil and commercial matters [2001] OJ L012/1–23.

particular attention to (a) whether or not the parties have excluded the possibility of joinder in their agreement; (b) whether the claims in the different proceedings have been made on the basis of the same arbitration agreement or—when based on different arbitration agreements—whether the different agreements are compatible; and (c) whether the proceedings involve the same parties and relate to disputes arising out of the same legal relationship. Further elements that will be taken into account are the progress made in the different arbitration proceedings (notably regarding the constitution of the arbitral tribunal) and the place of arbitration provided for in the different arbitration agreements. In making this decision, the appointments committee or the chairman will take into account the provisions on the appointment of arbitrators. Unless the parties have agreed otherwise, no consolidation may, however, be ordered if any decision regarding preliminary measures, admissibility, or the merits of the claim has already been made.

1.60 As discussed here, the BLA gives the president of the Court of First Instance a role in assisting the parties with the appointment of arbitrators, which is in many ways similar to the role of an arbitral institution. The question therefore arises of whether—although not explicitly provided for—the president of the Court of First Instance would (similarly to the case for the arbitration institution under, for example, the CEPANI Rules and in the light of the underlying principles of the BLA) also have the power to order joinder. No case law on this issue has been published to date, and no provision in this regard was included in the BLA as a result of the 2013 revision.

1.61 To ensure efficient resolution of related disputes among multiple parties, the BLA does provide for the possibility of intervention by third parties in the arbitral proceedings, on the initiative of the third party itself or of the parties in dispute. Any affected third party may address a written request to intervene in the arbitral proceedings to the arbitral tribunal, which shall communicate this request to the parties.[39] Also, a party involved in the arbitration proceedings may call upon a third party to intervene in the proceedings.[40]

1.62 In both situations, the intervention of a third party requires an arbitration agreement between the third party and the original parties to the dispute, as well as the unanimous consent of the arbitral tribunal.[41] The BLA does not provide for appeal before the courts when an arbitral tribunal refuses the intervention of a third party or cannot agree unanimously.

1.3 During the Arbitration

1.3.1 Role of courts in ruling on challenges to arbitrators

1.63 One of the cornerstones of an efficient justice system is the fundamental principle that disputes are settled by an independent and impartial judge. As part of the judicial nature of their role, the same applies to arbitrators. For this reason, article 1686(1) BCCP imposes a duty on arbitrators to disclose all relevant circumstances raising justifiable doubts as to their impartiality or independence, both before their appointment and throughout the proceedings.

[39] BCCP, art 1709(1).
[40] BCCP, art 1709(2).
[41] BCCP, art 1709(3).

When justifiable doubts exist as to an arbitrator's impartiality or independence, or when an arbitrator does not possess the qualities required by the parties' agreement, a party may bring a challenge.[42] Pursuant to article 1686(2) BCCP, a party may bring a challenge only for reasons of which it becomes aware *after* the appointment has been made. In other words, reasons for challenge known to a party at the pre-appointment stage (eg as a result of an arbitrator's disclosure in a statement of impartiality and independence) must be raised immediately at that stage. A failure to do so precludes that party from invoking such reasons as a ground for challenge after the establishment of the arbitral tribunal. **1.64**

Parties may agree on a challenge procedure.[43] Most often, this is done by reference to institutional arbitration rules. When the parties have agreed on a challenge procedure, the BLA precludes them from applying to the state courts, in order to prevent dilatory manoeuvres. In deviation from Article 13 of the Model Law, the BLA only permits parties to turn to the state courts for assistance in the challenge of arbitrators when no agreement regarding a challenging procedure exists.[44] This is the case for ad hoc arbitration, or when the parties have referred to rules that do not deal with challenges without specifically including a challenge procedure in their agreement. In these cases the BLA provides for a two-tier procedure in article 1687(2) BCCP. **1.65**

Within 15 days of becoming aware of the constitution of the arbitral tribunal, or after becoming aware of circumstances that may constitute a ground for challenge of an arbitrator, a party that wishes to challenge the arbitrator must send a written notice setting out the reasons for such challenge to the arbitrator in question as well as to the other members of the arbitral tribunal (if any). **1.66**

If the arbitrator in question does not resign within ten days after receiving a challenge notice, or if the other party does not accept the challenge, the challenging party will need to seek the assistance of the president of the Court of First Instance, again within ten days. To this end, the challenging party must summon the arbitrator in question, as well as the other parties, before the president of the Court. When an application to challenge is made to the Court of First Instance, the court will determine whether there are grounds to uphold the challenge. This decision is not subject to appeal.[45] Moreover, an application to challenge an arbitrator before the president of the Court neither suspends the arbitral proceedings *ipso jure*, nor prevents the arbitral tribunal from issuing an arbitral award. It is up to the arbitral tribunal to assess whether such a suspension would be necessary in the light of the relevant facts and circumstances.[46] **1.67**

The BLA provides for a similar procedure in situations where an arbitrator becomes *de jure* or *de facto* unable to perform his functions or fails to complete his mission without undue delay for any other reason. In this case, the arbitrator's mission ends on agreement of the parties, or when the arbitrator withdraws within the conditions set out by article 1685(5) BCCP.[47] In the case of disagreement between the parties regarding such a withdrawal, however, either party may summon the other party and the arbitrator before the president of the Court of **1.68**

42 BCCP, art 1686(2).
43 BCCP, art 1687(1).
44 *Travaux préparatoires*, DOC (Ch) 53 2743/001, pp 19–20.
45 BCCP, art 1680(2). See also *Travaux préparatoires*, DOC (Ch) 53 2743/001, p 14.
46 BCCP, art 1687(2). See also *Travaux préparatoires*, DOC (Ch) 53 2743/001, pp 19–20.
47 BCCP, art 1688(1).

First Instance, who will decide in accordance with article 1680(2) BCCP. Again, any such decision is final and not subject to appeal.

1.69 In the case of a resignation or successful challenge, the arbitrator will be replaced in accordance with the rules governing the initial appointment.[48] If this is not possible,[49] either party may make a request for the appointment of a substitute arbitrator to the president of the Court of First Instance, in accordance with article 1680(1) BCCP.[50] Once a substitute arbitrator has been appointed, the arbitral tribunal will, after consulting the parties, decide whether (parts of the) proceedings will have to be redone. However, any partial final awards or decisions taken cannot be revoked.[51]

1.70 In addition to assisting parties, courts may also assist arbitrators. In principle, once the arbitrator has accepted his mission he may not withdraw.[52] He may, however, apply to the president of the Court of First Instance to relieve him of his duties in the light of particular circumstances (such as the non-payment of his fees). The decision of the president of the Court of First Instance is not open to appeal.[53]

1.3.2 Role of courts in granting provisional relief in support of arbitration

1.71 Article 1691 BCCP gives arbitrators the power to order interim or protective measures, with the exception of the conservatory attachment of goods, which remains within the exclusive jurisdiction of the courts.

1.72 This provision does not, however, prevent the parties from bringing an action for interim or protective measures before the state courts, as the BLA also gives the courts power to grant provisional relief in support of arbitration proceedings.[54] Parties may, moreover, agree to restrict the possibility to order interim measures to courts only.[55] An application to the courts for interim or provisional relief is not considered to be a waiver of arbitration.[56]

1.73 Applications for interim or provisional relief are brought before the president of the Court of First Instance, or—in matters falling within the competence of the Commercial Court—before the president of the Commercial Court acting in summary proceedings (*référé/kortgeding*).[57] Pursuant to article 1698 BCCP, the president before whom the claim for interim or conservatory relief is brought, has the same powers as he has in relation to court proceedings, regardless of whether the arbitration is seated in Belgium or abroad. The president is to exercise this power in accordance with its own procedures[58] and with due consideration of the specific features of arbitration.[59] The president of the court may award interim or provisional relief within a timeframe appropriate under the circumstances, in case of urgency.[60] To this

48 BCCP, art 1689(1).
49 eg if the challenged arbitrator was named in the arbitration agreement, or if one of the parties refuses to cooperate in the appointment of an arbitrator.
50 BCCP, art 1689(2).
51 BCCP, art 1689(3).
52 BCCP, art 1685(7).
53 BCCP, art 1680(2).
54 BCCP, art 1683; BCCP, art 1691.
55 BCCP, art 1691.
56 BCCP, art 1683.
57 BCCP, art 1698.
58 These can be found in BCCP, arts 1035–1041.
59 BCCP, art 1698.
60 BCCP, art 584.

end, a party must demonstrate that, if no decision is made in the short term, its interests will suffer considerable harm, and that a regular application to the court (or in this case arbitral tribunal) will not lead to a timely solution. However, if the president finds—if necessary *ex officio*—that the matter is not urgent, he will dismiss the request.

The need to apply for interim relief to the courts may arise at an early stage in the proceedings. Following the arbitral tribunal's constitution, the court's power to grant provisional relief continues to exist in parallel with the tribunal's power.[61] Once the arbitral tribunal is appointed and in place, Belgian courts will in practice adopt a cautious approach to ordering interim relief, unless specific facts and circumstances warrant their intervention. This might be the case in situations of urgency, when it would be impractical or even impossible to convene a session of the arbitral tribunal in order to have emergency protective measures ordered and enforced in time. Furthermore, bearing in mind the lack of *imperium* of an arbitral tribunal, parties may need to turn to state courts in order to obtain immediately enforceable provisional measures. **1.74**

Courts may only order provisional or conservatory relief.[62] The final decision on the merits falls under the exclusive jurisdiction of the arbitral tribunal. Any provisional relief ordered prior to the constitution of the arbitral tribunal will in principle remain in force following the appointment of the arbitral tribunal. If the underlying facts have changed, however, a party may always apply to the arbitral tribunal (or, depending on the circumstances, the court) for new provisional relief or for a modification of the measures imposed.[63] **1.75**

Finally, as indicated here, the arbitral tribunal itself has the power to order interim measures. Unless the parties have agreed on any limitations, the arbitral tribunal can order the same relief as state judges.[64] The arbitral tribunal may require the party requesting the interim measure to provide appropriate security,[65] or impose on either party the duty to disclose any material change in circumstances relevant for the interim measures ordered.[66] One particular tool given to arbitrators under the BLA to ensure compliance is the power to impose a penalty on a non-complying party (*astreinte/dwangsom*), in accordance with the general provisions of articles 1385*bis* to *octies* BCCP.[67] The arbitral tribunal may order a party to pay a predetermined fine per infraction, or for each time period of non-compliance (eg per hour, day, or month). Such '*astreintes*' may not be imposed to ensure compliance with decisions ordering the payment of sums of money. Any difficulties that might arise in enforcing the *astreinte* against a party located in Belgium fall within the power of the attachments judge, a special judge linked to the Court of First Instance. **1.76**

Decisions on provisional relief by the arbitral tribunal, whether in the form of an order or an award, are binding and may be declared enforceable by the Court of First Instance. As the **1.77**

---

[61] BCCP, art 1683. It is worth noting, however, that for all interim measures or provisional measures relating to evidence, a party must obtain prior leave of the arbitral tribunal pursuant to BCCP, art 1708.

[62] BCCP, art 1683.

[63] In deviation of the Model Law, parties may always apply to the arbitral tribunal for a modification, suspension, or withdrawal of an interim measure, regardless of whether it was ordered by the arbitral tribunal itself or the (president of the) court, pursuant to BCCP, art 1692 (see *Travaux préparatoires*, DOC (Ch) 53 2743/001, p 25).

[64] BCCP, art 1691, second para.

[65] BCCP, art 1693.

[66] BCCP, art 1694.

[67] BCCP, art 1713(7).

enforcement of interim measures occurs at the risk of the requesting party,[68] the court may, however, require appropriate security.[69] Recognition and enforcement of an interim measure ordered by the arbitral tribunal may only be refused if, after a *prima facie* review, the court finds that one of the grounds to refuse enforcement of arbitral awards listed in paragraphs (i) to (v) of article 1721(1)(a) BCCP justifies a refusal; that an order of the arbitral tribunal to provide appropriate security has not been complied with; that the measure has been withdrawn or suspended by the arbitral tribunal or by the competent court; or that the one of the grounds listed in article 1721(1)(b) BCCP applies to the recognition and enforcement of the interim measure in question.[70]

1.3.2 Role of courts in compelling testimony and evidence

1.78 The arbitral tribunal has the power to determine the admissibility of evidence as well as its weight, unless the parties have agreed otherwise.[71]

1.79 While the taking of evidence is generally in the hands of the arbitral tribunal, state courts may grant evidentiary assistance. This is part of the courts' power to order provisional or conservatory relief in support of arbitration proceedings. It is worth recalling that an interlocutory application to the court to obtain provisional relief to obtain certain testimony or evidence is not inconsistent with the arbitration agreement, nor does it imply a waiver of the right to arbitrate.[72]

1.80 Court intervention may in particular be useful prior to the constitution of the arbitral tribunal, for example to obtain measures to preserve evidence that might otherwise disappear. Also during the arbitration proceedings, parties may file an application to the president of the Court of First Instance to take all measures necessary for the gathering of evidence. Given the arbitral tribunal's competence to determine the admissibility and weight of evidence, an application for court assistance in matters of gathering evidence requires prior approval of the arbitral tribunal.[73] The arbitral tribunal may refuse consent if it is of the opinion that the intended measures are inadmissible or irrelevant, or may impose a time limit within which the application to the courts must be made.

1.81 Court assistance may, in particular, be useful for certain types of measures falling outside the scope of the arbitral tribunal's power:

- First, as a matter of exception, arbitrators may not decide on claims regarding forgery of authentic deeds.[74] In this case, either party may file an application before the president of the Court of First Instance for a ruling. An application regarding the forgery of an authentic deed suspends the arbitration proceedings *ipso jure* until the arbitral tribunal receives notification of the final decision on the matter.[75] The decision of the president of the Court of Appeal, acting in summary proceedings, is final and not susceptible to appeal.[76] The

68 BCCP, art 1695.
69 BCCP, art 1696 (see *Travaux préparatoires*, DOC (Ch) 53 2743/001, p 26).
70 BCCP, art 1697.
71 BCCP, art 1700(3).
72 BCCP, art 1683.
73 BCCP, art 1680(4) with BCCP, art 1708.
74 BCCP, art 1700(5). According to BCCP, arts 1317ff, authentic deeds are documents drawn up by public officials in a legal format, which constitute full proof of the facts contained therein.
75 BCCP, art 1700(5).
76 BCCP, art 1680(4).

arbitral tribunal does have the power to rule on claims regarding forgery of any documents other than authentic deeds.[77]

- Second, unlike courts and given their lack of *imperium*, arbitral tribunals cannot order third parties to assist in gathering evidence. Consequently, court assistance may be necessary when a witness refuses to testify, or when a third party is presumed to hold a document in its possession.[78] In such cases, it is up to the arbitral tribunal to assess the need for suspension of the arbitral proceedings when allowing a party to turn to the competent court for assistance.

1.3.3 Ability of foreign practitioners to appear as counsel or arbitrator

The BLA provides for a very liberal system as to who may act as arbitrator or counsel in arbitrations with their seat in Belgium. **1.82**

First, parties are generally free to select the arbitrator of their choice, provided this person is capable of acting as an arbitrator[79] and meets the requirements of independence and impartiality. The BLA does not contain any requirements or limitations with regard to education, experience, residence, or nationality. In the light of the principle of party autonomy, parties are free to agree specific requirements for arbitrators in their agreement. This is specifically confirmed for the question of nationality: while the BLA starts from the principle of non-discrimination in the appointment of arbitrators, article 1685(1) BCCP confirms that parties are free to agree on certain exclusions based on nationality.[80] **1.83**

Second, the BLA does not contain any restrictions with regard to party representation: each party has the right to choose its representative in the arbitration proceedings. Parties may be represented either by a lawyer or by a specially empowered representative, including in-house counsel. No statutory restrictions limit foreign nationals in acting as arbitrators in Belgium. Moreover, the requirements and qualifications necessary for attorneys appearing in Belgian courts are not applicable to arbitration. Parties are therefore free to select counsel of their choice, regardless of nationality or admission to a bar or law society. **1.84**

1.3.4 Local requirements for conduct of arbitration hearings

Article 1699 BCCP subjects all arbitration proceedings to two fundamental principles: parties must be treated with equality and each party must be given a full opportunity to present its case. Within the limitations imposed by these general principles of due process and fair trial, however, the parties are free to organize the arbitral proceedings as they see fit.[81] If the **1.85**

[77] BCCP, art 1700(5).

[78] Under Belgian law parties can apply to the president of the court to obtain an order of production of this document under the conditions set out in BCCP, art 877. In principle, courts may only order production of (a) specific documents, (b) that bear proof of a pertinent fact, (c) provided there are precise, corresponding, and strong presumptions that a party has these documents in its possession. Orders for the production of broad categories of documents or American-style discovery are not available in Belgian court proceedings.

[79] Prior to the revision of 2013, BCCP, art 1680 provided that anyone capable of concluding an agreement was entitled to act as arbitrator, with the exception of minors, persons under the supervision of a legal administrator, or persons who do not enjoy full voting rights. While the revised BLA does not contain a provision in this regard, it appears that the same applies.

[80] See *Travaux préparatoires*, DOC (Ch) 53 2743/001, p 17. In practice, agreements regarding the nationality of arbitrators are rather rare. However, some institutional arbitration rules provide that the president of the arbitral tribunal shall in principle have a different nationality from the parties, in order to increase the sense of neutrality (see eg the ICC Rules, Art 13(5)).

[81] BCCP, art 1700(1).

parties have not agreed on specific procedural rules, these will be set by the arbitral tribunal.[82] The BLA contains few specific requirements in this regard.

Conduct and venue of hearings

1.86 In practice, it is the arbitral tribunal that decides, in consultation with the parties, how the actual hearing will be conducted. The chairman of the arbitral tribunal is responsible for setting the schedule for and presiding at the hearings.[83]

1.87 The arbitral tribunal must ensure that each party has a fair opportunity to substantiate its claims and to present its case.[84] Parties must submit their written arguments and corresponding evidence within the time limits agreed between the parties or set by the arbitral tribunal.[85] In case of default by a claimant, the arbitral tribunal shall terminate the arbitral proceedings, without prejudice to any counterclaim or cross-claim made by another party.[86] In case of default of a respondent, the arbitral tribunal may continue the arbitral proceedings, without, however, construing such default as an admission of the claimant's submissions.[87]

1.88 In addition to written submissions, the parties have a right to present their arguments at an oral hearing. They may, however, waive such right and agree to conduct the proceedings solely in writing.[88] If, without legitimate cause, a party that is properly summoned does not appear or does not present its case on the date fixed for the oral hearing, the arbitral tribunal may proceed on the basis of the information before it and render an award.[89]

1.89 Unless otherwise agreed by the parties, the arbitral tribunal may hold hearings and meetings at the venue it considers most appropriate, after consulting the parties.[90] The fact that the legal seat of the arbitration is Brussels does not therefore require that hearings take place there as well. For various reasons, it may be more appropriate to hold a hearing at another location. A decision to hold a hearing at a venue other than the seat has no legal consequences. Brussels remains the seat of the arbitration.

Language

1.90 While—as indicated in the preceding paragraphs—the use of languages in court proceedings in Belgium is governed by the strict rules of the Law of 1935, this law does not apply in arbitration. As expressly provided for in article 1703(1) BCCP, the parties are therefore entirely free to decide in which language or languages they wish the proceedings to take place. Failing an agreement on this point between the parties, the arbitral tribunal will make the decision.[91] In any case, the arbitral tribunal may order parties to file a translation of exhibits that are not in the language of the proceedings.[92]

---

82 BCCP, art 1700(2).
83 BCCP, art 1705(2).
84 BCCP, art 1699.
85 BCCP, art 1704(1).
86 BCCP, art 1706(a).
87 BCCP, art 1706(b).
88 BCCP, art 1705(2).
89 BCCP, art 1706(c).
90 BCCP, art 1701(1).
91 BCCP, art 1703(1).
92 BCCP, art 1704 (2).

Witnesses

Finally, the BLA does not restrict who can appear as witnesses and allows parties and arbitrators to organize the taking of evidence—including witness evidence—in the manner they consider most appropriate. The arbitral tribunal decides what weight to give the evidence submitted by the parties.[93] In arbitration proceedings, witnesses are not required to swear an oath or affirmation.[94] **1.91**

1.4 The Award

1.4.1 Mandatory rules as to form

The formal requirements for arbitral awards are found in article 1713 BCCP. An arbitral award must be rendered by an absolute majority of votes. The award must be made in writing and must be signed by the arbitrators, or at least by a majority of them. In the event that an arbitrator is unable or unwilling to sign, the reason for the omitted signature must be recorded in the award.[95] **1.92**

The award must contain the reasoning applied by the arbitrators in reaching their conclusion.[96] The parties may not relieve the arbitrators of the obligation to provide reasons, which is considered to be part of Belgian internal public policy. The BLA is stricter on this point than Article 31(2) of the Model Law, which permits parties to agree that no reasons need be given in the award. The requirement that reasons be given is not considered international public policy in Belgium, although this does not prevent the enforcement of foreign arbitral awards that are not reasoned if these are rendered in compliance with the applicable foreign law.[97] **1.93**

In addition to the decision itself, the award must contain the names and addresses of the arbitrators and the parties, and a description of the object of the dispute. The award must be dated, and the seat of the arbitration and place where the award was made must be indicated.[98] The place where an award is made generally coincides with the seat of arbitration, even though it may be physically signed elsewhere, in which case this should also be indicated. Failure to do so does not, however, expose the award to setting aside. **1.94**

Finally, although not explicitly provided in the BLA, an award should contain an operative part. This follows from the general duty of arbitrators to render an enforceable award, and taking into consideration that in many jurisdictions only the operative part (and not the reasoning) will be considered to have the authority of *res judicata*. In order for an award to be enforceable, the actual decisions of the arbitral tribunal should therefore be set out clearly (and preferably separately) in the arbitral award. **1.95**

1.4.2 Mandatory rules as to substance

Unless the parties have imposed limitations by agreement, the arbitral tribunal can order the same relief as state courts. **1.96**

---

93 BCCP, art 1700(3).
94 BCCP, art 1700(4), second para.
95 BCCP, art 1713(3).
96 BCCP, art 1713(4).
97 See *Travaux préparatoires*, DOC (Ch) 53 2743/001, p 37.
98 BCCP, art 1713(5).

1.97 Under Belgian law, the type of damages and interest that can be awarded is considered to be an issue of substantive law; hence, no specific provisions regarding this issue are included in the BLA. Under Belgian substantive law, damages are aimed at the reparation of harm incurred by a party. Punitive or exemplary damages are unlawful and in principle are not enforceable in Belgium.

1.98 In order to ensure full compensation, courts and arbitral tribunals may award interest, at the request of a party. Compound interest may be awarded under certain conditions: (a) interest must have been owed for at least one year, and (b) the parties must either have agreed that compound interest would be due, or the creditor must have requested compound interest by legal notice.[99]

1.99 The arbitral award must determine and allocate the costs of arbitration. This notion is broadly defined in the BLA: unless otherwise agreed between the parties, arbitration costs include the fees and costs of the arbitrators, defence costs, costs of the arbitration institutions, and all other costs incurred in relation to the arbitration proceedings.[100] No fixed rule of cost shifting exists. Generally, arbitral tribunals with a seat in Belgium will take into account the relative successes of the parties in their claims, but they have the discretion to consider other elements that they find relevant as well. It is worth noting that article 1022 BCCP, which limits compensation for a party's legal fees to a flat rate based on the amount in dispute, applies only to court proceedings and not to arbitration.

1.5 After the Award

1.5.1 Termination of the proceedings

1.100 Once the award is rendered, the chairman of the arbitral tribunal or sole arbitrator must notify the parties by sending them a signed original of the award, and deposit an original of the award with the registrar of the Court of First Instance of the place of the arbitration.[101] The parties may waive this deposit requirement. In institutional arbitration, the notification and deposit of the arbitral award may be taken care of by the arbitral institution.

1.101 The arbitral proceedings are terminated by the signing of the arbitral award, or by a decision of the arbitral tribunal. The latter might occur if a claimant withdraws its claim (and the respondent does not object to such withdrawal), or when both parties agree to terminate the arbitration.[102] The arbitrators' mandate terminates upon the termination of the arbitration proceedings, but this does not prevent the making of an application for correction, interpretation, or completion of the arbitral award.[103]

1.102 Unless the award violates public policy or the dispute was not capable of settlement by arbitration, and provided that the issue (or part of it) disposed of in the award may no longer be contested before the arbitrators, the notification to the parties gives the award in question the authority of *res judicata*.[104]

99 BCCP, art 1154.
100 BCCP, art 1713(6).
101 BCCP, art 1713(8).
102 BCCP, art 1717(2).
103 BCCP, art 1714(2).
104 BCCP, art 1713(9) with BCCP, arts 1714 and 1717(1).

For the sake of completeness, it is worth noting that the proceedings terminate *ipso jure* when the arbitral tribunal fails to render an award within the time period agreed between the parties or imposed by the president of the Court of First Instance, and no extension has been granted.[105] **1.103**

1.5.2 Appeal

Arbitral awards rendered in Belgium cannot be appealed before Belgian state courts, which may only hear applications to set aside an award pursuant to article 1717 BCCP. **1.104**

An appeal before a second arbitral tribunal is possible only in the rare event that the parties have expressly provided for this in their arbitration agreement.[106] Notwithstanding such an appeal, an award may be provisionally enforced if the arbitrators have so ordered. The arbitral tribunal may, however, subject any provisional enforcement of the award to the provision of security. **1.105**

Unless a different time limit has been agreed upon, an appeal against an award must be brought within one month of the notification of the award.[107] Other than for setting aside applications, the BLA does not restrict the grounds for appeal. **1.105**

In practice, it is exceptional for parties to agree on the possibility of appeal against an arbitral award, as this would undermine the greatest advantages of arbitration, the celerity and finality of resolution of the dispute. **1.107**

1.5.3 Local standards for setting aside/annulment

Arbitral awards may be challenged when the issues in dispute can no longer be contested before the arbitrators, and are therefore considered to have the authority of *res judicata*.[108] A challenge may target the award as a whole or in part, provided that this part can be separated from the rest of the award. **1.108**

An arbitral award may only be annulled on the basis of the limited grounds set out in article 1717 (3)(a) and (b) BCCP. Generally speaking, Belgian courts apply such grounds strictly. As an annulment action is not a full appeal, the court will review the arbitral award in the light of the grounds for annulment raised by the parties to determine whether there are any grounds to annul the award (or parts thereof). The court will, however, not review the merits of the dispute and may not substitute its own assessment for that of the arbitral tribunal. **1.109**

Grounds to be proven by a party

A party may request the setting aside of an arbitral award on the basis of the following grounds set out in article 1717(3)(a) BCCP. **1.110**

Lack of a valid arbitration agreement An arbitral award may be annulled if a party lacked capacity to conclude an arbitration agreement, or if no valid arbitration agreement exists.[109] **1.111**

First, an award may be annulled if the arbitral proceedings were based on an arbitration agreement concluded by a party lacking capacity to do so. As discussed previously, any **1.112**

---

105 BCCP, art 1713(2).
106 BCCP, art 1716.
107 BCCP, art 1716.
108 BCCP, art 1717(1).
109 BCCP, art 1717(3)(a)(i).

person capable of concluding a settlement agreement may conclude an arbitration agreement, which requires the capability to dispose of the objects included in the agreement.[110] Pursuant to article 1676(3) BCCP, public legal entities are also authorized to conclude an arbitration agreement, provided it relates to the settlement of contractual disputes, or—for disputes other than contractual disputes—that they are authorized by law or royal decree.

1.113 Second, the award may be annulled if no valid arbitration agreement exists. As discussed with respect to the enforcement of arbitration agreements, Belgian courts will primarily examine whether the parties had the intention to submit their disputes to arbitration. This ground also covers the question of whether the agreement to arbitrate was validly concluded under the applicable *lex contractus*. Failing a choice of law of the parties, the court will assess whether a valid arbitration agreement exists under Belgian law. For example, did both parties give their consent free of fraud, violence or error, and was it concluded before the dispute arose in a labour dispute?[111]

1.114 A party that was aware of any such ground during the course of the arbitration proceedings but that did not invoke it at the time is estopped from raising it as a ground for annulment pursuant to article 1717(5) BCCP.

1.115 **Violation of due process requirements** The award may be annulled if a party has been unable to defend its case, provided that the irregularity had a bearing on the decision.[112]

1.116 First, the award may be annulled if the parties were not properly notified of the appointment of an arbitrator, or of the arbitral proceedings. A notification requires the sending in writing of information through a means of communication or transmission that allows proof of sending.[113] Unless the parties provided differently, such notification must be addressed in accordance with article 1678 BCCP.

1.117 Second, an arbitral award may be set aside if a party has not been able to defend its case for any other reason. In this regard, it is worth recalling that article 1699 BCCP sets forth the general principle of equal treatment of the parties, and the requirement that each party be given a full opportunity to present its case. In practice, this requires that the parties must be given a reasonable opportunity to bring their case and to take a position regarding the arguments and evidence submitted by the other party. The parties must also be given a reasonable opportunity to take a position regarding all elements of procedure. Although the arbitral tribunal has the general power to decide on issues of procedure not agreed upon by the parties and has control over the conduct of the proceedings, it must consult the parties on all elements of procedure. It is sufficient that a reasonable opportunity be given: a party that does not make use of the opportunity cannot later raise this as a ground for annulment.[114]

1.118 A party that was aware of any such ground during the course of the arbitration proceedings but that did not invoke it at the time is estopped from raising it as a ground for annulment pursuant to article 1717(5) BCCP.

---

110 BCCP, art 1676(2) with BCC, art 2045.
111 BCCP, art 1676(5).
112 BCCP, art 1717(3)(a)(ii).
113 BCCP, art 1677(1)(2). This also includes electronic forms of communication or transmission.
114 See Court of Appeal Antwerp [1991] (1991) II *Pasicrisie belge* 108.

Decision *ultra petita* The arbitral award may be annulled if the arbitral tribunal exceeded either its jurisdiction[115] or its powers.[116] 1.119

An arbitral tribunal is considered to exceed its jurisdiction when it decides on an issue that was not envisaged by, or that falls outside the scope of, the arbitration agreement. This is, for example, the case when an arbitral tribunal awards more to one of the parties than it claimed, or when it decides on issues that were not raised by the parties. When the decisions that deal with matters not covered by the submission to arbitration can be separated from the other issues that were validly decided, only the former are liable to annulment. In that hypothesis, only a partial annulment of the arbitral award, limited to the parts decided *ultra petita*, will therefore be possible.[117] 1.120

A party that was aware of any such ground during the course of the arbitration proceedings but that did not invoke it at the time is estopped from raising it as a ground for annulment pursuant to article 1717(5) BCCP. 1.121

Lack of reasoning In deviation from the Model Law, an award may be set aside if it is not reasoned.[118] As previously mentioned, article 1713(4) BCCP requires an arbitral award to be motivated. The requirement to motivate any judicial act is part of Belgian internal public policy and therefore binding on arbitral tribunals with their seat in Belgium. However, this does not prevent the enforcement of a foreign arbitral award lacking reasons, if the award in question is rendered in compliance with the applicable procedural law.[119] 1.122

The reasoned award requirement is merely a formal requirement; on an application for annulment, the court must limit its review to formally ascertaining that reasons have been given. The court may not review the pertinence or sufficiency of the tribunal's reasons, or substitute its own assessment for that of the arbitral tribunal. This is implicitly confirmed in the *travaux préparatoires*, where it is stated that: 'The arbitral award will no longer be susceptible of being annulled because of contradictory provisions. Similarly, a contradiction in the motivation may not lead to the annulment of an arbitral award.'[120] 1.123

Finally, this ground does not permit the annulment of an arbitral award when the tribunal's reasoning is erroneous in fact or in law. Neither errors in law, nor errors in fact constitute grounds for annulment. 1.124

Irregularities in the composition of the arbitral tribunal or the conduct of the arbitral proceedings The award may be set aside if it was rendered by an arbitral tribunal that was irregularly constituted or if the arbitral proceedings were irregularly conducted.[121] This is the case if the composition of the arbitral tribunal or the arbitral proceedings did not comply with the parties' valid agreement or, alternatively, with the provisions of the BLA. Irregularities in the arbitral procedure may only constitute a ground for annulment to the 1.125

---

115 BCCP, art 1717(3)(a)(ii).
116 BCCP, art 1717(3)(a)(v).
117 BCCP, art 1717(3)(a)(iii).
118 BCCP, art 1717(3)(a)(iv).
119 See *Travaux préparatoires*, DOC (Ch) 53 2743/001, p 40.
120 See *Travaux préparatoires*, DOC (Ch) 53 2743/001, p 41. Before the 2013 revision, the old BCCP, art 1704(2)(j) allowed the annulment of an arbitral award that contained contradicting provisions. In the 2013 revision, however, only the lack of motivation element of the old art 1704(2)(i) was retained.
121 BCCP, art 1717(3)(a)(iv).

extent that they influenced the arbitral award. However, this limitation does not apply to an irregularity in the constitution of the arbitral tribunal.[122]

1.126 In any case, a party that was aware of any such ground during the course of the arbitration proceedings but that did not invoke it at the time, is estopped from raising it as a ground for annulment pursuant to article 1717(5) BCCP.

Grounds for setting aside that may be considered by the courts ex officio

1.127 Parties may request the setting aside of an arbitral award on the grounds set out in article 1717(3)(b) BCCP. Such grounds may be raised by the court on its own motion, on condition that the parties are given an opportunity to take a position on such grounds, in compliance with the principles of due process and fair trial. Article 1717(3)(b) BCCP lists non-arbitral disputes, violation of public policy, and fraud as grounds for annulment.

1.128 **Non-arbitrable dispute** The arbitral award may be annulled if the dispute was not arbitrable.[123] The basic rule on the objective arbitrability of disputes under Belgian law is set out in article 1676(1) BCCP, which provides that claims involving an economic interest, as well as disputes of a non-economic nature that may be the object of a settlement agreement, may be submitted to arbitration,[124] unless restrictions exist in specific legislation.[125]

1.129 Under this rule, most commercial disputes are arbitrable. This includes antitrust, intellectual property, and bankruptcy disputes, subject to the restrictions and limitations that are generally also found in other European jurisdictions, whereby the exclusive competence for certain issues that are considered essential is reserved for courts or authorities at the level of the European Union or at national level. For example, specific legislation restricting the arbitrability of disputes can be found with regard to labour law[126] and certain insurance contracts.[127]

1.130 Finally, some restrictions exist with regard to the arbitrability of disputes arising from the termination of exclusive distributorship agreements with an indefinite term. The Exclusive Distribution Law of 27 July 1961, which is of a mandatory character, sets out the conditions under which a supplier may terminate such agreements, and provides in article 4 that a distributor may bring disputes relating to the termination of an exclusive distribution agreement with territory in Belgium (or parts thereof) before the Belgian courts, which are to apply the mandatory provisions of Belgian law only. Unless parties have concluded an arbitration agreement *after* the dispute has arisen in which they choose a different applicable law, disputes relating to the termination of an exclusive distributorship with territory in Belgium are only considered to be arbitrable if the arbitrators are bound to apply the mandatory provisions of the Belgian Distribution Act of 1961. This has, however, been the subject of a lengthy legal controversy that remains unsettled. Similar, and equally controversial, case law has developed in recent years in respect of disputes relating to commercial

---

[122] BCCP, art 1717(3)(a)(iv) *in fine*. See *Travaux préparatoires*, DOC (Ch) 53 2743/001, p 41.

[123] BCCP, art 1717(3)(b)(i).

[124] BCCP, art 1676(1).

[125] BCCP, art 1676(4).

[126] See Law of 3 July 1978 on Employment Contracts, art 13 and BCCP, art 1676(5) pursuant to which an agreement to arbitrate labour disputes, that would normally fall within the competence of the Labour Courts pursuant to BCCP, arts 578–583, may be entered into only *after* a dispute has arisen.

[127] See Law of 25 June 1992 on Land Insurance Contracts, art 36.

agency agreements. When the agent has its principal place of business in Belgium and the applicable substantive law would not offer a protection equivalent to the mandatory provisions of Belgian law, an agency dispute falling within the scope of Belgian law may not be arbitrable.[128]

Violation of public policy An arbitral award may be set aside if it is contrary to public policy.[129] Under Belgian law, rules of public policy are considered to be those that touch upon the essential interests of the state or the community, or that introduce in private law fundamental legal principles on the basis of which the moral or economic order of a society is founded.[130] Such rules can be found in the constitution, in international conventions on human and civil rights to which Belgium is a party, and in general legal principles. **1.131**

The court before which an annulment proceeding is brought, will examine *ex officio* whether the arbitral award is contrary to public policy.[131] It is not settled whether in assessing the compliance of an arbitral award with public policy, a court may go further in its assessment than the limited scope of review that is possible for the assessment of other grounds (as already discussed).[132] **1.132**

Violation of public policy has been accepted as a ground for annulment in cases in which the arbitration proceedings were considered to violate Article 6 of the European Convention on Human Rights (ECHR), pursuant to which every party is entitled to a fair and public hearing within a reasonable time by an independent and impartial tribunal established by law. As many of the disputes submitted to arbitration concern commercial relationships, rules organizing the economic order (often imposed by international conventions or supranational bodies, for instance at European Community level) may also be a source of public policy. **1.133**

However, an incorrect application of, or manifest disregard for, the applicable law by the arbitral tribunal is no ground for annulment. Only if the error of law in itself violates public policy can the arbitral award be annulled. **1.134**

---

[128] Supreme Court [2011] (2010–11) *Rechtskundig Weekblad* 1646–50, w note D Mertens; Supreme Court [2012] (2012) 04 *Arresten van het Hof van Cassatie* 886.

[129] BCCP, art 1717(3)(b)(1).

[130] See Keutgen and Dal (n 21) 463.

[131] BCCP, art 1707(4).

[132] In *SNF v Cytec*, the Court of First Instance of Brussels annulled an award for violation of public policy (Court of First Instance Brussels [2007] *Rev Arb* 2007/2, 303–18). On the standard of review to be undertaken by an annulment court, the court held that while it is not up to state courts to reassess the merits of a case, a court should verify, upon reading the award, whether the arbitral tribunal complied with public policy in assessing the facts submitted to it and in the application of the law to these facts. The court recalled that (the old) BCCP, art 1704(2)(a) calls for the annulment of all violations of public policy, and not only obvious, effective, or concrete violations. In the court's opinion, the standard of such review therefore requires an assessment of the reasoning of the award, not only from a merely formal point of view, but also in terms of its contents. On appeal, however, this judgment was overturned by the Court of Appeal of Brussels on the finding that issues of damages and interest that arise out of the annulment of a contract for violation of a public law provision of European competition law, do not themselves form part of public policy (Court of Appeal Brussels [2009] (2009) 3 Rev arb 574–94). In the light of its finding that there was no ground for annulment, the Court of Appeal did not proceed to a detailed analysis of the question of whether an alleged violation of public policy requires a wider scope of review, as was suggested in first instance by the lower court. This question therefore remains unsettled. See O Caprasse, *La jurisprudence du code judiciaire commentée—Volume VI—arbitrage et médiation* (La Charte, 2010) 67.

1.135 Similarly, failure to correctly appreciate, interpret, or understand the scope and contents of the documents submitted to the arbitral tribunal does not constitute a violation of public policy, unless such failure constitutes proof of the partiality or lack of independence of the arbitral tribunal.[133]

1.136 While a violation of public policy is one of the grounds most often invoked by parties, very few arbitral awards have actually been annulled on this basis.

1.137 **Fraud** The award may be set aside if it was obtained by fraud.[134] This includes both fraud within the arbitration proceedings and fraud by the arbitration proceedings (eg when parties arbitrate a fictitious dispute, in order to circumvent a third party's rights).[135]

Suspension of the annulment proceedings to allow rectification of the arbitral award

1.138 The court before which an application to set aside is brought may suspend the annulment proceedings at the request of a party in order to allow the arbitral tribunal to reopen the arbitration proceedings or take any other measure that it considers useful to rectify any possible grounds for annulment.[136]

1.139 As indicated in the *travaux préparatoires*, this possibility is based on an argument of efficiency and on consideration that the annulment of an award should at all times be the last means to rectify a possible irregularity. If such irregularity can be corrected by the arbitral tribunal that rendered the award, this is to be preferred.[137]

1.140 When the case is referred back to the arbitral tribunal by the Court of First Instance in accordance with article 1717(6) BCCP, the provisions of article 1713 BCCP (on arbitral awards) and the requirements of article 1715 BCCP apply *mutatis mutandis*.[138] Article 1715 BCCP determines the conditions for applications regarding interpretation, correction, or additional awards.

1.141 First, unless the parties have agreed another term, either party may apply to the (same) arbitral tribunal within one month following receipt of the arbitral award for correction of calculation errors, material errors, spelling errors, or other similar mistakes.[139] Similarly, to the extent the parties have agreed on this possibility, a party may apply for interpretation of a certain point or passage of the arbitral award.[140] If the arbitral tribunal finds this application to be well founded, any correction or interpretation will become part of the arbitral award and must be issued by the arbitral tribunal within one month of receiving the application.[141] This term may, however, be extended by the arbitral tribunal itself if necessary.[142] Material errors may also be corrected by the arbitral tribunal on its own motion within one month of the date of the arbitral award[143]

[133] Court of First Instance Brussels [1975] (1976) *JT* 493.
[134] BCCP, art 1717(3)(b)(iii).
[135] Keutgen and Dal (n 21) 485.
[136] BCCP, art 1717(6).
[137] See *Travaux préparatoires*, DOC (Ch) 53 2743/001, pp 41–2.
[138] BCCP, art 1715(7).
[139] BCCP, art 1715(1)(a).
[140] BCCP, art 1715(1)(b).
[141] BCCP, art 1715(1)(b).
[142] BCCP, art 1715(4).
[143] BCCP, art 1715(2).

Second, an award may be completed by an additional award, when the arbitral tribunal decided *infra petita*. While the arbitral tribunal is not required to respond to every detail of the parties' arguments, it must deal with all issues in dispute. In a situation in which the arbitral tribunal omitted to decide on one or more claims brought in the arbitration,[144] and unless excluded by the parties, a party may apply to the (same) arbitral tribunal within one month of the receipt of the arbitral award for an additional award. If the arbitral tribunal finds this application to be well founded, any additional award must be rendered within two months from receipt of the application.[145] This term may, however, be extended by the arbitral tribunal itself if necessary.[146] The fact that the original deadline for rendering the arbitral award will have expired[147] does not prevent the issuing of an additional award.[148] **1.142**

Finally, as indicated here, applications for the correction or interpretation, or for an additional award must, as a principle, be brought before the same arbitral tribunal. However, when it is impossible to convene the same arbitral tribunal to decide on such application, parties may seek the assistance of the Court of First Instance, which will decide in accordance with article 1715(6) BCCP. This implies that in such a case, the Court of First Instance will itself correct, interpret, or complete the award, to the extent it finds that the request has merits. **1.143**

1.5.4 Local procedures for setting aside/annulment

Competent court

Proceedings for setting aside an award must be brought before the Court of First Instance of which the seat corresponds with that of the Court of Appeal that would have territorial jurisdiction over the seat of the arbitration. For arbitrations with a seat in Brussels, this is the Court of First Instance of Brussels.[149] **1.144**

Standing

In principle, an application for annulment may be brought only by the parties to the arbitration. Contrary to the situation before the courts, a third party whose rights are affected by a judgment may not rely on articles 1047ff BCCP in order to oppose an arbitral award. **1.145**

There is one notable exception with respect to arbitration proceedings affected by fraud: in an exceptional case in which the arbitral proceedings were found to be a sham aimed at circumventing a third party's rights, the third party not only successfully brought an action to oppose enforcement of the award, but also applied successfully for annulment of the award.[150] **1.146**

---

144 Prior to the 2013 revision, a failure to decide on issue(s) in dispute that cannot be separated from the issues on which the tribunal did decide, constituted a ground for annulment. See the old BCCP, art 1704(2)(e).

145 BCCP, art 1717(4).

146 BCCP, art 1715(4).

147 When the parties did not agree on a deadline for rendering the arbitral award and no award is rendered within six months after the appointment of the last arbitrator, BCCP, art 1713(2) allows the parties to apply to the Court of First Instance to set a deadline for rendering the award.

148 BCCP, art 1715(3). See *Travaux préparatoires*, DOC (Ch) 53 2743/001, p 39.

149 BCCP, art 1680(6) with BCCP, art 1717(2).

150 Van Houtte, Cox, and Cools (n 13) para 125.

Limitation periods

1.147 An application to set aside an arbitral award is admissible only when the decision can no longer be contested before the arbitral tribunal.[151] This is the case when and to the extent that the arbitral award finally disposes of one or more issues in dispute, regardless of whether this also entails the termination of the proceedings, and moreover, whether the parties did not provide for the option of an arbitral appeal in accordance with article 1716 BCCP.

1.148 An application to set aside an arbitral award must be brought within three months following the notification of the award in accordance with the requirements of article 1678(1)(a) BCCP.[152] The only exception is an application for annulment against a decision of an arbitral tribunal to assume jurisdiction: pursuant to article 1690(4) BCCP an annulment application against a decision on jurisdiction may only be brought at the same time as a decision on the merits. An award merely deciding on jurisdiction, even when this decision is final on the issue, is therefore not susceptible for appeal until a decision on the merits is taken. If, however, the issue of jurisdiction is finally dealt with in a partial award[153] together with a number of issues on the merits, an application for annulment is possible.

1.149 When a correction, interpretation, or additional award is issued on the basis of article 1715 BCCP, the notification thereof (and not the date of notification of the original award) is taken as starting point for the calculation of the three-month period.[154] Upon expiration of the three-month limitation period, the parties are estopped from invoking these grounds to challenge the award.

Course of annulment proceedings

1.150 The party wishing to bring an annulment action must serve a writ of summons on the other parties to appear before the Court of First Instance of the seat, unless these parties agree to appear voluntarily.[155] The writ is served by a bailiff and must include the names and addresses of the parties; the object and a short summary of the claims; the competent court; and the time, place, and location of the introductory hearing.[156]

1.151 At the introductory hearing, a procedural calendar for written submissions is adopted and a hearing date determined. Parties may agree on the procedural calendar among themselves. Failing an agreement, the court will determine the calendar.[157]

1.152 As discussed in the previous section, the award may be annulled only on the limited grounds set out in article 1717(3) BCCP. When reviewing an application for annulment, the Court will verify *ex officio* that the award does not contravene Belgian public policy, that the issues in dispute were arbitrable pursuant to Belgian law, and that the arbitral award was not obtained by fraud.[158]

1.153 Courts are only empowered to set aside an award whole or in part. When deciding to annul an arbitral award, the court may neither modify the content of the decision rendered by the

---

151 BCCP, art 1717(1).
152 BCCP, art 1717(4).
153 ie an award not finally disposing of all issues in dispute, and hence not terminating the arbitral proceedings.
154 See *Travaux préparatoires*, DOC (Ch) 53 2743/001, p 41.
155 BCCP, art 700.
156 BCCP, art 702.
157 BCCP, art 747(1).
158 BCCP, art 1717(3)(b).

arbitral tribunal, nor order that the award be sent back to the same or to another arbitral tribunal. As discussed earlier, article 1717(6) BCCP constitutes a notable exception to this rule. Pursuant to this article a court may—at the request of a party and before deciding on the application for annulment—suspend the annulment proceedings and refer the case back to the same arbitral tribunal, to allow the arbitral tribunal to take the necessary measures to correct any possible grounds for annulment within a certain term in accordance with article 1715 BCCP. Moreover, if the original arbitral tribunal can no longer convene, parties may apply to the court for assistance.[159]

An annulment decision of the Court of First Instance may not be appealed before the Court of Appeal. It is only subject to limited review by the Supreme Court, on limited grounds and limited to errors of law. **1.154**

An arbitral award preserves its full effect until a court decides to set it aside in whole or in part. An action to set aside does not therefore suspend ongoing arbitration proceedings or prevent enforcement of the award. **1.155**

The effect of a final decision setting aside an award (or part thereof) is that the award or part is annulled and no longer exists. It is then up to the parties to decide how to proceed. In principle, either party may commence new arbitral proceedings on the issues in respect of which the first award was set aside. **1.156**

Duration

Proceedings before the Court of First Instance generally last between 12 and 18 months. These decisions are not susceptible to appeal before the Court of Appeal.[160] **1.157**

Recourse against a judgment of the Court of First Instance is only possible before the Supreme Court on the basis of the general provision in article 609 °1 BCCP. As indicated earlier, however, recourse to the Supreme Court will not involve a full review, as it is limited to issues of law. Moreover, proceedings may be brought only on limited grounds. Generally, proceedings before the Supreme Court also last between 12 and 18 months. **1.158**

Exclusion of the possibility to set aside the award

The BLA permits foreign parties who wish to avoid any risk of finding themselves before the local courts in annulment proceedings to exclude this possibility by 'an express declaration' in the arbitration clause or in a later agreement. When none of the parties is a Belgian national or resident, or a legal person with its seat or a branch in Belgium, the parties may indeed exclude any right to apply for an arbitral award to be set aside.[161] This option is therefore only available when parties have chosen a location in Belgium, such as Brussels, as the seat of arbitration, but do not have any specific connection with Belgium themselves. The 'express declaration' requirement is, moreover, strictly interpreted: a reference by the parties in the arbitration agreement or in the terms of reference to institutional arbitration rules providing for a general waiver of any right of recourse is not sufficient. **1.159**

[159] BCCP, art 1717(6).
[160] BCCP, art 1680(5).
[161] BCCP, art 1718.

Costs

1.160 The cost of an action to set aside an award is fairly minimal. First, proceedings before the court itself entail barely any cost at all: a nominal filing fee not exceeding a few hundred euros at most must be paid by the party taking the initiative of the proceedings. Second, these and other procedural costs (eg costs those related to service of process) may be recovered by the prevailing party.

1.161 Similarly, compensation for defence costs may be claimed on the basis of article 1022 BCCP. As stated previously, only flat rate compensation is available in Belgian court proceedings, not the actual costs incurred.

1.6 Conclusion

1.162 With a global revision of the BLA in 2013 on the basis of the UNCITRAL Model Law, the Belgian legislature has successfully addressed the criticism of the old law. The result is a modern and progressive arbitration law, which is generally characterized by flexibility and demonstrates the will of the Belgian legislator to provide an efficient framework suitable for a modern business environment within which arbitration can proceed in the best possible circumstances. The fact that this revision has largely adopted the UNCITRAL Model Law—both in terms of content and in terms of wording—not only brings Belgium up to date with the world's most modern arbitration laws, but enhances the familiarity and accessibility of the law for an international audience.

1.163 The Belgian judiciary has demonstrated a favourable approach to arbitration. Generally, the courts will refrain from intervening in disputes, yet they are available to assist in the arbitral process when the need arises. Finally, the courts' attitude in proceedings for the setting aside or enforcement of arbitral awards is generally inclined in favour of arbitration. This trend should continue in the coming years in the light of the revision of the BLA, and due to the increased efficiency and specialization as a result of the centralization of all arbitration-related disputes before five Courts of First Instance. This is especially the case for the Brussels courts, which have extensive experience with international disputes in general, and with arbitration proceedings in particular.

1.164 The geographical position of Brussels, its status as an international administrative and business centre, and the relatively low cost of arbitrating in Brussels, further explain why Brussels is increasingly chosen as a seat for arbitration.

2

BUENOS AIRES

*Alejandro M Garro and Michael Fernández**

2.1 Background

2.1.1 History and development of arbitration in Argentina

2.01 Argentine law has long recognized alternative dispute resolution as a means of resolving disagreements.[1] However, Argentina's approach to arbitration has been and remains somewhat

* The authors wish to acknowledge and thank Lucila Hemmingsen for her assistance in the preparation of this chapter. Responsibility for all errors and omissions are our own.

[1] See A Spinillo and E Vogelius, 'Argentina' in N Blackaby et al (eds), *International Arbitration in Latin America* (Kluwer Law International, 2002) 20–1, noting that Argentina first adopted a law permitting alternative dispute resolution in 1812 and that arbitration was permitted under the Commercial Code of 1862 and the Civil and Commercial Code of Procedure of 1880.

ambivalent, due in large measure to contradictory and conflicting court decisions, but also because Argentina still lacks a modern statutory framework governing domestic and international commercial arbitration.[2]

2.1.2 Sources of arbitration law

2.02 Argentine internal arbitration law does not distinguish, by and large, between domestic and international commercial arbitration. The core provisions governing civil and arbitration proceedings before federal courts are found in articles 736–773 of the National (Federal) Code of Civil and Commercial Procedure (NCP).[3] Articles 517–519*bis* of the NCP, applicable to the enforcement of foreign judgments, also apply, by way of analogy, to the enforcement of foreign arbitral awards.

2.03 Argentina is a federation in which each province retains legislative jurisdiction to adopt its own rules of procedure.[4] To the extent that much of arbitration law is of a procedural nature, each of the Argentine provinces thus has its own rules applicable to arbitration proceedings conducted within its territorial boundaries. According to the supremacy clause of the Argentine Constitution, however, the rules found in the provincial rules of procedure are pre-empted in the international context by those found in international treaties and the federal rules of the NCP.[5]

2.04 Of the various multilateral treaties governing international commercial arbitration that Argentina has ratified, the most important are the 1958 United Nations Convention on the Recognition and Enforcement of Foreign Arbitral Awards (New York Convention),[6] and the 1975 Inter-American Convention on International Commercial Arbitration (Panama Convention).[7] Other international treaties of occasional relevance include the 1889 and 1940 Montevideo Treaties on Civil Procedure;[8] the 1979 Inter-American Convention on the Extraterritorial Efficacy of Foreign Judgments and Arbitral Awards (1979 Montevideo Foreign Judgments Convention);[9] the 1992 Mercosur Protocol on International

---

[2] On the many arbitration bills submitted to the Argentine Congress and speculations on their failure to become law, see RJ Caivano, 'La obsolescencia de la legislación argentina sobre arbitraje es cada vez más evidente' (9 January 2010) *Revista del Colegio de Abogados de la Ciudad de Buenos Aires*, available at <http://www.colabogados.org.ar/larevista/pdfs/id11/la-obsolescencia-de-la-legislacion-argentina.pdf>.

[3] Código Procesal Civil y Comercial de la Nación (Arg) (Cód Proc Civ y Com).

[4] See Constitución Nacional (Arg), art 121-24 (hereinafter 'Const Arg').

[5] See Const Arg, art 31, providing that in additional to the federal Constitution, federal laws and international treaties are 'the law of the land'.

[6] Law No 23619, 4 November 1988, BO (Arg) <http://www.infojus.gov.ar/index.php?kk_seccion=documento&registro=LEYNAC&docid=TRA%2520C%2520023619%25201988%252009%252028>, adopting reservations related to reciprocity and commercial disputes.

[7] Law No 24322, 17 June 1994, BO (Arg) <http://www.infojus.gov.ar/index.php?kk_seccion=documento&registro=LEYNAC&docid=TRA%2520C%2520024322%25201994%252005%252011>. Unlike the US, Argentina has not adopted implementing legislation to the New York and Panama conventions, so there is no express rule aimed at settling a potential conflict of application of the New York and Panama conventions. See JC Hamilton, 'Three Decades of Latin American Commercial Arbitration' (2009) 30 U PA J Intl L 1099, 1100.

[8] Respectively, Law No 3192, 6 December 1988, BO (Arg) <http://www.infojus.gov.ar/index.php?kk_seccion=documento&registro=LEYNAC&docid=TRA%2520C%2520003192%25201894%252012%252006> and Law No 7771, 8 May 1956, BO (Arg) <http://www.infojus.gov.ar/index.php?kk_seccion=documento&registro=LEYNAC&docid=TRA%2520C%2520007771%25201956%252004%252027>.

[9] Law No 22921, 27 September 1983, BO (Arg) <http://www.infojus.gov.ar/index.php?kk_seccion=documento&registro=LEYNAC&docid=TRA%2520C%2520022921%25201983%252009%252021>.

Jurisdictional Cooperation and Assistance in Civil, Commercial, Labor and Administrative Law Matters (Las Leñas Protocol);[10] the 1994 Mercosur Protocol on International Jurisdiction in Contractual Matters;[11] and the 1998 Mercosur International Commercial Arbitration Agreement (Mercosur Arbitration Agreement).[12]

If an arbitration proceeding involves the Republic of Argentina, or any of its centralized agen- **2.05**
cies or instrumentalities, the 1965 Washington Convention on the Settlement of Investment Disputes (ICISID Convention or Washington Convention) may be of relevance.[13] Other laws of potential relevance to arbitration proceedings include statutes authorizing the Argentine government to submit international loan disputes to arbitration,[14] a decree-law regulating commodities arbitration,[15] and several provisions regulating the arbitration of consumer disputes.[16] Many of the Argentine arbitration institutions also have their own internal statutes setting out procedural rules for arbitration proceedings conducted under their auspices. The Bolsa de Comercio de Buenos Aires[17] and the Cámara Arbitral de la Bolsa de Cereales de Buenos Aires[18] are among the more well-known arbitral institutions with their own arbitration rules.

2.1.3 *De jure* and *ex aequo et bono* arbitration

Depending on the substantive rules applicable to the merits of the dispute, the NCP distin- **2.06**
guishes between arbitration at law (*de jure* arbitration) and equitable arbitration (*amigable*

[10] Law No 24578, 27 November 1995, BO (Arg) <http://www.infojus.gov.ar/index.php?kk_seccion=documento&registro=LEYNAC&docid=TRA%2520C%2520024578%25201995%252010%252025>.

[11] Law No 24669, 2 August 1996, BO (Arg) <http://www.infojus.gov.ar/index.php?kk_seccion=documento&registro=LEYNAC&docid=TRA%2520C%2520024669%25201996%252007%252003>.

[12] Law No 25223, 5 January 2000, BO (Arg) <http://www.infojus.gov.ar/index.php?kk_seccion=documento&registro=LEYNAC&docid=TRA%2520C%2520025223%25201999%252011%252024>.

[13] Law No 24353, 2 September 1994, BO (Arg) <http://www.infojus.gov.ar/index.php?kk_seccion=documento&registro=LEYNAC&docid=TRA%2520C%2520024353%25201994%252007%252028>.

[14] Law No 20548, 9 November 1973, BO (Arg) <http://www.infojus.gov.ar/index.php?kk_seccion=documento&registro=LEYNAC&docid=LEY%2520C%2520020548%25201973%252010%252025>.

[15] Decree-Law No 6689/63:

> The Executive Power is authorized to pledge the public credit of the Nation, with a secondary or principal character, for the purposes and subject to the aforementioned conditions on behalf of public or private entities, and to submit eventual controversies with foreign parties to judges in other jurisdictions, arbitral tribunals who are impartially designated or the International Court of Justice in The Hague.

[16] Law No 26361, 7 April 2008, BO, art 29 (Arg):

> The enforcement authority shall organize arbitral tribunals that will act as amigables componedores or de jure arbitrators, depending on the case, to resolve the controversies that might arise as a result of this law. The enforcement authority may invite, in line with the conditions established in the law, all qualified persons proposed by consumer-advocate associations and chambers of commerce. <http://www.infojus.gov.ar/index.php?kk_seccion=documento&registro=LEYNAC&docid=LEY%2520C%2520026361%25202008%252003%252012>; Decree No 276/98, 13 March 1998, BO (Arg) <http://www.infojus.gov.ar/index.php?kk_seccion=documento&registro=DECRETOS&docid=DEC%2520C%2520000276%25201998%252003%252011>; Resolution No 212, Secretary of Trade, Dictámenes de la Procuración del Tesoro No 212, 2 November 1992 (Arg). <http://www.infojus.gov.ar/index.php?kk_seccion=documento&registro=DICTAMEN&docid=G0203034>.

[17] Bolsa de Comercio de Buenos Aires, Régimen Arbitral <http://www.bcba.sba.com.ar/tribunal/regimen.php>.

[18] Cámara Arbitral de la Bolsa de Cereales de Buenos Aires <http://www.cabcbue.com.ar/camara/index.php?option=com_content&task=view&id=466>.

composición). Both forms of arbitration share the same rules in terms of the capacity of the parties to arbitrate, the substance and form of submissions, the qualifications of arbitrators, the rules for their appointment, acceptance of appointment and replacement, and quorum and rules to be applied in making the award. However, arbitrators *de jure* are required to reach a decision based on the law applicable to that arbitration, while arbitrators *ex aequo et bono* (*amigables componedores* or *árbitros arbitradores*) must settle the dispute on the basis of principles of fairness and equity (*según su ciencia y conciencia*). In a major departure from most modern arbitration statutes, article 766(2) of the NCP provides that if the parties do not indicate the nature of the arbitration proceeding, or if the arbitrators have been authorized to decide the dispute according to equity, the arbitrators shall decide as *amigables componedores*.[19]

2.1.4 Formal distinction between pre-dispute and post-dispute arbitration agreements

2.07 The parties may agree to submit future disputes to arbitration by means of an arbitration clause (*cláusula compromisoria*) or may conclude an arbitration submission (*compromiso arbitral*) in order to submit to arbitration a dispute that has already arisen. The *cláusula compromisoria* can take the form of a clause within a contract, or an independent instrument by which the parties indicate that future disputes will be submitted to arbitration.[20] The *compromiso arbitral*, which is the only type of arbitration agreement formally recognized in the NCP, must 'bear the form of a public deed or a private instrument, or of a minute executed before the court or judicial tribunal that would entertain jurisdiction over the case if it were not brought to arbitration'.[21]

2.08 If the parties have agreed to an ad hoc arbitration under the rules of the NCP, even if there is an applicable arbitration clause, it is advisable to conclude an arbitral submission (*compromiso arbitral*) that includes, under penalty of nullity, the date, name and address of the parties and of the arbitrators, a statement of the issues submitted to arbitration, and the underlying circumstances of the dispute, as well as the amount of the fine that shall be paid by a party who does not comply with the acts necessary for the fulfilment of the arbitration agreement.[22] Further information, such as the applicable arbitration rules, place of arbitration, and language, may also be included. If the parties have agreed to institutional arbitration, they will not be required to execute a *compromiso arbitral*, and the relevant provisions of the institution's rules will apply.[23]

---

[19] cf UNCITRAL Arbitration Rules as revised in 2010, GA Res 65/22, Art 35, UN Doc A/RES/65/22 (6 December 2010): 'The arbitral tribunal shall decide as amiable compositeur or ex aequo et bono only if the parties have expressly authorized the arbitral tribunal to do so' (hereinafter 'UNCITRAL Rules').

[20] See eg CNCom, 26 September 1988, *Welbers SA, Enrique C v Extraktionstechnik Gesellschaft für Anlagenbay* [1989-E] La Ley 304 (Arg).

[21] NCP, art 739.

[22] NCP, art 741.

[23] See eg CNCom, 7 February 2011, *Sociedad de Inversiones Inmobiliarias del Puerto v Constructora Iberoamericana* (Arg), implicitly allowing the parties to use the rules of the ICC to set the terms of reference; but see CNCom, 21 December 1990, *Compañía Naviera Pérez Companc y otros v Ecofisa et al* 143 El Derecho 435 (Arg); Juzgado Contencioso Administrativo (1st Inst), 27 September 2004, *Entidad Binacional Yacyretá v Eriday et al* [2005-A] La Ley 12 (Arg), enforced, 18 April 2005 [2005-C] La Ley 651 (Arg).

2.1.5 Judicial attitudes towards arbitration

While many Argentine court decisions fail to demonstrate a clearly favourable attitude towards arbitration,[24] others have been very supportive.[25] Even where the courts have upheld an arbitration agreement or enforced an arbitral award, however, language can sometimes be found to the effect that arbitration agreements should be construed narrowly.[26] **2.09**

A 2004 decision of the Supreme Court of Argentina, *José Cartellone Construcciones Civiles SA v Hidroeléctrica Norpatagónica SA o HIDRONOR SA* (*Cartellone*),[27] alarmingly suggests that Argentine courts may be entitled to scrutinize awards at the enforcement stage on grounds of 'reasonableness'.[28] Referring to more recent decisions such as *Mobil v Gasnor*,[29] some legal commentators suggest that the judicial hostility towards arbitration evidenced in *Cartellone* has since been discarded.[30] Whether *Cartellone* is still 'good law', however, remains to be seen, particularly in cases in which the Argentine government is a party to arbitration proceedings.[31] **2.10**

2.1.6 Recent developments and anticipated changes

Commentators have long argued that Argentina's arbitration legislation should be replaced with a new and modern arbitration law.[32] Indeed, it would be a positive step for Argentina **2.11**

---

[24] See eg CNFed, 7 March 2007, *Estado Nacional—Procuración del Tesoro v Cámara de Comercio Internacional* (2007) IV Jurisprudencia Argentina 26 (Arg); CNCom, 3 March 2005, *Ogden Entertaiment Servs Inc v Eijo, Néstor E et al* LEXIS 35001029 (Arg); *Entidad Binacional Yacyretá* (n 23); CSJN, 1 June 2004, *José Cartellone Construcciones Civiles SA v Hidroeléctrica Norpatagónica SA o HIDRONOR SA* (2004) 327 Fallos 1881 (Arg).

[25] See eg CSJN, 24 May 2011, *Armada Holland BV Schiedam Denmark v Inter Fruit SA* (2011) 334 Fallos 552 (Arg); CNCiv y Com, 3 January 2011, *Smit Intl Argentina SA v Puerto Mariel* (Arg), recognizing the principal of seperability; CNCom, 19 October 2010, *Cemaedu SA v Envases EP SA* (Arg), extending the effects of the compromise clause to a guarantor; *Sociedad de Inversiones Inmobiliarias del Puerto v Constructora Iberoamericana*, CNCom, 7 February 2011, available at <http://fallos.diprargentina.com/2011/09/sociedad-de-inversiones-inmobiliarias.html>; CNCom, 8 August 2007, *Mobil Argentina SA v Gasnor SA* elDial.com–AA4188 (Arg), granted leave to appeal by, CNCom, 9 October 2007, remanded by CSJN, 26 May 2010, denied leave to appeal by, CNCom, 25 April 2011; Juzgado Comercial (1st Inst), 24 February 1988, *SA La Razón EEFIC & A v SA La Nación et al* 139 El Derecho 630 (Arg). See also *CNCom, 19 October 2012, Casanova Susana v Synthon Holding S.A. et al.*

[26] See eg CNCom, 15 March 2012, *Fe SA v Telefónica Móviles Argentina SA* (Arg); CNCom, 7 May 2010 *Medina Antonio v Pizza Rica SA* elDial.com, 4 April 2010 (Arg), holding that 'the jurisdiction of the arbitral tribunal is exceptional in relation to the jurisdiction of a judicial tribunal such that the clause that establishes arbitral jurisdiction should be interpreted restrictively. As a consequence, its reach should be limited to the interpretation of contractual clauses or the verification of factual questions, excluding those issues that are reserved for the exclusive review of a judge'; CNCom, 13 June 1972, *Vialco SA v El Fletero* 50 El Derecho 463, 15 Jurisprudencia Argentina 371, 152 La Ley 505 (Arg). See also CNCom, 19 October 2012, *Casanova Susana v Synthon Holding S.A. et al.*

[27] See *José Cartellone Construcciones Civiles* (n 24). The case concerned a dispute over a public works contract with an arbitration clause, resulting in an arbitral award rendered in Argentina in favour of the plaintiff, which the defendant sought to vacate. Plaintiff, José Cartellone Construcciones Civiles SA, was one of the leading Argentine construction companies, while the defendant, Hidroeléctrica Norpatagónica SA, was a state-owned company. The case eventually reached the Supreme Court of Argentina, which vacated the award on the grounds that it was 'unconstitutional, illegal or unreasonable'. See also Spinillo and Vogelius (n 1) 21–2; see also A Mourre, 'Perspectives on International Arbitration in Latin America' (2006) 17 Am Rev Intl Arb 597, 597–9.

[28] *José Cartellone Construcciones Civiles* (n 24).

[29] *Mobil Argentina SA* (n 25). The case concerned a dispute over a contract for the provision of natural gas. The case was arbitrated before the ICC. Notwithstanding the inclusion of a waiver of the parties' right to appeal in the underlying contract, Gasnor SA sought a review of the award based on the standard of review enunciated by the Supreme Court in *José Cartellone Construcciones* (n 24). A panel of the Cámara Nacional de Apelación rejected Gasnor's claim after heavily criticizing the Supreme Court's decision in *Cartellone*.

[30] cf Spinillo and Vogelius (n 1) 21; Mourre (n 27) 599–603 with 604–7.

[31] See Mourre (n 27) 604–7.

[32] See eg Caivano (n 2); RJ Caivano, 'Argentina necesita mejorar su legislación sobre arbitraje' [1994-A] La Ley 994; HG Naón, 'La ley modelo sobre arbitraje comercial internacional y el derecho argentino' [1989-E] La Ley 881.

to adopt a modern federal arbitration statute in line with the UNCITRAL Model Law on International Commercial Arbitration.[33] During the last two decades, several efforts to reform the legal regime governing arbitration have been elaborated and submitted to Congress. The latest reform efforts can be found in the provisions on the arbitration agreement set forth in a draft civil and commercial code recently submitted to Congress (2012 Draft Civil and Commercial Code).[34] This draft is intended to replace the Argentine Civil Code of 1872 and it includes for the first time an entire chapter dedicated to arbitration agreements.[35] At the time of writing, however, none of them has been successful.[36]

2.12 The draft provisions on arbitration in the 2012 Draft Civil and Commercial Code would introduce several positive changes.[37] For example, if the parties do not stipulate whether the arbitration is to be *de jure* or *ex aequo et bono*, the default rule provides that the arbitration shall be *de jure*.[38] While the current legislation does not specify the default number of arbitrators in cases in which the parties fail to agree, the draft indicates that the default number of arbitrators will be three.[39] Also, the draft expressly provides that the existence of an arbitration agreement excludes the jurisdiction of the courts.[40] Although this distinction between arbitral and judicial jurisdiction is already obtained under the New York Convention,[41] such a basic rule would be introduced for the first time in Argentine domestic law on arbitration. Be that as it may, the arbitration provisions included in the 2012 Draft Civil and Commercial Code fall short of the type of federal arbitration law regulating all procedural and substantive aspects of arbitration that would facilitate the use of arbitration in Argentina as a more readily accessible method of dispute resolution.

2.13 In large measure, Argentina's hostility to arbitration can be attributed to the economic crisis of the 1990s. Broad deregulation of the economy during the 1990s was followed by a flow of foreign investment under the umbrella of bilateral investment treaties (BITs). Most of the BITs gave foreign investors the chance to submit disputes to ICSID arbitration. The convertibility crisis gave rise—among other no less dramatic economic and institutional changes—to a flood of investment arbitration cases against Argentina, most of which pitted the investors' property rights against the state's regulatory powers. The proliferation of investment arbitration disputes in which Argentina was a losing respondent raised suspicions that arbitration tribunals nurtured an imperialistic bias against Argentina, tainting

[33] See UNCITRAL Model Law on International Commercial Arbitration, as revised in 2006 <http://www.uncitral.org/uncitral/en/uncitral_texts/arbitration/1985Model_arbitration.html>

[34] See Reforma del Código Civil y Comercial, <http://www.codigocivil.argentina.ar/dia-por-dia/>; see also Decree No 191/2011, providing for the establishment of a presidential commission (the leading members of this drafting committee were Chief Supreme Court Justice Ricardo Lorenzetti, Associate Justice Elena Highton, and former Chief Justice of the Supreme Court of the Province of Mendoza), in charge of the elaboration of a draft providing for the unification of the civil and the commercial codes.

[35] See Anteproyecto de Reforma del Código Civil y Comercial <http://www.codigocivil.argentina.ar/advf/documentos/4f997912226b8.pdf>.

[36] See Caivano (n 2).

[37] See PF Richards, 'Controversial Court Decisions. Forthcoming Legislation. An Opportunity to Change?' in *The Arbitration Review of the Americas 2013*, available at <http://www.globalarbitrationreview.com/reviews/48/sections/167/chapters/1864/argentina/#fono4>.

[38] 2012 Draft Civil and Commercial Code, art 1652.

[39] This is consistent with Model Law, Art 7, but it seems advisable to provide for a sole arbitrator as a default rule, indicating that if the amount in dispute exceeds a given threshold (eg US$100,000), the default number of arbitrators should be three. See eg International Chamber of Commerce, Arbitration and ADR Rules, Art 12.

[40] See Anteproyecto de Reforma del Código Civil y Comercial, art 1656.

[41] See Convention on the Recognition and Enforcement of Foreign Arbitral Awards, Art II(3), 7 June 1958, 330 UNTS 3 (hereinafter 'New York Convention').

the perception of arbitration in Argentina as a pro-capitalist and anti-Argentine conspiracy of greedy British, French, Spanish, and US-based multinationals. This negative image of arbitration has had an unfavourable impact in Argentina on the eventual expansion of arbitration as a successful alternative method of dispute resolution.

2.1.7 Comparison with other regional or national venues

Argentina, together with Uruguay, is one of the few Latin American countries without a modern arbitration law, the main provisions on arbitration remaining incorporated in a code of civil and commercial procedure. In contrast Chile, Costa Rica, the Dominican Republic, Guatemala, Honduras, Mexico, Nicaragua, Paraguay, Peru, and Venezuela, as reported on the UNCITRAL website in November 2012, have enacted modern arbitration legislation based on the UNCITRAL Model Law. Other Latin American jurisdictions, such as Brazil in 1996, have enacted arbitration legislation consistent with the UNCITRAL Model Law. **2.14**

Argentina lags behind other Latin American arbitration venues because it lacks a consistent and predictable line of decisions ensuring the cooperation of national courts. Although Argentine court decisions on arbitration are varied and conflicting, without a consistent jurisprudential bias in favour of arbitration, Buenos Aires remains an attractive and well-connected city, with all the logistical facilities necessary for the conduct of arbitral proceedings. **2.15**

2.2 Commencing the Arbitration

2.2.1 Court assistance in commencing arbitration

The main policy on 'arbitrability', understood as the type of disputes susceptible to be settled by arbitration, is incorporated into article 737 of the NCP, which provides that 'matters not capable of settlement cannot be submitted to arbitration'.[42] The exclusion generally comprises family law questions and rights and obligations, which cannot be the object or subject matter of a contract, as well as property rights that are 'out of commerce'.[43] Whether a given subject matter is susceptible of being submitted to arbitration is an issue that may be decided by the arbitral tribunal or, at the request of a party and in the ultimate instance, by a court of law, either at the seat of arbitration or at the place where the resulting award is to be enforced. Whether arbitrability presents an issue of admissibility or whether it touches upon the jurisdiction of the arbitration tribunal is a question that has not been expressly addressed by statute or settled by the courts.[44] **2.16**

Arbitration proceedings may be triggered as long as there is an arbitration agreement that is enforceable *prima facie*. If a party brings a suit before a court despite the existence of a *prima* **2.17**

---

42 NCP, art 737.

43 See Código Civil, art 2336 (Arg) (hereinafter 'Civil Code') <http://www.codigocivilonline.com.ar/codigo_civil_online_2311_2350.html> for a definition of *res extra commercium*.

44 See eg CNCom, Division F, 18 October 2010, *Re Vañesa Andrea Fabiana v Carballal Viviana Isel y otros*, divesting the arbitral tribunal of jurisdiction where the arbitration clause encompassed both arbitrable and non-arbitrable questions, see <http://www.abogados.com.ar/establecen-cuando-procede-la-exclusion-de-la-competencia-arbitral/9397>; CNCom, 6 May 2010, *Cri Holding Inc Sucursal Argentina v Cía Argentina de Comodoro Rivadavia Explotación de Petróleo SA* (Arg), a party declined to proceed with arbitration on a particular issue on the grounds that it was non-arbitrable on public policy grounds. The Court found that the issue was indeed non-arbitrable and refused to refer the matter to arbitration.

facie enforceable arbitration agreement, the national courts of state parties to the New York Convention must decline jurisdiction and refer the parties to arbitration.[45] The court must serve the summons and complaint on the other party, who may challenge the court's jurisdiction. Pursuant to Article II(3) of the New York Convention, the court must dismiss the case and refer the parties to arbitration. Under Argentine law, the right to submit the dispute to arbitration would be deemed waived if the challenge to the court's jurisdiction was not brought at the first opportunity.[46] Aside from the application of the New York Convention, the parties are bound by the arbitration agreement under general contract law, so in the presence of a dispute the subject matter of which is the subject of an arbitration agreement, the court will decline jurisdiction and refer the parties to arbitration.

2.18 Article 742 of the NCP outlines the steps that a party must follow, unless they agree otherwise, to initiate arbitral proceedings. This provision also addresses the role of the courts in deciding disputes between the parties regarding the existence and scope of an arbitral clause.[47] In order to start an arbitration, the claimant may file the claim or request arbitration before the court that would have been competent if the parties had not agreed to submit the dispute to arbitration. The court will notify the respondent and set a date for a hearing at which the parties will draw up and execute the *compromiso arbitral*, proceeding with the appointment of the arbitrators. This procedure is unlikely to be followed in international commercial arbitration, in which the parties generally agree to a speedier procedure to commence arbitration, serving the respondent directly without the need of court intervention.

2.19 Even if there is a *prima facie* enforceable arbitration clause, however, one of the parties may fail to cooperate with the establishment of the arbitral tribunal by refusing to execute a *compromiso arbitral*. In such a case, the other party may request the competent court, ie the court that would have decided the dispute in the absence of the arbitration agreement, to conclude the arbitration submission on behalf of the defaulting party.[48] Where the parties have concluded a *compromiso* but disagree as to its content, the courts may also intervene for the purpose of determining the substance of the *compromiso*, thus supporting the commencement of the arbitration and making it viable.[49]

---

45 See New York Convention, Art II(3).

46 See eg CNCom, 03 October 2012, *Captec S.R.L. v Constructora San José Argentina S.A.* (Arg.) (finding the right to arbitration waived where the party participated in a mediation proceeding without objection); CNCiv, 31 October 1975, *Signorelli, SA v Arriberos y Zavala, SCA* 66 El Derecho 232 (Arg).

47 The NCP, art 742 provides that:

> The constitution of an arbitral tribunal may be requested when one or more disputes are in need of settlement by arbitration. A request for arbitration must be submitted, subject to the relevant requirements of article 330, before the court that would have been the competent to hear the case. The court shall send a written communication to the respondent within 10 days, and a hearing shall be scheduled in order to proceed with a formal conclusion of the submission. In case of a groundless refusal to conclude a submission, the judge shall proceed pursuant to Article 740. If the objection raised against the composition of the tribunal is correct, the judge shall declare it so, and, if necessary, shall impose costs after a preliminary incidental proceeding. If the parties agree to conclude a submission, but disagree on the substance thereof, the court shall provide what is pertinent.

48 See eg CNCiv, 17 July 1998, *Calistri, LA v Chiron, JA* (Arg); CComCap, 20 April 1956, *Squery Atilio Lorenzo v Casas, Oscar y otros* 83 La Ley 719; (1956) III Jurisprudencia Argentina 280 (Arg); cf CNCom, 31 July 1948, *Corporación Cementera Argentina v Cía Deutz Argentina* 52 La Ley 23 (Arg).

49 See eg *Compañía Naviera Pérez Companc y otros* (n 23) ordering the trial judge to resolve a dispute over the terms of reference by imposing his own terms, even though the parties had submitted their dispute to an arbitral institution that already provided for a mechanism to fill gaps in the terms of reference; CNCiv, 25 February 2013, *Wallaby S.A. v Despegar.com.ar* (Arg.); *Entidad Binacional Yacyretá* (n 23).

Once a notice of arbitration has been submitted, the parties may need assistance if they are unable to agree on the constitution of the tribunal. Whether the courts should assist in the establishment of an arbitral tribunal and how is generally regarded as a matter of law.[50] Upon a party's request for assistance, Argentine courts will consider, among other things: (1) whether a valid arbitration clause exists between the parties; (2) whether the subject matter of the controversy is susceptible of being settled by arbitration; and (3) whether the matter under dispute falls within the scope of the arbitration clause.[51] If the court finds that these requirements are met, the arbitration may go forward without further interference from the Argentine courts. The involvement of the courts may be avoided, as noted before, by agreeing that the notice of arbitration may be served directly on the respondent, in which case the *compromiso* could be drawn up in the form of Terms of Reference under the ICC Rules, if necessary, or any other form. Such a spirit of cooperation, however, is not always forthcoming. At times, Argentine courts have unduly interfered with on-going arbitration proceedings. In *Compañía Naviera Pérez Companc y otros v Ecofisa y otros*,[52] for example, the National Court of Commercial Appeals ordered a trial judge to resolve a dispute pursuant to terms of reference outlined by the court itself, failing to relegate this to the arbitral institution to which the parties had entrusted the conduct of the arbitration.[53] Argentine courts have also intervened at times in order to frame the terms of a dispute submitted to arbitration and for the alleged purpose of addressing matters of public policy inviting the invalidation of the resulting arbitral award.[54] **2.20**

Other gateway issues, in the form of procedural requirements, have also led to the intervention of Argentine courts. For example, in a case in which the arbitration agreement provided that the dispute must be submitted to arbitration within a given time period, the court intervened in order to determine whether that period of time had elapsed.[55] In a case in which the notice of arbitration was filed after the end of the stipulated time period, it was held that a party which files a notice of arbitration after a time limit has expired is deemed to have waived its right to submit the dispute to arbitration.[56] **2.21**

2.2.2 Interim measures of protection

Most arbitration rules specifically empower the arbitrators to award preliminary relief,[57] yet Argentine law does not give arbitrators express authority to grant such relief.[58] More recent **2.22**

---

[50] See eg CNCom, 28 July 1954, '*Peruzzotti, Arturo A v Asociación Argentina de Criadores de Aves, Conejos, y Abejas* 76 La Ley 324 (Arg); CComCap, 3 November 1954, *Molinari, Atilio A y otro v Bacigalupe de Bordenave Lola* 77 La Ley 648 (Arg); *Cementera Argentina* (n 48).

[51] See eg CComCap, 19 September 1966, *Hadra y Cía (SA) v Ferrarini, Dardo* (1966) VI Jurisprudencia Argentina 36 (Arg); CNCom, 15 October 1957, *Atarrasagasti, Alberto y otros v Motti di Piazza y otros* 91 La Ley 59 (Arg); *Peruzzotti* (n 50); cf CNCom, 31 July 1948, *Corporación Cementera Argentina v Cía Deutz Argentina* 52 La Ley 23 (Arg).

[52] *Compañía Naviera Pérez Companc y otros* (n 23).

[53] For a well-deserved criticism of the national court's interference, see RJ Caivano, *Control Judicial en el Arbitraje* (AbeledoPerrot, 2011) 138–40.

[54] See eg *Compañía Naviera Pérez Companc y otros* (n 23).

[55] See eg *Signorelli, SA* (n 46).

[56] See eg CNFed, 29 October 1974, *Sargo SA v Gas del Estado* 66 El Derecho 585 (Arg) suggesting in dicta that a court would have jurisdiction in the event that the matter could not be submitted to an arbitral tribunal.

[57] See eg Bolsa de Comercio de Buenos Aires, Régimen Arbitral, art 33 <http://www.bcba.sba.com.ar/tribunal/regimen.php>.

[58] MB Noodt Taquela, 'El arbitraje internacional en Argentina' in *Derecho del Comercio Internacional. Temas y actualidades DeCITA, 02-2004*, 322.

case law has recognized the power of an arbitral tribunal to grant an injunction[59] or order the attachment of property,[60] but the issue remained controversial for some time. Argentine case law recognizes the prerogative of a party to bypass an arbitral tribunal while seeking interim relief if the parties' agreement expressly permits it to do so.[61] Such relief is likely to be available, however, even in the absence of an express provision in the arbitration agreement.

2.23 Admittedly, because arbitrators lack *imperium* or the power to enforce interim measures, court intervention is necessary if the party against whom the measure has been granted refuses to abide by the tribunal's order. Courts enforcing interim measures ordered by an arbitral tribunal are not expected to review the basis of the order. Parties may of course bypass the arbitration tribunal and resort directly to the courts in order to request interim or preliminary measures.

2.24 Regarding the enforcement of orders for interim relief issued by arbitration tribunals sitting abroad, the National Court of Commercial Appeals has refused to enforce such an order, on the ground that international arbitration treaties binding on Argentina provide for the recognition and enforcement of arbitral awards that are final, as opposed to an order granting interim relief, which is intrinsically temporary. The Court also mentioned the absence of express authorization in the arbitration agreement for the tribunal to grant such provisional injunctive relief.[62]

2.2.3 The role of courts in the appointment of arbitrators

2.25 The parties may appoint the arbitrators pursuant to the terms of the arbitration agreement or the rules of the arbitral institution designated by the parties.[63] Special care should be taken in the selection of the institution that the parties wish to administer the arbitration. In a case in which the parties mistakenly provided for an arbitral institution that turned out not to exist, the parties were held to have lost their right to submit the dispute to arbitration, and the otherwise competent court assumed jurisdiction over the case.[64]

2.26 In the event that the parties have not agreed on a specific procedure, or if they are unable to come to an agreement in an ad hoc arbitration, the arbitrators (both *de jure* arbitrators and *amigables componedores*), will be appointed by the court that would have heard the case if the parties had not agreed to submit the dispute to arbitration.[65] Also in the context of ad hoc

---

59 See eg CNCom, 20 November 2002, *Soletanche Bachy Arg SA v Victorio Americo Gualtieri SA* (Arg).

60 See eg CComCap, 27 October 1943, *Dreyfus y Cía, Ltda, Luis v Dunne, Guillermo J* 32 La Ley 667 (Arg).

61 See eg CNCom 22 September 2005, *Searle Ltd v Roemmers SA* [2006-A] La Ley 239; CNCom, 29 October 2002, *SRAA v Prime Argentina SA (Holdings)* [2003-C] La Ley 122) (Arg); CNCom, 12 December 2000, *Pérez Companc SA et al v Enersis SA et al* 192 El Derecho 142 (Arg).

62 See CNCom, 11 April 2002, *Forever Living Products Argentina SRL v Beas, Juan et al*, special procedural law, LEXIS 11/31228 (Arg), declining to recognize an injunction that would have prohibited a party from disclosing any confidential information previously obtained from its opponent.

63 See JC Rivera, *Arbitraje Comercial: Internacional y Doméstico* (Lexis Nexis, 2007) 216.

64 See eg CNCom, 24 August 2000, Boess, *Adriana et al v Discotecas Free Way SRL* [2001-B] La Ley 52 (Arg); CNCom, 27 August 1999, *Fernández Gallardo, Carlos M et al v Morales, Ana M et al* (2000) III Jurisprudencia Argentina 40 (Arg). This decision is misguided, and not in line with decisions in other jurisdictions, at least in those cases where it has been established beyond dispute that the parties sought to submit the dispute to arbitration, though failing to identify the institution in charge of administering the arbitration. If the parties' consent to submit the dispute to arbitration is well established, the default rules on the constitution of the arbitration tribunal may proceed with the arbitration, either under the applicable institutional rules or under the default rules governing ad hoc arbitration proceedings.

65 NCP, arts 742 and 743.

arbitration, the death of an arbitrator will not preclude a party from seeking arbitration as long as the deceased arbitrator's involvement was not a condition precedent to submitting the dispute to arbitration.[66] Similarly, it has been held that the resignation of an arbitrator does not preclude the appointment of a replacement arbitrator to carry on the proceedings to termination.[67] If a replacement arbitrator takes over, however, there is no statutory provision specifying whether the newly reconstituted arbitral tribunal would have to repeat any previously held hearings. Although many arbitration rules establish criteria for determining when the arbitration may carry on and when it must go back to an earlier stage, the NPC does not contemplate this situation.

2.2.4 The role of courts in resolving jurisdictional questions

Although Argentine law does not have a specific provision addressing the power of arbitrators to rule on their own jurisdiction, there is a consistent line of decisions, including pronouncements of the Supreme Court of Argentina, giving effect to the principle of *competence-competence*.[68] Some judicial decisions, however, have declined to recognize that the arbitral tribunal has such power.[69] In the light of these conflicting decisions, it seems advisable to incorporate into the arbitration agreement a clause providing expressly for the power of the arbitrators to decide on their own jurisdiction.[70] In *Reef Explorations Inc v Cía General de Combustibles*, a panel of the National Commercial Court of Appeals upheld an arbitral tribunal's finding that it had jurisdiction, rejecting a conflicting decision of another panel of the same court of appeals that had raised questions about the arbitral tribunal's power to rule on its competence.[71] **2.27**

Once an arbitral tribunal upholds its jurisdiction, the jurisdictional ruling may be challenged before the courts, which may stay the arbitration until the jurisdiction of the arbitration tribunal is sustained or overruled. Alternatively, a court may decline to take the case, referring the parties to arbitration or, conversely, the court may disagree with the arbitral tribunal and insist that the matter should be settled in court. In cases of conflict between arbitral and **2.28**

---

66 See eg *Peruzzotti* (n 50).

67 See eg CComCap, 18 December 1946, *Caul, Santiago v Cabec (Soc de Resp Ltda)* (1946) IV Jurisprudencia Argentina 841, 45 La Ley 198 (Arg).

68 See eg CSJN, 24 May 2011, *Armada Holland BV Shiedam Denmark v Inter Fruit SA* (2011) 334 Fallos 552 (Arg), holding that it was improper for a lower court to question an arbitral tribunal's finding of jurisdiction after the arbitrators had rendered a final award; CNCom, 1 April 2011, *Cubero Alberto Martin et al v Olman Argentina SA* (Arg); CNCom, 28 October 2009, *Harz Und Derivate et al v Akzo Nobel Coatings SA et al* (Arg); CNCom, 16 September 2008, *SP Relevamientos Catastrales SA Recovery SA v Municipalidad de la Ciudad de Cordoba* (Arg); CNCom, 25 August 2003, *Otondo, Cesar Alberto et al v Cortina Beruatto SA et al* elDial.com Año VI, No 1358 (Arg); CSJN, 5 April 2005, *Bear Service v Cerveceria Modelo SA* (Arg) citing Model Law, Art 16 for the proposition that an arbitral tribunal has competence to determine its own jurisdiction, subject to review by a competent court; CNCom, 5 November 2002, *Reef Explorations Inc v Cía General de Combustibles* (2003) III Jurisprudencia Argentina 90 (Arg). See generally Caivano (n 53) 27.

69 See eg CSJN, 11 May 2004, *Basf Argentina SA v Capevielle Kay y Cía SA* (2004) 327 Fallos 1450; CSJN, 10 November 1988, *Nidera Argentina v Rodriguez Álvarez de Canale* (1988) 311 Fallos 2300 [1990-A] La Ley 419 (Arg); CNCom, 23 September 1999, *Cía General de Combustibles* (2001) III Jurisprudencia Argentina 53 (Arg); CNCom, 30 September 1955, *Cimic SRL v Silva* 82 La Ley 402 (Arg).

70 See eg CNCom, 06 March 2013, *Grupo Propeller S.A. v Hincubu S.A.* (Arg.), respecting a clause contained in the parties' contract granting the arbitrator power to determine his own jurisdiction. The principle *kompetenz-kompetenz* is expressly recognized in the 1998 Mercosur International Commercial Arbitration Agreement, Arts 8 and 18. The Arbitration Rules of the Inter-American Commission of Commercial Arbitration Rules, Art 3, which applies in the absence of the parties' choice of the *lex arbitri* under the Panama Convention, Art 21(1), also acknowledges that the arbitral tribunal has the power to decide on its own jurisdiction.

71 cf *Reef Explorations Inc* (n 68) with *Cía General de Combustibles* (n 69) (Arg). See also Rivera (n 63) 422.

judicial jurisdiction, where an arbitral tribunal determines that it has jurisdiction and the court disagrees, or vice versa, there is no statute providing for a stay of the arbitral proceedings before either forum. The arbitral tribunal may stay the arbitration while a party brings a jurisdictional challenge or, alternatively, it may decide to go ahead with the arbitration while the challenge remains pending before the courts.[72] The final say on jurisdiction belongs to the courts. In the absence of a higher court to put an end to eventual jurisdictional conflicts, it falls to the Supreme Court of Argentina to decide the issue. The intervention of the Supreme Court may be triggered by one of the parties to the case,[73] or by the court or arbitral tribunal whose jurisdiction is being challenged.[74]

2.29 Argentine case law recognizes the negative application of the principle of *competence-competence*.[75] If an action is filed in court with regard to a dispute subject to an arbitration agreement, the party interested in pursuing arbitration may challenge the court's jurisdiction, requesting that the matter be referred to arbitration.[76] It has been held that the right to submit a dispute to arbitration is deemed to have been waived by a party that fails to raise a timely challenge to the court's jurisdiction.[77]

2.30 It bears repeating that Argentine courts have not given a clear message as to the standard to be applied with respect to the scope and breadth of arbitration clauses. While some courts have chosen to construe clauses broadly,[78] others have followed the more traditional approach of interpreting arbitration clauses narrowly.[79] A court will of course refuse to decline jurisdiction or to refer a matter to arbitration if finds that the subject matter of the dispute is not susceptible of being settled by arbitration.[80] Arbitral jurisdiction may also have to yield in cases where the dispute encompasses both arbitrable and non-arbitrable questions.[81]

2.31 There is no provision of Argentine law expressly addressing the issue of the separability or autonomy of the arbitration clause.[82] However, this principle has been established in the 1998 Mercosur International Commercial Arbitration Agreement (Article 7), in the 1958 New York Convention (Article II(3)), and in the 1980 Vienna Convention on Contracts for

---

72 NCP, art 12.

73 NCP, art 752.

74 See eg *Basf Argentina SA* (n 69) adopting the views of the *Procurador General* that the duty to settle jurisdictional disputes that arise between arbitral tribunals and trial courts falls upon the Supreme Court of Justice (CSJN); CN Civ y Com, 26 August 2003, *Administración de Usinas y Transporte Eléctrico del Uruguay v Centro Puerto SA* (Arg), holding that a jurisdictional dispute between the arbitral tribunal and the court must be resolved by the CSJN.

75 See Caivano (n 53) 27.

76 See eg CNCom, 14 August 1990, *Vázquez Torrielli, EN v Vázquez de Castro* 141 El Derecho 121, [1990-E] La Ley 148 (Arg).

77 See eg CComCap, 6 April 1967, *Iungman, Mauricio v Belgrano/Cía de seguros* (1967) IV Jurisprudencia Argentina 58 (Arg), holding that a party had waived the right to arbitration by failing to bring a timely motion before the Argentine Court to dismiss the action to the arbitral tribunal; cf CNCiv, 3 March 1966, *Garde Otto & Cía v Municipalidad de la Capital* 15 El Derecho 677, 122 La Ley 370 (Arg), to the effect that a party may waive the right to proceed to arbitration by submitting to the jurisdiction of a court.

78 See eg *SA La Razón EEFIC & A* (n 25).

79 See eg CNCom, 10 November 2011, *Esparrica Mario Roberto v Famiq SA* (Arg); *Vañesa Andrea Fabiana* (n 44); CNCom, 15 July 2010, *Araujo Osvaldo Gabriel v Frances Administradora de Inversiones SA et al* (Arg); CNCom, 5 May 2000, *Alquigas SA v Servinorte SA* [2000-E] La Ley 489 (Arg).

80 See eg CNCom, 6 May 2010, *Cri Holding Inc Sucursal Argentina v Cía Argentina de Comodoro Rivadavia Explotación de Petróleo SA* (Arg).

81 See eg *Vañesa Andrea Fabiana* (n 44).

82 See Caivano (n 53) 42–3.

the International Sale of Goods (Article 8(1)), all of which have been ratified by Argentina. The courts in Argentina have not, however, been consistent in applying this principle; some cases have recognized it[83] while others have not.[84] Recent decisions have enhanced the autonomy of the arbitration agreement. For example, the decision in *Smit International Argentina SA v Puerto Mariel SA* affirmed the doctrine of separability of the arbitration agreement, reasoning that the termination of a charter agreement did not affect the validity and effectiveness of an arbitration clause incorporated into the main contract. The court acknowledged that although the separability principle had not been incorporated in Argentine rules on arbitration, yet its application was warranted due to its worldwide acceptance in international conventions to which Argentina was a party and the scholarly support it enjoys.

2.2.5 The role of courts in enjoining arbitration

Although Argentine law does not include a specific provision empowering courts to enjoin arbitration proceedings, the courts have resorted to this type of injunction on more than one occasion, especially in cases in which the government, or a government instrumentality, was involved in the arbitration. **2.32**

In a case involving Entidad Binacional Yacyretá,[85] a bi-national state entity, Yacyretá sought an injunction against continuing arbitral proceedings in Buenos Aires under the ICC Arbitration Rules at the same time as an Argentine court was considering a challenge to the arbitrators and the terms of reference they had drafted. The recusal of the members of the arbitral tribunal was brought before the Argentine courts after the ICC Court of Arbitration rejected the challenge without disclosing its reasons. Yacyretá's request before the Argentine courts rested on allegations that the arbitral tribunal had: (1) disregarded Yacyretá's suggestions for changes in the terms of reference; (2) issued a procedural order announcing that the terms of reference would be sent to the International Chamber of Commerce for approval even if not signed by both parties; and (3) demonstrated its bias against Yacyretá by issuing this procedural order before an Argentine court could rule on Yacyretá's recusal motion. The court observed that the fact that arbitration was administered by an institution did not exempt the arbitral tribunal from its duty to provide the parties with equal treatment and due process, and ordered a stay of the arbitration proceedings based on the behaviour of the arbitrators and the lack of explanation for the ICC Court's decision to reject Yacyretá's recusal motion. The justification for the injunction was the absence of a reasoned decision, which the Argentine court regarded as a ground for vacating the ICC ruling, thus the need to prevent the eventual annulment of the award and unnecessary expenditures on the parties. The arbitration did not proceed after the court decision. **2.33**

[83] See eg CNCiv y Com, 3 January 2011, *Smit Intl Argentina SA v Puerto Mariel*; CNCom, 27 August 1999, *Camuzzi Argentina SA v Sodigas Sur, SA/sumario* 185 El Derecho 125 (Arg); citing CNCom, 26 September 1988, *Welbers SA, Enrique C v Extraktionstechnik Gesellschaft für Anlagenbay* [1989-E] La Ley 304 (Arg).

[84] See eg CNCom, 15 February 2008, *Miracle SA et al v Fernández, Juan Carlos* 228 El Derecho 280 (Arg); CNCom, 30 July 1965, *Hadra y Cía, SA, Pablo v Ferriarini, Dardo* 120 La Ley 322 (Arg).

[85] See AB Bianchi, 'Cuando los jueces vienen marchando' [2005-A] La Ley 27, discussing and criticizing the *Yacyretá* case. *Estado Nacional—Procuración del Tesoro* (n 24) issuing an injunction ordering the suspension of arbitral proceedings against the state, pending the consideration of a recusal motion; *Entidad Binacional Yacyretá* (n 23) issuing and subsequently enforcing an injunction against further proceedings by the arbitral tribunal pending judicial proceedings to determine the issues to be arbitrated.

2.34 In *National Grid*,[86] an investment arbitration governed by the UNCITRAL Rules, in which the arbitral tribunal sat in Washington, DC, the respondent—the Argentine government—sought to set aside a ruling by the ICC Court, acting as appointing authority, which rejected Argentina's challenge against an arbitrator without disclosing reasons. The court ordered the arbitration stayed, which the arbitral tribunal chose to disregard, because it refused to acknowledge the jurisdiction of the Argentine courts over arbitration proceedings conducted in Washington DC.[87]

2.35 *Yacyretá* and *National Grid* are the only reported cases in which the courts decided to enjoin arbitration proceedings. In both cases the Argentine government was a party to the proceedings and in both cases the injunction was granted in favour of the government. It is neither common nor customary in Argentina to issue unreasoned awards, and ICC decisions dismissing or confirming a challenge do not disclose the reasons behind the decision. Both cases, *Yacyretá* and *National Grid*, suggest that unreasoned awards and decisions, even though the parties agreed to abide by them, face an uncertain outcome before Argentine courts.

2.3 During the Arbitration

2.3.1 The role of courts in challenges to arbitrators

2.36 The two basic principles used by the courts to resolve challenges to would be arbitrators are that arbitrators may not be recused without cause and can be removed by agreement of the parties or a court decision. Party-appointed arbitrators may be recused only on grounds arising after their nomination, regardless of the party appointing them. However, there are basic statutory grounds for challenging arbitrators, which vary depending on whether the challenge is brought against arbitrators *de jure* as opposed to equity arbitrators or *amigables componedores*.

2.37 *De jure* arbitrators may be challenged on the same grounds applicable to the recusal of judges,[88] which include broad and clearly defined conflicts of interest, such as being related to any of the parties, sharing with the parties or their lawyers an interest in the dispute or in a business enterprise in which any of the parties or lawyers have an interest, participating in a pending lawsuit in which one of the parties is involved, or being a creditor or debtor of either party.[89] The grounds for challenging *amigables componedores* include having a direct or indirect interest in the matter; being related to one of the parties; and/or a manifest enmity with the parties on account of any specific incidents.[90] In addition, an arbitrator may be removed in accordance with the rules of an arbitral institution.

86 *National Grid v Republic of Argentina*, ICSID Case No ARB/07/17.

87 For a discussion of *National Grid v Argentina*, see (2009) 103 AJIL 722, available at <http://www.crowell.com/documents/National-Grid-plc-v-Argentina-case-comment.pdf>; and <http://lettersblogatory.com/2011/03/16/case-of-the-day-argentine-republic-v-natl-grid-plc/>.

88 See NCP, art 746 which provides that:

> Arbitrators appointed by the court may be challenged on the same grounds as judges. Arbitrators appointed by agreement of the parties may be challenged only for reasons of which the parties become aware after the appointment was made.
>
> Arbitrators may not be challenged without proper grounds. They shall be removed only with the consent of the parties and court approval.

89 See NCP, art 17.

90 See NCP, art 768 which provides that:

> *Amigable componedores* may be challenged only for reasons of which the parties become aware after the appointment has been made.

Any challenge to an arbitrator must be filed before the arbitral tribunal itself, but if the recused arbitrator refuses to step down, the challenge must be referred to the court that would have had jurisdiction over the dispute if it had not been submitted to arbitration. The arbitration is stayed until the challenge is decided.[91] **2.38**

2.3.2 The role of courts in compelling testimony/evidence

Rules applicable to the taking of evidence

The parties are free to choose the rules of procedure, including rules of evidence, applicable to the arbitration, but in the absence of the parties' agreement the arbitral tribunal must follow the procedural rules applicable to 'ordinary [judicial] proceedings' (*proceso ordinario*) or a more abbreviated procedure (*juicio sumario*), depending on the amount of material before the court and the complexity of the dispute.[92] *Amigables componedores*, in contrast, are free to select the rules of procedure they deem most suitable to the dispute.[93] **2.39**

Admissibility and weight of evidence

The arbitral tribunal enjoys broad powers to decide on the admissibility and weight of evidence, as well as the time, manner, and form in which evidence will be presented. It is only in the absence of the parties' agreement that ordinary rules of procedure are to be followed. Each party is bound to produce evidence in support of its own claims and defences.[94] If a substantive rule does not given any indication as to the party bearing the burden of producing evidential proof, the burden is most likely to fall on the party in the best position to have control and access to **2.40**

The only valid grounds for challenge shall be:

1) Direct or indirect interest in the matter;
2) Relationship with any of the parties of consanguinity within the fourth degree, or of affinity within the second degree;
3) Manifest enmity with the parties on account of any specific incidents.

On the incidental plea of challenge, the proceedings shall be conducted in accordance with the procedural rules provided for the challenge of *de jure* arbitrators.

[91] See NCP, art 747 which provides that:

The challenge shall be brought before the same arbitral tribunal within five days of the challenging party's becoming aware of the appointment of the arbitrators.

If the challenged arbitrator refuses to resign, the challenge proceeding shall be conducted by the judge before whom the submission was concluded or who should have been competent to take the case in the absence of the submission.

The provisions of article 17 and the following, when applicable shall apply.

The decisions of the judge shall be final.

The arbitration proceedings shall remain suspended, pending a decision on the challenge.

[92] See NCP, art 751 which provides that:

If rules of arbitral procedure have not been agreed upon in the arbitral clause, in the submission, or in a subsequent agreement by the parties, the arbitral tribunal shall decide whether to follow the rules for ordinary or summary judicial proceedings, taking into account the nature and economic importance of the case. This decision shall be final.

[93] See NCP, art 769 which provides that:

Amigables componedores are not bound by legal formalities; they shall limit themselves to receiving pleadings or documents submitted by the parties, request clarifications they deem proper, and render an award based on their knowledge and understanding.

[94] See NCP, art 387.

such evidence.[95] Arbitrators enjoy wide discretion to determine the standard, weight, and sufficiency of the evidence.

Compulsory production of evidence

2.41 If a party refuses to produce evidence, the arbitral tribunal must seek assistance from the courts, because the arbitration tribunal lacks the power to enforce compulsory measures. Argentine courts are expected to cooperate with arbitral tribunals to ensure that the arbitral process is carried out in the most rapid, effective, and practical manner.[96] Article 753 of the NCP provides that: 'Arbitators must address themselves to the courts for the compulsory summoning of witnesses and for obtaining an order for the forwarding of documentary pieces of evidence.'[97] Although there is no express provision allowing a party to seek judicial assistance from a court, such assistance is forthcoming and generally provided by the court of the seat of arbitration.

2.3.3 Requirements regarding the ability of foreign practitioners to appear as counsel or arbitrator

2.42 At least in principle, only lawyers admitted to the Buenos Aires bar may appear and submit filings before courts sitting in the federal district of the City of Buenos Aires. However, the only express requirements found in the NPC regarding the ability of foreign practitioners to serve as arbitrators are that *de jure* arbitrators and *amigable componedores* must be of age and fully able to exercise their civil rights.[98] There is no requirement that arbitrators be Argentine citizens or residents, and the rules of civil and commercial procedure do not expressly preclude foreign practitioners from serving as arbitrators.[99] Despite this, some courts have held that only lawyers are allowed to be *de jure* arbitrators.[100] Legal commentators believe that this requirement lacks a sound legal foundation and does not, in any event, seem to apply to international arbitration proceedings.[101] Foreign practitioners are not precluded from serving as counsel, and there are no reported cases regarding the ability of foreign lawyers to represent a client in arbitral proceedings taking place in Argentina.[102] As a practical matter, it is advisable to retain local counsel if court intervention becomes necessary.

2.3.4 Local requirements for the conduct of arbitration hearings

Oaths

2.43 Prior to the commencement of any arbitration proceedings, arbitrators and *amigables componedores* must be sworn in before the clerk of an Argentine court. There are judicial decisions acknowledging the right of the parties to waive the requirement that an *amigable componedor*

---

95 Spinillo and Vogelius (n 1) 43.

96 See NCP, art 753 which provides that:

> Arbitrators cannot issue orders of compulsion or enforcement. They must request compulsory measures from the court which shall lend its assistance in order to achieve the speediest and most efficient conduct of the arbitral proceedings.

97 Arbitration Law & Practice, ARG C-4-5.

98 See NCP, art 753.

99 Such a limitation, if imposed, may be in conflict with the equal protection clause embedded in the Argentine National Constitution, art 20.

100 See eg CCivCap, 21 May 1948, *Amura, Elso JC v Goglino, Emilio José y otros* II Jurisprudencia Argentina 540 (Arg).

101 See Rivera (n 63) 231; GS Tawil, 'Argentina' in P Sanders (ed), *International Handbook on Commercial Arbitration* (Supp, 2011) 13–14.

102 See Spinillo and Vogelius (n 1) 48.

(or *árbitro arbitrador*, as equity arbitrators are also called) be sworn,[103] but no federal case has created such an exception for *de jure* arbitrators.

2.44 The arbitral tribunal is empowered to swear in witnesses of fact and experts, informing them of the potential criminal consequences of making false statements. Perjury before an arbitral tribunal has been held not to constitute a criminal offence subject to prosecution.[104] This questionable decision[105] was rendered on the ground that an arbitral tribunal does not qualify as a 'competent authority' under article 275 of the Criminal Code of Argentina.[106]

Discretion to control the evidence and the evidentiary hearing

2.45 Arbitrators have broad discretion to decide the relevance, admissibility, materiality, and weight of evidence, and to control the conduct of the hearing. To the extent that the provisions of the NCP are applicable, an oral evidentiary hearing will take place in order to examine factual or expert witnesses.[107] There are no cases in point to indicate whether the parties can waive their right to a hearing, proceeding with the arbitration on the basis of documentary evidence alone.

2.46 The parties are not allowed to appear as witnesses, and their spouses and relatives are similarly excluded.[108] The arbitral tribunal may appoint an expert on its own motion or at the request of one of the parties.[109] Each party is also entitled to present its own party-appointed expert.[110]

Liability of arbitrators

2.47 Argentine law allows for the imposition of civil liability on *de jure* arbitrators and *amigables componedores*. Specifically, the NCP imposes liability for damages for failing to issue the award within the appropriate time limit. In evaluating whether an arbitrator or *amiable compositeur* is to be held liable for failing at his task, Argentine courts require circumstances reflecting negligence or bad faith.[111]

2.48 Argentine law also allows for the imposition of criminal liability on *de jure* arbitrators and *amigables componedores*. Article 269 of the Criminal Code imposes a fine on an arbitrator who does not rule in accordance with the law agreed to by the parties or who relies on false

---

[103] See eg CFedCap, 13 June 1949, *Matarazzo Ltda (Soc Paulista de Navegación) v Cassanello, Ángel SA* 56 La Ley 722 (Arg).

[104] See eg CNCrim and CNCorr, 8 February 1946, *Enquin, José* 44 La Ley 735 (Arg).

[105] See RJ Caivano, *Arbitraje* (Ad-Hoc, 2000) 234–5.

[106] The Criminal Code of Argentina, art 275 provides in its pertinent part:

> Any lay or expert witness or interpreter who, before a competent authority, makes an affirmatively false statement, denies the truth or fails to speak the truth in his testimony, in whole or in part, at his or her deposition, in his report, translation or interpretation, shall be subject to a prison term between one month and four years.

[107] NCP, art 360.

[108] See NCP, art 427: 'A party may not offer as a witness someone who is related to them by blood or in direct line, their spouse even if they are legally separated, unless the matter concerns the recognition of signatures.' Witnesses may be challenged for appearing to lack impartiality, such as when it is alleged that a given witness maintains a relationship of 'dependency' with one of the parties (eg current employees of a party, or a party's former employees asked to testify about events occurring during their employment by one of the parties). The court or arbitral tribunal may ultimately decide to admit their testimony, retaining the last word on the credibility and the weight to be attached to such evidence.

[109] See NCP, art 458.

[110] See NCP, art 462.

[111] See eg CNCiv, 26 May 1953, *Barredó, Antonio Oscar v Kutscher, Ascher y otro* (1953) IV Jurisprudencia Argentina 343 (Arg).

evidence. More significantly, article 265 of the Criminal Code imposes a prison term on an arbitrator who engages in self-dealing.

2.4 The Award

2.4.1 Time limit to render the award

2.49 If the parties have agreed to *de jure* arbitration, the arbitrators are required to render an award within the time designated in the arbitration agreement. In the absence of agreement by the parties, the court may fix such time period. Holidays are not counted for the purpose of determining whether an award has been rendered within the specified time.[112]

2.50 If the parties have agreed to equity arbitration, and unless the parties agree otherwise, the *amigables componedores* must render an award within three months. Courts will not interfere with the fixing of a time period in cases where the arbitration is being conducted under the auspices of an arbitration institution whose rules provide for extending the period of time that a tribunal has to render an award.[113] It is the principle of party autonomy and the absence of a mandatory time period that allows the parties to extend it by will.

2.4.2 Mandatory rules as to form

2.51 Articles 754[114] and 757[115] of the NCP set out the requirements that both *de jure* arbitrators and *amigables componedores* must follow in order to render a valid arbitral award. Thus, an arbitral award must address all of the issues submitted for decision,[116] including all ancillary matters such as fees and other costs arising from the proceedings. Awards must be rendered within the established deadline and be properly reasoned both in fact and in law.[117] The award must be made in writing, and state the place and date of its issuance.[118]

---

[112] See eg CCivCap, 19 July 1922, *Scotti v Naón*, 9 Jurisprudencia Argentina 74.

[113] See eg CNCom, 7 September 2007, *Papel de Tucumán SA v Banade* (Arg); see also RJ Caivano, 'El plazo para laudar y el carácter supletorio de las normas legales en el arbitraje institucional' (2008) 230 *Revista de Derecho Comercial y de las Obligaciones* 813.

[114] NCP, art 754 provides that:

> Arbitrators shall make the award on all matters submitted for their decision within the period of time provided in the submission, subject to any extension agreed upon by the parties.
> Ancillary disputes as well as those consented to by the parties shall also be deemed to have been included in the submission to arbitration.

[115] NCP, art 757 provides that:

> An award signed by a majority of the arbitrators shall be valid even if any members of the tribunal refuse to participate in the proceeding or in the making of the award.
> If a consensus cannot be reached because the opinions or the votes on each issue lead to situations that are irreconcilable with regard to all the issues submitted to arbitration, an additional arbitration shall be appointed to resolve the deadlock.
> If a majority agreement has been reached with regard to certain issues of the dispute, an award shall be made in respect thereof. The parties or the judge, as the case may be, shall appoint another arbitrator who shall make an award in respect of the remaining issues of the dispute within the period of time designated by the parties or judge, as the case may be.

[116] See eg CNCom, 3 June 2003, *Calles, Ricardo et al v General Motors Corps* [2004-B] La Ley 313 (Arg), partially setting aside an award for not addressing all the issues submitted to arbitration.

[117] See eg CNCom, 20 September 2004, *Ogden Entertainment Servs Inc v Eijo, Néstor E. y otro* [2005-B] La Ley 21 (Arg).

[118] See eg CNCom, 9 December 1959, *De Bodnar, Ricardo v Barbieri, José y otro* 99 La Ley 130 (Arg), holding that the arbitrator's vote must be signed to be valid.

In order for an award to be valid and enforceable, it must be signed by a majority of the arbitrators and, if a majority decision cannot be reached on one or more issues, a new arbitrator must be appointed.[119] The majority of arbitrators must rule on those issues on which consensus can be reached, leaving the undecided ones to be ruled on by the arbitral tribunal constituted with the newly-appointed arbitrator.[120] Dissenting opinions are allowed and must be signed and delivered to the parties as an annex to the award.[121] 2.52

2.4.3 Mandatory rules as to substance

Damages and interest

Punitive or exemplary damages are not allowed under Argentine law,[122] except in very specific situations under the Consumer Protection Act.[123] Arbitrators may award interest but, unless the parties agree otherwise, compound interest is not allowed.[124] 2.53

Costs

The parties are free to agree in advance, whether in an arbitration clause or in the *compromiso*, on the amount of costs and how these should be allocated. The term 'costs' includes not only the fees of the arbitrators and the arbitral institution, but also the parties' costs for legal representation (ie attorneys' fees). The arbitral tribunal will decide this issue in the absence of agreement by the parties. In principle, the rules applicable to the assessment and allocation of costs incurred in court proceedings apply equally to arbitration proceedings,[125] the general rule being that the losing party bears the costs of the successful party.[126] If an award is subject to appeal, the court will determine the costs of the arbitration without sending the case back to the arbitral tribunal.[127] 2.54

Arbitrators' fees

There is no specific legal provision addressing the level of fees paid to the members of the arbitral tribunal. In a case in which the parties had not reached agreement on this, the Supreme Court saw fit to resort to the rules and practice of the International Chamber of Commerce ICC regarding the assessment of fees.[128] 2.55

---

119 NCP, art 757.

120 NCP, art 757.

121 See eg *De Bodnar* (n 118).

122 See Argentine CivC, art 1083: 'Compensations for damages shall consist of restoring things to their prior state, except that monetary compensation shall do if such a restoration is impossible. Nevertheless, the aggrieved party retains the right to opt for compensation in money', available at <http://www.codigocivilonline.com.ar/codigo_civil_online_1066_1106.html>.

123 See Law No 26321, 7 April 2008, BO, art 25 (Arg):

> In the instance that a provider does not comply with its legal or contractual obligations to the consumer, the judge may upon request apply a civil fine for the benefit of the consumer. The amount of compensation shall be determined according to the magnitude of the damage and the circumstances of the case. If the fault of the wrongful act or the breach of the contract is attributable to more than one provider, all providers will be jointly responsible, with the proper reimbursements among them.

124 See Argentine CivC, art 623, providing that 'no interest shall be owed on interest . . .'. Compound interest is, however, allowed in many banking operations and commercial transactions in general (Argentine ComC, arts 569, 788, and 795).

125 NCP, art 772.

126 NCP, art 68.

127 See eg CNCom, 13 March 2009, *Nea Commerce SA v Sky Argentina SCA* (Arg).

128 See eg CSJN, 29 April 1997, *Blanco, Guillermo y otro v Petroquímica Bahía Blanca y otro* (1997) 320 Fallos 700 (Arg).

2.56 The parties are free to agree in advance on the determination of expert witnesses, attorneys, and consulting fees,[129] either by entering into an express agreement on the matter or by agreeing to follow the rules of an arbitral institution.[130] In the absence of such an agreement, it is for the arbitral tribunal to assess the attorneys' fees and the costs of the arbitration proceedings.[131] Ordinarily, the court will determine the amount of fees pursuant to the fee schedule provided in the law applicable to judicial proceedings,[132] calling for 'the application of its provisions, whenever they are compatible with the nature of the [arbitration proceeding]'. Thus, fees applicable to judicial proceedings would apply only if the arbitration were to evidence a format similar to court proceedings, meaning that the arbitration must include an exchange of written submissions, the production of evidence, and other steps characterizing judicial proceedings.[133] In some cases, the Supreme Court of Argentina has found that the statute regulating attorneys' fees did not apply, instead assessing arbitration fees pursuant to the ICC Rules.[134] In other cases the courts saw fit to apply the schedule of fees applicable to attorneys' fees, based on the amount at stake and the complexity of the case.[135] Even when that fee schedule is applicable, it has been held that courts may disregard it whenever the amount to be paid pursuant to the schedule would result in an unfair and insufficient amount of compensation or whenever such an amount would be excessive according to the court.[136]

---

[129] Law No 24432, 15 December 1994 (published 1 January 1995), art 14 (Arg): 'Professionals or experts in any activity shall be entitled to enter into agreement with their clients setting out their compensation, without regard to the schedule of fees set out in laws. If such fees pertain to services in judicial or arbitral proceedings, the general rule that such fees may be recovered from the losing party shall apply.' <http://www.infojus.gov.ar/index.php?kk_seccion=documento&registro=LEYNAC&docid=LEY%2520C%2520024432%25201994%252012%252015>.

[130] See eg RJ Caivano, 'Los honorarios de los abogados en el arbitraje' (1998-F) Jurisprudencia Argentina 167.

[131] See NCP, art 772 which provides that:

> Arbitrators and *amigables componedores* shall decide on the imposition of costs in accordance with articles 68 et seq.
>
> The party who fails to perform any actions indispensable to the successful completion of the arbitration shall pay costs, in addition to any fine provided under article 740. The fees of arbitrators, the secretary of the tribunal, attorneys, solicitors (*procuradores*), and other professionals shall be fixed by the court.
>
> The arbitrators may request the court to order the deposit of, or attachment for, an amount equivalent to their fees, unless the value of the property at stake in the arbitration is a sufficient guarantee.

[132] Law No 21839, 14 July 1978 (published on 20 July 1978) (Arg) <http://www.infojus.gov.ar/index.php?kk_seccion=documento&registro=LEYNAC&docid=LEY%2520C%2520021839%25201978%252007%252014>.

[133] See CSJN, 11 November 1997, *Yacimientos Carboníferos Fiscales re/arbitral tribunal* (1997) 320 Fallos 2379 (Arg); *Blanco, Guillermo y otro* (n 128).

[134] See *Yacimientos Carboníferos Fiscales* (n 133).

[135] See eg CNCom, 30 June 2011, *Igarzabal Claudio Adrian v Berries Premium SA* (Arg), distinguishing *Blanco Guillermo* and applying Law No 21839, regulating attorney fees in court proceedings, on the ground that arbitration proceedings have many similarities with judicial proceedings, including the formal presentation of the summons and complaint, a period of time to answer, an opportunity to file a motion to dismiss, etc.

[136] Law No 24432, 15 December 1994 (published on 1 January 1995), art 13 (Arg):

> Judges should regulate the fees of professionals, expert witnesses, receivers, liquidators and other auxiliaries of the court, for any work done in support of a judicial or arbitral proceedings, without regard to the minimum amounts or percentages established by the national or local laws governing such fees, in those cases in which the nature, reach, time, quality or result of the work done or the value of the property at stake suggests that strict application of the fee schedule is evidently and unjustifiably disproportionate in light of the importance of the work done and the compensation to be fixed under such fee regime. In such cases, the decision deciding not to apply said fee schedule must indicate, under pain of nullity, the reasons supporting setting aside the fee schedule.

2.5 After the Award

2.5.1 Local standards for setting aside/annulment

Domestic arbitral awards

2.57 Unless the parties have waived the right to appeal, arbitral awards rendered in ad hoc, institutional, or *de jure* arbitrations may be appealed by the parties on the same grounds as court judgments.[137] An appeal provides the courts with the power to review the finding of facts and application of law made by the arbitral tribunal. In contrast to the right to appeal, the parties are not allowed to waive the right to set aside an award or to request clarification.[138] Also in contrast with appellate review, the scope of review in an action to set aside is much more limited, as discussed at paragraph 2.58. It has been consistently held that the merits of arbitral awards cannot be reviewed, regardless of whether the award was rendered by arbitrators *de jure*[139] or by *amigables componedores*.[140]

Grounds for setting aside

2.58 There are significant differences between the grounds for setting aside an award rendered by *de jure* arbitrators,[141] and one rendered by *amigables componedores*.[142] According to articles 760–761 NCP, an Argentine court may set aside an award, rendered by arbitrators *de jure* if the award (a) manifested procedural errors that are considered fundamental;[143] (b) was rendered after the term for making the award had elapsed; (c) decides on issues that were not submitted

---

[137] See NCP, art 758 which provides that: 'Any recourse available against a court judgment is available against an arbitral award, unless such a recourse has been waived in the submission.'

[138] See NCP, art 760 which provides that:

> If recourse has been waived, any request for recourse against the award shall be rejected without further proceedings.
>
> The waiver of recourse shall not, however, prevent the parties from requesting reargument, nor shall it prevent a request for a declaration of nullity on the grounds that the award is based on substantial procedural defects, that the award has not been made within the applicable time period or that the award deals with a dispute that does not fall within the terms of the submission. In the latter case, the declaration of nullity shall be partial if the award is divisible.
>
> A request for an interpretation or a declaration of nullity of the award shall be decided without any substantiation.

[139] See eg CNCom, 09 December 2009, *EDF Intl SA v Endesa Internacional—España* (Arg); CNCom, 21 February 2008, *Nemesio Antonio y otros v Teledigital Cable SA* (Arg); *Mobil Argentina SA* (n 25); *Calles* (n 116).

[140] See eg CSJN, 18 August 1922, *Otto Frank v Provincia de Buenos Aires* 9 Jurisprudencia Argentina 190 (Arg); CNCom, 4 April 1989, *Salaberry, G et al v Natalío Alba SA* (1989) III Jurisprudencia Argentina 514 (Arg); *SA La Razón EEFIC & A* (n 25).

[141] NCP, arts 760–761.

[142] NCP, art 771 which provides that:

> The award made by *amigable componedores* shall be final. However, if the award was made after the designated period of time or in respect of matters not contemplated in the submission, the parties may request the annulment of the award within five days of the receipt of notice thereof.
>
> Upon receipt of the application, the court shall notify the other party, who shall have five days to reply. After the period of time has elapsed, the court shall give a final decision as to the validity or nullity of the award.

[143] See *Calles* (n 116) partially setting aside an award where the arbitral tribunal failed to decide all the issues it was called upon to decide; *Nemesio Antonio* (n 139) stating in dicta that the failure to rule on an issue amounted to the kind of essential procedural error that would permit an award to be set aside pursuant to the NCP, art 760; CNCom, 2 May 2008, *Red de Monitoreo SRL v ADT Security SA* (Arg), declining a party's request to set aside an arbitral award on the basis of alleged procedural errors because the party's memorandum of law did not identify any errors the arbitrators had committed. *Mobil Argentina SA* (n 25) rejecting a

to arbitration;[144] or (d) contains contradictory decisions.[145] Whether the award will be set aside in part or in full very much depends on whether the points or issues meriting annulment can be separated from the other parts of the award that were not affected by the part at fault.

2.59 A *de jure* arbitrator's award may also be set aside if any of the parties to the arbitration agreement lack capacity or if the subject matter of the dispute is not capable of settlement by arbitration.[146] In contrast, the only grounds for setting aside an arbitral award rendered by an *amigable componedor* are that it was rendered beyond the time limit provided by the agreement of the parties or by law, or that the award includes decisions on issues that were not submitted to the arbitrators.[147] It has been held that the parties are not allowed to expand by agreement on the limited grounds for reviewing awards rendered by *amigables componedores*.[148]

2.60 In addition to the statutory grounds for setting aside awards rendered by *de jure* arbitrators and *amigable componedores*, Argentine courts have long recognized that an arbitral award may be set aside on grounds of public policy. While the use of public policy as a ground for setting aside an award (or as an obstacle to its recognition and enforcement) should be used sparingly, the Argentine Supreme Court's loose manipulation of public policy in *Cartellone Construcciones Civiles v Hidroeléctrica Norpatagónica o HIDRONOR*, setting aside an arbitral award for being 'unconstitutional, illegal or unreasonable', creates uncertainty about the vulnerability of awards rendered or sought to be enforced in Argentina.[149] Regrettably, the *Cartellone* decision had an impact in a subsequent international case, *Ogden Entertainment Services v Eijo, Néstor E y otro ('Odgen Entertainment')*, in which the Chamber of the National Court of Commercial Appeals declined to recognize a foreign arbitral award on the ground that the award of attorneys' fees contained therein was excessive and thus a violation of public policy.[150] Although *Ogden Entertainment* did not refer expressly to *Cartellone*, it nonetheless utilized a *Cartellone*-like standard in declining to recognize a foreign arbitral award on the grounds that the award was excessive.[151]

2.61 Unsurprisingly, *Cartellone* has been the subject of strong criticism,[152] and some lower courts have openly criticized its manipulation of 'public policy' grounds to vacate an arbitral award.[153] Criticism of the *Cartellone* decision may explain why the Argentine Supreme

challenge against an award on this ground; CNCom, 12 July 2002, *Total Austral SA v Saiz, Francisco* (2003) II Jurispudencia Argentina 77 (Arg), CNCom, 21 November 2001, *Cortesfilms Argentina SA v Seb Argentina* 196 El Derecho 620 (Arg).

144 See CComCap, 15 July 1957, *Haigay Sary v Vesgan, Danielan et al* 89 La Ley 737 (Arg), setting aside an award where the arbitrator decided an issue he or she was not called upon to decide; *Mobil Argentina SA* (n 25); *Calles* (n 116). See also CSJN, 27 December 1974, *Yacimentos Petrolíferos Fiscales v SA Sargo Argentina* (1974) 290 Fallos 458 (Arg), setting aside an award, via a writ of error (*recurso extraordinario*), on the ground that that the appellate court denied an action to set aside against an award that failed to give reasons, rendering an award in US dollars rather than Argentine pesos, as required in the *compromiso*.

145 See *Calles* (n 116).

146 See NCP, art 740.

147 See eg CSJN, 24 August 1976, 'Carmen Alba v Adriana Chevy y otros,' (1976) 295 Fallos 597 (Arg); CSJN, 13 August 1907, *Provincia de Buenos Aires v Los herederos de Juan José Basavilbaso* (1907) 107 Fallos 126 (Arg).

148 See eg *Salaberry* (n 140).

149 *José Cartellone Construcciones Civiles* (n 24).

150 See *Ogden Entertainment* (n 24).

151 *Ogden Entertainment* (n 24).

152 See Rivera (n 63) 676 and fn 111.

153 See eg *Mobil Argentina SA* (n 25).

Court of Justice has not since issued a similar opinion, and why some lower courts have avoided its application and even criticized it openly in their decisions.[154]

In a relatively recent decision, *Mobil Argentina v Gasnor*, another panel of the National Commercial Court of Appeals confirmed once again that an express waiver to appeal an arbitration award does not violate public policy, because adequate judicial review is provided in the annulment procedure, which is not subject to waiver.[155] **2.62**

Foreign arbitral awards

Arbitral awards rendered outside Argentina are considered 'foreign' or 'international' awards, regardless of whether they were rendered in a country adhering to the New York Convention. Not having entered a reciprocity reservation to the New York Convention, Argentina does not discriminate, for the purpose of enforcing foreign arbitral awards, between countries that are parties to the New York Convention and the few that are not. There are no reported cases, to the authors' knowledge, of awards rendered in Argentina that were considered 'foreign', 'international', or 'non-domestic'. **2.63**

The enforcement of foreign or 'international' awards and foreign judgments is governed by applicable international treaties and, in the absence of a treaty, the rules of civil and commercial procedure embodied in articles 517 to 519*bis* NCP, laying out the grounds under which their recognition and enforcement may be refused. **2.64**

Applying the 1958 New York Convention, the Supreme Court of Argentina recently overturned a lower court decision that had declined to recognize an award by second-guessing the arbitral tribunal on the issue of whether the arbitration agreement had complied with the writing requirement called for by the New York Convention. Confirming the view of the lower court, the appellate court decided to set the award aside on the ground that the parties had not actually concluded the contract of carriage of goods in which the arbitration clause was incorporated.[156] The Supreme Court found that the parties had satisfied the requirement of Article IV of the Convention, submitting a copy of the arbitration agreement the formal validity of which had been confirmed by the arbitral tribunal.[157] **2.65**

2.5.2 Local procedures for setting aside/annulment

Domestic arbitral awards

A party that wishes to challenge a *de jure* arbitrator's award may bring a motion: (1) asking the arbitral tribunal to reconsider its decision; (2) appealing the arbitrator's decision to a court or second arbitral tribunal; and/or (3) requesting that the award be declared null and void in action to set aside. **2.66**

With the exception of the last ground for challenge, all of the grounds mentioned at paragraph 2.66 can be waived either by express agreement of the parties or implicitly by adopting the rules of an arbitral institution.[158] With the exception of a challenge to set aside the award, **2.67**

---

154 *Mobil Argentina SA* (n 25).

155 NPC, art 760. See also CNCom, 25 April 2011, *Mobil Argentina SA v Gasnor SA*, affirming CNCom, 8 August 2007, *Mobil Argentina SA v Gasnor SA* (n 25).

156 The decision of the court of appeal can be found at <http://ar.vlex.com/vid/-280301515>.

157 See *Armada Holland BV Schiedam Denmark* (n 25); see also the commentary at <http://fallos.diprargentina.com/2008/04/armada-holland-bv-schiedam-denmark-c.html>.

158 The waiver provision contained in the NCP has been found to be constitutional. See eg CSJN, 30 July 1974, 'UOM de la República Argentina' (1974) 289 Fallos 158 (Arg); *Sociedad de Inversiones Inmobiliarias del Puerto* (n 23) rejecting a party's argument that a waiver of the right to appeal constituted a violation of public policy.

which cannot be waived, the parties may agree to the imposition of a fine against a party that challenges the award. Such a fine must be paid by the party challenging the award before the court renders its decision on the challenge.[159]

2.68 To appeal a *de jure* arbitrator's award, a party must bring a motion before the arbitral tribunal within five days of being notified of the award.[160] Thus, the arbitral tribunal's jurisdiction may include its authority to decide the availability of this appeal, by way of exception to the general principle that it becomes *functus officio* once the award is rendered. If the tribunal grants the application, the file is transferred to the court of appeals with territorial and subject matter jurisdiction over the seat of arbitration. If the arbitral tribunal does not grant leave to appeal, the losing party retains the option to directly seek leave from a court of appeals, within five days of being notified of the tribunal's decision. Before ruling on this leave for appeal, the court must first hear the other party.[161] The Court may then reach a decision solely on the basis of the record of the arbitral proceedings, without the need of further exchange of briefs or evidence.[162] The scope of appellate review of arbitral awards encompasses *de novo* review of both facts and the law, obviously addressing the merits of the case. Thus, if a party wishes to avoid judicial scrutiny of the merits of the arbitrator's decision, a waiver of the right to appeal will be necessary. If the award is in conflict with federal law, a writ of error (*recurso extraordinario*) may also lie before the Supreme Court of Argentina.[163] If the court of appeals dismisses the appeal or reverses the award, the aggrieved party is still formally entitled to seek further recourse by bringing a writ of error before the Supreme Court.

2.69 A party challenging an award rendered by an *amigable componedor* can do so only by means of a setting-aside action seeking the award's nullification. This cannot be brought before the arbitral tribunal, but such an action can only be brought before the competent court of first instance, which must decide the matter within five days after hearing the opposing party.[164] When evaluating whether to set aside an arbitral award rendered by *amigables componedores*, the court may hear new evidence or accept new written submissions, though this is not common because a decision based on fairness (*ex aequo et bono*) is unlikely to be set aside on grounds other than manifest and outrageous arbitrariness. In any event, the court's decision on an action to set aside may in turn be subject to appeal.[165] No stay of execution will be granted pending an appeal against an award rendered by *amigables componedores*.[166]

---

[159] NCP, arts 741(4) and 762.

[160] See NCP, arts 759–763.

[161] See eg CNCom, 30 August 2001, *Industrial e Inversiones Orión SA y otra v Arcor SAIC* 198 El Derecho 460 (Arg), held to be unconstitutional on due process grounds a ruling on leave of appeal without having heard first the other party to the arbitraition.

[162] See eg Spinillo and Vogelius (n 1) 53; cf *Nemesio Antonio* (n 139) explaining that the court will limit itself to considering whether the arbitral award exhibits the defects that have been pleaded.

[163] See Law No 48, 14 September 1863, BO, art 16 (Arg) <http://www.infoleg.gov.ar/infolegInternet/anexos/115000-119999/116296/texact.htm>. See eg CSJN, 28 July 1983, *Gas del Estado v EPTM et al* (1983) 305 Fallos 963 (Arg); *Yacimentos Petrolíferos Fiscales* (n 144); cf CSJN, 24 August 2006, *Cacchione, Ricardo Constantino v Urbaser Argentina SA* [2007-A] La Ley 552 (Arg), outlining the procedure that must be followed to bring a writ of error before the Supreme Court.

[164] NCP, art 771. See eg *SA La Razón EEFIC & A* (n 25).

[165] A fine may not be imposed on a party that brings a challenge against the award of an *amiable compositeur*. CNCom, 30 April 1952, *Toricella, Lorenzo v Alberto, Serafín, y otros* 68 La Ley 264 (Arg).

[166] See eg CNCom, 24 October 1960, *Gerola e Iriart, SA v Delta Industrial y Comercial, SA* 102 La Ley 581 (Arg) adopting the reasoning of the trial court that 'an arbitral award which cannot be challenged by means of

De jure awards may be set aside on limited grounds, similar to those providing for the nullity of judicial decisions, including inconsistencies of the award or cases of evident partiality or misconduct on the part of the arbitrators, for example exceeding their powers or not showing sufficient deference to due process.[167] **2.70**

If an award is set aside, the courts may reconvene a new arbitral tribunal to resolve the parties' dispute.[168] Once the time period for attacking the award has elapsed, the award acquires the force of *res judicata*.[169] Generally, the first level of judicial review of an arbitral proceeding should be concluded within a year from the date of filing,[170] subject to much longer delay if the intervention of the Supreme Court of Justice is sought and obtained.[171] **2.71**

Foreign arbitral awards

Article 518 of the NCP outlines the procedure for seeking the enforcement of foreign arbitral awards. The enforcement action must be commenced before a competent court of appeals, accompanied by 'a certified copy and translation of the judgment, along with the documents showing that the judgment is enforceable and that all requirements have been complied with, if such compliance is not evidence from the face of the judgment'. Thus, unless expressly noted in the code itself, the provisions applicable to the enforcement of foreign judgments also apply to the enforcement of arbitral awards. Depending on the complexity of the case, the annulment proceedings may take between one and two years. Occasionally, Argentine courts have granted a stay of the enforcement of a foreign award pending further consideration of questions presented before the court.[172] **2.72**

2.6 Conclusion

Arbitration in Argentina has its pitfalls, in particular due to a generalized perception of discredit brought about by numerous investor complaints against Argentina and the fact that the country continues to operate with an obsolete statutory framework in matters of arbitration **2.73**

---

a motion is enforceable... [based on the principle] that a judicial act which is not manifestly null is presumed to be presumed to be valid'.

[167] See NCP, art 761:

> *Vacatur of the award.* An award shall be void if its resolutory part were to include decisions that are incompatible *inter se*. Code provisions applicable to the nullity of judicial proceedings shall apply in order to fill existing gaps. If the proceedings were conducted without problems and the nullity were to affect the award only, the judge may, upon petition, render a judgment, which shall be subject to challenge in accordance with the ordinary procedure.

[168] See eg CSJN, 20 October 1908, '*Basavilbaso, JJ y R (su sucesión) v Provincia de Buenos Aires*,' (1908) 110 Fallos 185 (Arg) convening a new tribunal of *amiable compositeurs* to resolve the parties' dispute.

[169] See eg CNCom, 2 July 2011, *Pelatti, Juan Bautista v Curcija SA* (Arg).

[170] See eg *Red de Monitoreo SRL* (n 143) issuing a judgment on a motion to nullify the award of *de jure* arbitrators within two months; *Industrial e Inversiones Orión SA* (n 161) issuing a judgment on a motion to nullify the award of *de jure* arbitrators within seven months. *SA La Razón EEFIC & A* (n 25) issuing a judgment in an action for nullification of *amiable compositeurs* within seven months.

[171] eg it took the Supreme Court of Justice almost two and half years to render a judgment in *Mobil Argentina SA v Gasnor SA* (n 25).

[172] See eg CNCiv y Com, 26 August 2003, *Administración de Usinas and Transporte Eléctrico del Uruguay v Centro Puerto SA* (Arg), enjoining enforcement of an arbitral award until a jurisdictional dispute between the Arbitral Tribunal and the Court could be resolved by the CSJN; CNFed, 5 May 2005, *Estado Nacional—Procuración del Tesoro v Tribunal Arbitral-Laudo* (Arg), enjoining enforcement of an award under the New York Convention, Art 5(1) until the petitioner's request that the award be nullified by an Argentine court could be adjudicated.

in general, with very little attention paid to the singularity of international commercial arbitration. While the current environment does not seem openly or even consistently hostile to arbitration, arbitration law in Argentina fails to embrace, comparatively speaking, a positive approach towards the enforcement of domestic as well as foreign arbitration agreements and arbitral awards.

2.74 Due to the many gaps in the arbitration provisions found in the National Code of Civil and Commercial Procedure, it is particularly advisable for the parties to either choose arbitration rules especially geared towards international commercial arbitration or, if the arbitration is ad hoc, to provide in the contract itself for every possible instance in which either an obsolete provision can be waived or an issue can be clarified.

3

CAIRO

Karim Hafez

3.1 Introduction

3.1.1 Arbitration in Cairo

Cairo is a major regional and, increasingly, international, centre for international commercial arbitration. **3.01**

The choice of seat of the arbitration is always an important and strategic decision. The courts of the seat will be competent in relation to any action in support of the arbitral process. This applies, for instance, to the constitution of the arbitral tribunal or the ordering of provisional or conservatory measures. The courts of the seat will also have jurisdiction over any application to set aside the award. **3.02**

An arbitration may be seated in Cairo by agreement of the parties or by decision of the arbitral tribunal. The Egyptian Arbitration Act distinguishes between the legal meaning of the place of arbitration (the seat of the arbitration) and its geographical meaning. It expressly empowers the arbitral tribunal to convene in places other than the seat of the arbitration whenever appropriate. This distinction is confirmed by Egyptian scholars. **3.03**

3.1.2 The Egyptian arbitration experience

3.04 Two developments have been instrumental in establishing Cairo as a centre for international arbitration: the establishment of an arbitral institution that serves as an international venue for arbitration, and the adoption of pro-arbitration legislation.

3.05 The Egyptian Act on Arbitration in Civil and Commercial Matters (Law No 27/1994) (the 'Arbitration Act') was promulgated on 18 April 1994. It is based on the 1985 UNCITRAL Model Law on International Commercial Arbitration. The Arbitration Act applies to arbitral proceedings conducted in Egypt and to proceedings conducted abroad when the parties have expressly agreed to subject them to the provisions of the Act.

3.06 The Arbitration Act puts Egypt on the list of arbitration-friendly countries. It empowers the arbitral tribunal to examine its own jurisdiction and to make a broad range of decisions and orders. It further limits the ability of the local courts to interfere with the arbitral process while allowing them to assist and support it; a role of *juge d'appui* as consecrated by the French courts.

3.07 The main arbitral institution in Cairo is the Cairo Regional Centre for International Commercial Arbitration (the 'Cairo Centre' or 'CRCICA'), established in 1979.[1] The Cairo Centre publishes its own set of arbitration rules (the 'CRCICA Rules'), based on the UNCITRAL Arbitration Rules. The latest version of the CRCICA Rules—which mirrors, with minor modifications, the 2010 revision of the UNCITRAL Arbitration Rules—came into force on 1 March 2011.[2]

3.08 Domestic arbitration, international arbitration, and other forms of alternative dispute resolution (mediation, conciliation, and mini-trial) may all be conducted under the auspices of the Cairo Centre. The Cairo Centre also administers ad hoc arbitration and provides technical assistance when the parties so request.

3.1.3 Recent developments and anticipated changes

3.09 The last two decades have seen marked increases in the number of arbitrations based in Cairo, as reflected in the statistics of the Cairo Centre. Major developments in relation to prominent arbitral issues have also occurred over the last decade.

CRCICA Rules

3.10 In 2011, the Cairo Centre published its new version of the CRCICA Arbitration Rules, which came into effect on 1 March 2011. The rules reflect the 2010 revision of the UNCITRAL Arbitration Rules, with some modifications reflecting international best practices and, in particular, the role of the Centre as administering institution.

Sports arbitration

3.11 In July 2012, the Cairo Centre entered into an agreement with the International Court of Arbitration for Sport (ICAS) and has subsequently been appointed as an Alternative Hearing Centre for the court.

---

[1] The CRCICA is located at 1 El Saleh Ayoub Street, Zamalek, Cairo. Tel (202) 27 35 13 33, (202) 27 35 13 35; fax (202) 27 35 13 36; email: info@crcica.org.eg; website <http://www.crcica.org.eg>.

[2] <http://www.crcica.org.eg/arbitration_rules.html>.

Mediation law

A law on mediation is now being examined before the Egyptian Parliament and specifically discussed by the Senate. It is expected to be adopted shortly. **3.12**

3.2 Judicial Assistance in the Commencement of Arbitration

3.2.1 Enforcing agreements to arbitrate

The Egyptian Arbitration Act expressly stipulates that parties to an arbitration agreement may commence arbitral proceedings, or continue them if commenced, even in the event that court proceedings are pending or subsequently initiated. The Act also expressly empowers the arbitral tribunal to issue an award in these circumstances. **3.13**

The Act further directs a court to declare inadmissible those claims filed in breach of an arbitration agreement. The court cannot, however, dismiss the claim *sua sponte*. The party seeking the dismissal of the proceedings must raise its objection to the jurisdiction of the court, pointing to the existence of an arbitration agreement, before taking any other action with regard to the proceedings, including any request or defence. The court must act upon such a request. **3.14**

The relevant provision of the Act, article 13(1), was challenged as unconstitutional before the Egyptian Constitutional Court. The Constitutional Court rejected the contention that article 13(1) violates the right of access to justice and held that it merely gives effect to the parties' agreement to settle their dispute through arbitration.[3] **3.15**

The Arbitration Act gives effect to two key principles of international arbitration: the principle of autonomy of the arbitration agreement and the principle of *competence-competence*. Any jurisdictional objections, in particular those based on the non-existence, expiry, or nullity of the arbitration clause, will thus be determined by the arbitral tribunal once constituted. The arbitral tribunal is also competent to decide issues related to the scope of the arbitration agreement or the arbitrability of the claims. **3.16**

3.2.2 Judicial intervention in jurisdictional matters

As set out earlier in this chapter, the arbitral tribunal has the full power to decide any objection relating to its jurisdiction. **3.17**

Objections to jurisdiction must be raised *in limine litis*. Unless it satisfies the tribunal that its delay was justified in the circumstances, a respondent will be deemed to have waived its right to object if it failed to raise its objections on or before the filing of its statement of defence. **3.18**

The arbitral tribunal may decide on its jurisdiction in a separate decision or in the final award on the merits. The tribunal's decision on jurisdiction, whether issued in the form of a partial award or otherwise, cannot be challenged until issuance of the final award. **3.19**

The provisions of the CRCICA Rules on these issues are broadly the same. **3.20**

[3] Arbitration Act, art 13.1. provides that:

> The court before which an action is brought concerning a disputed matter which is the subject of an arbitration agreement shall hold this action inadmissible provided that the respondent raises this objection before submitting any demand or defence on the substance of the dispute.

3.2.3 Judicial appointment of arbitrators

3.21 Pursuant to the Arbitration Act, arbitrators must be appointed in the manner agreed upon by the parties. The parties may agree to empower a third person or an arbitral institution, in Egypt or abroad, to appoint the arbitrators on their behalf.

3.22 In the absence of any agreement between the parties as to the manner of appointment of the arbitral tribunal, the Arbitration Act applies. If the parties have agreed that their dispute will be resolved by a sole arbitrator, the sole arbitrator may be appointed by the competent court, upon a party's request. In the case of a three-member tribunal, each party selects an arbitrator within 30 days from the date of receipt of the other party's request to appoint an arbitrator. Following the appointment of the second arbitrator, the two party-appointed arbitrators must appoint a chairperson within 30 days.

3.23 In the event that a party fails to appoint its arbitrator according to the agreement between the parties, or if the two party-appointed arbitrators fail to select the chairperson, or, in institutional arbitration, if the institution agreed upon by the parties fails to do so, either party may ask the competent court to proceed with the appointment. The court seised with such request must proceed expeditiously.

3.24 In the absence of any agreement between the parties regarding the number of arbitrators, the Arbitration Act stipulates that the arbitral tribunal shall comprise three members.

3.25 The Act requires that any arbitral tribunal be composed of an odd number of members. This requirement is mandatory.

3.2.4 Judicial termination of the arbitration

3.26 The court may, at the request of any party, terminate the arbitration proceedings in the event that the tribunal fails to render an award within the time limit agreed by the parties, or that provided by the institutional rules selected by the parties, or, failing any agreement, within a period of 12 months from the date of the commencement of the arbitral proceedings.

3.27 In the case of termination of the proceedings, either party may file its original claim before the court that would have been competent in the absence of an arbitration agreement.

3.28 The Court of Cassation has now firmly settled an earlier controversy as to whether the time limit set forth by the Arbitration Act is mandatory.[4] The Court restated that the parties' agreement prevails. When the parties have agreed to apply the CRCICA Rules, which empower the tribunal to determine various time limits during the course of the proceedings,[5] the arbitral tribunal is bound by the time limit it has fixed or upon which the parties have agreed.

---

[4] Court of Cassation, Civil Chamber, challenge nos 5745 and 6467/75J (13 December 2005), available at <http://www.eastlaws.com/AhkamView.aspx?I=127074&H=&HM=0>.

[5] CRCICA Arbitration Rules, art 19 provides that:

> 1. In the absence of an agreement by the parties, the arbitral tribunal shall, promptly after its appointment, determine the language or languages to be used in the proceedings.
> 2. The arbitral tribunal may order that any documents annexed to the statement of claim or statement of defence, and any supplementary documents or exhibits submitted in the course of the proceedings, delivered in their original language, shall be accompanied by a translation into the language or languages agreed upon by the parties or determined by the arbitral tribunal.

CRCICA Arbitration Rules, art 20 provides that:

The Court of Cassation confirmed its position in a later decision relating to proceedings under the UNCITRAL Rules.[6] The Court held that the UNCITRAL Rules conferred upon the tribunal the power to fix the time limit to issue the award. Accordingly, the 12-month time limit stipulated by the Arbitration Act did not apply to the proceedings. The Court set aside the order for termination granted by the lower court pursuant to article 45(2) of the Arbitration Act.[7] **3.29**

The Court of Cassation has also ruled that the failure of a party to object, before the arbitral tribunal, to the expiry of the time limit to render the award, amounts to a waiver of its rights in this regard under article 8 of the Act.[8] That party cannot subsequently request the setting aside of the award on this basis. **3.30**

---

1. The claimant shall communicate its statement of claim in writing within a period of time to be determined by the arbitral tribunal. The claimant may elect to treat its notice of arbitration referred to in article 3 as a statement of claim, provided that the notice of arbitration also complies with the requirements of paragraphs 2 and 3 of this article.
2. The statement of claim shall include the following particulars:
   a. The names and contact details of the parties;
   b. A statement of the facts supporting the claim;
   c. The points at issue;
   d. The relief or remedy sought; and
   e. The legal grounds or arguments supporting the claim.
3. The statement of claim should, as far as possible, be accompanied by all documents and other evidence relied upon by the claimant, or contain references to them.

CRCICA Arbitration Rules, art 22 provides that:

> During the course of the arbitral proceedings, a party may amend its claim, defence, counterclaim or a claim for the purpose of a set-off, unless the arbitral tribunal considers it inappropriate to allow such amendment having regard to the delay in making it or prejudice to other parties or any other circumstances. However, a claim, defence, counterclaim or a claim for the purpose of a set-off may not be amended in such a manner that the amended claim or defence falls outside the jurisdiction of the arbitral tribunal.

CRCICA Arbitration Rules, art 23 provides that:

1. The arbitral tribunal shall have the power to rule on its own jurisdiction, including any objections with respect to the existence or validity of the arbitration agreement. For that purpose, an arbitration clause which forms part of a contract shall be treated as an agreement independent of the other terms of the contract. A decision by the arbitral tribunal that the contract is null shall not entail automatically the invalidity of the arbitration clause.
2. A plea that the arbitral tribunal does not have jurisdiction shall be raised no later than in the statement of defence or, with respect to a counterclaim or a claim for the purpose of a set-off, in the reply to the counterclaim or to the claim for the purpose of a set-off. A party is not precluded from raising such a plea by the fact that it has appointed, or participated in the appointment of, an arbitrator. A plea that the arbitral tribunal is exceeding the scope of its authority shall be raised as soon as the matter alleged to be beyond the scope of its authority is raised during the arbitral proceedings. The arbitral tribunal may, in either case, admit a later plea if it considers the delay justified.
3. The arbitral tribunal may rule on a plea referred to in paragraph 2 either before ruling on the merits or in its award on the merits. The arbitral tribunal may continue the arbitral proceedings and make an award, notwithstanding any pending challenge to its jurisdiction before a court.

[6] Court of Cassation, Civil Chamber, challenge no 11248/65J (27 November 2006), available at <http://www.eastlaws.com/AhkamView.aspx?I=289105&H=&HM=0>.

[7] Arbitration Act, art 45.2 provides that:

> If the arbitral award is not rendered within the period referred to in the preceding paragraph, either of the two parties to arbitration may request the president of the court referred to in Article 9 of this Law to issue an order either extending the period of time or terminating the arbitral proceedings. In the latter case, either party may bring the dispute to the court having initial jurisdiction to adjudicate the case.

[8] Arbitration Act, art 8 provides that:

3.3 During the Arbitration

3.3.1 Judicial role in deciding arbitrator challenges

3.31 The Arbitration Act empowers the courts to hear and decide applications to challenge an arbitrator or terminate his mandate. The mandatory nature or otherwise of the relevant provisions of the Act in this regard is an issue that has yet to be decided by the courts.

Grounds for challenge

3.32 An arbitrator may be challenged when circumstances give rise to serious doubts as to his impartiality or independence. A party cannot challenge the arbitrator it has appointed unless new circumstances are discovered after the appointment.

3.33 The courts have defined impartiality as 'a mental or psychological bias of the arbitrator in favour of one of the parties or against one of them' and 'a mere feeling by the challenging party which does not rely on real or true facts but which can be observed or noticed by an ordinary person who is not involved in the ongoing dispute and which gives reasonably justifiable doubts as to the arbitrator's impartiality'.[9]

3.34 An arbitrator should not be a former counsel or employee of a party, or otherwise under a party's influence, nor can he have any financial interest in relation to any of the parties.

Challenge procedure

3.35 A challenge must be made in writing, and set out the reasons upon which it is based. It must be submitted to the arbitral tribunal within 15 days from the date when the requesting party first became aware of the constitution of the arbitral tribunal or of the facts underlying the challenge. The challenged arbitrator has 15 days from the date of submission of the challenge to give notice of his resignation, failing which the arbitral tribunal must refer the challenge to the competent court.

3.36 A challenge cannot be formulated prior to the constitution of the arbitral tribunal; it cannot be submitted directly by the requesting party to the state court. The court's decision is final and not subject to appeal. A party cannot challenge the same arbitrator twice in the same arbitral proceedings.

3.37 A challenge does not result in the suspension of the arbitral proceedings. However, if the challenge is accepted and the arbitrator is removed, all the procedures undertaken before the arbitrator's removal will be void *ab initio*. This applies even in the event that the tribunal has already issued an award or is in the process of doing so.

3.38 The parties, or the arbitrators, cannot follow a new procedure for the appointment of the replacement arbitrator; the procedure that governed the appointment of the challenged arbitrator applies to the designation of his replacement.

If either party to a dispute knows that any requirement under the arbitration agreement has been violated or a non-mandatory provision of this Law has not been complied with, yet proceeds with the arbitration without invoking his objection to the violation or noncompliance within the period agreed upon, or without undue delay in the absence of such agreement, the party shall be deemed to have waived his right to object.

[9] Cairo Court of Appeal 342/120J, 91 commercial circuit (22 November 2003), unpublished.

Institutional rules, such as the CRCICA Rules, contain their own provisions governing the challenge of arbitrators. Pursuant to the CRCICA Rules, the challenge of an arbitrator is decided by an ad hoc committee constituted by the Cairo Centre from among members of its Advisory Committee, whose decision is final and subject to no appeal. The question of whether the institutional rules agreed upon by the parties prevail over the provisions of the Arbitration Act remains to be considered and decided by the Egyptian Court of Cassation. **3.39**

Termination of the arbitrator's mandate

An arbitrator's mandate may be terminated upon his resignation, or by agreement of the parties. Any of the parties may also request the competent court to terminate an arbitrator's mission in circumstances where the arbitrator is no longer able to perform his mission, fails to perform it, acts in a way leading to unjustified delay in the proceedings, and fails to withdraw or is not removed by agreement between the parties. **3.40**

Like most institutional rules, the CRCICA Rules also address the removal of an arbitrator. Article 12 entitles any of the parties to request the termination of the arbitrator's mission on grounds similar to those stipulated by the Arbitration Act. The decision is made by an ad hoc committee constituted from among members of the Cairo Centre's Advisory Committee. The committee's decision is final.[10] **3.41**

It is unclear whether the provisions of the Arbitration Act have a mandatory character and would prevail over any institutional rules and procedures agreed upon by the parties. **3.42**

3.3.2 Judicial intervention in obtaining documentary and physical evidence

Documentary and physical evidence are dealt with in the procedural matters section of the Arbitration Act. As the Act accords the parties and, failing agreement between them, the arbitral tribunal, the broadest powers to determine the rules applicable to their proceedings, provisions concerning evidence are limited. The evidence provisions specifically address witnesses, party-appointed and court-appointed experts, and documentary evidence. **3.43**

As a general proposition, the Arbitration Act provides that each party is entitled to receive a copy of all pleadings and all evidence submitted by the other party, and, generally, of all materials provided to the tribunal. **3.44**

Witnesses and experts

The Arbitration Act accords the broadest powers to the arbitral tribunal with regard to witnesses and experts. However, the courts may lend their support to the arbitral tribunal when so requested. **3.45**

Thus, pursuant to article 37 of the Act, the court may sanction a witness who refuses or fails to appear before the arbitral tribunal.[11] An order compelling witnesses to appear may also **3.46**

---

[10] CRCICA Arbitration Rules, art 12 provides:

> In the event that an arbitrator fails to act or in the event of de jure or de facto impossibility of his or her performing his or her functions, or in the event that he or she deliberately delays the commencement or the continuation of the arbitral proceedings, said arbitrator may be removed, at the request of a party, and after giving him or her and the other party(s) the opportunity to express their views in this respect, by a decision from an impartial and independent tripartite ad hoc committee to be composed by the Centre from amongst the members of the Advisory Committee.

[11] Arbitration Act, art 37 provides that:

be issued in 'urgent circumstances'. Whether particular circumstances satisfy the 'urgency' requirement is decided by the judge on a case-by-case basis.

3.47 The courts have also confirmed that the arbitral tribunal is entitled to determine the admissibility, relevance, materiality, and weight of any evidence offered, including witness testimonies.

Documentary evidence

3.48 The parties submit supporting evidence with their main submissions and statements before the arbitral tribunal. The parties do not have to produce the originals of documents with their submissions. Copies of the documents relied upon are acceptable, subject to the arbitral tribunal's right to demand the production of the originals in due course.

3.49 Upon the request of any of the parties, the arbitral tribunal may order the production of documents. Though confirmed by doctrine, it is unclear whether, in the absence of an agreement by the parties, the Arbitration Act confers upon the arbitral tribunal a general power to order the production of documents. Article 35 of the Act addresses the consequences of a party's failure to produce documents when so requested.[12] In one view, article 35 implicitly recognizes the arbitral tribunal's general power to order the production of documents, on its own initiative or upon a party's request; a more restrictive construction of this provision would limit its interpretation to the express power granted to the tribunal to order originals of documents submitted by the parties, or to the situation in which the parties have expressly agreed to empower the arbitral tribunal to order the production of documents.

3.50 The Arbitration Act does not grant the courts any powers to compel the production of documents, should a party fail to do so. Article 35 provides that in the event that a party fails to submit documents when required to do so, the arbitral tribunal may proceed on the basis of the evidence before it. The arbitral tribunal is thus implicitly entitled to draw appropriate inferences from the failure to submit documents, as part of its responsibility and discretion in assessing the weight and materiality of the evidence.

3.51 Under the CRCICA Rules, an arbitral tribunal has broad and specific powers to order the production of documents, exhibits, or other evidence within a specified period of time. This order can be made by the tribunal at the request of either party or on its own initiative. Failure by a party to comply with the tribunal's order to produce specific documents or evidence entitles the arbitral tribunal to draw appropriate inferences.

3.3.3 Judicial power to issue interim measures of protection

3.52 The Arbitration Act entitles the parties to apply to the competent court for provisional or conservatory measures before the commencement of, or at any time during, the arbitration proceedings. The parties may, in addition, request the arbitral tribunal to order any such

The president of the court referred to in Article 9 of this Law is competent, upon the request of the arbitral panel, to do the following:

a) Condemn any of the witnesses who refrain from attending or decline to reply, by inflicting the sanction prescribed in Articles 78 and 80 of the Law of Evidence in Civil and Commercial Matters.
b) Order a rogatory commission.

[12] Arbitration Act, art 35 provides that: 'If either party fails to appear at any of the meetings or to submit the documents required from it, the arbitral tribunal may continue the arbitral proceedings and make the award on the dispute based upon the elements of evidence before it.'

provisional or conservatory measures. The selection of the CRCICA Rules automatically imports such an agreement.

The Arbitration Act does not specify the type of interim measures that an arbitral tribunal may order. Scholars refer in this regard to the general rules of the Egyptian Code of Civil Procedure regarding provisional measures, as set out in article 45.[13] Article 45 imposes the following conditions for the issuance of any interim measures: there is an imminent danger or risk of substantial prejudice to the right of the requesting party; delay in the final decision may prejudice the right or the legal status that the measure aims to protect; or the required measure will not have an impact on the outcome or the merits of the dispute. These conditions apply to interim measures issued by both the arbitral tribunal and the competent court. **3.53**

The arbitral tribunal may require security for the costs of the interim measure. The interim measure may be ordered in the form of an interim award. **3.54**

In the event of non-compliance with the interim measure ordered by the arbitral tribunal, the other party can apply to the competent court for an enforcement order. It may also request the arbitral tribunal to allow it to take the necessary measures for execution of the order. **3.55**

The CRCICA Rules contain fairly detailed provisions governing interim measures. They provide a definition of 'interim measures' and set forth the conditions that must be satisfied for their issuance. The arbitral tribunal is empowered to order such measures at the request of any of the parties, subject to security for costs if appropriate. It may also, at the request of a party or, in exceptional cases, on its own initiative, modify, suspend, or terminate an interim measure previously granted. To this end, the arbitral tribunal may request any of the parties to disclose material changes to the circumstances on the basis of which the interim measure was granted. **3.56**

The Rules expressly stipulate that an application to the courts for interim measures does not constitute a waiver of the arbitration agreement. This position is also implicit under the Arbitration Act. **3.57**

3.3.4 Treatment of foreign arbitrators and counsel

Arbitrators

Article 16(2) of the Arbitration Act stipulates that an arbitrator may be of any sex or nationality, unless otherwise agreed by the parties or provided by law.[14] **3.58**

An arbitrator may be any person having legal capacity. However, persons under curatorship, guardianship, bankruptcy, or convicted of a crime affecting honour, cannot act as arbitrators, **3.59**

---

[13] Egyptian Code of Civil Procedure, art 45 provides that:

> One of the Court of First Instance judges will be assigned to rule on a temporary basis and without prejudice to the rights of urgent issues, of which the time expiration is of concern.
>
> In case of this being outside the Court of First Instance's district, this falls under the Partial Court jurisdiction.
>
> This does not preclude the jurisdiction of the competent court [with jurisdiction over the subject matter], if raised [before such court as secondary or subsidiary matters to claims within its jurisdiction].

[14] The Arbitration Act, art 16.2 provides that: 'The arbitrator is not required to be of a given gender or nationality, unless otherwise agreed upon between the two parties or provided for by law.'

unless and until they are restored to the full exercise of their rights. No specific legal or technical qualifications are otherwise required.

3.60 In the context of proceedings under the CRCICA Rules, when the Centre is called upon to appoint a sole arbitrator or to make a default appointment of the chairman, it must give consideration to the appointment of an arbitrator of a nationality other than that of the parties in the case where the parties are not nationals of the same country.

Counsel

3.61 Article 5 of the CRCICA Rules provides that the parties may be represented or assisted by any person of their choice.[15] The Arbitration Act is silent on this matter.

3.3.5 Local requirements for conduct of arbitration hearings

3.62 Unless the parties agree otherwise, the arbitration proceedings begin on the day when the respondent receives the request for arbitration filed by the claimant.

3.63 The arbitration proceedings are conducted in accordance with the rules agreed upon by the parties or, failing such agreement, in the manner determined by the arbitral tribunal. When choosing the applicable rules, the arbitrators must take into consideration rules of public policy as stipulated by the Arbitration Act. This would include rules such as the general rule that all the parties should be treated on an equal footing and accorded an equal and full opportunity to present their case.

3.64 According to the majority of Egyptian scholars, the parties have the right to choose a national law to govern the procedure of the arbitration. The choice of a foreign law, or of institutional rules, will exclude the application of the provisions of the Act except for those pertaining to public policy.

3.65 The only exchanges of pleadings prescribed by the Arbitration Act are a statement of claim and a statement of defence (and counterclaim if applicable).

3.66 The Arbitration Act does not mandate the convening of oral hearings by the arbitral tribunal; an arbitral award may thus be rendered on the basis of written statements and written documents alone without any hearing held for purposes of listening to the parties' arguments and statements.

3.67 If a party fails to attend one of the hearings, in the event that a hearing is indeed held, or to submit a document that has been requested, the arbitral tribunal may continue the proceedings and issue an award based on the evidence available before it, excluding any evidence that party might have in its possession.

Language of the proceedings

3.68 The language of the proceedings is determined by the parties, or failing agreement between them, by the arbitral tribunal. One or more languages may be selected to apply to the pleadings, testimonies, communications, decisions, and awards. Failing any agreement on this

---

[15] CRCICA Arbitration Rules, art 5 provides that:

> In the cases where this Law permits the two parties to the arbitration to select the procedures which must be followed in a given matter, this also includes their right to allow third parties to make such selection. In this respect, any arbitration organization or centre in the Arab Republic of Egypt or abroad shall be deemed a third party.

issue, Arabic is the default language of the proceedings pursuant to the Arbitration Act. It will apply to all aspects of the proceedings.

Witnesses and experts

Witnesses and experts are not heard under oath. The tribunal may seek the assistance of the courts to sanction a witness's refusal or failure to appear before it and testify or to compel a witness to appear in 'urgent circumstances'. The Arbitration Act does not prescribe any specific procedure for the hearing of witnesses. The procedure is determined by the parties' agreement or, in the absence of such agreement, by the arbitral tribunal itself. **3.69**

The arbitral tribunal may decide, *sua sponte* or at a party's request, to hold a hearing to hear the testimony of a tribunal-appointed expert. Unless otherwise agreed by the parties, the parties may cross-examine the tribunal-appointed expert in the manner and to the extent directed by the arbitral tribunal. The parties may also present their own expert to express views about the issues addressed in the report of tribunal-appointed expert. **3.70**

Under the CRCICA Rules, the arbitral tribunal does not have the power to act *sua sponte*; the hearing of the tribunal-appointed expert must be requested by one of the parties. **3.71**

The parties are entitled to rely upon expert evidence, regardless of whether the arbitral tribunal has decided to appoint an expert. **3.72**

3.4 The Award

3.4.1 Types of award

The arbitral tribunal may issue both interim (interlocutory), partial and final awards, unless otherwise agreed by the parties. Interim awards deal with incidental matters, such as a request for interim measures. Partial awards are awards that dispose of some, but not all, of the issues in dispute. They may include issues as to the jurisdiction of the tribunal or the arbitrability of the dispute. A partial award does not put an end to the tribunal's jurisdiction. The Arbitration Act does not expressly address the enforcement of interim awards. **3.73**

The arbitral tribunal must issue a final award at the end of the proceedings. Final awards are awards that end the dispute between the parties finally and completely. **3.74**

A party may, within 30 days of receipt of the award, request the tribunal to issue an additional award on any claim submitted by such party in the course of the proceedings that the arbitral award fails to determine. A request may be made even after the time limit for the proceedings has expired. This request must be notified to the other party before it is presented to the tribunal. **3.75**

Additional awards may only be requested in respect of claims related to the merits, and made by a party to the dispute. The claim may be an alternative or ancillary claim. The tribunal's failure to address one of the parties' arguments or defences in the award does not constitute a valid ground to request the issuance of an additional award. **3.76**

Requests to issue additional awards cannot be made if their purpose and effect is to re-litigate issues that have been previously decided by the tribunal. This has been confirmed by many CRCICA tribunals. This also applies if the effect of those requests is to amend the award, or to raise a claim that was not presented before the tribunal in the course of the proceedings. **3.77**

3.78 The arbitral tribunal must issue its decision within 60 days of submission of the request. It may extend this time limit by a further period of 30 days.

3.79 Under the CRCICA Rules, a party has 30 days from receipt of either the termination order or the award, to submit a request for an award or an additional award in relation to claims presented in the arbitral proceedings but not decided by the arbitral tribunal. The other party and the Cairo Centre must be notified of the request. The arbitral tribunal may invite the other party to comment on the request within 15 days.

3.80 The tribunal's decision must be issued within 60 days of receipt of the non-requesting party's comments, subject to any extension that the tribunal may deem necessary. The additional award must satisfy the requirements of form for awards stipulated by the Rules.[16]

3.4.2 Mandatory rules as to form

3.81 Two sets of rules govern the form of the award and how it is rendered. The Arbitration Act and the CRCICA Rules prescribe rules as to the form of the award. They also contain rules governing the pre-award phase.

Making of the award

3.82 **Majority awards** The Arbitration Act stipulates that awards rendered by an arbitral tribunal comprising more than one arbitrator must be based on a majority decision following deliberation, unless the parties agree that a unanimous decision is required. The CRCICA Rules also prescribe a majority decision.

3.83 **Time limits** The arbitral tribunal is required to render its award within the time limit agreed by the parties (including any time limit provided for in the applicable institutional rules) or, failing any agreement, within a period of 12 months from the date of the commencement of the arbitral proceedings. The arbitral tribunal may, at its discretion, extend the time limit agreed by the parties or prescribed by the Act, as applicable, by a period not exceeding six months, unless the parties have agreed on a longer period.

3.84 Upon the tribunal's failure to render an award within the foregoing time limits, either party may request the competent court to issue an order either to extend the time limit or to terminate the arbitration proceedings. If the court orders the termination of the proceedings, either party may file its claim before the court that would have had jurisdiction in the absence of an arbitration agreement.

---

[16] CRCICA Arbitration Rules, art 39 provides that:

1. Within 30 days after the receipt of the termination order or the award, a party, with notice to the other party(s) and the Centre, may request the arbitral tribunal to make an award or an additional award as to claims presented in the arbitral proceedings but not decided by the arbitral tribunal. The arbitral tribunal may invite the other party(s) to comment on the said request within 15 days.
2. If the arbitral tribunal considers the request for an award or additional award to be justified, it shall render or complete its award within 60 days after the expiry of the date of commenting on the request. The arbitral tribunal may extend, if necessary, the period of time within which it shall make the award.
3. When such an award or additional award is made, the provisions of article 34, paragraphs 2 to 5, shall apply.

The Court of Cassation has consistently held that these provisions of the Arbitration Act are not mandatory.[17] 3.85

Form of award

Pursuant to the Arbitration Act, an award must satisfy several requirements of form. The award must be in writing, it must state reasons for the decision, and it must refer to the place and date of the award. Failure to fulfil any of these conditions could result in the setting aside of the award.[18] 3.86

Writing The award must be in writing and signed by the arbitrators, or by the majority of them. The position is similar under the CRCICA Rules. Where an arbitral award is not signed by an arbitrator, it must state the reasons for this. 3.87

Reasons The award must be reasoned. Article 43(2) of the Act provides that the reasons for the decision must be stated in the award, unless the parties have agreed otherwise or the law applicable to the proceedings does not mandate a reasoned award. Under the CRCICA Rules, the award must state the reasons upon which it is based, unless the parties have agreed otherwise. 3.88

The Cairo Court of Appeal has previously annulled unreasoned awards in cases in which the parties did not agree to forgo reasons.[19] The court has held that summary reasons or 'reasons that are not serious' amount to an absence of reasons. 'Reasons that are not serious' include unclear or unjustifiable reasons, or reasons that are not based on true facts. The Court of Appeal has also held that contradictory reasons do not amount to an absence of reasons, and therefore cannot justify the setting aside of arbitral awards.[20] 3.89

Contents of the award The award must record the date and the place of the award, the names and addresses of the parties, and the names, addresses, and nationalities of the arbitrators. It must include the arbitration agreement, a summary of the parties' claims, a summary of the parties' statements, an operative part ('*dispositif*'), and the underlying reasons (if a reasoned award is required). The Court of Cassation has set aside an award for failure to include 3.90

---

[17] Court of Cassation, Civil Chamber, challenge nos 5745 and 6467/75J (13 December 2005), available at <http://www.eastlaws.com/AhkamView.aspx?I=127074&H=&HM=0>; Court of Cassation, Civil Chamber, challenge no 11248/65J (27 November 2006), available at <http://www.eastlaws.com/AhkamView.aspx?I=289105&H=&HM=0>.

[18] Arbitration Act, art 43 provides that:

1. The arbitral award shall be made in writing and shall be signed by the arbitrators. If the arbitral tribunal consists of more than one arbitrator, the signatures of the majority of the arbitrators shall suffice, provided that the award states the reasons for which the minority did not sign.
2. The arbitral award shall state the reasons upon which it is based, unless the two parties to arbitration have agreed otherwise or the law applicable to the arbitral proceedings does not require the award to be supported by reasons.
3. The arbitral award shall include the names and addresses of the parties, the names, addresses, nationalities and titles of the arbitrators, a copy of the arbitration agreement, a summary of the parties' requests, submissions, documents, the dispositive part of the award, date and place of making, as well as the reasons whenever their inclusion is required.

[19] Cairo Court of Appeal, case no 130/123J (20 June 2007); Cairo Court of Appeal, case no 26/114J (18 February 1998), (2004) 7 Journal of Arab Arbitration 183; Cairo Court of Appeal case no 2240/11J (22 February 1995), (2003) 6 Journal of Arab Arbitration 157.

[20] Cairo Court of Appeal, case no 69/119J, 91 commercial circuit (26 June 2003), unpublished; Cairo Court of Appeal case nos 11, 14, and 24/119J (23 April 1997), unpublished; Cairo Court of Appeal, case no 32/113J (27 November 2002), (2004) 7 Journal of Arab Arbitration 185; Cairo Court of Appeal, case no 66/120J (26 May 2004), (2005) 8 Journal of Arab Arbitration 167.

the arbitration agreement. The Court held that this requirement is essential to enable the tribunal to assess whether the arbitrators have exceeded the scope of the arbitration agreement.[21]

3.91 **Additional awards** The Arbitration Act does not prescribe the form of an additional award. Scholars take the view that additional awards are governed in all respects by the provisions applicable to arbitral awards. This position is expressly reflected in article 39(3) of the CRCICA Rules.[22]

3.4.3 Mandatory rules as to substance

Costs

3.92 The Arbitration Act is silent on the allocation of costs. The provisions of articles 184 to 189 of the Egyptian Code of Civil Procedure therefore apply. They stipulate that the court determines costs in its final decision, and that these include the cost of legal assistance. Generally, the losing party bears the costs. The court may, however, make an order for costs against the winning party when it has caused unnecessary costs, or failed to inform the other party of a decisive document in its possession.

3.93 When a party is only successful on some of its claims, the court makes an appropriate order for costs: it may order each party to bear its own costs, or a proportion of the costs, or order that one party bear all the costs.

3.94 Under CRCICA Rules,[23] the tribunal must similarly determine the costs of arbitration in its final award. The Rules define the term 'costs' to include registration fees, administrative fees, the arbitral tribunal's fees and expenses, the fees and expenses of experts or other assistance sought by the tribunal in relation to the proceedings (translation costs for instance), and the parties' legal costs and expenses, including travel costs for witnesses in appropriate cases.

3.5 Post-Award Judicial Intervention

3.5.1 Deposit of awards for enforcement purposes

3.95 The winning party must deposit the original of the award, or a signed copy or certified translation, as a condition for its enforcement.

3.96 An award rendered in a domestic arbitration must be deposited at the registry of the court that has original jurisdiction to hear the dispute. For international arbitration proceedings, the relevant registry is that of the Cairo Court of Appeal or such other court of appeal as the parties may have designated. Failure to deposit the award has no effect on its validity, and does not constitute a ground for setting it aside.

3.97 The deposit of the award is formally recorded and the document issued in relation thereto must be submitted upon filing a request for enforcement. The deposit of the award is thus a prerequisite to enforcement. There is no time limit for the deposit of the award.

---

[21] Court of Cassation, Civil Chamber, challenge no 4623/66J (18 December 1997). The court reached this decision in circumstances where the arbitration agreement had been deposited with the award and was available to the court, see <http://www.eastlaws.com/AhkamView.aspx?I=13992&H=&HM=0>.

[22] CRCICA Arbitration Rules, art 39.3 provides that: 'When such an award or additional award is made, the provisions of article 34, paragraphs 2 to 5, shall apply.'

[23] CRCICA Arbitration Rules, art 42.1 provides that: 'The arbitral tribunal shall fix the costs of arbitration in the final award and, if it deems appropriate, in another decision.'

Since 2008, deposited awards have been subject to the scrutiny of a special section of the Ministry of Justice. The Ministry of Justice satisfies itself that the award does not violate Egyptian public policy, that the arbitration did not involve non-arbitrable matters, and that the court in which the party is seeking to deposit the award has jurisdiction for the purposes of deposit. **3.98**

The Ministry of Justice issues an opinion, which is not binding upon the registry of the court. The registry of the court may accept the deposit of the award before or after the opinion is rendered and regardless of its content. **3.99**

There is no requirement that an award rendered in the context of institutional proceedings be deposited with the institution under the auspices of which it was rendered. **3.100**

3.5.2 Enforcement of the award

In 2005, the Court of Cassation held that foreign awards are enforceable under the Arbitration Act.[24] The Court held that since the enforcement mechanism for awards prescribed in the Arbitration Act is less onerous than that contemplated by the Egyptian Code of Civil Procedure, the provisions of the former should govern the enforcement of foreign awards. In reaching its decision, the court first highlighted the principle of Egyptian law that international agreements have precedence over national laws. It relied in this regard on the reference in article 1 of the Arbitration Act[25] to its provisions being 'without prejudice to the provisions of international conventions in force in the Arab Republic of Egypt' and noted that this included the provisions of the New York Convention. The Court also referred to article 23 of the Egyptian Civil Code and article 301 of the Egyptian Code of Civil Procedure,[26] which also provide that international agreements have precedence over national laws. The court then noted the provisions of Article III of the New York Convention, which specifically direct that 'there shall not be imposed substantially more onerous conditions or higher fees or charges on the recognition or enforcement of arbitral awards to which this convention applies than are imposed on the recognition or enforcement of domestic arbitral awards'. The Court concluded accordingly that the more onerous provisions of the Egyptian Civil Code of Procedure should not apply to foreign awards. **3.101**

However, if the claimant so chooses, the court can proceed with enforcement in accordance with the Egyptian Code of Civil Procedure. The enforcement regime may thus differ depending upon the enforcement mechanism adopted. **3.102**

---

[24] Court of Cassation, Civil Chamber, challenge no 966/73J (10 January 2005), available at <http://www.eastlaws.com/AhkamView.aspx?I=64448&H=&HM=0>.

[25] Arbitration Act, art 1 provides that: 'The provisions of the annexed Law shall apply to any arbitration pending at the time of its entry into force or which commences thereafter, even if it is based on an arbitral agreement concluded before the entry into force of this Law.'

[26] Egyptian Civil Code, art 23 provides that: 'The provisions of the aforementioned articles shall not be applicable in case of the existence of other contradicting provisions in any other laws or international agreements applicable in Egypt.' Egyptian Code of Civil Procedure, art 301 provides that: 'The aforementioned provisions shall be applicable without prejudice to all International Agreements—to which Egypt is a signatory—related to the implementation of judgments and orders.'

3.103 According to the Arbitration Act, enforcement may be ordered by the president of the competent court as defined in article 9 of the Arbitration Act,[27] at the request of one of the parties.[28]

3.104 An application for enforcement is submitted in an *ex parte* application to a judge in chambers after the expiry of the time limit to request the setting aside of the award[29] (90 days from the date of the notification of the award to the party against whom it is rendered).[30] Applications submitted before expiry of that time limit will be declared inadmissible.

3.105 An award may be denied enforcement if it conflicts with a prior decision of the Egyptian courts in the subject matter of the dispute, if it is contrary to Egyptian public policy, or if it has not been properly notified to the party against whom it was rendered.[31]

3.106 Decisions denying recognition and enforcement are reviewable within 30 days.[32] Decisions ordering enforcement are reviewable within either ten or 30 days. This uncertainty as to the applicable time limit arises from the fact that decisions granting exequatur were originally final, while those denying enforcement were reviewable. The Constitutional Court declared the discrepancy unconstitutional, holding that both types of decisions should be reviewable to afford the parties equal rights.[33] The court did not explain whether the same time limit applies in each case. The better view is that it does, again to maintain equality between the

---

27 Pursuant to the Arbitration Act, art 9 the competent court is the Cairo Court of Appeal in the case of international commercial arbitration, and otherwise the court that would have had jurisdiction in the absence of an arbitration agreement.

28 Arbitration Act, art 56 provides that:

> Jurisdiction to issue an enforcement order of arbitral awards lies with the president of the court referred to in Article 9 of this Law or with the member of said court who has been mandated for this purpose by delegation from said president. The application for enforcement of the arbitral award shall be accompanied by the following: 1. The original award or a signed copy thereof. 2. A copy of the arbitration agreement. 3. An Arabic translation of the award, certified by a competent organism, in case the award was not made in Arabic. 4. A copy of the procès-verbal attesting the deposit of the award pursuant to Article 47 of this Law.

29 Arbitration Act, art 58.1 provides that: 'Application for the enforcement of an arbitral award shall not be admissible before the expiration of the period during which the action for annulment should be filed in the court registry.'

30 Arbitration Act, art 54.1 provides that:

> The action for annulment of the arbitral award must be brought within ninety days of the date of the notification of the arbitral award to the party against whom it was made. The admissibility of the action for annulment shall not be prevented by the applicant's renouncement of its right to request the annulment of the award prior to the making of the arbitral award.

31 Arbitration Act, art 58.2 provides that:

> The application to obtain leave for enforcement of the arbitral award according to this Law shall not be granted except after having ascertained the following:
> a) That it does not contradict a judgment previously rendered by the Egyptian Courts on the subject matter in dispute;
> b) That it does not violate the public policy in the Arab Republic of Egypt; and
> c) That it was properly notified to the party against whom it was rendered.

32 Arbitration Act, art 58.3 provides that:

> The order granting leave for enforcement is not subject to appeal. However, the order refusing to grant enforcement may be subject to a petition lodged, within thirty days from the date thereof, before the competent court referred to in Article 9 of this Law.

33 Supreme Constitutional Court, case no 92/21J (6 January 2001), available at <http://www.eastlaws.com/AhkamView.aspx?I=37085&H=&HM=0>.

parties. Some, however, argue that, in the absence of a specific provision in the arbitration Act, the default ten-day time limit under the Egyptian Code of Civil Procedure applies.[34]

Under the Egyptian Code of Civil Procedure, the enforcement of foreign awards is governed by the rules governing the enforcement of foreign judgments. It is sought through an ordinary action before the Court of First Instance in whose district enforcement is sought. The enforcement action is by means of an originating summons, followed by a full hearing.[35] The following conditions must be satisfied for an *exequatur* to be granted: the dispute must not fall within the exclusive jurisdiction of the Egyptian courts; the parties must have been properly notified and represented in the proceedings; the award must have the effect of *res judicata* pursuant to the governing law; the award must not be contrary to a previous decision rendered by the Egyptian courts on the subject matter of the dispute; the award must not be contrary to Egyptian public policy; and the subject matter of the dispute must be arbitrable under Egyptian law.[36] **3.107**

3.5.3 Publication of the award

An arbitral award may be published only with the prior approval of the parties to arbitration. **3.108**

The Cairo Centre may (and does), under its Rules, publish awards, provided that the award does not disclose the identity of any of the parties. **3.109**

3.5.4 No appeal on the merits

Appeal to a second arbitral instance

Neither the Arbitration Act nor the CRCICA Rules provide for an appeal or challenge before a second arbitral instance. While a leading Egyptian scholar has taken the view that the **3.110**

---

[34] Egyptian Code of Civil Procedure, art 197 provides that:

> The concerned party has the right to appeal to the competent court, unless the law stipulates otherwise.
>
> The appeal shall be brought by the usual procedures for bringing a case before the court within 10 days from the day of the issuance of redetection or from the date of execution of the order or declaration depending on the circumstances.
>
> And the court shall issue the order or confirm the validity of the issued order, or modify or revoke it. The appeal also needs to have cause or it will be considered null.

[35] Egyptian Code of Civil Procedure, art 297 provides that: 'The application for enforcement is submitted to the circuit of the court of First Instance in which the enforcement is requested by the usual procedures for bringing a case before the court.'

[36] Egyptian Code of Civil Procedure, art 298 provides that:

An enforcement order may not be issued before the verification of the following:

1. The Republic's courts do not have jurisdiction to examine the dispute in which a judgment or order has been rendered; and that the foreign courts which rendered the judgment have jurisdiction in accordance with international judicial rules relevant to jurisdiction as prescribed in their laws.
2. The parties to the dispute in which a judgment has been rendered have been invited to attend the hearings and have been properly represented.
3. That the judgment or order has *res judicata* in accordance with the law of the court which rendered it.
4. That the judgment or order does not contradict a previous judgment which has been issued by the Egyptian courts, and does not violate public policy or morality.

Egyptian Code of Civil Procedure, art 299 provides that: 'The provisions of the foregoing articles apply on arbitral awards issued in a foreign country; the subject matter of the award must be arbitrable according to the Republic's law.'

parties could by express agreement provide for appeal or challenge,[37] the question has yet to be considered by the courts.

Appeal to a court

3.111 The parties cannot challenge an arbitral award on the merits. The Arbitration Act does not provide for any such challenge; furthermore, it expressly excludes the means of recourse stipulated in the Egyptian Code of Civil Procedure (namely appeal to the Court of Appeal, challenge before the Court of Cassation, and petition for review).

3.5.5 Annulment of award

Local standards for setting aside

3.112 **Grounds for setting aside** The Arbitration Act lists exhaustively the grounds upon which an award may be set aside. These grounds are as follows:

- there was no arbitration agreement, it was void, voidable or its duration had elapsed;
- either party to the arbitration agreement was, at the time of the conclusion of the arbitration agreement, fully or partially incapacitated according to the law governing its legal capacity;
- either party to the arbitration was unable to present its case as a result of not being given proper notice of the appointment of an arbitrator or of the arbitral proceedings, or for any other reason beyond its control;
- the arbitral award failed to apply the law agreed upon by the parties to govern the subject matter in dispute;
- the composition of the arbitral tribunal or the appointment of the arbitrators was made other than in accordance with the provisions of the Arbitration Act or the parties' agreement;
- the arbitral award dealt with matters that do not fall within the scope of the arbitration agreement or exceed the limits of this agreement—when matters falling within the scope of the arbitration can be separated from the matters outside it, the nullity affects exclusively the parts of the award relating to the latter; or
- either the arbitral award itself or the arbitration procedures affecting the award contain a legal violation that causes nullity.[38]

---

[37] M Shafik, *International Commercial Arbitration* (Dar Al Nahda Al Arabeyya, 1997) 303.

[38] Arbitration Act, art 53 provides that:

1. An arbitral award may be annulled only:
    a) If there is no arbitration agreement, if it was void, voidable or its duration had elapsed;
    b) If either party to the arbitration agreement was at the time of the conclusion of the arbitration agreement fully or partially incapacitated according to the law governing its legal capacity;
    c) If either party to the arbitration was unable to present its case as a result of not being given proper notice of the appointment of an arbitrator or of the arbitral proceedings, or for any other reason beyond its control;
    d) If the arbitral award failed to apply the law agreed upon by the parties to govern the subject matter in dispute;
    e) If the composition of the arbitral tribunal or the appointment of the arbitrators was in conflict with this Law or the parties' agreement;
    f) If the arbitral award dealt with matters not falling within the scope of the arbitration agreement or exceeding the limits of this agreement. However, in the case when matters falling within the scope of the arbitration can be separated from the part of the award which contains matters not included within the scope of the arbitration, the nullity affects exclusively the latter parts only;

A party is deemed to have waived any objection to a procedural irregularity that it has failed to raise within the applicable time limit or, in the absence of any such time limit, within a reasonable time during the course of the proceedings; such procedural irregularity can thus no longer be invoked to ground an application to set aside. **3.113**

Reconsidering the merits Both the Court of Cassation[39] and the Cairo Court of Appeal[40] have held that the action to set aside is not an appeal; thus the court cannot reconsider the merits of the dispute; it cannot review the award, verify the findings of the arbitrators, or assess the correctness of their decision. **3.114**

Moreover, an error of law does not justify the setting aside of an award. The Cairo Court of Appeal rejected an application to set aside an award in a case in which the applicant claimed that the arbitral tribunal failed to comply with the provisions of the contract, breached the provisions of the tender law, and failed properly to apply the provisions of the Civil Code.[41] **3.115**

Public policy Violation of public policy is a ground for setting aside an award, and one that the court must invoke *ex officio*. The court should not, under cover of setting aside the award for violation of public policy, review the merits of the case. **3.116**

Violation of Egyptian public policy will result in the setting aside of a domestic award and a refusal to enforce a foreign award. Thus, awards rendered in connection with disputes relating to the possession of real estate and to the validity of a sale of real estate were set aside as being inarbitrable as regards the former[42] and as amounting to an attempt to circumvent Egyptian public policy provisions as regards the latter.[43] **3.117**

International public policy The court must set aside *ex officio* any award that does not comply with, or is contrary to, Egyptian public policy. In their decisions regarding the enforcement of foreign judgments and the application of foreign laws, the courts have drawn a distinction between domestic and international public policy. **3.118**

This distinction is further stated in the Explanatory Note to article 28 of the Civil Code, which provides that foreign laws that would otherwise apply according to the Egyptian rules of conflict of laws will be excluded if they violate public policy.[44] The Note states that public policy, as envisaged by article 28, differs from public policy in a domestic context. **3.119**

---

g) If the arbitral award itself or the arbitration procedures affecting the award contain a legal violation that causes nullity.

2. The court adjudicating the action for annulment shall *ipso jure* annul the arbitral award if it is in conflict with the public policy in the Arab Republic of Egypt.

[39] Court of Cassation, Civil Chamber, challenge no 7307/76J (8 February 2008), (2009) 1(4) Intl J Arab Arbitration 150.

[40] Cairo Court of Appeal, case no 6/124J (16 April 2007); Cairo Court of Appeal, case no 120/120J (28 February 2004) unpublished; Cairo Court of Appeal, case no 46/119J (22 November 2003) unpublished; Cairo Court of Appeal, case no 17/119J (26 June 2002) (2003) 6 Journal of Arab Arbitration 175; Cairo Court of Appeal, case no 61/115J (21 April 1999) unpublished.

[41] Cairo Court of Appeal, case no 4/119J (30 December 2002) unpublished.

[42] Court of Cassation, Civil Chamber, challenge no 61/126 J (8 June 2010), (2011) 9 Arbitration Journal 547.

[43] Cairo Court of Appeal, case nos 17 and 142/124 (2 February 2010), (2012) 13 Global Arbitration Journal 408; Cairo Court of Appeal, case nos 33/123J, and 130 and 133/124J (2 February 2010), (2010) 8 Global Arbitration Journal 448; Cairo Court of Appeal, case no 50/123J (8 April 2010), (2011) 10 Global Arbitration Journal 546.

[44] Egyptian Civil Code, art 28 provides that: 'The provisions of a foreign law applicable by virtue of the preceding articles shall not be applied if these provisions are contrary to public policy or to morality in Egypt.'

3.120 The Egyptian Court of Cassation has defined public policy as 'the social, political, economic or moral bases of the nation, which pertain to the nation's consciousness or fundamental public interests of society'. The court emphasized that the provisions of a foreign law are not contrary to public policy as defined in the preceding commentary for the mere reason that they differ from, or are less favourable than, those of the *lex fori*.[45]

3.121 In another case, the Court of Cassation restated in clear terms that a mere contradiction between foreign law and a mandatory provision of Egyptian law does not amount to a breach of public policy and preclude the application of the foreign law. The foreign law must violate the social, political and moral bases of the state to be excluded on grounds of public policy. In that case, the alleged violation was directly relevant to article 502(3) of the Code of Civil Procedure which mandates that the names of the arbitrators be specified in order for the arbitration agreement to be valid.[46] The court held that this requirement was not a matter of international public policy[47] and that the validity of the arbitration agreement is properly governed by the applicable law (in this instance English law, being the law of the seat of the arbitration). English law does not mandate that the names of the arbitrators be stipulated in the arbitration agreement, and the arbitration agreement was accordingly found to be valid.

3.122 The same violation was alleged in a subsequent case, and the court affirmed its earlier decision.[48]

3.123 In summary, some, but not all, mandatory provisions of Egyptian law reflect public policy within the meaning of article 28 of the Egyptian Civil Code;[49] whether the violation of a particular provision results in the exclusion of the applicable foreign law is therefore an issue to be decided by the courts on a case-by-case basis.

3.124 **Waivers** A party's right to request the setting aside of the award can only be excluded after the issuance of the arbitral award. The waiver of this right before the issuance of the award is ineffective and will not cause the inadmissibility of a subsequent application to set aside the award.

3.125 The question of whether the parties may restrict the grounds for setting aside is not addressed in the Arbitration Act and has yet to be considered by the courts. This should be possible as a matter of principle, because such an agreement would merely constitute a partial waiver by the parties of their right to set aside.

3.126 **Effects of setting aside an award** After it is set aside, the award ceases to have legal effect, in whole or as regards the part that has been set aside. Any decision regarding the correction or the interpretation of the award loses its effect accordingly.

---

45 Court of Cassation, Civil Chamber, challenge no 371/32J (5 April 1967), available at <http://www.eastlaws.com/AhkamView.aspx?I=3199&H=&HM=0>.

46 This provision pre-dates the Arbitration Act.

47 Court of Cassation, Civil Chamber, challenge no 714/47J (26 April 1982), available at <http://www.eastlaws.com/AhkamView.aspx?I=7734&H=&HM=0>.

48 Court of Cassation, Civil Chamber, challenge no 1259/49J (13 June 1983), available at <http://www.eastlaws.com/AhkamView.aspx?I=8112&H=&HM=0>.

49 The Egyptian Civil Code, art 28 provides that: 'The provisions of the foreign law applicable by operation of the preceding articles will not be applied if they are contrary to public policy or to morality in Egypt.'

If the award is set aside on grounds that are unrelated to the arbitration agreement, the agreement remains valid and in force between the parties. 3.127

Local procedures for setting aside an arbitral award

An action to set aside must be brought within 90 days following the date of notification of the award by to the losing party.[50] This time limit applies to all actions for setting aside, regardless of the grounds upon which the action is based. Like all court actions the action to set aside begins with the filing of an originating summons and includes, in due course, a full hearing. 3.128

Proceedings to enforce the award may be initiated or continued pending the rendering of the court's decision on the application to set aside. 3.129

Egyptian law does not stipulate or contemplate the possibility that an arbitral tribunal might be requested, by a party or the court, to eliminate possible grounds for setting aside the award it has rendered. 3.130

3.6 Conclusion

Since the promulgation of the Arbitration Act, inspired by the UNCITRAL Model Law, Cairo has become an attractive venue for international commercial arbitration. The Egyptian courts are generally favourable to arbitration. They exercise minimal control over awards in actions for setting aside. Both the Court of Cassation[51] and the Cairo Court of Appeal[52] have consistently held that the action to set aside is not an appeal and refused to reconsider the merits of the dispute or the tribunal's findings. As judges become more familiar with arbitration, they understand and perform their role better, be it in assisting the parties during the proceedings or in exercising their control in actions for the setting aside of awards. 3.131

The desirability of Cairo as a venue for international arbitration is further enhanced by the existence and activities of the Cairo Centre. The Centre administers proceedings at very competitive rates compared with those of other arbitral institutions, and regularly updates its rules to reflect best international arbitration practices. The Centre also offers all the facilities required in connection with modern arbitration proceedings. 3.132

The uprising of January 2011, despite the instability that has followed it, does not seem to have negatively influenced the choice of Cairo as a seat for arbitration. In 2011, 66 arbitration cases were filed before the Centre. This number increased to 78 new arbitration cases in 2012, which is the highest number of cases filed before the Centre in a single year.[53] In 3.133

[50] In a case where there is no clear loser, both parties will have the right to notify the award for the purpose of triggering the 90-day period.

[51] Court of Cassation, Civil Chamber, challenge no 7307/76J (8 February 2008), (2009) 1(4) Intl J Arab Arbitration 150.

[52] Cairo Court of Appeal, case no 6/124J (16 April 2007) unpublished; Cairo Court of Appeal, case no 120/120J (28 February 2004) unpublished; Cairo Court of Appeal, case no 46/119J (22 November 2003) unpublished; Cairo Court of Appeal, case no 17/119J (26 June 2002), (2003) 6 Journal of Arab Arbitration 175; Cairo Court of Appeal, Case no 61/115J (21 April 1999) unpublished.

[53] See CRCICA Newsletter No 4/2012, available at <http://crcica.org.eg/newsletters/nl201204/crnl42012a001.html> (accessed 30 April 2013).

the first quarter of 2013, 15 new arbitration cases were filed. The total number of arbitration cases filed before the centre has thus reached 885 cases. The new cases relate to disputes arising out of services, supply, investment, construction, and petroleum concession agreements, hotel management and transfer of technology, and other commercial and financial activities.[54]

[54] See CRCICA Newsletter no 1/2013, available at <http://crcica.org.eg/newsletters/nl012013/nl012013.html> (accessed 30 April 2013).

4

CHINA

Jingzhou Tao

4.1 Background

4.1.1 Historical development of arbitration in China

China has a long history of using amicable dispute resolution, the rise of which is closely **4.01** associated with traditional Chinese culture. Deeply influenced by Confucian philosophy, people in ancient China regarded a dispute as an evil, disturbing the harmony that governed the social order. Litigation was also considered negative, particularly given that China's traditional judicial system did not make a distinction between civil and criminal law, so a person involved in any kind of litigation would be considered as having done bad deeds.[1] Going to court was long considered the last resort of parties to a dispute. In this cultural context, early

[1] See JV Feinerman, 'The History and Development of China's Dispute Resolution System' in C Hunter (ed), *Dispute Resolution in China: A Practical Guide to Litigation & Arbitration in China* (Asia Law & Practice, 1995) 7. See also J Zhou, 'Arbitration Agreements in China: Battles on Designation of Arbitral Institution and Ad Hoc Arbitration' (2006) 23(2) J Intl Arb 147.

alternative dispute resolution, such as mediation or conciliation,[2] gradually arose in China. One popular type of mediation in ancient China was conducted by town officials, who were appointed by the relevant local governments. For example, during the Zhou Dynasty (circa BC1100–256), the town official in charge of mediation was known as *tiaoren* (which means 'mediator'). The duty of *tiaoren* as described in a book from the Zhou Dynasty was 'resolving the difficulties of thousands of people through conciliation and mediation'.[3] However, mediation by town officials in ancient China was substantially different from the modern concept of mediation, because the town officials were endowed with powers of administration, by which they probably imposed decisions upon disputants.[4]

4.02 China did not, however, have a concept of 'arbitration' in its language until it began to adopt Western-style legislation in the early 1900s. In 1912, the government of the Qing Dynasty promulgated the Constitution for Business Arbitration Office, followed in 1913 by the Working Rules for Business Arbitration Office, which permitted parties to submit their disputes to the Business Arbitration Office for settlement. Under the rules, an arbitration award would not become legally binding without the consent of the disputing parties; if consent could not be obtained, a disputing party could choose to file civil proceedings in court. The Business Arbitration Offices accepted both disputes between Chinese parties and disputes involving foreigners. In 1930, the then Chinese government promulgated the Law for Settling Disputes between Labor and Management, setting forth conciliation and arbitration procedures for employment disputes.[5]

4.03 Following the founding of the People's Republic of China (the 'PRC') in 1949, China gradually established a dual-track arbitration system, under which domestic disputes and foreign-related disputes were distinguished and treated differently. As a result, two arbitration systems—domestic and foreign-related—have evolved and developed in parallel.

4.1.2 Arbitration law prior to 1994 legislation[6]

Domestic arbitration system

4.04 China's modern domestic arbitration system originated in the early 1950s, when arbitration and conciliation were promoted by the government as a preferred way for resolving domestic commercial disputes. From the early 1960s, various rules and regulations were adopted requiring arbitration as a preliminary mandatory step before the litigation of economic contractual disputes.[7] During that period, the domestic arbitration system consisted of various

---

[2] In the context of Chinese law, the method is known as *tiaojie*, in which a dispute is resolved by a third party designated by the litigants, by reconciling them either before or while they resort to litigation before a court or an arbitral tribunal. Either 'mediation' or 'conciliation' can be a translation of the Chinese word *tiaojie*. Conversely, *tiaojie* can be the Chinese translation of both 'mediation' and 'conciliation'. In this chapter, these two words are not distinguished and are used interchangeably.

[3] In the Zhou Dynasty this book was known as *Zhouli, Diguansitu, Tiaoren*.

[4] See Dr JS Mo, *Arbitration Law in China* (Sweet & Maxwell, 2001) 10–11.

[5] See J Tao, *Arbitration Law and Practice in China* (3rd edn, Kluwer Law International, 2012) 1.

[6] The Arbitration Law of the PRC, promulgated at the 9th session of the Standing Committee of the 8th National People's Congress, 31 August 1994, effective 1 September 1995 (hereinafter the 'Arbitration Law 1994').

[7] Draft Working Rules for the State-Owned Industrial Enterprises, adopted by the State Council, September 1961; Draft Opinions of the State Economic Commission Concerning the Arbitration of Disputes Arising from Defaulting on Loan Payments Among the State-Owned Industrial Enterprises by the Economic Commissions at Various Levels, adopted by the State Economic Commission, 30 August 1962; Notice Concerning the Strict Implementation of Basic Construction Procedure and the Strict Implementation of Economic Contract, promulgated by the State Council, 10 December 1962.

arbitration commissions,[8] which exercised their jurisdiction over disputes between Chinese legal and/or natural persons[9] arising from economic contracts, labour matters, patents, technology transfer contracts, urban property rights, and other matters. The then-existing commissions had little independence in that they were subordinate to or affiliated with governmental administrative authorities such as the Administration for Industry and Commerce (the 'AIC'), and the arbitrators were mainly drawn from the government.[10] The commissions accepted arbitration applications based on administrative law and regulations rather than an arbitration agreement voluntarily signed by the parties, and the parties were not allowed to select the arbitration commission of their own choice. The principle of party autonomy was not adequately recognized in China at the time. Another main feature of China's domestic arbitration regime was that domestic arbitration awards did not have a binding effect on the parties. A dissatisfied party could appeal against the arbitral award before a higher arbitration body, and initiate civil proceedings with the people's court.[11]

From 1966 to 1976, during the chaos of the Cultural Revolution, domestic arbitration practice almost completely ceased. However, a revival followed in the wake of the Open Door and Reform Policy launched in 1979. From then on, many of the key elements of the domestic arbitration system were gradually restored and further developed. **4.05**

In 1983, the Economic Contract Law of the PRC 1981 (the 'Economic Contract Law') was promulgated,[12] establishing the basic legal framework for contractual relationships among domestic PRC entities within China's socialist system.[13] This was the statutory underpinning for the pre-1994 domestic arbitration regime. It stipulated that parties to any dispute arising from an economic contract should first consult with each other to resolve the dispute. It further provided that where the parties failed to reach a resolution of their dispute via consultation, a disputing party could apply to the competent contract administrative authorities for conciliation or arbitration, or alternatively file a lawsuit directly before the people's court. This provision furnished parties with the choice between arbitration and litigation and, as a result, arbitration was no longer a compulsory preliminary step. However, if a party refused to accept the arbitral award, it had the right to challenge it on the merits before the people's court within 15 days of receipt. Domestic arbitral awards therefore still lacked binding effect and could be undermined by the initiation of a lawsuit. **4.06**

In summary, during the period 1978–94, arbitration was widely and almost compulsorily used for the resolution of domestic commercial disputes in China. However, arbitration **4.07**

[8] Arbitration commissions under Chinese law are essentially arbitration institutions. In fact, only institutional arbitration is possible in China. Although ad hoc arbitration is not expressly prohibited, the Arbitration Law 1994, art 16(2) specifically requires that an arbitration commission be designated in the arbitration agreement; otherwise, the arbitration agreement may be null and void.

[9] Foreign invested enterprises, such as equity joint ventures, cooperative joint ventures, and wholly foreign-owned enterprises, which are established partially or wholly by foreign capital, were deemed to constitute Chinese legal persons under Chinese law, and accordingly, disputes between such entities and other domestic legal and natural persons generally fell within the exclusive ambit of the domestic arbitration system, rather than the foreign-related arbitration regime.

[10] See Tao (n 5) 4.

[11] See W Wang, 'Distinct Features of Arbitration in China: A Historical Perspective' (2006) 23(1) J Intl Arb 62.

[12] The Economic Contract Law of the PRC 1981, promulgated by the Standing Committee of the National People's Congress, 13 December 1981, effective 1 July 1982, repealed by the Contract Law of the PRC, effective 1 October 1999.

[13] See Tao (n 5) 2.

practice at that time was different from the modern concept of arbitration in the Western world in many aspects, given the absence of many internationally recognized principles, such as independence, party autonomy, and the binding effect of arbitral awards.

Foreign related arbitration system

4.08 Chinese modern foreign-related arbitration had its beginning with the Protocol for General Conditions of Delivery of Goods between China and the Soviet Union in April 1950, under which any dispute arising from a contract was to be submitted for arbitration. If the respondent was a Chinese enterprise or organization, the arbitration would take place in China. The implementation of the Protocol called for the establishment of a dedicated arbitration body dealing with foreign-related disputes, separate and distinct from the domestic arbitration commissions.[14]

4.09 In May 1954, the China Council for the Promotion of International Trade (CCPIT)[15] was authorized under a Decision of the PRC State Council[16] to establish the Foreign Trade Arbitration Commission (FTAC), which in 1988 became the China International Economic and Trade Arbitration Commission (CIETAC). The FTAC (or CIETAC) was empowered to exercise jurisdiction based on the agreement of the parties, and the parties could appoint a sole arbitrator or the two co-arbitrators in a three-member arbitral tribunal. The Decision also provided that the Chinese courts were to treat awards made by the FTAC as final and enforceable.

4.10 In 1958, the Maritime Arbitration Commission (MAC), another special arbitration commission handling foreign-related disputes, was established. It was renamed in 1988 as the China Maritime Arbitration Commission (CMAC). At that time, CIETAC and CMAC were the only two arbitration institutes empowered to accept foreign-related disputes; they were not allowed to handle domestic disputes until this monopoly over foreign-related disputes was abolished by the Arbitration Law 1994.

4.11 In fact, from 1949 to the late 1970s only a small number of cases were handled by the two foreign-related arbitration commissions, because of China's limited commercial interaction with other countries. In the 1980s, however, following the adoption of the Open Door and Reform policy, the foreign-related arbitration regime underwent rapid growth, as various laws dealing with foreign-related dispute resolution were enacted. In July 1979, China adopted the Sino-Foreign Equity Joint Venture Law, which provided that if the board of an equity joint venture[17] failed to resolve a dispute between the parties to the venture through

---

[14] See Tao (n 5) 8.

[15] CCPIT is the national state body charged with the promotion of international trade in China. There are more than 20 administrative departments falling within the charge of CCPIT, including the following: the CCPIT General Office; the Department of Sub-Council Affairs; the Personnel Department; the Department for Exhibitions Abroad; the Economic Information Department; the Department of Media and Press; the Department of Legal Affairs; the China Trademark Agency; the China Patent Agency; CIETAC; CMAC; the Economic and Trade Coordination Committee for the Two Sides of the Straits; and the China Maritime Law Association.

[16] The Decision of the Government Administration Council of the Central People's Government Concerning the Establishment of a Foreign Trade Arbitration Commission within the China Council for the Promotion of International Trade, promulgated by the State Council, 6 May 1954.

[17] An equity joint venture is a vehicle allowing a foreign partner to participate in a limited liability company with a Chinese party by contributing a minimum of 25% of the registered capital. Equity joint venture partners share profits and bear risks and losses in proportion to their contributions to the registered capital.

consultation, the dispute could be resolved by mediation or arbitration. In March 1982, the Civil Procedure Law of the PRC (for Trial Implementation) (the 'Trial Civil Procedure Law') was adopted,[18] which included a chapter entitled 'Arbitration', specifically addressing foreign-related arbitration. In March 1985, the Foreign Economic Contract Law of the PRC[19] was adopted, serving as the primary legislative instrument governing contracts with foreign elements. It stipulated in its article 37 that if the parties failed to settle their dispute via consultation or mediation, they could submit it to a Chinese arbitration institution or other arbitration institution. In September 1986, China acceded to the 1958 New York Convention[20] with both the reciprocal and commercial reservations,[21] and the Convention became effective in the PRC as of 22 April 1987. In order to implement the Convention, on 10 April 1987, the Supreme People's Court (the 'SPC') issued the Notice of the Supreme People's Court Regarding the Implementation of the Convention on the Recognition and Enforcement of Foreign Arbitral Awards acceded to by China, which detailed the reservations and defined the extent of judicial jurisdiction over recognition and enforcement applications. In 1991 and 1992, the Civil Procedure Law of the PRC (the 'Civil Procedure Law')[22] and the SPC Opinions relating to the Civil Procedure Law were adopted, replacing the Trial Civil Procedure Law. They laid down many important provisions in relation to foreign-related arbitration concerning the consensual nature of China's foreign-related arbitration, the jurisdiction of courts, the property and evidence preservation procedures in connection with ongoing arbitration proceedings, the finality of arbitration awards, and their enforcement.[23]

This legislation set up a foreign-related arbitration regime more in line with international **4.12** practice than the Chinese domestic arbitration system. For example, the principle that arbitration is a consensual process based on the agreement of the parties was emphasized, and the arbitration could be conducted in China or elsewhere, provided that the place of arbitration was agreed upon by the disputing parties.[24]

---

[18] The Civil Procedure Law of the PRC was implemented on a trial basis at the 22nd session of the Standing Committee of the 5th National People's Congress, 1 October 1982. It was subsequently repealed by the Civil Procedure Law of the PRC, promulgated at the 4th Session of the 7th National People's Congress, 9 April 1991, effective 9 April 1991 (hereinafter the 'Civil Procedure Law').

[19] The Foreign Economic Contract Law of the PRC, promulgated at the 10th session of the Standing Committee of the 6th National People's Congress, March 1985, effective 1 July 1985, repealed by the Contract Law of the PRC, promulgated 15 March 1999, effective 1 October 1999 (hereinafter the 'Contract Law 1999').

[20] Convention on the Recognition of Foreign Arbitral Awards, New York, 10 June 1958, 330 UNTS 38 (the New York Convention).

[21] Under the reciprocity reservation, China agreed to apply the New York Convention to the recognition and enforcement of foreign arbitral awards rendered by an arbitration institution in the territory of another contracting state only; under the commercial reservation, China applies the New York Convention only to disputes arising from legal relationships, whether contractual or not, which are considered *commercial* under Chinese law.

[22] The Civil Procedure law was revised by the Decision Regarding the Revision of the Civil Procedure Law of the PRC, promulgated at the 30th session of the Standing Committee of the 10th National People's Congress, 28 October 2007, effective 1 April 2008. It was then revised by another Decision, promulgated at the 25th session of the Standing Committee of the 11th National People's Congress, 31 August 2012, effective 1 January 2013 (hereinafter the 'Civil Procedure Law 2013').

[23] Civil Procedure Law 2013, arts 271–274.

[24] eg the Sino-Foreign Equity Joint Venture Law of the PRC, art 14 promulgated at the 3rd Session of the 7th National People's Congress, 4 April 1990; the Regulations of the PRC on the Exploration of Offshore Petroleum Resources in Cooperation with Foreign Enterprises, art 27; and the Foreign Economic Contract Law of the PRC, art 37.

4.1.3 Arbitration law after 1994

Unification of domestic arbitration system

4.13 Prior to the entry into effect of the Arbitration Law 1994 on 1 September 1995, both the domestic and the foreign-related arbitration systems were regulated by diverse legal documents, in the absence of a uniform arbitration law. It is estimated that by 1994, provisions regarding arbitration had been introduced in 14 laws, 82 administrative rules and regulations, and 190 local regulations.[25] One of the most important purposes of the Arbitration Law 1994 was therefore to unify the commercial arbitration legal framework.[26]

4.14 The new legislation released the domestic arbitration commissions from direct government control and thus arbitration became, to a certain extent, a service offered by arbitration commissions. Article 8 of the Law emphasizes the independence of arbitration, stipulating that arbitration shall be carried out independently according to law and shall be free from interference by administrative authorities, social organizations, or individuals. Article 14 requires arbitration commissions to be independent from, or not to subordinate to, any administrative authorities or other arbitration commissions. Article 77 expressly exempts from the law's scope of application the arbitration of labour disputes[27] and disputes arising from farm contract work within collective agricultural organizations.[28]

4.15 For the implementation of the Arbitration Law 1994, article 79 required that the previously established arbitration commissions be organized in accordance with the law, and that arbitration commissions that were not reorganized were to terminate within one year from the effective date of the Law. The then-existing institutions established within the AIC, and other administrative organs of the local governments, were therefore automatically dissolved on 1 September 1996. Since then, around 215 domestic arbitration commissions have been reorganized or established throughout China.[29] The majority of arbitration commissions were established through consolidation of the then-existing institutions, the only exceptions being labour dispute arbitration commissions and farming dispute arbitration commissions.[30] Thus, the current domestic arbitration system in China consists of three types of

---

[25] See 'Illustration Regarding the Arbitration Law of PRC (Draft)', SCNPC Legislative Affairs Commission, 28 June 1994, available at <http://www.npc.gov.cn/wxzl/gongbao/2001-01/02/content_5003212.htm> (accessed 8 March 2013).

[26] Mo (n 4) 27.

[27] Labor Law of the PRC, promulgated by the Standing Committee of the National People's Congress, 5 July 1994, effective 1 January 1995, revised by the Decision of the Standing Committee of the of the National People's Congress on the Amendment of Some Laws, 27 August 2009, effective 27 August 2009; Labor Contract Law of the PRC, promulgated by the Standing Committee of the National People's Congress, 29 June 2007, effective 1 January 2008; Law on Labor Dispute Mediation and Arbitration of the PRC, promulgated by the Standing Committee of the National People's Congress, 29 December 2007, effective 1 May 2008.

[28] Interpretation of the Supreme People's Court on Some Issues Concerning the Trial of Cases Involving Disputes Over Agricultural Contracts, promulgated by the Supreme People's Court on 28 June 1999, effective 8 July 1999, repealed by Decision of the Supreme People's Court on Abolishing Relevant Judicial Interpretations (the Seventh Batch) Promulgated before the End of 2007, promulgated by the Supreme People's Court, 18 December 2008, effective 24 December 2008; Law of the PRC on the Mediation and Arbitration of Rural Land Contract Disputes, promulgated by the Standing Committee of the National People's Congress on 27 June 2009, effective 1 January 2010.

[29] Y Li, *Continue to Implement the Arbitration Law and to Further Improve the Arbitration Legal System*, Vol 5 (Arbitration & Law, 2000); S Shen and J Shen, 'Features and Self-innovation of China Commercial Arbitration System' (2010) 12 Legal Science Monthly 31.

[30] C Ying, *The Science of Law of Arbitration* (House of China University of Politics & Law, 2001).

arbitration: commercial arbitration under the Arbitration Law 1994, labour arbitration, and the arbitration of farming disputes.

Introduction of international practices

The Arbitration Law 1994 consists of 80 articles divided into eight chapters, successively dealing with general provisions (Chapter I), arbitration commissions and arbitration associations (Chapter II), arbitration agreements (Chapter III), arbitration proceedings (Chapter IV), applications for setting aside arbitral awards (Chapter V), enforcement (Chapter VI), special provisions on foreign-related arbitration (Chapter VII), and supplementary provisions (Chapter VIII). To bring domestic arbitration into line with international practice, the Arbitration Law 1994 embodies many of the internationally recognized principles of modern arbitration. For example, a valid arbitration agreement excludes the jurisdiction of courts,[31] and without the *prima facie* existence of an arbitration agreement, the arbitration commission will refuse to accept the case.[32] Arbitration must be conducted independently,[33] and an arbitral award is final and binding on both parties, has *res judicata* effect,[34] and is enforceable by the courts. **4.16**

Distinction between domestic and foreign-related arbitration

Before adoption of the Arbitration Law 1994, foreign-related arbitration in China was monopolized by CIETAC and CMAC, with domestic cases restricted exclusively to domestic arbitration institutions, and foreign-related cases to the two foreign-related arbitration institutions. Although not expressly stipulated in the law, the Arbitration Law 1994 has in fact blurred the historical distinction between domestic arbitration and foreign-related arbitration. According to the Notice of the General Office of the State Council of 8 June 1996, which clarified certain issues around implementation of the Arbitration Law 1994, domestic arbitration commissions are entitled to handle foreign-related cases if so entrusted by the parties. Subsequently, in its Arbitration Rules 2000 (effective as of 1 October 2000), CIETAC extended its jurisdiction to domestic cases that the parties submit by agreement, based on the autonomy of the parties and the practical needs of the business community. As a result, China has now abolished the rigid separation between domestic and foreign-related arbitration, and parties can choose a domestic arbitration commission to administer foreign-related arbitration, and CIETAC to administer domestic arbitration. **4.17**

Nevertheless, differences between domestic and foreign-related arbitration remain under the Arbitration Law 1994, which contains a Chapter VII entitled 'Special Provisions on Foreign-related Arbitration'. Under the Law, different sets of rules are provided for domestic arbitration and foreign-related arbitration. The qualifications necessary empanelment with any arbitration commission is provided for by article 13 for domestic arbitration, and for foreign-related arbitration by article 67. The application for preservation of evidence in domestic disputes is set forth in article 46, and in article 68 for foreign-related disputes. Articles 58 to 64 apply to setting aside or refusing to enforce an award made in a domestic dispute, and articles 70 and 71 apply to awards made in a foreign-related dispute. The Chinese courts exercise wider control and supervision over awards made in a domestic dispute than **4.18**

[31] Arbitration Law 1994, art 5.
[32] Arbitration Law 1994, art 4.
[33] Arbitration Law 1994, art 8.
[34] Arbitration Law 1994, art 9.

they do over awards made in a foreign-related dispute. In other words, it is easier to set aside or resist the enforcement of a domestic award than a foreign-related award,[35] as the grounds for refusing to enforce foreign-related awards are broadly similar to the New York Convention grounds.

4.1.4 Recent developments in arbitration in China

CIETAC and its Arbitration Rules 2012

4.19 CIETAC is certainly the most well-known arbitration body in China, and also one of the busiest arbitration centres in the world. In 2010 alone, CIETAC handled 1,352 cases, of which 418 were foreign-related.[36] It has its headquarters in Beijing, and four sub-commissions in Shanghai, Shenzhen, Chongqing, and Tianjin.[37]

4.20 After its establishment in 1956, CIETAC's arbitration rules were amended and supplemented several times. The 2005 amendments to its arbitration rules introduced many significant changes to CIETAC, which bring its practice into line with international standards. Among other things: (1) the parties may select arbitrators outside the CIETAC panel; (2) the parties may agree on a seat of arbitration outside China; (3) the tribunal can conduct either inquisitorial or adversarial proceedings; and (4) arbitrators are—for the first time—required to disclose any facts that may affect their independence and impartiality.

4.21 As from 1 May 2012, a new set of arbitration rules came into force for arbitrations administered by CIETAC, which replaced the 2005 Rules (the 'CIETAC Rules 2012'). The main new developments in the CIETAC Rules 2012 include the following:

(1) CIETAC is empowered to designate the place of arbitration when the parties fail to do so. This is highly controversial, since Shanghai and other branches were very reluctant to give such power to CIETAC headquarters.
(2) If the claimant fails to comply with the formality requirements when filing the request for arbitration and further fails to rectify the problem in due course, it will be deemed not to have submitted a request for arbitration.
(3) The Secretariat of CIETAC is empowered to decide whether to grant extensions to parties for their submissions when the arbitral tribunal has not yet been constituted.
(4) A mechanism of consolidation of arbitration was introduced. Article 17 of the CIETAC Rules 2012 reads:

    1. At the request of a party and with the agreement of all the other parties, or where CIETAC believes it necessary and all the parties have agreed, CIETAC may consolidate two or more arbitrations pending under these Rules into a single arbitration.
    2. In deciding whether to consolidate the arbitrations in accordance with the preceding Paragraph 1, CIETAC may take into account any factors it considers relevant in respect of the different arbitrations, including whether all of the claims in the different arbitrations are made under the same arbitration agreement, whether the different arbitrations

---

[35] Mo (n 4) 59.

[36] A Ross, 'An Interview with Yu Jianlong', Global Arbitration Review, 5 September 2011, available at <http://www.globalarbitrationreview.com/journal/article/29794/an-interview-yu-jianlong> (accessed 8 March 2013).

[37] The four sub-commissions are, respectively, the CIETAC Shanghai Sub-Commission, the CIETAC South China Sub-Commission in Shenzhen, the CIETAC Financial Arbitration Centre in Tianjin, and the CIETAC Southwest Sub-Commission in Chongqing.

are between the same parties, or whether one or more arbitrators have been nominated or appointed in the different arbitrations.

3. Unless otherwise agreed by all the parties, the arbitrations shall be consolidated into the arbitration that was first commenced.

(5) The arbitral tribunal is empowered to grant interim measures in the form of a procedural order or interim award.

(6) The procedure of suspension of arbitration was introduced by article 43 of the CIETAC Rules 2012, which reads:

1. Where parties request a suspension of the arbitration proceedings, or under circumstances where such suspension is necessary, the arbitration proceedings may be suspended.
2. The arbitration proceedings shall resume as soon as the reason for the suspension disappears or the suspension period ends.
3. The arbitral tribunal shall decide whether to suspend or resume the arbitration proceedings. Where the arbitral tribunal has not yet been formed, the decision shall be made by the Secretary General of CIETAC.

(7) The parties may choose to conduct conciliation before the arbitral tribunal, or enter into a settlement themselves; the latter will no longer be deemed to be conciliation conducted by the arbitral tribunal.

In general, the CIETAC Rules 2012 have taken further steps forward in following predominant international arbitration practice, which reflects China's determination and efforts to become an international arbitration centre. **4.22**

CIETAC Shanghai and Shenzhen's split

On 1 May 2012, the same day when the CIETAC Rules 2012 came into force, the CIETAC Shanghai sub-commission announced that it had split from CIETAC Beijing, declaring itself an independent arbitral institution. CIETAC Shanghai then published a new set of arbitration rules and formed its own panel of arbitrators, separate from those of CIETAC Beijing. Following Shanghai's announcement, CIETAC Shenzhen also declared its independence and the application of its own arbitration rules as of 1 December 2012. It also changed its name from CIETAC South China Commission to the South China International Economic and Trade Arbitration Commission (the 'SCIETAC') and gave itself a second official name, the Shenzhen Court of International Arbitration (the 'SCIA'). **4.23**

CIETAC Shanghai, as one of the four CIETAC sub-commissions, decided to split from CIETAC Beijing because the new CIETAC Rules largely centralized CIETAC's powers in its Beijing headquarters. In particular, article 2.3 of the new Rules describes the sub-commissions as 'CIETAC's branches'. Moreover, article 2.6 provides that the Secretariat of CIETAC (Beijing) will administer the case whenever a general reference to 'CIETAC arbitration' is made or the parties' agreement is ambiguous. As a consequence, the number of cases handled by the sub-commissions would be greatly reduced. **4.24**

In response to Shanghai's announcement, CIETAC released its own announcement on the same day, rejecting Shanghai's intention to break away and accusing it of violating China's arbitration law and of 'seriously affecting parties' exercise of their arbitration rights'.[38] On 1 August 2012, CIETAC released another announcement, suspending CIETAC's **4.25**

[38] The Statement announced by CIETAC is available at <http://cn.cietac.org/notes/notes088.shtml> (accessed 8 March 2013).

authorization of the CIETAC Shanghai sub-commission and the CIETAC South China sub-commission to accept and administer arbitration cases. In response to the announcement, the CIETAC Shanghai sub-commission and South China sub-commission jointly issued another statement, announcing that they had been independent arbitration institutions since their establishment and their rights to accept requests for arbitration were not dependent on CIETAC's authorization. Currently, the two sub-commissions are continuing to accept and manage cases submitted to them. The main implications concern jurisdictional challenges and enforcement problems regarding cases administrated by the CIETAC Shanghai sub-commission and CIETAC South China sub-commission.

4.1.5 Arbitration and the courts

Judicial interpretation

4.26 The SPC has issued decisions interpreting the Arbitration Law 1994, the Civil Procedure Law, and other relevant laws and regulations that are in fact binding on lower courts. Lower courts are not authorized to engage in judicial interpretation in the constitutional sense. However, in practice some courts, such as the Shanghai Municipal High Court, Beijing Municipal High Court, and Shenzhen Municipal High Court, have made judicial pronouncements concerning the validity of arbitration agreements and the setting-aside of arbitral awards. These interpretations, usually in the form of 'Provisions' or 'Opinions', are binding only on lower courts within the same jurisdiction, and only as long as they do not contradict the laws, regulations, or interpretations of the SPC.

Court assistance to arbitration

4.27 The courts provide assistance to arbitration in many aspects. Under the Arbitration Law 1994, if the jurisdiction of an arbitral tribunal is challenged, the arbitration institution or a competent court decides the jurisdiction issue. In addition, the courts are empowered to decide on requests for the preservation of evidence and property.

Court supervisory power over arbitral awards

4.28 Although article 9 of the Arbitration Law 1994 establishes the principle of finality of the arbitral award, a party may still request the court to set aside the award or to refuse its enforcement in specific circumstances. In respect of the enforcement of foreign awards, Article V(2) of the New York Convention and accordingly article 274(2) of the Civil Procedure Law 2013, provides that the court may—upon the approval of the SPC—refuse on public policy grounds to recognize an award. Notably, the courts can examine only the procedural aspects of a foreign or foreign-related award. For domestic awards, courts can scrutinize from both procedure and substance perspectives.

4.2 Commencing the Arbitration

4.2.1 Role of courts in commencing the arbitration and resolving jurisdictional issues

4.29 Articles 5 and 26 of the Arbitration Law 1994 establish the principle that a valid arbitration agreement excludes the jurisdiction of the courts. When the parties have concluded an arbitration agreement and a party files a lawsuit in court, the court may not accept the case, unless the arbitration agreement is invalid. If the court has accepted the case without knowing that there was a valid arbitration agreement, the court must dismiss the case, provided the other party submits the arbitration agreement prior to the first hearing. If the other party fails to raise an objection prior to the first hearing, it will be deemed to have waived its right to refer to arbitration, and the court may proceed with the matter.

4.30 Though the Arbitration Law 1994 does not expressly reject the principle of *competence-competence* of the arbitral tribunal, it can be inferred from the relevant provisions that the principle has not been accepted by Chinese law. Article 5 of the Arbitration Law 1994, which provides that a valid arbitration agreement excludes the jurisdiction of the court, does not lay down who—the court or the arbitral tribunal—has the final say on the validity of the arbitration agreement. Thus, this article does not provide the arbitral tribunal with the power to determine its own jurisdiction under the *competence-competence* principle.

4.31 The second paragraph of article 19 of the Arbitration Law 1994 stipulates that 'the arbitral tribunal shall have the power to affirm the validity of a contract'. However, this stipulation is generally interpreted as failing to answer the question of who is competent to determine the validity of the arbitration agreement, given that the separability doctrine regarding the arbitration clause is expressly recognized in the first paragraph of article 19. In view of the doctrine of separability, the arbitral tribunal that is empowered to decide on the validity of the contract does not necessarily have the competence to decide on the validity of the arbitration clause.

4.32 It appears that article 20 of the Arbitration Law 1994 answers the question regarding *competence-competence* more directly, providing:

> If a party challenges the validity of the arbitration agreement, such party may request the arbitration commission to make a decision or apply to the People's Court for a ruling. If one party requests an arbitration commission to make a decision while the other party applies to the People's Court for a ruling, the People's Court shall give a ruling.
>
> A challenge to the validity of an arbitration agreement shall be raised by the parties prior to the first hearing before the arbitration tribunal.

4.33 Article 20 deprives the arbitral tribunal of the competence to decide on the validity of an arbitration agreement, since it provides only for recourse to either the arbitration commission or the court. Moreover, it makes it clear that if one party requests the arbitration commission to decide and the other party applies to the court, the court's decision will prevail, provided that (a) the concerned party has raised the objection prior to the first hearing of the arbitral tribunal and (b) the arbitration commission has not yet made a decision. If the commission finds that the tribunal has jurisdiction, there is no immediate recourse to the courts, which must refuse any application to rule on arbitral jurisdiction.[39]

4.34 The Arbitration Law 1994 therefore leaves no room for the *competence-competence* principle, and the court has the last word on the validity of an arbitration agreement and resulting arbitral jurisdiction. As a result, the court is given the power to intervene at the commencement of arbitration proceedings. The lack of *competence-competence* calls into doubt the independence of the arbitral tribunal, because it is hard to say that a tribunal is independent from the arbitration commission if it is deprived of the right to decide its own jurisdiction.

[39] Reply of the Supreme People's Court to Several Issues Arising from the Determination of the Validity of Arbitration Agreements, art 3, promulgated 5 November 1998, effective 5 November 1998.

4.2.2 Role of courts in appointing arbitrators

4.35 Under the Arbitration Law 1994, an arbitral tribunal may consist of either a sole arbitrator or three arbitrators.[40] If the parties agree to have a sole arbitrator, they jointly appoint the arbitrator or entrust the appointment to the chairman of the arbitration commission. If the parties agree to have a three-member arbitral tribunal, the claimant and respondent each appoint one arbitrator, while the presiding arbitrator is jointly selected by the parties or appointed by the chairman of the arbitration commission.[41]

4.36 Unlike many jurisdictions that allow the parties to raise objections before the courts to the appointment of an arbitrator or to seek judicial assistance in appointing arbitrators, China's arbitration law does not give the courts a role in this regard. Pursuant to the Arbitration Law 1994, only the parties and the chairman of the arbitration commission have the power to appoint arbitrators. Although the court can later examine the impartiality of an arbitrator in the context of setting aside or enforcing an arbitral award, it is not allowed to step in during the arbitration proceedings to appoint arbitrators.

4.37 As China has not yet recognized ad hoc arbitration, the fact that the court lacks competence to appoint arbitrators does not cause much practical difficulty. However, if China should decide to introduce ad hoc arbitration in the future, it will be necessary to empower the courts to appoint arbitrators in certain situations.

4.2.3 Role of the court in enjoining arbitration

4.38 The question of whether the court has power to enjoin arbitration is closely related to the arbitrability of the dispute. In some jurisdictions, the court is empowered to enjoin an arbitration or issue an injunction terminating a pending arbitration, if it determines that the dispute was not subjected to arbitration or is not arbitrable. Chinese law had never defined the scope of arbitrability until the enactment of the Arbitration Law 1994, which sets this out in its articles 2, 3, and 77.[42]

4.39 A question that is not answered under Chinese law is who should decide on the arbitrability of disputes—the court or the arbitral tribunal. It also leaves open the question of whether the court has the power to enjoin arbitration when it considers the dispute to fall outside the scope of arbitrable matters. In spite of this legislative lacuna, the following cases may provide some clues.

4.40 In *China National Technical Import & Export Corporation v Swiss Industrial Resources Corporation* of 1988,[43] the court of appeal concluded that since the dispute between the

---

[40] Arbitration Law 1994, art 30.

[41] Arbitration Law 1994, art 31.

[42] Arbitration Law 1994, art 2 lays down a general principle that arbitrable disputes must be of a contractual or non-contractual nature and relate to property rights and interests between citizens, legal persons or other organizations that are equal civil subjects. Art 3 sets out the types of disputes that cannot be submitted to arbitration, including (a) disputes pertaining to marriage, adoption, guardianship, child maintenance, and inheritance and (b) disputes arising from administrative management by the government, between governmental organs *inter se*, or between governmental organs and other social organizations or individuals. Additionally, art 77 excludes labour disputes and agricultural disputes from being submitted to either the domestic or foreign-related arbitration commissions for arbitration, by stipulating that regulations concerning these two types of dispute shall be formulated separately.

[43] *China National Technical Import & Export Corp v Swiss Industrial Resources Corp* [1989] 1 Gazette of the Supreme People's Court of the PRC 26, 27 (Intermediate People's Court of Shanghai Municipality, 1988).

parties was not of a contractual nature but a tortious dispute, the appellee had the right to raise an action of trespass before the court, rather than being bound by the arbitration clause concluded between the parties. The court of appeal then confirmed the jurisdiction of the court of first instance. Regardless of the hotly-debated issue of whether a tortious dispute was arbitrable under the then Chinese law, the Court's ruling shows that it had a determining say in whether a dispute was subject to arbitration or not, though it did not issue an order directly to enjoin the arbitration.

Another case relating to arbitrability is *Textile & Other Light Industries Co Ltd of the Commodities Group v Topcapital Holdings Ltd and Prince Development Ltd*.[44] The court of first instance (the Higher People's Court of Jiangsu Province) rejected the defendants' objection to jurisdiction based on the existence of a valid arbitration clause, holding that the parties were not bound by the contractual arbitration clause because the dispute arose in tort. The court of appeal (the Supreme People's Court) held that disputes of a tortious nature fall within the scope of arbitrable matters under article 2 of the Arbitration Law 1994 and article 2 of the then applicable CIETAC Arbitration Rules. Therefore, the Court, concluding that the parties were bound by the arbitration clause and the people's court had no jurisdiction over the dispute, reversed the decision of the lower court. **4.41**

The people's courts do, in practice, actually decide on arbitrability. If a court decides that a dispute is non-arbitrable and that it should therefore exercise jurisdiction, the arbitration proceedings will be made impossible or enjoined *de facto*. More importantly, one of the reasons for the absence of provisions regarding enjoining arbitration is that the principle of *competence-competence* is not recognized under Chinese law; in practice it is the courts that have the final say on arbitral jurisdiction at the outset of the arbitration. As such, there is no need to empower the courts to enjoin arbitration proceedings. **4.42**

4.3 During the Arbitration

4.3.1 Role of court during the arbitration

During the stage from the constitution of the tribunal until the issuance of the award, the tribunal is expected to perform its function to the utmost, which naturally leaves open the question of whether a court should intervene in the arbitration at this stage. **4.43**

General international practice restricts court interference during the arbitration under most circumstances, except where this is necessary to guarantee procedural fairness and provide assistance to the parties and the arbitral tribunal, as exemplified by the role of the *juge d'appui* in the French arbitration regime.[45] Following this practice, Chinese legislation allows only minimal court intervention[46] during arbitration compared to the practice in jurisdictions **4.44**

---

[44] *Textile & Other Light Industries Co Ltd of the Commodities Group v Topcapital Holdings Ltd and Prince Development Ltd* [1998] 3 Gazette of the Supreme People's Court of the PRC 109-10 (Supreme People's Court of PRC, 1998).

[45] A Redfern, M Hunter, N Blackaby, and C Partasides, *Law and Practice of International Commercial Arbitration* (4th edn, Sweet & Maxwell, 2004) 353–4 (Chinese version translated by L Yifei and S Lianbin and published in China by Peking University Press, 2005).

[46] W Shengchang, 'CIETAC's Perspective and Conciliation Concerning China' in A van den Berg (ed), *New Horizons in International Commercial Arbitration and Beyond* (ICCA Congress Series no 12, Kluwer Law International, 2005). See also C von Wunschheim, P Tercier, and G Ajani, *Enforcement of Commercial Arbitral Awards in China: Business Laws in China* (West, 2011) 42–3.

with similar cultural backgrounds, such as Hong Kong and Singapore. Except for exclusive jurisdiction over evidence and property preservation measures, no other power to intervene is available to the people's courts. This is, of course, explained in part by the primacy of the arbitration commissions and their broad powers in supervising arbitration.

Challenge of arbitrator

4.45 The court has no legal basis for removing an arbitrator. The Arbitration Law 1994 sets forth four grounds for removing an arbitrator from a tribunal and two grounds for removing an arbitrator from a commission's panel,[47] and makes the arbitration commission or its chairman the sole decision-maker.[48] The courts play no role in arbitrator challenges, and are empowered only to impose liability on arbitrators for illegal private interaction with the parties, acceptance of bribes, deception for personal gain, or intentional misapplication of the law.[49]

4.46 In comparison with the widely-adopted terms of the UNICITRAL Model Law, according to which the party's agreement on the conduct of the arbitration prevails over non-mandatory legislative provisions and arbitration rules,[50] the Chinese mechanism dilutes the parties' autonomy in choosing a tribunal, as it provides no legal basis for handling a challenge pursuant to the parties' agreement. Unlike other venues,[51] where the courts are empowered to hear appeals against unsuccessful challenges and to make the decision, in China, it is the arbitration commission that makes the sole and final decision regarding challenge of an arbitrator.[52] Because of the commissions' control over the parties' choice of arbitrators in China,[53] the public tends to believe that commissions are reluctant to remove an arbitrator, for all arbitrators are selected from the commissions' arbitrator panels and the tribunals are formed indirectly under the will of the commission or appointed by the chairman of the commission. Although the situation has improved and certain commissions like CIETAC now allow parties to choose arbitrators outside the panel, this practice has not yet been adopted by many arbitration commissions and depends on the commission involved.[54]

Evidence

4.47 With respect to assisting the tribunal in obtaining evidence, the law sets no legal basis for the court to compel testimony or evidence but only to preserve evidence, an area where the court's intervention renders indispensable support to the arbitral proceedings.[55] Pursuant

---

[47] Arbitration Law 1994, arts 34 and 38.

[48] Arbitration Law 1994, art 36.

[49] Arbitration Law 1994, art 58.

[50] UNCITRAL Model Law on International Commercial Arbitration (the UNCITRAL Model Law) (1985, 24 ILM 1302), Art 13(1).

[51] Examples of countries and regions that allow the court to accept a party's appeal against the tribunal's or arbitration institution's decision on an application for removing an arbitrator include but are not limited to Hong Kong, Singapore, and the UK.

[52] Arbitration Law 1994, art 36; CIETAC Rules 2012, art 30(6).

[53] In China, the parties must choose the arbitrators from among the panel of arbitrators of the relevant arbitration commission (who must meet certain criteria) and on most occasions are not free to appoint arbitrators not on the list of the panel. See also von Wunschheim, Tercier, and Ajani (n 46) 62; Arbitration Law 1994, arts 31 and 32.

[54] G Weixia, 'The China-Style Closed Panel System in Arbitral Tribunal Formation: Analysis of Chinese Adaption to Globalization' (2008) 25(1) J Intl Arb 121, 131; F Kun, 'Arbitration in China: Practice, Legal Obstacles and Reforms' (2008) 19(2) ICC International Court of Arbitration Bulletin 39.

[55] Redfern, Hunter, Blackaby, and Partasides (n 45) 354.

to article 46 of the Arbitration Law 1994, a party may apply to the tribunal seeking an evidence preservation order where evidence the party relies on is at a risk of destruction, loss, or difficulty in later collection. The arbitral commission must submit the application to the people's court at the place where the evidence is located for review and determination.[56] The evidence preservation mechanism for foreign-related arbitration shares the basic criteria and principles used for domestic arbitration, while the competent court is the Intermediate People's Court at the place where the evidence is located. Hence, preservation applications in foreign-related cases are likely to be handled with greater efficiency and correctness compared to those in domestic arbitrations, due to the fact that the intermediate courts have considerably more experience.

China's evidence preservation mechanism in arbitration has long been criticized because initiation of arbitration was a precondition for making an evidence preservation application. The new Civil Procedure Law 2013 dispenses with this precondition, providing in article 81 that where it is likely that evidence may be destroyed, lost, or become difficult to obtain later on, an interested party may, prior to instituting a lawsuit or applying for arbitration, apply to the people's court at the place where the evidence is located or the domicile of the party against which the application is made, or the people's court with jurisdiction over the case, to preserve the evidence. **4.48**

4.3.2 Restrictions/requirements regarding the ability of foreign practitioners to appear in arbitration as counsel or arbitrator

When entering into an arbitration agreement, the parties should choose an arbitration institution that allows them freedom in appointing arbitrators and choosing counsel; this is fundamental in guaranteeing the parties' autonomy. The arbitration commissions in China has been making progress in expanding the parties' choice of arbitrators and counsel, yet restrictions still exist. **4.49**

The restrictions on counsel lie mainly with their nationality. Over the years, both Chinese and foreign lawyers were permitted to represent clients in foreign-related arbitrations,[57] until a regulation issued in 2002[58] expressly denied foreign law firms and foreign practitioners[59] the right to provide legal advice concerning 'Chinese legal matters'. This regulatory restriction was further clarified in 2003:[60] foreign practitioners are not forbidden from acting as counsel in arbitrations in China that involve Chinese legal matters, but may not issue legal opinions or represent clients on Chinese legal matters. A party with foreign counsel must therefore engage a local practitioner to deal with Chinese law issues. This restriction was originally intended to protect parties from receiving unqualified legal services regarding local **4.50**

[56] Arbitration Law 1994, art 46.

[57] Arbitration Law 1994, art 29.

[58] Regulations on the Administration of the Operation of the Offices of Foreign Law Firms in China, art 15, promulgated by the State Council, 22 December 2001, effective 1 January 2002.

[59] Lawyers employed by foreign law firms in China are not considered Chinese practitioners according to the Regulations on the Administration of the Operation of the Offices of Foreign Law Firms in China, art 16 which provides that 'Representing offices of the foreign law firms in China are forbidden from hiring licensed Chinese lawyers'.

[60] Clarification Issued by the Administrative Office of the Ministry of Justice to Confirm that Representative Offices of Foreign Law Firms and Their Representatives can Serve as Legal Agents in International Arbitration in China, promulgated by the Ministry of Justice of the PRC, 6 January 2003, effective 6 January 2003.

law, but is becoming unnecessary, as more and more locally qualified lawyers join foreign law firms.

4.51 In comparison, nationality is not a major barrier when it comes to arbitrators. Both Chinese arbitrators and arbitrators from Hong Kong, Macao, Taiwan, or other countries and regions may be appointed in a foreign-related arbitration in China.[61] Furthermore, since May 2008 CIETAC no longer distinguishes between its arbitrator panels for domestic cases and foreign-related cases, so foreign practitioners may act as arbitrators in domestic arbitrations as well. Rather than the practitioners' nationality, it is the panel system that limits parties autonomy in appointing arbitrators. Although the parties are now allowed to choose outside the panels in CIETAC cases, any such unconventional appointment must be confirmed by CIETAC,[62] and only a few commissions in China have followed CIETAC's lead. It is undeniable that this reform is a positive step in expanding the pool of arbitrators and facilitating the practice of choosing presiding arbitrators of a third nationality, but the parties' autonomy in appointing arbitrators is still overshadowed by the arbitration commissions' will.

4.3.3 Other local requirements for the conduct of arbitration hearings

4.52 The Arbitration Law 1994 provides that an arbitral tribunal must hold an oral hearing unless the parties have agreed otherwise.[63] Nevertheless, due to the influence of litigation proceedings on arbitration, it is only on rare occasions that a tribunal will decide a case solely on the basis of written submissions and other documents.

4.53 There are limitations on the language used during an oral hearing. The parties may choose a specific language to be used during the arbitral proceedings. If there is no agreement, Chinese was the default language under the 2005 CIETAC Rules,[64] while the 2102 CIETAC Rules follow the more common practice of empowering the arbitration commission to decide whether languages other than Chinese may be used and whether the translation of documents is needed.[65] Foreign parties are advised to specify a language in their arbitration clauses; Chinese parties often require all documents to be translated into Chinese despite the widespread use of English for conducting business.

4.54 With regard to the introduction of evidence during an oral hearing, the tribunal may require a party to provide evidence either on the tribunal's own initiative or at the other parties' request,[66] and may even collect evidence on its own where it deems this to be necessary.[67]

4.55 Several issues regarding witness testimony require attention. For instance, although in theory all evidence, including the testimony of witnesses, must be examined in order to establish a legal basis for the facts of the case,[68] in practice, witnesses are rarely cross-examined in

---

61 Stipulations for the Appointment of Arbitrators Jointly Issued by CIETAC and CMAC, promulgated 1 September 1995, amended 1 September 2000 and 2 March 2005.

62 CIETAC Rules 2005, art 21(2); CIETAC Rules 2012, art 24(2).

63 Arbitration Law 1994, art 39.

64 CIETAC Rules 2005, art 67.

65 CIETAC Rules 2012, art 71.

66 Arbitration Law 1994, art 44.

67 Arbitration Law 1994, art 43(2).

68 Several Provisions of the Supreme People's Court on the Evidence for Civil Actions, art 47, promulgated at the 1201st session of the Judicial Committee of the Supreme People's Court, 6 December 2001, promulgated by the Supreme People's Court, 21 December 2001, effective 1 April 2002 (hereinafter 'SPC on the Evidence for Civil Actions'). This provision, regulating the introduction of evidence in civil lawsuits before the People's

China. The arbitral tribunal usually questions witnesses directly. Moreover, while both the tribunal and the parties may call experts,[69] the cross-examination of third-party experts is conditioned on the tribunal's consent.[70] Witnesses are not required to swear an oath before giving testimony, but are simply informed of their obligation to tell the truth and the legal consequences of perjury.[71]

There is also an important limitation as to choice of law in China. The parties to a foreign-related contract generally have autonomy in selecting the law governing the dispute, yet certain types of foreign-related contracts are compulsorily subject to Chinese law.[72] Hence, it is important for foreign investors to have a thorough knowledge of relevant Chinese regulations prior to making an actual investment in China.[73] **4.56**

4.3.4 Conciliation during the arbitration

Despite the foregoing restrictions, the parties' autonomy is reinforced by the practice of conciliation outside arbitration proceedings, which is a conspicuous feature of arbitration in China. While CIETAC sets the 'combination of arbitration and conciliation' as a principle,[74] all Chinese commissions allow the combination of the two dispute resolution methods and frequently use them.[75] Parties benefit from the flexibility of conciliation, as it may be conducted prior to or in parallel with an ongoing arbitration, with or without the involvement of the tribunal,[76] and an enforceable award may be rendered according to the settlement agreement.[77] Conciliation is also popular in China due to its high success rate. There are two types of conciliation during arbitration in China: conciliation within arbitration proceedings and conciliation outside arbitration proceedings. In the former case, the arbitrator will act as a conciliator, and assume the position of arbitrator to carry on the arbitration proceeding if the parties fail to reach a settlement; in the latter case, the parties reach a settlement by themselves without an arbitrator serving as conciliator. **4.57**

4.4 The Award

4.4.1 Introduction

The tribunal must endeavour to ensure not only the correctness but also the effectiveness and enforceability of its award in accordance with the governing law.[78] To fulfil this responsibility, **4.58**

Court, is an important reference for the introduction of evidence in arbitral proceedings before the tribunal, as it is widely expected that this provision will gradually be adopted into the practice of arbitration in China, and will ultimately be incorporated into the next amendment to the Arbitration Law 1994.

[69] Arbitration Law 1994, art 44(2).

[70] CIETAC Rules 2005, art 39; CIETAC Rules 2012, art 42(3).

[71] SPC on the Evidence for Civil Actions, art 54.

[72] Contract Law 1999, art 126.

[73] See generally, World Bank Group, 'Ease of Doing Business in China' <http://doingbusiness.org/data/exploreeconomies/china/>.

[74] CIETAC Rules 2012, art 45; CIETAC Rules 2005, art 40.

[75] von Wunschheim, Tercier, and Ajani (n 46) 69.

[76] Arbitration Law 1994, arts 49 and 51.

[77] Arbitration Law 1994, art 51.

[78] Redfern, Hunter, Blackaby, and Partasides (n 45) 405.

the tribunal must render an award within the time limit, in a proper manner, in accordance with the mandatory format, and containing the necessary content. Where all requirements are met, an arbitral award takes legal effect from the date it is rendered.[79]

4.59 The tribunal must render an award within the time limit. Under the 2012 CIETAC Rules, except in a summary proceeding,[80] a tribunal must render an award within six months following the formation of the tribunal in a foreign-related arbitration,[81] and within four months following the formation of the tribunal in a domestic arbitration.[82]

4.60 The award also must be rendered in accordance with an opinion duly reached within the tribunal. In general, a tribunal should render an award according to the tribunal's majority opinion, or the opinion of the presiding arbitrator if no majority opinion is reached.[83] In addition, an award may also be rendered following a settlement agreement reached between the parties within or outside a tribunal-sponsored conciliation, unless the parties agree otherwise.[84]

4.4.2 Requirements on the form and content of the award

4.61 An award must meet the form and content requirements in order to be final and binding. Article 54 of the Arbitration Law 1994 provides that an award must be rendered in writing with the arbitrator's signatures and the arbitration commission's seal affixed. The signature of an arbitrator holding a dissenting view is not mandatory.[85]

4.62 The award must cover (a) the arbitration claims, (b) the facts in dispute, (c) the reasoning upon which the award is based, (d) the result of the award, (e) the allocation of arbitration costs, and (f) the date on which and the place where the award was made.[86]

4.63 One exception set forth in the 2012 CIETAC Rules is that the facts in dispute and the reasons for reaching the decision may be omitted if the parties have so agreed, or if the award is rendered in accordance with a settlement agreement reached between the parties.[87] Therefore, in a country that encourages conciliation as China does, reaching agreement or settlement is a practical way to accelerate the process of rendering an award and to highlight arbitration's advantages in flexibility and party autonomy.

4.64 Three issues concerning the content of an award are worth noting. First, a tribunal may award interest provided the claimant has requested it;[88] CIETAC usually follows the rate

---

[79] Arbitration Law 1994, art 57.

[80] CIETAC Rules 2012, art 60 and CIETAC Rules 2005, art 56 provide that where summary proceedings are adopted, the time limit is three months commencing from the tribunal's formation for a document-based arbitral proceeding.

[81] CIETAC Rules 2012, art 46.

[82] CIETAC Rules 2012, art 69.

[83] Arbitration Law 1994, art 63.

[84] Arbitration Law 1994, arts 49 and 51.

[85] Arbitration Law 1994, art 54.

[86] Arbitration Law 1994, art 54.

[87] CIETAC Rules 2012, art 47(3); CIETAC Rules 2005, art 43(2).

[88] General Principles of the Civil Law of the PRC, art 112(2) provides that the parties may specify in a contract that upon breach of the contract, a breaching party shall pay the non-breaching party a certain amount of damages; they may also specify in the contract the method of assessing the compensation for any losses resulting from a breach of contract.

of loan interest of financial institutions determined by the court.[89] Further, the tribunal is empowered to allocate the arbitration costs by ordering the losing party to reimburse the winning party's reasonable expenses, based on factors such as the outcome and complexity of the case, the workload of the winning party, and the amount in dispute.[90] Finally, a dissenting opinion may be included in the award for record-keeping purposes only.[91]

The foregoing requirements on format and content largely follow international practices, thereby increasing a Chinese award's acceptability for the international community. This is especially relevant when the award needs to be enforced by a court outside China. **4.65**

4.4.3 Correction and supplementation of the award

There is a remedial measure available with respect to awards in China. If an arbitral award includes any typographical or calculation errors, or omits a decision on any of the issues in dispute, the tribunal must correct the mistakes or supplement the award.[92] This may be initiated either upon a party's written request or the tribunal's own finding.[93] The corrected and the supplemental award must be issued in writing, and constitutes an integral part of the arbitral award.[94] **4.66**

It must be clarified that the correction and supplementation mechanism does not breach the principle of finality of the arbitral award, because the tribunal is not allowed to have a second look at its findings and substantive decisions. The only recourse against an award rendered in China is to request the People's Court to set it aside or to refuse enforcement. **4.67**

4.5 After the Award

4.5.1 Introduction

Upon termination of the tribunal's mandate, the court plays the main role. Under the Arbitration Law 1994, a party dissatisfied with an award may apply to the court to set it aside,[95] or ask the court to refuse the winning party's application for enforcement.[96] The Arbitration Law 1994 provides two types of recourse against a domestic award: setting aside and refusal of enforcement.[97] Refusal of enforcement has particular consequences in China: if enforcement is refused, the parties may initiate new litigation or arbitration proceedings with respect to the same dispute. Thus, refusal of enforcement results in the *de facto* setting aside of the award. In other words, in China, a court's decision to set aside and a court's decision to refuse enforcement of a domestic award have the same effect: the **4.68**

[89] K Ligeng, 'The Interests in International Arbitration' (2005) 3 Arbitration and Law 129–130, re-published on the official website of CIETAC <http://cn.cietac.org/TheoryResearch/Theory.asp?stitle=%B9%FA%BC%CA%D6%D9%B2%C3%D6%D0%B5%C4%C0%FB%CF%A2> (accessed 29 July 2012).

[90] CIETAC Rules 2012, art 50(2); CIETAC Rules 2005, art 46(2).

[91] Arbitration Law 1994, art 53.

[92] Arbitration Law 1994, art 56.

[93] The rules regarding the correction of an award are set forth in the CIETAC Rules 2012, art 51 and the CIETAC Rules 2005, art 47, while the rules regarding supplementing an award are set forth in the CIETAC Rules 2012, art 52 and the CIETAC Rules 2005, art 48.

[94] Arbitration Law 1994, arts 58, 63, 70, and 71.

[95] Arbitration Law 1994, arts 58 and 70.

[96] Arbitration Law 1994, arts 62 and 71.

[97] Arbitration Law 1994, art 9(2).

annulment of the award within China.[98] There has been criticism of this system on the basis that the decision rejecting enforcement, as a procedural order, should simply terminate the enforcement proceedings, rather than eliminate the effectiveness of an award.[99] Article 9(2) of the Arbitration Law 1994 also indicates that an arbitration agreement becomes invalid upon the annulment of an award rendered pursuant to it, which has also been criticized for ignoring the independence of the arbitration agreement.[100]

4.69 The Arbitration Law 1994 establishes a dual-track review mechanism for domestic disputes and foreign-related disputes at the post-award stage. In the case of domestic arbitration, the legislation adopts an overall supervision mechanism,[101] whereby article 237 of the Civil Procedure Law 2013 provides seven grounds for refusing an award and mandates that the court review both procedural issues and the merits of the case. The court's review of the substance may not be excluded by the parties' agreement. This is similar to the supervision system established by the English Arbitration Act 1950. In contrast, in foreign-related arbitration, article 274 of the Civil Procedure Law 2013 provides four grounds for refusing the enforcement an award, and the court is limited to procedural supervision[102] by looking only at due process. This practice, which is also the choice of the UNCITRAL Model Law[103] and the New York Convention,[104] follows the most widely-accepted modern approach.

4.5.2 **Local standards for setting aside an award**

4.70 Although foreign-related arbitration used to be an area exclusively reserved for CIETAC and CMAC, domestic arbitral institutions are now also permitted to handle foreign-related arbitrations,[105] and the standards and procedures for setting aside foreign-related arbitral awards rendered by domestic arbitral institutions are identical to those applicable to CIETAC and CMAC awards.

4.71 The Arbitration Law 1994 borrows directly from the Civil Procedure Law's grounds for setting aside a foreign-related award.[106] In order to set aside an award, a party must apply to a competent court providing evidence sufficient to prove (a) the non-existence of a valid arbitration agreement; (b) lack of due process; (c) irregularity in arbitration procedure; or (d) exceeding the scope of the arbitration agreement. There is in fact a fifth ground in

---

98 von Wunschheim, Tercier, and Ajani (n 46) 182.

99 Y Xifu, *The Judicial Supervision and Assistance in International Commercial Arbitration* (1st edn, Intellectual Property Publishing House, 2006) 399.

100 D Huanfang, 'Reflection regarding the Perfection of the Annulment System of Foreign-related Arbitral Awards' (CIETAC, 2007) available at <http://cn.cietac.org/TheoryResearch/Theory.asp?stitle=%B4%D3%CA%B5%C0%FD%BF%B4%D6%D0%B9%FA%C9%E6%CD%E2%D6%D9%B2%C3%B2%C3%BE%F6%B3%B7%CF%FA%B5%C4%CD%EA%C9%C6> (accessed 29 July 2012).

101 W Exiang and Y Xifu, 'Re-discussion on the Relationship between Judicial System and Arbitration: Legislation, Practice and the Theories Regarding Whether the Court Should Supervise over the Substantive Issues in Arbitration' (2004) 3 Law Review 60, republished on the website of the Law School of Renmin University of China, the International Law Department (RUC International Law), <http://www.rucil.com.cn/article/default.asp?id=461> (accessed 29 July 2012).

102 Exiang and Xifu (n 101).

103 UNICITRAL Model Law, arts 34 and 36.

104 New York Convention, Art 5.

105 Notice of the General Office of the State Council regarding Some Problems Which Need to Be Clarified for the Implication of the Arbitration Law of the PRC, promulgated 8 June 1996.

106 Arbitration Law 1994, art 70.

article 274(2) of the Civil Procedural Law 2013, according to which the court is obliged to set aside a foreign-related arbitral award *ex officio* if it finds that the award contravenes the social and public interest.[107] These five globally recognized grounds are consistent with the UNCITRAL Model Law and the New York Convention, and the Chinese courts have revealed a leaning towards narrow interpretation.

The examination of the validity of an arbitration agreement falls mainly to the arbitration commission, but the parties may also resort to the competent court. When no specific arbitration commission is expressly provided for or implied by the arbitration agreement, and the parties fail to reach an agreement subsequently, the arbitration clause is considered invalid.[108] In a representative case, the arbitration agreement fixed China as the seat of arbitration without naming a specific arbitration commission. After an award was rendered under the auspices of CIETAC, a party applied to the court for setting aside based on invalidity of the arbitration agreement. The court found that a commission could not be selected by implication, and the parties had failed to reach agreement on a commission. The court reported the case to the SPC, and the SPC declared the arbitration agreement invalid and affirmed the lower court's decision to set aside the award.[109] In addition, an arbitration agreement giving a party a choice between litigation and arbitration once a dispute arises is invalid.[110] Invalidity of the arbitration agreement can only be invoked as a ground for setting aside if the applicant has raised it prior to the first arbitration hearing.[111] **4.72**

Numerous recent cases involve attempts to set aside a CIETAC award on grounds of lack of due process and procedural irregularity. Judging from past cases, an award is likely to be set aside on these grounds in the following five situations: (a) a party was deprived of sufficient opportunity to present its case by the tribunal's failure to hold a supplementary hearing; (b) the tribunal incorrectly accepted documents after the deadline for making such submissions; (c) the successful party presented forged documentary evidence to the tribunal, regardless of whether this had any impact on the tribunal's decision. **4.73**

An award may also be set aside if it decides matters that exceed the scope of the arbitration agreement or are beyond the arbitral authority of the arbitration commission.[112] The courts' attitude in two common scenarios can be derived from SPC decisions holding that a tribunal does not exceed the arbitration agreement or its jurisdiction where the award (a) addresses disputes arising from contracts or agreements supplementary to a main contract that contains an arbitration clause, or (b) addresses disputes arising from contracts or agreements subsequently entered into by the parties in contemplation of a contract that contains an arbitration clause or thereby further detailing the duties and obligations pursuant to that contract. In comparison, in a typical case successfully setting aside an award, the SPC held that an award exceeded the arbitration agreement because it addressed disputes arising from **4.74**

[107] Civil Procedure Law 2013, art 274(2).

[108] Interpretation of the Supreme People's Court Concerning Some Issues on Application of the Arbitration Law of the PRC, promulgated on 23 August 2006 and effective 8 September 2006, arts 3–6 (hereinafter 'SPC Interpretation on the Arbitration Law').

[109] Reply of the Supreme People's Court to the Request for Instructions on the Case of Application of Changsha Xinzhi Industry Ltd and American Metal Plus International Ltd for Revocation of the Arbitral Award, promulgated 18 November 2008, effective 18 November 2008.

[110] SPC Interpretation on the Arbitration Law, art 7.

[111] SPC Interpretation on the Arbitration Law, art 13.

[112] Civil Procedure Law 2013, art 274.

a consulting fee agreement between the parties, while the arbitration agreement was limited to disputes related to their joint venture.[113] Partial annulment may be available where only part of an award exceeds an arbitration agreement and that part is separable from the rest of the award.[114] However, if an award exceeds the arbitration commission's jurisdiction, the dispute is not arbitrable and the tribunal violates the mandatory law, so the entire award must be set aside.

4.75 The last ground, contravention of public policy, though widely accepted and applied by countries as a ground for refusing enforcement of an award is subject to divergent interpretation.[115] Different countries define public policy differently, and the terminology China has adopted, 'social and public interest',[116] is vague, due to the lack of transparency in legislation and changing Chinese national policies. The SPC's decisions indicate that this phrase must be interpreted narrowly, and its application limited to a breach of the interests of China's 'fundamental legal principles', which refers to the interests of the Chinese as a whole rather than the interests of part of society or a group of individuals.[117] Some SPC judges espouse the view that an award violates public policy if it (a) violates the principles provided or implied by the Constitution or Four Fundamental Principals of China;[118] (b) damages the sovereignty or state security of China; (c) violates fundamental rules of Chinese law; or (d) contravenes China's obligations under international treaties or the fairness or justice recognized in international law.[119]

4.76 This is a clear indication that public policy is closely entwined with politics in China, which makes it difficult to predict the outcome of setting aside applications. In this situation, the SPC's judgments help parties to form strategies to attack awards by setting out unsuccessful examples in the past. For instance, the SPC deems that certain kinds of fraud, and mere procedural unfairness or injustice covered by lack of due process or procedural irregularities, are insufficient to constitute conflict with the social and public interest.[120] The SPC has also held that a violation of mandatory law does not necessarily contravene the social and public

---

113 Reply of the Supreme People's Court to the Request for Instructions on the Application of Hui Ying Media Sales Limited for Revocation of the Arbitral Award, [2003] Da Zhong Zi No 083, promulgated 14 September 2004, effective 14 September 2004.

114 SPC Interpretation on the Arbitration Law, art 19.

115 Z Xianchu, 'The New Development in the Theories and Practice of the Judicial Supervision over Arbitral Awards in Foreign Commercial Arbitration in respect of Public Policy' (2005) 4 Arbitration and Law 23, re-published on the official website of the CIETAC, <http://cn.cietac.org/TheoryResearch/Theory.asp?stitle=%CD%E2%B9%FA%C9%CC%CA%C2%D6%D9%B2%C3%B2%C3%BE%F6%CB%BE%B7%A8%C9%F3%B2%E9%D6%D0%A1%B0%B9%AB%B9%B2%D5%FE%B2%DF%A1%B1%C0%ED%C2%DB%D3%EB%CA%B5%BC%F9%B5%C4%D0%C2%B7%A2%D5%B9> (accessed 29 July 2012).

116 Civil Procedure Law 2013, art 274(2).

117 von Wunschheim, Tercier, and Ajani (n 46) 283, citing the Standing Committee of the National People's Congress Legislative Affairs Commission/CIETAC, 'Complete Works on Arbitration Law of the People's Republic of China', 62 and 125.

118 Supreme People's Court Third Five-Year Plan 2009–2013, s I.3 provides seven principles for reformation of the People's Court, where four are considered the Fundamental Principles of China: to adhere to the socialist road, to adhere to the people's democratic dictatorship, to adhere to the leadership of the Communist Party, and to adhere to Marxism-Leninism and Mao's thought.

119 von Wunschheim, Tercier, and Ajani (n 46) 283, citing Judge Gao Xiaoli of the Supreme People's Court. See also G Xiaoli, *Use of Public Policy in International Private Law* (China Democracy & Legality Publishing House, 2008) 336.

120 von Wunschheim, Tercier, and Ajani (n 46) 283, citing Judge Gao Xiaoli of the Supreme People's Court). See also Xiaoli (n 119) 285.

interest, and that the fairness of the award is irrelevant.[121] In general, like courts in other jurisdictions, the SPC is cautious in upholding the social and public interest, and rarely sets aside awards on this ground.

In practice, China's judicial acuity in setting aside foreign-related awards pursuant to the Arbitration Law 1994 has been questioned, because the lower courts have shown a tendency to set these aside erroneously. This has been attributed to local protectionism, which is a serious challenge to judicial independence. The situation is now improving, due to the establishment of the prior reporting system, discussed in detail in paragraph 4.88. **4.77**

4.5.3 Local procedures for setting aside an award

An application to set aside an award must be made to the competent court, which is the Intermediate People's Court at the location of the arbitration commission.[122] The request must be made within six months of the applicant's receipt of the award,[123] which is longer than the three-month time limit in the UNICITRAL Model Law and the limits in effect in most countries.[124] Moreover, the court must reach a decision within two months of receipt of the application,[125] leading to a potential eight-month period during which the effectiveness of the award remains pending. This not only goes against the basic legal principle of timely justice, but also sabotages parties' preference for arbitration due to its purported efficiency. This is especially problematic when enforcement proceedings are suspended because of the initiation of the setting aside proceedings.[126] **4.78**

An award enforcement proceeding may be delayed by the setting aside proceeding: if the winning party applies for enforcement of the award, and the losing party applies for setting aside the award before the court renders its enforcement/non-enforcement decision, the enforcement proceeding will be suspended until the court denies the application for setting aside; in the event that the court actually sets aside the award, the court will terminate the enforcement proceeding. The court may refuse to enforce a foreign-related award on the following grounds: (1) lack of a valid arbitration agreement in the parties' contract or subsequent agreement; (2) failure to provide the respondent notice inviting him to appoint an arbitrator or informing him of the commencement of the arbitration proceeding, or his inability to present his views for other reasons; (3) the composition of the tribunal or arbitration procedure being inconsistent with the applicable arbitration rules; (4) rendering a decision on issues that exceed the scope of the arbitration agreement or are beyond the authority of the arbitration commission; and (5) conflict with the public interest.[127] In respect of domestic awards, there are seven grounds for non-enforcement. In addition to the previously-mentioned grounds, the court may refuse to enforce a domestic award based on the impact on the award of forged evidence or a party's concealing of important evidence, or based on arbitrator corruption, such as accepting bribes.[128] **4.79**

[121] von Wunschheim, Tercier, and Ajani (n 46) 283 (citing Judge Gao Xiaoli of the Supreme People's Court). See also Xiaoli (119) 284–5.
[122] Arbitration Law 1994, art 70.
[123] Arbitration Law 1994, art 59.
[124] Du Huanfang (n 100).
[125] Arbitration Law 1994, art 60.
[126] Arbitration Law 1994, art 64.
[127] Civil Procedure Law 2013, art 274.
[128] Civil Procedure Law 2013, art 237(2).

4.80 Instead of setting aside or refusing to set aside an award, the court may decide on its own motion that the dispute should be re-arbitrated. The setting-aside proceeding is suspended in cases of re-arbitration, and may be resumed if the tribunal declines to re-arbitrate.[129] No detailed grounds for re-arbitration are provided, but in the case of a foreign-related award, only procedural issues are subject to re-arbitration.[130] According to SPC decisions, where the errors in the award are not serious enough for setting aside,[131] or are capable of being rectified by means of re-arbitration,[132] and initiation of a new arbitration would not unnecessarily burden the parties,[133] re-arbitration is likely to be invoked. Re-arbitration is undertaken by the same tribunal that rendered the original award, unless there are special circumstances precluding this.[134]

4.81 Before the Intermediate People's Court renders a decision to set aside or to re-arbitrate a foreign-related award, it must file it with the High People's Court for approval within 30 days following its acceptance of the application.[135] If the High People's Court concurs, it files an Approval Advice with the SPC within 50 days following its receipt of the report from the Intermediate People's Court for approval. Only after the SPC has confirmed the findings may the Intermediate People's Court issue its decision.[136] This is known as the prior reporting system, a special centralized reporting and review system that applies to court decisions in respect of awards other than domestic awards.[137] The prior reporting system is considered the most notable intervention of the SPC in arbitration, and functions as a shield against the influence of local protectionism on lower courts in setting aside awards. There have been comments that this system diminishes the independence of the lower courts by making the SPC the final decision-maker. It is, however, undeniable that it effectively safeguards the rights and interests of a successful party by raising the bar on the annulment of awards and eliminating local influence, and thereby greatly increases foreign investor confidence in arbitration in China.

[129] Arbitration Law 1994, art 61.

[130] Du Huanfang (n 100).

[131] Reply of the Supreme People's Court to the Request for Instructions on the Case of Application of Sichuan Hua Hang Construction Ltd for Revocation of an Arbitral Award, promulgated 15 June 2005, effective 15 June 2005.

[132] Reply of the Supreme People's Court to the Request for Instructions about Whether to Revoke the Arbitral Award No 0140 [2007] of China International Economic and Trade Arbitration Commission, promulgated 7 April 2008, effective 7 April 2008.

[133] Reply of the Supreme People's Court to the Request for Instructions about Whether to Revoke an Arbitral Award Rendered by Dalian Arbitration Commission, promulgated 23 February 2006, effective 23 February 2006.

[134] The special circumstances include, but are not limited to, those where an arbitrator cannot further perform his or her obligation as an arbitrator due to illness, death, or other similar reasons, or should be removed based on the situations set forth in the Arbitration Law 1994, art 34.

[135] Notice of the Supreme People's Court on Relevant Issues Relating to the Cancellation by the People's Courts' of Foreign-Related Arbitral Awards, promulgated by the Supreme People's Court, 23 April 1998, revised by Decision of the Supreme People's Court on Adjustment of Serial Number of Articles of the Civil Procedure Law of the People's Republic of China Cited in Judicial Interpretation and Other Documents, promulgated 16 December 2008, effective 31 December 2008.

[136] Notice of the Supreme People's Court on Several Issues Regarding the Handling by the People's Courts of Certain Issues Pertaining to Foreign-Related Arbitration and Foreign Arbitration, promulgated by the Supreme People's Court, 28 August 1995, effective 28 August 1995, revised by Decision of the Supreme People's Court on Adjustment of Serial Number of Articles of the Civil Procedure Law of the People's Republic of China Cited in Judicial Interpretation and Other Documents, promulgated 16 December 2008, effective 31 December 2008.

[137] Circular of the Supreme People's Court on Issues in the People's Courts' Revocation of Foreign-related Arbitral Awards, promulgated on and effective since 23 April 1998.

The cost of setting aside an award consists of two parts. The first part is the actual expense incurred, for instance payments to translators or experts. The second part is the application fee, which is calculated according to the monetary value of the case as follows:[138] 4.82

> Where there is no monetary value, the cost shall be determined by the court within the range of 50 to 500 CNY.
>
> Where there is a monetary value, the cost is calculated cumulatively based on the following ranges.
>
> i. The cost is 50 CNY where the amount subject to annulment does not exceed 10,000 CNY;
> ii. Where the amount subject to annulment is between 10,000 CNY and 500,000 CNY, the cost is 1.5%;
> iii. Where the amount subject to annulment is between 500,000 CNY and 5 million CNY, the cost is 1.0%;
> iv. Where the amount subject to annulment is between 5 million CNY and 10 million CNY, the cost is 0.5%;
> v. Where the amount subject to annulment is over 10 million CNY, the cost is 0.1%.
> vi. Where the amount subject to annulment is between 10,000 CNY and 500,000 CNY, the cost is 1.5%.

4.6 Conclusion

Arbitration has a long history in China, and the establishment of the modern arbitration system with the promulgation of the Arbitration Law in 1994 was a key step in modernizing the dispute resolution system in China. For foreign investors seeking to resolve disputes in China, arbitration is a better choice than litigation. Choosing a Chinese arbitration commission instead of the People's Court not only provides the common advantages of arbitration, but also better shields the foreign party from the strong local protectionism in the local judiciary and from the professional incompetence of some judges in China. 4.83

More importantly, arbitral awards rendered by arbitration institutions in China are more easily recognized and enforced in other countries than judgments issued by Chinese courts, as China is a signatory to the New York Convention, but has not yet entered into judgment recognition and enforcement treaties with most of the major world economies.[139] Unlike many less-developed and developing countries, China has not adopted the UNCITRAL Model Law into its arbitration regime. It has developed certain unique features based on its own culture, such as the encouragement of a combination of arbitration and conciliation, and the establishment of a prior reporting system in setting aside foreign-related and foreign awards in order to prevent local protectionism. Meanwhile, there is still room for improvement in the system. For example, there is a call for the expansion of the arbitrator pool, and the elimination of the current practice limits on foreign counsel in the arbitration proceedings, and of the compulsory application of Chinese Law in certain circumstances. 4.84

[138] State Council Measure on Litigation Cost, art 13, promulgated by the State Council 8 December 2006, effective 1 April 2007.

[139] Examples of countries with which China has concluded treaties include France, Poland, Mongolia, Romania, Russia, Belarus, Cuba, and Spain. Moreover, Mainland China has recently concluded two arrangements providing for the recognition and enforcement of court judgments rendered by courts in Macao and Hong Kong. On the other hand, major economies with which China has not concluded treaties include the US, the UK, and Japan.

5

DUBAI

Essam Al Tamimi and Robert Karrar-Lewsley

5.1 Introduction

The Dubai International Financial Centre (DIFC) is an English-language, common law jurisdiction in the heart of Dubai, United Arab Emirates (UAE). It has its own civil and commercial laws distinct from those of the rest of the UAE, and an English-style common law court system. The DIFC adheres to the New York Convention and has a modern arbitration law based on the UNCITRAL Model Law. It also hosts an international arbitration centre, the DIFC-LCIA. **5.01**

Despite being less than ten years old, the DIFC has quickly become one of the most advanced legal jurisdictions in the Middle East. It was designed to attract global investors and international business, and in order to do so adopted laws and institutions based on international best practice and Western models (in particular those of England). As this chapter will explore, many aspects of the DIFC arbitration regime are likely to appear familiar to a Western practitioner, although this can result in important aspects being overlooked. Furthermore, being a new jurisdiction, the DIFC has a limited track record and only a small body of case law. Practitioners will therefore have to consider carefully before choosing the DIFC above other more established arbitral seats, but those who do may find it offers a rare balance between international standards and regional convenience. **5.02**

This chapter will begin by giving an overview of the DIFC and its legal system, before reviewing its arbitration law and the practical considerations that need to be taken into account when choosing the DIFC as an arbitral seat. The chapter will conclude by considering the DIFC in its local and regional context. **5.03**

5.2 Background

5.2.1 The United Arab Emirates

The UAE is a country situated on the southeast of the Arabian Peninsula. It was created in 1971 and is a federation of seven emirates,[1] the largest of which is Abu Dhabi (the capital), followed by Dubai. Each emirate is governed by a ruling monarch, with the country as a whole having a national president (who by convention is the Ruler of Abu Dhabi, with the Ruler of Dubai being the country's Prime Minister).[2] **5.04**

Each of the emirates has the power to create its own laws, although these are not to conflict with federal laws. Dubai and Ras Al Khaimah have their own court systems, while the other emirates use the federal court system based in Abu Dhabi. The Federal Supreme Court of Cassation adjudicates on constitutional issues.[3] **5.05**

The UAE is a civil law system that closely follows Egyptian law, itself modelled on the Napoleonic Code (albeit with some significant differences to reflect the influence of **5.06**

---

[1] The seven emirates are Abu Dhabi, Dubai, Sharjah, Ras Al Khaimah, Ajman, Fujairah, and Umm Al Quwain.

[2] E Al Tamimi, *Practical Guide to Litigation and Arbitration in the United Arab Emirates* (1st edn, Kluwer Law International, 2003) 3.

[3] Al Tamimi (n 2) 16.

sharia—Islamic law—principles). UAE Courts do not normally hear oral arguments and precedents are not binding, although they can be persuasive.[4]

5.2.2 The Dubai International Financial Centre

5.07 The DIFC was established in 2004 as a Federal Financial Free Zone. In order to create this new jurisdiction, the UAE constitution had to be amended so as to exempt the DIFC from all civil and commercial federal laws. The Ruler of Dubai[5] and the President of the DIFC[6] have the power to issue laws, rules, and regulations within the DIFC.[7] The DIFC's three core independent bodies are the DIFC Authority, the Dubai Financial Services Authority, and the DIFC Judicial Authority (DIFC Courts). The currency used in the DIFC is the US dollar.

5.08 The DIFC Courts comprise the Court of First Instance and the Court of Appeal.[8] There is also a Small Claims Tribunal for claims under $28,000 (or $136,000 if both parties consent in writing). The courts have exclusive jurisdiction over all civil and commercial disputes within the DIFC,[9] including any arbitration seated there.[10] The DIFC Courts have judges from England, Singapore, Malaysia, and New Zealand, as well as three UAE judges. A number of the DIFC court judges are also prominent international arbitrators, such as the current Chief Justice, Michael Hwang SC.

5.2.3 The development of arbitration in the DIFC

Before the 2008 Arbitration Law

5.09 The DIFC has always had an arbitration law. The initial arbitration law, DIFC Law No 8 of 2004 (the 2004 Law), was passed shortly after the DIFC was created. Although the DIFC modelled the bulk of its laws on those of England, its arbitration law is based on the UNCITRAL Model Law on International Commercial Arbitration (the Model Law), and not the English Arbitration Act 1996.

5.10 The 2004 Law was a marked improvement on the pre-existing UAE arbitration law, which is found in a handful of provisions in the UAE Procedural Law.[11] However it suffered from a number of issues, the most significant being that it did not allow non-DIFC entities to seat an arbitration in the DIFC. Article 7(3) of the 2004 Law stated: 'Unless otherwise agreed in writing, this Law applies to Arbitration in relation to disputes arising out of or in connection with the DIFC and to which at least one party is an Arbitration Party'.

5.11 An 'Arbitration Party' was defined as 'any person who would be entitled to bring an action in the Court in relation to a matter which is to be the subject of an Arbitration'.[12] Therefore, in order to be seated in the DIFC an arbitration had to relate to a dispute that had a connection

---

[4] Al Tamimi (n 2) 5.

[5] Sheikh Mohammad Bin Rashid Al Maktoum.

[6] Sheikh Maktoum Bin Mohammed Bin Rashid Al Maktoum, the Deputy Ruler of Dubai and the third son of Sheikh Mohammad.

[7] The Law of the Dubai International Financial Centre, Dubai Law No 9 for the year 2004, art 2.

[8] There is also the Small Claims Tribunal for claims of less than (approximately) $28,000, but this tribunal does not hear claims related to arbitration.

[9] The Law of the Judicial Authority at Dubai International Financial Centre, Dubai Law No 12 of 2004, art 5.

[10] DIFC Law No 1 of 2008 (hereinafter the 'DIFC Arbitration Law of 2008').

[11] UAE Civil Procedure Code, Federal Law No 11 of 1992, arts 203–218. An English translation is available at <http://www.diac.ae/idias/rules/uae> (accessed 8 July 2012).

[12] DIFC Law No 8 of 2004, Schedule Interpretation 3.

to the DIFC, and to which at least one party was an entity who would have a right to bring an action in the DIFC Courts in relation to the matter.

The 2008 Arbitration Law

On 1 September 2008, a new arbitration law was introduced, DIFC Law No 1 of 2008 (the '2008 Law'). As with the old law, the 2008 Law is based on the UNCITRAL Model Law (including the 2006 amendments adopted in the meantime). The 2008 Law repealed the 2004 Law in its entirety[13] and introduced important changes. The most significant change was that article 7(3) of the 2004 Law was removed, effectively opening the DIFC to world-wide use as an arbitral seat. **5.12**

The 2008 Law also allowed for the confidentiality of arbitral proceedings (unless the parties agree otherwise),[14] which was a reversal of the position under the 2004 Law under which parties had to agree explicitly to confidentiality. The 2008 Law does depart from the Model Law in some material respects, as discussed in the following commentary in more detail. The new law was well received by legal practitioners in the UAE, and was reviewed as a 'good arbitration law' and 'cutting edge' by one commentator.[15] **5.13**

The DIFC-LCIA

The 2008 Law was one of two major developments in 2008 which significantly enhanced the DIFC as an arbitral seat. In February of that year a new international arbitral institution opened, the 'DIFC-LCIA'. This institution is a strategic partnership between the DIFC and the London Court of International Arbitration. Its rules and services are almost identical to those of the LCIA, providing a robust framework for arbitration. The LCIA assists in the management of cases and is responsible for constituting the tribunal,[16] which allows parties access to the LCIA's substantial list of arbitrators. **5.14**

The close relationship between the DIFC and the DIFC-LCIA has given rise to the mistaken assumption that the use of the DIFC-LICA is limited to those parties with a connection to the DIFC, or that those that want to use the DIFC as their seat must use (or will gain some advantage from using) the DIFC-LCIA.[17] This is not the case. The DIFC-LCIA is simply located in the DIFC, and parties are free to use it regardless of where they, or the seat of arbitration, are located.[18] Furthermore, parties using the DIFC as their seat are free to use any institution they choose, or none. **5.15**

---

[13] DIFC Arbitration Law of 2008, art 5.

[14] DIFC Arbitration Law of 2008, art 14.

[15] SR Luttrell, 'Commentary on the 2008 Arbitration Law of the Dubai International Financial Centre' (2009) 2(1) Intl J Private L 31.

[16] Arbitration Rules of the DIFC-LCIA Arbitration Centre, arts 5–12 (hereinafter the 'DIFC-LCIA Arbitration Rules').

[17] eg R Ashraf, J Brown, and V Lysenko, 'Enforcement of Foreign Arbitral Awards Against UAE Counterparties: DIFC-LCIA Awards Versus New York Convention Awards' (Hadef & Partners, 12 March 2012) available at <http://www.hadefpartners.com/News/pageid/120-137/default.aspx?mediaid=215> (accessed 4 March 2013); and R Bell and L Chicken, 'Enforcing DIFC-LCIA Arbitral Awards' (Clyde & Co, 8 March 2012) available at <http://www.clydeco.com/insight/articles/enforcement-of-arbitral-awards-in-the-uae-part-ii-enforcing-difc-lcia-arbit> (accessed 4 March 2013), both erroneously using the phrase 'DIFC-LCIA award' to mean 'DIFC award'.

[18] If, however, the parties do not agree a seat, then under art 16 of the DIFC-LCIA Arbitration Rules, the seat shall be the DIFC.

5.16 This position has been explicitly recognized by the DIFC Courts. In the case of *Dhir v Waterfront Property Investment Ltd*,[19] the agreement in dispute contained an arbitration clause stating that any arbitration was to be administered by the DIFC-LCIA and that the arbitration 'shall take place in the Emirate of Dubai'. The claimant attempted to argue, among other things, that the seat of the arbitration was the DIFC because the parties had chosen the DIFC-LCIA to administer the arbitration. In rejecting this argument Michael Hwang DCJ, sitting in the Court of First Instance, stated that there was 'no significant connection with the DIFC because the DIFC-LCIA Arbitration Centre can administer an arbitration with a seat outside the DIFC',[20] and that there is 'no inexorable or symbiotic link between the DIFC-LCIA Arbitration Centre and the DIFC'.[21] Since the parties had stated the place of arbitration to be Dubai, the seat was Dubai and not the DIFC.

5.17 The only official involvement the DIFC-LCIA has with DIFC-related disputes is with regard to the Financial Markets Tribunal. This tribunal is overseen by the Dubai Financial Services Authority (DFSA) and is charged with hearing and determining proceedings relating to any alleged breaches of laws, rules, or legislation administered by the DFSA. The President of the Financial Markets Tribunal has appointed the DIFC-LCIA to provide the services of the Financial Market Tribunal Registrar.

5.2.4 Treaties

5.18 The DIFC is not a sovereign or political entity and does not have the capacity to enter into international treaties. It is a jurisdiction within the UAE and as such is bound by any treaty that the UAE has signed and ratified. This is made clear in article 42(1) of the 2008 Law, which states: 'For the avoidance of doubt, where the UAE has entered into an applicable treaty for the mutual enforcement of judgments, orders and awards the DIFC Court shall comply with the terms of such treaty.'

The New York Convention

5.19 The UAE ratified the New York Convention on 13 June 2006[22] and it came into force on 19 November 2006. There has been some confusion as to whether, when the UAE ratified the New York Convention, it did so with the reservation that it would only apply the convention in respect of awards from other signatory states.[23] The UAE, however, made no reservations to the New York Convention whatsoever (in contrast to other states such as France, the United Kingdom, the United States, and Germany).

5.20 The fact that the UAE has not made reservations to the New York Convention means that the DIFC Courts should treat all foreign awards equally, irrespective of whether they emanate from a signatory state or not. This approach appears to be confirmed in the 2008 Law, which states in article 42(1) that: 'An arbitral award, *irrespective of the State of jurisdiction in which it was made*, shall be recognised as binding within the DIFC...' (emphasis added).

---

[19] *Dhir v Waterfront Property Investment Ltd* CFI 011/2009 [2006-09] DIFC CLR 12 (Judicial Authority of the Dubai International Finance Centre, Court of First Instance).

[20] *Dhir* (n 19) para 85.

[21] *Dhir* (n 19) para 91.

[22] Federal Decree No 43 of 2006 Concerning the Accession of the United Arab Emirates to the New York Convention on the Recognition and Enforcement of Foreign Arbitral Awards, art 1.

[23] eg Gordon Blanke and Karim Nassif, 'Arbitration in the UAE 2011' (Habib Al Mulla & Company, 2011) available at <www.habibalmulla.com/Mediaresource/bdad3ca9-e25b-42f7-a6cd-bec9b24d6ab7.pdf> (accessed 4 March 2013).

The ICSID Convention

The UAE is a signatory to the ICSID Convention and has entered into bilateral investment treaties (BITs) with the following states: Algeria (2002), Austria (2002), Azerbaijan (2007), Belarus (2001), Belgium-Luxembourg Economic Union (2005), China (1994), Czech Republic (1995), Egypt (1998), Finland (1997), Germany (1998), Italy (1995), Jordan (2009), Korea (2004), Lebanon (1998), Malaysia (1992), Mongolia (2002), Morocco (1999), Pakistan (1996), Poland (1994), Romania (1996), South Korea, Sudan (2002), Sweden (2000), Switzerland (1999), Syria (1999), Tajikistan (2000), Tunisia (1997), Turkey (2006), Turkmenistan (1999), Ukraine (2004), the United Kingdom (1993), the United States (1992), Uzbekistan (2008), Vietnam (2009), and Yemen (2001). **5.21**

GCC Convention

Under the Gulf Cooperation Council (GCC) Convention for the Execution of Judgments, Delegations and Judicial Notifications 1987,[24] each of the countries in the GCC are bound to execute the final judgments issued by the courts of any member state in civil, commercial, and administrative cases and cases involving personal matters, save in a limited number of situations (such as a violation of the sharia). **5.22**

Despite its name, the GCC Convention also covers arbitral awards. The grounds on which the enforcement of an award can be refused are the same as those for judgments, but also include any other 'applicable rules in the state where the award is required to be executed' (Article 12). Since all GCC countries except Yemen are now signatories to the New York Convention, using the GCC Convention only adds further requirements to those found in the New York Convention. The GCC Convention is therefore of limited use when it comes to arbitral awards. **5.23**

The Riyadh Convention

The Riyadh Convention on Judicial Cooperation 1983 replaced the 1952 Arab League Convention on enforcement of judgments and awards. It has a very wide scope and specifically provides for the reciprocal enforcement of arbitral awards. Signatory counties are obliged to enforce arbitral awards from other Riyadh Convention countries unless: **5.24**

- the subject matter is not capable of being arbitrated in the state in which enforcement is sought;
- the arbitration clause was void or the award is not yet final;
- the arbitrators were not competent according to the arbitration clause or under the law governing the award; or
- the parties were not correctly notified of the arbitration.[25]

The party seeking enforcement will also need to produce a copy of the relevant contract and a certified copy of the award and a statement of the local judicial authority certifying that it has become *res judicata*. **5.25**

---

[24] A full translation of this treaty is available at <http://www.diac.ae/idias/rules/GCC/> (accessed 11 February 2013).

[25] An unofficial translation of this treaty is available at <http://www.unhcr.org/refworld/docid/3ae6b38d8.html> (accessed 11 February 2013).

5.26 The Riyadh Convention is of greater importance than the GCC Convention because it has been ratified by Iraq, Yemen, Somalia, and Libya, all of which are yet to ratify the New York Convention.

Bilateral treaties

5.27 Over the years the UAE has entered into bilateral treaties with the following states regarding judicial matters, some of which cover the enforcement of arbitral awards: Afghanistan (2009), Algeria (1984), Armenia (2003), Azerbaijan (2007), China (2004), Egypt (2000), France (1992), India (2000), Jordan (1999), Kuwait (2008), Morocco (2006), Pakistan (2005), Somalia (1982), Sudan (2005), Syria (2002), Tajikistan (2007), Tunisia (1975), and the United Kingdom (2007).

5.2.5 Important recent developments and anticipated changes

5.28 At the time of writing there are no anticipated changes to the arbitral regime in the DIFC, although it is likely that a small clarifying amendment to the 2008 Arbitration Law will be made this year (see paragraph 5.57).

5.29 In terms of recent developments, the most important has been the announcement that a DIFC-LCIA award seated in the DIFC was successfully enforced in Dubai, having been ratified by the DIFC Courts.[26] The enforcement of the award by the Dubai Courts was effected without a re-examination of the award and in accordance with a Protocol between the Dubai and DIFC courts (this Protocol is discussed in more detail in the following commentary). The successful use of the Protocol for enforcement has greatly increased the credibility of the DIFC as an arbitral seat by demonstrating its effectiveness.

5.30 Generally speaking, the DIFC Courts have experienced a significant expansion to their jurisdiction in that the courts will now accept jurisdiction over cases that have no connection to the DIFC, provided the parties have agreed in writing to submit to the jurisdiction of the DIFC Courts.[27] This means the court is now available to all, and it is expected that international parties across the region will seek to use the DIFC Courts for their disputes. This enhances the DIFC as a jurisdiction for international disputes and—with the expected increase in work—will lead to a more tested and robust system.

5.3 The DIFC Courts

5.3.1 Using the DIFC Courts

5.31 The DIFC Courts have jurisdiction over all civil and commercial disputes in the DIFC, and will hear non-DIFC disputes provided the parties have agreed in writing to submit to the jurisdiction of the DIFC Courts. Although the DIFC Courts have a separate jurisdiction from that of the Dubai Courts, they remain courts of Dubai. DIFC judges swear the same oath to the Ruler of Dubai, Sheikh Mohammad bin Rashid Al Maktoum, as Dubai judges. The DIFC Courts are considered to be among the most efficient and transparent courts in

[26] 'DIFC Courts and Dubai Courts Achieve New Arbitration Enforcement Landmark', DIFC Courts Press Release, 5 April 2011, available at <http://difccourts.complinet.com/en/display/display_main.html?rbid=2725&element_id=4492> (accessed 4 March 2013).

[27] Dubai Law No 16 of 2011 Amending Certain Provisions of Law No 12 of 2004 Concerning Dubai International Financial Centre Courts, art 5(A)(2).

the region. The Courts make extensive use of technology. Claims are filed electronically, and communications are primarily undertaken by email. Hearings are both videotaped and digitally tape-recorded, and the modern courtrooms allow for attendance by video-link (if the court deems it appropriate). All court judgments and orders are published on the Courts' website and can be freely accessed.[28]

The DIFC Courts have been engaged in agreeing memorandums of understanding with local and regional courts to promote collaboration and cooperation among judicial bodies in the region. At present, they have Memorandums of Understanding with the Dubai Courts, the Abu Dhabi Courts, the Ras Al Khaimah Courts, and the Jordanian Ministry of Justice.[29] In 2012 the DIFC Courts signed a 'Memorandum of Guidance as to Enforcement' with the English Courts, which explains how the courts are to enforce each other's judgments without review.[30] The courts also have a pro bono programme that is the first of its kind in the Middle East.[31] **5.32**

To date, the DIFC Courts have only had a modest workload since, until recently, they were only able to handle cases related to the DIFC.[32] Given the modest workload, the DIFC Courts only sit for one week a month,[33] which can give rise to timetabling issues. Furthermore, there are only two full-time resident judges, all the others being part-time and based overseas. The infrequency with which these judges deal with DIFC court matters and the long distances many of them must travel to get to the Court can lead to a perception that their performance level is not as high as would be expected from conventional judges in other jurisdictions who are involved permanently and on a daily basis in the court matters of their jurisdiction. No doubt this will change in the future when the court gets busier and when DIFC judges are appointed from the pool of DIFC practitioners who are resident in the UAE. Finally, the diversity of backgrounds that make up the DIFC court judiciary means that it is not always easy to anticipate how an issue will be determined, since judges will be strongly influenced by their own domestic experience. It will take some time for an independent DIFC jurisprudence to develop. **5.33**

Nonetheless the DIFC Courts provide a high level of service comparable to that of the English courts on which they are based, and so are an attractive option when compared to local courts in the region. A significant difference is that, unlike the UAE Courts, the DIFC Courts will order costs in favour of the successful party, which strongly deters weak cases and appeals. **5.34**

---

28 All court decisions are available at <http://www.difccourts.ae>. This is in stark contrast to most jurisdictions in the region where the reporting of judgments is irregular and obtaining copies of court judgements can be difficult.

29 'DIFC Courts and Ras Al Khaimah Courts Sign Landmark Co-operation Memorandum', DIFC Courts Press Release, 22 June 2010, available at <http://difccourts.complinet.com/en/display/display_main.html?rbid=2725&element_id=4254> (accessed 4 March 2013).

30 A copy of this guidance is available on the DIFC Courts website at <http://www.difccourts.ae/Admin/Content/C5917_MOG%20FINAL%20PROTOCOL%20VERSION%20AAA-HWANG%2023%20Jan%202013.pdf> (accessed 4 March 2013).

31 'DIFC Courts Host First Pro Bono Clinic', DIFC Courts Press Release, 7 February 2012, available at <http://difccourts.complinet.com/en/display/display_main.html?rbid=2725&element_id=9016> (accessed 4 March 2012).

32 DIFC Courts can now deal with non-DIFC cases provided the parties involved have agreed to submit to the Courts' jurisdiction.

33 Nevertheless, urgent matters can be dealt with over the telephone or by video conference.

5.3.2 Relationship with the Dubai World Tribunal

5.35 Dubai World is an investment company responsible for managing a range of businesses and projects for the Dubai government. This includes its property arm, Nakheel, which built the Palm Islands and The World developments. Nakheel suffered greatly following the decline in Dubai's property market after the global financial crisis hit Dubai in 2008. In order to satisfy creditors that their claims would be resolved efficiently and in a neutral forum, the Dubai World Tribunal (DWT)[34] was created in 2009 to hear all disputes brought by or against Dubai World and its subsidiaries.[35]

5.36 The DWT is seated in the DIFC (it uses the DIFC Courts' facilities) and has its own rules, which are merely a variation of the DIFC court rules. The Tribunal consists of two DIFC court judges (Sir John Chadwick and Chief Justice Michael Hwang) and is led by former DIFC court Chief Justice Sir Anthony Evans. There is no appeal from its decisions.

5.37 Although the DWT's jurisdiction is wholly independent of the DIFC, because its judges are current or former DIFC judges, the judgments made by the Tribunal give a strong indication of how similar issues may be decided by the DIFC Courts.

5.4 DIFC Law

5.4.1 Relationship between DIFC law and English law

5.38 The DIFC has a common law legal system based primarily on English law, although there are significant deviations to account for international best practices and local requirements. The importance of English law can be seen at section 8(2) of Dubai Law 12 of 2004, which explains that English law is the ultimate fall-back law to be applied:

> The relevant [law to be applied by the DIFC court or tribunal] is to be the one first ascertained under the following paragraphs:
> (a) so far as there is a regulatory content, the DIFC Law or any other law in force in the DIFC; failing which,
> (b) the law of any Jurisdiction other than that of the DIFC expressly chosen by any DIFC Law; failing which,
> (c) the laws of a Jurisdiction as agreed between all the relevant persons concerned in the matter; failing which,
> (d) the laws of any Jurisdiction which appears to the Court or Arbitrator to be the one most closely related to the facts of and the persons concerned in the matter; failing which,
> (e) the laws of England and Wales.[36]

5.39 The DIFC court system is based on the English commercial court system. The first Chief Justice, Sir Anthony Evans (2005–10), was an English Court of Appeal judge and oversaw the creation of the DIFC Courts. The Rules of the DIFC Court were drafted by English barristers and closely modelled on the English Civil Procedure Rules 1998. Although English law exerts a strong influence on DIFC law, it would be wrong to assume that the DIFC law inevitably follows English law. The DIFC Arbitration law, for example, is based on

34 Further information is available at <http://dubaiworldtribunal.ae> (accessed 4 March 2013).

35 In 2011, Nakheel was removed from the jurisdiction of the DWT and is now covered again by the Dubai Courts. Other Dubai World entities remain covered by the DWT.

36 Since this law was passed in 2004, DIFC law has become far more comprehensive, making it rare for the Courts to apply English law directly.

international best practice as reflected in the Model Law and not the English Arbitration Act 1996. Another notable deviation is that disclosure under the DIFC court rules is modelled on international arbitration practice, so that parties only disclose what they wish to rely on or have been ordered to disclose,[37] rather than on the English rule, which requires that all relevant material be disclosed even if it is harmful to the party's case.

5.4.2 Relationship between DIFC law and the sharia

The sharia is a source of UAE law but is not applied in the DIFC. As discussed in more detail later, there has been concern that because the public policy of the UAE applies in the DIFC, sharia will be applied indirectly and cause problems when enforcing arbitral awards. These concerns are, however, baseless, and there is no evidence of sharia being applied in the DIFC. **5.40**

5.5 General Aspects of the 2008 DIFC Arbitration Law

The DIFC Arbitration Law 2008 covers all aspects of arbitration, including default provisions regarding procedure (some of which are mandatory), the involvement of the DIFC court in supporting the arbitral process, and rules regarding enforcement. The 2008 Law is substantially based on the UNCITRAL Model Law, albeit with certain omissions and additions described here. Notably, the 2008 Law does not replicate article 1(1) and (3)–(5) of the Model Law, which restricts the Model Law to 'international' arbitration. The 2008 Law therefore applies to both domestic and international arbitration. **5.41**

What follows here is not an article-by-article comparison between the 2008 Law and the Model Law (although some significant deviations will be highlighted). This is not only because such a comparison would be of limited practical value, but also because the 2008 Law is a free-standing arbitration law that should be assessed on its own terms. This is underlined by the fact that the 2008 Law does not replicate article 2A of the Model Law, which states that 'regard is to be had to [the law's] international origin and the need to promote uniformity in its application and the observance of good faith'. By omitting this section, the 2008 Law implies that although interpretations of Model Law provisions in other states will no doubt be of some relevance, their relevance is limited because the DIFC does not recognize a need to promote uniformity of interpretation. **5.42**

5.5.1 The Scope of the 2008 Law's application

As stated earlier, the 2008 Law covers both domestic and international arbitration in the DIFC. The law states in article 3 that it 'applies in the jurisdiction of the Dubai International Financial Centre', and although the entire law applies when the seat is the DIFC, according to article 7(2) only the following provisions apply when the seat is outside the DIFC: **5.43**

- article 14, regarding the confidentiality of the arbitral proceedings;
- article 15, regarding interim measures and the arbitration agreement;
- part 4, regarding the recognition and enforcement of awards; and
- the Schedule to the 2008 law (rules of interpretation and defined terms).

[37] In particular, the rules regarding disclosure have been borrowed from the 1999 version of the IBA Rules on the Taking of Evidence in International Commercial Arbitration, art 3.

5.44 It has been said that article 3 of the 2008 Law does not fit comfortably with the rest of the 2008 Act because although it states that the 2008 Law only applies within the jurisdiction of the DIFC, article 27(2) allows for DIFC-seated arbitrations to physically take place outside the DIFC, which would appear to give the 2008 Law extra-territorial application.[38] However, this apparent inconsistency arises only from confusion between the juridical place of arbitration (which is abstract) and the physical location of the hearings. The 2008 Law allows parties to choose the DIFC as their seat and so opt into the jurisdiction of the DIFC and by extension its arbitration law, without having to have the proceedings physically located in the DIFC. This is in keeping with the Model Law and generally accepted international arbitration practice.

5.5.2 Definition of 'seat' in the 2008 Law

5.45 In the Schedule to the 2008 Law is a list of defined terms to be used 'unless the context indicates otherwise'. The Schedule defines 'seat' as 'the juridical seat which indicates the procedural law chosen by the parties to govern their arbitration as designated in article 27 of this Law'. This definition is consistent with the seat theory of international arbitration, which holds that arbitration is governed by the arbitration law of the place in which it is held.[39]

5.46 In *Dhir v Waterfront Property*,[40] the Court observed that the 2008 Law makes a distinction between the terms 'seat' and 'place'. The term 'seat' is defined in the 2008 Law whereas the term 'place' is not. After considering the use of the term 'place' in article 24(3) of the 2008 Law, Michael Hwang DCJ found that 'place' in the 2008 Law means 'physical place', as distinct from the juridical seat. This is despite the fact that 'place' is often used by drafters of arbitral clauses as a synonym for 'seat'.

Mandatory aspect

5.47 Article 27 of the 2008 Law states that the parties are free to agree on the seat of the Arbitration but that, in the absence of such agreement and when the dispute is governed by DIFC Law, the seat of the arbitration shall be the DIFC. This is in contrast to the equivalent Model Law section, which provides that in the absence of agreement the Tribunal is to decide the seat 'having regard to the circumstances of the case, including the convenience of the parties'.[41] The 2008 Law does not afford any such discretion to the tribunal and so parties who agree to DIFC law must be aware that under that law the seat will be the DIFC unless agreed otherwise.

5.5.3 Involvement of the DIFC court

5.48 Article 10 of the 2008 Law is based on Article 5 of the Model Law and states that 'no DIFC Court shall intervene except to the extent so provided in this Law'. Article 11 then details which functions must be performed by the DIFC Courts, and which functions will be performed by the DIFC Courts unless agreed otherwise by the parties. This is a helpful deviation from the Model Law as it means parties have greater autonomy and can contract out of the DIFC court's involvement with regard to:

---

38 Luttrell (n 15) 33.

39 A Redfern and M Hunter, *Redfern & Hunter on International Arbitration* (5th edn, OUP, 2009) para 3.51.

40 *Dhir v Waterfront Property Investment Ltd* CFI 011/2009 [2006-09] DIFC CLR 12 (Judicial Authority of the Dubai International Finance Centre, Court of First Instance), para 74.

41 UNCITRAL Model Law on International Commercial Arbitration (the UNCITRAL Model Law) (1985) 24 ILM 1302, art 20(1).

- confidentiality (article 14);
- the role of the DIFC Courts in appointing arbitrators (articles 17(3)–(5), 20(1), and 21(2));
- determining issues of jurisdiction (article 23(3)); and
- determining the fees of the arbitrator (article 39(5)).

Functions that the DIFC Courts must perform include: **5.49**

- hearing challenges to arbitrators (article 19(3));
- enforcing interim measures granted by a Tribunal (article 24(2));
- assisting with the taking of evidence (article 34); and
- hearing applications to set aside or recognize an award (articles 41–44).

In *Dhir*, it was confirmed that the DIFC Courts would abide by the widely accepted international practice that only the courts at the seat have jurisdiction to oversee an arbitration, so unless the DIFC is the seat, the DIFC Courts will not intervene.[42] **5.50**

5.5.4 Arbitration agreements

The 2008 Law follows the Model Law provisions in relation to the definition and form of an arbitration agreement. The agreement must be in a 'recorded form', which may include electronic communications 'provided the information contained therein is accessible so as to be usable for subsequent reference'.[43] Only oral agreements are excluded. **5.51**

Arbitration clauses in standard form agreements are acceptable, as are agreements incorporated by reference.[44] When in an exchange of pleadings one party alleges that there is an arbitral agreement and the other party does not dispute it, this will also constitute a written arbitration agreement.[45] **5.52**

As regards clauses that grant only one party the right to elect arbitration, it would appear that in principle such clauses are acceptable. The case of *Injazat Capital Ltd v Denton Wilde Sapte & Co*[46] involved such a clause and there was no suggestion by the court that it posed a problem. **5.53**

5.5.5 Recognizing arbitration agreements

Under article 13 of the 2008 Law, if an action is brought before the DIFC court in a matter that is subject to an arbitration agreement, the DIFC court must (if requested by a party no later than when submitting its first statement) dismiss or stay such an action unless it finds that the arbitration agreement is null and void, inoperative, or incapable of being performed. **5.54**

Whether arbitration agreements with non-DIFC seats will be recognized by the DIFC court has been the subject of some controversy. Article 13 is one of the articles which, by virtue of article 7 of the 2008 Law, only applies when the seat of the arbitration is the DIFC. In *Injazat*, it was held that when the seat is not the DIFC the court is under no obligation to stay the proceedings on the bias of an arbitration agreement.[47] The court acknowledged that this **5.55**

---

[42] *Dhir* (n 40) para 69.
[43] DIFC Arbitration Law of 2008, art 12(5).
[44] DIFC Arbitration Law of 2008, art 12(7).
[45] DIFC Arbitration Law of 2008, art 12(6).
[46] *Injazat Capital Ltd v Denton Wilde Sapte & Co* CFI 019/2010 (Dubai International Financial Centre Courts, Court of First Instance).
[47] In *Injazat* (n 46) the seat was Dubai, and not the DIFC.

was a failure to implement Article II(3) of the New York Convention.[48] The judge in *Injazat*, Sir David Steel, held that the inherent jurisdiction of the court could not be used to stay the proceedings because the court had no residual discretion in matters explicitly covered by statute, in this case the 2008 Law.[49]

5.56 This reasoning was not followed by Justice Williams QC in the case of *International Electromechanical Services v Al Fattan Engineering*.[50] Justice Williams QC, sitting in the DIFC Court of First Instance, found that the the DIFC court did retain a discretion to stay proceedings due to the court's inherent jurisdiction to stay proceedings which is 'wide-ranging and fundamental'.[51] Unlike Sir David Steel, he did not believe that the issue had been legislated upon to such a degree so as to negate this inherent jurisdiction. Article 7 merely fails to provide that the mandatory stay provision applies, and it takes more than an inference from silence to oust the court's inherent jurisdiction.

5.57 The case of *International Electromechanical Services* has helpfully re-affirmed the DIFC as a seat fully supportive of arbitration and keen to comply with the New York Convention. Indeed, one of the reasons given by Justice Williams QC in his decision was that to hold otherwise would 'thwart the promotion of the DIFC as a jurisdiction supportive of arbitration as an expeditious and cost effective dispute resolution process'.[52] In order to put this issue firmly to rest, the DIFC will shortly be issuing a small amendment to the 2008 Arbitration Law to make it clear that article 13 applies where the seat is the DIFC, where the seat is not the DIFC, and where no seat is designated.

5.5.6 Arbitrability of disputes

5.58 The 2008 Law does not detail any types of disputes that cannot be arbitrated, stating only that the dispute must arise out of a 'defined legal relationship'.[53] However, since DIFC law only covers civil and commercial matters, it may be presumed that criminal and family matters cannot be arbitrated.

5.59 As regards consumer contract claims and employment disputes, the 2008 Law states in article 12(2) that these may not be subject to arbitration, unless:

- the employee or consumer provides written consent after the dispute has arisen; or
- the employee or consumer has submitted to arbitral proceedings in the past (irrespective of whether this relates to the current dispute); or
- the DIFC Courts have made an order declaring article 12(2) inapplicable on the basis that it is not detrimental to the employee or consumer for the dispute to be referred to arbitration.

5.5.7 Liability of the arbitral tribunal and others

5.60 Article 22 of the 2008 Law provides that no arbitrator or arbitral institution shall be liable for any act or omission in connection with the arbitration unless the damage has been caused

48 *Injazat* (n 46) paras 20–21.
49 CFI 019/2010 (Dubai International Financial Centre Courts, Court of First Instance) para 38.
50 *International Electromechanical Services Co LLC v Al Fattan Engineering LLC* CFI 004/2012 (Dubai International Financial Centre Courts, Court of First Instance).
51 *International Electromechanical Services* (n 50) para 101.
52 *International Electromechanical Services* (n 50) para 116.
53 DIFC Arbitration Law of 2008, art 12(1). This follows the UNCITRAL Model Law.

by conscious and deliberate wrongdoing. This is not a provision found in the Model Law. It is important to note that this exclusion of liability does not apply where the arbitrator has resigned.

5.5.8 Plain English

The 2008 Law is largely drafted in plain English and this makes it particularly accessible. Whereas the Model Law uses technical jargon such as *amiable compositeur*, *ex aequo et bono*, *ipso jure*, *de jure*, and *de facto*, the 2008 Law uses plain English equivalents (ie 'principles of equity and good conscience',[54] 'by itself',[55] and 'as a matter of fact or law').[56] **5.61**

The use of plain English in this instance has been criticized on the basis that the non-English phrases are 'neutral terms more suited to use in international disputes than their Anglo approximation'.[57] While it is certainly the case that the non-English phrases are more often used in international arbitration documents (such as the Model Law), it would be wrong to suggest that they are 'neutral terms'. The phrases are specifically grounded in Western legal tradition and the fact that they are found in documents regarding international arbitration merely reflects that these documents were drafted primarily by Western lawyers. They have been incorporated by many non-Western countries either because their legal systems have already been heavily influenced by Western legal systems due to colonialism or because they wish to attract Western business. By incorporating such phrases, the 2008 Law would merely be perpetuating this, but by avoiding them the DIFC enhances its international neutrality while creating a more readily understood document. **5.62**

The use of non-English phrases is also of little practical use. As described previously, although the 2008 Law aims to be consistent with international best practice, it does not have as a stated priority the uniform interpretation of the Model Law across the various countries that have adopted it. Since most lawyers and business people around the world will not understand these non-English phrases, they will use their own equivalent anyway. Foreign phrases merely become jargon and the removal of jargon should be welcomed. **5.63**

5.6 Commencing an Arbitration

5.6.1 Composition of the tribunal

The 2008 Law states that the parties can only agree to an odd number of arbitrators and that in the absence of agreement the number of arbitrators shall be one.[58] There is no requirement that an arbitrator be a UAE national or have any particular characteristics, and the law allows parties to agree to exclude people of a particular nationality. Arbitrators must, however, disclose any circumstances likely to give rise to justifiable doubts as to their independence or impartiality, and may be challenged on this basis if any such circumstances arise.[59] **5.64**

[54] DIFC Arbitration Law of 2008, art 35(3). This follows the UNCITRAL Model Law, Art 28(3).
[55] DIFC Arbitration Law of 2008, art 23(1). This follows the UNCITRAL Model Law, Art 16(1).
[56] DIFC Arbitration Law of 2008, art 20(1). This follows the UNCITRAL Model Law, Art 14(1).
[57] Luttrell (n 15) 39.
[58] DIFC Arbitration Law of 2008, art 16. This is in contrast to the UNCITRAL Model Law, Art 10 which states that the parties are free to determine the number of arbitrators, failing which the number shall be three.
[59] DIFC Arbitration Law of 2008, art 18.

5.65 In situations in which there is difficulty constituting the tribunal, the DIFC court has the power, under article 17 of the 2008 Law, to assist. Article 17 allows the DIFC court to make appointments where a party fails to do so within 30 days.[60]

5.66 The 2008 Law also grants an additional power to the DIFC Courts not found in the Model Law. When the dispute involves more than two parties and each party is to appoint an arbitrator but the parties have not agreed in writing that the parties represent two separate sides for the formation of the tribunal, the DIFC court will appoint the tribunal without regard to any party's nomination. In order to avoid any challenge to a subsequent award on the basis that the tribunal was not formed in accordance with the agreement of the parties, article 17(3)(d) states that when the DIFC court exercises such power, the arbitral agreement is to be treated for all purposes as a written agreement for the appointment of the arbitral tribunal by the DIFC court.

5.67 This rule, found in articles 17(3)(c) and (d) of the 2008 Law, has been lifted from the LCIA Rules (article 8) and is a practical solution to the problems posed by multi-party arbitration. However, this arguably creates an inconsistency in the 2008 Law. Under article 16 of the 2008 Law the parties are allowed to determine the number of arbitrators provided the number is odd, but this power is then restricted by article 17 because even if, for example, three parties enter into an agreement and provide for five arbitrators (each party choosing an arbitrator with two neutrals, one of whom is chairman), then according to article 17(3)(c) the DIFC court must appoint all the arbitrators unless the parties agree to artificially designate themselves claimant or respondent. Since article 17(3)(c) states that the DIFC court 'shall' appoint the tribunal rather than 'may', the DIFC court would not appear to have the ability to refuse to exercise this power even if it wished to respect the agreement of the parties.

5.68 Of course, this is a hypothetical example and not one likely to occur in practice. It does, however, show that despite affording parties a great number of freedoms, the 2008 Law has nonetheless been drafted with conventional arbitration in mind and anything unusual will be likely to encounter problems. The insistence that parties be identified as either claimant or respondent in relation to multi-party disputes restricts creativity in dealing with such matters, although perhaps this is the trade-off necessary to have an accessible arbitration law.

5.6.2 Role of courts in deciding challenges to arbitrators

5.69 As regards challenging arbitrators, the 2008 Law adopts the relevant Model Law provisions. Under article 18, parties can challenge an arbitrator only if circumstances exist that give rise to a justifiable doubt as to his impartiality or independence, or if he does not possess qualifications agreed to by the parties. Unless agreed otherwise, a party has 15 days after becoming aware of the constitution of the arbitral tribunal or the relevant circumstances to send a written statement of the reasons for the challenge. If unsuccessful, the party may, within 30 days of the decision, refer the matter to the DIFC Court of First Instance, from which there is no appeal. While the decision of the DIFC court is pending the arbitration may proceed.

60 This incorporates the UNCITRAL Model Law, Art 11.

5.6.3 Role of courts in resolving jurisdictional questions

Under article 23 of the 2008 Law the arbitral tribunal has the power to determine its own jurisdiction. This provision reflects the principle of *competence-competence* and will be familiar to international practitioners. **5.70**

5.6.4 Role of courts in consolidating arbitrations

There are no provisions in the 2008 Law regarding the joining of arbitrations and no case law has considered the issue. Since the DIFC court will only become involved to the extent allowed for in the 2008 Law, it is probable that the DIFC Courts would decline an application to consolidate multiple arbitrations forcibly. **5.71**

5.6.5 Role of courts in enjoining arbitration

There have not been any cases of the DIFC court being asked to make an order staying an arbitration, either domestic or foreign. The 2008 Law does not address such a scenario, so presumably if minded to, the DIFC court could make such an order. **5.72**

5.7 Interim Measures

Article 24 of the 2008 Law gives the tribunal the power to grant interim measures unless the parties have agreed otherwise. The tribunal may, at the request of a party, order any party to take such interim measures as the tribunal considers necessary in relation to the arbitration. These can include security for costs and orders to preserve goods or evidence. **5.73**

When seeking an interim measure, a party must satisfy the tribunal that the harm that it will suffer if the order is not granted will outweigh the harm the other party will suffer if it is granted, and that the harm is not adequately reparable by an award of damages. The applicant must also show that it has a reasonable possibility of success on the merits of the case. On granting an interim measure, the tribunal may request that the applicant provide security in relation to the measure ordered. **5.74**

Article 24 also provides that a party may request from the DIFC court an order enforcing the tribunal's order or any part of it, and may recover the costs of doing so in the arbitration. **5.75**

The DIFC court may also, under article 24(3), grant interim measures in relation to arbitral proceedings 'irrespective of whether their place [physical not juridical location] is in the DIFC'. In *Dhir*,[61] Michael Hwang DCJ considered in detail how the DIFC Courts would approach such applications for interim measures. According to *Dhir*, the court has jurisdiction to grant an injunction only where: **5.76**

- the seat of the arbitration is the DIFC; or
- the court otherwise has jurisdiction over the person against whom it is sought (this follows the principle set out in the English case *Fourie v Le Roux* [2007] UKHL 1); or
- strong factors justify the grant of an injunction (usually involving fraud); or
- the defendant has substantial assets in the DIFC which demonstrates a sufficiently strong link between the defendant and the DIFC (this follows the English case *Mobil Cerro Negro Ltd v Petroleos de Venezuale SA* [2008] APP LR 03/18).

[61] *Dhir v Waterfront Property Investment Ltd* CFI 011/2009 [2006-09] DIFC CLR 12 (Judicial Authority of the Dubai International Finance Centre, Court of First Instance), paras 108–141.

5.77 In accordance with the earlier DIFC judgment of *Ithmar Capital Ltd v 8 Investment*,[62] the applicant must produce evidence that satisfies the court that:

- it has a good arguable case;
- the respondent may have assets available to satisfy the award against him;
- there is a real risk that the award will not be satisfied by reason of an unjustifiable disposal of those assets; and
- it is just and convenient in the circumstances for the order to be made.

5.78 If the application is made without notice to the defendant, the applicant must disclose to the Court all material facts, including any defense the defendant has or may raise. Failure to do so will jeopardize the integrity of any order made and likely be punished by an adverse costs order.

5.79 With regard to the test for determining whether there is a risk of the defendant dissipating assets, the court in *Ithmar Capital* referred to the approach of the English Court's decision in *Mobil*:

(1) Freezing orders are not granted in order to provide security for a claim (although that may be their effect).
(2) The question is whether a particular course of conduct in relation to assets by the defendant, actual or feared, is conduct which should or may lead the court to conclude that the grant of a freezing order is just and convenient.
(3) The actual or feared conduct must be unjustifiable, ie the assets will be used otherwise than for normal and proper commercial purposes. What is unjustifiable depends on the purpose of the injunction.
(4) The risk of dissipation must involve a risk of impairing the claimant's ability to enforce the award. The claimant must produce solid evidence to support his assertion that there is a real risk of the assets being dissipated, which may include the following factors:
    (a) The nature of the assets and the ease with which they may be disposed of;
    (b) The nature and financial standing of the defendant's business;
    (c) The length of time the defendant has been in business;
    (d) The domicile or residence of the defendant;
    (e) If the defendant is a foreign company, the ease with which any judgment or arbitral award may be enforced in that country;
    (f) The defendant's past or existing credit record;
    (g) Any intention expressed by the defendant about future dealings with his assets (in and outside of the country); and
    (h) Connections between a defendant company and other companies which have defaulted on arbitration awards or judgments.

5.8 During the Arbitration

5.8.1 Written communications

5.80 Article 8 of the 2008 Law describes how parties are to effect written communications and when these are deemed to have been received. This replicates Article 3(1) of the Model Law,

[62] *Ithmar Capital Ltd v 8 Investment* CA 1/2008 (Judicial Authority of the Dubai International Finance Centre, Court of Appeal).

while Article 3(2) of the Model Law (which states that the provisions relating to the written communications between the parties do not apply to court proceedings) has not been replicated. This has led to speculation that the deemed receipt provisions in the 2008 Law will bind the DIFC Courts even if they are inconsistent with the Courts' own rules.[63] They do not, however, appear to be inconsistent,[64] and in any event the 2008 Law applies only to arbitration proceedings and not to court proceedings so there can be no conflict.

5.8.2 Waiver of right to object

Article 9 of the 2008 Law states that any party who knows that any provision of the 2008 Law or requirement under the arbitration agreement has not been complied with and yet proceeds with the arbitration without raising an objection will be deemed to have waived the objection.[65] **5.81**

5.8.3 Role of courts in compelling testimony/evidence

Under article 34 of the 2008 Law the tribunal (or a party if it has the approval of the tribunal) can request from the DIFC court assistance in taking evidence. This would be likely to extend to using the court's powers to compel a witness to give evidence under the DIFC Court Rules 30.15, although this has not been tested. **5.82**

5.8.4 Ability of foreign practitioners to appear in arbitration as counsel or arbitrator

There are no provisions under DIFC law that prevent foreign practitioners from appearing as counsel or arbitrator. The parties are free to choose who they are represented by and to choose their arbitrator as they wish. The parties do not have to be legally represented, but if they are it is recommended that powers of attorney authorizing their representatives be submitted as although this is not necessary under DIFC law, such documents can often be needed when enforcing awards through local courts in the region. **5.83**

5.8.5 Requirements for the conduct of the hearing

Article 25 of the 2008 Law requires that the parties be treated equally and that each party be given a full opportunity to present its case. This is derived from Article 18 of the Model Law. The 2008 Law also provides that the parties are free to agree on the procedure to be followed by the arbitral tribunal in conducting the proceedings, failing which the tribunal can conduct the arbitration as it sees fit.[66] **5.84**

Article 29 of the 2008 Law states that the parties are free to agree on the language or languages that are to be used, and, in the absence of agreement, the tribunal shall determine this. **5.85**

As with the Model Law, article 32 of the 2008 law allows proceedings to continue despite a party's failure to attend a hearing or produce evidence. **5.86**

5.8.6 Experts

The are no provisions in the 2008 Law preventing parties from relying on experts. The law also grants the tribunal the power to appoint its own expert. The 2008 Law differs from the **5.87**

---

63 Luttrell (n 15) 32.

64 cf the Rules of the Dubai International Finance Centre Court of 2007, Pt 9 (hereinafter 'RDC').

65 UNCITRAL Model Law, Art 4 regarding the waiver of rights to object is replicated here.

66 This replicates the UNCITRAL Model Law, Art 10.

Model Law slightly in that it expressly states that the costs of a tribunal expert form part of the arbitration costs to be borne by the parties in accordance with any allocation made by the arbitral tribunal.[67]

5.9 The Award

5.9.1 Mandatory rules as to form

5.88 The award must be in writing and signed by the arbitrators.[68] When there is more than one arbitrator a majority of the members will suffice, provided that the reason for any omitted signature is stated.[69] The award must state its date and the seat of the arbitration.[70] Once made, a copy must be sent to each party.[71] Unless otherwise agreed, the award must state the reasons upon which it is based.[72]

5.9.2 Mandatory rules as to substance

5.89 Article 38(5) of the 2008 Law states that the tribunal must fix the costs of the arbitration in its award. It defines the term 'costs' as including only:

- the fees of the arbitral tribunal to be stated separately as to each arbitrator;
- the properly incurred travel and other expenses incurred by the arbitrators;
- the costs of expert advice and of other assistance required by the arbitral tribunal;
- the travel and other expenses of witnesses to the extent that such expenses are approved by the arbitral tribunal;
- such other costs as are necessary for the conduct of the arbitration;
- the legal costs and assistance of the successful party if claimed and only to the extent that they are reasonable;
- any fees and expenses of any arbitral institution or appointing authority.

5.90 The mandatory nature of this provision appears to rule out costs incurred in taking pre-arbitral steps such as formal mediation. It also appears to overlook article 24(2) of the 2008 Law, which states that costs incurred in applying to the DIFC court to enforce a tribunal's order for interim measures may be recovered in the arbitration.

5.10 After the Award

5.10.1 Lien

5.91 The 2008 law allows the tribunal to refuse to deliver the final award or the order for termination until its fees are paid in full.[73] The DIFC court can assist by assessing the appropriate amount should there be a disagreement.[74]

---

67 DIFC Arbitration Law of 2008, art 33.
68 DIFC Arbitration Law of 2008, art 38(1).
69 DIFC Arbitration Law of 2008, art 38(1).
70 DIFC Arbitration Law of 2008, art 38(3).
71 DIFC Arbitration Law of 2008, art 38(4).
72 DIFC Arbitration Law of 2008, art 38(2).
73 DIFC Arbitration Law of 2008, art 39(4).
74 DIFC Arbitration Law of 2008, art 39(5).

5.10.2 Corrections

The default position under the law is that any request for clerical corrections, interpretation of a specific point or part of the award, or that the tribunal make an additional award in respect of claims omitted from the award, must be made within 30 days of receipt of the award.[75] **5.92**

5.10.3 Setting aside a DIFC award

The 2008 Law makes clear that any application to set aside an award made in the DIFC must be made to the DIFC Courts only.[76] From the DIFC Courts' perspective, no other court is competent to set aside a DIFC award. This again affirms that the DIFC follows the seat theory of international arbitration, rather than the transnational theory. **5.93**

The criteria for setting aside an award are substantially the same as the criteria for refusing enforcement under the New York Convention. The party making the application must do so within three months of receiving the award (unless the parties have agreed otherwise in writing) and must furnish proof that: **5.94**

- the party was under some incapacity, or the agreement to arbitrate was not valid, either under the law the parties subjected it to or under DIFC law;
- the party was not given proper notice of the appointment of an arbitrator or of the proceedings or was otherwise unable to present his case;
- the award covers matters outside the scope of reference given to the tribunal (although the rest of the award may be enforced); or
- the composition of the tribunal or the arbitral procedure was not in accordance with the agreement of the parties or with the DIFC law.

An award may also be set aside by the DIFC court if: **5.95**

- the matter is not arbitrable under DIFC law;
- the dispute was expressly referred to a different body or tribunal for resolution under DIFC law; or
- the award is in conflict with the public policy of the UAE.

This last provision has caused some debate. First, there is a concern that by stating that the public policy enforced in the DIFC is UAE public policy, the 2008 Law is making clear that international awards will be subject to local standards of public policy, rather than the narrower 'international' or 'transnational' standards that some commentators believe should apply in international arbitration.[77] It is perhaps unreasonable, however, to expect any sovereign state to enforce an award it finds contrary to its own public policy simply because it does not offend the public policy of other nations. **5.96**

The second concern is that UAE public policy is essentially 'Islamic public policy' and that non-Muslims will be prejudiced by this. The argument[78] is that the DIFC Courts, bound as they are under article 42(1) of the 2008 Law to comply with all treaties entered into by the UAE, will be at least partially guided by the Riyadh Convention. Under Article 3(a) **5.97**

[75] DIFC Arbitration Law of 2008, art 40(1).
[76] DIFC Arbitration Law of 2008, art 41(2).
[77] Luttrell (n 15) 40.
[78] Luttrell (n 15) 41.

of the Riyadh Convention, signatories are to refuse to enforce foreign judgments that are 'contrary to the Sharia principles, the Constitution or the public policy of the country where the [enforcement] application [is] made'. Because the words preceding the phrase 'public policy' refer to Islam (the sharia being part of Islamic law and the UAE Constitution at article 7 stating that sharia is a main source of law), this frames the phrase 'public policy' in religious terms, thereby creating 'Islamic public policy'. This gives rise to concern that 'awards that conflict with Islamic public order and morals will not be enforceable in the wider UAE . . . [and] are liable to be set aside by DIFC Courts also'.[79]

5.98 There are, however, a number of significant flaws in this argument that render the concern tenuous. First, given the fact that under article 2(1) of the 2008 Law the DIFC Courts are to comply with all treaties signed by the UAE, there is no reason to believe that the DIFC Courts will favour the Riyadh Convention over the New York Convention, especially if the Riyadh Convention is more restrictive.

5.99 Second, even if the Riyadh Convention were followed, the interpretation of Article 3(a) could not sensibly be said to produce a concept of 'Islamic public policy'. The convention states that awards will not be enforced if they are 'contrary to the Sharia principles, the Constitution or the public policy of the country where the [enforcement] application [is] made', thereby explicitly distinguishing between the sharia and national public policy.

5.100 Third, even if 'Islamic public policy' existed and applied in the DIFC, it is unlikely that it would have detrimental effects. It has been suggested that an award relating, for example, to a licensing agreement for the sale of alcohol would be at risk of being set aside.[80] However, alcohol is legally sold to non-Muslims in the UAE (including in the DIFC), and arbitrations have been conducted in relation to agreements regarding its supply.[81] There is then no reason to believe that an arbitral award concerning alcohol would have difficulty being enforced in the DIFC.

5.101 Interest is another commonly misunderstood issue. It is widely believed that interest is forbidden under sharia and it would therefore be contrary to the public policy of the UAE to enforce an award providing for the payment of interest. In fact, the UAE courts have found that the use of interest in commercial dealings is necessary and therefore in the public interest, and does not violate public policy.[82] If, however, the interest awarded is excessive, this may be an issue during enforcement, but the remaining elements of the award will be enforceable. The DIFC Courts allow interest to be claimed, so there is no reason to believe that an award providing for the payment of interest would be unenforceable in whole or in part.

5.102 It should be noted that the DIFC Courts have three local judges, part of whose role is to inform the non-UAE judges of what may be considered contrary to UAE public policy. It is expected that public policy will be given a narrow meaning and only applied in the most obvious and clear circumstances.[83]

---

[79] Luttrell (n 15) 41.

[80] Luttrell (n 15) 41.

[81] In the past three years, the author's law firm has been involved in at least one such arbitration.

[82] eg Union Supreme Court Decision 1/Judicial Year 20 (24 October 2000) and Decision 61/Judicial Year 28 (16 May 2007).

[83] The only foreign award that is likely to be refused outright is an Israeli award since the UAE has had a boycott of Israel since 1972.

5.10.4 Enforcing a DIFC award

In the early years of the DIFC, the issue of how to enforce a DIFC award gave rise to much debate among practitioners. Without confidence that a DIFC award will be enforced there is little reason to use the DIFC as a seat. However, these fears have been substantially allayed by two recent developments: the reported enforcement of a DIFC arbitration award in the UAE; and the publication of a paper by the DIFC Courts detailing how to enforce DIFC judgments (which includes ratified DIFC awards). **5.103**

Enforcing a DIFC award in the DIFC

Enforcing a DIFC award in the DIFC is relatively straightforward. A party must make an application to the DIFC Court of First Instance under Part 43 of the DIFC Court Rules to have the award enforced. **5.104**

The application may be made without notice.[84] The Court of First Instance may specify the parties on whom the arbitration claim form must be served, although under the general rules regarding arbitration claim forms[85] the form must be served by the claimant on the defendant within 30 days of its issue,[86] and all parties to the arbitration must be made a defendant to the arbitration claim (not simply the party against whom enforcement is sought).[87] Although the tribunal does not need to be notified of the action, the rules do allow an arbitrator to make written representations to the Court.[88] **5.105**

The application must be supported by written evidence and have attached to it the original arbitration award and the original arbitration agreement, or certified copies. If not in English a translation of these documents must be provided. The applicant must also state to what extent, if any, the award has been complied with.[89] It is also necessary for a draft order in English and Arabic to be submitted with the application, unless the court orders otherwise.[90] **5.106**

The defendant has 14 days from receiving the order for the enforcement of the award to apply for it to be set aside.[91] The enforcement of the order can only take place once this 14-day period has expired, or if an application is made to set aside an award, once any application has been finally disposed of.[92] The grounds on which the award can be set aside are detailed at paragraphs 5.94 and 5.95. **5.107**

If an application to set aside the order is made, the respondent to the application has seven days in which to file any written evidence. Once any application has been dealt with or the 14 days have expired, the award may be enforced in the same manner as a court judgment or order, and the court may enter judgment in the terms of the award.[93] **5.108**

The rules on confidentiality state that, unlike conventional claim forms (which are published on the DIFC Court website), an arbitration claim form may only be inspected with the **5.109**

---

84 RDC 43.61.
85 RDC 43.62.
86 RDC 43.9.
87 RDC 43.17.
88 RDC 43.23.
89 RDC 43.65.
90 RDC 43.66. It is not clear why the expense of providing a draft award in Arabic is necessary given that English is the language of the DIFC.
91 RDC 43.69.
92 RDC.
93 RDC 43.74.

permission of the court.[94] The court will also hear arbitration claims in private unless there is a good reason for not doing so.[95]

5.110 The foregoing demonstrates the speed in which an arbitral award may be enforced in the DIFC. The time limits for each stage are minimal and the process should not take more than a few months even if contested. The costs of taking enforcement action through the DIFC Courts can also be recovered and added to the judgment debt.

Enforcing a DIFC award in Dubai

5.111 The method to be used when seeking to enforce a DIFC award in Dubai was initially established under Dubai Law 12 of 2004. It was then supplemented in 2009 by a Protocol of Enforcement between the Dubai and DIFC courts. The method was amended again in 2011 when Dubai Law 16 of 2011 significantly amended Dubai Law 12 of 2004. The method is now largely settled following the successful enforcement of a DIFC award in Dubai in 2011.[96]

5.112 The mechanism for enforcement is as follows:

- the award must be final, ratified by the DIFC courts, and endorsed with an executory clause;[97]
- the DIFC courts must issue a letter requesting enforcement to the chief justice of the Dubai Court of First Instance and explaining the enforcement action to be taken;[98]
- the applicant must apply to the execution judge of the Dubai Courts, enclosing a copy of the award, the order of the DIFC court ratifying the award (with a certified translation) and the letter requesting enforcement from the DIFC Courts;
- the Dubai execution judge will then execute the award as if it were a Dubai court judgment, ie the execution judge will not review the substance of the award, but will follow the usual procedure applicable to Dubai court judgments, allowing objections to the enforcement to be heard.[99]

5.113 The effect of this is that a ratified DIFC award can be sent directly for execution in Dubai without any investigation into its merits. As with any enforcement process, the defendant will have an opportunity to object to enforcement in the usual manner and this will be processed accordingly. The winning party is therefore spared from having to prosecute a claim for recognition through the Dubai Courts (as would be necessary in respect of a foreign award), a process that can take many months.

Enforcing a DIFC award in the wider UAE

5.114 The system for enforcing DIFC awards in the wider UAE is not as clear as the method for enforcing such awards in Dubai, nor has it been tested. It is anticipated that if a DIFC award were to be taken directly to the courts in the wider UAE, there is a real risk that when

---

[94] RDC 43.25.

[95] RDC 43.41.

[96] The case in question was *Proprty Concepts FZE v Lootah Network Real Estate & Commercial Brokerage* ARB001/2010 (Dubai International Financial Centre Courts, Court of First Instance) and involved the enforcement of award approximately US$7.2m, including interest and costs.

[97] Dubai Law No 16 of 2011 Amending Certain Provisions of Law No 12 of 2004 Concerning Dubai International Financial Centre Courts, art 7(2).

[98] Dubai Law No 16 of 2011, art 7(3)(a).

[99] Dubai Law No 16 of 2011, art 7(3)(c).

reviewing the award the local judge may attempt to review the merits rather than merely the procedural aspects of the award. This is because the rules for ratifying a local award give the courts the ability to set aside an award if 'an invalidity occurs in the ruling or in the procedures which influences the ruling'.[100] This is not therefore a recommended route. Having the award ratified first by the DIFC Courts is a safer process. Federal Law 11 of 1973 (Judicial Relationships Amongst Emirates) states that each emirate must respect the judgments of the other emirates and enforce them without reviewing the merits of the case.

Under article 221 of the UAE Law of Civil Procedure 1992, when a court judgment from one emirate is to be enforced in another, the process is for the execution judge of the jurisdiction in which the judgment has been made to contact the execution judge in whose jurisdiction the judgment is to be enforced, sending all the legal documents necessary for the implementation of the judgment. **5.115**

The execution judge in the jurisdiction in which enforcement is sought will then take the necessary decisions to enforce the judgment (such decisions being susceptible to appeal). Anything seized (ie located by the authorities and confiscated) is then sent back to the enforcement judge in the jurisdiction where the judgment was made. Alternatively, if enforcement is not possible for practical or legal reasons, the execution judge of the jurisdiction where the judgment was made is informed of this. **5.116**

Having the DIFC Courts ratify the award is therefore a recommended step. The grounds for setting aside an award under the 2008 Law are much narrower than those under UAE law and the DIFC court judges are more supportive of arbitration. **5.117**

The final issue for practitioners once the award has become a DIFC judgment is whether this is enough, or whether the DIFC court judgment must be converted into a Dubai court judgment before being sent to the relevant court for enforcement. One of the amendments implemented by Dubai Law No 16 of 2011 was that any 'arbitral awards ratified by the [DIFC] Courts shall be executed by the competent entity having jurisdiction outside DIFC in accordance with the procedure and rules adopted by such entities in this regard'.[101] This would seem to suggest that a direct approach is appropriate. However, although the DIFC Courts have a relationship with the other UAE courts and indeed other courts in the region (such as the Jordanian courts), the Dubai courts have a long-established practice with the other emirate courts with regard to the enforcement of judgments. It is therefore recommended that the Dubai courts be used as an intermediary. A case can be filed before the Dubai courts for enforcement of the DIFC judgment, which will enable the Dubai courts to use their established methods for enforcing judgments in the other emirates. Although this adds a further layer of administration, it should greatly reduce the risk of unforeseen problems. **5.118**

Enforcing a DIFC award outside the UAE

A DIFC award is in principle as enforceable abroad as any UAE award. The DIFC is constitutionally part of the UAE and is covered by the New York Convention, to which the UAE made no reservations. Any such award should therefore be enforceable in the 145 other states that are signatories to the New York Convention. **5.119**

---

[100] UAE Civil Procedure Code, Federal Law No 11 of 1992, art 216(1)(c).

[101] Dubai Law No 16 of 2011 Amending Certain Provisions of Law No 12 of 2004 Concerning Dubai International Financial Centre Courts, art 7(2).

5.120 Although most countries in the GCC and the wider region have ratified the New York Convention, there are a few exceptions (such as Iraq, Libya, Sudan, Somalia, and Yemen). In the GCC states, DIFC arbitral awards are covered by the GCC Convention, and non-GCC states in the region are covered by the Riyadh Convention (see paragraphs 5.24–5.26). Given the recent establishment of the DIFC, however, it remains advisable to have any award ratified by the DIFC Courts and then recognized by the Dubai Courts, so that it becomes a Dubai court judgment. This additional process should then smooth the enforcement process.

5.11 Comparison with other Regional Seats

5.121 Arbitration in the GCC has changed dramatically in recent years. In addition to the developments detailed previously regarding the DIFC, there have been new arbitration laws in Qatar, Bahrain, and most recently in Saudi Arabia. There has also been a flurry of new arbitral institutions, including the BCDR-AAA, the Qatar International Center for Arbitration, and the revised Dubai International Arbitration Centre.

5.122 In the following commentary is a brief description of how the DIFC compares with three regional seats: the UAE, Qatar, and Bahrain.

5.11.1 The UAE

5.123 The UAE does not have an independent arbitration law, although a draft has been circulated and will hopefully be enacted in the near future. The law of arbitration is found in the UAE Procedural Law 1992,[102] a federal law that applies throughout the emirates. It is not based on the Model Law, nor is it modern or comprehensive. This does not, however, make it unusable, and in recent years hundreds of arbitrations, including international arbitrations, have been successfully seated in Dubai or other emirates of the UAE.

5.124 The law does, however, contain a number of local requirements that can cause problems for the uninitiated. For example, in order to be recognized, an arbitral award must be signed on every page—simply having the final page containing the order signed by the arbitrator is insufficient because the arbitrator must also sign off on the reasoning. Another issue is that although the law states that arbitrators are not bound by legal procedures,[103] witnesses must swear an oath.[104] If the oath is not made the award may be set aside, since it is a matter of public policy that witnesses give evidence on oath (irrespective of whether they have any religious belief). This issue came to international attention in the 2004 case of *International Bechtel Co Ltd v Department of Civil Aviation of the Government of Dubai*,[105] when a $25 million arbitral award was set aside on this basis.

5.125 The primary difficulty with arbitration in the UAE is the unpredictability of the UAE courts. Very few judges in the UAE courts are UAE nationals. The vast majority are from

---

102 For a more systematic analysis of UAE arbitration law, please see the chapter on the UAE by E Al Tamimi and C Clutterham in JW Rowley (ed), *Arbitration World* (3rd edn, European Lawyer Reference, 2010).

103 UAE Civil Procedure Code, Federal Law No 11 of 1992, art 212(1).

104 UAE Civil Procedure Code, Federal Law No 11 of 1992, art 212(1).

105 *International Bechtel Co Ltd v Department of Civil Aviation of the Government of Dubai*, Dubai Court of Cassation, Petition No 503/2003, Judgment dated 15 May 2005.

Egypt, Syria, Lebanon, and Sudan,[106] and many are on temporary secondment with limited experience. This gives rise to inconsistent and sometimes ill-informed judgments. These inconsistencies are compounded by the existence of three court systems in the UAE (the federal system based in Abu Dhabi, and the independent systems of Dubai and Ras Al Khaimah) that can differ in matters of procedure and substantive law. There is also no system of precedent, so judges are free to exercise broad discretion. Finally, limited court reporting means that many judgments are reported by word of mouth, which results in the spread of misinformation.

In comparison, the DIFC courts offer a much more uniform and predictable judicial system, with greater transparency and a system of precedent. The DIFC court judges are supportive of arbitration and knowledgeable about it, additionally the DIFC Arbitration Law of 2008 is comprehensive and covers many more aspects of the arbitral process than the UAE law. **5.126**

5.11.2 Qatar

Dubai is not the only regional jurisdiction to have radically changed its legal framework to appeal to international business. Like Dubai with the DIFC, Qatar has set up its own financial centre, the Qatar Financial Centre (QFC), with its own laws and courts that follow the common law. Unlike the DIFC, however, the QFC is not a physical location but a purely legal jurisdiction. This means that Qatar has two separate and independent civil legal systems coexisting in the same territory. Provided the parties are either QFC-registered companies or have agreed to be governed by QFC law, they will fall within the QFC jurisdiction and the arbitration will be seated there. **5.127**

The QFC has a modern arbitration law based on the Model Law.[107] Like Dubai, Qatar itself does not have an independent arbitration law but relies on a handful of provisions in the general Civil and Commercial Procedure Law 1990.[108] These provisions have come to be seen as inadequate for modern needs.[109] **5.128**

The conduct of arbitration in Qatar was enhanced in 2006 when the Qatar International Center for Conciliation and Arbitration (QICCA)[110] was established within the Qatar Chamber of Commerce and Industry. In May 2012, QICCA adopted a new set of rules based on the UNCITRAL Rules as modified in 2010. **5.129**

Practical concerns regarding arbitration in Qatar and the QFC mainly relate to the fact that much of its new arbitral framework has yet to be tested. It is said that there have yet to be any arbitrations conducted under the QFC law,[111] and the QFC courts have only decided a **5.130**

[106] Al Tamimi (n 2) 6.

[107] Qatar Financial Centre reg No 8 of 2005.

[108] Qatari Law No 13 of 1990, arts 190–210.

[109] S Maleh, 'Is it Time to Amend the Articles Regulating Arbitration in Qatar?', Kluwer Arbitration Blog, 30 June 2011, available at <http://kluwerarbitrationblog.com/blog/2011/06/30/is-it-time-to-amend-the-articles-regulating-arbitration-in-qatar/> (accessed 4 March 2013).

[110] This institution is also referred to as the Qatar Centre for International Arbitration (QICA).

[111] F Nesheiwat, 'New rules Issued by Qatar International Centre for Arbitration', Lexology, 9 July 2012, available at <http://www.lexology.com/library/detail.aspx?g=f40f9d90-f561-4de7-b02f-a8ade75a3718> (accessed 4 March 2013).

small number of cases.[112] There has not been any time for the new QICCA rules to be tested, although being based on the UNCITRAL rules they are expected to function well.

5.131 The fact that the QFC does not physically exist means that it is possibly the only arbitral seat in which it is impossible to hold a hearing. It is a purely abstract seat. If the term 'seat' has its common international meaning of being a juridical place rather than a geographical place, the fact that it is physically impossible for an arbitration to occur within the QFC should not be an issue. Since there do not appear to have been any awards made under QFC law it remains to be seen whether the abstract existence of the QFC will create problems with enforcement. It has been suggested that although Qatar has ratified the New York Convention, the QFC is not covered by this international instrument because it is not a state.[113] It is possible, however, that since the QFC is a jurisdiction within Qatar, it will be covered by the New York Convention.

5.11.3 Bahrain

5.132 Bahrain has historically been seen as one of the most supportive jurisdictions for arbitration. In recent years this has been underlined by the passing of a new arbitration law, Decree No 30 of 2009. This introduced three developments: the creation of the Bahrain Chamber for Dispute Resolution; a new domestic dispute resolution process; and an 'arbitration free zone'.

5.133 The Bahrain Chamber for Dispute Resolution (the BCDR) was created to handle domestic and international arbitrations. It was created in partnership with the American Arbitration Association (AAA), forming the BCDR-AAA. The influence of the AAA on the BCDR is strong, since not only are the rules of the BCDR almost identical to those of the International Centre for Dispute Resolution (the international division of the AAA), but the AAA is assisting with the running of the institution and the training of staff. As with the DIFC-LCIA, the BCDR-AAA is free to administer arbitrations seated outside Bahrain.

5.134 The major innovation, however, comes under article 25 of the Decree, which established what has been called the world's first 'arbitration free zone'. It provides that:

> ...parties to the dispute shall not be entitled to challenge on nullity base [sic] against the award issued by the Dispute Resolution Tribunal [under Chapter 2, Section 2, of the Decree], if the parties have agreed in writing [1] to choose a foreign law concerning the dispute, [2] [that] they shall not be entitled to challenge the award before Bahrain's Courts, and [3] that the challenge against the award shall be before the competent authority in another state.

5.135 This means that parties who use Bahrain as their seat can agree to disempower the Bahraini courts from hearing challenges against the award. The parties can therefore have confidence that the Bahraini courts will not set aside an award, even though they are the curial courts by virtue of being the seat of the arbitration. This means that parties no longer have to wait a number of years to determine whether the Bahraini courts will respect arbitral awards issued in their country.

5.136 At present, however, the BCDR-AAA has yet to have any cases, so it remains to be seen whether this experimental approach will work in practice. There are considerable obstacles

---

112 QFC civil and commercial court judgments are available at <http://www.qfccourt.com/Judgement.html>.

113 Norton Rose Group, 'Arbitration in the Middle East' (July 2008) 13, available at <http://www.nortonrose.com/files/qatar-25751.pdf> (accessed 4 March 2013).

in that, if the courts of the jurisdiction nominated by the parties to review the award refuse to accept such a mission because they are not the courts of the seat, there will be no forum in which to annul an award no matter how defective. It also seems that the Bahraini courts will remain the curial courts during the arbitral process and so may be involved to some degree.

5.12 Practical Matters Regarding Arbitration in the DIFC

5.12.1 The DIFC as a location for hearings

One of key benefits of the DIFC as a seat for arbitration is that it provides a modern, efficient, stable, and convenient place for arbitration in an important region that has few jurisdictions, if any, that have such qualities. **5.137**

The UAE is one of the most politically stable countries in the region and has been largely untouched by the 'Arab Spring', which began in 2011. The country has actually benefited from the recent regional upheavals as international businesses and banks have sought to move their investments from troubled areas, such as Egypt and Bahrain, to the more secure UAE. Parties can therefore have confidence that by agreeing on DIFC as the seat of their arbitration, there is little risk of domestic problems occurring that might disrupt the process. **5.138**

The UAE, and by extension the DIFC, is well connected for international travel. It also has an abundance of quality hotels, many of which have conference rooms with recording equipment (although independent transcription services are available). The UAE also has a fully developed domestic legal services industry. Almost all the major international law firms have a presence in the UAE and there is a large pool of experienced arbitrators resident in the country. **5.139**

5.12.2 Drafting DIFC arbitral clauses and the meaning of 'Dubai'

The fact that the DIFC is a jurisdiction within Dubai has created an ambiguity as to the meaning of 'Dubai' and whether, when used in an arbitration clause, it refers simply to Dubai or includes the DIFC. **5.140**

In the case of *Dhir*, the arbitration clause stated that the arbitration was to be administered by the DIFC-LCIA and that the arbitration was to take place in the Emirate of Dubai. The claimant attempted to argue that this was not a reference to the seat but merely to the physical location of any hearings, and therefore the DIFC should be the seat as dictated by article 16.1 of the DIFC-LCIA Rules (which states that in the absence of agreement the seat shall be the DIFC). This was, however, firmly rejected by Michael Hwang DCJ, who was satisfied that the Emirate of Dubai was agreed by the parties as the seat. Since, among other things, the dispute had no connection to the DIFC (other than the use of the DIFC-LCIA) and had strong connections with Dubai, he inferred that the intention of the parties was for the seat to be Dubai and not the DIFC. He commented that 'the DIFC is within the Emirate of Dubai but the two terms are clearly not synonymous or interchangeable'[114] since they have different laws. He warned that 'the moral of this case is that, if parties want the DIFC **5.141**

[114] *Dhir v Waterfront Property Investment Ltd* CFI 011/2009 [2006-09] DIFC CLR 12 (Judicial Authority of the Dubai International Finance Centre, Court of First Instance), para 87.

Arbitration Law to apply and the DIFC Court to have jurisdiction over an arbitration, they should expressly select the DIFC as the seat in the arbitration agreement'.[115]

5.142 This seemed to make clear that a reference to Dubai was not to the DIFC, a position affirmed in the case of *Hardt v Damac (DIFC)*,[116] in which it was held that the natural and ordinary meaning of 'Courts of Dubai' was the courts of non-DIFC Dubai. However, in *National Bonds Corporation PJSC v Taaleem PJSC*,[117] the Court of Appeal held that the meaning of 'Dubai' depended on the circumstances, so that although the parties agreed to the 'Courts of Dubai', this was a vague term that incorporated both the DIFC courts and the non-DIFC Dubai courts. The court would therefore have to look to the intention of the parties and the circumstances to determine what was meant. In the circumstances of that particular case, which related to a property in the DIFC and the regulation of interests under a trust (a concept which does not exist under Dubai law), the phrase 'Courts of Dubai' was found to mean 'Courts of DIFC'.[118]

5.143 When preparing arbitral clauses therefore, practitioners must make absolutely clear that the DIFC is the seat, and avoid any reference to Dubai or the UAE. This will minimize the risk of the DIFC courts refusing jurisdiction. A possible phrasing would be: 'The seat or legal place of the arbitration will be the Dubai International Financial Centre.'

5.13 Conclusion

5.144 The DIFC provides a good, if relatively untested, seat for arbitration. It has a comprehensive and modern Model Law-based arbitration law, and an efficient and pro-arbitration English language court system to act as the curial court. It has a developed legal services industry and quality amenities to cater for hearings. Although the method of enforcing DIFC awards has been a subject for debate, in the past few years this debate has subsided. DIFC awards have been enforced within the UAE and should be readily enforceable outside the DIFC pursuant to the New York Convention. The DIFC also benefits from being covered by the GCC and Riyadh Conventions, meaning that the awards of arbitrations seated in the DIFC are enforceable in a number of states that are not signatories to the New York Convention.

---

[115] *Dhir* (n 113) para 92.

[116] *Hardt v Damac (DIFC) Co Ltd* CFI 036/2009 (Judicial Authority of the Dubai International Financial Centre, Court of First Instance).

[117] *National Bonds Corp PJSC v Taaleem PJSC* CA 001/2011 (Dubai International Finance Centre Courts, Court of Appeal).

[118] *National Bonds Corp* (n 116).

6

DUBLIN

Klaus Reichert

6.1 Background

6.1.1 History and development of arbitration

The history and development of arbitration in Ireland mirrors, in many respects, the history of the country. The long and sometimes complex relationship with England has left its mark on the Irish legal system in general and on arbitration in particular. **6.01**

The use of arbitration to resolve disputes has a long and sometimes picturesque history in Ireland. Until the seventeenth century, much of Ireland was subject to the native Brehon laws with the 'Pale' (Dublin and its surrounding hinterland) subject to the common law. Brehon law was administered by Brehons (or *brithem*). They were the successors to Celtic druids and, while similar to judges, their role was closer to that of an arbitrator. From the early seventeenth century, Brehon law was completely supplanted by the common law throughout Ireland. **6.02**

6.03 In 1698, arbitration law in Ireland swung decidedly towards England with the passing of An Act for Determining Differences by Arbitration.[1] That Act provided, in colourful terms:

> ... itt shall and may be lawfull for all Merchants and Traders & others desiring to end any Controversie Suit or Quarrel Controversies Suits or Quarrels (for which there is no Remedy but by Personal Action or Suit in Equity) by Arbitration to agree that their Submission of their Suit to the Award or Umpirage of any person or persons should be made a Rule of any of His Majesties Courts of Record which the Parties shall choose and to insert such their Agreement in their Submission...

6.04 In the eighteenth century, an arbitration body established in Dublin—the Ouzel Galley Society—had a short but successful and agreeable life (it was famed for its entertainment). The society resolved commercial disputes and its arbitrators comprised men such as Arthur Guinness and John Jameson, whose commercial exploits and products resonate to this day.[2]

6.05 The 1698 statute remained in place until 1954, when it was repealed by the Arbitration Act of that year. By that time, Ireland was no longer in the United Kingdom, but it still drew heavily upon English statutes as a template for much of its legislative activity. So it was with the Arbitration Act 1954, which was all but identical to the English Arbitration Act 1950. Until 1998, Irish arbitration law and practice continued to substantially reflect English law, with reliance on English case law and texts, particularly that of Mustill and Boyd.

6.1.2 Modern and recent developments

6.06 With the adoption of the Arbitration Act 1980, the New York and Washington Conventions became part of Irish law, but in terms of the ordinary practice and law of arbitration, the close tracking of the law in England continued, save in one respect: Ireland did not pass a law similar to England's Arbitration Act 1979, as it was generally felt that the 'case stated' procedure under the 1954 Act was operating satisfactorily. The 'case stated' procedure allowed an arbitrator to refer a question of law to the courts for resolution, and also allowed a party to apply to the courts to compel an arbitrator to make such a reference.

6.07 One of the strongest and most famous (among Irish practitioners) statements of support from the uppermost ranks of the judiciary came from Mr Justice McCarthy when he set the tone for the correct judicial approach to arbitral awards under the 1954 Act in *Keenan v Shield Insurance Company Ltd*:

> Arbitration is a significant feature of modern commercial life; there is an International Institute of Arbitration and the field of international arbitration is an ever expanding one. It ill becomes the courts to show any readiness to interfere in such a process; if policy considerations are appropriate as I believe they are in a matter of this kind, then every such consideration points to the desirability of making an arbitration award final in every sense of the term. *Church v Connolly*... itself is an example of the type of fine-combing exercise which courts should not perform when it is sought to review an arbitration award.[3]

6.08 In 1998, Ireland took the first of two decisive swings away from the preceding three hundred years of closely tracking English arbitration law, with the passing of the Arbitration (International Commercial) Act. This act prescribed the UNCITRAL Model Law on

---

1 Statutes of the Realm: Vol 7, 367–70.

2 <http://www.irishtimes.com/newspaper/features/2005/1101/1130406921448.html>.

3 *Keenan v Shield Insurance Co Ltd* [1988] IR 89, 96.

International Commercial Arbitration (1985 version) for all international arbitration taking place in Ireland. Domestic arbitration continued to be governed by the Arbitration Act 1954. This distinction did, however, give rise to occasional boundary disputes as to which Act governed a particular case.[4]

Finally, the Arbitration Act 2010 (hereinafter 'the Act') swept all previous arbitration laws away, and the UNCITRAL Model Law (2006 version) (hereinafter 'the Model Law') was adopted for all arbitrations taking place in Ireland, without distinction between domestic and international actions. English cases and textbooks[5] continue to be relied upon but only on issues where that country's Arbitration Act 1996 and the Model Law are similarly framed. Case law from other Model Law jurisdictions (Canada, Australia, and New Zealand in particular) is now regularly cited in arbitration applications before the Irish courts. **6.09**

The Act has a simple structure; there is a short series of sections that give force of law in Ireland to the Model Law and also continue in force, among others, the New York and Washington Conventions. The Act makes some very minor changes and additions to the Model Law.[6] **6.10**

6.1.3 Comparison with other regional or national venues

Ireland is unique in being an independent common law jurisdiction in Europe, faithfully adopting the Model Law for all arbitration conducted within its borders. **6.11**

6.2 Commencing the Arbitration

6.2.1 Stay of litigation

The Act is quite clear as regards the law on stay applications before the Irish courts when there is an arbitration agreement: the orthodox and international standard found in either Article II of the New York Convention or Article 8 of the Model Law applies without any variation. Either can be invoked by a party seeking a stay of litigation, however, in practice, since the passing of the Act the normal and usual approach is to rely upon Article 8 of the Model Law: **6.12**

> Article 8. Arbitration agreement and substantive claim before court
> (1) A court before which an action is brought in a matter which is the subject of an arbitration agreement shall, if a party so requests not later than when submitting his first statement on the substance of the dispute, refer the parties to arbitration unless it finds that the agreement is null and void, inoperative or incapable of being performed.
> (2) Where an action referred to in paragraph (1) of this article has been brought, arbitral proceedings may nevertheless be commenced or continued, and an award may be made, while the issue is pending before the court.

The other pertinent issue in such circumstances is what, as a matter of Irish law and the Act in particular, constitutes an 'arbitration agreement'. The definitions section of the Act **6.13**

[4] Occasionally in practice there were preliminary points disputed before the courts as to which Act applied to a particular case, with close attention being paid to the UNCITRAL Model Law, Art 1, and whether or not the agreement or the parties were in fact 'international'.

[5] A new text on the Act has rapidly become the *vade mecum* of all practitioners in Ireland working in the field of arbitration. B Mansfield, *Arbitration Act 2010 and Model Law: A Commentary* (Clarus Press, 2012).

[6] For completeness, there is a short annex to this chapter outlining those variations.

(section 2) requires the term 'arbitration agreement' to be construed in accordance with option 1 of Article 7 of the Model Law. Option 1 provides:

> Article 7. Definition and form of arbitration agreement
> (1) 'Arbitration agreement' is an agreement by the parties to submit to arbitration all or certain disputes which have arisen or which may arise between them in respect of a defined legal relationship, whether contractual or not. An arbitration agreement may be in the form of an arbitration clause in a contract or in the form of a separate agreement.
> (2) The arbitration agreement shall be in writing.
> (3) An arbitration agreement is in writing if its content is recorded in any form, whether or not the arbitration agreement or contract has been concluded orally, by conduct, or by other means.
> (4) The requirement that an arbitration agreement be in writing is met by an electronic communication if the information contained therein is accessible so as to be useable for subsequent reference; 'electronic communication' means any communication that the parties make by means of data messages; 'data message' means information generated, sent, received or stored by electronic, magnetic, optical or similar means, including, but not limited to, electronic data interchange (EDI), electronic mail, telegram, telex, or telecopy.
> (5) Furthermore, an arbitration agreement is in writing if it is contained in an exchange of statements of claim and defence in which the existence of an agreement is alleged by one party and not denied by the other.
> (6) The reference in a contract to any document containing an arbitration clause constitutes an arbitration agreement in writing, provided that the reference is such as to make that clause part of the contract.

Option 1 is drawn in wide terms and eliminates debate as to whether electronic communications can constitute 'in writing'.

6.14 Stay applications are, in the main, routine matters before the Irish courts and are dealt with fairly readily (and usually rapidly) by means of a two-stage process: first, a written application requesting a stay is filed with the court backed up by an affidavit exhibiting the relevant agreement (there may then be further exchanges of affidavit evidence if the party that has commenced the litigation wishes to contest the matter or the evidence filed); second, there is an oral argument phase before the court. In practice, stay applications tend to be quite short as there is usually little real debate as to whether or not there is an arbitration agreement; once the arbitration agreement has been put before the court and it appears to cover the matters at issue in the litigation, a stay is mandatory. This is neither surprising nor indeed particularly unusual for any well-developed legal system that has adopted the Model Law (or has similar principles in its arbitration regime).

6.15 A feature of the Act in relation to stay applications is that there is no appeal from any determination of the court:

> [Section]11.—There shall be no appeal from—
> (a) any court determination of a stay application, pursuant to Article 8(1) of the Model Law or Article II(3) of the New York Convention

This means that the delay inherent in any appeal process, regardless of how efficient appellate courts might be, is simply not a factor in Ireland.

6.16 Perhaps the more interesting question relates to the situation in which the party that brings the litigation decides to put up a spirited fight against the stay application. These fall into two broad theoretical categories: (a) that there is, in fact, no arbitration agreement in place between the parties; or (b) that the arbitration agreement is null and void, inoperative, or incapable of being performed.

Barnmore Demolition *case*

The first of these categories was the subject of one of the first cases heard and decided under the Act. The High Court considered the appropriate standard of review to be applied when determining whether or not a party that has commenced litigation is a party to an arbitration agreement for the purposes of Article 8 of the Model Law.[7] **6.17**

In *Barnmore Demolition and Civil Engineering Ltd v Alandale Logistics Ltd and ors*,[8] Mr Justice Feeney had to decide an application brought by two of the defendants to stay the litigation pursuant to Article 8 of the Model Law. **6.18**

The defendants bringing the application to stay the proceedings alleged that there was an arbitration agreement in place between the parties. The plaintiff's position was that there was no such agreement in existence. The issue canvassed by the parties before the High Court was whether there should be either a full trial or investigation by the judge on whether there was such an agreement (which is comparable to the English position) or whether the court should conduct a *prima facie* review. **6.19**

The factual background to the case stemmed from works carried out at the new terminal at Dublin Airport. The judgment refers to a thicket of correspondence back and forth about contractual entities, incomplete forms of contract, who was paying whom, conditions, authority, and alleged ratification, among other matters. **6.20**

At the outset, the judgment discussed the concept of the separability of arbitration agreements, which is found in Article 8, Option 1 of the Model Law. The House of Lords decision in *Lesotho Highlands Development Authority v Impregilo SpA and ors*[9] in that regard, with its famous passage on separability,[10] was described as being equally applicable to the position in Ireland. **6.21**

Mr Justice Feeney then examined the provisions of the Model Law in Article 16 concerning *competence-competence*, which brought him to the core issue in the application before him: **6.22**

> The entitlement of both the Court and the arbitral tribunal to rule on the existence of an arbitration agreement has given rise to extensive discourse. In light of the fact that both a court and the arbitral tribunal have jurisdiction to consider and rule on the existence of an arbitration agreement the issue arises as to the standard of judicial review which should be applied by the Court in exercising its jurisdiction on this matter under the Model law. This matter is summarized in the textbook by Gary B. Born entitled *International Commercial Arbitration* at Chapter 6, p. 881, where he deals with the issue of prima facie versus full judicial consideration of interlocutory jurisdictional challenges under the Model Law.

[7] Discussed by G Born at <http://kluwerarbitrationblog.com/blog/2010/12/13/irish-high-court-on-full-versus-prima-facie-judicial-consideration-of-whether-an-arbitration-agreement-exists>.

[8] *Barnmore Demolition and Civil Engineering Ltd v Alandale Logistics Ltd and ors* [2010] No 5910P (11 November 2010).

[9] *Lesotho Highlands Development Authority v Impregilo SpA and ors* [2005] UKHL 43 (30 June 2005).

[10] 'It is part of the very alphabet of arbitration law, as explained in *Harbour Assurance Co (UK) Ltd v Kansa General International Insurance Co Ltd* [1993] QB 701, 724–725, per Hoffmann LJ (now Lord Hoffmann) and spelled out in section 7 of the Act, that the arbitration agreement is a distinct and separable agreement from the underlying or principal contract.' *Lesotho Highlands* (n 9) opinion of Lord Steyn.

6.23 Mr Justice Feeney went on to quote Born:

> When a party seeks an interlocutory judicial determination of jurisdictional objections, prior to any arbitral award on the subject, there is uncertainty regarding the standard of judicial review that should be applied by a court under the Model Law. As discussed here, the text of the Model Law, and many judicial authorities, strongly suggest that full judicial review of the jurisdictional objection is appropriate, at least in some circumstances. In contrast, as also discussed here, some judicial authority, and some aspects of the Model Law's drafting history, suggest that only *prima facie* interlocutory judicial consideration is ever appropriate.

6.24 Ultimately Mr Justice Feeney did not have to decide between the two approaches as, following a careful analysis, he found that even on a *prima facie* standard the defendants did not succeed in showing that there was an arbitration agreement in place between the parties. He took, by way of example, on the *prima facie* standard, the legal test applied by Irish courts in deciding whether an application to summarily dismiss a case at the conclusion of a plaintiff's case:[11]

> ... whether assuming that the tribunal of fact was prepared to find that all the evidence of the plaintiff was true, and in other words treating the plaintiff's case at its highest, whether in those circumstances the tribunal of fact would be entitled to arrive at the conclusion that making those assumptions ... the defendant had a case to meet.[12]

The stay was refused and the litigation continued.

6.25 The issue, therefore, as to the standard of judicial review under a contested application pursuant to Article 8(1) of the Model Law remains to be determined as a matter of Irish law. The sense one gets from this decision is that the views of Born in favour of a full judicial review may well carry the day if the matter arises in the future. However, the approach of a full judicial review in all circumstances does have its powerful critics, most notably David Joseph QC.[13] Joseph advocates a more nuanced approach whereby the difference should be recognized between a stay in respect of an arbitration agreement subject to the same law as that of the court, and a stay in respect of an arbitration agreement subject to a different law (ie an overseas seat).[14]

6.26 This seems to reflect an approach that would be more sensitive to the wide diversity of international standards for the conclusion of arbitration agreements. It is hoped the High Court will adopt it in future.

6.27 For present purposes, Mr Justice Feeney's decision has interesting features, particularly given that it is one of the very first decisions of the High Court under the Act. It demonstrates a very high degree of receptiveness to leading international authority (Born and *Lesotho Highlands*), and was rendered expeditiously: oral arguments concluded on 4 November 2010, and only seven days later Mr Justice Feeney rendered a detailed judgment.

Stay based on invalidity of arbitration agreement

6.28 The second avenue for the enthusiastic litigant seeking to resist a stay is to attempt to demonstrate that the arbitration agreement is null and void, inoperative, or incapable of being

[11] This standard does *not* apply to arbitrators. There is no reference in the Act to summary dismissal; this was an approach used by Mr Justice Feeney for the purpose of the Model Law, Art 8.

[12] *Barnmore Demolition* (n 8) para 16, quoting Keane CJ in *O'Donovan v The Southern Health Board* [2001] 3 IR 385, 386.

[13] D Joseph, *Jurisdiction and Arbitration Agreements and Their Enforcement* (2nd edn, Sweet & Maxwell, 2010).

[14] Joseph (n 13).

performed. These grounds have not been the subject of judicial scrutiny in Ireland under the Act, however, as was the case in *Barnmore Demolition*, it is perhaps overwhelmingly likely that the Irish courts would follow case law from other Model Law jurisdictions (particularly common law jurisdictions) on the issue; equally possible would be the path of following case law (again from common law jurisdictions) on the same phraseology as that in Article II(3) of the New York Convention.

In summary, the Irish Courts adopt an orthodox and straightforward approach to the staying of litigation commenced notwithstanding the presence of an arbitration agreement. **6.29**

6.2.2 Judicial assistance in constituting the arbitral tribunal

If the parties cannot agree on the arbitrator and do not make provision for a default mechanism (such as by means of an agreed procedure under institutional rules), the default appointing authority is the High Court. The court will exercise its powers pursuant to Article 11 of the Model Law if the relevant circumstances set out in that article have been triggered. The decision of the High Court appointing an arbitrator is not subject to appeal, although the court is obliged by Article 11(5) of the Model Law to have regard to any qualifications required of the arbitrator by the parties' agreement, and to such considerations as are likely to secure the appointment of an independent and impartial arbitrator, including the advisability of appointing arbitrators of a nationality different from that of any of the parties. **6.30**

In practice, it is not particularly usual for the High Court to make appointments, as most arbitration agreements in the Irish context have a default appointing authority provided for, whether through one of the major institutions (the ICC being the most common international arbitration institution) or through local bodies (such as the Law Society or Bar Council). However, when the High Court is called upon to make such an appointment, this is usually done without difficulty or delay. By way of example from relatively early in the life of the Act, an application was made to appoint an arbitrator in the matter of *Munster Football Club Ltd v Football Association of Ireland*,[15] and the relevant papers to commence the arbitration application to the High Court were filed on 18 January 2011. The application was given a date before the High Court on 31 January 2011 and on that date an order was made appointing a former Chair of the Bar Council of Ireland as arbitrator. **6.31**

6.2.3 Role of court in resolving jurisdictional questions

The Model Law strikes a particular balance as to the sequence for the resolution of jurisdictional questions: **6.32**

> Article 16. Competence of arbitral tribunal to rule on its jurisdiction
> (1) The arbitral tribunal may rule on its own jurisdiction, including any objections with respect to the existence or validity of the arbitration agreement. For that purpose, an arbitration clause which forms part of a contract shall be treated as an agreement independent of the other terms of the contract. A decision by the arbitral tribunal that the contract is null and void shall not entail *ipso jure* the invalidity of the arbitration clause.
> (2) A plea that the arbitral tribunal does not have jurisdiction shall be raised not later than the submission of the statement of defence. A party is not precluded from raising such a plea by

[15] The underlying dispute between the applicant, with the corporate name of Limerick City FC—a football club in that city—and the governing body of football in Ireland, the respondent, was widely reported in the Irish media at the time and involved a proposed friendly match between the applicant and FC Barcelona. There was no written judgment of the High Court. The author was counsel for Limerick City FC.

the fact that he has appointed, or participated in the appointment of, an arbitrator. A plea that the arbitral tribunal is exceeding the scope of its authority shall be raised as soon as the matter alleged to be beyond the scope of its authority is raised during the arbitral proceedings. The arbitral tribunal may, in either case, admit a later plea if it considers the delay justified.

(3) The arbitral tribunal may rule on a plea referred to in paragraph (2) of this article either as a preliminary question or in an award on the merits. If the arbitral tribunal rules as a preliminary question that it has jurisdiction, any party may request, within thirty days after having received notice of that ruling, the court specified in article 6 to decide the matter, which decision shall be subject to no appeal; while such a request is pending, the arbitral tribunal may continue the arbitral proceedings and make an award.

6.33 In the most straightforward of situations, the party seeking to challenge jurisdiction does so before the arbitral tribunal and then, if it chooses to do so (when it has been unsuccessful), it can bring an application to the High Court for a final decision. This is the structure of the Model Law and informs the approach normally taken.

6.34 Complications might arise, as foreshadowed by the *Barnmore Demolition* case, when a party brings litigation and then meets a stay application with the 'I never bargained for arbitration' argument. That argument is then, in turn, countered with 'you can run that jurisdictional objection before the arbitrators as is your right under Article 16'.

6.35 It cannot yet be said where the High Court will ultimately draw the line as between a full judicial review or *prima facie* review in determining the existence of an arbitration agreement. However, the *Barnmore Demolition* case does indicate that the mere assertion of the existence of an arbitration agreement will not be sufficient to persuade the courts to pass the jurisdictional baton to the arbitral tribunal.

6.36 A subsidiary question concerns the nature and extent of the judicial review to be undertaken by the High Court when called upon to decide a jurisdictional question under Article 16(3) of the Model Law after a determination by the arbitral tribunal. There is presently no case law that offers guidance as to the type of judicial exercise the High Court would conduct if called upon to make a ruling on a tribunal's substantive jurisdiction or the scope of its authority. Since the Act provides that all applications thereunder are to be dealt with by way of summary procedure,[16] it is unlikely that the High Court would direct a full trial with oral examination of witnesses. Although it would of course be free to reach its own conclusion, the High Court may be assisted by the tribunal's findings on the issue, and in practice a well-reasoned decision by the tribunal is likely to carry significant persuasive weight.

6.2.4 Role of court in enjoining arbitration

6.37 The issue of the court enjoining arbitration has never arisen in Ireland as far as the author's research has been able to ascertain. It also seems a remote prospect given the provisions of Article 5 of the Model Law, which limits court intervention to the situations expressly provided for in the Model Law.[17]

---

[16] All High Court applications under the Act are made by summary procedure as per s 9(3). Summary proceedings in the High Court are dealt with by means of oral argument based on affidavit evidence only (and any documentary exhibits to such affidavits) and live witness testimony is not usually presented. The procedural rules of the High Court under the Act (Order 56 of the Rules of the Superior Courts) set out a clear and robust timetable for the filing of affidavits and the speedy disposition of applications.

[17] Model Law, Art 5. 'Extent of court intervention: In matters governed by this Law, no court shall intervene except where so provided in this Law.'

6.2.5 Interim measures

The Act has adopted the Model Law's provisions on interim measures in full. Thus, its provisions on interim measures, preliminary orders, and the recognition and enforcement thereof,[18] are available to arbitral tribunals sitting in Ireland. As regards the obtaining of interim measures from the High Court, the Model Law's provisions[19] in that respect apply and allow for relief to be obtained in respect of an arbitration regardless of where it is located. **6.38**

6.3 During the Arbitration

6.3.1 Role of courts in ruling on challenges to arbitrators

The standard Model Law role for the courts in relation to challenges to arbitrators applies in Ireland without any variation or change. For ease of reference the relevant articles of the Model Law are set out in full: **6.39**

> Article 12. Grounds for challenge
>
> (1) When a person is approached in connection with his possible appointment as an arbitrator, he shall disclose any circumstances likely to give rise to justifiable doubts as to his impartiality or independence. An arbitrator, from the time of his appointment and throughout the arbitral proceedings, shall without delay disclose any such circumstances to the parties unless they have already been informed of them by him.
>
> (2) An arbitrator may be challenged only if circumstances exist that give rise to justifiable doubts as to his impartiality or independence, or if he does not possess qualifications agreed to by the parties. A party may challenge an arbitrator appointed by him, or in whose appointment he has participated, only for reasons of which he becomes aware after the appointment has been made.
>
> Article 13. Challenge procedure
>
> (1) The parties are free to agree on a procedure for challenging an arbitrator, subject to the provisions of paragraph (3) of this article.
>
> (2) Failing such agreement, a party who intends to challenge an arbitrator shall, within fifteen days after becoming aware of the constitution of the arbitral tribunal or after becoming aware of any circumstance referred to in article 12(2), send a written statement of the reasons for the challenge to the arbitral tribunal. Unless the challenged arbitrator withdraws from his office or the other party agrees to the challenge, the arbitral tribunal shall decide on the challenge.
>
> (3) *If a challenge under any procedure agreed upon by the parties or under the procedure of paragraph (2) of this article is not successful, the challenging party may request, within thirty days after having received notice of the decision rejecting the challenge, the court or other authority specified in article 6 [the High Court] to decide on the challenge, which decision shall be subject to no appeal*; while such a request is pending, the arbitral tribunal, including the challenged arbitrator, may continue the arbitral proceedings and make an award. [Emphasis added.]
>
> Article 14. Failure or impossibility to act
>
> (1) If an arbitrator becomes de jure or de facto unable to perform his functions or for other reasons fails to act without undue delay, his mandate terminates if he withdraws from his office or if the parties agree on the termination. Otherwise, *if a controversy remains*

[18] Arbitration Act, Ch IVA.

[19] Model Law, Art 17J. 'Court-ordered interim measures: A court shall have the same power of issuing an interim measure in relation to arbitration proceedings, irrespective of whether their place is in the territory of this State, as it has in relation to proceedings in courts. The court shall exercise such power in accordance with its own procedures in consideration of the specific features of international arbitration.'

concerning any of these grounds, any party may request the court or other authority *specified in article 6 [the High Court] to decide on the termination of the mandate, which decision shall be subject to no appeal.* [Emphasis added.]

(2) If, under this article or article 13(2), an arbitrator withdraws from his office or a party agrees to the termination of the mandate of an arbitrator, this does not imply acceptance of the validity of any ground referred to in this article or article 12(2).

6.40 There has been no reported case in Ireland under these articles; however, as with all other aspects of the Act, the High Court can have regard to the *travaux préparatoires* in interpreting the Act. It is likely that the High Court would also have regard to decided cases in other common law Model Law jurisdictions or to guidelines such as those promulgated by the International Bar Association (IBA).[20]

6.3.2 Role of courts in compelling testimony and evidence

6.41 The Act strikes a rigorous note in regard to the powers of the High Court to compel testimony or evidence.

6.42 First, one looks to Article 27 of the Model Law:

> The arbitral tribunal or a party with the approval of the arbitral tribunal may request from a competent court of this State assistance in taking evidence. The court may execute the request within its competence and according to its rules on taking evidence.

6.43 Second, one looks to section 10 of the Act:

(1) Subject to subsection (2), the High Court shall have the same powers in relation to Articles 9 and 27 as it has in any other action or matter before the Court.

(2) When exercising any powers in relation to Articles 9 or 27, the High Court shall not, unless otherwise agreed by the parties, make any order relating to security for costs of the arbitration or make any order for discovery of documents.

6.44 The combination of these two provisions makes it clear that in Ireland there is no room for applications to the High Court on evidentiary matters, save with the express permission of the arbitral tribunal. It is also clear that the obtaining or discovery of documents via the High Court is only possible with the consent of the parties. This combination also ensures that the arbitral tribunal remains in full control of the evidence-taking in any arbitration.

6.45 In section 15 of the Act, there is an interesting extension of the scope of Article 27: 'The reference in Article 27 to an arbitral tribunal includes a reference to an arbitral tribunal conducting arbitral proceedings in a place other than the State.' This means that, subject to the gateway provisions of Article 27 being satisfied (namely the approval of the arbitral tribunal wherever seated), the High Court will be able to assist with evidence-taking in Ireland in aid of a foreign arbitration.

6.46 Assuming that the permission of the arbitral tribunal is forthcoming, the question arises in practice as to what evidence is actually compellable via the High Court.

6.47 As already noted, if the parties do not agree among themselves that discovery of documentation is permissible through the High Court, then the court has no jurisdiction to make such orders. If, on the other hand, the parties agree that the High Court can make discovery

[20] <http://www.ibanet.org/LPD/Dispute_Resolution_Section/Arbitration/Projects.aspx#guidelines>.

orders and they persuade the arbitral tribunal to give them permission to apply (by means of Article 27), the Irish procedural law standard on discovery will apply. There is a two-fold requirement, relevance and necessity.[21]

Relevance is determined by the following test: **6.48**

> It seems to me that every document relates to the matters in question in the action, which not only would be evidence upon any issue, but also which, it is reasonable to suppose, contains information which may—not which must—either directly or indirectly enable the party requiring the affidavit either to advance his own case or to damage the case of his adversary. I have put in the words 'either directly or indirectly,' because, as it seems to me, a document can properly be said to contain information which may enable the party requiring the affidavit either to advance his own case or to damage the case of his adversary, if it is a document which may fairly lead him to a train of inquiry.[22]

Necessity is determined by the following test: **6.49**

> The crucial consideration is, in my judgment, the meaning of the expression 'disposing fairly of the cause or matter'. Those words direct attention to the question whether inspection is necessary for the fair determination of the matter, whether by trial or otherwise. The purpose of the rule is to ensure that one party does not enjoy an unfair advantage or suffer an unfair disadvantage in the litigation as a result of a document not being produced for inspection. It is, I think, of no importance that a party is curious about the contents of a document or would like to know the contents of it if he suffers no litigious disadvantage by not seeing it and would gain no litigious advantage by seeing it. That, in my judgment, is the test.[23]

This is similar to the traditional test for discovery in England. Any party agreeing to empower **6.50** the High Court to make discovery orders in aid of an arbitration should do so with knowledge of the foregoing tests. A further matter to consider is that the High Court requires full compliance with its discovery orders and any breach will render the party concerned liable to attachment and committal for contempt.

In the absence of a party agreement in relation to discovery, the power of the High Court **6.51** most commonly invoked is aimed at obtaining oral testimony of a witness. The closest analogy in Irish law is the power of the High Court to execute a Letter of Request from a foreign court seeking to obtain the evidence of a witness within the jurisdiction. This power is not a vehicle for obtaining documents in the possession of a witness. The High Court is quite alert to attempts to obtain discovery from custodians of documents who have, in fact, no personal knowledge of the matters in issue in the foreign litigation.[24] The orders that are usually made are to direct the presence of a witness who has personal knowledge of the matters in issue in the underlying litigation (or arbitration) to attend before an officer of the court (or person designated in that regard) to give their oral testimony. The only documents that person needs to produce during the course of their testimony are those they have in their possession and which touch upon their testimony. This is a restriction that often catches parties used to broad court discovery unaware.

---

21 *Ryanair plc v Aer Rianta Cpt* [2003] IESC 62 (2 December 2003).

22 *Ryanair* (n 21).

23 *Ryanair* (n 21).

24 *Sabretech Inc v Shannon Aerospace Ltd* [1999] IEHC 234 (1 July 1999).

6.3.3 Ability of foreign practitioners to appear as counsel or arbitrator

6.52 There are no restrictions imposed by the Act or the local bar. Foreign practitioners frequently sit as arbitrators and appear as counsel in Dublin-based arbitrations.

6.3.4 Local requirements for the conduct of arbitration hearings

6.53 There are no procedural requirements or restrictions imposed by the Act. All that is necessary is that Chapter V of the Model Law is followed with, by way of pertinent example, the basic requirements of equal treatment.[25]

6.4 The Award

6.4.1 Mandatory rules as to form

6.54 The Act does not add to or subtract from the Model Law in relation to the form of the award:

> Article 31. Form and contents of award
> (1) The award shall be made in writing and shall be signed by the arbitrator or arbitrators. In arbitral proceedings with more than one arbitrator, the signatures of the majority of all members of the arbitral tribunal shall suffice, provided that the reason for any omitted signature is stated.
> (2) The award shall state the reasons upon which it is based, unless the parties have agreed that no reasons are to be given or the award is an award on agreed terms under article 30.
> (3) The award shall state its date and the place of arbitration as determined in accordance with article 20(1). The award shall be deemed to have been made at that place.
> (4) After the award is made, a copy signed by the arbitrators in accordance with paragraph (1) of this article shall be delivered to each party.

6.4.2 Mandatory rules as to substance (including cost-shifting, interest, etc)

6.55 In addition to the requirement in Article 31(2) of the Model Law that the award be reasoned, noted previously, the arbitral tribunal must follow the provisions of Article 28 as regards the substance:

> Article 28. Rules applicable to substance of dispute
> (1) The arbitral tribunal shall decide the dispute in accordance with such rules of law as are chosen by the parties as applicable to the substance of the dispute. Any designation of the law or legal system of a given State shall be construed, unless otherwise expressed, as directly referring to the substantive law of that State and not to its conflict of laws rules.
> (2) Failing any designation by the parties, the arbitral tribunal shall apply the law determined by the conflict of laws rules which it considers applicable.
> (3) The arbitral tribunal shall decide *ex aequo et bono* or as *amiable compositeur* only if the parties have expressly authorized it to do so.
> (4) In all cases, the arbitral tribunal shall decide in accordance with the terms of the contract and shall take into account the usages of the trade applicable to the transaction.

These articles have not been the subject of judicial scrutiny.

6.56 With regard to both costs and interest, the Act does not have any mandatory provisions and full support is given to party autonomy to agree such terms as they see fit. However, this

[25] Model Law, Art 18.

autonomy is likely to be subject to a public policy caveat as regards interest if the relevant provisions of the contract concerned lead to a penalty or an *in terrorem* clause. It is worth noting, particularly by way of contrast to section 60 of the English Arbitration Act 1996, that section 21(1) of the Act allows parties to agree in their arbitration agreement that regardless of the outcome of any case, each side will bear its own legal costs. This is a facility which parties from the United States may wish to bear in mind in particular given the historical favour in that country for such types of cost-allocation clauses.

6.5 After the Award

6.5.1 Local standards for setting aside/annulment

The sole grounds in Ireland by which an award *may* be set aside are those set out in Article 34 of the Model Law: **6.57**

> Article 34. Application for setting aside as exclusive recourse against arbitral award
> (1) Recourse to a court against an arbitral award may be made only by an application for setting aside in accordance with paragraphs (2) and (3) of this article.
> (2) An arbitral award may be set aside by the court specified in article 6 only if:
> (a) the party making the application furnishes proof that:
> (i) a party to the arbitration agreement referred to in article 7 was under some incapacity; or the said agreement is not valid under the law to which the parties have subjected it or, failing any indication thereon, under the law of this State; or
> (ii) the party making the application was not given proper notice of the appointment of an arbitrator or of the arbitral proceedings or was otherwise unable to present his case; or
> (iii) the award deals with a dispute not contemplated by or not falling within the terms of the submission to arbitration, or contains decisions on matters beyond the scope of the submission to arbitration, provided that, if the decisions on matters submitted to arbitration can be separated from those not so submitted, only that part of the award which contains decisions on matters not submitted to arbitration may be set aside; or
> (iv) the composition of the arbitral tribunal or the arbitral procedure was not in accordance with the agreement of the parties, unless such agreement was in conflict with a provision of this Law from which the parties cannot derogate, or, failing such agreement, was not in accordance with this Law; or
> (b) the court finds that:
> (i) the subject-matter of the dispute is not capable of settlement by arbitration under the law of this State; or
> (ii) the award is in conflict with the public policy of this State.
> (3) An application for setting aside may not be made after three months have elapsed from the date on which the party making that application had received the award or, if a request had been made under article 33, from the date on which that request had been disposed of by the arbitral tribunal.
> (4) The court, when asked to set aside an award, may, where appropriate and so requested by a party, suspend the setting aside proceedings for a period of time determined by it in order to give the arbitral tribunal an opportunity to resume the arbitral proceedings or to take such other action as in the arbitral tribunal's opinion will eliminate the grounds for setting aside.

6.58 The Act does make one slight change to article 34, but only in respect of the limitation period:

> 12.—Notwithstanding Article 34(3), an application to the High Court to set aside an award on the grounds that the award is in conflict with the public policy of the State shall be made within a period of 56 days from the date on which the circumstances giving rise to the application became known or ought reasonably to have become known to the party concerned.

6.59 These provisions of the Model Law have not been subject to judicial scrutiny. As suggested here, it is likely that international case law and the *travaux préparatoires* would significantly influence the approach of the High Court.

6.60 Some significant guidance can be gleaned from a decision of the High Court in relation to the public policy exception of the New York Convention (which is similar to the public policy ground in Article 34 of the Model Law). In *Broström Tankers AB v Factorias Vulcano SA*,[26] the public policy ground is very narrowly construed:

> I am satisfied that a broad interpretation such as is contended for by the defendant would defeat the Convention's purpose of permitting parties to international transactions to promote neutral dispute resolution. The issue is dealt with in this fashion in Redfern and Hunter under the heading 'Public Policy'. This is at Paragraph 10(46), and I quote:
>
> 'Recognition and enforcement of an arbitral award may also be refused if it is contrary to the public policy of the enforcement state. It is understandable that a state may wish to have the right to refuse to recognise and enforce an arbitration award that in some way offends the state's own notions of public policy. Yet, when reference is made to public policy, it is difficult not to recall the skeptical comment of the English judge who said more than a century ago:
>
> "'It is never argued at all but where other points fail.' Certainly, the national Courts in England are reluctant to excuse an award from enforcement on grounds of public policy. Indeed, according to one learned commentator:
>
> 'There is no case in which this exception has been applied by an English Court.'"
>
> Indeed, in most countries this pro-enforcement bias of the New York Convention has been faithfully observed.'
>
> I am of opinion that I would only be justified in refusing enforcement if there was, (as is stated Cheshire and North's Private International Law in the 13th Edition):
>
> 'Some element of illegality, or that the enforcement of the award would be clearly injurious to the public good, or possibly that enforcement would be wholly offensive to the ordinary responsible and fully informed member of the public.'

6.61 It would certainly appear from this judgment that the public policy exception under Article 34 of the Model Law would similarly be narrowly construed.

6.62 Further indication of the likely approach of the High Court under Article 34 of the Model Law can be found in *Kastrup Trea-Aluvinduet A/S v Aluwood Concepts Ltd*.[27] This case concerned the enforcement in Ireland under the New York Convention of an award of the Danish Arbitration Board for the Construction Industry. The losing party, Aluwood Concepts Ltd, resisted enforcement on the basis of alleged procedural irregularities. These arguments were

[26] *Broström Tankers AB v Factorias Vulcano SA* [2004] 2 IR 19 (19 May 2004).

[27] *Kastrup Trea-Aluvinduet A/S v Aluwood Concepts Ltd* [2009] IEHC 577 (13 November 2009).

dismissed, in trenchant terms, by the High Court, and the concluding paragraph of the judgment of Mr Justice MacMenamin is worthy of repetition in full:

> Finally, it is to be noted that there is an onus upon the party opposing enforcement to prove to the Court that it raised grounds upon which it resists enforcement at the earliest opportunity before the arbitral forum. (See the judgment of Colman J. in *Minmetals Germany Gmbh v. Ferco Steel Ltd* [1999] All E.R. (Comm.) 315). In this case the lateness of all the 'procedural' claims raised by the respondents before the Danish Arbitration Board speak for themselves. It was too late. The issue as to jurisdiction was raised at the eleventh minute of the eleventh hour on the evening prior to the arbitration itself. The point was devoid of merit. I would imagine the force of such a claim before the Arbitrator was in reverse ratio to its timeliness. The same observation is true here also. The respondent fails in its defences. The applicant is entitled to the relief it seeks.

The point to be made is that clever, after-the-fact lawyering will get short shrift from the High Court.

There is no standard of 'manifest disregard of the law' or review of the substance of the award. Either there is a route of challenge under Article 34 of the Model Law or there is not. Those who wish to have a wider possibility of challenging an arbitral award should not seat their arbitration in Ireland. **6.63**

6.5.2 Local procedures for setting aside/annulment

Order 56 of the Rules of the Superior Courts, headed 'Arbitration', sets out a rigorous timetable for the filing of evidence in any court application related to an arbitration. In particular, the following extract from order 56(6) is pertinent: **6.64**

> ...
>
> (2) Every originating notice of motion[28] shall be grounded upon an affidavit sworn by or on behalf of the moving party. Each such grounding affidavit shall set out the basis upon which the moving party alleges that the Court has jurisdiction to grant the relief sought in the notice of motion.
>
> (3) Copies of the originating notice of motion and of the grounding affidavit and of any exhibits thereto shall be served upon each respondent and, where required or directed under rule 2(1), shall be delivered to the arbitral tribunal, not later than fourteen days before the date fixed for the hearing of the said motion.
>
> (4) Any respondent may deliver a replying affidavit. Any such replying affidavit shall be filed in the Central Office and a copy served upon the applicant and upon every other respondent within seven days of the service by the applicant of the originating notice of motion and the applicant's grounding affidavit upon the said respondent.
>
> (5) Any replying affidavit shall set out concisely the grounds relied upon by the respondent to resist the applicant's claim for the reliefs set out in the originating notice of motion as against such respondent.
>
> (6) The applicant shall be at liberty to file a further affidavit replying to any matter raised by a respondent in a replying affidavit, which further affidavit shall be filed in the Central Office and a copy delivered to each respondent within seven days after the service upon the applicant of the respondent's replying affidavit.
>
> (7) An affidavit giving the names and addresses of, and the places and dates of service on, all persons who have been served with the originating notice of motion, grounding affidavit and exhibits (if any) shall be filed before the motion is heard. If any person who ought

[28] A notice of motion is the formal court document in which the relevant relief is sought.

under this Order to have been served has not been so served, the affidavit shall state that fact and the reason for it.

6.65 While there is no direct experience of the length of time required for an Article 34 challenge, the foregoing provisions of the High Court procedural rules make certain that the filing of evidence in support of such a challenge must be completed in very short order. The experience of the Irish Commercial Court (a division of the High Court dedicated to the rapid disposal of commercial litigation of substance) since its foundation in 2004 has pointed to complex cases being finally disposed of in a matter of a few months as opposed to years.

6.66 It is simply impossible to state with any degree of certainty what costs would be involved with a challenge to an award before the High Court. Ireland does not have significant court filing fees and the lodging of documents and affidavits with the High Court Central Office involves very modest charges. The principal costs involved are the legal costs of both sides, and there is a robust system of costs-follow-the-event as a matter of Irish law. Thus, a failed challenge will invariably result in the legal costs of both sides being borne by the loser.

6.6 Conclusion

6.67 There is an interesting conundrum facing every practitioner who is asked whether his jurisdiction is a good venue for international arbitration. Struggle as one might with the aim of being objective, there is unquestionably a sense of viewing one's home jurisdiction in a favourable light. The assessment of Ireland and its place in the world of arbitration can be taken from the foregoing discussion, but when it comes to a conclusion, the author shall defer to the following description:

A. Dublin
   1. Ireland is a party to the New York Convention.
   2. Ireland has just passed a new Arbitration Act (2010), which is a virtually pure form of the UNCITRAL Model Law. It provides for a dedicated arbitration judge in the High Court, and there is no appeal from the High Court on arbitration matters.
   3. Ireland has a high-quality, independent judicial system and a high-quality bar. The necessary facilities in the form of conference space, hotels, and restaurants in Dublin are ample and convenient.
   4. Dublin should be considered a low-cost alternative to London, with many of the same advantages, but at lower cost. It might serve as an alternative to London in a situation in which one party wants London but the other party, for whatever reason, resists London itself.[29]

Annex

The changes to the Model Law are as follows:

1. The default number of arbitrators is set at one rather than three—a change to Article 10(2).[30]

[29] Debevoise & Plimpton LLP, *Annotated Model Arbitration Clause for International Contracts* (New York, 2011) 68.

[30] Arbitration Act, s 13.

2. The reference in Article 27 of the Model Law (court assistance with the taking of evidence) is extended to include arbitrations with seats outside Ireland.[31]
3. Decisions of the High Court under the provisions of the Model Law are not subject to appeal to the Supreme Court.[32]
4. The time limit for the making of an application to set aside an award based upon a public policy argument per Article 34(3) of the Model Law shall be made within 56 days from the date on which the circumstances giving rise to the application became known or ought reasonably to have become known to the party concerned.[33]
5. Articles 35 and 36 of the Model Law do not apply in respect of an award rendered in Ireland.[34] Enforcement by the High Court of an award made in Ireland is pursuant to section 23(1) of the Act by means of a simple application which does not permit the raising of the various grounds in Article 36 by a defendant. This means that the potential for two bites at the cherry[35] by a recalcitrant defendant has been completely removed.

The *additions* to the Model Law are as follows:

1. The arbitral tribunal is empowered,[36] unless otherwise agreed by the parties, to administer an oath to a witness—but this is not a mandatory provision.
   Consolidation of arbitrations is permitted but only upon the consent of the parties.[37]
2. The parties can agree the powers of the arbitral tribunal to award interest; in default of such agreement there is a power to award simple or compound interest from the dates, at the rates, and with the rests which are considered fair and reasonable.[38]
3. The arbitral tribunal can (unless otherwise agreed by the parties) order a party to provide security for costs.[39]
4. The arbitral tribunal has (unless otherwise agreed by the parties) the power to make an award requiring specific performance of a contract (other than a contract for the sale of land).[40]
5. The parties are free to make such agreement as to the costs of the arbitration as they see fit whether before or after a dispute breaks out. In default of agreement on costs or in the absence of an agreed procedural power to award/withhold costs, the arbitral tribunal can determine by award those costs as it sees fit.[41]
6. There is a full and unqualified protection[42] from liability in respect of arbitrators[43] and arbitral institutions[44] for anything done or omitted in the discharge or purported discharge of their functions.

---

[31] Arbitration Act, s 15.

[32] Arbitration Act, s 11.

[33] Arbitration Act, s 12.

[34] Arbitration Act, s 23(4).

[35] First bite: a set aside application under the Model Law, Art 34; second bite, resisting enforcement under the same grounds again in Art 36. If a losing party sits on its hands and does not challenge an award under Art 34, it will be shut out from complaint when confronted with a High Court enforcement application.

[36] Arbitration Act, s 14.

[37] Arbitration Act, s 16.

[38] Arbitration Act, s 18.

[39] Arbitration Act, s 19.

[40] Arbitration Act, s 20.

[41] Arbitration Act, s 21. The form of an Arbitral Tribunal's determination is prescribed in s 21(5) and requires specification of the grounds, the items of recoverable costs, fees, or expenses, the amount referable to each and by and to whom they shall be paid.

[42] Arbitration Act, s 22.

[43] This includes an employee, agent, adviser, or tribunal-appointed expert.

[44] Arbitration Act, s 22(3).

7. An arbitration agreement or the authority of an arbitral tribunal is not discharged by the death of any party.[45]
8. In the event of the bankruptcy of a party there is a prescribed mechanism in order to allow the arbitration to move forward.[46]
9. The Act applies to an arbitration agreement under which a state authority is a party.[47]

There are some further provisions:

1. The Act carries on the pre-existing force of law in Ireland of the New York[48] and Washington[49] Conventions and the Geneva Protocol.[50]
2. When considering any application under the Model Law the High Court shall take judicial notice of the UNCITRAL *travaux préparatoires* and its working group relating to the preparation of the Model Law.[51]
3. The Act appoints[52] the president[53] of the High Court (or such judge of the High Court as may be appointed by the president) to deal with all applications[54] under the Model Law, save for stay applications.
4. Unless otherwise agreed by the parties, the Act specifically prohibits[55] the High Court from ordering the discovery of documentation or security for costs when exercising its powers under article 9 or 27 of the Model Law.
5. The Act does not apply to an arbitration under an agreement providing for the resolution of any question relating to the terms or conditions of employment or the remuneration of any employees.[56]

---

[45] Arbitration Act, s 26.

[46] Arbitration Act, s 27:

(1) Where an arbitration agreement forms part of a contract to which a bankrupt is a party, the agreement shall, if the assignee or trustee in bankruptcy does not disclaim the contract, be enforceable by or against him or her insofar as it relates to any dispute arising out of, or in connection with, such a contract.

(2) Where—(*a*) a person who has been adjudicated bankrupt had, before the commencement of the bankruptcy, become a party to an arbitration agreement, and (*b*) any matter to which the agreement applies requires to be determined in connection with or for the purposes of the bankruptcy proceedings, and (*c*) the case is one to which *subsection (1)* does not apply, then, any other party to the agreement or the assignee or, with the consent of the committee of inspection, the trustee in bankruptcy, may apply to the court having jurisdiction in the bankruptcy proceedings for an order directing that the matter in question shall be referred to arbitration in accordance with the agreement and that court may, if it is of the opinion that having regard to all the circumstances of the case, the matter ought to be determined by arbitration, make an order accordingly.

(3) In this section 'assignee' means the Official Assignee in Bankruptcy.

[47] Arbitration Act, s 28.

[48] Reproduced in full in the Arbitration Act, Sch 2.

[49] Reproduced in full in the Arbitration Act, Sch 3.

[50] Reproduced in full in the Arbitration Act, Sch 4.

[51] Arbitration Act, s 8.

[52] Arbitration Act, s 9(2).

[53] The most senior judge of the Irish High Court and second only to the chief justice in the judicial hierarchy.

[54] All applications are to be made in a summary fashion (Arbitration Act, s 9(3)), which means that evidence in support of the relief sought is tendered by way of affidavit and not by live testimony. The procedural rules of the High Court under the Act (Order 56 of the Rules of the Superior Courts) set out a clear and robust timetable for the filing of affidavits and the speedy disposition of applications.

[55] Arbitration Act, s 10.

[56] Arbitration Act, s 30.

6. In relation to consumers, such a party shall not be bound by an arbitration agreement (unless they agree after the dispute has arisen) where the agreement between the parties contains such a term which has not been individually negotiated and the dispute involves a claim not exceeding €5,000.00.[57]
7. The High Court and Circuit Court[58] can of their own motion adjourn proceedings to enable the parties to consider whether any or all of the matters in dispute might be determined by arbitration.[59]

While the Act contains the entirety of Ireland's arbitration law, there is a provision in another statute that is also relevant. Section 17 of the Defamation Act 2009 gives absolute privilege to a statement made in the course of proceedings before an arbitral tribunal where the statement is connected with those proceedings.

The Arbitration Act 2010 relates to both domestic and international arbitration in Ireland without distinction.

[57] Arbitration Act, s 31. There is also a provision in s 31 which specifically excludes the protection afforded to consumers from amateur sports persons who are parties to arbitration agreements involving their sporting bodies. This is particularly aimed at supporting the arbitration system under the auspices of the Gaelic Athletic Association, which is the major amateur sporting body in Ireland with a very large number of participants.

[58] The Circuit Court deals with smaller civil claims and sits in most towns of any size in Ireland. The High Court sits, almost exclusively, in Dublin.

[59] Arbitration Act, s 32.

7

GERMANY

*Richard Happ**

7.1 Background

7.1.1 History and development

7.01 Arbitration, particularly in commercial matters, has a long history in Germany. Although Prussia's legislature included provisions on arbitration in its 1794 *Allgemeines Preussisches Landrecht*, the roots of arbitration in Germany seem to be grounded in the middle ages.[1] As in many other legal systems, the state court system actually developed from ad hoc tribunals based on plain consent.[2] The first comprehensive codification of German arbitration law took place in 1879, only eight years after the creation of Germany as an independent unified state. Since then, it has been part of the German Code of Civil Procedure (*Zivilprozessordnung* or ZPO) as its tenth book. It was reformed in 1998.

7.02 Even the 'old law'—from a current perspective—can be considered quite modern: arbitration agreements were enforced, which led to the dismissal of claims before the state courts,

* The author gratefully acknowledges the assistance of Ms Anna Bashkova in the finalization of the manuscript.

[1] H Krause, *Die geschichtliche Entwicklung des Schiedsgerichtswesens in Deutschland* (C Heymann, 1930) 3.

[2] Krause (n 1) 4.

and arbitral awards were enforced without review on the merits. Other principles, however, including a default number of two arbitrators if the parties did not provide otherwise, became increasingly out of touch with international practice.[3]

Shortly after adoption of the UNCITRAL Model Law in 1985, the German Institute for Arbitration established a working group to consider a revision of German arbitration law. One of the main purposes was to increase Germany's attractiveness as a venue for international arbitration by adhering to international standards. The resulting report was published in 1989. In 1991, the Federal Ministry of Justice established an official commission that led to a report with a draft Bill published in 1994. After three more years, the Bill was passed by parliament and finally entered into force on 1 January 1998.[4] **7.03**

The revised German arbitration law deviates only slightly from the UNCITRAL Model Law. It has a wider scope of application, as it applies to both domestic and international arbitration. The main condition for its applicability is that the seat of the arbitration be in Germany.[5] It is less strict than the Model Law as regards the form of the arbitration agreement, also accepting agreements contained in bills of lading.[6] As will be set out in more detail in the following commentary, it also provides for broader forms of court assistance than the Model Law; these are basically remnants of the German legal tradition. **7.04**

The law also concentrates jurisdiction over arbitration matters in the higher regional courts (*Oberlandesgerichte* or OLGs), the instance directly subordinate to the Federal Court of Justice. In the 14 years since the reform, most OLGs have created special chambers for arbitration matters, thus ensuring the necessary expertise. **7.05**

Parallel to that, two German arbitration institutions merged in 1998 to create the German Institution for Arbitration (*Deutsche Institution für Schiedsgerichtsbarkeit* or DIS). The DIS has over a thousand members and also offers an organization for young arbitration practitioners and professionals, the DIS40, which itself has nearly a thousand members all over Germany. The DIS's caseload has been steadily increasing. In 2005, 72 new cases were registered, 16 of them international, with a total value of €282 million. In 2011, 178 new cases were registered, 55 of which were international, with a total value of €3.33 billion.[7] **7.06**

7.1.2 Recent developments and anticipated changes

Book Ten of the ZPO has not been amended since 1998. The case law of the Federal Court of Justice (*Bundesgerichtshof* or BGH) and of the higher regional courts, however, has clarified certain aspects relevant to the application of the law. **7.07**

With its decision of 6 April 2009 (*Schiedsfähigkeit II*),[8] the BGH paved the way for arbitration of disputes between the shareholders of limited liability companies. The main obstacle **7.08**

[3] For more detail see K-H Böckstiegel, S Kröll, and P Nacimiento, 'General Overview' in K-H Böckstiegel et al (eds), *Arbitration in Germany: The Model Law in Practice* (Wolters Kluwer, 2007) (hereinafter '*Arbitration in Germany*') 5.

[4] For a more in-depth report, see K-H Böckstiegel, 'Einführung zum neuen Recht der Schiedsgerichtsbarkeit in Deutschland' in DIS (ed), *Neues Deutsches Schiedsverfahrensrecht* (DIS-MAT IV, 1998) 1.

[5] § 1025(1) ZPO.

[6] § 1031(4) ZPO.

[7] Further information is available at <http://www.dis-arb.de/en/39/content/statistics-id53>.

[8] Bundesgerichtshof [BGH] (Federal Court of Justice) Case No II ZR 255/08, 6 April 2009, published with an English summary in [2009] *SchiedsVZ* 233.

to this had been an earlier judgment of 29 March 1996 (*Schiedsfähigkeit I*),[9] in which the BGH had held that shareholder disputes were not arbitrable, because they could not have the same effect on non-party shareholders as court proceedings. Whereas a court judgment, for example invalidating a shareholders' resolution, would have effect vis-à-vis shareholders who did not participate in the proceedings, an arbitral award would have effect only between the parties to the arbitration agreement. With its 2009 decision, the BGH held that shareholder disputes were arbitrable, as long as (a) the arbitration agreement bound all shareholders, (b) all shareholders had notice of the institution of arbitration proceedings, and (c) all shareholders had the opportunity to participate in the proceedings. These requirements for a 'class action' type of arbitration were soon implemented into existing arbitration clauses and adapted by the DIS into special rules for the arbitration of corporate disputes.

7.09 In a decision rendered on 11 April 2012,[10] the OLG Munich confirmed that under German law, attorneys' fees exceeding those in the German Attorneys' Fees Act (*Rechtsanwaltsvergütungsgesetz* or RVG) can be reimbursed, at least in international arbitrations. The question was whether costs exceeding RVG fees could be defined as being 'necessary'. With regard to whether the fees of foreign correspondence lawyers who act in domestic court proceedings were eligible for reimbursement, the BGH had decided that the fees of foreign lawyers were eligible for reimbursement only insofar as they were 'necessary', and did not exceed the statutory RVG fees for German lawyers.[11] Whether this also applied to foreign and domestic lawyers in arbitral proceedings was disputed.[12] The OLG's 2012 decision held that an international arbitral award (under the DIS Arbitration Rules, but rendered in Switzerland) reimbursing higher fees than the statutory RVG fees was indeed enforceable.

7.1.3 Regional venues

7.10 Due to Germany's history, the country has not developed a dominant economic and political hub such as London for the United Kingdom or Paris in France. Rather, several cities are focal points of industry and commerce in Germany, and thus potential arbitration venues. In practice, however, five cities (Cologne and Düsseldorf are counted together because of their proximity) play a major role for arbitration proceedings:

- Frankfurt;
- Cologne/Düsseldorf;
- Hamburg;
- Munich; and
- Stuttgart.

7.11 While arbitration proceedings can be held in any city in Germany, this is not advisable. As set out in paragraph 7.05, jurisdiction for arbitration-related court proceedings is vested in the

---

9 Bundesgerichtshof, Case No II ZR 124/95, 29 March 1996, [1996] *Neue Juristische Wochenschrift* 1753.

10 Oberlandesgericht [OLG München] (Higher Regional Court Munich) Case No 34 SCH 21/11, 11 April 2012, [2012] *SchiedsVZ* 156.

11 Bundesgerichtshof, Case No VIII ZB 55/04 (OLG Stuttgart), 8 March 2005, [2005] *Neue Juristische Wochenschrift* 1373.

12 Against: J Risse and M Altenkirch, 'Kostenerstattung im Schiedsverfahren: fünf Probleme aus der Praxis' [2012] *SchiedsVZ* 10; F von Schlabrendorff and A Sessler, in Böckstiegel et al (eds), *Arbitration in Germany* § 1057, para 30. In favour: JP Lachmann, *Handbuch für die Schiedsgerichtspraxis* (3rd edn, O Schmidt, 2008) para 1947; also J Münch, in T Rauscher et al (eds), *Münchener Kommentar zur Zivilprozessordnung: ZPO* (3rd edn, Beck, 2008) § 1057, para 7 (hereinafter '*MünchKommZPO*').

higher regional courts. While nearly all of them now have specialized arbitration senates,[13] their expertise can differ greatly depending on the cases submitted to them. Courts in cities with major law firms and considerable international business will automatically be better suited to supervise and support international arbitration proceedings, and more inclined to be familiar with foreign languages such as English. It can be helpful—and cost-effective—not to have to translate every English document into German. Although German is the official language for court proceedings, judges in large cities often waive the requirement that English-language documents be translated into German unless the documents are particularly complicated.[14]

7.2 Commencing Arbitration Proceedings

German courts will intervene in arbitral proceedings only to the extent provided for in Book Ten of the ZPO.[15] They assist in the enforcement of arbitration clauses, appoint arbitrators where necessary, and may, in a peculiarity of German law, determine, before the arbitral tribunal is constituted, whether or not arbitral proceedings are 'admissible'.[16] 'Admissibility' may relate to the existence of a valid arbitration agreement, whether it is operative or capable of being performed, or whether the subject matter is arbitrable.[17] **7.12**

7.2.1 Enforcing arbitration agreements

Paralleling Article 8(1) of UNCITRAL Model Law, German arbitration law provides that the existence of an arbitration agreement constitutes a jurisdictional objection that, only if raised, leads to the dismissal of the claim before the court. Section 1032(1) ZPO provides: **7.13**

> A court before which an action is brought in a matter which is the subject of an arbitration agreement shall, if the respondent raises an objection prior to the beginning of the oral hearing on the substance of the dispute, reject the action as inadmissible unless the court finds that the arbitration agreement is null and void, inoperative or incapable of being performed.

Pursuant to section 1032(3) ZPO, arbitral proceedings can be commenced or continued while proceedings pursuant to section 1032(1) ZPO are pending. This can lead to potential conflicts. Should the arbitral tribunal confirm its jurisdiction (in either a final award on the merits or a preliminary ruling pursuant to section 1040(3) ZPO) before the court decides, that decision will not bind the court.[18] The principle of *competence-competence* is applied cautiously in Germany—the final competence to decide about the tribunal's jurisdiction lies with the courts, not the tribunal. **7.14**

However, should the court decide that the tribunal does not have jurisdiction, it must nevertheless stay its proceedings in order to allow proper recourse against the tribunal's decision or award (see paragraph 7.13).[19] If the court decides before the arbitral tribunal and finds **7.15**

[13] The chambers of Higher Regional Courts are referred to as the 'Senate'.

[14] Two German federal States (Hamburg and Northrhine-Westphalia) have sponsored a draft bill to enable German Regional Courts establish special chambers for international commercial cases ('*Kammern für Internationale Handelssachen*') which would hold the proceedings in English. The draft bill has not yet passed the *Bundestag*.

[15] § 1026 ZPO.

[16] § 1032(2) ZPO.

[17] P Huber, in Böckstiegel et al (eds), *Arbitration in Germany* § 1032, para 52; Münch, in Rauscher et al (eds), MünchKommZPO § 1032(2), para 24.

[18] Huber, in Böckstiegel et al (eds), *Arbitration in Germany* § 1032, para 30ff.

[19] R Geimer, in R Zöller (ed), *Zivilprozessordnung* (29th edn, O Schmidt, 2012) § 1032, para 14.

that the arbitration agreement cannot be invoked, any award rendered by the tribunal will be null and void, not merely capable of being set aside.[20] It might, however, in such a case, be advisable to institute setting aside proceedings to be on the safe side.

7.16 The scope of German arbitration law is broader than the scope of the UNCITRAL Model Law. While the Model Law applies only to 'international commercial' arbitration, under German law 'any claim involving an economic interest' is arbitrable.[21] It need not be commercial. What is more, under German law, arbitration agreements are valid that would not satisfy the Model Law's 'in writing' requirement. While Article 7(2) of the Model Law requires an exchange of documents in order to constitute an agreement in writing, section 1031(2) ZPO provides that:

> The form requirement of subsection 1 shall be deemed to have been complied with if the arbitration agreement is contained in a document transmitted from one party to the other party or by a third party to both parties and—if no objection was raised in good time—the contents of such document are considered to be part of the contract in accordance with common usage.

7.17 Thus, arbitration clauses contained in unilateral contract confirmation letters, if not objected to, can be valid under German law. Section 1031(4) ZPO also explicitly accepts agreements contained in bills of lading.

7.2.2 The courts' role in appointing arbitrators

7.18 Generally, the parties are free to determine the number of arbitrators as well as the method of their appointment. If there is no agreement, the tribunal will consist of three arbitrators. The courts will intervene only when the arbitration agreement does not give equal rights to both parties[22] or when problems arise in the appointment of arbitrators.[23]

7.19 Section 1034(2) ZPO is not based on the Model Law, but on a comparable provision of the 1879 arbitration law:

> If the arbitration agreement grants preponderant rights to one party with regard to the composition of the arbitral tribunal which place the other party at a disadvantage, that other party may request the court to appoint the arbitrator or arbitrators in deviation from the nomination made, or from the agreed nomination procedure. The request must be submitted at the latest within two weeks of the party becoming aware of the constitution of the arbitral tribunal. Section 1032 subs. 3 applies mutatis mutandis.

7.20 The purpose of this provision is to ensure that the principle of equality of parties is upheld as early as the time of constitution of the tribunal.[24] A predominance for one party exists, for example, when that party has a greater influence than the other on the appointment of the sole arbitrator or chairman of the tribunal.[25] Examples might include an arbitration clause in general terms and conditions naming a specific sole arbitrator, or the appointment of arbitrators from the roster of an association of which only one party is a member.[26] Similarly, a

---

[20] Geimer, in Zöller (ed), *Zivilprozessordnung* § 1032, para 15.

[21] § 1030 ZPO.

[22] § 1034(2) ZPO.

[23] § 1035 ZPO.

[24] Münch, in Rauscher et al (eds), *MünchKommZPO* § 1034(2), para 2; P Nacimiento and A Abt, in Böckstiegel et al (eds), *Arbitration in Germany* § 1034, para 6.

[25] Münch, in Rauscher et al (eds), *MünchKommZPO* § 1034 (2), para 8; Lachmann (n 12) paras 932ff.

[26] Geimer, in Zöller (ed), *Zivilprozessordnung* § 1034, para 11; see also Nacimiento and Abt, in Böckstiegel et al (eds), *Arbitration in Germany* § 1034, paras 13–17.

clause that would transfer the right of appointment to the other party if a party fails to make a timely appointment would also be invalid.[27]

Depending on the reasons for the predominance, the court may substitute the 'affected' arbitrator with a neutral arbitrator, replace the entire tribunal, or determine a new mechanism for the appointment of arbitrators, using the statutory default mechanism.[28] **7.21**

The subsidiary role of the court in appointing arbitrators is regulated by section 1035(3) to (5) ZPO. The pertinent parts read: **7.22**

> ... If a party fails to appoint the arbitrator within one month of receipt of a request to do so from the other party, or if the two arbitrators fail to agree on the third arbitrator within one month of their appointment, the appointment shall be made, upon request of a party, by the court.
> (4) Where, under an appointment procedure agreed upon by the parties, a party fails to act as required under such procedure, or if the parties, or two arbitrators, are unable to reach an agreement expected of them under such procedure, or a third party fails to perform any function entrusted to it under such procedure, any party may request the court to take the necessary measure, unless the agreement on the appointment procedure provides other means for securing the appointment.
> (5) The court, in appointing an arbitrator, shall have due regard to any qualifications required of the arbitrator by the agreement of the parties and to such considerations as are likely to secure the appointment of an independent and impartial arbitrator. In the case of a sole or third arbitrator, the court shall take into account as well the advisability of appointing an arbitrator of a nationality other than those of the parties.

Parties are free to opt-out of section 1035 ZPO by agreeing on a different procedure, either expressly or by reference to a set of arbitration rules. **7.23**

The default mechanism of section 1035(3) ZPO is simple: each party appoints one arbitrator, and the two party-appointed arbitrators together appoint the third, presiding, arbitrator.[29] Section 1035(3) ZPO regulates the role of the court when the parties have not agreed on a different appointment mechanism, while subsection (4) is applicable when the parties have agreed on the appointment procedure, but failed to include a default mechanism to secure the constitution of the tribunal. **7.24**

When faced with an application for the appointment of an arbitrator, the court will incidentally review whether a valid arbitration agreement exists. As this is a *prima facie* review only, the decision will not have binding effect, either for the tribunal or in subsequent court proceedings.[30] In selecting an appropriate arbitrator, the court must consider any requirements agreed on by the parties, and—in international arbitrations—ensure that the arbitrator is impartial and independent. In the light of the *Jivraj* **7.25**

[27] Bundesgerichtshof, Case No VII ZR 31/69, 5 November 1970, 54 BGHZ 392.

[28] Nacimiento and Abt, in Böckstiegel et al (eds), *Arbitration in Germany* § 1034, para 30; according to Lachmann (n 12) para 955, the arbitrator of the disadvantaged party will never be replaced.

[29] It is to be noted that the 'request' mentioned in § 1035(3) ZPO need not be in writing: Geimer, in Zöller (ed), *Zivilprozessordnung* § 1035, para 14. Even after an oral request, the time period of one month for appointing an arbitrator starts to run. Whether the oral request can be proven, however, is a different issue.

[30] Geimer, in Zöller (ed), *Zivilprozessordnung* § 1035, paras 17, 18. The respondent party in that proceeding would be free to file a 'counter-application' requesting to determine the inadmissibility of arbitral proceedings pursuant to § 1032(2) ZPO.

case decided in the UK courts and currently in the hands of the European Commission,[31] it remains to be seen whether the inclusion of a mandatory 'third nationality rule' can be upheld in future.[32]

7.26 Appointing an arbitrator is an enormous responsibility for the court. When the dispute is international, the court must select someone suitably qualified. This is one of the best arguments for selecting the place of arbitration with care. The OLGs are responsible for nominating arbitrators. Only an OLG in a city with considerable international business and an active arbitration scene is likely to be able to appoint suitable arbitrators.

7.27 Section 1035 ZPO does not regulate the appointment of arbitrators in multi-party arbitrations, in particular in a case with several respondent parties (the '*Dutco* problem' situation).[33] Both academic writing and court cases have, however, clarified that when two or more respondents cannot agree on an arbitrator, not only that arbitrator but the entire tribunal is to be appointed by the court (*Vollneutralisierung*).[34] It would be a breach of the principle of equality of parties to appoint an arbitrator for the respondents only. Although this is said not to apply when multiple respondents do not have conflicting interests,[35] it is unclear in practice how the courts should determine whether conflicting or parallel interests exist.[36] With the exception of a few clear cases, this will usually require a round of written submissions.

7.2.3 The role of courts in resolving jurisdictional questions

7.28 As explained previously, the principle of *competence-competence* is applied restrictively in Germany. It is not the arbitral tribunal, but rather the courts that have the final say. Consequently, German law offers two mechanisms for invoking the courts' competence to finally determine questions of jurisdiction.

---

[31] See *Jivraj v Hashwani* [2011] UKSC 40. The UK Supreme Court has confirmed that arbitrators are not 'employees' within the meaning of UK anti-discrimination laws and therefore a 'discriminatory' arbitration clause was held to be valid. In its decision, the Supreme Court overruled the decision of the Court of Appeal and also refused to refer the certain points to the ECJ. A complaint has been lodged by the former claimant, Mr Hashwani, with the European Commission under the Treaty on the Functioning of the European Union (TFEU), Art 258. In this complaint he indicates that the Supreme Court should have referred certain questions of his case to the ECJ in the first place. The complaint essentially requests the Commission to commence infringement proceedings against the UK and asking them to rectify the situation.

[32] J Koepp, 'Staatliche Diskriminierungsverbote bei der Auswahl von Schiedsrichtern?' [2011] *SchiedsVZ* 306; Nacimiento and Abt in Böckstiegel et al (eds), *Arbitration in Germany* § 1035, para 31.

[33] In *BKMI and Siemens v Dutco* (*Siemens AG and BKMI Industrieanlagen GmbH v Dutco Construction Co (Dubai)*) the claimant had appointed its arbitrator while the respondents could not reach an agreement, arguing that their interests were too different. Nevertheless, the ICC Court insisted that they needed to appoint an arbitrator jointly. The respondents made the required joint nomination, but raised an objection to the necessity of such joint appointment of the arbitrator. The French Court of Cassation (7 January 1992, (1992) 3 *Revue de l'Arbitrage* 470–2, English translation (1993) 18 YB Commercial Arbitration 140) agreed with the respondents' position and refused to recognize the ICC decision, stating that the violation of the equal rights of the parties in regard to the appointment of the arbitrator was contrary to *ordre public*.

[34] See the discussion in Bundesgerichtshof, Case No II ZR 124/95, 29 March 1996, [1996] *Neue Juristische Wochenschrift* 1753, 1755; Oberlandesgericht [OLG Frankfurt], Case No 26 Sch 13/05, 24 November 2005, [2006] *SchiedsVZ* 219; W Voit, in H-J Musielak, *Kommentar zur Zivilprozessordnung mit Gerichtsverfassungsgesetz* (9th edn, Vahlen 2012) (hereinafter '*Kommentar zur ZPO*') § 1035, para 7. A full 'neutralization' is also provided for in art 12(8) of the 2012 ICC Rules.

[35] Münch, in Rauscher et al (eds), *MünchKommZPO* § 1035, para 69. Oberlandesgericht Case No 26 Sch 13/05, 24 November 2005, [2006] *SchiedsVZ* 219. See also VIAC-Rules, art 5(7) and in contrast SCC, art 13(4) and the 2012 Swiss Rules, art 8(5).

[36] Münch, in Rauscher et al (eds), *MünchKommZPO* § 1035, para 72.

7.29 The first is section 1032(2) ZPO. Deviating from the UNCITRAL Model Law, section 1032(2) allows a party to an arbitration agreement to apply to the court to determine the admissibility or inadmissibility of arbitration proceedings: 'Prior to the constitution of the arbitral tribunal, an application may be made to the court to determine whether or not arbitration is admissible.'

7.30 This provision allows a party to apply to the court for a ruling on jurisdiction without having to initiate court proceedings on the merits of the dispute and wait for the other party to raise the existence of an arbitration agreement. This application can be filed before arbitration has been initiated if, for example, the threat of arbitration is imminent or the other party denies the admissibility of a contemplated arbitration.[37] This possibility ends, however, once the tribunal has been constituted.[38] A section 1032(2) application does not block the commencement of arbitration proceedings. This is to prevent a party from delaying arbitration proceedings by raising potentially unfounded jurisdictional objections in court. After constitution of the arbitral tribunal, ie when all arbitrators have accepted their appointments,[39] any claims of inadmissibility for lack of jurisdiction must be raised before the arbitral tribunal. The commencement of the arbitral proceedings, however, does not end pending court proceedings, the two can proceed simultaneously.[40] What is decisive is the time at which the application is made.

7.31 The issue of admissibility covers the questions of whether a valid arbitration agreement exists, whether it is operable, and whether the dispute is arbitrable and within the scope of the arbitration clause.[41] It is not entirely settled whether a section 1032(2) application must relate to the admissibility or inadmissibility of the arbitration as a whole, or whether it can relate to specific aspects of potential arbitration proceedings only. For example, certain claims might fall within or outside the scope of the arbitration agreement.[42] The statutory wording does not indicate any limitation, and it is arguable that an application can refer to the admissibility of specific claims in an arbitration, as well as the validity of the arbitration agreement as such. Limiting section 1032(2) to the entire arbitration would deprive it of much of its scope of application, as such objections could in any case be raised in the arbitration, and section 1032(2) is meant to give the courts the final say on this.

7.32 As explained, court proceedings and arbitration can proceed in parallel. The arbitral tribunal is bound by the decision of the court, whether it declares arbitration proceedings admissible or inadmissible. If the tribunal renders an award while section 1032(2) proceedings are pending and the court declares the arbitration proceedings inadmissible, the award will be void *ipso jure*.[43] It is nevertheless advisable in such cases to commence setting aside proceedings. There is a risk that enforcement courts in other jurisdictions might assess the impact of

[37] Münch, in Rauscher et al (eds), *MünchKommZPO* § 1032, para 22.

[38] In contrast, the UK Arbitration Act 1996, s 72 allows for applications even after the tribunal is constituted and up until the final award has been rendered.

[39] Münch, in Rauscher et al (eds), *MünchKommZPO* § 1032 (2), para 22.

[40] This follows from § 1032(3) ZPO, which explicitly states that arbitral proceedings may nevertheless start or be continued, and an arbitral award be rendered, while the issue is pending before the court.

[41] See eg Huber, in Böckstiegel et al (eds), *Arbitration in Germany* § 1032, para 52; Münch, in Rauscher et al (eds), *MünchKommZPO* § 1032(2), para 24.

[42] Huber, in Böckstiegel et al (eds), *Arbitration in Germany* § 1032, paras 53–56.

[43] Münch, in Rauscher et al (eds), *MünchKommZPO* § 1032(2), para 34; I Saenger, in I Saenger (ed), *Zivilprozessordnung* (5th edn, Nomos 2013) § 1032, para 17.

the court's decision incorrectly and, for example, order recognition and enforcement because the award has not been set aside by a German court.[44]

7.33 German law also gives parties an immediate remedy against a decision on jurisdiction by the arbitral tribunal.[45] If a party raises jurisdictional objections with the arbitral tribunal, section 1040(3) ZPO provides:

> If the arbitral tribunal considers that it has jurisdiction, it rules on a plea referred to in subsection 2 of this section in general by means of a preliminary ruling. In this case, any party may request, within one month after having received written notice of that ruling, the court to decide the matter. While such a request is pending, the arbitral tribunal may continue the arbitral proceedings and make an award.

7.34 That the ruling is treated as 'preliminary' does not mean that the tribunal renders a decision that is not binding on it. From the perspective of the arbitration, the tribunal's decision is final and binding, ie it cannot be revisited in the award. From the perspective of the court, the tribunal's decision is preliminary, as the court can fully review whether the tribunal has jurisdiction.[46] The wording indicates that any party can file a request for review with the court. For the potential claimant this can be interesting, as a court judgment confirming jurisdiction will have *res judicata* effect in a subsequent or parallel arbitration and thus might make the arbitration simpler.

7.35 The court's decision on jurisdiction is binding on the arbitral tribunal, which may not render an award on the merits and must terminate the arbitral proceedings at once. If the tribunal nevertheless renders an award (or has rendered an award), commentators suggest that the award will be void *ipso jure* (see discussion of section 1032(2) ZPO at paragraph 7.32).[47] As with section 1032, in order to ensure proper treatment in foreign courts, it is advisable in this situation to institute setting aside proceedings against the final award, asserting lack of jurisdiction.[48]

7.36 The last sentence of section 1040(3) ZPO makes clear that the tribunal can continue with the arbitral proceedings while a jurisdictional challenge is pending. This is to prevent delay in the arbitral proceedings being caused by unfounded applications to the courts.[49] It might, however, be advisable for a tribunal to stay arbitral proceedings in questionable cases, to avoid unnecessary costs in the event the court rejects the tribunal's jurisdiction.

7.37 Failure to invoke section 1040(3) ZPO will lead to waiver. A party will be precluded from raising lack of jurisdiction in setting aside or enforcement proceedings.[50]

---

44 Huber, in Böckstiegel et al (eds), *Arbitration in Germany* § 1032, para 60.

45 As a side note, the reader might be interested to learn that one of the most prominent proceedings of that kind was the application against the decision on jurisdiction in the BIT proceeding in *Eureko v Poland* decided in May 2012 by the Higher Regional Court, Frankfurt.

46 Voit, in Musielak, *Kommentar zur ZPO* (n 34) § 1040, para 12; Huber, in Böckstiegel et al (eds), *Arbitration in Germany* § 1040, para 2.

47 Huber, in Böckstiegel et al (eds), *Arbitration in Germany* § 1040, para 40.

48 Huber, in Böckstiegel et al (eds), *Arbitration in Germany* § 1040, paras 40, 41. According to Geimer, in Zöller (ed), *Zivilprozessordnung* § 1040, para 14, the application under § 1040 ZPO becomes inadmissible and the applicant in any case has to file setting aside proceedings against the award.

49 See Bill of the Arbitration Law Reform Act, BT-Drs 13/5274, 44.

50 Münch, in Rauscher et al (eds), *MünchKommZPO* § 1040 (3), para 50; Geimer, in Zöller (ed), *Zivilprozessordnung* § 1040, para 11.

7.2.4 The role of courts in enjoining arbitration

Both the Model Law and the ZPO limit the role of courts to matters expressly provided for. Where an arbitration clause provides for arbitration in Germany, any party wishing to avoid arbitration can request the competent court to determine the admissibility or inadmissibility of arbitration proceedings. German courts will not intervene beyond this. **7.38**

7.3 Court Assistance Before or During Arbitration

7.3.1 Interim measures

The German Code of Civil Procedure (ZPO) offers two routes for obtaining interim measures. On the one hand, arbitral tribunals have the competence to grant interim measures themselves. On the other hand, state courts remain competent to grant interim measures both before and after the arbitral tribunal has been constituted.[51] Courts also remain competent to enforce interim measures ordered by the arbitral tribunal. **7.39**

Parallel powers of state courts and arbitral tribunals

The right to seek interim measures in court is codified in section 1033 ZPO, which provides: **7.40**

> An arbitration agreement does not rule out that a court may order, before or after arbitration proceedings have commenced, and upon a party having filed a corresponding petition that a provisional measure or one serving to provide security be taken with regard to the subject matter of the dispute being dealt with in the arbitration proceedings.

The existence of an arbitration agreement cannot, therefore, be used as an objection to the court's jurisdiction to order interim measures. It is not entirely clear whether parties can opt out of this provision by agreement. However, commentators and the courts tend towards the view that section 1033 ZPO is of a compulsory nature.[52] **7.41**

Pursuant to section 1025(2) ZPO, German courts can also order interim measures when the arbitration proceedings take place outside Germany. There are no special requirements, for example that there must be German parties or property located in Germany.[53] **7.42**

In principle, arbitral tribunals also have the power to issue interim measures, as codified in section 1041 ZPO: **7.43**

> (1) Unless otherwise agreed by the parties, the arbitral tribunal may, at the request of a party, order such interim measures of protection as the arbitral tribunal may consider necessary in respect of the subject-matter of the dispute. The arbitral tribunal may require any party to provide appropriate security in connection with such measure.

---

[51] eg unlike the provisions of the 1996 Arbitration Act, where the primary power of the court to issue interim measures ceases once the arbitral tribunal has been duly constituted. See the UK Arbitration Act 1996, s 44.

[52] Münch, in Rauscher et al (eds), *MünchKomm ZPO* § 1033, para 18; Voit, in Musielak, *Kommentar zur ZPO* § 1033, para 3; R Kreindler and J Schäfer, in Böckstiegel et al (eds), *Arbitration in Germany* § 1033, paras 7–8; Oberlandesgericht Munich Case No U (K) 3208/00, 26 October 2000 [2001] *Neue Juristische Wochenschrift*-RR 711, 712; but see Geimer, in Zöller (ed), *Zivilprozessordnung* § 1033, para 6. Rules such as DIS-Sports-Arbitration, art 21.1 which specifies that once the arbitral tribunal is fully constituted, interim measures are no longer admissible before the court and may only be served before the arbitral tribunal thus very likely only have *inter partes* effect and do not bind the court.

[53] However, the normal rules for establishing jurisdiction apply, see R Kreindler and J Schäfer, in Böckstiegel et al (eds), *Arbitration in Germany* § 1033, para 10.

(2) The court may, at the request of a party, permit enforcement of a measure referred to in subsection 1, unless application for a corresponding interim measure has already been made to a court. It may recast such an order if necessary for the purpose of enforcing the measure.
(3) The court may, upon request, repeal or amend the decision referred to in subsection 2.
(4) If a measure ordered under subsection 1 proves to have been unjustified from the outset, the party who obtained its enforcement is obliged to compensate the other party for damage resulting from the enforcement of such measure or from his providing security in order to avoid enforcement. This claim may be put forward in the pending arbitral proceedings.

7.44 As a result of these provisions, parallel proceedings in court and before an arbitral tribunal are possible and occur with some regularity. State court proceedings, however, enjoy priority. While an interim decision of the arbitral tribunal does not bind or otherwise pre-judge the state court when deciding an application for an interim relief,[54] a court application will render an application to enforce an interim measure of the arbitral tribunal inadmissible.[55]

Obtaining interim measures from arbitral tribunals

7.45 An application for interim measures from an arbitral tribunal requires that the tribunal be fully or partially constituted (see paragraph 7.46). As the constitution of a tribunal may take several months, this reduces the instances in which interim measures can be obtained from the tribunal. In most cases, prompt and effective relief will be available only from the state courts.

7.46 A request for interim measures may be considered even if the tribunal is not yet fully constituted, for example if the arbitration agreement pre-emptively appoints a sole arbitrator or if the applicable arbitration rules provide for an emergency arbitrator.[56] Experience with emergency arbitrators remains limited and only time will tell whether they are a useful and effective tool. Parties may also consider referring, in the arbitration agreement, to a special mechanism for provisional measures, such as the ICC Pre-Arbitral Referee Procedure, to bridge the time until the arbitral tribunal is sufficiently established to act in its own capacity.

7.47 Faced with an application for interim measures, the tribunal must decide whether to grant or reject it.[57] One of the reasons a party might chose an arbitral tribunal over a state court is that the former has more flexibility in issuing interim measures. Section 1041 ZPO allows an arbitral tribunal to order 'any provisional measure . . . it deems fit', while state courts are restricted by an enumerated list of measures and therefore may not always offer the most suitable toolkit for the situation at hand.

7.48 There is some controversy in German literature as to whether the measure for which application has been made need only be necessary, or whether the applicant must substantiate a reason (*Anordnungsgrund*) and a right pursued with the application (*Anordnungsanspruch*), as is required before state courts. This academic discussion has little practical relevance. A measure will be necessary if it protects a certain right and if there is a good reason for

---

54 Kreindler and Schäfer, in Böckstiegel et al (eds), *Arbitration in Germany* § 1041, para 3.

55 § 1041(2) ZPO.

56 The Stockholm Chamber of Commerce (SCC) and the International Chamber of Commerce (ICC) have made provisions for '*Emergency Arbitrators*': SCC-Rules App II, arts 1–10 in force as of 1 January 2010 and ICC-Rules, art 29, App V, arts 1–8 in force as of 2012. These will be nominated within days and serve the purpose of giving immediate relief via the arbitration route and before constitution of the arbitral proceedings.

57 Geimer, in Zöller (ed), *Zivilprozessordnung* § 1041, para 1; R Happ, 'Schiedsverfahren' in D Kleveman (ed), *Anwaltshandbuch Einstweiliger Rechtsschutz* (2nd edn, O Schmidt, 2013) § 8, para 21.

implementing it, such as an impending risk of loss. It may nevertheless be advisable to structure the application along the lines of an application before state courts, particularly if the arbitrators have limited arbitration experience.[58]

Availability of ex parte *measures*

Although German state courts may order interim measures on an *ex parte* basis, it is contested in legal literature and commentary whether arbitral tribunals may do so.[59] One of the main arguments against such a power is the absence of an appellate track for such interim measures in the ZPO. It is argued that the parties must be heard prior to the order if they cannot be heard afterwards (ie by way of appeal).[60] The parties must at least have their 'day in court', either before or after the interim measure has been ordered. **7.49**

Ex parte measures would therefore appear to be available if the arbitral tribunal is obliged to hear the parties in the immediate aftermath of an order. This should be sufficient to guarantee the parties' right to be heard. If the tribunal failed to hear the other party shortly afterwards, the interim measure would not be enforceable in state courts, thus providing sufficient safeguards against abuse of the tribunal's power. This is the solution adopted by article 26(3) of the 2012 Swiss Arbitration Rules. Despite strong arguments that arbitral *ex parte* measures are indeed permissible, the legal discussion is still very much in a state of flux. For example, the DIS Arbitration Rules expressly require that the parties be heard in advance.[61] The safest route, at least for the time being, would therefore be to seek *ex parte* measures in state courts,[62] rather than running the risk of the tribunal's order being unenforceable. **7.50**

Content and enforceability of interim measures

The content of arbitral interim relief is not limited by the power of the national courts to grant interim measures according to section 916 ZPO.[63] The tribunal may grant any provisional relief that it deems necessary. The scope of interim measures can be demonstrated by the following non-exhaustive list: **7.51**

- securing evidence;
- imposing restrictions on the sale of assets;
- specific performance;
- freezing injunctions;
- security for costs; and
- seizure of assets.

Since the arbitral tribunal lacks the power to declare its interim measures enforceable, it will be necessary to seek the assistance of state courts, consuming time and costs that might cause **7.52**

[58] Happ (n 57) § 8, paras 23–24; I Hanefeld, 'Germany' in F-B Weigand (ed), *Practitioner's Handbook on International Commercial Arbitration* (2nd edn, OUP, 2009) paras 7.136–7.137.

[59] Against the possibility of *ex parte* injunctions: RA Schütze, 'Einstweiliger Rechtsschutz im Schiedsverfahren' [1998] *Betriebs-Berater* 1650, 1651. In favour of *ex parte* injunctions by arbitral tribunals: Geimer, in Zöller (ed), *Zivilprozessordnung* § 1042, para 3; Hanefeld (n 58) para 7.139; G Walter and KH Schwab, *Schiedsgerichtsbarkeit* (7th edn, Beck, 2005) ch 17a, para 20.

[60] Schütze (n 59) 1651; P Hartmann, in A Baumbach, W Lauterbach, J Albers, and P Hartmann (eds), *Zivilprozessordnung* (70th edn, Beck, 2012) § 1041, para 2.

[61] See also U Theune, 'DIS-Schiedsordnung' in Schütze (ed), *Institutionelle Schiedsgerichtsbarkeit* (2nd edn, Heymann, 2011) 193.

[62] P Hobeck and M Weyreuther, 'Anordnung von vorläufigen oder sichernden Maßnahmen durch Schiedsgerichte in ex-parte-Verfahren' [2005] *SchiedsVZ* 238, 240.

[63] Kreindler and Schäfer, in Böckstiegel et al (eds), *Arbitration in Germany* § 1041, para 21.

detrimental delay to one of the parties. Where speed is of the essence in obtaining an interim measure, obtaining interim relief from an arbitral tribunal is therefore not the best option.

7.53 In order to bridge the time between the application and the eventual enforcement order, it is possible and indeed advisable to obtain an *ex parte* order from the court that the measure is 'provisionally enforceable'.[64] The court has discretion regarding whether or not to grant provisional enforceability.[65] The other party may cancel the effect of provisional enforceability by providing security to the court. An application for provisional enforceability, if granted, will therefore provide the requisite protection one way or the other.

7.54 When the tribunal orders a party to refrain from taking certain actions, any application for enforcement of the order must be supplemented by an application for a coercive fine.[66] The reason is that under German law, the enforcement of this type of order requires that the court's warning of a coercive fine, in case of failure to comply, be served on the other party.[67]

7.3.2 The role of courts in deciding challenges to arbitrators

7.55 According to section 1036(2) ZPO, an arbitrator may be challenged if circumstances exist giving rise to justifiable doubts as to his impartiality or independence. The challenge procedure is regulated in section 1037 ZPO. Section 1036 provides as follows:

> *Challenge of an arbitrator*
>
> (1) When a person is approached in connection with his possible appointment as an arbitrator, he shall disclose any circumstances likely to give rise to justifiable doubts as to his impartiality or independence. An arbitrator, from the time of his appointment and throughout the arbitral proceedings, shall without delay disclose any such circumstances to the parties unless they have already been informed of them by him.
>
> (2) An arbitrator may be challenged only if circumstances exist that give rise to justifiable doubts as to his impartiality or independence, or if he does not possess qualifications agreed to by the parties. A party may challenge an arbitrator appointed by him, or in whose appointment he has participated, only for reasons of which he becomes aware after the appointment has been made.

7.56 A person who is proposed as arbitrator must disclose all circumstances that could give rise to doubts as to his impartiality or independence. The disclosure obligation also includes circumstances that might not give rise to a challenge, which is possible only in the case of *justifiable* doubts regarding impartiality or independence. Disclosure does not therefore automatically mean that a ground for challenge exists.[68] Also, failing to disclose circumstances that are not sufficient for a challenge (see paragraph 7.57) does not itself give rise to a challenge.[69] The International Bar Association (IBA) Guidelines on Conflicts of Interest in International

---

64 § 1063(3) ZPO.

65 § 1041(2) ZPO.

66 Under the German Code of Civil Procedure, interim measures obliging the debtor to do something or to cease doing something must be accompanied by the court's warning that failure to comply might result in a coercive fine of up to €250,000.

67 Happ (n 57) § 8, para 38.

68 Saenger, in Saenger (ed), *Zivilprozessordnung* § 1036, para 3; Geimer, in Zöller (ed), *Zivilprozessordnung* § 1036, para 9.

69 Oberlandesgericht [OLG Naumburg] (Higher Regional Court Naumburg) Case No 10 SchH 3/01, 19 December 2001, [2003] *SchiedsVZ* 134, 136.

Arbitration[70] are increasing in practical importance for assessing disclosure obligations, but do not authoritatively concretize the specific domestic German requirements.[71]

Pursuant to section 1036(2) ZPO, a challenge requires circumstances that give rise to justifiable doubts about the arbitrator's impartiality or independence. While Book Ten does not explicitly refer to the reasons set forth in sections 41ff ZPO that would justify the challenge of a judge in civil court proceedings stated in sections 41ff ZPO, circumstances that would justify the challenge of a judge always justify the challenge of an arbitrator.[72] An arbitrator can also be challenged if he does not fulfil the requirements or qualifications agreed between the parties. In addition, a party may challenge an arbitrator appointed by it—or in whose appointment the party has participated—only for reasons of which the party was unaware at the time of appointment[73] **7.57**

The parties may, within certain limits, restrict the grounds for challenge,[74] and may without limitation include specific qualifications in the arbitration agreement.[75] **7.58**

Challenge procedure

Section 1037 sets forth the challenge procedure: **7.59**

> (1) The parties are free to agree on a procedure for challenging an arbitrator, subject to the provisions of subsection 3 of this section.
> (2) Failing such agreement, a party who intends to challenge an arbitrator shall, within two weeks after becoming aware of the constitution of the arbitral tribunal or after becoming aware of any circumstance referred to in section 1036 subs. 2, send a written statement of the reasons for the challenge to the arbitral tribunal. Unless the challenged arbitrator withdraws from his office or the other party agrees to the challenge, the arbitral tribunal shall decide on the challenge.
> (3) If a challenge under any procedure agreed upon by the parties or under the procedure of subsection 2 of this section is not successful, the challenging party may request, within one month after having received notice of the decision rejecting the challenge, the court to decide on the challenge; the parties may agree on a different time-limit. While such a request is pending, the arbitral tribunal, including the challenged arbitrator, may continue the arbitral proceedings and make an award.

As section 1037(1) makes clear, the parties may agree on a challenge procedure, and the procedure in section 1037(2) applies only where no such agreement has been reached. It provides that a party must first turn to the arbitral tribunal to rule on a challenge of one of its members. This application must be made no later than two weeks after the constitution of the tribunal or after the applicant becomes aware of any circumstance referred to in section 1037(2) ZPO. Failure to raise a challenge in the arbitral proceedings precludes a party from **7.60**

---

[70] The full text is available on the International Bar Association website, at <http://www.ibanet.org/ENews_Archive/IBA_July_2008_ENews_ArbitrationMultipleLang.aspx>.

[71] cf. Voit, in Musielak, *Kommentar zur ZPO* § 1046, para 2; Münch, in Rauscher et al (eds), *MünchKommZPO* § 1036, para 13; Hanefeld (n 58) para 7.59.

[72] Oberlandesgericht Case No 10 SchH 3/01, 19 December 2001, [2003] *SchiedsVZ* 134,136; KG Berlin (Higher Regional Court Berlin) Case No 20 SchH 2/10, 7 July 2010, [2010] *SchiedsVZ* 225; Münch, in Rauscher et al (eds), *MünchKommZPO* § 1036, para 30; Geimer, in Zöller (ed), *Zivilprozessordnung* § 1036, para 10.

[73] § 1036(2) ZPO.

[74] Geimer, in Zöller (ed), *Zivilprozessordnung* § 1036, para 10; stricter (no limitation): Nacimiento and Abt, in Böckstiegel et al (eds), *Arbitration in Germany* § 1036, para 4.

[75] For 'discriminatory' clauses, see n 31.

raising the same grounds later in setting aside or enforcement proceedings.[76] The applicant must state the reasons for the challenge. From a purely practical point of view, the threshold for removal will be rather high for collegial tribunal members.

7.61 If a challenge is rejected under a procedure agreed on by the parties (eg in applicable institutional arbitration rules) or by the tribunal under section 1037(2), the applicant may, within one month of having received the rejection, apply to the courts to decide the challenge.[77] While the challenge before the court is under way, the tribunal, including the challenged arbitrator, may continue the proceedings and even make an award. Where serious reasons for a challenge are submitted, prudent tribunals will consider staying the proceedings until the court decides. If the tribunal does not stay the proceedings and renders an award, and the court then upholds the challenge, the award can be set aside.[78]

7.62 The decision of the court will have *res judicata* effect: a court faced with an enforcement or setting aside action will be bound by the first court's decision.[79]

7.3.3 The role of courts in compelling testimony/evidence

7.63 German courts will support both domestic and foreign[80] arbitral tribunals in the taking of evidence. Section 1050 ZPO provides:

> The arbitral tribunal or, with the consent of the arbitral tribunal, a party may file a petition that the court provide support by taking evidence or by taking any other actions reserved for judges that the arbitral tribunal is not authorized to take. The court shall deal with the petition, unless it deems it to be inadmissible, in accordance with its procedural rules as applying to the taking of evidence or any other actions reserved for judges. The arbitral judges are entitled to attend the court hearing at which evidence is taken and to ask questions.

7.64 This provision allows tribunals to request the assistance of courts for official service in foreign countries (when a postal/courier service is unavailable), official inquiries with public authorities, examining witnesses who do not want to appear voluntarily, or examining witnesses under oath.[81] The court can also fix the amount in dispute where the parties disagree and the applicable arbitration rules do not allow the tribunal to do this (this is an 'action reserved for judges which the tribunal is not authorized to do').[82] While it is argued that the scope also encompasses requiring the parties or third parties to produce documents or objects, or to consent to the examination of objects by experts (which is possible under German procedural law),[83] the courts can do little more than an arbitral tribunal. If a party refuses to produce certain documents, the court may draw adverse inferences but does not have the

[76] Geimer, in Zöller (ed), *Zivilprozessordnung* § 1037, para 6.

[77] §1037(3) ZPO. Here, too, failure to comply with the time limit will lead to preclusion in later proceedings, see Voit, in Musielak, *Kommentar zur ZPO* § 1037, para 5. However, if the reasons for a challenge become public only after the award has been rendered, they may still be brought forward if an egregious and serious reason exists, see Voit, in Musielak, *Kommentar zur ZPO* § 1037, para 6 and Geimer, in Zöller (ed), *Zivilprozessordnung* § 1037, para 7; Saenger, in Saenger (ed), *Zivilprozessordnung* § 1037, para 7.

[78] Voit, in Musielak, *Kommentar zur ZPO* § 1037, para 7.

[79] Geimer, in Zöller (ed), *Zivilprozessordnung* § 1037, para 6.

[80] See §1025(2) ZPO.

[81] See Voit, in Musielak, *Kommentar zur ZPO* § 1050, para 2.

[82] See AG Stuttgart (Municipal Court Stuttgart) Case No 18 C 7402/07, Decision of 8 April 2008, [2012] *SchiedsVZ* 54.

[83] Münch, in Rauscher et al (eds), *MünchKommZPO* § 1050, para 6.

power to compel document production, for example by way of coercive fines.[84] A refusal does not amount to contempt of court.

Pursuant to section 1050 ZPO, the court will give effect to a request for evidentiary assistance in accordance with its procedural rules, unless it regards the application as inadmissible. An application is inadmissible if the requested assistance is not possible under the ZPO, for example if document discovery is requested.[85] The court is not, however, empowered to review the usefulness of the requested assistance (eg whether the taking of evidence is necessary).[86] **7.65**

Unlike for other types of judicial assistance in arbitration, the competent court for judicial assistance in obtaining evidence is the local court (*Amtsgericht*) in whose district the assistance is requested.[87] This tracking to the local courts has a helpful side-effect: a party that is represented in the arbitral proceedings by foreign counsel need not necessarily retain German counsel, as it is not mandatory to be represented by counsel before the local courts. **7.66**

Experience with this procedure, insofar as available, seems to be positive. *Wirth* and *Hoffmann-Nowotny* recall that in a complex multi-party arbitration, from the filing of the request until the hearing of witnesses just three months passed. They concluded that the mechanism was fast and unbureaucratic, in particular in comparison with the situation under Swiss law.[88] **7.67**

7.3.4 Foreign practitioners as counsel

German procedural law does not impose any restrictions on foreign counsel in arbitral proceedings. It is, however, necessary to be represented by German counsel in proceedings before the Higher Regional Court in most arbitration-related matters. **7.68**

7.3.5 Local requirements for the conduct of proceedings

As Germany has adopted the UNCITRAL Model Law, there are few local requirements for the conduct of proceedings. The general rules of procedure are contained in section 1042 ZPO: **7.69**

> Section 1042 General rules of procedure
> (1) The parties shall be treated with equality and each party shall be given a full opportunity of presenting his case.
> (2) Lawyers may not be excluded from acting as authorized representatives.[89]
> (3) Otherwise, subject to the mandatory provisions of this Book, the parties are free to determine the procedure themselves or by reference to a set of arbitration rules.

[84] A Stadler, in *Kommentar zur ZPO* § 142, para 7; but see H Wöstmann, in I Saenger (ed), *Zivilprozessordnung* § 142, para 2, arguing that disclosure requests made to third parties can be enforced by penal notices if the third party is obliged under substantive law to disclose the documents.

[85] Geimer, in Zöller (ed), *Zivilprozessordnung* § 1050, para 6.

[86] K Sachs and T Lörcher, in Böckstiegel et al (eds), *Arbitration in Germany* § 1050, para 4.

[87] § 1062(4) ZPO.

[88] M Wirth and UH Hoffmann-Nowotny, 'Rechtshilfe deutscher Gerichte zugunsten ausländischer Schiedsgerichte bei der Beweisaufnahme—ein Erfahrungsbericht' [2005] *SchiedsVZ* 66.

[89] While there is no requirement to be represented by lawyers in arbitration proceedings, whether they are German *Rechtsanwälte* or foreign lawyers (unlike the situation before the Regional Courts), a tribunal may not exclude lawyers from acting as authorized representatives in proceedings. This is mandatory law; the parties cannot deviate from it.

(4) Failing an agreement by the parties, and in the absence of provisions in this Book, the arbitral tribunal shall conduct the arbitration in such manner as it considers appropriate. The arbitral tribunal is empowered to determine the admissibility of taking evidence, take evidence and assess freely such evidence.

7.70 No one would consider these rules to be strange or a deviation from international practice. According to section 1042(3) ZPO, the parties may shape the procedure according to their wishes, as long as mandatory rules are adhered to. It would, for example, be possible to conduct an arbitration like a German court proceeding, albeit with the arbitrator acting as a 'private judge', or like a common-law arbitration with witness statements and full cross-examination. There is no requirement to hold an oral hearing, unless one of the parties expressly requests this.[90] There are few mandatory rules; these include sections 1042(1) (equal treatment and due process) and 1042(2) (counsel as authorized representative) and the rules on the court's control over jurisdiction (see paragraphs 7.28–7.37).

7.71 With the exception of somewhat restricted *competence-competence*, none of the German rules should surprise a foreign party. However, there are some dispositive rules of Book Ten that the parties might wish to consider modifying in their agreement.

7.72 According to section 1043 ZPO, the parties are free to agree on the place of arbitration. Failing such agreement, the place of arbitration shall be determined by the arbitral tribunal having regard to the circumstances of the case, including the convenience of the parties. The place of arbitration in Germany determines which OLG has jurisdiction over the arbitration.[91] It may therefore be of greater relevance in Germany to carefully consider the place of arbitration, as opposed to such countries as France, Sweden, and the United Kingdom, in which judicial supervision of arbitration tends to be centralized in the capital.

7.73 Section 1049 ZPO provides:

(1) Unless otherwise agreed by the parties, the arbitral tribunal may appoint one or more experts to report to it on specific issues to be determined by the arbitral tribunal. It may also require a party to give the expert any relevant information or to produce, or to provide access to, any relevant documents or property for his inspection.
(2) Unless otherwise agreed by the parties, if a party so requests or if the arbitral tribunal considers it necessary, the expert shall, after delivery of his written or oral report, participate in an oral hearing where the parties have the opportunity to put questions to him and to present expert witnesses in order to testify on the points at issue.

Tribunals will of course treat party-appointed experts and their reports as means of evidence, but parties should not be surprised if the tribunal wants to appoint its own expert.

7.74 There is another aspect that is not explicitly regulated in Book Ten. In German court proceedings, the courts will—and are in fact legally required to—explore chances for a settlement and make settlement proposals, irrespective of whether the parties request the court's assistance. This established legal tradition has no relevance for arbitration proceedings. However, in purely domestic proceedings, parties and counsel will expect tribunals to make settlement proposals. While experienced German arbitrators in international proceedings (ie those with foreign parties) will address this issue very carefully (if at all), foreign parties should be aware

90 See § 1047 ZPO.
91 § 1062(1) ZPO.

of this and not mistake it for bias on the part of the tribunal. A challenge against an arbitrator for making settlement proposals is unlikely to be successful.[92]

7.4 The Award

Although German law does not establish the meaning of the terms 'award' or 'final award', the latter may be defined as an award that finally disposes of all or part of the as yet undecided issues presented in the proceedings. Consequently, such an award has the effect of *res judicata* with regard to all claims and counterclaims that have been decided in the award and terminates the arbitral proceedings pursuant to section 1056(1) ZPO. **7.75**

Within the scope of its jurisdiction, an arbitral tribunal may make the same orders in its award as could be made in a court judgment. In particular, the arbitral tribunal can order a party to make payments, to deliver goods, to make a declaration of will,[93] or to determine the existence or non-existence of a legal relationship. **7.76**

The arbitral tribunal has the discretion to issue a partial award that disposes of certain parts of the issue, for example one of several claims or a certain part of a specific claim. Partial awards must satisfy the same formal requirements as final awards, which are laid down in section 1054 ZPO. Partial awards can be separately challenged according to section 1059 ZPO or enforced against a party according to sections 1060ff ZPO. In contrast to final awards (which may include partial awards), interim awards do not decide finally on a separate part of the dispute but on certain issues related to the claim, for example the limitation of a claim or special admissibility criteria. Unlike partial awards, interim awards may not be challenged or enforced. They are binding solely on the arbitral tribunal with regard to its subsequent final decision.[94] **7.77**

7.4.1 Form of award

The formal requirements for an award are regulated in section 1054 ZPO: **7.78**

(1) The award shall be made in writing and shall be signed by the arbitrator or arbitrators. In arbitral proceedings with more than one arbitrator, the signatures of the majority of all members of the arbitral tribunal shall suffice, provided that the reason for any omitted signature is stated.
(2) The award shall state the reasons upon which it is based, unless the parties have agreed that no reasons are to be given or the award is an award on agreed terms under section 1053.
(3) The award shall state its date and the place of arbitration as determined in accordance with section 1043 subs. 1. The award shall be deemed to have been made on that date and at that place.
(4) A copy of the award signed by the arbitrators shall be delivered to each party.

[92] See Hanefeld (n 58) para 7.192; Nacimiento and Abt, in Böckstiegel et al (eds), *Arbitration in Germany* § 1036, para 40.

[93] Under German law, a judgment (or an award) may order a party to make a declaration of will, eg to make an offer or accept an offer, to consent to land charges being entered into the land registry or to the change of articles of association of a company. The judgment/award obliging the debtor to make such declaration replaces/constitutes that declaration once the judgment/award has become enforceable.

[94] cf Voit, in Musielak, *Kommentar zur ZPO* § 1055, para 2–4.

There are thus four formal requirements for awards under German law: they must be in writing, they must state reasons, include the date and place of arbitration, and be signed at least by the majority of members of the tribunal.

7.79 At a minimum, the statement of reasons requires that the arbitral tribunal should comment at least briefly, but not necessarily comprehensively, on the substance of the claims and defences. A complete and exhaustive account of all relevant considerations is not required,[95] but in practice, most arbitral awards include exhaustive and detailed reasoning. A largely incomplete, or entirely absent, account of reasons leaves the award open to challenge under section 1059 ZPO.

7.80 According to section 1054 (3) ZPO, the arbitral award must state the date on which it was rendered and the place of arbitration. The specification of the date proves the date on which the arbitral award came into existence. The specification of the place of arbitration is of considerable legal importance. For example, the question of whether an arbitral award is foreign depends on the place of arbitration. The place of arbitration also determines which OLG is competent to assist and supervise the arbitral proceedings.

7.81 The award can be served on the parties by post (if possible). It is not necessary to register it first with the court or a notary public. There is also no stamp duty or similar levy on awards.

7.4.2 Substance of award

7.82 The substance of an arbitral award is primarily determined by the claims of the parties. With regard to deciding those claims, section 1051 ZPO provides:

> (1) The arbitral tribunal shall decide the dispute in accordance with such rules of law as are chosen by the parties as applicable to the substance of the dispute. Any designation of the law or legal system of a given State shall be construed, unless otherwise expressed, as directly referring to the substantive law of that State and not to its conflict of laws rules.
> (2) Failing any designation by the parties, the arbitral tribunal shall apply the law of the State with which the subject-matter of the proceedings is most closely connected.
> (3) The arbitral tribunal shall decide *ex aequo et bono* or as *amiable compositeur* only if the parties have expressly authorized it to do so. The parties may so authorize the arbitral tribunal up to the time of its decision.
> (4) In all cases, the arbitral tribunal shall decide in accordance with the terms of the contract and shall take into account the usages of the trade applicable to the transaction.

7.83 These provisions are basically self-explanatory. Paragraph 1 makes clear that parties may choose not only a particular national law, but also 'rules of law'. This allows them to agree on the application of the CISG[96] or the UNIDROIT Principles of International Commercial Contracts.[97]

7.84 It is disputed whether this also covers applying the *lex mercatoria*, or whether applying the *lex mercatoria* amounts to deciding *ex aequo et bono*, for which the tribunal must be expressly

---

[95] Saenger, in Saenger (ed), *Zivilprozessordnung* § 1054, para 5; Voit, in Musielak, *Kommentar zur ZPO* § 1054, para 4.

[96] United Nations Convention on Contracts for the International Sale of Goods, Vienna, 11 April 1980 (entry into force 1 January 1988), 1487 UNTS 3.

[97] The full text of UNIDROIT Principles of International Commercial Contracts 2010 is available at <http://www.unidroit.org/english/principles/contracts/main.htm>. See Hanefeld (n 58) para 7.176.

authorized under subsection (3). To be on the safe side, a tribunal should only apply the *lex mercatoria* if expressly authorized to do so by the parties.[98]

The only provision regulating the substance of the award is section 1057 ZPO: **7.85**

(1) Unless the parties agree otherwise, the arbitral tribunal shall allocate, by means of an arbitral award, the costs of the arbitration as between the parties, including those incurred by the parties necessary for the proper pursuit of their claim or defense. It shall do so at its discretion and take into consideration the circumstances of the case, in particular the outcome of the proceedings.
(2) To the extent that the costs of the arbitral proceedings have been fixed, the arbitral tribunal shall also decide on the amount to be borne by each party. If the costs have not been fixed or if they can only be fixed once the arbitral proceedings have been terminated, the decision shall be taken by means of a separate award.

The Tribunal thus has to allocate of the costs of the proceedings, unless the parties agree otherwise. This means that section 1057 is not mandatory. Any rule of cost allocation, for example as provided for in institutional arbitration rules, will prevail over section 1057.

The 'necessary' costs for the proper pursuit of claim or defence of course encompasses lawyers' fees. For international proceedings taking place in Germany, and in particular where non-German lawyers are retained as counsel, it is generally accepted that the amount of reimbursable lawyers' fees is not limited by German statutory rules.[99] For proceedings involving German parties and German lawyers, it seems arguable that fees exceeding the statutory rules can be compensated where the applicable arbitration rules do not contain this limitation.[100] As regards interest on costs, this needs to be specifically requested and requires a substantive legal basis for the claim.[101] **7.86**

The tribunal has a reasonable amount of flexibility in deciding which party bears the costs of the proceedings. While the general rule is that 'costs follow the event', ie that the unsuccessful party bears the costs, the tribunal may deviate from this rule and may even shift costs to the winning party. However, this should be done only in exceptional cases.[102] **7.87**

7.5 After the Award

Arbitral awards are subject to attack in the German courts under section 1059 ZPO, regardless of whether they were made according to national, foreign, or international procedural rules, as long as the place of arbitration was in Germany.[103] In contrast, German courts do not have jurisdiction to set aside foreign awards. With regard to foreign awards, German courts are limited to refusing recognition and enforcement in Germany under section 1062 ZPO. **7.88**

[98] The full text of UNIDROIT Principles of International Commercial Contracts 2010 is available at <http://www.unidroit.org/english/principles/contracts/main.htm>. See Hanefeld (n 58) para 7.183 with further references.

[99] Oberlandesgericht Case No 34 Sch 19/11, 23 July 2012, [2012] *SchiedsVZ* 282; Risse and Altenkirch (n 12) 5ff; cf Saenger, in Saenger (ed), *Zivilprozessordnung* § 1057, para 6.

[100] Oberlandesgericht Case No 34 Sch 19/11, 23 July 2012, [2012] *SchiedsVZ* 282.

[101] K Gerstenmaier, 'Zur Verzinslichkeit von Kostenerstattungsforderungen im Schiedsverfahren' [2012] *SchiedsVZ* 1–4.

[102] Münch, in Rauscher et al (eds), *MünchKommZPO* § 1057, para 13; Geimer, in Zöller (ed), *Zivilprozessordnung* § 1056, para 2.

[103] § 1025 ZPO.

7.89 Under certain circumstances, an award might be void *ipso jure*, for example if it was rendered while the tribunal's jurisdiction was still being challenged in the local courts.[104] In such a case, a party nevertheless has a legitimate interest in setting aside the award, which formally exists.[105] Similarly, while foreign arbitral awards cannot be set aside,[106] it has been suggested that a party should at least be able to seek declaratory relief that the award is null and void.[107] This would usually require that the award has been set aside by the courts of the seat of the arbitration.

7.90 The parties may stipulate in their arbitration agreement that each party has the right to commence state court proceedings for an appeal-like review of the award within a certain time after receipt of the award. While in the past German state courts did not accept such agreements as valid, the Federal Court of Justice has held that the parties may agree in their arbitration agreement that the binding effect of the arbitral award is subject to neither party having initiated court proceedings within a specific period of time.[108] Arbitration agreements with this provision tend to be the exception.

7.5.1 Local standards for setting aside/annulment

7.91 The arbitration award can be set aside only at the request of one of the parties and on the grounds listed in section 1059(2) ZPO. This provision is based on Article 34 of the UNCITRAL Model Law and distinguishes between grounds that have to be pleaded by the applicant (section 1059(2)(1)) and those which are taken into account *ex officio* (section 1059(2)(2)).

7.92 Section 1059(2)(1) ZPO provides:

> An arbitral award may be set aside only if:
> 1. the applicant shows sufficient cause that:
>   a) a party to the arbitration agreement referred to in sections 1029 and 1031 of the German Code of Civil Procedure was under some incapacity pursuant to the law applicable to him; or the said agreement is not valid under the law to which the parties have subjected it or, failing any indications thereon, under German law; or
>   b) he was not given proper notice of appointment of an arbitrator or of the arbitral proceedings or was otherwise unable to present his case; or
>   c) the award deals with a dispute not contemplated by or not falling within the terms of the submission to arbitration, or contains decisions on matters beyond the scope of the submission to arbitration; provided that, if the decisions on matters submitted to arbitration can be separated from those not so submitted, only that part of the award which contains decisions on matters not submitted to arbitration may be set aside; or
>   d) the composition of the arbitral tribunal or the arbitral procedure was not in accordance with a provision of this Book or with an admissible agreement of the parties and this presumably affected the award.

---

104 See discussion of § 1040 ZPO at para 7.14.
105 S Kröll and P Kraft, in Böckstiegel et al (eds), *Arbitration in Germany* § 1059, para 16.
106 See § 1061(2) and (3) ZPO.
107 Geimer, in Zöller (ed), *Zivilprozessordnung* § 1059, para 14.
108 Hanefeld (n 58) para 7.227; Bundesgerichtshof Case No III ZB 7/06, 1 March 2007, [2007] *SchiedsVZ* 160, 162, para 19.

The grounds in section 1059(2)(1) are mainly concerned with procedural defects and must be pleaded by the applicant, who needs to show sufficient cause for his allegations.[109] Under section 1059(2)(1)(a) to (d), an arbitral award may be set aside on account of an invalid arbitration agreement, violations of the right to be heard and to fairly present one's case, excess of jurisdiction by the tribunal, improper constitution of the arbitral tribunal, or other procedural irregularities. It is important to recall that because of the tribunal's limited *competence-competence*, its findings on jurisdiction are not binding on the court.[110] **7.93**

Section 1059(2)(2) ZPO reads:

> An arbitral award may be set aside only if:
>
> ...
>
> 2. the court finds that
>   a) the subject matter of the dispute is not capable of settlement by arbitration under German law; or
>   b) recognition and enforcement of the award leads to a result which is in conflict with public policy (*ordre public*)....

This second category of grounds for setting aside therefore deals with cases of non-compliance with procedural and substantive law requirements that are so serious they must be considered by the court *ex officio*. These grounds, and in particular, the *ordre public* ground, are construed narrowly. German courts tend to apply international *ordre public* as a yardstick, which is not automatically violated even if the award violates mandatory German law.[111] **7.94**

A party will be precluded from raising in setting aside proceedings any objection that it could have raised during the arbitration, but omitted to do so.[112] **7.95**

7.5.2 Local procedures for setting aside/annulment

An application for setting aside an award can generally only be made within three months from the day on which the party making the application received notification of the award.[113] The jurisdiction for challenges to arbitral awards lies with the OLG at the place of arbitration. According to section 1059(4) ZPO, the court can set the award aside and refer the matter back to the arbitral tribunal. The proceedings would then be continued with the original arbitral tribunal in place, as it is presumed that the original arbitration agreement is revived. Referring the matter back to the original tribunal is, however, the exception. If the award is set aside without the matter being referred back to the arbitral tribunal, pursuant to section 1056(3) ZPO, a new arbitral tribunal must be constituted because in such cases the mandate of the original arbitral tribunal will have ended. **7.96**

The duration of setting aside proceedings will, of course, very much depend on the specific grounds raised, and on the caseload of the OLG concerned. Generally, a duration between six to twelve months should be expected. **7.97**

---

109 Geimer, in Zöller (ed), *Zivilprozessordnung* § 1059, para 33.

110 See Kröll and Kraft, in Böckstiegel et al (eds), *Arbitration in Germany* § 1059, para 55.

111 Geimer, in Zöller (ed), *Zivilprozessordnung* § 1059, para 47 (but see para 65, according to which intentional misapplication of the law is a breach of *ordre public*); Kröll and Kraft, in Böckstiegel et al (eds), *Arbitration in Germany* § 1059, paras 78–79. As to the international ordre public, see Bundesgerichtshof Case No XI ZR 377–97, 21 April 1998, [1998] *Neue Juristische Wochenschrift* 2358.

112 § 1027 ZPO.

113 § 1059(3) ZPO.

7.6 Conclusion

7.98 Germany offers a modern and effective legal framework for international arbitration. As in other popular arbitration jurisdictions such as the UK, there are deviations from the UNCITRAL Model Law regarding the courts' control of and assistance in the proceedings. However, they do not affect Germany's general suitability as arbitration venue. It is also well connected by plane (Frankfurt is Europe's third busiest airport) and offers excellent infrastructure in terms of hotels and hearing facilities.

7.99 Nevertheless, a German venue is not always on the shortlist of counsel and arbitral tribunals. Whether it is more attractive to spend a week in Geneva or Paris, rather than in Munich or Hamburg, is debatable. What may be an obstacle in the minds of foreign lawyers is that there is not a single German arbitration venue akin to London for the United Kingdom or Paris for France. Instead, there are at least six suitable venues in Germany. The ability to choose should not be seen as an obstacle, but rather as an advantage. The text of the German arbitration law is available in English,[114] the courts have specialized arbitration chambers, and there is an abundant and flourishing arbitration scene. That court proceedings cannot (yet) be conducted in English should not be a problem as this is no different from the situation in Paris, Geneva, or Zurich—all popular arbitration venues.

[114] Available at <www.dis-arb.de>.

8

HONG KONG

Michael J Moser and John Choong

8.1 Background[1]

8.1.1 Introduction

Hong Kong is a Special Administrative Region of the People's Republic of China (PRC). **8.01**
British rule ended in 1997, with the PRC assuming sovereignty under the 'one country, two

[1] For more detailed discussion of the issues mentioned in this chapter, see 'Hong Kong SAR' in MJ Moser and J Choong (eds), *Asia Arbitration Handbook* (OUP, 2011), which formed the basis for this chapter.

systems' principle. The Hong Kong Special Administrative Region's constitutional document is the Basic Law,[2] which is akin to a mini-constitution, and ensures that the current political situation will remain in effect for 50 years.

8.02 Under the Basic Law, Hong Kong enjoys a high degree of autonomy, except in areas relating to foreign affairs and defence. In particular, the Hong Kong Special Administrative Region exercises executive, legislative, and independent judicial power, including that of final adjudication.

8.03 The Basic Law ensures that laws previously in force in Hong Kong (ie the common law, rules of equity, ordinances, subordinate legislation, and customary law) will, in general,[3] be maintained. The national laws of the People's Republic of China do not apply in Hong Kong, save for a few exceptions.[4]

8.04 Hong Kong has long been one of the leading arbitral seats in Asia. Hong Kong's prominence as a leading arbitral seat is due in large part to the establishment of the Hong Kong International Arbitration Centre (HKIAC) in 1985 and Hong Kong's adoption in 1990 of the United Nations Commission on International Trade Law (UNCITRAL) Model Law on International Commercial Arbitration.

8.05 In 1997, the PRC resumed sovereignty over Hong Kong. Importantly, arbitration law and practice in Hong Kong has remained unaffected by the handover,[5] and today Hong Kong continues to be widely regarded as one of the leading arbitral venues in Asia, particularly for China-related disputes. In addition, Hong Kong is also increasingly seen as one of the leading international arbitration seats worldwide.

8.1.2 Arbitration in Hong Kong

8.06 For many years, there has been strong support for arbitration in Hong Kong, both from the courts and from regional users of arbitration. The courts are respectful of party autonomy, and recognize that when parties have agreed to arbitration, the courts should uphold this agreement and provide support to ensure that disputes are effectively resolved by arbitration. In addition, the Hong Kong courts regularly enforce arbitral awards, both foreign and domestic, in Hong Kong.

8.07 The users of Hong Kong arbitration typically come from Hong Kong and the PRC, although given Hong Kong's international links, a significant number also come from further afield.

8.08 Hong Kong is the leading international arbitration venue for PRC-related disputes, with many Hong Kong-affiliated arbitrators having the necessary expertise, cultural background, and language skills to handle such disputes. In addition, Hong Kong is also seen as a leading arbitration venue for disputes relating to the wider Asian region.

---

[2] Basic Law of the Hong Kong Special Administrative Region of the People's Republic of China 1990.

[3] Save for laws which contravene the Basic Law, and subject to subsequent amendment by the Hong Kong legislature.

[4] In general, laws relating to defence and foreign affairs listed in Annex III to the Basic Law apply.

[5] Save for the recognition and enforcement of Hong Kong awards in the PRC and vice versa, which is discussed later.

8.1.3 The Hong Kong Arbitration Ordinance

In November 2010, Hong Kong passed its long-awaited new Arbitration Ordinance (Arbitration Ordinance).[6] The Ordinance takes into account the 2006 amendments to the Model Law and largely abolishes the previous distinction between international and domestic arbitrations. **8.09**

Schedule 2 to the Ordinance, which is based on provisions previously applied to domestic arbitrations under the old regime, allows the court to deal with preliminary questions of law, provides for challenges to the award on grounds of serious irregularity, and allows for appeals on questions of law.[7] Parties may expressly opt into Schedule 2. More significantly, Schedule 2 also automatically applies (unless the parties opt out) to: **8.10**

- arbitration agreements entered into before the commencement of the Ordinance that provide for domestic arbitration; or
- agreements entered into *within six years* after commencement of the Ordinance that provide for domestic arbitration.

In practice, parties to domestic arbitrations often fail to opt out of Schedule 2, with the result that the schedule applies by default to such arbitrations. More significantly, Schedule 2 does not by default apply to non-domestic arbitrations, including Hong Kong 'international' arbitrations. **8.11**

As in other Model Law countries, the Ordinance does not provide a complete code for the conduct of arbitrations, but is intended to provide a framework within which all kinds of ad hoc and institutional arbitrations may be carried out in Hong Kong. **8.12**

In addition to adopting the Model Law articles, the Arbitration Ordinance also contains a number of helpful amendments and clarifications. Proportionately, there are many such provisions although, in reality, many of these are less significant, and the Ordinance retains the original intent and approach of the Model Law. **8.13**

Apart from the Arbitration Ordinance, the High Court Ordinance[8] and Rules of the High Court[9] also contain relevant provisions dealing with arbitration-related court proceedings. **8.14**

The Arbitration Ordinance does not expressly list which provisions are mandatory. In line with the general approach under the Model Law, many of its provisions allow, either expressly or by implication, for the parties to contract out of them. Nonetheless, there are a number of key provisions in the Arbitration Ordinance that are mandatory. These include, for example, Article 18 of the UNCITRAL Model Law, the 'Magna Carta of arbitral procedure'.[10] **8.15**

Structurally, the Ordinance is divided into 14 parts: **8.16**

- Part 1 deals with preliminary issues;
- Parts 2 to 9 are based on Articles 1 to 34 of the Model Law, with various modifications to the Model Law provisions, as well as additional sections supplementing the Model Law provisions;

---

[6] Cap 609.

[7] All with various limitations; see the Arbitration Ordinance, Sch 2.

[8] Cap 4.

[9] Cap 4A.

[10] See P Binder, *International Commercial Arbitration and Conciliation in UNCITRAL Model Law Jurisdictions* (3rd edn, Sweet & Maxwell, 2010) 282.

- Part 11 sets out opt-in provisions as well as those that automatically apply in certain cases; and
- Parts 12 to 14 set out miscellaneous provisions.

8.17 Compared to the legislation in other jurisdictions in Asia, the Arbitration Ordinance is a lengthy statute, containing over 100 sections. One of its unusual features is that in most cases, the drafters have chosen to reproduce the full text of each Model Law provision in the Ordinance proper, followed by subsections under each article that modify or supplement the Model Law provision. The advantage of this approach is that readers can easily see the extent to which a Model Law provision has been adopted in Hong Kong.

8.18 Parties to Hong Kong international arbitrations typically agree to arbitrate under a set of arbitration rules. These rules usually contain more detailed provisions governing the procedure, which often prevail over the default provisions in the Arbitration Ordinance.

8.19 As already noted, although the Arbitration Ordinance adopts many provisions found in the Model Law, it also contains additional provisions that clarify or supplement the Model Law provisions. Most importantly, the Arbitration Ordinance:

- applies the Model Law to both international and domestic arbitrations;[11]
- omits the provision that the default number of arbitrators is three;[12]
- states that the parties shall have a 'reasonable opportunity' to present their cases, rather than a 'full opportunity';[13]
- adds confidentiality provisions that apply to information relating to arbitral proceedings, awards, and related court proceedings;[14]
- adds provisions providing for mediator-arbitrators;[15]
- expressly lists the general powers exercisable by the tribunal, and by the courts;[16]
- allows arbitrators to limit the amount of recoverable costs;[17]
- adds more extensive provisions dealing with costs, the taxation of costs, and disputes over the tribunal's fees and expenses;[18]
- adds more extensive provisions dealing with the enforcement of various categories of awards which are relevant to Hong Kong;[19]
- adds a Schedule 2, dealing with provisions that parties may opt into or opt out of;[20] and
- adds provisions limiting the liability of the tribunal and related parties.[21]

8.20 There are no significant legislative amendments to the Arbitration Ordinance on the horizon.

[11] See Arbitration Ordinance, s 5. But note that the provisions of Sch 2 will often still apply to domestic arbitrations.

[12] Arbitration Ordinance, s 23.

[13] Arbitration Ordinance, s 46(3)(b).

[14] Arbitration Ordinance, ss 16–18.

[15] Arbitration Ordinance, ss 32 and 33.

[16] Arbitration Ordinance, ss 56 and 60.

[17] Arbitration Ordinance, s 57.

[18] Arbitration Ordinance, ss 74–77.

[19] Arbitration Ordinance, Pt 10.

[20] Read with Arbitration Ordinance, Pt 11.

[21] Arbitration Ordinance, ss 104 and 105.

8.1.4 The HKIAC

The HKIAC is the leading arbitral institution in Hong Kong. It was established in 1985 to promote the use of arbitration and other forms of alternative dispute resolution. Formed as a non-profit making company limited by guarantee under Hong Kong law, the HKIAC was originally funded by contributions from the business community and the Hong Kong government. Today the HKIAC is completely independent of both business and government and operates with its own budget and funds. It has grown to become a major international arbitration institution and in its current role, it provides the focus for arbitration activity in Hong Kong. **8.21**

The role of the HKIAC has grown substantially over the last decade. In 1993 the HKIAC (acting either in an administrative capacity or as an appointing authority) handled 139 cases, rising to 218 in 1997, 257 in 1999, 307 in 2001, and 448 in 2007. **8.22**

In 2011, the HKIAC handled 502 dispute resolution matters.[22] These included: **8.23**

- 275 arbitration cases;
- 127 domain name cases; and
- 100 mediations.

Of the 275 arbitration cases in 2011, 65 per cent were international in nature and 35 per cent were domestic. Of the total, 41 cases were fully administered by the HKIAC in accordance with its own rules. Of all the arbitration cases, 14 per cent were construction disputes, 29 per cent were commercial disputes, 15 per cent were corporate disputes, 4 per cent were insurance disputes, and 38 per cent were maritime disputes.

In practice, a significant number of cross-border commercial contracts, including many PRC-related contracts, provide for arbitration instead of litigation. This is for a variety of reasons, including the belief that a Hong Kong arbitral tribunal is more impartial than the PRC courts or a PRC tribunal, and because a Hong Kong arbitral award is more easily enforceable in the PRC than a Hong Kong court judgment. **8.24**

The more distinctive features of arbitration under the HKIAC Administered Arbitration Rules include the following:[23] **8.25**

- *a 'light touch' approach*: the HKIAC adopts a 'light touch' role in administering arbitrations, compared to other rules which provide for a more institutionalized process, such as those of the International Chamber of Commerce (ICC) and the Singapore International Arbitration Centre—for example the HKIAC rules do not provide for a scrutiny process for the award;
- *no time limit*: there is no time limit within which a tribunal must render its award;
- *confidentiality*: the rules contain strict confidentiality provisions imposed on the parties, the arbitrators, the HKIAC, and other involved parties;
- *expedited procedure*: the rules provide for an expedited procedure which applies where the aggregate value of the amounts in dispute is less than US$250,000, unless the parties agree or the HKIAC Secretariat decides otherwise; and

22 HKIAC Annual Report 2011 <http://hkiac.org/images/stories/hkiac/2011_Annual_Report.pdf> (accessed 6 July 2012).

23 HKIAC Arbitration Rules and Guidelines, available at <http://www.hkiac.org/index.php/arbitration/arbitration-rules> (accessed 25 January 2013).

- *flexibility on costs*: the HKIAC rules give the parties considerable flexibility on the issue of costs, and the parties may opt to have the fees calculated according to the HKIAC's scale of fees, or in accordance with fee arrangements agreed with the arbitrator(s).

8.26 The Arbitration Ordinance authorizes the HKIAC to carry out two significant statutory functions:

- determining whether the tribunal should have one or three arbitrators;[24] and
- appointing arbitrators when (a) parties fail to agree or designate an appointing authority or (b) the designated appointing authority fails to carry out its function.[25]

8.27 It is also worth noting that in 2008, the ICC opened an Asia office of the ICC Court's Secretariat in Hong Kong. The office is the ICC Court Secretariat's first branch outside Paris and has a case management team which administers cases in the region under the ICC Rules of Arbitration. Also, in September 2012, the China International Economic and Trade Arbitration Commission (CIETAC) opened its Hong Kong Arbitration Center—its first branch outside Mainland China.

8.1.5 Comparison with alternative seats

8.28 Given Hong Kong's status as a leading regional arbitration venue, it is unsurprising that most Hong Kong-related arbitration disputes are arbitrated in Hong Kong itself. Even when only one of the parties is connected to Hong Kong, informed foreign parties do not view this as a major concern, given the large pool of impartial international arbitrators available in Hong Kong.

8.29 When there is a concern over a perceived lack of neutrality, and if parties do not agree that Hong Kong should be the place of arbitration, popular alternatives include Singapore (if a regional seat is sought, and if none of the parties are connected to Singapore) or, further afield, seats such as London or Stockholm.

8.30 Which seat is eventually chosen depends largely on the backgrounds of the parties and their lawyers. When all the parties to the transaction are based in the region, it is likely that there will be a preference for arbitration in the region (particularly in Singapore); if there are foreign parties that are not based in the region, there may be a stronger likelihood of a venue outside Asia (such as London); and when Chinese parties are involved and they agree to arbitrate outside Asia, some may incline towards Stockholm (partly for historical reasons).

8.31 Given Hong Kong's close integration with the PRC, a significant number of Hong Kong transactions involve the PRC. When both parties have connections to Hong Kong or the PRC (even if the ultimate parent companies are not based there), there is often less of a concern with agreeing to arbitration in Hong Kong. However, when one of the parties has particularly close connections with the PRC and Hong Kong, and the other does not, the alternatives already mentioned may also be considered.

8.32 Hong Kong and Singapore are often compared as leading venues for arbitration in the region. They share many of the same attributes that make for successful arbitral venues, including modern arbitral legislation based on the Model Law, a supportive judiciary, modern

---

[24] Arbitration Ordinance, s 23(3). For further discussion, see para 8.54.

[25] Arbitration Ordinance, ss 13(2) and 24(1). For further discussion, see paras 8.55–8.65.

facilities, and good infrastructural support. However, whereas Hong Kong has very much become the leading venue for PRC-related arbitrations, Singapore has come into its own in handling South Asia-related arbitrations.

8.2 Commencing the Arbitration

8.2.1 Requirements for a valid arbitration agreement

The Arbitration Ordinance adopts option I of Article 7 of the Model Law (as amended in 2006),[26] which provides that an 'arbitration agreement' is an agreement by the parties to submit to arbitration all or certain disputes which have arisen or which may arise between them in respect of a defined legal relationship, whether contractual or not. **8.33**

The arbitration agreement may be in the form of an arbitration clause in a contract or in the form of a separate agreement. The agreement must be in writing and, for this purpose, it may be recorded in any form, whether the arbitration agreement or contract has been concluded orally, by conduct, or by other means. The writing requirement is met even when electronic communications are used (as further detailed in Article 7 of the Model Law), and the agreement may be contained in an exchange of statements of claim and defence in which the existence of an agreement is alleged by one party and not denied by the other. **8.34**

In addition, section 19 of the Arbitration Ordinance expressly clarifies that the writing requirement is met if the arbitration agreement is contained in a document, whether or not it is signed by the parties, and when the agreement, although not in writing, is recorded by one of the parties to the agreement or by an authorized third party. The effect of this amendment is to extend the meaning of 'written agreement'. **8.35**

However, it seems that arbitration agreements that are entirely oral fall outside the Ordinance. In the rare event that a party should seek to commence arbitral proceedings based on a wholly oral arbitration agreement, the proceedings would be governed by the common law.[27] **8.36**

8.2.2 Legal capacity

In general, under Hong Kong law, any person who has the capacity in law to enter into contracts may also enter into an arbitration agreement. Whether persons have or lack such capacity is determined under general contract law; legal infants (persons under 18 years of age) and persons lacking mental capacity do not have contractual capacity. Different rules may apply to certain categories of persons, including bankrupts,[28] partners, personal representatives, and trustees; these are subject to the principles ordinarily applicable to such persons. **8.37**

---

[26] Model Law, Art 7 is given effect by the Arbitration Ordinance, s 19.

[27] Unless, of course, there is an exchange of statements of claim and defence in which the existence of an agreement is alleged by one party and not denied by the other: the Model Law, Art 7(5) given effect by the Arbitration Ordinance, s 19. The old Arbitration Ordinance, s 2AC(2)(f) brings such an agreement within the scope of the 'writing' requirement.

[28] This used to be dealt with under the old Arbitration Ordinance (cap 341), s 5 in relation to domestic arbitrations, but the provision has been deleted from the current Arbitration Ordinance, in line with the recommendations of the *Report of Committee on Hong Kong Arbitration Law* (2003) that the subject should more appropriately be dealt with by the legislation on insolvency.

8.38 Of greater practical importance, it must be noted that under Hong Kong law[29] a person dealing as a consumer[30] may not, in general,[31] agree to submit future disputes to arbitration. Instead, consent will be binding only if it is made after the disputes in question have arisen, or when the consumer himself or herself invokes the arbitration agreement.

8.39 Outside such situations, in most ordinary commercial transactions parties have the capacity to agree to, and be bound by, arbitration agreements they enter into.

8.2.3 Arbitrability

8.40 Hong Kong law adopts a broad view of the types of dispute that are arbitrable. Generally, any dispute affecting the civil interests of parties is arbitrable. This includes claims for breach of contract, tort, breach of trust, and claims relating to real or personal property. This broad approach is also suggested by the decision[32] in Hong Kong to extend the scope of the Model Law beyond just 'international commercial arbitrations', to cover all arbitrations 'under an arbitration agreement'[33] (as the term is defined in the Ordinance).[34]

8.41 The Hong Kong courts are also strongly supportive of international arbitration, and regard a broad range of matters as arbitrable, including tort claims. Recent English authorities have highlighted a trend of construing arbitration clauses broadly and of moving away from technical constructions based on the precise wording of the clause.[35] This approach has been viewed favourably in Hong Kong.[36]

8.42 That said, under Hong Kong law, pre-dispute agreements to arbitrate consumer disputes are generally not valid. In addition, restrictions apply in the case of employment disputes. In particular, the Court of Final Appeal has held that claims falling within the scope of the Employees' Compensation Ordinance (c 282) fall within the jurisdiction of the district court, to the exclusion of arbitration. Accordingly, the court has no power to stay such proceedings in favour of arbitration.[37]

8.43 In the case of matters that fall within the jurisdiction of the Labour Tribunal,[38] section 20(2) of the Arbitration Ordinance provides that the court may, if a party so requests, refer the parties to arbitration if there is 'no sufficient reason' why the parties should not be so referred, and provided the party requesting arbitration is ready and willing to do all things necessary in the arbitration.

---

[29] Control of Exemption Clauses Ordinance (cap 71), s 15.

[30] 'Dealing as a consumer' is defined in the Control of Exemption Clauses Ordinance (cap 71), s 4 and generally includes situations where the 'consumer' does not make the contract in the course of a business and the counterparty does.

[31] The limitation imposed on arbitration agreements with consumers does not apply in certain cases: see the Control of Exemption Clauses Ordinance (c 71), Sch 1 read together with s 15(2)(b).

[32] See the Consultation Paper: 'Reform of the Law of Arbitration in Hong Kong' (Department of Justice, 2007) 6ff.

[33] Arbitration Ordinance, s 5.

[34] See Arbitration Ordinance, s 19.

[35] *Fiona Trust and Holding Corp and ors v Privalov and ors* [2007] UKHL 40 (HL).

[36] *UDL Contracting Ltd v Apple Daily Printing Ltd and Lai Chee Ying Jimmy* HCA 1209/2007; 厦門新景地集團有限公司 *v Eton Properties Ltd* et al HCA 961/2008 (16 March 2010, CFI).

[37] See generally Arbitration Ordinance, s 20(2) and the CFA decision in *Paquito Lima Buton v Rainbow Joy Shipping Ltd Inc* [2008] 4 HKC 14, 55.

[38] The Labour Tribunal Ordinance (c 25), s 7 and Schedule set out the contracts within the Labour Tribunal's jurisdiction. These cover a range of claims, including those based on breach of a term in a contract of employment.

In addition, and in the absence of direct Hong Kong authority, it is generally believed that the usual restrictions on arbitrability that apply under English law also apply in Hong Kong. Thus, for example, disputes relating to family (marriage, divorce, children), intellectual property (when third-party rights are affected—in particular, the validity of copyrights, patents, registered designs, or trademarks), and criminal activity are unlikely to be arbitrable. **8.44**

8.2.4 Court enforcement of multi-tiered dispute resolution clauses

In many international contracts with a connection to Hong Kong, it is common for parties to include a proviso that the parties should endeavour to settle their disputes by negotiation before commencing arbitration. A provision for mediation prior to arbitration is considerably less common. However, this may become more commonplace, given the current push for mediation by the Hong Kong courts. **8.45**

Clauses that envisage more than one form of dispute resolution are known as multi-tiered or stepped clauses, since they usually envisage that parties will attempt to resolve their dispute using the first 'tier' or step in the dispute resolution process, and if that fails, proceed to the next step. **8.46**

In Hong Kong, it is common for there to be a time limit imposed on the negotiation component of multi-tiered dispute resolution clauses, with a typical period being 30 days (or 45 or 60 days). Often, the clause will provide that if no settlement is reached within the stipulated period, parties may (or shall) then proceed to the next step in the dispute resolution process, such as arbitration. Such clauses are usually straightforward, and experienced parties will often issue a formal written notice to the other disputant(s) referring to the dispute resolution clause, when they begin negotiations. This ensures that there is no subsequent dispute over whether the parties have fulfilled the negotiation step prior to moving on to the next step in the procedure. **8.47**

More difficult issues arise, however, when the clause provides that the parties should carry out such negotiations 'in good faith', using their 'best endeavours' or other similar wording, and no time limit is specified. In England, the courts have historically been reluctant to enforce obligations to negotiate in good faith, holding that these are merely agreements to agree.[39] In recent years, however, they have been more prepared to enforce agreements to engage in an alternative dispute resolution process, provided that the process is sufficiently identified and defined by objective criteria.[40] In Hong Kong, in one case, the Court of Appeal held that the clause in question lacked sufficient precision in not defining any specific steps that had to be taken. On this basis, the provision was held to be imprecise and unenforceable.[41] **8.48**

8.2.5 Stay of proceedings

Hong Kong has adopted Article 8 of the Model Law, with a few supplementary provisions.[42] If a party to an arbitration agreement commences court proceedings in respect of a dispute that is subject to an arbitration agreement, the other party (usually the defendant) may apply **8.49**

---

39 See generally *Walford v Miles* [1992] 2 AC 128.
40 See generally *Cable & Wireless plc v IBM UK Ltd* [2003] 1 BLR 89.
41 *Hyundai Engineering and Construction Co Ltd v Vigour Ltd* [2005] 1 HKC 579.
42 Model Law, Art 8 is given effect by the Arbitration Ordinance, s 20.

to the Court of First Instance for an order to stay those proceedings. The only significant limitations on a defendant's right to obtain a stay of court proceedings are that:

- the request must be made not later than when the defendant submits its first statement on the substance of the dispute; and
- the court is entitled to refuse to grant a stay if it finds that the arbitration agreement is null and void, inoperative, or incapable of being performed.

8.50 If the defendant files a defence (or other pleading) without requesting a stay in favour of arbitration, it will be unable to move to stay the court proceedings at a later stage. Otherwise, if the request is timely and the arbitration agreement is enforceable, the court must order a stay. Section 20(5) of the Arbitration Ordinance also makes it clear that when the court refers the parties to arbitration, it must also make an order staying the legal proceedings in that action.

8.51 In the unusual case in which the plaintiff is the party seeking a stay of its own court proceedings, there is case authority suggesting that the court may have inherent jurisdiction to grant the stay, and it may do so even when the plaintiff has already taken a substantive step in the proceedings.[43]

8.52 The Hong Kong courts have made it clear that the court's role is not to investigate whether the defendant has an arguable basis for disputing the claim. If a claim is made in a matter that is the subject of an arbitration agreement and the defendant does not admit the claim, there is a dispute within the meaning of the article. If the defendant seeks a stay of the action, the court must grant a stay unless these limitations apply.[44]

8.53 A decision of the court to refer the parties to arbitration under Article 8 of the Model Law is not subject to appeal.[45] In contrast, if the court refuses to refer the parties to arbitration, an appeal is allowed with leave of the court.[46] This indicates the pro-arbitration stance taken by the Ordinance. In addition, it is clear that Article 8 applies regardless of whether the agreed place of arbitration is in or outside Hong Kong.[47]

8.2.6 Number of arbitrators

8.54 Under the Arbitration Ordinance, the parties have the freedom to determine the number of arbitrators. This determination may be set out in the parties' arbitration agreement. By agreeing to adopt specific arbitration rules, the parties may have accepted the default number in the rules or authorized an arbitral institution to make the determination on their behalf. Failing agreement, section 23(3) of the Arbitration Ordinance provides that the number of arbitrators is to be either one or three, as decided by the HKIAC. This is the case unless section 1 of Schedule 2 to the Arbitration Ordinance applies (primarily in domestic arbitration, as discussed). Section 1 of Schedule 2 provides for a sole arbitrator.

---

[43] See *Chok Yick Interior Design & Engineering Co Ltd v Fortune World Enterprises Ltd HCA 2394/2008*; HCA 280/2009.

[44] *Tai Hing Cotton Mill Ltd v Glencore Grain Rotterdam BV and anor* [1996] 1 HKC 363 (CA).

[45] Arbitration Ordinance, s 20(8).

[46] Arbitration Ordinance, s 20(9).

[47] Arbitration Ordinance, s 5(2) expressly provides that s 20 applies when the place of arbitration is outside Hong Kong.

8.2.7 Appointment of arbitrators

The Arbitration Ordinance largely adopts Article 11 of the Model Law, dealing with the appointment of arbitrators. A number of supplementary provisions have also been included to deal with less common situations. **8.55**

Article 11 sets out the general principle that no person shall be precluded by reason of his nationality from acting as an arbitrator, unless otherwise agreed by the parties. In practice, it is not unusual for parties to Hong Kong arbitrations to include a nationality prohibition on the chairman or sole arbitrator, either expressly or by agreeing to arbitrate under arbitral rules that include such a prohibition. **8.56**

Article 11 further allows the parties the freedom to agree on a procedure for appointing the arbitrator or arbitrators. When they have agreed to adopt certain arbitration rules, the rules will set out the appointment procedure. **8.57**

Failing such agreement, the default appointment procedure is: **8.58**

- in an arbitration with three arbitrators, each party appoints one arbitrator, and the two arbitrators thus appointed appoint the third arbitrator; if a party fails to appoint the arbitrator within 30 days of receipt of a request to do so from the other party, or if the two arbitrators fail to agree on the third arbitrator within 30 days of their appointment, the appointment will be made, upon request of a party, by the HKIAC; and
- in an arbitration with a sole arbitrator, if the parties are unable to agree on the arbitrator, the arbitrator will be appointed, upon request of a party, by the HKIAC.

Hong Kong has also adopted the fallback provision in Article 11(4). Under an appointment procedure agreed upon by the parties, when (a) a party fails to act as required under that procedure, or (b) the parties or two arbitrators are unable to reach the agreement expected of them under that procedure, or (c) a third party, including an institution, fails to perform any function entrusted to it under that procedure, any party may request the HKIAC to take the necessary measures (unless the agreement on the appointment procedure provides another means for securing the appointment). **8.59**

Under Article 11(5), the HKIAC's decision is not subject to appeal. The HKIAC, in appointing an arbitrator, must have due regard to any qualifications required of the arbitrator by the agreement of the parties, to such considerations as are likely to secure the appointment of an independent and impartial arbitrator, and, in the case of a sole or third arbitrator, also take into account the advisability of appointing an arbitrator of a nationality other than that of a party. **8.60**

In this regard, the Arbitration (Appointment of Arbitrators and Umpires) Rules set out criteria to be taken into account by the HKIAC in making appointments.[48] In practice, the HKIAC will attempt to appoint an arbitrator who is on the HKIAC's Panel of Arbitrators. When the appointment sought requires skills and experience not readily available on the Panel, the HKIAC may appoint non-panelists. **8.61**

[48] These are: (a) the nature of the dispute; (b) the availability of arbitrators or umpires, as the case may be; (c) the identity of the parties; (d) the independence and impartiality of the arbitrator or umpire; (e) any stipulation in the relevant arbitration agreement; and (f) any suggestions made by the parties themselves. See the Arbitration (Appointment of Arbitrators and Umpires) Rules, s 7.

8.62 Section 24 of the Arbitration Ordinance, which gives effect to Article 11 of the Model Law, also sets out certain supplementary provisions dealing with arbitrations with an even number of arbitrators, and an uneven number of arbitrators greater than three. Both situations are rare.

- In an arbitration with an even number of arbitrators:
  (a) if the parties have not agreed otherwise, each party is to appoint the same number of arbitrators; or
  (b) if the parties have agreed otherwise and (in effect) there is a default in the appointment process, then the HKIAC must make the necessary appointment upon a request to do so from any party.
- In an arbitration with an uneven number of arbitrators greater than three:
  (a) if the parties have not agreed otherwise, each party is to appoint the same number of arbitrators; and unless otherwise agreed, the HKIAC must appoint the remaining arbitrator or arbitrators; or
  (b) if the parties have agreed otherwise and (in effect) there is a default in the appointment process, then the HKIAC must make the necessary appointment upon a request to do so from any party.

8.63 Section 24(4) of the Arbitration Ordinance addresses the appointment of arbitrators in multi-party arbitrations and provides that in a deadlock situation, the HKIAC shall step in.

8.64 Finally, section 24(5) of the Arbitration Ordinance makes it clear, among other things, that where an appointment is made by the HKIAC, the appointment has effect as if it were made with the agreement of all the parties.

8.65 Under the Arbitration Ordinance, as already noted, it is the HKIAC and not the court that steps in to appoint arbitrators when there is a deadlock. In practice, this procedure has proved to be efficient and cost-effective, and has helped progress arbitrations expeditiously in Hong Kong.

8.2.8 Appointment of arbitrators—Hong Kong considerations

8.66 Apart from the usual considerations that apply in choosing arbitrators, in the context of Hong Kong arbitrations, there are a number of factors that are particularly important:

- *Language:* many Hong Kong disputes involve more than one language, particularly the Chinese language. Foreign parties are not always comfortable choosing ethnic Chinese arbitrators as their party-appointed arbitrator. If this is the case, they may turn to the (limited) pool of well-established non-ethnic Chinese arbitrators who are fluent in Chinese;
- *Cultural affinity*: as in many other jurisdictions, cultural affinity is an important trait for a successful arbitrator. In Hong Kong, there have in previous cases been difficulties in some Sino-foreign disputes where parties have appointed arbitrators from very different backgrounds. Thus, a PRC party may appoint an eminent arbitrator who is familiar with PRC law (which places a greater emphasis on equity and justice), whereas the foreign party may appoint an arbitrator from its home jurisdiction (who may take a strictly 'black letter law' approach to the case). In such cases, unfortunate disagreements can occur among the arbitrators; a presiding arbitrator who has the necessary cultural affinity can help to bridge the gap.
- *PRC law*: a significant number of contracts that provide for Hong Kong arbitration are governed by PRC law. Even where the governing law is not PRC law, when the subject matter relates to the PRC, questions of PRC law often arise. Appointing an arbitrator who

has the necessary experience in dealing with PRC law issues can be important, since the arbitrator is able to draw on his or her past experience and, in certain cases, realize when parties are overstating the position under PRC law.

Experienced parties are often very careful in appointing their arbitrators, and it is increasingly common for parties to substantial international arbitrations to interview prospective arbitrators, particularly when counsel are less familiar with them. This is a practice that some Hong Kong arbitrators are comfortable with, provided various safeguards are in place,[49] while others, as well as certain counsel, are less accepting. **8.67**

8.2.9 Jurisdictional objections

Article 16 of the Model Law, which embodies the *competence-competence* doctrine, applies in Hong Kong. Accordingly, the arbitral tribunal is authorized to rule on its own jurisdiction, including on the existence or validity of the arbitration agreement. In addition, the Arbitration Ordinance specifically provides that the arbitral tribunal has the power to decide whether the tribunal is properly constituted, and what matters have been submitted to arbitration in accordance with the arbitration agreement.[50] **8.68**

As for the actual procedure, Article 16 provides that any objection to jurisdiction must be raised not later than the submission of the statement of defence. Where the plea relates to the tribunal exceeding the scope of its authority, this must be raised as soon as the matter alleged to be beyond the scope of authority is raised during the arbitration. In both cases, the tribunal may admit a later plea, if justified. **8.69**

The tribunal is entitled to rule on the objection either as a preliminary question, or in an award on the merits. If the tribunal rules as a preliminary question that it has jurisdiction, any party may, within 30 days after the ruling, request the Court of First Instance to decide the matter, which decision is not subject to appeal. While the request is pending, the tribunal may continue the arbitral proceedings and make an award.[51] Any such application to the courts can usually be dealt with in several months. **8.70**

Conversely, the Ordinance makes it clear that a ruling of the tribunal that it does *not* have jurisdiction cannot be referred for review to the Court of First Instance.[52] **8.71**

8.2.10 Anti-suit injunctions

The Hong Kong courts recognize that they are able to grant anti-suit injunctions, and have in a small number of cases granted such orders outside the arbitration context.[53] In the context of anti-suit injunctions granted in relation to arbitral proceedings, it has been suggested that in addition to their general power, the courts may also be empowered by section 45(2) of the Arbitration Ordinance to grant such an injunction.[54] This would be on the basis that **8.72**

49 See eg *Guideline on the Interviewing of Prospective Arbitrators*, published by the Chartered Institute of Arbitrators; although in practice, not all arbitrators agree with or consider that the guidelines should be applied in their entirety.

50 Arbitration Ordinance, s 34, which also gives effect to the Model Law, Art 16.

51 Model Law, Art 16(3) given effect by Arbitration Ordinance, s 34.

52 See Arbitration Ordinance, s 34(4).

53 See eg *China Light & Power Co Ltd v Wong To Sau Heung and ors* [1993] 2 HKC 238 (CA), involving an interim anti-suit injunction.

54 On the face of it, this might include arbitral proceedings taking place outside Hong Kong, although the fact that there are no substantive proceedings taking place in Hong Kong would be a significant hurdle.

an anti-suit injunction qualifies as an 'interim measure', which the court is empowered to order.[55]

8.73 Applications for anti-suit injunctions have failed in a number of Hong Kong cases. In the context of arbitrations, it is suggested that the Hong Kong courts may be prepared to grant such orders more readily, particularly where it is clear that a party has commenced court proceedings overseas in clear breach of an agreement to arbitrate in Hong Kong. Relevant factors would be whether the application has been brought promptly and how far advanced the foreign proceedings are. In this regard, the Hong Kong courts are likely to apply the general principles set out in English cases.[56]

8.74 PRC parties involved in Hong Kong court proceedings have sometimes commenced parallel court proceedings in the PRC. Thus far, the Hong Kong courts have been prepared to consider granting anti-suit injunctions in connection with such proceedings, on normal principles. However, in practical terms this may raise difficult issues of comity, given the relationship between Hong Kong and the PRC under the Basic Law.

8.75 There is no published Hong Kong case where an anti-arbitration injunction has been granted to restrain a party from proceeding with an arbitration.[57] In principle, there is no clear prohibition to such an order being made, although the actual test applied by the courts may differ.

8.3 During the Arbitration

8.3.1 Challenges to arbitrators

8.76 Section 25 of the Arbitration Ordinance gives effect to Article 12 of the Model Law, which sets out the grounds for challenging an arbitrator. It provides that a prospective arbitrator must disclose any circumstances likely to give rise to justifiable doubts as to his impartiality or independence, and that an arbitrator, from the time of his appointment and throughout the arbitral proceedings, must without delay disclose any such circumstances to the parties, unless the arbitrator has already informed the parties of the circumstances.

8.77 Correspondingly, an arbitrator may be challenged only if circumstances exist that give rise to justifiable doubts as to his impartiality or independence, or if he does not possess qualifications agreed to by the parties. A party may challenge an arbitrator appointed by him, or in whose appointment he has participated, only for reasons the party becomes aware of after the appointment has been made.

8.78 Although parties and tribunals in Hong Kong often refer to the International Bar Association (IBA) Guidelines on Conflict of Interest in International Arbitrations for guidance, the extent to which the Guidelines reflect Hong Kong law is less clear. In one case involving

[55] 'Interim measures' that a Hong Kong court is able to order are defined by reference to 'interim measures' that an arbitral tribunal may grant: Arbitration Ordinance, s 45(9). Correspondingly, it would seem that the reference to 'interim measures' in Model Law, Art 17(2)(b) is broad enough to cover an anti-suit injunction: see Binder (n 10) 244, summarizing the views of the UNCITRAL Working Group.

[56] Although, of course, the complications raised by the Brussels Regulation regime are not relevant to Hong Kong.

[57] See also the discussion in *Lin Ming and anor v Chen Shu Quan and ors* HCA 1900/2011.

a challenge to an arbitrator, the Court of First Instance held that the 'apparent bias' test, which applies to judges, also applies to arbitrators: namely, whether a hypothetical, objective, fair-minded, and informed observer, having considered the relevant facts, would conclude that there was a real possibility that the tribunal was biased.[58]

Section 26 of the Arbitration Ordinance gives effect to Article 13 of the Model Law, and sets out the procedure for challenging an arbitrator. Article 13 recognizes that the parties are free to agree on a procedure for challenging an arbitrator, subject to oversight from the courts. This agreement would, in practice, be set out in any arbitration rules agreed upon by the parties. **8.79**

Failing such agreement, a party who intends to challenge an arbitrator must, within 15 days after becoming aware of the constitution of the arbitral tribunal or after becoming aware of any ground for challenge, send a written statement of the reasons for the challenge to the arbitral tribunal. Unless the challenged arbitrator withdraws from his office or the other party agrees to the challenge, the arbitral tribunal decides on the challenge. **8.80**

Article 13(3) then sets out the court's overriding powers when a challenge has been unsuccessful: in such a situation, the challenging party may, within 30 days of notice of the tribunal's decision rejecting the challenge, request that the Court of First Instance decide on the challenge, which decision is not subject to appeal. While the request is pending, the tribunal, including the challenged arbitrator, may continue the arbitral proceedings and make an award. **8.81**

Section 26 further supplements Article 13, by providing, among other things, that: **8.82**

- although Article 13 allows the tribunal to continue with the proceedings pending a challenge, the court may refuse to grant leave to enforce any resulting award, pending the challenge;
- an arbitrator who is challenged is entitled voluntarily to withdraw from office;[59] and
- the mandate of a challenged arbitrator terminates in certain specified situations, consequent upon a challenge.

In recent years, and consistent with the increasingly adversarial nature of arbitration proceedings, there have been more challenges made to Hong Kong arbitrators. However, the challenges have generally not been successful, and the number of actual challenges is still relatively small. **8.83**

8.3.2 Liability of arbitrators

The Arbitration Ordinance provides that an arbitral tribunal is liable in law for acts done or omitted to be done by it (or an employee or agent) in relation to the exercise or performance, or purported exercise or performance, of the tribunal's functions only if it is proved that the act was done or omitted to be done dishonestly.[60] **8.84**

---

[58] *Jung Science Information Technology Co Ltd v ZTE Corp* [2008] 4 HKLRD 776 (CFI); see also *Gao Haiyan and anor v Keeneye Holdings Ltd and anor* CACV No 79 of 2011 which touches on similar issues in the context of an application to enforce an award.

[59] Model Law, Art 14(2) provides that such a withdrawal does not imply acceptance of the validity of the challenge.

[60] Arbitration Ordinance, s 104.

8.85 The Ordinance[61] also includes provisions dealing with the immunity of arbitral institutions and related parties.[62]

8.86 To date, there have been no reported court decisions in Hong Kong dealing with the authority or immunity of arbitrators, or of institutions such as the HKIAC.

8.3.3 Legal representation

8.87 The Arbitration Ordinance enshrines the principle that the parties to an arbitration have complete freedom to choose their own representatives, advisers, and advocates regardless of their qualifications or nationality.[63] Thus, parties are fully permitted to, and often do instruct foreign lawyers to represent them in international arbitrations conducted in Hong Kong.

8.88 This freedom contrasts with the requirement that only Hong Kong-admitted barristers and solicitors may conduct litigation in the Hong Kong courts, and must therefore be retained to present any arbitration-related applications in the courts.

8.89 In Hong Kong, the legal profession is divided into two distinct branches—barristers and solicitors. Solicitors have limited rights of audience before the courts whereas barristers have unlimited rights of audience. Conversely, barristers can generally only accept instructions from a firm of solicitors (or members of other recognized professional bodies). Lawyers practising within one branch of the profession are not allowed to practice within the other.

8.90 In virtually all substantial international arbitration cases heard in Hong Kong, parties are represented by solicitors or foreign lawyers. As for barristers, the practice varies among firms, and also depends on what is at stake. In law firms with a more substantial arbitration practice, it is increasingly the case that advocacy is done by solicitors instead of barristers. It is argued that the solicitors who have been conducting the case will present the case in a more consistent manner, without incurring the additional fees associated with briefing barristers. Conversely, it is argued that barristers often have specialist knowledge; they have considerably more experience with advocacy; and are often able to bring a fresh perspective to the case.

8.91 In some cases, there may also be an element of one-upmanship: when one party engages a Queen's Counsel or Senior Counsel, the other party may feel obliged to do the same.

8.3.4 Party autonomy

8.92 Article 19(1) of the Model Law[64] recognizes that, subject to the provisions of the Model Law, the parties are free to agree on the arbitral procedure. Section 3(2)(a) also provides that, subject to the public interest, the parties are free to agree on how the dispute should be resolved.

8.93 In practice, the principle of party autonomy is widely followed by Hong Kong tribunals. Thus, the parties may opt for an elaborate, full-blown court-type proceeding with solicitors, barristers, extensive written submissions, and lengthy oral hearings involving the presentation of evidence and the examination and cross-examination of witnesses, or they may choose to conduct the proceedings by the simple exchange of written statements without any hearings at all.

---

[61] Arbitration Ordinance, s 105.

[62] Note, however, the UK Supreme Court decision of *Jones v Kaney* [2011] UKSC 13 which abolished the longstanding immunity from suit afforded to expert witnesses. The case may be persuasive in Hong Kong, particularly with respect to the position of party-appointed experts.

[63] Arbitration Ordinance, s 63.

[64] Given effect in Hong Kong by the Arbitration Ordinance, s 47.

8.3.5 Equality of treatment

Although Article 18 of the Model Law has not been adopted wholesale in Hong Kong, section 46(2) of the Arbitration Ordinance provides that the parties must be treated with equality. In practice, this principle is of paramount importance and has been carefully followed by tribunals in Hong Kong. 8.94

8.3.6 Reasonable opportunity to present their case

Section 46(3) of the Arbitration Ordinance provides that the arbitral tribunal is required: 8.95

- to be independent;
- to act fairly and impartially as between the parties, giving them a reasonable opportunity to present their cases and to deal with the cases of their opponents; and
- to use procedures that are appropriate to the particular case, avoiding unnecessary delay or expense, so as to provide a fair means for resolving the dispute to which the arbitral proceedings relate.

Notably, section 46(3) deliberately departs from Article 18 of the Model Law, which refers to each party's entitlement to be given a 'full opportunity of presenting his case'. Instead, the Arbitration Ordinance refers to a 'reasonable opportunity to present their cases'. In practice, this distinction has not been material. It is thought by some commentators that the use of 'reasonable opportunity' rather than 'full opportunity' merely underscores the objective of the Arbitration Ordinance to facilitate the fair and speedy resolution of disputes while preserving the rules of natural justice. 8.96

Article 24 of the Model Law has been adopted wholesale in Hong Kong. It expressly provides that unless the parties have agreed that no hearings shall be held, the arbitral tribunal is obliged to hold hearings at an appropriate stage of the proceedings, if so requested by a party. In practice, it is certainly rare for an entire international arbitration of any complexity to be conducted on a 'documents only' basis without oral hearings, and this would certainly not happen if at least one of the parties requested a hearing. 8.97

8.3.7 Language

The Arbitration Ordinance has adopted Article 22 of the Model Law wholesale, which gives parties the freedom to agree on the language or languages to be used in the arbitral proceedings. 8.98

Failing such agreement, the arbitral tribunal will determine the language or languages to be used in the proceedings. This agreement or determination, unless otherwise specified therein, will apply to any written submission by a party, any hearing, and any award, decision or other communication by the arbitral tribunal. 8.99

In addition, Article 22(2) provides that the arbitral tribunal may order that any documentary evidence be accompanied by a translation into the language or languages agreed upon by the parties or determined by the arbitral tribunal. 8.100

In practice, the most common languages encountered in Hong Kong arbitrations are English and Chinese. This is because foreign parties are often reasonably conversant with English, and many of their documents are likely to be in English, whereas PRC parties often prefer Chinese, and many of their internal documents are in Chinese. 8.101

8.102 A significant number of arbitrators and counsel in Hong Kong are bilingual in English and Chinese. However, in practice, there will often be only one working language in the arbitration. As between Chinese and English, this will often be the latter, because one or more of the arbitrators may not be familiar with Chinese; or even if they are bilingual, their primary working language may still be English. In some cases, barristers from outside Hong Kong are engaged, who are unfamiliar with Chinese.

8.103 In these situations, it might appear logical for English to be the only language of the arbitration. In practice, however, this may not happen. First, it is fairly common practice for Sino-foreign contracts to provide expressly that the languages of the arbitration are English and Chinese. This is often considered an acceptable compromise by both parties, and little thought is given at the drafting stage to the cost consequences of such a decision. Secondly, many disputes arbitrated in Hong Kong have a strong PRC connection, with the subject matter of the dispute often being in the PRC, the governing law being the PRC law (or otherwise subject in some way to PRC law principles), the core documentation being in Chinese, and the agreements being in both languages.

8.104 As a result of these factors, a number of Sino-foreign disputes in Hong Kong are conducted in both English and Chinese, notwithstanding that English may still be the main working language. This can result in significant amounts being spent on translating the submissions and conducting the oral hearings in both languages, and translating the eventual award. Fortunately, with respect to documentary evidence, tribunals may not always require full translations (much less certified or official translations) of all disclosed documents.

8.3.8 Confidentiality

8.105 Section 18 of the Arbitration Ordinance contains a confidentiality provision. Even if these express provisions do not apply, there may be an implied duty of confidentiality. Under English law, such a duty is an implied term of an arbitration agreement,[65] and it is likely that the Hong Kong courts would be influenced by the English authorities to this effect.[66]

8.3.9 Oaths and affirmations

8.106 Section 56(8) of the Arbitration Ordinance expressly empowers the tribunal to:

- administer oaths to, or take the affirmations of, witnesses and parties; and
- examine witnesses and parties on oath or affirmation.

The tribunal has this power unless the parties have agreed otherwise, but such an agreement is rare in practice.

8.3.10 Role of courts in compelling testimony/evidence

8.107 In Hong Kong international arbitrations, documentary evidence is of considerable importance and, in many cases, may be given greater weight than witness testimony.

---

[65] See generally *Hassneh Insurance Co of Israel v Stuart J Mew* [1993] 2 Lloyd's Rep 243; cf the more liberal Australian position expressed by the High Court of Australia in *Esso Australia Resources Ltd v Plowman* (1995) 183 CLR 10.

[66] See generally *Hong Kong Housing Authority v Sui Chong Construction & Engineering Co Ltd and anor* [2008] 1 HKLRD 84; *Nam Tai Electronics Inc v PricewaterhouseCoopers* [2008] 1 HKLRD 666 for a discussion of some of the general confidentiality issues.

Under Article 27 of the Model Law, which is given effect by section 55 of the Arbitration Ordinance, the tribunal or a party with the approval of the tribunal may request assistance from a Hong Kong court in taking evidence. The court may execute the request within its competence and according to its rules on taking evidence. **8.108**

Section 55(2) of the Ordinance builds on this, by making it clear that the court may order a person, including a person who is not a party to the arbitration agreement,[67] to attend proceedings before an arbitral tribunal to testify or to produce documents or other evidence. Furthermore, section 55(3) provides that these powers may be exercised by the court irrespective of whether or not similar powers may be exercised by a tribunal under the Ordinance. This power is exercised by the Court of First Instance, and section 55(4) provides that the court's decision or order is not subject to appeal. **8.109**

In practice, it is relatively uncommon for parties to invoke this provision, in part because it is a relatively time-consuming, cumbersome procedure, and also because it is less effective against parties which are outside the court's jurisdiction. **8.110**

Under the Arbitration Ordinance, the tribunal is also empowered to make an order directing the discovery of documents, and to direct the attendance of witnesses before the tribunal in order to testify or to produce documents or other evidence.[68] In turn, section 61 of the Arbitration Ordinance provides that, with the leave of the Court of First Instance, an order or direction made in relation to arbitral proceedings by a tribunal is enforceable in the same manner as an order or direction of the court that has the same effect. If leave is granted, the court may enter judgment in terms of the order or direction. This can be useful given that the court has more extensive powers for ensuring compliance with an order or direction. This provision also applies, with some limitations, to orders or directions made outside Hong Kong.[69] **8.111**

8.3.11 Evidence

When conducting arbitral proceedings, an arbitral tribunal is not bound by the rules of evidence and may receive any evidence (excluding evidence protected by privilege) that it considers relevant to the arbitration. However, it must give the evidence the weight 'that it considers appropriate'.[70] Thus, for example, evidence that is hearsay carries less weight than direct evidence. **8.112**

In practice, in most Hong Kong international arbitrations, tribunals will not apply strict court rules of evidence, although principles underlying the court rules of evidence may still influence tribunals' evidentiary findings. **8.113**

Under the Arbitration Ordinance, a tribunal may take the initiative to ascertain the facts relevant to the proceedings.[71] However, the arbitrator or tribunal should not decide solely on the basis of evidence obtained through their own investigations without sharing such evidence with the parties beforehand. If an award is based in whole or in part on evidence **8.114**

---

[67] See *Hong Kong Civil Procedure* (Sweet & Maxwell, 2013), Vol 2, para G1/55/4. The Arbitration Ordinance, s 55(5) also specifies the court's power to compel a prisoner to testify.

[68] Arbitration Ordinance, s 56(1)(b) and (8)(c).

[69] Arbitration Ordinance, s 61(1), cf s 61(2).

[70] Arbitration Ordinance, s 47(3).

[71] Arbitration Ordinance, s 56(7).

ascertained through the arbitral tribunal's own investigations or specialized knowledge, the tribunal must first put that evidence before the parties for comment, otherwise the award may be set aside or refused enforcement because the parties have not been given a reasonable opportunity to present their case.[72]

8.3.12 Default by a party

8.115 The Arbitration Ordinance contains provisions that extend the powers of the tribunal granted under Article 25 of the Model Law to deal with a defaulting party. This was a deliberate decision when the Ordinance was drafted[73] and is in line with the current trend in international arbitral practice to ensure that proceedings move along more quickly.

8.116 Section 53 of the Arbitration Ordinance gives effect to the Article 25 Model Law provisions, which generally allow the tribunal:

- to terminate the proceedings, if the claimant fails to communicate its statement of claim;
- to continue the proceedings if the respondent fails to communicate its statement of defence (albeit without treating such failure as an admission of the claimant's allegations); and
- to continue the proceedings and to make the award on the evidence before it, if any party fails to appear at a hearing or to produce documentary evidence.

8.117 Importantly, as noted in paragraph 8.116, even if the respondent fails to submit its statement of defence, or to appear at the hearing, Article 25 of the Model Law envisages that the tribunal should still continue with the proceedings to reach a final decision. In practice, this is the approach taken by most tribunals in Hong Kong, and while proceedings may move more quickly in a default situation, there would still be no automatic 'default award' in the claimant's favour.

8.118 Sections 53(3) and (4) of the Arbitration Ordinance expand on the previous discussion, by providing that:[74]

- if, without sufficient cause, a party fails to comply with any order or direction of the tribunal, the tribunal may make a 'peremptory order' prescribing the time for compliance; and
- if a party fails to comply with a peremptory order, the tribunal may:
  (a) direct that the party is not entitled to rely on any allegation or material which was the subject matter of the peremptory order;
  (b) draw any adverse inferences that the circumstances justify;
  (c) make an award on the basis of materials properly provided to the tribunal; or
  (d) make any order that the tribunal thinks fit as to payment of the costs of the arbitration consequent upon the non-compliance.

8.119 In the past, Hong Kong tribunals, as with tribunals elsewhere in Asia, have generally been reluctant to impose draconian consequences on defaulting parties. However, with the increasing emphasis on cost and efficiency in arbitrations, as well as more dilatory tactics being emplyed by parties in recent years, Hong Kong tribunals have been taking a tougher

[72] See *Brunswick Bowling & Billiards Corp v Shanghai Zhonglu Industrial Co Ltd and Chen Rong* HCCT 66/2007 (10 February 2009).

[73] See generally, 'Report of Committee on Hong Kong Arbitration Law' (2003) paras 25.21ff.

[74] Arbitration Ordinance, s 53(3) and (4) do not apply in relation to an application for security for costs: s 53(2).

stance. The latest provisions found in section 53 are consistent with this, although it remains to be seen how often they will be used.

8.3.13 Settlement

Article 30 of the Model Law applies in Hong Kong.[75] During the arbitration, if the parties settle the dispute, the tribunal will terminate the proceedings and may, if requested by the parties, record the settlement in the form of an arbitral award on agreed terms. **8.120**

In addition, section 66(2) of the Arbitration Ordinance provides that settlement agreements entered into by the parties are also, for purposes of enforcement, to be treated as an arbitral award. **8.121**

Section 33 of the Arbitration Ordinance expressly recognizes that if all parties consent, an arbitrator may act as a mediator after the arbitration has commenced. In such a situation: **8.122**

- the arbitration must be stayed to facilitate the mediation;
- the arbitrator-mediator:
  (a) may communicate with the parties collectively or separately, and
  (b) must treat the information obtained as confidential, unless otherwise agreed; and
  (c) if the mediation proceedings terminate without a settlement, the arbitrator must disclose to all parties as much of the confidential information received as is considered material.

Section 33(5) provides that no objection may be made against the conduct of the arbitral proceedings by an arbitrator solely on the ground that he or she acted previously as a mediator. **8.123**

In practice, mediation-arbitration has not been used much in international arbitrations in Hong Kong. **8.124**

8.4 The Award

8.4.1 Types of Awards

In Hong Kong, two types of awards are generally recognized: **8.125**

- a final award, which disposes of all the issues currently before the tribunal; and
- an interim or partial award, in which the tribunal deals with some of the issues, such as jurisdiction.

If the parties have reached a settlement, the terms can be incorporated into the form of an award on agreed terms.

In substantial international arbitrations, it is not uncommon for a Hong Kong tribunal to render more than one award. In such cases, separate awards on jurisdiction and liability are common. **8.126**

[75] Given effect by the Arbitration Ordinance, s 66.

8.4.2 Form of arbitral award

8.127 Under the Arbitration Ordinance, there are no detailed statutory requirements for a valid arbitral award, although the basic requirements set out in Article 31 of the Model Law apply, whereby the award must:[76]

- be in writing;
- be signed by at least a majority of the tribunal, provided that the reason for any omitted signature is stated;
- state the reasons, unless the parties have agreed otherwise; and
- state the date and place of arbitration.

8.128 Other basic requirements are provided by the common law. These are, essentially, that the award must be final in relation to the issues dealt with, in a manner that is cogent, consistent, clear and unambiguous, and capable of enforcement by a court. If it is a final award, it must deal with all matters in dispute.

8.129 In substantial international arbitrations, detailed reasons for the decision are usually set out, and it is rare for parties to agree for these to be dispensed with. The award may run into a hundred pages or more, with close analysis of the facts, evidence, and law.

8.130 In Hong Kong, a dissenting arbitrator cannot insist that dissenting reasons form part of the award, unless the arbitration agreement or arbitration rules provide for this. In practice, at the dissenting arbitrator's request, the dissenting opinion will usually be included with the award.

8.131 The Arbitration Ordinance does not specify any time limit for the making of an international award. However, if an arbitrator fails to act in a timely manner, he or she can be removed by agreement of the parties or by order of the Hong Kong courts.[77] In such a situation, a substitute arbitrator will be appointed in accordance with the rules that applied to the original appointment.

8.132 There is no requirement under Hong Kong law for Hong Kong awards to be registered in order to be effective. However, the HKIAC does provide an authentication service for Hong Kong awards. This can be useful if a party is seeking to enforce a Hong Kong award overseas.

8.4.3 *Ex aequo et bono* and *amiable compositeur*

8.133 The Arbitration Ordinance expressly envisages that the arbitral tribunal may decide *ex aequo et bono* or as *amiable compositeur*, only if the parties have expressly authorized it to do so.[78] Such agreement is rare in practice.

8.4.4 Remedies

8.134 In general, a Hong Kong tribunal may award any remedy or relief that could have been ordered by a court if the dispute had been the subject of civil proceedings.[79] Thus, the tribunal is empowered to grant a wide range of remedies. In practice, the primary remedy in Hong

---

[76] Given effect by the Arbitration Ordinance, s 67.

[77] Model Law, Art 14(1) given effect by Arbitration Ordinance, s 27.

[78] Model Law, Art 28(3) given effect by Arbitration Ordinance, s 64.

[79] Arbitration Ordinance, s 70; save for specific performance relating to land: s 70(2).

Kong is for damages, although declarations and specific performance are also available, and are granted in appropriate situations.

8.4.5 Interest

In Hong Kong, as in many other jurisdictions, questions relating to interest in international arbitrations may be subject to different laws. For example, when a party is claiming interest based on a contractual provision, this will usually be subject to the governing law of the contract. In contrast, post-award interest is usually a matter of procedural law. **8.135**

In practice, Hong Kong tribunals frequently rely on the relevant provisions in the Arbitration Ordinance, which give an arbitral tribunal the discretion to award simple or compound interest on the principal sum awarded (or on an amount claimed in the arbitration but paid before the award is made) from such dates, and at such rates as it considers appropriate for any period up to the date of payment.[80] Unless the award provides otherwise, simple interest is payable on the amount of the award from the date of the award at the same rate as for a judgment debt (as determined from time to time by the Chief Justice).[81] Interest is also payable on costs awarded or ordered by the tribunal at the judgment rate, unless otherwise provided.[82] **8.136**

Interest may be awarded in a foreign currency, provided that the award has been made in that currency. Such interest is commonly awarded where appropriate. **8.137**

8.4.6 Costs

Section 74(1) of the Arbitration Ordinance empowers the tribunal to include in an award directions with respect to the costs of arbitral proceedings (including the fees and expenses of the tribunal). Section 74(2) further provides that the tribunal may, having regard to all the relevant circumstances (including any settlement offer), direct in the award to whom and by whom and in what manner the costs are to be paid. Subject to any agreement by the parties to have the costs of arbitral proceedings taxed by the court, the tribunal must assess the amount of costs to be awarded or ordered to be paid (other than the fees and expenses of the tribunal), and award or order those costs (including the fees and expenses of the tribunal).[83] **8.138**

However, the tribunal's discretion is not unfettered. It must only allow costs that are reasonable having regard to all the circumstances, although (unless otherwise agreed by the parties) it may allow costs incurred in the preparation of the arbitral proceedings prior to the commencement of the arbitration. Subject to the foregoing, the tribunal is not obliged to follow the scales and practices adopted in court taxation of costs.[84] **8.139**

A provision in an arbitration agreement that the parties must pay their own costs is void,[85] unless contained in an agreement to submit present disputes to arbitration. In the course of the arbitration, the tribunal is also entitled to direct that the recoverable costs of proceedings be limited to a specified amount, although this provision is rarely used in substantial international arbitrations.[86] **8.140**

[80] Arbitration Ordinance, s 79.
[81] Arbitration Ordinance, s 80(1).
[82] Arbitration Ordinance, s 80(2).
[83] Arbitration Ordinance, s 74(5).
[84] Arbitration Ordinance, s 74(6) and (7).
[85] Arbitration Ordinance, s 74(8).
[86] Arbitration Ordinance, s 57.

8.4.7 Allocation of costs

8.141 Hong Kong tribunals apply a wide range of factors in deciding how costs should be awarded. Many of these principles are similar to those applied in international arbitrations seated elsewhere. In the context of Hong Kong, parties do not always take equal care in preparing their cases, or hire counsel who are from the same jurisdiction. As a result, tribunals have sometimes had to consider whether it is relevant that the parties incurred significantly disproportionate costs in the preparation of their cases.

8.142 In recent years, with the rising complexity of disputes, cost recovery has become an increasingly contentious issue. Many international arbitrators in Hong Kong decline to apply the court scale in awarding costs,[87] but typically, when costs are awarded in favour of a successful party, the recovery is ordinarily significantly more than 50 per cent of actual costs, subject to reasonableness.

8.143 The decision on costs may either be included as part of the award, or issued as a separate costs award. In both cases, the tribunal will typically invite the parties to make submissions on who should be liable for costs, and on the quantum of costs, following which it will render its decision. When proceedings are carried out in stages, separate costs awards may also be issued at each stage.

8.144 If the parties have agreed that costs are taxable by the court, the tribunal must direct accordingly in its award (other than for the tribunal's fees and expenses); and on taxation by the court, it must make an additional award of costs reflecting the result of such taxation.[88]

8.145 If there is a dispute over the tribunal's fees and expenses, the tribunal may refuse to deliver an award, and a party may apply to the court, which:

- may order the tribunal to deliver the award on the payment into court of all or part of the fees and expenses specified by the court; and
- may order that the tribunal's fees and expenses are to be determined by the means and on terms the court may direct, and then paid to the tribunal from the amount paid into court.[89]

The arbitrator is entitled to appear and be heard on the determination.[90]

8.146 This procedure is not available if there is an available arbitral process for appeal or review of the fees or expenses demanded, or the total amounts of fees and expenses have been fixed by a written agreement between a party and the arbitrators.[91] In practice, both situations are uncommon.

8.4.8 Correction, interpretation, and supplementation of awards

8.147 Article 33 of the Model Law applies in Hong Kong. Accordingly:

- within 30 days of receipt of the award, a party may request the tribunal:

---

[87] Arbitration Ordinance, s 74(6) recognizes that the tribunal is, in general, not obliged to follow the scales and practices in court taxation.

[88] Arbitration Ordinance, s 75.

[89] Arbitration Ordinance, s 77.

[90] Arbitration Ordinance, s 77(8).

[91] Arbitration Ordinance, s 77(4).

(a) to correct in the award any errors in computation, clerical, or typographical, or other similar errors,
(b) to give an interpretation of a specific point or part of the award, if the parties so agree;

- if the tribunal considers the request justified, it shall make the correction or give the interpretation within 30 days of the request, and the interpretation shall form part of the award;
- the tribunal may also correct any error of the this type on its own initiative.

When claims have been presented in the proceedings but omitted from the award, a party may also, within 30 days, request an additional award. If the tribunal considers the request justified, it must make the additional award within 60 days. The tribunal may, however, extend the period for making a correction or interpretation, or for issuing an additional award.[92] **8.148**

In addition, section 69 of the Arbitration Ordinance sets out supplemental provisions empowering the tribunal to: **8.149**

- change the award when this is necessitated by or a consequence of the correction or interpretation process just discussed; and
- review an award of costs within 30 days if, when making the award, the tribunal was not aware of any information relating to costs (including any offer for settlement) which it should have taken into account. Following a review, the tribunal may confirm, vary, or correct the award of costs.

8.5 After the Award

8.5.1 Overview

A Hong Kong award may be set aside in the following circumstances: **8.150**

- under section 81 of the Arbitration Ordinance, which gives effect to Article 34 of the Model Law, setting out grounds that mirror those found in the New York Convention; and
- under section 26(5) of the Arbitration Ordinance, following a successful challenge to an arbitrator who has participated in proceedings resulting in an award.

A Hong Kong award may also be: **8.151**

- the subject of a challenge under section 4 of Schedule 2 to the Arbitration Ordinance, for serious irregularity; and
- appealed against on a question of law under section 5 of Schedule 2; in the limited circumstances in which those provisions apply, as just explained.

In addition, a decision or award on jurisdiction may also be challenged under Article 16 of the Model Law, as explained in paragraph 8.70.

However, the court does not otherwise have jurisdiction to set aside or remit an arbitral award for errors of fact or law on the face of the award, or to deal with appeals on the law or on the merits.[93] **8.152**

[92] Model Law, Art 33(4) given effect by Arbitration Ordinance, s 69.
[93] Arbitration Ordinance, s 81(3).

8.5.2 Setting aside

8.153 The Arbitration Ordinance adopts the narrow setting-aside grounds found in the Model Law, which are essentially based on the New York Convention grounds[94] for resisting enforcement. In essence, an arbitral award may be set aside only for procedural defects, lack of jurisdiction, or on public policy grounds:[95]

- the arbitral award may be set aside by the court of its own volition if it finds that:
  - (a) the subject matter of the dispute is not capable of settlement by arbitration under the laws of Hong Kong; or
  - (b) the award is in conflict with the public policy of Hong Kong;
- an award may also be set aside if the losing party proves that:
  - (a) a party to the arbitration was under some incapacity or the arbitration agreement is not valid under Hong Kong law—there is therefore no valid agreement or arbitration agreement;
  - (b) the applicant was not given proper notice of the appointment of an arbitrator or of the arbitral proceedings, or the applicant was otherwise unable to present its case—thereby being in breach of rules of natural justice or due process;
  - (c) the award deals with a dispute not contemplated by or not falling within the terms of the submission to arbitration, or contains decisions on matters beyond the scope of the submission to arbitration—the arbitrator exceeded the jurisdiction given to him or her, and if that part of the award can be severed it would be severed so as to preserve the rest of the award which does not exceed jurisdiction; or
  - (d) the composition of the arbitral tribunal or the arbitral procedure was not in accordance with the agreement of the parties or was not in accordance with the Model Law—thereby not preserving party autonomy and being in breach of the arbitration agreement/arbitration law.

8.5.3 Case law

8.154 *Brunswick v Shanghai Zhonglu*[96] is a leading authority on applications to set aside an arbitral award under Article 34 of the Model Law. In *Brunswick*, in construing a particular clause in the contract in dispute, the tribunal relied on certain PRC law requirements dealing with the validity of contracts, even though this approach had not been considered by the parties. The applicant argued that the tribunal ought to have canvassed with the parties its 'secret view' on contractual requirements under PRC law before deciding the issue. In contrast, the respondent argued that the arbitrators were entitled to rely on their own expertise on PRC law.

8.155 The Court decided that the requirement of contractual validity under PRC law had to be decided on the evidence before the tribunal, and that on primary factual disputes, the tribunal has to act on evidence and give a reasonable opportunity to the parties to put forward their respective cases on such evidence. On the facts, the Court held that the tribunal's failure to do so was a breach of Article 34(2)(a)(ii) of the Model Law (the party was 'unable to present his case').

---

[94] New York Convention, Art V.

[95] Model Law, Art 34.

[96] *Brunswick Bowling & Billiards Corp v Shanghai Zhonglu Industrial Co Ltd and Chen Rong* HCCT 66/2007 (10 February 2009).

Despite this, the Court held that it still had to consider whether the award should be set aside as a matter of discretion. The Court declined to import the English law requirement that a party applying to set aside an award has to show that a violation under Article 34(2) has caused 'substantial injustice'. **8.156**

Instead, it held that the test was whether the violation would affect the outcome of the dispute, or the tribunal would have reached a different conclusion but for the matter complained of. On the facts, the Court held that the violation had no real impact on the result, and even in the absence of the violation, the tribunal would have reached the same conclusion, in the light of the other reasons in its award. Therefore, the Court in *Brunswick* declined to set aside the award on this ground. **8.157**

In addition, the applicant also complained about a conversion issue, in which both parties had argued the matter on the basis that Illinois law was the governing law for the claim. In its award, however, the tribunal considered that the conversion claim should be governed by PRC law, and decided the matter by reference to PRC law, even though neither party had adduced any evidence of PRC law applicable to the claim. **8.158**

Again, the Court held that the tribunal was not entitled to apply its secret view on PRC law without giving the parties an opportunity to address it. On the facts, the Court held that the applicant was successful in establishing that it had been deprived of the opportunity to present its case on PRC law pertaining to the conversion claim, leading the Court to partially set aside the award. **8.159**

In *Pacific China Holdings Ltd v Grand Pacific Holdings Ltd*,[97] the Hong Kong Court of Appeal overturned a decision of the Court of First Instance setting aside an ICC award under Article 34(2) of the Model Law. The Court of Appeal made it clear that in order to establish a ground for setting aside, it must be shown that the tribunal's conduct was of such a 'serious' or 'egregious' nature as to amount to a denial of due process, which was not the case here. The Court of Appeal recognized that the tribunal is given wide discretionary case management powers, and acknowledged that the court has discretion *not* to set aside an award even when there are grounds for setting aside under Article 34(2)(a), if it is satisfied that the result would not have been different. In February 2013, the Hong Kong Court of Final Appeal refused Pacific China's application for leave to appeal against the Court of Appeal judgment.[98] **8.160**

8.5.4 Substantive challenges

In addition to a setting aside application, a Hong Kong arbitral award may also be the subject of: **8.161**

- a challenge under section 4 of Schedule 2 to the Arbitration Ordinance, for serious irregularity affecting the tribunal, the arbitral proceedings, or the award; or
- an appeal on a question of law arising out of an award made in the arbitral proceedings under section 5 of Schedule 2.

[97] *Pacific China Holdings Ltd v Grand Pacific Holdings Ltd* [2012] HKEC 645.

[98] *Pacific China Holdings Ltd (in liquidation) v Grand Pacific Holdings Ltd* [2013] HKEC 248. The Court of Final Appeal stated that 'the rulings complained of were made by the tribunal in the proper exercise of its procedural and case management discretions' and could not be of 'great general or public importance' for granting leave under the Court of Final Appeal Ordinance (Cap 484), s 22(1)(b).

8.162 Significantly, the provisions of Schedule 2 do *not* apply, unless:

- the parties expressly opt in to these provisions; or
- it is a domestic arbitration, and the arbitration agreement was entered into before, or within six years of, commencement of the Arbitration Ordinance.[99]

In practice, parties to international arbitrations will rarely opt in to the provisions of Schedule 2. This is in part because they are often reluctant to increase the degree of oversight by the Hong Kong courts. Accordingly, the Schedule 2 provisions are, in practice, only of significance to domestic arbitrations.

8.5.5 Procedure

8.163 An application to set aside an arbitration award under section 81 of the Arbitration Ordinance is made by originating summons to the judge in charge of the Construction and Arbitration List. An application must be made within three months of the date on which the applicant received the award or, if a request has been made to correct or interpret the award (or for an additional award), from the date on which that request has been disposed of by the arbitral tribunal.[100]

8.164 The court, when asked to set aside an award may, 'where appropriate' and if requested by a party, suspend the setting-aside proceedings in order to give the tribunal an opportunity to resume the arbitral proceedings or to take such other action as will eliminate the grounds for setting aside.[101]

8.165 Apart from an application to set aside an award under section 81, the award may also be set aside as part of a challenge to an arbitrator. When a challenge to an arbitrator is upheld, the court 'may', as part of that application, set aside any award that was made with the participation of the challenged arbitrator. In practice, this provision is not often relied on, and most applications for setting aside are made pursuant to section 81.

8.166 A typical setting aside application will take several months to resolve at first instance, assuming that it is contested. The cost varies significantly, depending on the complexity of the arguments and the materials before the court. In fairly complex applications, the cost is likely to be in the six-figure US dollar range.

8.6 Conclusion

8.167 With the coming into effect of the new Arbitration Ordinance in 2011, arbitration in Hong Kong has entered a new era. Having largely abolished the distinction between domestic and international arbitrations, the Arbitration Ordinance has created a unitary regime based on the UNCITRAL Model Law, which is familiar to participants from both civil and common law jurisdictions. This allows parties to draw on and benefit from a vast amount of international experience. Together with its supportive judiciary, good infrastructure, and first class legal and arbitration professionals, the Arbitration Ordinance further cements Hong Kong as a world-class arbitration centre for resolving international disputes.

---

99 See also Arbitration Ordinance, s 101, which deals with the specific case of Hong Kong construction subcontracting cases.

100 Model Law, Art 34(3).

101 Model Law, Art 34(4).

9

INDIA

Ciccu Mukhopadhaya

9.1 Background

9.1.1 History and development of arbitration in India

Background to the 1940 Act

In essence, the Indian traditional system of justice included the concept of arbitration. Hindu mythology may also be said to have adopted arbitration (and conciliation) to resolve disputes, as seen in the attempt of Lord Krishna to bring peace between the warring *Kaurvas* and *Pandvas*.[1] **9.01**

Long before arbitration in its current form came to be firmly embedded as an alternative mode of settlement of disputes, disputes were being settled at the village level by village *panchayats*. The word *panch*, a Hindi word, literally means 'five' and *ayat*—'assembly'. Authors have used the term *panchayat* loosely to mean 'five arbitrators'. Although *panchayats* had a broader role, one of their essential roles was to resolve all disputes among the villagers, **9.02**

[1] The Mahabharata <http://www.sacred-texts.com/hin/maha>.

including domestic disputes, whether matrimonial or property-related. Their decisions were binding on the parties, and where social or caste issues were raised, binding on all the villagers, although in most cases the declarations or decisions of the *panchayats* were not given in writing but orally.[2]

9.03 Arbitration in the international sense was first introduced in India during British Rule as an adjunct to the British court system. This may be divided into three key periods, pre-1858, 1858 to 1940, and post-1940.

The pre-1858 period

9.04 The Bengal Regulations of 1772 and 1780 contained a provision that 'in all cases of disputed accounts, it shall be recommended to the parties to submit the decision of their cause to arbitration, the award of which shall become a decree of the court'.[3]

9.05 Sir Elijha Impey's Regulation of 1781[4] included a provision whereby a judge could recommend without compulsion and persuade parties to submit their disputes to arbitration before a mutually agreed person and that no such award would be set aside, except upon testimony, fully proved by oath, of two credible witnesses that the arbitrator had been guilty of gross corruption or partiality in making the award.

9.06 The 1781 Regulation for the Administration of Justice provided for the referral of suits to arbitration with the consent of parties. This was amended by Regulation XVI of 1793 to enable the referral of specific existing disputes to arbitration, such as disputes relating to accounts, non-performance of contracts, partnerships, etc. It also detailed the procedure for referring disputes to arbitration and for the setting aside of awards.[5]

9.07 In 1813, the Regulations were further amended to enable suits in respect of rights in land to be referred to arbitration. As territories acceded, such provisions were extended from Bengal to other areas such as Banaras and Bombay (now Mumbai).

1858–1940

9.08 The first enactment of the legislative council for India to regulate civil procedure in courts (under British Rule), was the Procedure of Civil Code was passed in 1859. This Code contained sections 312 to 327, which enabled the courts to refer existing disputes (as opposed to future disputes) to arbitration.

9.09 The Indian Contract Act of 1872 recognized and gave effect to arbitration agreements by incorporating in section 27 an exception to the general rule that agreements in restraint of legal proceedings were void. It also extended the exception to agreements that limited recovery to the amount awarded in arbitration.

9.10 The Procedure of Civil Code (or as it later came to be known, the Code of Civil Procedure) was amended from time to time, retaining these provisions for arbitration, all of which enabled the referral of existing disputes to arbitration, but not future disputes.

9.11 In 1877, the Specific Relief Act was introduced, wherein section 21 barred a suit when the parties had contracted to refer disputes to arbitration. While this provision did not directly

---

[2] BP Saraf and SM Jhunjhunwala, *Law of Arbitration and Conciliation* (6th edn, Snow White, 2012) Preface.

[3] The Bengal Regulation Act 1772.

[4] Sir Elijha Imphey's Regulation 1781.

[5] The Bengal Regulation XVI 1793.

enable the referral of future disputes to arbitration and did not provide for the right to seek specific performance of an arbitration agreement, it sought to give effect to such agreements by precluding civil proceedings in respect of matters agreed to be referred to arbitration.

Finally, in 1899, an Indian Arbitration Act along the lines of the English Arbitration Act 1889 was enacted. For the first time, specific provision was made for the referral of disputes, both existing and future, to arbitration without the intervention of courts.[6] However this legislation was limited in its effect to the three Presidency towns, ie Bombay (now Mumbai), Madras (now Chennai), and Calcutta (now Kolkata). **9.12**

When the Civil Procedure Code was extensively revised in 1908, provisions relating to arbitration were included in the Second Schedule. At the time, it became clear that this legal mechanism was not the most satisfactory method of providing for arbitration and that new and comprehensive legislation on arbitration was required. This was the view expressed by the Special Committee (a committee constituted by the British government to recommend legislative changes to the Civil Procedure Code in India) presided over by Sir Erle Richards.[7] **9.13**

Comments had been made on the unsatisfactory state of affairs regarding arbitration and the lack of an independent statute governing it on other occasions as well. In the case of *Dinkarrai Lakshmiprasad v Yeshvantrai Hariprasad*, the Bombay High Court, referring to the express intent and hope for a comprehensive arbitration act in the near future, stated: 'Unfortunately that hope has not yet been realized. I think it is high time that those responsible for legislation in this country should seriously consider the advisability of taking early steps to revise the law of arbitration.'[8] **9.14**

While the this position prevailed in respect of domestic arbitrations until 1940, in 1937 India enacted the Geneva Protocol and Convention Act to give effect to the 1927 Geneva Convention on the Execution of Foreign Arbitral Awards.[9] This was the first legislation giving effect to international arbitration agreements and foreign awards in India. **9.15**

The 1940 Act

The objective and rationale for the Arbitration Act of 1940 (the '1940 Act') were to consolidate the two then-existing enactments: the Indian Arbitration Act of 1899, which applied only to presidency towns,[10] and the Second Schedule to the Civil Procedure Code, 1908. **9.16**

The 1940 Act set down an exhaustive code relating to domestic arbitration.[11] It was seen as a substantial development in the law of arbitration, and was considered arbitration-friendly. In *Société de Traction et d'électricite SA v Kamani Engineering Co Ltd* it was held to be a complete code in itself.[12] In other words, the courts took the view that provisions of other procedural statutes such as the Civil Procedure Code, save to the extent expressly provided in the 1940 Act, were not applicable. It provided for referral of both existing and future **9.17**

[6] The Arbitration Act 1899.

[7] Book on the Code of Civil Procedure (first published 1908, Universal Law Publishing Co. 2012 edn).

[8] *Dinkarrai Lakshmiprasad v Yeshvantrai Hariprasad* AIR [1930] Bom 98, para 105; 124 IC 119; 31 Bom LR 1403; ILR [1930] 54 Bom 197.

[9] Arbitration (Protocol and Convention) Act 1937.

[10] Presidency towns in British India were the administrative units under the direct control of the British East India Company. The three presidency towns were Madras, Bombay, and Calcutta.

[11] The Act did not extend to the State of Jammu and Kashmir, which state enacted its own Arbitration Act of 1940 largely following the (Indian) Arbitration Act 1940.

[12] *Société de Traction et d'électricite SA v Kamani Engineering Co Ltd* AIR [1964] SC 558.

disputes to arbitration. If two arbitrators differed, an umpire was to be appointed, ie a sole arbitrator (other than the two) would decide issues on which the two arbitrators could not reach consensus. The authority of an arbitrator could be revoked, but only with the leave of the court.[13] An arbitration agreement was not discharged by the death of a party.[14]

9.18 The court was empowered to appoint arbitrators or umpires, if the parties did not concur on their appointment or if an arbitrator refused to act or a vacancy was not filled by the parties.[15] If a party failed to appoint an arbitrator despite notice, the arbitrator appointed by the first party could act as the sole arbitrator.[16] If arbitrations were not conducted with reasonable dispatch or the arbitrators failed to conducted the proceeding properly, the court could, on an application of any of the parties to the reference, remove an arbitrator or umpire.[17]

9.19 In such circumstances, the court could also replace the arbitrator or umpire. Arbitrators were empowered to state a special case to the court for its opinion.[18] The formal requirements for an award included the requirement that it be signed, that notice be given in writing to the parties, and that on the request of any party, the arbitrators or umpire, as the case may be, were obliged to file the award in court.[19] The court was specifically empowered to modify or remit an award to the arbitrator for fresh consideration[20] and, if no such power was exercised and the award was not set aside, to render judgment in terms of the award.[21] The court was empowered to make interim orders in aid of arbitration and to supersede (ie declare that the dispute could no longer be arbitrated but must be tried in court) an arbitration if the award became void or was set aside.[22]

9.20 The court was empowered to refer the parties to arbitration on the application of a party, even when there was no suit pending on the subject matter.[23] Where there was no arbitration agreement to refer future disputes to arbitration but a suit was filed and all parties to the suit agreed that the subject matter of the suit should be referred to arbitration, the court was empowered to do so.[24] Arbitrators were empowered to make interim awards and to grant interest on awards.[25]

9.21 The grounds for setting aside an award under the 1940 Act were broad and included situations in which the arbitrator or umpire failed to conduct himself or the proceedings in a proper manner; or an award was improperly procured or otherwise invalid.[26] The term 'otherwise invalid' was construed broadly to include errors of law appearing on the face of the record. An error of law could be established when the court was of the view that findings of fact were perverse, ie when

[13] (Indian) Arbitration Act 1940, s 5.
[14] (Indian) Arbitration Act 1940, s 6.
[15] (Indian) Arbitration Act 1940, s 8.
[16] (Indian) Arbitration Act 1940, s 9.
[17] (Indian) Arbitration Act 1940, s 11.
[18] (Indian) Arbitration Act 1940, s 13(b). The arbitrator would need to set out the specific question of law on which the opinion of the Court was required and the Parties would then file an application to the concerned court of jurisdiction for the Court to gives its opinion which would then be binding on the Arbitrator and the Parties.
[19] (Indian) Arbitration Act 1940, s 14.
[20] (Indian) Arbitration Act 1940, s 15, 16.
[21] (Indian) Arbitration Act 1940, s 17.
[22] (Indian) Arbitration Act 1940, ss 18, 19.
[23] (Indian) Arbitration Act 1940, s 20.
[24] (Indian) Arbitration Act 1940, ss 21, 22, 23.
[25] (Indian) Arbitration Act 1940, s 29.
[26] (Indian) Arbitration Act 1940, s 30.

the finding was contrary to evidence on record. Challenges to the existence and validity of an arbitration agreement or the jurisdiction of the arbitrator could be made under sections 31 and 33 of the 1940 Act. Under the 1940 Act, it was discretionary for a court to refer legal proceedings to arbitration even when the parties had entered into an arbitration agreement in respect of the subject matter of the suit.[27] Appeals could be filed against specific orders, including an order modifying or correcting an award, staying or refusing to stay legal proceedings where there was an arbitration agreement, or setting aside or refusing to set aside an award.[28]

The implied terms of an arbitration agreement as provided in the First Schedule to the 1940 Act included that, in a reference to an even number of arbitrators, the arbitrators would appoint an umpire not later than one month from the second arbitrator's appointment, and that an award must be made within four months of entering upon the reference. Arbitrators were said to have entered upon the reference when they could be said to have first applied their mind to the issues involved. **9.22**

The 1940 Act was found to provide for excessive court interference and indeed to require substantial court interference. For example, hardly ever would an arbitration be concluded within four months, and if any party to the arbitration did not consent to an extension of time, only the court could order an extension.[29] Therefore, it was considered necessary to revise the Arbitration Law with a view to reducing court interference. **9.23**

Post-1940

In 1961, having signed the 1958 New York Convention on the Recognition and Enforcement of Foreign Arbitral Awards (the 'New York Convention'), India enacted the Foreign Awards (Recognition and Enforcement) Act, 1961 to give effect to the Convention. **9.24**

Thus, at the time, there were three legislative instruments covering arbitration in India—two dealing with international arbitration to give effect both to the Geneva Convention and the New York Convention, and one dealing exclusively with domestic arbitration. While the Indian judiciary was largely supportive of arbitration, there were several judicial pronouncements that attracted substantial criticism as being anti-arbitration—including anti-international arbitration—and demonstrative of excessive interference by the Indian courts. **9.25**

In the realm of domestic arbitrations, ie India-seated arbitrations governed by the 1940 Act, the primary criticisms concerned (a) the wide scope for challenge of awards based on section 30 of the 1940 Act; (b) the discretionary power, and apparent reluctance, of the courts to refer disputes to arbitration when suits were filed in breach of an arbitration agreement; (c) the initial view taken by the Supreme Court that an arbitrator had no jurisdiction or power to grant interest for a period prior to the arbitration, and *pendente lite* interest[30] (which was, however, subsequently overruled by a larger bench in *Executive Engineer v NC Bhudharaj*);[31] (d) the requirement of filing suits, which took a long time to be disposed of, to refer disputes to arbitration when the mechanism of appointing the arbitrator had not been **9.26**

[27] (Indian) Arbitration Act 1940, s 34.
[28] (Indian) Arbitration Act 1940, s 39.
[29] (Indian) Arbitration Act 1940, First Sch: '3. The arbitrators shall make their award within four months after entering on the reference or after having been called upon to act by notice in writing from any party to the arbitration agreement or within such extended time as the Court may allow.'
[30] Executive Engineer (Irrigation), *Balimela and ors v Abhaduta Jena* [1988] 1 SCC 418.
[31] *Executive Engineer v NC Bhudharaj* AIR [2001] SC 260.

agreed in the arbitration clause; and (e) in the absence of agreement by the parties, limiting the power to order an extension of time for making an award exclusively to the courts.

9.27 As far as international arbitration is concerned, a positive step was found in three judgments rendered in the late 1980s and early 1990s in the *Renusagar Power Co Ltd v General Electric*[32] cases, which concerned a foreign-seated arbitration governed by New York substantive law. In *Renusagar 1*, the Supreme Court held, inter alia, that challenges to the existence and validity of an arbitration agreement could be made before the arbitral tribunal (although the final decision would rest with the Court), and that if the arbitration clause was broad enough, even tortious claims arising out of a contract could be referred to arbitration. It was held that words such as 'arising out of' or 'in connection with' were of the widest scope. When Renusagar failed in its attempt to avoid an international arbitration by challenging the existence and validity of the arbitration agreement invoked by General Electric, it filed a suit in a local court where the power plant subject to the dispute was located. In *Renusagar 2*, the suit was stayed by the Supreme Court under section 3 of the Foreign Awards Act. Finally, when General Electric was successful in the London-based arbitration and sought to enforce the award in India, Renusagar mounted several challenges based on public policy, including that the grant of interest on interest or compound interest was contrary to the public policy of India. In *Renusagar 3*, the court dismissed these objections and granted an order for enforcement of the foreign award. However, as can be seen from the dates of the judgments, it was a long battle of over ten years.

9.28 Delay is one of the constant criticisms of the Indian judicial system. It is often felt that the Indian court system has ultimately failed in giving effect to arbitration, the whole purpose of which is an expeditious resolution of disputes. This purpose is defeated if, before, and/or after the award, lengthy court battles ensue.

9.29 One of the most criticized judgments in the history of the Indian judiciary and international arbitration has been the case of *National Thermal Power Corporation v Singer Co*,[33] in which an Indian Court held that an award rendered in London in an ICC arbitration seated in London could be amenable to setting aside proceedings in the Indian courts. The Court held that the challenge was available under the 1940 Act because section 9(b) of the Foreign Awards Act provided that the Act would not apply to an arbitration agreement governed by the laws of India. The Court found that the contractual choice of Indian law to govern the dispute was broad enough to encompass the law relating to the arbitration agreement and the curial law. The Court failed to consider the distinction between the clauses in the contract providing for domestic or international arbitration depending on the domicile of the contractor, ie Indian or foreign, respectively, and that in the case of a foreign contractor, the Indian Act was not intended to apply and only the ICC Rules were applicable, including in relation to challenging the award. Once the Supreme Court had held that the award was amenable to challenge, the Delhi High Court, in the case of *National Thermal Power v Singer*, set aside the award on the ground that the claims were time-barred.[34]

---

[32] *Renusagar Power Co Ltd v General Electric* [1984] 4 SCC 679 ('Renusagar 1'), [1987] 4 SCC 137 ('Renusagar 2'), and [1994] Supp (1) 644 ('Renusagar 3').

[33] *National Thermal Power Corp v Singer Co* [1992] 3 SCC 551.

[34] *National Thermal Power Corp v Singer Co* [1997] 1 Arb LR 466.

While the decision in *National Thermal Power v Singer* was misguided, an overview of the enforcement of foreign awards in India does not suggest that India is an arbitration-unfriendly jurisdiction. From a statistical point of view, a large majority of foreign awards have in fact been enforced, the main difficulty being the time taken to enforce them. **9.30**

9.1.2 Current legislation and the attitude of the Indian judiciary

The 1996 Act

It was widely felt that the 1940 Act had fallen out of step with developments in the law of arbitration, particularly as reflected in the work of the United Nations Commission on International Trade Law (UNCITRAL) adopting the Model Law on International Commercial Arbitration. It was also felt that economic reforms taking place in the country would not be fully effective if the law dealing with the settlement of both domestic and international commercial disputes remained out of sync with such reforms. Finally, it was also felt that it was time to give statutory support to conciliation proceedings. This lead the Law Commission of India, trade and industry representatives, and experts in the field of arbitration to propose amendments to the 1940 Act over a period of time, primarily from the early 1990s. **9.31**

In order to consolidate and amend the law relating to international commercial arbitration and enforcement of foreign arbitral awards, and to provide a law relating to conciliation, on 16 January 1996, the President of India promulgated the Arbitration and Conciliation Ordinance, 1996.[35] Subsequently, with effect from 16 August 1996, the Arbitration and Conciliation Act, 1996 (the '1996 Act') entered into force. **9.32**

The 1996 Act is divided into four parts, with Part I limited to domestic and international arbitrations seated in India; Part II giving effect to arbitration agreements and awards falling under the New York and Geneva Conventions; Part III providing for conciliation; and Part IV containing supplementary provisions. **9.33**

Although the 1996 Act is quite clear and unambiguous, a series of decisions (mostly applicable to Indian-seated arbitrations and some foreign-seated arbitrations) rendered under the 1996 Act may, in effect, have made the administration of arbitration law worse than that existing prior to the 1996 Act. **9.34**

Soon after the 1996 Act came into force, the Supreme Court of India construed its provisions on the appointment of a sole or third arbitrator in an international commercial arbitration in a pro-arbitration spirit by holding that although section 11(9) of the 1996 Act provided that in a case of the appointment of a sole or third arbitrator in an international arbitration, the Chief Justice of India 'may' appoint an arbitrator of a nationality other than the nationality of the parties, the word, 'may' should be read as 'shall' in order to ensure neutrality.[36] In the subsequent case of *Malaysian Airlines Systems BHD (II) v Stic Travels (P) Ltd*,[37] however, without considering the earlier judgment, the court read 'may' as being discretionary and not mandatorily requiring the sole or third arbitrator to be of a neutral nationality. Therefore, unless the arbitration clause in a contract for an Indian-seated arbitration expressly requires the sole or a third arbitrator to be of a neutral nationality, it is not essential for the Supreme **9.35**

[35] The Parliament not being then in session.

[36] *Dolphin Intl Ltd v Ronak Enterprises Inc* [1998] 5 SCC 724.

[37] *Malaysian Airlines Systems BHD (II) v Stic Travels (P) Ltd* [2001] 1 SCC 509.

Court to appoint a neutral national. In practice, more often than not, the court continues to appoint Indian nationals as the sole or presiding arbitrator.

9.36 A decision that was probably rendered with good intentions but has wrongly led to chaos in terms of intervention by Indian courts in arbitrations seated outside India is the decision of the Supreme Court in *Bhatia International v Bulk Trading SA*, rendered in the context of a petition seeking interim measures in aid of arbitration under section 9 of the 1996 Act.[38] Although section 2(2) in Part I of the 1996 Act expressly provides that Part I applies where the place of arbitration is in India, the court held that unless necessarily implied or expressly excluded, Part I would apply to all arbitrations including those outside India. It did not at all consider the curial law applicable to the arbitration agreement and its effect. It went into convoluted reasoning as to why Part I would apply to a foreign-seated arbitration, conspicuously omitting the language of the arbitration clause or the applicable curial law. Since section 9 is found in Part I of the 1996 Act, in order to hold section 9 applicable to a foreign-seated arbitration, the court necessarily had to find that Part I as a whole applied to foreign-seated arbitrations.

9.37 If *Bhatia International* had been limited in its application to interim measures of protection rather than the whole of Part 1, although the judgment was wrong, as a matter of law, its practical effect might not have been drastic. However, soon after it was rendered, the decision was extended by various High Courts entertaining petitions to set aside awards under section 34 of the 1996 Act, which also falls under Part I of the Act, even though they were in fact 'foreign awards' not subject to setting aside in India. Some High Courts looked into the applicable substantive law of the contract and, where the substantive law was also foreign and the arbitration was seated outside India, the Court in *Max India Ltd v General Binding Corporation* held that by implication, the applicability of Part I would be excluded.[39] However, where the substantive law was Indian law, notwithstanding the foreign curial law by reason of the seat being outside India, the High Courts, applying *Bhatia International*, continued to hold, incorrectly, that setting aside could be sought under section 34.[40]

9.38 Shortly after the judgment in *Bhatia International* came a series of decisions dealing with Indian-seated arbitrations, both domestic and international, that set back the clock. First, *ONGC v SAW Pipes Ltd* (a domestic arbitration case),[41] broadly construed the public policy ground in section 34 of the 1996 Act.[42] Apart from the narrow meaning given in *Renusagar 3*, the Court added that an award could be set aside as contravening the public policy of India if it was 'patently illegal' and if it was so unfair or unreasonable that it would shock the conscience of the court. While it explained that the illegality must go to the root of the matter and would not apply to trivial illegalities, the Court nevertheless set aside the award in *ONGC v SAW Pipes* even though it could hardly be said to satisfy the requirement of patent illegality. As a consequence, a new ground was introduced: the award would be set aside if it was contrary to the 'express' terms of the contract. In practice, the test has become a subjective one for the particular judge hearing

[38] *Bhatia Intl v Bulk Trading SA* [2002] 4 SCC 105.

[39] *Max India Ltd v General Binding Corp* [2009] 3 Arb LR 162.

[40] See *Max India Ltd v General Binding Corp* (OS) No 193/2009, para 1.50 (16 July 2009).

[41] *Oil & Natural Gas Corp v SAW Pipes Ltd* [2003] 5 SCC 705.

[42] *ONGC* (n 41) para 31: '... award could be set aside if it is contrary to: (a) fundamental policy of Indian law; or (b) the interest of India; or (c) justice or morality; or (d) in addition, if it is patently illegal'.

the matter to determine whether any part of the award can be said to be contrary to the express terms of the contract.

9.39 The second significant post-*Bhatia* case was *Sukanya Holdings (P) Ltd v Jayesh H Pandya*,[43] in which the Supreme Court held that if a suit was filed against a number of parties, some of whom were parties to an arbitration agreement with the plaintiff while others were not, none of the parties could be referred to arbitration. While this case related to an Indian-seated domestic arbitration, the principle has since been frequently misused in both domestic and international arbitrations whether seated in or outside India. Parties have been filing suits naming multiple defendants, including those with whom there is no arbitration agreement, in order to claim the benefit of *Sukanya*. Although the principles articulated in *Sukanya* were the subject of reconsideration before the three-member bench of the Supreme Court in 2012,[44] the Court side-stepped the issue by holding that since the particular case involved section 45 of the Act which was in Part II, rather than section 8 which was in Part 1, the decision in *Sukanya* was not relevant. *Sukanya* therefore remains good law for Indian-seated arbitrations, domestic and international.

9.40 On a positive note, in 2002 the Supreme Court held, in *Konkan Railways Corporation Ltd v Rani Construction Pvt Ltd*,[45] that the power of the chief justice of the High Court in domestic arbitration and the Supreme Court in international commercial arbitration to appoint an arbitrator under section 11[46] of the 1996 Act was a purely administrative function, and the judge was not required to decide on the existence or validity of the arbitration agreement or any other jurisdictional matters, all of which should be decided by the arbitrator according to the *competence-competence* principle.

9.41 However, in 2005, seven judges of the Supreme Court overruled *Konkan* and held that, when appointing an arbitrator, the chief justice was acting as a court; the function was not administrative, and issues relating to jurisdiction or time-bar must be decided in a petition under section 11. The court is therefore also required to finally decide these issues when an application is filed under section 8 of the 1996 Act to refer an action to arbitration, as well as on a *prima facie* basis in section 9 proceedings for interim relief. This was a change to the Supreme Court's prior jurisprudence, which had held, in *Hindustan Petroleum Corporation Ltd v Pinkcity Midway Petroleums*,[47] that when a petition was filed under section 8, if on the face of it there was an arbitration agreement, the court was bound to refer the parties to arbitration and any issues of jurisdiction had to be decided by the arbitral tribunal under section 16 of the 1996 Act.

9.42 In *Venture Global Engineering v Satyam Computer Services Ltd*,[48] the Supreme Court held that in a case in which the substantive law was the law of Michigan and the seat was London, Part I and section 34 for setting aside of the award would apply. The court failed to consider the relevant issues as to the applicable curial law and its effect. Similarly, in *Phulchand Exports Ltd v OOO Patriot*,[49] the Supreme Court extended the broader interpretation of public policy

[43] *Sukanya Holdings (P) Ltd v Jayesh H Pandya* [2003] 5 SCC 351.
[44] *Choloro Controls (I) P Ltd v Severn Trent Water Purification Inc and ors* Civil Appeal Nos 7135–7136 of 2012; 2013(1) CTC 418.
[45] *Konkan Railways Corp Ltd v Rani Construction Pvt Ltd* [2002] 2 SCC 388.
[46] *SBP & Co v Patel Engineering* [2005] 8 SCC 618.
[47] *Hindustan Petroleum Corp Ltd v Pinkcity Midway Petroleums* [2003] 6 SCC 503.
[48] *Venture Global Engineering v Satyam Computer Services Ltd* [2008] 4 SCC 190.
[49] *Phulchand Exports Ltd v OOO Patriot* [2011] 10 SCC 300.

to foreign awards by applying the *ONGC v SAW Pipes* test, ignoring that decision's express observation that the test of public policy in respect of foreign awards should be narrower. The Court held that awards made outside India can also be set aside by Indian courts under section 34 of the 1996 Act for violating Indian statutory provisions and being contrary to Indian public policy. The only saving grace was that the Supreme Court also held that parties can put suitable language in their contracts to exclude the applicability of Part I of the 1996 Act.

9.43 Following the *Bhatia International* principle, in *Indtel Technical Services v WS Atkins plc* in which the contract was governed by the laws of England and Wales but there was no express seat of arbitration, the Supreme Court held that a petition could be brought under section 11 of the 1996 Act for the appointment of an arbitrator.[50] In *TDM Infrastructure (P) Ltd v UE Development India (P) Ltd*,[51] another decision that has come in for criticism in relation to international commercial arbitration seated in India, the Supreme Court held that a section 11 petition could not be maintained directly to the Supreme Court when both parties were Indian, notwithstanding that one of them was a wholly-owned subsidiary of a foreign company, whose central management and control were exercised from outside India, and despite the express definition of international commercial arbitration in section 2(f) of Part I of the 1996 Act (which defines international commercial arbitration as including the situation in which the central management and control of a party, is exercised in a country other than India). The Court held that two Indian parties could not contract for international arbitration, as this would be against public policy. The Court did not consider a prior decision of a larger bench in *Atlas Export Industries v Kotak & Company*,[52] where the two Indian parties had contracted for a GAFTA or FOSFA arbitration with English law, and the very contention accepted in *TDM Infrastructure* had been rejected. The Court's attention was, of course, not drawn to its earlier judgment. *TDM* is not, therefore, good law and the view of the larger bench decision in *Atlas Export* should prevail.

9.44 The negative trend has continued since then. In *Indian Oil Corporation Ltd v Raja Transport Pvt Ltd*,[53] a domestic arbitration seated in India, the Supreme Court was called upon to consider whether an employee of one of the parties could be objected to as an arbitrator, on the ground that this violated the requirement of impartiality and independence. It is common for Indian public sector contracts, and in fact many private party contracts where there is inequality of bargaining power, to provide that an employee of one of the parties may be an arbitrator and that the other party has no objection to such an appointment. The Court made an artificial distinction between contracts between a public sector or government entity or the government itself and a private party, and between two private parties. It upheld such clauses where public sector and government were concerned but held such clauses to be without effect where both parties were private entities. In other words, notwithstanding section 12 of the 1996 Act, which provides that an arbitrator may be challenged if circumstances exist that give rise to justifiable doubts as to his independence and impartiality and impose on arbitrators the obligation to disclose in writing any

[50] *Indtel Technical Services v WS Atkins plc* [2008] 10 SCC 308. See also *Infowares Ltd v Equinox Corporation* [2009] 7 SCC 220 (contract governed by Californian Law with no express seat).

[51] *TDM Infrastructure (P) Ltd v UE Development India (P) Ltd* [2008] 14 SCC 271.

[52] *Atlas Export Industries v Kotak & Co* [1999] 7 SCC 61.

[53] *Indian Oil Corp Ltd v Raja Transport Pvt Ltd* [2009] 7 SCC 696.

circumstances likely to give rise to such doubts, an employee drawing salary from a company (that may even be a listed company in which the employee holds shares) could be an arbitrator. However, one exception that the court made was that an employee of a public sector corporation who had dealt with the contract or whose superior officers had dealt with the contract could not legitimately be an arbitrator.

More recently, in *N Radhakrishnan v Maestro Engineers*,[54] another domestic arbitration case, the Supreme Court held that where allegations of fraud were made, arbitration was not available, despite the existence of an arbitration agreement in the contract in question. **9.45**

With regard to international arbitration after *Venture Global*, the Supreme Court and the High Courts have nevertheless held that Part I and section 34 would be excluded, at least where there was an express choice of foreign law governing the substance of the dispute and a seat outside India,[55] or an express choice of foreign law governing the arbitration agreement with a seat outside India,[56] even if Indian law was applicable law to the substance.[57] A major step in the right direction was the decision of the Supreme Court, in *Bharat Aluminium Co v Kaiser Aluminium Technical Service Inc*,[58] to refer *Bhatia International* and *Venture Global* to a larger bench of five judges (Constitution Bench) for reconsideration. The matter was heard at length over January and February 2012 and judgment was delivered on 6 September 2012. The judgment overruled *Bhatia International* and *Venture Global*, but unfortunately and surprisingly only prospectively, with respect to arbitration agreements entered into after 6 September 2012. An otherwise well-written and positive judgment has, for all practical purposes, been rendered useless for the next ten to twenty years. It is hoped that the Court will quickly review this aspect. **9.46**

After *SAW Pipes* and *Bhatia International*, the Indian government from time to time sought to introduce amendments to the 1996 Act to minimize the extent of judicial intervention in arbitration. Based on the 176th Report of the Law Commission of India, the Arbitration and Conciliation (Amendment) Bill, 2003 was introduced in Parliament in December 2003. The Bill proposed the introduction of a new section 34A, which would allow an award to be set aside 'where there is an error apparent on the face of the arbitration award giving rise to a substantial question of law'. Although the proposed ground for setting aside was narrower in definition than the *SAW Pipes* ruling, it would still have afforded losing parties an opportunity to approach courts in an attempt to seek judicial review of arbitral awards. However, after additional review by the Standing Committee on Personnel, Public Grievances, Law and Justice, which concluded that the Bill still allowed for excessive judicial intervention in arbitration, the Bill was withdrawn from Parliament with the expectation that new legislation would be introduced in its place. With a view to introducing a new Bill, in April 2010, the Union Ministry of Law and Justice released a consultation paper proposing key amendments to the 1996 Act. The consultation paper was candid in admitting that in some cases, courts have interpreted the provisions of the Act in a way that defeats the main objectives of the legislation. The main amendment proposed by the **9.47**

---

54 *N Radhakrishnan v Maestro Engineers* [2010] 1 SCC 72.
55 *Dozco India P Ltd v Doosan Infracore Co Ltd* [2011] 6 SCC 179.
56 *Videocon Industries Ltd v Union of India* [2011] 6 SCC 161.
57 *Bharat Aluminium Co v Kaiser Aluminium Technical Service* [2012] 6 SCC 552.
58 *Bharat Aluminium Co v Kaiser Aluminium Technical Service Inc* [2012] 9 SCC 552.

consultation paper was to exclude the applicability of Part I of the Act to arbitrations held outside India (except for the provisions for courts to grant interim measures and court assistance in obtaining evidence). The aim behind this proposed change was to nullify the effect of *Bhatia International* and *Venture Global*. Another significant change proposed by the consultation paper was to nullify the effect of *SAW Pipes* by narrowing the scope and meaning of 'public policy' as a ground for setting aside arbitral awards. According to the proposed amendment, an award would be considered in conflict with public policy only when it was contrary to a fundamental policy of India, the interests of India, or justice and morality. The consultation paper, however, proposed the introduction of an additional ground for setting aside in purely domestic arbitrations: the 'patent and serious illegality' of an arbitral award.

9.48 The general consensus of the legal community was that the consultation paper did not adequately make the amendments that were required to set right the law of arbitration and make India a more friendly seat for arbitration—domestic and international. A review of the consultation paper was contemplated. More than two years have elapsed since then and no attempt has been made by the government to table a Bill in Parliament.

Attitude to arbitration in India

9.49 The general view in India is that barring few exceptions, the bar, the bench, and arbitrators have not supported arbitrations as they should. The majority of the bar do not look at arbitration as a full-time practice area. Rather, practitioners in India prefer to do court work during the day, and arbitrations after normal working hours and at the weekends. There is generally no resolve to set a procedural timetable right at the inception of an arbitration, fixing firm dates for evidence and submissions over a continuous period with equal time for both parties. This happens only where at least one or more arbitrators are from an outside jurisdiction and sometimes not even then.

9.50 Indian arbitrators, again barring a few exceptions, similarly have no resolve for the expeditious and cost-efficient disposal of arbitrations. Dates are set again and again and arbitrations can drag on for years. Even less complex arbitrations that could be completed in six months often go on for two years or more, with the respondents enjoying the benefit of the delay.

9.51 The bench, again barring some exceptions, is not quick to dispose of arbitration matters. In the field of international arbitration, due to a lack of judicial experience and training, there is a particular lack of understanding of the complexities and particularly the effect of the various laws that could be applicable. While this may sound pessimistic, it is expected that either the law will be amended or judicial precedent will be corrected.

9.1.3 Comparison with other regional or national venues

9.52 If one considers the immediate neighbourhood—comprising Pakistan, Bangladesh, Sri Lanka, and Nepal—India is far ahead in being pro-arbitration. However, if one looks at the larger region—including countries such as Dubai, Singapore, and Malaysia—India has a long way to go to improve both logistical aspects such as hearing facilities and other support, and the attitude of courts in terms of discouraging them from interfering with arbitration, in particular international and foreign-seated arbitration.

9.2 Commencing the Arbitration

9.2.1 The arbitration agreement as a bar to court proceedings

The 1996 Act requires courts to refer parties to arbitration if the subject matter of a suit or court proceedings is the subject matter of an arbitration agreement.[59] Although under Indian law, the existence of an arbitration agreement by itself does not bar a suit,[60] if a court proceeding is initiated in breach of an arbitration agreement, the other party has the option to file an application under section 8 of the 1996 Act to have the matter referred to arbitration, or to waive the arbitration agreement by participating in the suit by filing its written statement on the merits of the case and not raising the existence of the arbitration agreement. **9.53**

The 1996 Act even provides that an arbitration may be commenced or continued and an arbitral award made even where an application is pending to the court to refer the action brought in court to arbitration. There is, however, a technical requirement that an application under section 8 be accompanied by the original arbitration agreement or a duly certified copy. **9.54**

Under section 7 of the 1996 Act, the requirements of an arbitration agreement are fulfilled if there is an arbitration agreement in writing, which may be evidenced either by a document signed by the parties or an exchange of letters, telex, telegrams, or other means of telecommunication that provide a record of the agreement, such as electronic mail or even an exchange of a statement of claim and a defence in which the existence of an agreement is alleged by one party and not denied by the other. An arbitration agreement may also be incorporated in a contract or a document by reference. The mandatory nature of section 8 of the 1996 Act has been recognized by the Supreme Court in several judgments, including *P Anand Gajapathi Raju and ors v PVG Raju*; *Rashtriya Ispat Nigam Ltd and anor v Verma Transport Company*; and *Hindustan Petroleum Corporation Ltd v Pinkcity Midway Petroleums*.[61] In practice, originals are hardly ever produced. Parties certify a copy of the arbitration agreement, which they produce in court as being a true copy of the original. In the case of emails, this is usually considered sufficient; if the other party disputes the authenticity of the email, the exchange would have to be proved in the usual way. However, in view of the decision of seven judges of the Supreme Court in *SBP & Co v Patel Engineering*,[62] the judicial authority before whom an application is filed under section 8 must now finally decide in those proceedings, ie in a binding manner, whether a valid arbitration agreement in fact exists. The court decides the issue by taking evidence, if necessary, on affidavits and determines the existence of an arbitration agreement by applying the section 7 tests. If the existence is admitted but the validity challenged, the court would examine the legal and/or factual grounds on which the validity is challenged. **9.55**

---

59 Arbitration and Conciliation Act, 1996, s 8.

60 Save in cases where the arbitration agreement is not governed by the Indian Arbitration Act of 1940, and now by implication by Part I of the Arbitration and Conciliation Act, 1996. In view of the language of the Specific Relief Act, s 21(h) which provides that the existence of an arbitration agreement to which the 1940 Act does not apply (hence by implication to which Part I of the 1996 does not apply) bars a suit in respect of a subject matter agreed to be referred to arbitration.

61 *Anand Gajapathi Raju and ors v PVG Raju* [2000] 4 SCC 539; *Rashtriya Ispat Nigam Ltd and anor v Verma Transport Co* [2006] 7 SCC 275; *Hindustan Petroleum Corp Ltd v Pinkcity Midway Petroleums* [2003] 6 SCC 503.

62 *SBP* (n 46).

9.56 While the Supreme Court has explained that since the determination is a final and binding one, the court is entitled to take evidence on the issue, the court also decides issues relating to existence and validity, in practice, in a summary fashion, ie by affidavit evidence, although theoretically it is open for the court to take oral evidence on the point.

9.57 The effect of this judgment is that in all matters in which a party raises the existence or validity of an arbitration agreement, the court must decide that issue finally, and the principle of *competence-competence* reflected in section 16 is to that extent rendered nugatory. This is particularly so as the Supreme Court also held that once the court has determined this issue, it cannot be re-adjudicated before the arbitrator.

9.58 Additionally, in the light of the judgment of the Supreme Court in *Sukanya Holdings (P) Ltd v Jayesh H Pandya*,[63] when a proceeding is filed in court against a number of defendants, some of whom are party to an arbitration agreement while others are not, the court cannot refer the dispute to arbitration, because if there is a common cause of action against all of the parties, it cannot be split into multiple proceedings. This decision was to be the subject of reconsideration in *Chloro Controls (I) Pvt Ltd v Severn Trent Water Purification Inc*,[64] decided on 28 September 2012. As, unlike *Sukanya*, *Chloro Controls* involved an international arbitration seated outside India, the Court held that *Sukanya*, which dealt with section 8 in Part I of the 1996 Act, was not applicable to section 45 in Part II of the Act, which implemented the provisions of the New York Convention. The Court held that as far as international arbitrations were concerned, the party relying on the arbitration agreement would still be entitled to be referred to arbitration notwithstanding the fact that there were other parties to the suit who were not subject to arbitration.[65] The Court went further, even referring to arbitration parties who were not parties to the arbitration agreement, by interpreting the words in section 45 'persons claiming through or under a party' to be wide enough, as long as there was a connection between the contracts concerned.

9.59 While the court would still need to be satisfied that there is an arbitration agreement in existence between two principal parties, and that the arbitration agreement is not null and void, inoperative, or incapable of being performed, it essentially held that international arbitration seated outside India would not be defeated merely by certain parties to the suit not directly being parties to the arbitration agreement, as long as the contract under which the dispute was raised was connected with the principal agreement between the principal parties.

9.60 *SBP* and *Sukanya* have both had an adverse impact on arbitration generally. One often finds that a party wishing to avoid arbitration files a civil proceeding on the subject matter of the arbitration but includes in those proceedings parties who are not party to the arbitration agreement, and when an application under section 8 of the 1996 Act is filed, takes shelter in *Sukanya*. This has had an impact on both domestic and international arbitrations seated in India, as the rationale of *Chloro Control* applies only to arbitrations seated outside India when there is a principal agreement pursuant to which other agreements are entered into—and not in all circumstances. Similarly, when faced with a mandatory referral to arbitration, parties rely on *SBP* to raise objections to the existence, validity, and scope of the arbitration

---

63 *Sukanya Holdings (P) Ltd v Jayesh H Pandya* [2003] 5 SCC 531.

64 *Chloro Controls (I) Pvt Ltd v Severn Trent Water Purification Inc* [2013] 1 SCC 641.

65 In *Chloro Controls* a reference was made to the judgment dated 4 March, 2010, whereby the Division Bench of the Honourable Bombay High Court allowed the Notice of Motion No 778 of 2004 and made reference to arbitration under the Arbitration and Conciliation Act, 1996, s 45.

agreement in order to delay proceedings. Section 8(3) of the 1996 Act, which permits the arbitration to be commenced and concluded notwithstanding proceedings in court, is hardly ever resorted to, and when attempts have been made to use it on various occasions, interim injunctions were granted restraining the arbitration from proceeding, despite the clear terms of section 8(3).

9.2.2 The role of courts in appointing arbitrators

When the arbitration agreement does not provide for an institution to appoint an arbitrator and the parties are unable to agree on a sole arbitrator or the presiding arbitrator (or where the two appointed arbitrators are unable to agree on the presiding arbitrator), section 11 of the 1996 Act provides for the chief justice of the High Court concerned or his designate (in the case of domestic arbitrations) and the Chief Justice of India or his designate (in the case of international arbitrations) to appoint the required arbitrator. **9.61**

The question of whether the power to appoint under section 11 is an administrative or a judicial power has been the subject of considerable debate in the Indian courts. Section 11 applies to all Indian-seated arbitrations whether domestic or international. When the question first came up, the Supreme Court in *Ador Samia Pvt Ltd v Peekay Holdings Ltd* held that the chief justice acted under section 11 in his administrative capacity and the resulting orders were administrative rather than judicial.[66] Subsequently, a larger bench of three judges confirmed this view,[67] holding that even if contentious issues as to jurisdiction and other matters were raised, these had to be decided by the arbitral tribunal, and the court should simply appoint the arbitrator so that the arbitration proceedings could commence expeditiously. **9.62**

In the subsequent case of *Konkan Railway Corporation Ltd v Rani Construction*,[68] the issue was referred for reconsideration to a Constitution Bench of five judges which affirmed the decision in *Konkan Railway Corporation Ltd and ors v Mehul Construction Co*, holding that the function performed by the Chief Justice or his designate was not judicial in nature. It further held that since the powers of the Chief Justice were administrative in nature. It was not even required that the Chief Justice or his designate hear the respondent before making an appointment, although in the ordinary course, notice of the application should be given. It was further held that orders passed under section 11 were not appealable. **9.63**

This decision was seen as a positive step in favour of arbitration. It gave full effect to section 16 of the 1996 Act, which incorporates the principle of *competence-competence* and enables the arbitral tribunal to determine its own jurisdiction. Soon thereafter, however, the issue was referred to seven judges in the *SBP* case.[69] The Court reversed *Konkan* and, ignoring the clear language of section 11, held that the power of the chief justice or his designate to appoint arbitrators was a judicial one. Accordingly, if issues as to jurisdiction (ie the existence or validity of an arbitration agreement) or whether there was a live claim (ie a claim which was not barred by limitation) that could be referred to arbitration were raised, they had to be finally decided by the court, and could not thereafter be raised before the arbitral tribunal. Similarly, whether there had been a settlement agreement that discharged the arbitration agreement would also be a matter for the court to decide before appointing an **9.64**

---

66 *Ador Samia Private Ltd v Peekay Holdings Ltd* [1999] 8 SCC 572.

67 *Konkan Railway Corporation Ltd & ors. v Mehul Construction Co.*, [2000] 7 SCC 201.

68 *Konkan Railway Corp Ltd v Rani Construction* [2000] 8 SCC 159.

69 *SBP* (n 62).

arbitrator. The rationale of this decision extended not only to proceedings under section 11 in respect of the role of the court in appointing arbitrators but also, as explained previously, to proceedings under section 8 of the 1996 Act to refer court actions to arbitration and significantly—on a *prima facie* standard or possibly even finally if the court so decided—to applications for interim measures of protection under section 9.[70] The Court in the *SBP* case expressly referred to section 8 and held so. As far as section 9 is concerned, the Court did not expressly refer to section 9 but that was the necessary inference, and subsequent judgments have applied this principle.

9.65 Subsequent Supreme Court decisions have narrowed the strict application of the *SBP* principles. In *National Insurance Co Ltd v Boghara Polyfab Pvt Ltd*,[71] the Supreme Court recognized three separate categories of issues that may arise in a section 11 application. The first category included the question of whether the application had been made to the appropriate high court[72] and whether there was an arbitration agreement to which the applicant was a party. In this category, the chief justice or his designate was required to decide before appointing the arbitrator. In the second category, with regard to matters such as whether the claim was time-barred or live, and whether there had been an accord and satisfaction, the court held that the chief justice or his designate may choose to decide the issues or leave them to be decided by the arbitral tribunal. The third category included the merits of any claims in the arbitration and whether they fell within the scope of the arbitration agreement, as well as allegations that a claim fell within the exclusive jurisdiction of a departmental authority and was therefore excepted or excluded from arbitration. For this category, the chief justice or his designate should leave the decision exclusively to the arbitral tribunal. In *Indian Oil Corporation Ltd v SPS Engineering Ltd*,[73] a recent case applying this principle, the Court held that even if an objection were raised that the claim was barred by *res judicata*, it was a matter for the arbitral tribunal to decide and therefore the court would simply appoint the arbitrator.

9.66 One of the conditions to be satisfied before an application for the appointment of an arbitrator under section 11 can be made is that there must be a failure of the agreed procedure for appointment of an arbitrator, failure by an institution to appoint an arbitrator in accordance with its rules, or failure of the parties to reach agreement in the absence of any agreed procedure. Although section 11 of the 1996 Act does not provide a time period within which such failure must be established, the courts, applying the 'reasonable time' principle, have held that failure to agree or to appoint an arbitrator within 30 days of the appointment being sought, can trigger an application under section 11(6).[74] It has been further held in some cases that a party that has a right to appoint an arbitrator may lose this right by failing to do so within a reasonable time, ie 30 days.[75]

9.67 Another issue involves allegations that an arbitral tribunal has been unilaterally appointed by a party or institution. When legal proceedings have been instituted to enjoin such a tribunal

---

70 *Perma Container (UK) Line Ltd v Perma Container Line (India) Pvt Ltd* [2010] 2 Bom CR 419.

71 *National Insurance Co Ltd v Boghara Polyfab Pvt Ltd* [2009] 1 SCC 267.

72 As each state has a high court and application under the Arbitration and Conciliation Act, 1996, s 11 can only be made to a high court where part of the cause of action in respect of the arbitration raises issues including where the seat of the arbitration is.

73 *Indian Oil Corp Ltd v SPS Engineering Ltd* [2011] 3 SCC 507.

74 *Dattar Switchgear v Tata Finance Ltd* [2000] 8 SCC 151.

75 *Punj Lloyds Satellite Public Co Ltd v Jain Studios Ltd* [2006] 2 SCC 680.

from proceeding, the courts have declined to do so, and upheld the *competence-competence* principle, whereby it is for the tribunal to decide its own jurisdiction. In a recent domestic arbitration case, *MIC Electronics Ltd v International Techno Media Pvt Ltd*,[76] the Court held that section 5 of the 1996 Act prevented the courts from interfering in an arbitration except as expressly provided in the Act, and that the applicant had to go through the arbitration proceedings, raise the objections before the arbitrator, and if unsuccessful in such objections, challenge the award when made. An interesting question is currently pending before the Supreme Court as to whether a tribunal constituted under the ICC Rules could be displaced by a party contesting the constitution of that tribunal by filing an application under section 11 of the 1996 Act for the constitution of a tribunal in accordance with such contesting parties' interpretation of the arbitration agreement.[77]

9.2.3 The role of courts in resolving jurisdictional questions

When parties raise issues of jurisdiction before the arbitral tribunal, the *competence-competence* principle is fully applicable and the arbitrator is empowered to make a decision under section 16 of the 1996 Act. This principle applies to all Indian-seated arbitrations, whether domestic or international. A decision that the tribunal has jurisdiction is not considered as an interim award[78] and hence is not amenable to attack under section 34 of the 1996 Act. However, a decision of the arbitral tribunal that there is no arbitration agreement in existence or accepting any other plea as to the scope or validity of the arbitration agreement is amenable to appeal under section 37 of the 1996 Act. **9.68**

When issues of jurisdiction arise in court proceedings, whether under section 11 (appointment of arbitrator), section 8 (referral to arbitration), or section 9 (interim measures) of the 1996 Act, it is largely dependent upon the judge hearing the matter whether the issue is to be decided by the arbitral tribunal or the court. In domestic arbitration, it is now only when the existence or validity of the arbitration agreement is called into question that the court must decide the issue and not leave it to the tribunal. Given the decision in *Boghara Polyfab*, in all other cases a judge can leave the jurisdictional issue—including whether the dispute is within the scope of the arbitration agreement—to the tribunal to decide. **9.69**

A slightly different situation arises under section 45 (Part II) of the 1996 Act. Here, following *Chloro Controls*, the court must decide on the existence of an arbitration agreement or whether it is inoperative or incapable of being performed before referring the matter to arbitration. While in an earlier case, *Shin Itsu Chemical Co Ltd v Akash Optifibre Ltd*,[79] the Supreme Court had held (by a decision of two to one) that if the court comes to a *prima facie* view that there exists an arbitration agreement and that it is not inoperative or incapable of being performed, then it would refer the parties to arbitration. Without expressly overruling *Shin Itsu*, *Chloro Controls* holds that these issues must be finally decided. To that extent, *Chloro Controls* may be said to have implicitly overruled *Shin Itsu*. **9.70**

[76] *MIC Electronics Ltd v Intl Techno Media Pvt Ltd* [2012] 3 Arb LR 313, [2012] 1 ALT 527, affirmed by Supreme Court *vide* order dated 12 March 2012, in SLP (Civil) No 8143 of 2012.

[77] *Antrix Corp Ltd v Devas Multimedia P Ltd* [2011] Arbitration Petition No 20.

[78] *Union of India v East Coast Boat Builders and Engineers Ltd* [1998] 2 Delhi 797; *Rajnigandha Cooperative Group Housing Society Ltd v M/S Chand Construction Co and anor* [2001] 94 DLT 636.

[79] *Shin Itsu Chemical Co Ltd v Akash Optifibre Ltd* [2005] 7 SCC 234.

9.2.4 The role of courts in enjoining arbitration

9.71 The 1996 Act does not contemplate any judicial intervention enjoining arbitrations.[80] In the author's view, the policy of the law is that arbitration should not be enjoined, in particular with international arbitration, except possibly where there is an allegation of serious fraud and/or forgery, etc whereby the very existence of the contract including the arbitration agreement is assailed.[81] In a purportedly foreign-seated arbitration, the argument raised to support enjoining when a serious issue of fraud/forgery is raised, is that Part I does not apply and therefore section 16 providing for the separability of the arbitration agreement does not apply. Further, the argument raised is often that the arbitration agreement itself is vitiated by fraud/forgery and hence non-existent. In practice, however, there may be no other jurisdiction that interferes as much by granting orders enjoining pending arbitration proceedings, particularly in international arbitrations seated outside India. More often than not this has the practical effect of completely stalling the arbitration, as the international parties do not wish to be seen to disobey the orders of the courts given their investments or businesses in India and the possibility of contempt proceedings. This is despite the fact that the Supreme Court has, in *Dresser Rand SA v KG Khosla Compressors Ltd*, observed that international arbitrations should not ordinarily be enjoined,[82] and that another bench of the Supreme Court has, in *Svenska Handelsbanken v Indian Charge Chrome*, held that the right of international arbitration is an indefeasible right.[83]

9.2.5 Interim measures

9.72 Section 17 of the 1996 Act empowers the arbitral tribunal to order interim measures of protection in respect of the subject matter of the dispute. Section 17 applies to all Indian-seated arbitrations, whether domestic or international. An order passed under section 17 is appealable to the court under section 37 of the 1996 Act. It is to be noted that there is no provision in the 1996 Act to compel compliance with an order passed under section 17. However, if an appeal is filed and the order is confirmed, it will be an order of the court and non-compliance could lead to contempt proceedings. In practice, while the Delhi High Court has taken the view that non-compliance would amount to contempt, a subsequent coordinate bench has disagreed with this view in *Intertoll ICS Cecons O&M Co Pvt Ltd v National Highways Authority of India*.[84] Other High Courts have also taken the view that an order under section 17 is not enforceable, and the Supreme Court has also so observed in *MD, Army Welfare Housing Organisation v Sumangal Services (P) Ltd*.[85]

9.73 Section 9 of the 1996 Act provides for a party's right to approach a court for interim measures of protection, including injunctions, the appointment of receivers, and securing an amount in dispute to provide for a security for the amount in dispute in arbitration. Such security can be granted in respect of a debt but not simply for a claim in damages unless it is established that the party is trying to dissipate assets to avoid enforcement of an eventual award.

---

[80] *Oval Investment P Ltd v Indiabulls Financial Service Ltd* [2009] 4 Arb LR 282, para 13.

[81] *N Radhakrishnan v Maestro Engineers* [2010] 1 SCC 72 (see para 9.45).

[82] *Dresser Rand SA v KG Khosla Compressors Ltd* [1995] Supp (3) SCC 181.

[83] *Svenska Handelsbanken v Indian Charge Chrome* [1994] 2 SCC 155, para 43.

[84] *Intertoll ICS Cecons O&M Co Pvt Ltd v National Highways Authority of India* [2012] Arbitration Application No 5, decided on 4 February 2013.

[85] *MD, Army Welfare Housing Organisation v Sumangal Services (P) Ltd* [2004] 9 SCC 619.

9.3 During the Arbitration

9.3.1 The role of courts in deciding challenges to arbitrators

Under the 1996 Act, the role of courts in deciding challenges to arbitrators is minimal during the arbitration. Section 12(3) of the 1996 Act which applies to both domestic and international arbitrations seated in India, provides that an arbitrator may be challenged if circumstances exist that give rise to justifiable doubts as to his independence and impartiality or if he does not possess the qualifications agreed to by the parties. Section 12(4) of the 1996 Act provides that a party may challenge an arbitrator appointed by him, or in whose appointment he has participated, only for reasons of which he becomes aware after the appointment has been made. **9.74**

Section 13 of the 1996 Act lays down the challenge procedure in respect of the grounds set out in section 12(3) of the 1996 Act. It provides that parties are free to agree on a procedure for challenging an arbitrator. If no such procedure has been agreed, for example by reference to a set of arbitration rules regulating challenges, in accordance with section 13(2), a party who intends to challenge an arbitrator must, within 15 days of becoming aware of the constitution of the arbitral tribunal or of the circumstances giving rise to the challenge, send a written statement of the reasons for the challenge to the arbitral tribunal. If the challenged arbitrator does not withdraw from his office and the other party does not agree to the challenge, it is for the tribunal, in the first instance, to decide on the challenge. The challenged arbitrator participates in this decision. Very often, it is a sole arbitrator whose independence is challenged and he/she must decide the issue in the first instance. **9.75**

If a challenge under an agreed procedure or under the this procedure is not successful, section 13(4) of the 1996 Act provides that the arbitral tribunal shall continue the arbitral proceedings and make an arbitral award. However, in terms of section 13(5) of the 1996 Act, if an arbitral award is made by such a tribunal or an arbitrator who has been challenged, the party challenging the arbitrator may make an application for setting aside in accordance with section 34 of the 1996 Act which includes among the grounds for setting aside an award, that the composition of the arbitral tribunal or the arbitral procedure was not in accordance with the agreement of the parties or, failing such an agreement, was not in accordance with Part I of the Act. **9.76**

Section 14 of the 1996 Act which also applies to both domestic and international arbitrations seated in India, provides that the mandate of an arbitrator shall terminate if he becomes *de jure* or *de facto* unable to perform his functions or for other reasons fails to act without undue delay. Additionally, the mandate of the arbitrator terminates if he withdraws from his office or the parties agree to the termination of his mandate. Section 14 also provides for court assistance in this respect. If a controversy remains concerning whether the mandate of an arbitrator has terminated either because he was *de jure* or *de facto* unable to perform his functions or failed to act without undue delay, a party may (unless otherwise agreed by the parties) apply to the court to decide on the termination of the mandate. **9.77**

This has led to some debate as to whether section 14(1)(a) could also be applied to allow for court intervention with respect to an unsuccessful challenge based on justifiable doubts as to independence and impartiality or lack of qualifications agreed to by the parties. **9.78**

One view is that if an arbitrator lacks independence or impartiality, he is legally, and therefore *de jure* or *de facto*, not in a position to perform his functions as an arbitrator and hence **9.79** an aggrieved party may file a petition under section 14 of the 1996 Act to have the court declare the tribunal or the arbitrator's mandate as terminated, instead of waiting for the award and then raising a challenge. The Delhi High Court initially accepted this analysis in a number of judgments,[86] with some benches of the Delhi High Court taking a conflicting view.[87] A Division Bench of the Delhi High Court reviewed the law and ultimately came to the conclusion that section 14 did not empower the court to terminate the mandate of an arbitrator when a section 13 challenge had failed.[88]

9.80 Other courts have also taken different views on this issue. The Calcutta High Court has held that a section 14 petition would not be maintainable,[89] as has the Jharkhand High Court.[90] On the other hand, the Punjab and Haryana High Court and a Division Bench of the Guwahati High Court have found that a petition under section 14 would be maintainable.[91]

9.81 In India, where in a large number of public sector corporation and even private contracts, the appointed arbitrators are employees of one party, or retired judges appointed repeatedly, the better practice would be that section 14 applications to terminate an arbitrator's mandate due to lack of independence or impartiality should be maintainable. Obviously, in each case the court would have to decide on the facts whether justifiable doubts as to independence or impartiality had been established (not difficult in the case of an employee, which should per se be a disqualification). The question is whether it serves the purpose of expeditious arbitration to await the award before a challenge can be mounted under section 34, or whether it would be more efficient to decide on the termination at the threshold and have an independent arbitrator appointed so that the grounds for challenge to the award would be minimized. One way or the other, such cases are inevitably going to call for court involvement

9.3.2 The role of courts in compelling testimony/evidence

9.82 Section 27 of the 1996 Act provides for court assistance in taking evidence. Section 27 also applies to both domestic and international arbitrations seated in India. An arbitral tribunal or a party with the approval of the arbitral tribunal may apply to the court to compel a witness to appear and give evidence, ie testimony. The court is empowered to order that the evidence be provided directly to the arbitral tribunal and to issue a summons to the witness to attend the arbitral hearing to provide evidence on particular dates.

9.83 Section 27(5) further provides that persons failing to attend in accordance with such process or refusing to give evidence are subject to the same disadvantage, penalties, and punishment as they would have incurred for a similar offence in a suit tried by the court. In other words, the court could hold such a person guilty of contempt of court. This provision ensures that witnesses who are directed to give testimony/evidence in arbitrations cannot avoid doing so. There is no recourse available to the courts if a tribunal does not order the production of

---

[86] *Interstate Constructions v NPCC Ltd* [2004] 3 RAJ 672 (Del); *Indira Rai and anor v Vatika Plantations (P) Ltd and ors* [2006] 127 DLT 646; *Alcove Industries Ltd v Oriental Structural Engineers Ltd* [2008] 1 Arb LR 393; *National Highways Authority of India v Mr KK Sarin and ors* [2009] 159 DLT 314.

[87] *Shri Pinaki Das Gupta v Publicis (India) Communications and ors* [2004] 115 DLT 345.

[88] *Progressive Career Academy Pvt Ltd v FIIT JEE Ltd* [2011] 180 DLT 714.

[89] *Jas Enterprises v Karanpara Development Co Ltd* [1997] 2 CLT 277.

[90] *State of Jharkhand v Indian Builders* [2003] 3 JCR 718.

[91] *State of Arunachal Pradesh v Subhash Projects and Marketing Ltd and anor* [2007] 1 Arb LR 564; *OPBK Construction Pvt Ltd v Punjab Small Industries & Export Corp Ltd* [2008] 3 Arb LR 189.

documents by parties. Section 27 of the 1996 Act can be used to compel non-party representatives and party representatives to give evidence if relevant on the issue of arbitration.

9.3.3 Restrictions/requirements regarding the ability of foreign practitioners to appear in arbitration as counsel or arbitrator

The 1996 Act does not place any restriction on foreign practitioners appearing in arbitrations seated in India, whether as counsel or arbitrators. However, invoking the provisions of the Advocates Act, 1961, certain Indian lawyers have challenged the right of foreign practitioners to practice in India, including in arbitrations. The Bombay High Court, in *Lawyers' Collective v Bar Council of India*,[92] has held that the practice of law in India without a licence issued by the Bar Council under the Bar Council Act and Rules is illegal. It did not specifically deal with the question of international arbitration and international practitioners participating in international arbitrations seated in India, whether as counsel or arbitrator, but some lawyers have taken the view that the judgment is sufficiently broad in its prohibition to cover arbitration. However, the Madras High Court has, in the case of *AK Balaji v The Government of India*, held that there could be no bar to foreign practitioners appearing in international arbitrations seated in India, whether as counsel or arbitrator.[93] A special leave petition has been filed with the Supreme Court against the Madras High Court judgment, which is currently pending. The interim order passed by the Supreme Court does not expressly prohibit foreign practitioners from appearing in international arbitrations and therefore such practice is not currently barred or illegal. **9.84**

9.3.4 Local requirements for the conduct of arbitration hearings

The 1996 Act does not require an arbitration to be conducted in any specific language. It is open to the parties to agree to a language to be used in the arbitration proceedings. If there is no such agreement between the parties, the arbitral tribunal is empowered to determine the language to be used.[94] In practice, most arbitrations are conducted in English, as are proceedings in the Supreme Court and in most of the High Courts. **9.85**

Rules for the swearing in of witnesses are informal and vary from tribunal to tribunal. Section 19 of the 1996 Act expressly provides that the tribunal is not bound by the Code of Civil Procedure, 1908 or the Evidence Act, 1872, and that the parties are free to agree on the procedure to be followed by an arbitral tribunal in conducting its proceedings. As a matter of practice, most tribunals do not insist on the swearing in of a witness unless one of the parties insists. **9.86**

In the absence of applicable procedural rules being agreed by the parties, ad hoc tribunals do not, as a matter of practice, adopt any particular procedural rules of institutions, etc; this is particularly so in purely domestic arbitrations seated in India. On the other hand, in the case of international arbitrations seated in India where the tribunal is chaired by experienced international arbitrators, the parties are often persuaded to adopt a set of procedural rules of institutions acceptable to them. Therefore, in purely domestic arbitrations in India the tribunals follow basic principles of natural justice and, in a general way, the principles embodied in the civil procedure code. **9.87**

92 *Lawyers' Collective v Bar Council of India* [2010] 2 Bom LR 32.
93 *AK Balaji v The Government of India* AIR [2012] Mad 124.
94 Arbitration and Conciliation Act, 1996, s 22(2).

9.4 The Award

9.4.1 Mandatory rules as to form

9.88 The only mandatory rules as to the form of an award are those found in section 31 of the 1996 Act. This applies to both domestic and international arbitrations seated in India. The arbitral award must be in writing and must be signed by all members of the tribunal. If the award is not unanimous, the signatures of a majority of the tribunal are sufficient, as long as the reason for any omitted signature is stated.[95] The award must state the reasons upon which it is based, unless the parties have agreed that no reasons need be given or the award is a consent award, ie on agreed terms following a settlement. The arbitral award must state the date and place of arbitration, and a signed copy of the award must be delivered to each of the parties.

9.89 A unique feature of arbitral awards made in India is the requirement that they be stamped in accordance with the Indian Stamp Act, 1899. Each state has its own rates of stamp duty, which can vary from a fixed nominal stamp duty in some states to *ad valorem* duty. For example, in Delhi, based on article 12 of Schedule 1A to the Indian Stamp (Delhi Amendment) Act, 2001, an award must bear a stamp duty of 0.01 per cent of the value of the amount awarded. However, in the author's view, the provision does not apply to a purely monetary award but only where the award effects the transfer of immovable property. This issue has not been tested in the courts. In practice, arbitrators usually issue the award on a stamp paper of INR 100 and direct in the award for one or other party (usually the winning party) to get the award adjudicated by the Collector of Stamps and to have it stamped accordingly. As it is necessary for the award to be stamped in accordance with law for the same to be enforced, a winning party would usually comply with this requirement.

9.90 Another important aspect of an award delivered under Part I is that a signed copy of the award must be served on the party and not just an agent of a party, including the lawyer representing the party. In other words, if a signed copy of the award was not sent to a party, the limitation period to challenge the award would not begin to run. In *Benarsi Krishna Committee v Karmyogi Shelters Pvt Ltd*,[96] the Supreme Court held that when a copy of the award is sent to the lawyer acting for a party and not to the party itself, the period of limitation to challenge the award (90 days) would not begin to run and that it is only when a signed copy of the award was received by the party itself, that the period of limitation would begin to run.

9.4.2 Mandatory rules as to substance

9.91 The mandatory rules as to the substance of an award include that it must be made in accordance with the substantive law applicable to the contract. Where all parties are domestic, the substantive law must be Indian.[97] In an international commercial arbitration, however, the substantive law will be the law designated by the parties, or failing such designation, as may be determined by the arbitral tribunal to be the appropriate law given the circumstances of the dispute. An arbitral tribunal cannot act *ex aequo et bono* or as *amiable compositeur* unless

[95] Arbitration and Conciliation Act, 1996, s 31(2).

[96] *Benarsi Krishna Committee v Karmyogi Shelters Pvt Ltd* [2012] 9 SCC 496.

[97] Arbitration and Conciliation Act, 1996, s 28(1)(a).

the parties have expressly authorized it to do so, and must decide the dispute in accordance with the terms of the contract.

It is not mandatory for a tribunal to grant interest on an award; this is at the discretion of the tribunal.[98] Similarly, costs are entirely at the discretion of the tribunal unless agreed otherwise by the parties. It is not mandatory to award costs but, if awarded, the costs are to be reasonable and can include the fees and expenses of the arbitrators and witnesses, legal fees and expenses, administrative fees of the institution, or other expenses incurred in connection with the arbitral proceedings. **9.92**

The practice in relation to awarding costs varies from tribunal to tribunal. Many tribunals do not award costs in favour of the successful party but rather order each party to bear its own costs and the tribunal's fees and costs equally. This is particularly so in domestic arbitrations seated in India. In some domestic arbitrations and in most international arbitrations seated in India with an international tribunal, the successful party is usually awarded a reasonable share of the costs incurred by it. **9.93**

9.5 After the Award

9.5.1 Local standards for setting aside/annulment

With respect to the setting aside or annulment of awards considered to be domestic under Part I of the 1996 Act, section 34 of the Act incorporates the provisions of the Model Law. The grounds specifically stipulated are: **9.94**

(a) where a party was under some incapacity;
(b) where the arbitration agreement is invalid under its applicable law;
(c) when a party is unable to present its case due to lack of notice of the appointment of an arbitrator, or the arbitration proceedings, or for other reasons;
(d) where the arbitral award is made beyond the scope of the arbitration agreement (if such an award is severable from the rest of the award, then there would be a limited setting aside only to such offending severable extent);
(e) where the composition of the arbitral tribunal was not in accordance with the agreement of parties or, in the absence of such agreement, not in accordance with Part I of the Act;
(f) where the subject matter of the dispute is not capable of settlement by arbitration; and lastly
(g) if the award is contrary to the public policy of India.

Therefore, the intent of the statute was to allow for setting aside or annulment only on internationally accepted standards. Initially, certain High Courts had applied these standards strictly, construing narrowly the public policy ground for challenging an award.[99] However, when the issue arose before the Supreme Court in *ONGC v SAW Pipes*, the court expanded the interpretation of the public policy ground beyond its earlier interpretation in *Renusagar 3* by holding that the 'patent illegality' of the award violated public policy. Although the court clarified that patent illegality did not include trivial illegalities, but only illegality going **9.95**

[98] Arbitration and Conciliation Act, 1996, s 31(7).

[99] *Housing & Urban Development Corp v Leela Hotels* Order dated 20 January 2003, passed by the Single Judge of the Delhi High Court in OMP No 308/2002.

to the root of the matter, it added another public policy ground that could be read as being independent of patent illegality: the award 'could also be set aside if it is so unfair and unreasonable that it shocks the conscience of the Court'.[100]

9.96 In practice at all levels, ie in the Supreme Court of India and various High Courts, the result of *ONGC v SAW Pipes* has been that courts undertake a review of the substance of the award in one way or the other. A common ground for setting aside awards that has emerged is that the award is contrary to an express term of the contract under the head of 'patent illegality'.

9.97 It has been widely felt that *ONGC v SAW Pipes* needs reconsideration but there is currently no case in which reconsideration appears to be pending. *ONGC v SAW Pipes* has had a significant deleterious impact on arbitrations in India. Nearly every domestic award is now subjected to challenge under section 34. Public sector companies in particular tend to raise challenges under section 34, when in fact the majority of these awards should never be challenged in court. In many cases, for all practical purposes, the court sits in appeal over arbitral awards, although it has been held time and again that this was not the intent of section 34.[101]

9.98 The impact of *ONGC v SAW Pipes* is not limited to domestic awards, but has found its way to foreign awards as well. In *Renusagar 3* (which preceded the 1996 Act), the Supreme Court of India had occasion to consider the scope of the public policy exception to enforcement of a foreign award under section 7(1)(b)(ii) of the Foreign Awards Act, 1961 which is *para materia* to section 48(2)(b) of the 1996 Act. *Renusagar 3* interpreted the public policy exception as being limited to (a) fundamental policy of India law; or (b) the interest of India; or (c) justice or morality.

9.99 Recently, however, in *Phulchand Export Ltd v OOO Patriot*,[102] the Supreme Court has extended the expansive definition of public policy from *ONCG v Saw Pipes* to the enforcement of foreign awards. Nevertheless, as far as foreign awards are concerned, the overall status quo is that very seldom has the Indian court refused enforcement. In nearly all cases, enforcement has been granted; the problem has been the time it has taken for the party concerned to recover the amount awarded.

9.5.2 Local procedures for setting aside/annulment

9.100 A party that wishes to challenge an award must file a petition under section 34 of the 1996 Act with the competent court, within 90 days of having received a copy of the award. There is, however, provision for a 30-day extension for sufficient cause. It has been held that this period of time is not open to extension by application of the (Indian) Limitation Act, 1963. Any court where part of the cause of action for the main claims in the arbitration arose has jurisdiction. In many states, this could be a lower, or district, court. However, in presidency towns and Delhi, the High Courts have original jurisdiction to entertain such petitions if the amount in dispute exceeds certain values (eg in the Delhi High Court, the equivalent of approximately US$40,000 at current rates of exchange) or, as in the Calcutta High Court, by virtue of a certain territorial application of the High Court's jurisdiction.

---

100 See *Oil & Natural Gas Corp v SAW Pipes Ltd* [2003] 5 SCC 705, para 31.

101 *Power Grid Corp of India Ltd v Klen and Marshalls Manufacturers and Exporters Ltd* Judgment dated 8 April 2010, passed by the Delhi High Court in OMP 262/2003 and 88/2006 (MANU/DE/1011/2010).

102 *Phulchand Export Ltd v OOO Patriot* [2011] 10 SCC 300.

The court has jurisdiction to dismiss the petition on the basis that no ground under section 34 has been established. In practice, this is seldom done. The court will usually issue notice, and give the respondent an opportunity to file a reply. The petition will then be heard on its merits. The time taken to dispose of a section 34 petition varies from court to court. In some courts it can take as long as three to five years. Depending on the particular judge, the process may be much quicker. Section 34 petitions are currently being disposed of in some instances (eg in the Delhi High Court) within a few months. **9.101**

If a section 34 petition is rejected, this results in a deemed decree of the court, which is then executable. However, pursuant to section 37 of the 1996 Act, an appeal can be filed against an order of dismissal or setting aside of the award. The normal trend is that when an appeal is filed against an order of dismissal in respect of a monetary award, the court requires the deposit of the awarded sum in court, which can be withdrawn pending the appeal subject to suitable security being provided. **9.102**

Against any order passed by the court in any appeal preferred against the judgment dismissing an application to set aside an award or upholding the award, it is always open for a party to file a petition for leave to appeal (commonly called a Special Leave Petition or SLP) to the Supreme Court of India. Again, if the stakes are reasonably high (by Indian standards), the Supreme Court will ordinarily grant leave and hear the matter, unless both lower courts have dismissed the challenge. The overall time taken in the ultimate disposal of a challenge to an award can therefore be anything from two to five years, or even more at times. The costs can also vary significantly, depending on the lawyers involved. **9.103**

9.6 Conclusion

Many practitioners dedicated to arbitration practice in India are of the view that the state of affairs is not a happy one. Delays are common at nearly every stage of arbitration, from the very constitution of the tribunal, when recourse is needed to section 11 of the 1996 Act, to the conduct of the arbitration proceedings, where unusually large numbers of hearings or sittings often take place, and the delivery, challenge, and enforcement of awards. Much needs to be done, but there are definite signs of progress. Undoubtedly, there are a handful of judges in the various High Courts and the Supreme Court who try their best to dispose of matters expeditiously and to decide cases based on the true spirit of the arbitration law. It is often felt that practitioners representing clients are also to blame, as they do not usually wish to conduct arbitrations on weekdays during normal working hours, but would rather hold hearings after court hours and at weekends. This is a major factor that delays the conduct of an arbitration. **9.104**

India is not equipped with good hearing centres. Hearings are usually held in luxury hotels, adding to cost. Transcription facilities are not available, and usually hearings are not even recorded for transcription purposes. When evidence is recorded, it is a slow and laborious process where, through ordinary computer systems, the questions and answers are typed on screen with much attention being paid to grammar, ie the questions and answers are corrected. Often the whole purpose of cross-examination is lost. However, interpreters, if required, are usually available for the well-known foreign languages at least. **9.105**

10

LONDON

Stephen Jagusch and Epaminontas E Triantafilou

10.1 Introduction

10.01 Long considered a leading centre for arbitration, England and Wales—and London in particular—has become firmly established as a pre-eminent venue[1] for international arbitration worldwide.[2] Several factors account for this, most prominently the highly competent and independent English courts and the modern, arbitration-friendly domestic legislation, as

[1] We use the terms 'seat' and 'venue' interchangeably for purposes of this chapter, although parties have sought to distinguish the two terms before the English courts. See *Shashoua and ors v Sharma* [2009] EWHC 957 (Comm), ruling, *inter alia*, that the designation of London as the 'venue' of the arbitration in an ICC arbitration clause was sufficient to hold that London was the juridical seat of arbitration intended by the parties.

[2] See eg Queen Mary University of London and White & Case LLP, '2010 International Arbitration Survey: Choices in International Arbitration' (2010) 19, reporting that 30% of the corporate counsel that participated in the survey prefer London as the seat of arbitration, with other widely-used seats such as Geneva and Paris trailing by a substantial margin. These findings are substantially the same as those in a similar survey undertaken in 2006 (Queen Mary School of International Arbitration, 'International Arbitration: Corporate Attitudes and Practices' (2006)). This trend is reflected, among others, in the substantial caseload of

well as the superb and business-oriented infrastructure. Another factor is the convenient physical location of London, situated as it is at the crossroads of three continents and within reach from every major business centre on the planet.

The pages that follow summarize the key aspects of the English legal system with respect to the role of courts in arbitrations seated in England and Wales. The discussion proceeds in three parts. First, it highlights the key provisions of relevant English legislation, mainly of the English Arbitration Act of 1996 ('1996 Act' or 'Act'),[3] and the principal court decisions arising under that legislation.[4] Second, it describes the manner in which English law as the law of the seat affects the role of English courts in the course of three discrete stages: before the award, after the award, and during recognition and enforcement. In the process and where necessary, it addresses and ultimately rejects recently articulated concerns questioning the supremacy of England and Wales as an arbitration seat. **10.02**

10.1.1 Relevant legislation

Given its repeated use before and by the English courts, and the abundant commentary it has engendered, it is no longer appropriate to consider the 1996 Act a 'new' piece of legislation. More than 15 years after its enactment, it is widely praised for the balance it strikes between the arbitration parties' autonomy and the English courts' role as gatekeepers of justice.[5] A recent review of the Act, based on a survey of the legal community and conducted by a private committee consisting of leading legal professionals and academics, concluded that changes to the 1996 Act were not 'necessarily desirable'.[6] **10.03**

The 1996 Act was drafted by the UK government's Departmental Advisory Committee on Arbitration Law (the 'DAC'), under the chairmanship of Lord Justice Saville.[7] It is influenced by the UNCITRAL Model Law on International Commercial Arbitration, but differs **10.04**

London-based arbitral institutions such as the London Court of International Arbitration, to which more than 200 cases are referred annually, with 80% of parties based outside England and Wales. See generally London Court of International Arbitration, Annual Reports at <http://www.lcia.org/LCIA/Casework_Report.aspx>; similarly, the London Maritime Arbitrators' Association has reported that 'more maritime disputes are referred to arbitration in London than to any other place where arbitration services are offered'. London Maritime Arbitrators Association, 'Introduction', at <http://www.lmaa.org.uk/about-us-Introduction.aspx>.

[3] Arbitration Act 1996 (c 23) <http://www.legislation.gov.uk/ukpga/1996/23>. It is worth noting that the Act does not purport to 'codify' English arbitration law in the sense the term is used in civil law systems; several court decisions that have followed the enactment of the Arbitration Act have established fundamental principles of English arbitration law. Recognizing the importance of pre-existing and future common law, the Act preserves any such law consistent with the Act's provisions. 1996 Act, s 81(1).

[4] Reference will be made to other applicable statutes, such as the Supreme Court Act 1981, where appropriate. Parties lodging arbitration-related applications before the English courts also may need to consult the Civil Procedural Rules of 1998, as amended—especially Pt 62 and the associated Practice Direction. See D St John Sutton, J Gill, and M Gearing, *Russell on Arbitration* (Sweet & Maxwell 2007) s 7-009.

[5] For an excellent overview of the Act and the manner in which it operates both procedurally and substantively, see St John Sutton, Gill, and Gearing (n 4).

[6] B Harris, 'Report on the Arbitration Act 1996' (2007) 23(3) Arb Intl 437, 451 (hereinafter the '2007 Report'). The Report, intended to commemorate the ten years from the Act's entry into force, also commented that: 'The conclusions reached in this Report are an enormous tribute to the Act and, by extension, to those responsible for its authorship. . . ': at 437. But see MM Cohen, 'A Missed Opportunity to Revise the Arbitration Act 1996' (2007) 23(3) Arb Intl 461, arguing that reforms to the 1996 Act are necessary and that the 2007 Report 'represents a missed opportunity' to enact such reforms.

[7] In September 1996, the DAC issued its Report on the Arbitration Bill 1996 (hereinafter the 'DAC Report'). Departmental Advisory Committee on Arbitration Law, 'Report on Arbitration Bill 1996', 28 September 1996, available at <http://arbitration.practicallaw.com/5-205-4994#sect1pos2res1>. The DAC Report provides useful guidance on the procedural and policy considerations underlying the Act's provisions.

from it in several important respects. Unlike the Model Law, it constitutes a single legislative framework governing all arbitrations seated in England, Wales, and Northern Ireland, not just international commercial arbitrations.[8] Moreover, while the 1996 Act does not codify the law completely,[9] it contains most of the important provisions of English arbitration law.

10.05 Before the Act, English law had been criticized for allowing the courts to intervene too readily in the arbitral process. The legislation preceding the 1996 Act, namely the Arbitration Act 1979 and the Arbitration Act 1950, resulted in a combined framework that generally protected party autonomy; however, because the 1979 Act did not address arbitral procedure, the more 'interventionist' provisions of the 1950 Act still governed important contingencies. For example, before the 1996 Act parties to arbitration were obligated to resort to the courts if one party refused to cooperate with the proceedings. Moreover, the courts retained residual powers to invalidate the arbitration agreement, dismiss the arbitrators, or remand an award to a tribunal due to 'procedural mishap'—a term that courts were at liberty to interpret.[10]

10.06 The drafters of the 1996 Act sought to address these issues through a requirement that the courts not intervene except as provided in Part I of the 1996 Act, and by giving powers to the arbitral tribunal, rather than the courts, wherever possible. Under the Act, the tribunal has the power to decide all procedural and evidentiary matters, appoint experts, order security for costs, and give directions in relation to property or for the preservation of evidence.[11] The Act confers on the courts powers of both a supportive nature (eg to appoint arbitrators where an agreed process fails, enforce a 'peremptory order' made by the tribunal, or summon a witness to appear before the tribunal) and a supervisory nature (eg to hear challenges to arbitrators and applications to set aside awards).

10.07 The courts, furthermore, retain some powers that are unusual compared to those of other jurisdictions. For example, a party to arbitral proceedings may appeal to the courts on a point of English law, although this right may be excluded by agreement and, is rarely exercised in practice. The courts have also emphasized that a major purpose of the 1996 Act was to reduce drastically the extent of court intervention in the arbitral process. This policy has influenced their approach in applying the Act.

10.08 The Act consists of four parts. Part I contains the main provisions applicable to arbitration under an arbitration agreement, which agreement must be 'in writing'.[12] Part II contains provisions relating to consumer arbitration agreements, statutory arbitrations, and the exceptional

[8] Arbitration Act 1996, s 2(1), providing that: 'The provisions of [Part I of the Act, which are mandatory] apply where the seat of arbitration is in England and Wales or Northern Ireland.' Sections 85–87, which modify Part I in the case of a 'domestic arbitration agreement', have never been brought into force. As a result, English law operates a unified regime for both domestic and international arbitration.

[9] Arbitration Act 1996, s 81(1) preserves any common law rule consistent with the Act's provisions, including on matters that are not capable of settlement by arbitration and the refusal of recognition of an arbitral award on grounds of public policy. The confidentiality of the arbitral process under English law likewise remains governed by the common law; see also DAC Report (n 7) ch 2, paras 9–17.

[10] For an overview of the historical background to the 1996 Act, see R Merkin and L Flannery, *Arbitration Act 1996* (4th edn, Informa, 2008) 2–3; Lord Saville, 'The Origin of the New English Arbitration Act 1996: Reconciling Speed With Justice in the Decision-Making Process' (1997) 13(3) Arb Intl 237.

[11] See Arbitration Act 1996, ss 34, 37, 38.

[12] 1996 Act, s 5. The requirement under the Act that the arbitration agreement be 'in writing' is construed broadly under the Act to encompass recording by any means. The manner of recording may be similarly broad, eg via a unilateral recording by one of the parties or by a third party with the permission of the parties; by exchange of communications between the parties; or by some medium other than writing that refers to an

appointment of a judge as arbitrator.[13] Part III concerns the recognition and enforcement of certain foreign awards,[14] while Part IV sets out a number of general provisions.[15]

The 1996 Act also sets out the principles that underlie arbitration law and procedure. Thus, the object of arbitration is defined in section 1 as 'the fair resolution of disputes by an impartial tribunal without unnecessary delay or expense'. Under the same section, 'the parties should be free to agree how their disputes are resolved, subject only to such safeguards as are necessary in the public interest'. In this regard, the Act draws a sharp distinction between provisions whose public policy importance renders them mandatory, ie superseding any agreement between the parties to arbitration, and those from which the parties can diverge by agreement or by adopting institutional arbitration rules.[16] According to Schedule 1 to the Act, the mandatory provisions of Part I are sections 9 to 13, 24, 26, 28, 31 to 33, 37, 40, 43, 56, 60, 66, 67, 68, and 70 to 75. The remaining sections may be excluded by agreement. **10.09**

Most proceedings under the 1996 Act must be taken to the High Court, the senior of the two levels of court exercising civil jurisdiction at first instance. Two specialist courts within the High Court hear most arbitration-related cases: the Commercial Court, which hears general commercial arbitration matters; and the Technology and Construction Court, which deals with construction disputes. This allocation of expertise results in the more efficient disposal of cases. **10.10**

10.2 Role of Courts Prior to the Commencement of Arbitral Proceedings

We now turn to the question of the powers that the Act's provisions confer upon English courts when the venue of the arbitration is England and Wales. Notably, the provisions of the 1996 Act discussed do not necessarily apply only during the phase of the proceedings in the context of which they are first mentioned. For example challenges under section 72 of the Act, described at paragraphs 10.16–10.17, may actually be raised at any suitable time before the rendering of the award, and possibly also thereafter. To avoid repetition, we will provide appropriate cross-references where necessary. **10.11**

Before the commencement of an arbitral proceeding seated in England and Wales, the law of the seat may be invoked with respect to the establishment of the proceedings—including the existence and enforceability of an arbitration agreement, the law of limitations, the constitution of the arbitral tribunal, anti-suit injunctions, and interim or emergency measures. **10.12**

10.2.1 The tribunal's jurisdiction

One of the first questions to consider when commencing arbitration is whether there is a valid arbitration agreement.[17] It is well established under the principle of *competence-competence*, **10.13**

agreement that is in writing. In any event, the agreement need not be signed by the parties. The same standards apply to other agreements under the Act, including those carving out non-mandatory provisions. See generally Arbitration Act 1996, s 5; St John Sutton, Gill, and Gearing (n 4) s 2-039.

[13] Arbitration Act 1996, ss 89–91, 94–98, and 93 respectively.

[14] 1996 Act, ss 99–104.

[15] 1996 Act, ss 105–110.

[16] See 1996 Act, s 4(1) and Sch 1; see also s 4(2).

[17] Importantly, the law of the seat does not apply automatically to this question. Pursuant to the House of Lords ruling in *Fiona Trust v Privalov*, the law of the arbitration clause is legally distinct from the contract of

a principle that the 1996 Act recognizes and supports explicitly,[18] that the arbitral tribunal is empowered to interpret the arbitration agreement and to rule on its own jurisdiction.

10.14 However, under the 1996 Act, the validity of the arbitration agreement and by extension the jurisdiction of the tribunal is not entirely immune from collateral challenge before the English courts. Such a challenge can be brought under limited circumstances and subject to strong procedural protections meant to minimize disruption and costs.

10.15 Specifically, the validity and scope of the arbitration agreement can be challenged under section 72, which provides:

> A person alleged to be a party to arbitral proceedings but who takes no part in the proceedings may question—
> (a) whether there is a valid arbitration agreement,
> (b) whether the tribunal is properly constituted, or
> (c) what matters have been submitted to arbitration in accordance with the arbitration agreement
> by proceedings in the court for a declaration or injunction or other appropriate relief.

10.16 Section 72 covers a broad array of challenges to the establishment of the arbitration, including whether the applicant is a proper party to the arbitration agreement, and whether the facts giving rise to the action in arbitration are covered by the arbitration agreement. The section also allows challenges to the constitution of the arbitral tribunal.[19]

10.17 Despite the permissive wording of section 72, English courts have interpreted it restrictively in light of the Act's stated policy of favouring *competence-competence*.[20] In this regard, parties must remain cognizant of the limits of 'taking part' in an arbitration proceeding for purposes of this section. For instance, correspondence with an arbitral institution in an attempt to

---

which it forms a part: *Fiona Trust and Holding Corp v Privalov* [2007] UKHL 40 (Comm). English jurisprudence has been somewhat unsettled on the question of whether English law governs the arbitration agreement, in the absence of a clear choice of law, when the seat is England and Wales. In a decision rendered on 16 May 2012, the Court of Appeal adopted a two-pronged approach to determine which law should apply to the arbitration agreement under such circumstances: first, one cannot assume that the proper law of the arbitration agreement will follow the law of the contract; second, there should be a 'three-stage enquiry' into (a) express choice of law; (b) implied choice of law; and (c) to which law the arbitration agreement has the 'closest and most real connection'. *Sulamerica CIA Nacional De Seguros SA and ors v Enesa Engenharia SA and ors* [2012] EWCA Civ 638.

[18] See eg Arbitration Act 1996, s 30, providing that, unless otherwise agreed by the parties, and subject to challenge by any available arbitral process of appeal or review or in accordance with the provisions of Part I of the 1996 Act, an arbitral tribunal may rule on its own substantive jurisdiction; s 32, providing for limited circumstances under which a party can challenge in court the tribunal's substantive jurisdiction, and discussed at paras 10.19–10.22; cf UNCITRAL Model Law on International Commercial Arbitration (1985), Art 16(1): 'The arbitral tribunal may rule on its own jurisdiction, including any objections with respect to the existence or validity of the arbitration agreement.' Nonetheless, consistently with the Act's oft-repeated aim of protecting the interests of parties that dispute their participation in the arbitration agreement itself, the English courts will examine *de novo* the arbitral tribunal's jurisdiction if a party, for example, resists enforcement under the 1996 Act or the New York Convention as a non-party to the arbitration agreement. See *Dallah Real Estate and Tourism Holding Co v The Ministry of Religious Affairs, Government of Pakistan* [2010] UKSC 46.

[19] The DAC Report states the policy rationale for this provision in the following terms:

> A person who dispute [sic] that an arbitral tribunal has jurisdiction cannot be required to take part in the arbitration proceedings or to take positive steps to defend his position, for any such requirement would beg the question whether or not his objection has any substance and thus be likely to lead to gross injustice.

DAC Report (n 7) para 275.

[20] See *Fiona Trust* (n 17).

dismiss the case, correspondence to the tribunal notifying it of objections to its jurisdiction, or the provisional appointment of an arbitrator do not constitute 'taking part' in the proceeding, and therefore do not preclude an application under section 72.[21]

Alternatively, and more rarely, a party may challenge the jurisdiction of the arbitral tribunal under section 32 of the Act, prior to the commencement of proceedings.[22] According to that section: 'The court may, on the application of a party to arbitral proceedings (upon notice to the other parties), determine any question as to the substantive jurisdiction of the tribunal.'[23] Notably, lack of participation is not required in order to lodge a challenge under this section. **10.18**

Section 32 challenges are rare, however, because of the stringent prerequisites the applicant must meet: either all parties to the arbitration must consent, or the arbitral tribunal must grant leave for the application to be filed. In the latter case, the courts must also be satisfied that the applicant acted without delay, the resolution of the application is likely to result in substantial cost savings, and overall that 'there is good reason why the matter should be decided by the court'.[24] **10.19**

To minimize disruption from a section 32 application (and its potential abuse), unless the parties to the arbitration agree otherwise, the Act allows the arbitral proceedings to continue and an award to be made while the application is pending.[25] After the court's decision on the application is issued, the applicant cannot appeal against the court's ruling with respect to the filing requirements imposed by section 32(2) without leave from the court.[26] An appeal on the merits of the decision similarly requires leave from the court, which under the Act cannot be granted unless the court finds that the question of law underlying its decision is 'of general importance' or should be considered by the Court of Appeal 'for some special reason'.[27] **10.20**

Parties contemplating a jurisdictional challenge prior to the commencement of the proceedings should be mindful of section 73 of the 1996 Act. Under section 73(1)(a), a party that fails to raise an objection to the arbitral tribunal's substantive jurisdiction: **10.21**

> ... either forthwith or within such time as is allowed by the arbitration agreement or the tribunal or by any provision of [Part I of the Act] ... may not raise that objection later, before the tribunal or the court, unless he shows that, at the time he took part or continued to take part in the proceedings, he did not know and could not with reasonable diligence have discovered the grounds for the objection.

21 *Law Debenture Trust Corp plc v Elektrim* [2005] 2 Lloyd's Rep 755, para 18. The courts have also noted that an application under s 72(1) should be decided only *after* a motion under s 9 of the Act, which allows a party to an arbitration agreement to apply for a stay of court proceedings brought against it on a matter covered by the arbitration agreement.

22 A third possibility is for a party to refuse to participate in the arbitration and challenge the resulting award under the 1996 Act, s 67, which is discussed at para 10.99.

23 Arbitration Act 1996, s 32(1). According to s 30(1)(a)–(c), 'substantive jurisdiction' is defined in terms of 'whether there is a valid arbitration agreement, whether the tribunal is properly constituted, and what matters have been submitted to arbitration in accordance with the arbitration agreement'; see also s 82(1).

24 Arbitration Act 1996, s 32(2)(a)–(b).

25 1996 Act, s 32(4).

26 1996 Act, s 32(5).

27 1996 Act, s 32(6). Parties should note that provisions in the Act that vest the first instance court with discretion as to whether to grant an appeal may not hold if the Court of Appeal finds that the first instance court did not have jurisdiction to make its determination in the first place; or that determination was arbitrary or unfair. In such rare instances, the Court of Appeal will exercise its jurisdiction *sua sponte*. See St John Sutton, Gill, and Gearing (n 4) s 7-201.

10.22 A court injunction against arbitral proceedings based on the sections just mentioned is limited to exceptional circumstances, as in most cases it would contravene not only the principal policy of the Act, but potentially also the United Kingdom's international legal obligations under the New York Convention.[28] According to commentary on the Act, it is 'virtually impossible' to enjoin an arbitration under section 72; an injunction application under section 32 may stand higher chances if submitted jointly by all parties to arbitration.[29] Finally, an anti-arbitration injunction may lie in favour of a party that commences court proceedings disputing the validity of an arbitration agreement and successfully defends against the opposing party's application for a stay of the court proceedings under section 9 of the Act.[30]

10.2.2 Commencement of proceedings and service of process

10.23 According to section 14, entitled 'Commencement of arbitral proceedings':

> (1) The parties are free to agree when arbitral proceedings are to be regarded as commenced for the purposes of this Part and for the purposes of the Limitation Acts.
> (2) If there is no such agreement the following provisions apply.
> (3) Where the arbitrator is named or designated in the arbitration agreement, arbitral proceedings are commenced in respect of a matter when one party serves on the other party or parties a notice in writing requiring him or them to submit that matter to the person so named or designated.
> (4) Where the arbitrator or arbitrators are to be appointed by the parties, arbitral proceedings are commenced in respect of a matter when one party serves on the other party or parties notice in writing requiring him or them to appoint an arbitrator or to agree to the appointment of an arbitrator in respect of that matter.
> (5) Where the arbitrator or arbitrators are to be appointed by a person other than a party to the proceedings, arbitral proceedings are commenced in respect of a matter when one party gives notice in writing to that person requesting him to make the appointment in respect of that matter.

10.24 This provision allows the parties to agree on the event that will initiate arbitration proceedings for purposes of the Limitation Acts. Another notable feature of this provision is the use of the term 'matter' instead of 'dispute'; according to the DAC Report, this is to allow the provision to cover not only disputes, but also claims.[31] Finally, there has been some disagreement among courts with respect to the meaning of 'requiring' as used in section 14(3) and (4), specifically whether the service of a notice of arbitration 'requires' the respondent to submit the matter to a single arbitrator or to appoint an arbitrator, thereby initiating the proceedings. The majority view is that a notice of arbitration is sufficient, but a mere statement alluding to the possibility of arbitration is not.[32]

---

[28] New York Convention on the Recognition and Enforcement of Foreign Arbitral Awards 1958, Art II(3): 'The court of a Contracting State, when seized of an action, in a matter in respect of which the parties have made an agreement within the meaning of this article shall, at the request of one of the parties refer the parties to arbitration, unless it finds that the said agreement is null and void, inoperative or incapable of being performed.'

[29] St John Sutton, Gill, and Gearing (n 4) s 7-058; *accord* T Raphael, *The Anti-Suit Injunction* (OUP, 2008) 255. An additional wrinkle is whether the injunction sought is interim or permanent. The former may be comparatively more difficult to obtain, as 'it will interfere with the arbitration without finally determining the question of jurisdiction' Raphael, at 257.

[30] See Raphael (n 29); see also n 21.

[31] DAC Report (n 7) para 76.

[32] Merkin and Flannery (n 10) 51–2.

The Act, moreover, allows a court to extend any agreed time limit by which a party must initiate arbitration or lose the right to do so. According to section 12 (which is mandatory): **10.25**

(1) Where an arbitration agreement to refer future disputes to arbitration provides that a claim shall be barred, or the claimant's right extinguished, unless the claimant takes within a time fixed by the agreement some step—
   (a) to begin arbitral proceedings, or
   (b) to begin other dispute resolution procedures which must be exhausted before arbitral proceedings can be begun, the court may by order extend the time for taking that step.
(2) Any party to the arbitration agreement may apply for such an order (upon notice to the other parties), but only after a claim has arisen and after exhausting any available arbitral process for obtaining an extension of time.
(3) The court shall make an order only if satisfied—
   (a) that the circumstances are such as were outside the reasonable contemplation of the parties when they agreed the provision in question, and that it would be just to extend the time, or
   (b) that the conduct of one party makes it unjust to hold the other party to the strict terms of the provision in question.
(4) The court may extend the time for such period and on such terms as it thinks fit, and may do so whether or not the time previously fixed (by agreement or by a previous order) has expired.
(5) An order under this section does not affect the operation of the Limitation Acts (see section 13).
(6) The leave of the court is required for any appeal from a decision of the court under this section.

Despite the broad power it confers on the courts, section 12 is subject to strict constraints. Thus, section 12(2) requires the applicant to exhaust its arbitral remedies, which in turn renders it unlikely that a court would order an extension when an arbitral tribunal has previously denied it.[33] Section 12 is further limited in scope by the operation of subsection (3)(a), which requires that 'circumstances are such as were outside the reasonable contemplation of the parties' at the time of fixing the time limitation on which an extension is sought. Furthermore, a court is not authorized to extend time limits set under the Limitations Acts, which section 13 of the 1996 Act renders applicable to arbitration proceedings.[34] **10.26**

Equally importantly for purposes of initiating proceedings, the Act confers a role on courts in supervising the proper service of process to implicated parties. Under section 77(2), and unless otherwise agreed by the parties, the court 'may make such order as it thinks fit—(a) for service in such a manner as the court may direct, or (b) dispensing with service of the document'.[35] **10.27**

10.2.3 Constitution of the tribunal

As noted previously, section 72(1)(b) allows a party to challenge the constitution of the arbitral tribunal (which is governed by sections 15 to 20 of the Act). Generally the parties to an **10.28**

---

33 Merkin and Flannery (n 10) 46, citing *Marc Rich Agriculture Trading SA v Agrimex Ltd* [2000] 1 All ER (Comm) 951.

34 See para 10.66.

35 In the rare instance where the parties have contracted out of this provision, and are unable to comply with the process service requirements of the 1996 Act, s 76 (which provides for the ways service may be effected), the arbitration 'may be halted in its tracks' with the Act providing no further guidance. Merkin and Flannery (n 10) 181.

arbitration are at liberty to set the number of arbitrators,[36] the procedure for their appointment,[37] and the procedure for resolving appointment-related disputes.[38] The Act contains its own default appointment procedure for cases in which no pre-agreed procedure exists.[39]

10.29 The courts may become involved in arbitrator appointments in three instances: first, when each party must appoint an arbitrator and one party defaults. In that case, the non-defaulting party may provide notice that its chosen arbitrator shall serve as sole arbitrator in the dispute.[40] The defaulting party can challenge this appointment in court, which may set it aside—although it would do so only upon showing a good cause for the default, such as an invalid arbitration agreement. No appeal can be filed from this decision without leave from the trial court.[41] This procedure applies, *mutatis mutandis,* when there are three arbitrators to be appointed and the procedure for the appointment of one of them fails, either by inaction of the appointing party or, if the third arbitrator serves as chairperson, due to irresolvable disagreement between the two party-appointed arbitrators.

10.30 Second, under section 18 of the Act the courts may appoint an arbitrator if the appointing authority specified in the arbitration agreement refuses, neglects, or otherwise fails to do so. The courts may proceed with the appointment after a reasonable period (eg seven days)[42] has elapsed from the time the appointing authority received the request to appoint from one of the parties.[43]

10.31 Third, the courts may direct the appointment of arbitrators upon the application of any party to the arbitration agreement when the parties have not agreed in advance on the appointment procedure. Under section 18(3) of the 1996 Act, the courts are empowered:

(a) to give directions as to the making of any necessary appointments;
(b) to direct that the tribunal shall be constituted by such appointments (or any one or more of them) as have been made;
(c) to revoke any appointments already made;
(d) to make any necessary appointments itself.

10.32 Under section 18(5), 'leave of the court is required for any appeal from a decision of the court under this section'.[44] Finally, section 19 of the Act requires the courts, in making appointments under sections 16 and 18, to take into account any specific qualifications of arbitrators agreed upon by the parties.

---

[36] Arbitration Act 1996, s 15(1): 'The parties are free to agree on the number of arbitrators to form the tribunal and whether there is to be a chairman or umpire.' The Act, however, creates the presumption that where an arbitration agreement provides for an even number of arbitrators, it 'shall be understood as requiring the appointment of an additional arbitrator as chairman of the tribunal': 1996 Act, s 15(2).

[37] 1996 Act, s 16(1): 'The parties are free to agree on the procedure for appointing the arbitrator or arbitrators, including the procedure for appointing any chairman or umpire.'

[38] 1996 Act, s 18(1): 'The parties are free to agree what is to happen in the event of a failure of the procedure for the appointment of the arbitral tribunal.'

[39] 1996 Act, s 16(2)–(7). The Act provides for the appointment of arbitrators in common configurations, such as a sole arbitrator or a three-member panel, but also in rarer combinations such as two-arbitrator panels, or panels consisting of two arbitrators and one umpire.

[40] 1996 Act, s 17(1)–(2).

[41] 1996 Act, s 17(3)–(4). Note the common law exceptions to this type of provision discussed in n 27.

[42] The 1996 Act, s 18 does not mention a time limit, but seven days is adopted as a reasonable such limit in s 17(2). St John Sutton, Gill, and Gearing (n 4) s 7–102.

[43] 1996 Act, s 18(2).

[44] Note the common law exceptions to this type of provision discussed in n 27.

10.2.4 Interim measures

Before the constitution of the arbitral tribunal, parties may initiate court proceedings to obtain interim measures, for example to preserve the status quo or to prevent the destruction of evidence. A party may be irreparably harmed if it must wait until the arbitral tribunal is constituted before seeking relief,[45] because the process of constituting an arbitral tribunal is time-consuming and, during that time, critical evidence or assets may disappear. **10.33**

Section 44 of the 1996 Act enumerates the powers of the English courts in support of arbitration proceedings and provides in this regard: **10.34**

> (1) Unless otherwise agreed by the parties, the court has for the purposes of and in relation to arbitral proceedings the same power of making orders about the matters listed here as it has for the purposes of and in relation to legal proceedings.
> (2) Those matters are—
> (a) the taking of the evidence of witnesses;
> (b) the preservation of evidence;
> (c) making orders relating to property which is the subject of the proceedings or as to which any question arises in the proceedings—
> (i) for the inspection, photographing, preservation, custody or detention of the property, or
> (ii) ordering that samples be taken from, or any observation be made of or experiment conducted upon, the property; and for that purpose authorising any person to enter any premises in the possession or control of a party to the arbitration;
> (d) the sale of any goods the subject of the proceedings;
> (e) the granting of an interim injunction or the appointment of a receiver.
> (3) If the case is one of urgency, the court may, on the application of a party or proposed party to the arbitral proceedings, make such orders as it thinks necessary for the purpose of preserving evidence or assets.
> (4) If the case is not one of urgency, the court shall act only on the application of a party to the arbitral proceedings (upon notice to the other parties and to the tribunal) made with the permission of the tribunal or the agreement in writing of the other parties.
> (5) In any case the court shall act only if or to the extent that the arbitral tribunal, and any arbitral or other institution or person vested by the parties with power in that regard, has no power or is unable for the time being to act effectively.
> (6) If the court so orders, an order made by it under this section shall cease to have effect in whole or in part on the order of the tribunal or of any such arbitral or other institution or person having power to act in relation to the subject-matter of the order.
> (7) The leave of the court is required for any appeal from a decision of the court under this section.

This reflects the interim powers the Act grants to the courts in support of arbitral proceedings—powers that may be limited by agreement of the parties under section 44(1). Parties should be mindful of the wording they employ in carving out such limitations. For example, a provision establishing the 'exclusive jurisdiction' of arbitrators may not suffice to preclude court intervention under section 44, because it is presumed to apply to matters of substance rather than procedure.[46] By contrast, a clause granting the arbitrators exclusivity with **10.35**

[45] G Born, *International Commercial Arbitration* (Wolters Kluwer, 2009) 1931, 'there are circumstances where court-ordered discovery can be considered a form of provisional relief, necessary in order to prevent imminent, irreparable harm, because the tribunal has not yet been constituted'.

[46] Merkin and Flannery (n 10) 108.

respect to substantive matters and 'other legal proceedings' has been interpreted as precluding recourse to the courts under this section.[47]

10.36 Section 44(2)(a) and (b) identifies the taking and preservation of evidence, including documents and witness evidence, as within the scope of court orders under this section. Section 44(2)(c) to (e) covers the equally important contingencies of surveying and securing property, ordering the sale of goods at issue (a power not possessed by the arbitral tribunal), and granting interim injunctions or appointing a receiver in cases of insolvency.

10.37 Section 44(2)(e) refers generally to an 'interim injunction', reflecting the courts' broad power to issue equitable relief in the form of freezing orders and/or directions to parties to act or refrain from acting as required to protect the arbitration agreement and the arbitral process (an example of the latter order is an anti-suit injunction).[48] Parties that wish to avail themselves of this provision should, however, act in a timely fashion and marshal sufficient evidence to show that in the absence of the injunction, irreparable harm will accrue to them, as for example when an opposing party attempts to relocate its assets outside the jurisdiction of the English courts.[49]

10.38 Section 44(3) complements section 44(2)(e) by empowering courts to issue orders as necessary to 'preserv[e] evidence or assets'. Importantly, the scope of section 44(2)(e) is not limited by that of section 44(3)—the former provides wide discretion to grant interim relief in contrast with the latter, which applies only to the narrower subject matters of 'evidence' and 'assets'.

10.39 Moreover, in instances in which a party to arbitration wishes to elicit the testimony of or evidence from a third party witness, over whom the arbitral tribunal does not have personal jurisdiction,[50] the party can petition the courts under section 43. Under that section: 'A party to arbitral proceedings may use the same court procedures as are available in relation to legal proceedings to secure the attendance before the tribunal of a witness in order to give oral testimony or to produce documents or other material evidence.'[51] To obtain such an order, however, the applicant must either secure permission from the tribunal or agreement from the other parties.[52]

---

[47] Merkin and Flannery (n 10) 108.

[48] Arbitration Act 1996, s 44 also may apply when the seat of the arbitration is outside England and Wales. See CPR 62.5(1)(b): 'The court may give permission to serve an arbitration claim form out of the jurisdiction if... the claim is for an order under section 44 of the 1996 Act.' Courts, however, will typically offer assistance in terms that are consistent with or similar to the practice in England. For example, s 44 was deemed inapplicable in a case where it was invoked in support of a US arbitration, and specifically of US-style depositions, which are viewed as 'fishing expeditions' in the English system. *Commerce and Industry Insurance Co of Canada v Lloyd's Underwriters* [2002] 1 Lloyd's Rep 219. Similarly, and just as importantly, English courts would be reluctant to enjoin arbitration proceedings in foreign-seated arbitrations because doing so would contravene both the New York Convention, which is enshrined in the Act, as well as the policies underlying the latter. See *Weissfisch v Julius and ors* [2006] EWCA 218, para 33; see also St John Sutton, Gill, and Gearing (n 4) s 7-062.

[49] The power to grant freezing injunctions may lie outside the powers of the arbitral tribunal even if the parties have agreed otherwise. Merkin and Flannery (n 10) 109, citing *Kastner v Jason* [2005] 1 Lloyd's Rep 397.

[50] Generally, English law does not allow a party to be bound by an arbitration agreement without its consent; in other legal systems, however, the courts are more amenable to binding non-parties if, for example, they belong to the same 'group of companies' as a party to the arbitration agreement. See generally B Hanotiau, *Complex Arbitrations: Multiparty, Multicontract, Multi-issue and Class Actions* (Kluwer Law International, 2005).

[51] Arbitration Act 1996, s 43(1).

[52] 1996 Act, s 43(2).

It is worth noting that similarly to the provisions of the 1996 Act, the rules of major arbitral institutions also recognize the importance of effective injunctive relief prior to the commencement of arbitration proceedings, and envisage explicitly the involvement of courts in support of arbitration proceedings prior to the commencement of arbitration.[53] In an attempt to provide an arbitration-based solution to relief needed prior to the tribunal's constitution, certain institutional rules have adopted the concept of the 'emergency arbitrator'. **10.40**

For example, under the 2012 ICC Rules, the President of the ICC Court may appoint an 'Emergency Arbitrator' before the arbitral tribunal is constituted, to whom the parties may apply for interim measures.[54] The ICC Rules, however, reserve the right of parties to seek interim measures from courts before the arbitral tribunal is constituted.[55] The arbitration rules of the International Centre for Dispute Resolution also allow for the appointment of an 'Emergency Arbitrator' with powers similar to those under the ICC Rules, and likewise expressly reserve the right of parties to seek interim measures from courts.[56] **10.41**

10.2.5 Staying parallel proceedings

Section 9 of the 1996 Act governs the frequently occurring scenario of a party commencing court proceedings parallel to the arbitration, usually in the early stages. Section 9(1) of the Act provides: **10.42**

> A party to an arbitration agreement against whom legal proceedings are brought (whether by way of claim or counterclaim) in respect of a matter which under the agreement is to be referred to arbitration may (upon notice to the other parties to the proceedings) apply to the court in which the proceedings have been brought to stay the proceedings so far as they concern that matter.

According to section 9(4): 'On an application under this section the court shall grant a stay unless satisfied that the arbitration agreement is null and void, inoperative, or incapable of being performed.' **10.43**

---

53 A notable exception to this observation is the World Bank's International Centre for Settlement of Investment Disputes (ICSID), where the ICSID Convention effectively 'insulates ICSID proceedings from the application of national procedural law'. L Reed, J Paulsson and N Blackaby, *Guide to ICSID Arbitration* (2nd edn, Kluwer Law International, 2010) 49; see Convention for the Settlement of Investment Disputes between States and Nationals of Other States (1963), art 26, at <https://icsid.worldbank.org> providing that: 'Consent of the parties to arbitration under this Convention shall, unless otherwise stated, be deemed consent to such arbitration to the exclusion of any other remedy.'

54 ICC Rules, art 29.1–29.2 (in force as of 1 January 2012) <http://www.iccwbo.org/court/arbitration/id4199/index.html> 'A party that needs urgent interim or conservatory measures that cannot await the constitution of an arbitral tribunal ("Emergency Measures") may make an application for such measures pursuant to the Emergency Arbitrator Rules in Appendix V . . . The parties undertake to comply with any order made by the emergency arbitrator.' This provision applies if the parties' arbitration agreement was concluded before the date on which the Rules came into force, ie 1 January 2012: ICC Rules, art 29.6(a); see also Netherlands Arbitration Institute Rules, art 42, providing for the NAI's appointment of an arbitrator to resolve interim measure issues prior to the arbitral tribunal's constitution.

55 ICC Rules, art 29.7: 'The Emergency Arbitrator Provisions are not intended to prevent any party from seeking urgent interim or conservatory measures from a competent judicial authority at any time prior to making an application for such measures, and in appropriate circumstances even thereafter, pursuant to the Rules.'

56 ICDR Rules, art 37 (as amended 1 June 2009) <http://www.adr.org/sp.asp?id=33994>. The arbitration rules of the Stockholm Chamber of Commerce adopted in 2010 also provide for interim relief by an emergency arbitrator. SCC Rules (2010) Appendix 2. The LCIA Rules provide for the 'expedited formation' of the arbitral tribunal. LCIA Rules, art 9(1), providing that: 'In exceptional urgency, on or after the commencement of the arbitration, any party may apply to the LCIA Court for the expedited formation of the Arbitral Tribunal, including the appointment of any replacement arbitrator under Articles 10 and 11 of these Rules.'

10.44 The Act allows a party to apply for a stay even if the relevant arbitration agreement conditions recourse to arbitration on the exhaustion of 'other dispute resolution procedures'.[57] Simultaneously, it requires the applicant to recognize the court proceedings against it, but not to take steps towards answering the substantive claim in those proceedings as such steps constitute a *de facto* waiver of the objection to the proceedings that animates the section 9 application.[58]

10.45 If an application under section 9 fails, or cannot be maintained under that section (eg if the court proceedings are located abroad), the party may apply to the English courts to issue an injunction under section 44(2)(e), discussed at paragraph 10.37, prohibiting the opposing party from pursuing a court action in violation of an arbitration agreement.

10.46 It is important to reiterate here that injunctions under section 44(2)(e) are temporary, but a party may be required to show a 'high degree of probability' that the underlying arbitration agreement is valid in order to obtain such an injunction.[59] Permanent anti-suit injunctions may be issued under section 37 of the Supreme Court Act 1981, which also applies to arbitrations seated outside England and Wales.[60] Such injunctions, either temporary or permanent, may also be issued at any point in the arbitral proceedings but, similarly to section 9 remedies, are usually sought early, when objecting parties seek to delay or derail the arbitration.[61] Notably, a party may obtain an anti-suit injunction even if it has no intention of commencing arbitration to protect its contractual right not to be sued in any forum other than arbitration.[62]

---

57 Arbitration Act 1996, s 9(2).

58 1996 Act, s 9(3); cf s 73.

59 *Midgulf International Ltd v Groupe Chimique Tunisien* [2009] EWHC 963, ultimately denying an interim anti-suit injunction after a brief hearing on evidence showing the validity of an arbitration agreement.

60 The Supreme Court Act 1981, s 37 provides:

> (1) The High Court may by order (whether interlocutory or final) grant an injunction or appoint a receiver in all cases in which it appears to the court to be just and convenient to do so.
>
> (2) Any such order may be made either unconditionally or on such terms and conditions as the court thinks just.
>
> (3) The power of the High Court under subsection (1) to grant an interlocutory injunction restraining a party to any proceedings from removing from the jurisdiction of the High Court, or otherwise dealing with, assets located within that jurisdiction shall be exercisable in cases where that party is, as well as in cases where he is not, domiciled, resident or present within that jurisdiction.
>
> (4) The power of the High Court to appoint a receiver by way of equitable execution shall operate in relation to all legal estates and interests in land; and that power—
>
> (a) may be exercised in relation to an estate or interest in land whether or not a charge has been imposed on that land under section 1 of the Charging Orders Act 1979 for the purpose of enforcing the judgment, order or award in question; and
>
> (b) shall be in addition to, and not in derogation of, any power of any court to appoint a receiver in proceedings for enforcing such a charge.
>
> (5) Where an order under the said section 1 imposing a charge for the purpose of enforcing a judgment, order or award has been, or has effect as if, registered under section 6 of the Land Charges Act 1972, subsection (4) of the said section 6 (effect of non-registration of writs and orders registrable under that section) shall not apply to an order appointing a receiver made either—
>
> (a) in proceedings for enforcing the charge; or
>
> (b) by way of equitable execution of the judgment, order or award or, as the case may be, of so much of it as requires payment of moneys secured by the charge.

61 St John Sutton, Gill, and Gearing (n 4) s 7-011.

62 *AES-UST Kamenogorsk Hydropower Plant LLP v UST Kamonogorsk Hydropower Plant JSC* [2010] EWHC 772 (Comm).

The arbitration-friendly attitude of English courts often leads parties that wish to resist arbitration to file suit in a foreign court. Historically, English courts have issued injunctions against participation in foreign court proceedings in violation of an agreement to arbitrate.[63] This trend has been stemmed considerably, however, by the European Court of Justice's decision in *West Tankers*, which all but restrained the ability of courts throughout the European Union to enjoin court proceedings in favour of arbitration when those proceedings are instituted in another EU Member State. Perhaps unsurprisingly, *West Tankers* arose from an anti-suit injunction issued by an English court, and was referred to the ECJ by the House of Lords.[64] **10.47**

According to the ECJ in *West Tankers*, anti-suit injunctions between courts of EU Member States are incompatible with Council Regulation (EC) 44/2001 on jurisdiction and the enforcement of judgments in civil and commercial matters (the 'Brussels Regulation').[65] The ECJ reasoned that anti-suit injunctions constitute an unwarranted interference in the jurisdiction of the national courts of EU Member States and violate the mutual trust principle of the Brussels Regulation.[66] Still, anti-suit injunctions remain available in EU courts where court proceedings brought in breach of an arbitration agreement are commenced outside the European Union.[67] **10.48**

The *West Tankers* decision appears to have generated several unwelcome side-effects, including the situation in which a judgment from the courts of an EU Member State may render invalid an arbitration agreement that is considered enforceable by the (EU-based) courts of the seat. The European Commission's proposed remedy of seeking an early declaration from the courts of the seat as to the validity of the arbitration agreement has been criticized by countries where declaratory relief is unavailable. In this sense, however, England and Wales is a favourable jurisdiction because, as discussed earlier, the courts are empowered under Section 32 of the 1996 Act to declare the arbitration agreement valid even before the proceedings commence. **10.49**

Responding to the ECJ's highly controversial interpretation of the Brussels Regulation,[68] the English courts in *West Tankers* have held that despite the ECJ's ruling, EU law does not **10.50**

63 See eg *OT Africa Line Ltd v Magic Sportswear Corp* [2005] EWCA Civ 710.

64 Case C-185/07 *Allianz SpA v West Tankers Inc* [2009] ECR I-663. The House of Lords' decision to refer the case is reported at [2007] UKHL 4. The House of Lords made clear when referring the case that it would have reached a different decision to that later taken by the ECJ.

65 Council of the European Union, Council Regulation (EC) 44/2001 of 22 December 2000, available at <http://curia.europa.eu/common/recdoc/convention/en/c-textes/2001R0044-idx.htm>; see also *Allianz SpA v West Tankers* (n 64). The arbitration agreement in *West Tankers* specified London as the seat of arbitration and the contract provided for the application of English law.

66 *Allianz SpA v West Tankers* (n 64).

67 See eg *Shashoua and ors v Sharma* [2009] EWHC 957 (Comm), granting an injunction to restrain proceedings commenced in a Delhi court in breach of an arbitration agreement; *Shell v Coral Oil* [1999] 1 Lloyd's Rep 72; *AES-UST Kamenogorsk Hydropower Plant LLP v UST-Kamonogorsk Hydropower Plant JSC* [2010] EWHC 722 (Comm); *Midgulf International Ltd v Groupe Chimique Tunisien* [2010] EWCA Civ 66; *Bankers Trust v Jakarta International* [1999] 1 Lloyd's Rep 910.

68 See eg AR Markus and S Giroud, 'A Swiss Perspective on *West Tankers* and Its Aftermath'(2010) 28(2) ASA Bulletin 230, 238: 'As a decision exclusively related to arbitration, the English anti-suit injunction is undoubtedly excluded from the scope of the Brussels I Regulation and so is the examination of the jurisdiction issue in the Italian proceedings. In this respect, the ECJ's opinion according to which the validity of the arbitration agreement should be verified as an incidental question pursuant to the Brussels I Regulation appears problematic'; *accord* A Bělohlávek, '*West Tankers* as a Trojan Horse with Respect to the Autonomy of Arbitration Proceedings and the New York Convention 1958' (2009) 27(4) ASA Bulletin 646; M Schöll, 'Brussels I/

pre-empt the jurisdiction of the arbitral tribunal to award damages against the party that breaches an arbitration agreement by initiating proceedings before an EU Member State's court.[69] Moreover, the arbitral award may be enforced while the related EU Member State court proceeding is pending, thus establishing the primacy of the award over any later inconsistent judgment by that court.[70]

10.51 As the date of writing, the European Parliament has voted to amend the Brussels Regulation so as to address its adverse effects with respect to arbitral proceedings. The new Regulation is poised to exclude arbitration completely, and to contain specific directions as to how the courts of EU Member States should handle applications concerning the validity of arbitration agreements.[71]

10.3 Role of Courts Before the Issuance of the Award

10.3.1 The tribunal's jurisdiction

10.52 After the commencement of the proceedings, the tribunal's jurisdiction may be challenged under section 32 of the 1996 Act. However, after the commencement of the proceedings, the timing of such a challenge is governed by section 31, a mandatory provision of the Act, which provides:

> (1) An objection that the arbitral tribunal lacks substantive jurisdiction at the outset of the proceedings must be raised by a party not later than the time he takes the first step in the proceedings to contest the merits of any matter in relation to which he challenges the tribunal's jurisdiction.

10.53 A party is not precluded from raising such an objection by the fact that he has appointed or participated in the appointment of an arbitrator.

> (2) Any objection during the course of the arbitral proceedings that the arbitral tribunal is exceeding its substantive jurisdiction must be made as soon as possible after the matter alleged to be beyond its jurisdiction is raised.
> (3) The arbitral tribunal may admit an objection later than the time specified in subsection (1) or (2) if it considers the delay justified.
> (4) Where an objection is duly taken to the tribunal's substantive jurisdiction and the tribunal has power to rule on its own jurisdiction, it may—
> (a) rule on the matter in an award as to jurisdiction, or

Lugano and Arbitration: Problems and Perspectives' in C Müller and A Rigozzi (eds), *New Developments in International Commercial Arbitration 2009* (Schulthess Editions Romandes, 2009) 43. The ensuing controversy raised concerns about the desirability of the law of EU Member States as the law of the seat. See D Rainer, 'The Impact of West Tankers on Parties' Choice of A Seat of Arbitration' (2010) 95 Cornell L Rev 431, 435–6: 'The availability of antisuit injunctions to enforce arbitration agreements is one factor that may influence parties choosing a seat and the law that shall govern their arbitration . . . the European Union could lose some of its traditional appeal as a forum for international commercial arbitration.'

[69] *West Tankers Inc v Allianz SpA v Generali Assicurazioni Generali SpA* [4 April 2012] EWHC 854. This is consistent with previous English jurisprudence, see St John Sutton, Gill, and Gearing (n 4) s 7-021.

[70] *West Tankers, Inc v Allianz SpA v Generali Assicurazione Generali SpA* [24 January 2012] EWCAS Civ 27; see also *African Fertilizers and Chemical Nig v BD Shipsnavo GmbH and Co Reederei Kg* [2011] EWHC 2452 (Comm), enforcing under the 1996 Act, s 66 the arbitral tribunal's declaration on its jurisdiction while a collateral challenge to tribunal's jurisdiction was pending before the Romanian courts.

[71] European Commission, Memorandum: European Parliament backs rules to do away with 27 national rules for recognising judgments in cross-border court cases (20 November 2012) available at <http://europa.eu/rapid/press-release_MEMO-12-875_en.htm>.

(b) deal with the objection in its award on the merits.
If the parties agree which of these courses the tribunal should take, the tribunal shall proceed accordingly.

(5) The tribunal may in any case, and shall if the parties so agree, stay proceedings whilst an application is made to the court under section 32 (determination of preliminary point of jurisdiction).

As mentioned earlier, section 73 of the Act renders failure to raise a jurisdictional objection at the appropriate juncture as a waiver of that objection. Consequently, a party may face a claim of waiver on two separate yet overlapping grounds, namely sections 31 and 73. Such a waiver operates to negate any objection raised after the rendering of the award under section 67 of the Act, discussed at paragraph 10.99. **10.54**

10.3.2 Appeal on a question of law

Section 45(1) of the 1996 Act permits a party to the arbitration (but not the arbitral tribunal acting *sua sponte*) to appeal to the English courts a question of law that affects the rights of one or more of the parties: **10.55**

> Unless otherwise agreed by the parties, the court may on the application of a party to arbitral proceedings (upon notice to the other parties) determine any question of law arising in the course of the proceedings which the court is satisfied substantially affects the rights of one or more of the parties.

The 'question of law' need not be limited to a specific municipal law[72] or subject matter, and may include questions of construction of a contract or other instrument, and issues of arbitral procedure. Applicants under this section, however, should be mindful of the preclusive effect of other sections of the 1996 Act on the 'catch-all' nature of section 45. For example, a jurisdictional challenge is governed by sections 32 and 67 (depending on its timing) while a challenge regarding arbitrator appointment arises under section 18. Similarly, section 45 does not cover questions that the Act places squarely within the discretion of the arbitral tribunal, such as the admissibility of evidence.[73] **10.56**

Applications under this section are extremely rare in practice because of the 1996 Act's stringent prerequisites. The Act requires that all parties to the arbitration consent to such application, or that the tribunal grant the applicant leave to file, and the court hearing the application must be satisfied that the application was made without delay and that its resolution will result in 'substantial savings in costs'.[74] In fact, even if all the requirements under section 45 are satisfied, the court retains discretion to decline to decide the issue of law presented thereunder—although such a decision would be rare in practice.[75] **10.57**

Moreover, similarly to section 32, discussed previously, while the 'decision of the court on the question of law shall be treated as a judgment of the court for purposes of an appeal', no appeal **10.58**

---

[72] The DAC Report indicates that the drafters of the Act intended s 45 to apply to a broad array of disputes, mentioning 'the closure of the Suez Canal or the United States embargo on the export of soya beans' as illustrative examples: DAC Report (n 7) para 218. Moreover, the DAC rejected a proposal to restrict the applicability of s 45 only to domestic arbitrations: DAC Report, para 221.

[73] See Arbitration Act 1996 Act, s 34(2)(f).

[74] 1996 Act, s 45(2)(a)–(b). Section 45(3)–(5) ensures further that applications under this section will not disrupt arbitral proceedings by allowing such proceedings to continue while the application is pending; and disallowing any appeal based on the court's finding that the requirements under s 45(2) have been met.

[75] St John Sutton, Gill, and Gearing (n 4) s 7-173.

can be filed unless the court grants leave because it considers the question 'of general importance' or one that must be considered by the Court of Appeal 'for some other special reason'.[76]

10.59 Finally, as noted earlier, parties to an arbitration agreement may contract out of this section by entering into an 'exclusion agreement' or by agreeing that the resulting arbitral award need not contain reasons, which has been interpreted as a *de facto* exclusion agreement.[77] The adoption of certain arbitral rules, such as those of the London Court of International Arbitration, or the International Chamber of Commerce, also has the effect of precluding judicial review of alleged errors of law.[78]

10.60 Notably, applications under section 45, as well as under section 32 (discussed at paragraphs 10.19–10.22) can also be used in support of arbitration, namely to request a declaration by the courts that an arbitration agreement is valid.

10.3.3 Interim measures

10.61 Once an arbitral tribunal is in place, the parties should direct to the tribunal, and not to a court, any request for interim measures that falls within the tribunal's power under section 38 of the 1996 Act. This course of action, although not mandatory, is consistent with the spirit and policy aims of the Act.[79] As a practical matter, however, resorting directly to a court may result in swifter relief than the sometimes arduous process of obtaining a tribunal order or award and attempting to enforce it through the courts.[80] Moreover, a court order or injunction may bind third parties that are not part of the arbitration agreement, and therefore that are beyond the *in personam* jurisdiction of the arbitrators.[81]

10.62 Section 38 provides:

> (1) The parties are free to agree on the powers exercisable by the arbitral tribunal for the purposes of and in relation to the proceedings.
> (2) Unless otherwise agreed by the parties the tribunal has the following powers.
> (3) The tribunal may order a claimant to provide security for the costs of the arbitration. This power shall not be exercised on the ground that the claimant is—
> (a) an individual ordinarily resident outside the United Kingdom, or
> (b) a corporation or association incorporated or formed under the law of a country outside the United Kingdom, or whose central management and control is exercised outside the United Kingdom.
> (4) The tribunal may give directions in relation to any property which is the subject of the proceedings or as to which any question arises in the proceedings, and which is owned by or is in the possession of a party to the proceedings—
> (a) for the inspection, photographing, preservation, custody or detention of the property by the tribunal, an expert or a party, or

[76] Arbitration Act 1996 Act, s 45(6).
[77] St John Sutton, Gill, and Gearing (n 4) s 7-166.
[78] See LCIA Rules, art 26.9; ICC Rules (2010) art 34(6); ICC Rules (1998), art 34(6).
[79] See Arbitration Act 1996, s 42(3): 'The court shall not act [to enforce a tribunal peremptory order] unless it is satisfied that the applicant has exhausted any available arbitral process in respect of failure to comply with the tribunal's order'; see also DAC Report (n 7) para 189: 'Wherever a power could properly be exercised by a tribunal rather than the Court, provision has been made for this, thereby reducing the need to incur the expense and inconvenience of making applications to Court during arbitral proceedings.'
[80] St John Sutton, Gill, and Gearing (n 4) s 5-078.
[81] See *Star Reefers Pool Inc v JFC Group Co Ltd* [2012] EWCA Civ 14, holding that the court has jurisdiction to grant an anti-suit injunction against a non-party to an arbitration for using court proceedings to undermine an arbitration agreement; similarly, *BNP Paribas SA v OJSC Russian Machines* [2011] EWHC 308 (Comm).

(b) ordering that samples be taken from, or any observation be made of or experiment conducted upon, the property.

(5) The tribunal may direct that a party or witness shall be examined on oath or affirmation, and may for that purpose administer any necessary oath or take any necessary affirmation.

(6) The tribunal may give directions to a party for the preservation for the purposes of the proceedings of any evidence in his custody or control.

If a party obtains a peremptory order from the arbitral tribunal, for example ordering the respondent to refrain from selling any of the property in dispute, the courts have authority to enforce such an order—in addition, of course, to the tribunal's own power under the Act to do so. According to recent case law, this authority extends to negative declarations by the arbitral tribunal.[82] **10.63**

According to Section 42: **10.64**

(1) Unless otherwise agreed by the parties, the court may make an order requiring a party to comply with a peremptory order made by the tribunal.

(2) An application for an order under this section may be made—
   (a) by the tribunal (upon notice to the parties),
   (b) by a party to the arbitral proceedings with the permission of the tribunal (and upon notice to the other parties), or
   (c) where the parties have agreed that the powers of the court under this section shall be available.

(3) The court shall not act unless it is satisfied that the applicant has exhausted any available arbitral process in respect of failure to comply with the tribunal's order.

(4) No order shall be made under this section unless the court is satisfied that the person to whom the tribunal's order was directed has failed to comply with it within the time prescribed in the order or, if no time was prescribed, within a reasonable time.

(5) The leave of the court is required for any appeal from a decision of the court under this section.

To request interim measures directly from a court after the proceedings have commenced, parties can avail themselves of section 44 of the Act, which, as shown earlier, covers a broad array of requests for relief.[83] Such relief, however, may be denied in the presence of a '*Scott v Avery*' clause,[84] precluding any judicial remedy before the case has been heard by the arbitral tribunal.[85] **10.65**

---

[82] *West Tankers Inc v Allianz SpA* [2012] EWCA Civ 27.

[83] Note, however, that security for costs can be granted only by the arbitral tribunal: Arbitration Act 1996, s 38(3). It is also important to ensure that certain kinds of remedy are not precluded by specific provisions within the Act. In admiralty proceedings, for example, the protection of property in dispute may be ordered under the 1996 Act, s 11.

[84] This is the reference to an 1856 case before the English courts, where Lord Campbell departed from the then customary practice of continuing arbitration proceedings despite the existence of a valid arbitration clause. Nowadays the term is employed to describe an obligation to arbitrate that sets the conclusion of the arbitration as a precondition to access to the courts.

[85] See *B v S* [2011] EWHC 691 (Comm), holding that contractual language precluding legal proceedings prior to arbitration encompassed ancillary proceedings to grant a freezing injunction under the 1996 Act, s 44(2)(e). The relevant contractual language in *B v S* read as follows: 'Neither party hereto, nor any persons claiming under either of them, shall bring any action or other legal proceedings against the other of them in respect of any such dispute until such dispute shall first have been heard and determined by the arbitrators…'. But see *Alfred C Toepfer International GmbH v Société Cargill France* [1997] APP LR, 25 November, 33: 'Our finding in relation to the Scott v. Avery clause rejects the argument that the English Court is precluded, by the terms of the contracts, from entertaining the present proceedings.'

10.3.4 Time limitations and extensions

10.66 Under section 13(1) of the 1996 Act: 'The Limitation Acts apply to arbitral proceedings as they apply to legal proceedings.' Section 13 goes on to provide as follows:

> (2) The court may order that in computing the time prescribed by the Limitation Acts for the commencement of proceedings (including arbitral proceedings) in respect of a dispute which was the subject matter—
> (a) of an award which the court orders to be set aside or declares to be of no effect, or
> (b) of the affected part of an award which the court orders to be set aside in part, or declares to be in part of no effect,
> the period between the commencement of the arbitration and the date of the order referred to in paragraph (a) or (b) shall be excluded.
> (3) In determining for the purposes of the Limitation Acts when a cause of action accrued, any provision that an award is a condition precedent to the bringing of legal proceedings in respect of a matter to which an arbitration agreement applies shall be disregarded.
> (4) In this Part 'the Limitation Acts' means—
> (a) in England and Wales, the Limitation Act 1980, the Foreign Limitation Periods Act 1984 and any other enactment (whenever passed) relating to the limitation of actions;
> (b) in Northern Ireland, the Limitation (Northern Ireland) Order 1989, the Foreign Limitation Periods (Northern Ireland) Order 1985 and any other enactment (whenever passed) relating to the limitation of actions.

10.67 The most important consequence of this provision is that it applies the time limitations imposed by the Limitation Act 1980 to arbitration proceedings. For example, the limitation for a contract case is six years from the time of the breach.[86] An action for the enforcement of an award must be brought, according to section 7 of the Limitation Act, within six years from the date 'the cause of action accrued'. This has been held to signify the date on which the award should have been paid.[87] It is also worth noting that section 35 of the Limitation Act 1980, which allows the addition and 'backdating' of a new claim to litigation proceedings, does not apply to arbitration.[88]

10.68 Section 13(2) and (3) resolve time lapse issues that arise in special circumstances: in the former case, when a court sets aside or modifies an award, and in the latter case when a contract contains a '*Scott v Avery*' clause that preconditions resort to the courts on the completion of the arbitration proceedings.

10.69 The 1996 Act, moreover, empowers the courts to 'extend any time limit agreed by them in relation to any matter relating to the arbitral proceedings or specified in any provision of [Part I of the Act] having effect in default of such agreement'.[89] Section 79 of the Act further provides:[90]

> (2) An application for an order may be made—
> (a) by any party to the arbitral proceedings (upon notice to the other parties and to the tribunal), or

---

[86] Limitations Act 1980, s 5.

[87] *Argomet Motoimport Ltd v Maulden Engineering Co (Beds) Ltd* [1985] All ER 436. Moreover, in *National Ability SA v Tinna Oils & Chemicals Ltd* [2009] EWCA Civ 330, the Court of Appeal held that whether a party seeks to enforce an award as a debt or under the procedure outlined in the 1996 Act, s 66, the applicable time limit would be the same.

[88] *Kenya Railways v Antares Pte Ltd* [1987] 1 Lloyd's Rep 424.

[89] Arbitration Act 1996, s 79(1).

[90] 1996 Act, s 79(1) explicitly notes that it 'does not apply to a time limit to which section 12 applies (power of court to extend time for beginning arbitral proceedings, &c.)'.

(b) by the arbitral tribunal (upon notice to the parties).
(3) The court shall not exercise its power to extend a time limit unless it is satisfied—
(a) that any available recourse to the tribunal, or to any arbitral or other institution or person vested by the parties with power in that regard, has first been exhausted, and
(b) that a substantial injustice would otherwise be done.
(4) The court's power under this section may be exercised whether or not the time has already expired.
(5) An order under this section may be made on such terms as the court thinks fit.
(6) The leave of the court is required for any appeal from a decision of the court under this section.

There are two principal issues to note with respect to section 79—in addition to its being non-mandatory. First, although the courts enjoy wide discretion in extending time limits, including those imposed by other provisions of the Act except section 12, they will rarely impinge upon a decision by the arbitral tribunal not to provide an extension in the first place.[91] Second, the section imposes two conditions on a court-mandated time extension: first, that all avenues open to the arbitrators to extend time have been exhausted; and second, that inaction on the court's part would result in a 'substantial injustice'.[92] **10.70**

Similarly, the English courts may extend the time provided in an arbitration agreement for the issuance of an arbitral award. According to Section 50(2), an application for such extension may be made '(a) by the tribunal (upon notice to the parties) and (b) by any party to the proceedings (upon notice to the tribunal and the other parties)'. The only condition attached to the court's action under this Section is the 'substantial injustice' test[93] discussed at paragraph 10.70 in the context of section 79. In reaching its decision, the court is not bound by prior time limitations either contractual or subsequently agreed upon by the parties, and its order can be appealed only by the court's leave.[94] **10.71**

10.3.5 Challenging or replacing an arbitrator

The 1996 Act allows parties to petition the English courts to remove an arbitrator. The circumstances under which a court may effect such a removal are listed in some detail in section 24(1) of the Act, which provides: **10.72**

(1) A party to arbitral proceedings may (upon notice to the other parties, to the arbitrator concerned and to any other arbitrator) apply to the court to remove an arbitrator on any of the following grounds—
(a) that circumstances exist that give rise to justifiable doubts as to his impartiality;
(b) that he does not possess the qualifications required by the arbitration agreement;
(c) that he is physically or mentally incapable of conducting the proceedings or there are justifiable doubts as to his capacity to do so;
(d) that he has refused or failed—
(i) properly to conduct the proceedings, or
(ii) to use all reasonable despatch in conducting the proceedings or making an award,
and that substantial injustice has been or will be caused to the applicant.

[91] DAC Report (n 7) para 309: 'As we have said in other contexts, it would be a rare case indeed where we would expect the Court to grant an extension where such has not been obtained through that process.'
[92] A plea of 'substantial injustice' requires the court to take into account 'relative fault, the sum at stake and the consequences of the failure to act': Merkin and Flannery (n 10) 183 (citations omitted).
[93] Arbitration Act 1996, s 50(3).
[94] 1996 Act, s 50(4)–(5).

10.73 Notably, section 24(1)(a) makes reference only to 'impartiality' and not to 'independence', the term that often accompanies it.[95] Apparently this was deliberate, in order to avoid protracted litigation over the standard of independence, which under the Act becomes relevant only insofar as it affects impartiality.[96] Impartiality may be questioned, for example, where the arbitrator maintains a commercial relationship with one of the parties, or when the arbitrator maintains an interest in the outcome of the arbitration.[97]

10.74 The reference to arbitrator 'qualifications' in section 24(1)(b) concerns the background and skills of the appointed arbitrator as contractually agreed upon between the parties, while section 24(1)(c) permits the removal of an arbitrator due to metal or physical incapacity. Finally, section 24(1)(d) represents an open-ended provision, which:

> ...should only be available where the conduct of the arbitrator is such as to go so beyond anything that could reasonably be defended that substantial injustice has resulted or will result. The provision is not intended to allow the Court to substitute its own view as to how the arbitral proceedings should be conducted.[98]

An arbitrator's excess of his or her jurisdiction may constitute a 'serious irregularity' under section 24(1)(d), as may do, *inter alia*, unequal treatment of the parties; unilateral communications; and refusal to act.[99] In any event, the evidence of misconduct must be accompanied by a showing of prejudice sufficient to constitute a 'substantial injustice'.[100]

10.75 Section 24 further provides that a party petitioning to remove an arbitrator ought to exhaust any remedies it may have under the arbitral rules or institutional framework of the arbitration,[101] and that the petition for removal should not derail the arbitral proceedings, which may continue to the issuance of an award.[102] Finally, the courts may order the parties to pay the removed arbitrator's fees,[103] and the arbitrator him- or herself may appear before the courts to defend against his or her removal.[104] As with several other sections, leave of the court is required to appeal against a decision under section 24.[105]

10.76 The courts may also grant relief to an arbitrator who resigns voluntarily. Under section 25, if an arbitrator resigns and is unable to reach agreement with the parties, he or she may petition the courts 'to grant him relief from any liability thereby incurred by him, and to make such order as it think fit as to his entitlement (if any) to fees and expenses or the repayment of any

---

95 See eg UNCITRAL Model Law on International Commercial Arbitration 1985, Art 12; see also International Bar Association, *Guidelines on Conflicts of Interest in International Arbitration* (2004) at <http://www.ibanet.org>; American Bar Association, *The Code of Ethics for Arbitrators in Commercial Disputes* (2004) at <http://www.americanbar.org>.

96 See DAC Report (n 7) para 101: 'It seems to us that lack of independence, unless it gives rise to justifiable doubts about the impartiality of the arbitrator, is of no significance.'

97 See Merkin and Flannery (n 10) 66; *Norbrook Laboratories v Tank* [2006] EWHC 1055, removing an arbitrator who had disregarded a party's timely request to terminate the short form procedure and had also contacted witnesses unilaterally.

98 See DAC Report (n 7) para 106.

99 See St John Sutton, Gill, and Gearing (n 4) ss 7-117–7-122.

100 See n 92.

101 Arbitration Act 1996, s 24(2).

102 1996 Act, s 24(3).

103 1996 Act, s 24(4); cf s 28(3), providing that the court may require arbitrators to repay fees they have received that are subsequently adjudged as excessive by the court.

104 1996 Act, s 24(5).

105 1996 Act, s 24(6). Note the common law exceptions to this type of provision discussed in n 27.

fees and expenses already paid'.[106] To obtain such relief, the arbitrator must show that it was reasonable for the arbitrator to resign.[107] Under Section 27, vacancies on the tribunal by reason of removal, death, etc may be filled pursuant to sections 16 and 18, discussed previously.

10.3.6 Costs

Under section 28 of the 1996 Act, the parties are jointly and severally liable to the tribunal for fees and expenses, and the courts retain jurisdiction to amend such fees and expenses as they see fit. In fact, under section 59, the arbitral tribunal may withhold the award until it has received payment for its services—a payment that it has discretion to allocate between the parties under section 61 of the Act.[108] If the parties dispute the arbitrators' fees and expenses, they may petition the courts to intervene and either set the fees and costs directly, or determine the manner in which they should be calculated.[109] **10.77**

10.4 Arbitration under the English Arbitration Act

10.4.1 Arbitration rules

The 1996 Act gives the tribunal discretion to decide all procedural and evidentiary matters, subject to the right of the parties to agree any matter.[110] Such matters include whether to apply strict rules of evidence (or any other rules) regarding the admissibility, relevance, or weight of any material produced.[111] Moreover, the tribunal must decide on the scope and content of document production.[112] This discretion is not absolute; it must be exercised subject to the general duty under the 1996 Act to act fairly and impartially, and to adopt procedures that are suitable to the circumstances of the case.[113] **10.78**

Procedures regulating document production are set out in the IBA Rules and may be adopted by agreement of the parties or by order of the tribunal. In the absence of such an agreement, tribunals frequently look to the IBA Rules for guidance in any event. Parties generally produce those documents upon which they rely and, if necessary, request the production of certain documents or categories of documents from the opposing party. If a party fails to comply with a peremptory order for document production, the tribunal may, *inter alia*, draw adverse inferences and/or make appropriate orders as to costs.[114] **10.79**

10.4.2 Limitation periods

The 1996 Act provides that the UK Limitation Act 1980 and the UK Foreign Limitation Periods Act 1984, as well as 'any other enactment (whenever passed) relating to the limitation **10.80**

[106] 1996 Act, s 25(3).

[107] 1996 Act, s 25(4).

[108] 1996 Act, s 61(1): 'The tribunal may make an award allocating the costs of the arbitration as between the parties, subject to any agreement of the parties.' The tribunal's cost allocation may be challenged in court as a 'serious irregularity' under s 68 (discussed at paras 10.103–10.104), but the high evidentiary burden set by that section renders such challenges—let alone sustained applications—quite rare.

[109] 1996 Act, s 64(2)(a)–(b).

[110] 1996 Act, s 34(1).

[111] 1996 Act, s 34(2)(f).

[112] 1996 Act, s 34(2)(d).

[113] 1996 Act, s 33.

[114] 1996 Act, s 41(7).

of actions', apply to arbitral proceedings as they apply to legal proceedings.[115] A claimant in arbitration proceedings must therefore commence arbitration within the same time periods as a claimant in litigation.

10.4.3 The arbitration agreement

10.81 The 1996 Act does not list or delimit matters which are not capable of settlement by arbitration.[116] Commercial disputes arising under a valid arbitration agreement are generally arbitrable; non-arbitrable matters may include criminal and family law disputes.

10.82 Under English law, a third party cannot be bound by an arbitration clause without its consent, and may participate in an arbitration only with the consent of all parties concerned. Consent may be given by adopting institutional rules that provide for joinder (eg the LCIA Rules). A tribunal may only consolidate proceedings with the consent of all parties concerned.[117] Parties may provide for consolidation in the relevant contract(s) or agree to consolidation once a dispute has arisen.[118]

10.83 Unless otherwise agreed by the parties, an arbitration agreement is treated as a distinct agreement and is not regarded as invalid, non-existent, or ineffective merely because the wider contract never came into existence or is subsequently found to be invalid.[119] However, in certain limited circumstances (eg in cases of forgery) the arbitration agreement may be declared invalid on the same grounds as the wider contract.[120]

10.4.4 The arbitral tribunal and procedural issues

10.84 The principle of *competence-competence* is recognized in the 1996 Act and empowers the tribunal to rule on the question of whether it has jurisdiction.[121] Unless otherwise agreed by the parties, the tribunal may rule on whether there is a valid arbitration agreement, whether the tribunal is properly constituted, and what matters have been submitted to arbitration.[122] Where one party denies that the tribunal has jurisdiction to determine the dispute, it must raise the objection at the outset of the proceedings.[123]

10.85 Unless the parties agree otherwise (eg by adopting institutional rules that provide for a different procedure), arbitral proceedings are commenced by written notice to the other party/parties or (if applicable) the appointing authority.[124] The parties are free to agree on the number of arbitrators and the procedure for their appointment.[125] If there is no agreement on the number of arbitrators, the 1996 Act provides that the tribunal shall consist of a sole arbitrator.[126]

---

[115] 1996 Act, s 13(1).
[116] 1996 Act, s 81(1)(a).
[117] 1996 Act, s 25(2).
[118] 1996 Act, s 25(1).
[119] 1996 Act, s 7.
[120] *Fiona Trust Corp and ors v Privalov and ors* [2007] All ER (D) 233.
[121] Arbitration Act 1996, s 30.
[122] 1996 Act, s 30(1).
[123] 1996 Act, s 31(1).
[124] 1996 Act, s 14(2)–(5).
[125] 1996 Act, ss 15 and 16.
[126] 1996 Act, s 15(3).

If there is no agreement on the procedure, then the 1996 Act provides that: 10.86

- in the case of a sole arbitrator, the parties shall jointly appoint an arbitrator within 28 days of a request by either party to do so;[127]
- if the tribunal is to consist of two arbitrators, each party shall appoint one arbitrator not later than 14 days after a request in writing by either party to do so;[128]
- if the tribunal is to consist of three arbitrators, each party shall appoint one arbitrator within 14 days of a written request by either party, and the two appointed arbitrators shall appoint the third member of the tribunal forthwith;[129]
- if the tribunal is to consist of two arbitrators and an umpire, each party shall appoint one arbitrator within 15 days of a written request by either party and the two appointed arbitrators shall appoint an umpire at any time before any substantive hearing or forthwith if they cannot agree on any matter relating to the arbitration.[130]

When one party fails to appoint an arbitrator within the time specified, the other party may give notice in writing to the defaulting party that it proposes to appoint its arbitrator as sole arbitrator. If the defaulting party does not make the required appointment and notify the other party that it has done so within seven days, the other party may appoint its arbitrator as sole arbitrator, whose award will be binding on both parties.[131] An arbitrator can be removed by the parties acting jointly or by a relevant arbitral institution.[132] 10.87

Where a respondent fails to participate in an arbitration, the tribunal may proceed to an award on the basis of the evidence before it.[133] The party in default will typically be given every opportunity to participate before the tribunal allows the arbitration to proceed in its absence. The tribunal may ask the non-defaulting party to attend a merits hearing and present its case (including witness evidence) in order that the tribunal is able to render a fully-reasoned award. It remains open to the defaulting party subsequently to challenge the award on the usual grounds. 10.88

10.4.5 Interim measures

The first source of a tribunal's powers is the arbitration agreement between the parties under which the tribunal has been appointed. These can be incorporated from the rules of an arbitration institution or contained in an express agreement. If there is no express agreement, the 1996 Act states that the tribunal has the power to grant interim relief,[134] including, *inter alia*, security for costs[135] and directions regarding the inspection, preservation, custody, or detention of the subject matter of the dispute.[136] The tribunal may also make interim awards, including a provisional order for the payment of money between the parties.[137] The tribunal has no power to direct the taking of witness evidence, or to compel a witness to attend, but 10.89

[127] 1996 Act, s 16(3).
[128] 1996 Act, s 16(4).
[129] 1996 Act, s 16(5).
[130] 1996 Act, s 16(6).
[131] 1996 Act, s 17.
[132] 1996 Act, s 23.
[133] 1996 Act, s 41(4).
[134] 1996 Act, s 38.
[135] 1996 Act, s 38(3).
[136] 1996 Act, s 38(4).
[137] 1996 Act, s 39.

may direct that a party or witness shall be examined under oath or affirmation (and may for that purpose administer any necessary oath or affirmation).[138]

10.90 If the claimant fails to comply with an order requiring security for costs, the tribunal can dismiss the claim.[139] The tribunal may also refuse delivery of an award if its fees and expenses have not been met.[140] If a party fails to comply with an order of the tribunal without good cause, the tribunal may issue a peremptory order to the same effect.[141]

10.4.6 Award and costs

10.91 The award must be rendered in accordance with the substantive law chosen by the parties. Unless the parties agree otherwise, where there are three or more arbitrators, decisions are made by majority.[142] Where the tribunal is unable to reach a majority decision, the chairman's vote will prevail.[143] The parties are free to agree on the remedies or relief that the tribunal may grant.[144] Accordingly, subject to public policy restrictions, parties can provide that a remedy not available under English law (eg punitive damages) may be awarded by the tribunal.[145]

10.92 The parties are free to agree on the form of the award.[146] The default position under the 1996 Act is that the award must be in writing and signed by all arbitrators (or those assenting to it), contain reasons (unless it is an agreed award or the parties have agreed to dispense with the reasons), and state the seat of the arbitration and the date on which it is made.[147]

10.93 The tribunal is not subject to a fixed time limit in rendering its award. The tribunal may correct an award on its own initiative or on the application of either party. Any application must be made within 28 days of the award.[148] Any correction must be made within 28 days of receipt of the application or, where made by the tribunal of its own motion, within 28 days of the award.[149] The parties are free to agree on different time limits (eg by adopting institutional rules).[150]

10.94 Costs are either determined by the relevant arbitral institution or, in ad hoc arbitrations, on the basis of an hourly rate agreed in advance between the parties and the tribunal. The parties usually share the costs of the tribunal in the first instance (and any costs of the arbitral institution). Each party pays the costs of its own lawyers and other advisers, subject to any recovery that it might make from the other party.

10.95 Unless otherwise agreed, the tribunal may make an award allocating the costs of the arbitration (including legal fees) between the parties and will generally require the unsuccessful party to pay the reasonable costs of the successful party.[151] In awarding costs, the tribunal

---

138 1996 Act, s 38(5).
139 1996 Act, s 41(6).
140 1996 Act, s 56(1).
141 1996 Act, s 41(5).
142 1996 Act, s 20(3).
143 1996 Act, s 20(4).
144 1996 Act, s 48(1).
145 1996 Act, s 48(2)–(5).
146 1996 Act, s 52(1).
147 1996 Act, s 52(3)–(5).
148 1996 Act, s 57(3)–(4).
149 1996 Act, s 57(5).
150 1996 Act, s 79.
151 1996 Act, s 61(1)–(2).

must specify the basis on which it has acted, and the items of recoverable costs and the amount referable to each.[152] The tribunal may take into account offers to settle made by the parties where, for example, the tribunal's award is less than an amount offered by a party in settlement prior to the award.

The parties are free to agree on the power of the tribunal to award interest.[153] The default position under the 1996 Act is that the tribunal may award simple or compound interest from such dates and at such rates as it considers meets the justice of the case.[154] No mandatory or customary rate of interest is applicable, although where interest is claimed it will generally be awarded unless there is good reason not to (such as inordinate delay in prosecuting the claim). **10.96**

10.5 Role of Courts After the Issuance of the Award

According to the Act: 'Unless otherwise agreed by the parties, an award made by the tribunal pursuant to an arbitration agreement is final and binding both on the parties and on any persons claiming through or under them.'[155] 'This', the Act goes on to provide, 'does not affect the right of a person to challenge the award by any available arbitral process of appeal or review or in accordance with the provisions of this Part.'[156] This section outlines the grounds on provisions on recognition and enforcement, along with some comments and pointers. **10.97**

10.5.1 Challenges to the award

According to section 67 of the 1996 Act: **10.98**

(1) A party to arbitral proceedings may (upon notice to the other parties and to the tribunal) apply to the court—
   (a) challenging any award of the arbitral tribunal as to its substantive jurisdiction; or
   (b) for an order declaring an award made by the tribunal on the merits to be of no effect, in whole or in part, because the tribunal did not have substantive jurisdiction.

   A party may lose the right to object (see section 73) and the right to apply is subject to the restrictions in section 70(2) and (3).
(2) The arbitral tribunal may continue the arbitral proceedings and make a further award while an application to the court under this section is pending in relation to an award as to jurisdiction.
(3) On an application under this section challenging an award of the arbitral tribunal as to its substantive jurisdiction, the court may by order—
   (a) confirm the award,
   (b) vary the award, or
   (c) set aside the award in whole or in part.
(4) The leave of the court is required for any appeal from a decision of the court under this section.

---

152 1996 Act, s 63.
153 1996 Act, s 49.
154 1996 Act, s 49(3).
155 1996 Act, s 58(1).
156 1996 Act, s 58(2).

10.99 Section 67, which is mandatory, allows a challenge against an award that has been issued by a tribunal without the power to do so.[157] The Act allows objections as to substantive jurisdiction, including the scope and validity of the arbitration agreement and the constitution of the tribunal, to be raised both before and during the arbitration proceedings. Meanwhile, section 73 imposes a waiver over objections that are not raised in a timely manner, as also noted in section 67(1). Consequently, a challenge to jurisdiction under section 67 will lie in two instances: first, where a party refused to participate in arbitral proceedings from the outset,[158] and second, where a party lodged a timely objection to the tribunal's jurisdiction that was not resolved by a preliminary ruling.

10.100 Additional constraints imposed by this section are the 'restrictions in section 70(2) and (3)'. Section 70(2) provides that: 'An application or appeal may not be brought if the applicant or appellant has not first exhausted—(a) any available arbitral process of appeal or review, and (b) any available recourse under section 57 (correction of award or additional award).' This provision, in other words, requires the applicant to have previously availed itself of the tribunal's ability to provide relief as provided for under the Act.

10.101 Section 70(3) sets a time limitation on a party's ability to raise a claim under section 67: 'Any application or appeal must be brought within twenty-eight days of the date of the award or, if there has been any arbitral process of appeal or review, of the date the applicant or appellant was notified of the result of that process.'

10.102 Challenges under section 67 typically are resolved in fully-fledged trials, where the courts review *de novo* the evidence of fact and law (as they pertain to substantive jurisdiction) that was initially submitted to the arbitral tribunal, on the theory that the courts should be as well placed as the arbitrators to resolve the issue of jurisdiction before them.[159] It follows that a party may not freely introduce evidence that was not submitted in the arbitration proceedings in the course of a plea under section 67; if it wishes to do so, it should obtain consent from the opposing side or leave of the court seised of the action at an appropriate interlocutory hearing.[160]

---

[157] The term 'substantive jurisdiction' is defined in s 30(1)(a)–(c) of the Act. See n 23.

[158] In fact, the rights of a non-participating person are explicitly reserved under the 1996 Act, s 72 which provides as follows:

> (1) A person alleged to be a party to arbitral proceedings but who takes no part in the proceedings may question—
> (a) whether there is a valid arbitration agreement,
> (b) whether the tribunal is properly constituted, or
> (c) what matters have been submitted to arbitration in accordance with the arbitration agreement,
>
> by proceedings in the court for a declaration or injunction or other appropriate relief.
>
> (2) He also has the same right as a party to the arbitral proceedings to challenge an award—
> (a) by an application under section 67 on the ground of lack of substantive jurisdiction in relation to him, or
> (b) by an application under section 68 on the ground of serious irregularity (within the meaning of that section) affecting him;
>
> and section 70(2) (duty to exhaust arbitral procedures) does not apply in his case.

[159] For an overview of the practical steps necessary to lodge a s 67 application, see CPR pt 62.

[160] *Primetrade AG v Ythan Ltd* [2006] 1 Lloyd's Rep 457.

In addition to a challenge to the tribunal's substantive jurisdiction, the Act permits an appeal based on a 'serious irregularity' that affects the tribunal, the proceedings, or the award. Section 68 provides, in this regard: 10.103

> (2) Serious irregularity means an irregularity of one or more of the following kinds which the court considers has caused or will cause substantial injustice to the applicant—
> (a) failure by the tribunal to comply with section 33 (general duty of tribunal);
> (b) the tribunal exceeding its powers (otherwise than by exceeding its substantive jurisdiction: see section 67);
> (c) failure by the tribunal to conduct the proceedings in accordance with the procedure agreed by the parties;
> (d) failure by the tribunal to deal with all the issues that were put to it;
> (e) any arbitral or other institution or person vested by the parties with powers in relation to the proceedings or the award exceeding its powers;
> (f) uncertainty or ambiguity as to the effect of the award;
> (g) the award being obtained by fraud or the award or the way in which it was procured being contrary to public policy;
> (h) failure to comply with the requirements as to the form of the award; or
> (i) any irregularity in the conduct of the proceedings or in the award which is admitted by the tribunal or by any arbitral or other institution or person vested by the parties with powers in relation to the proceedings or the award.

Section 68(3) goes on to provide the remedies that the courts can adopt in the presence of a 'serious irregularity', including remittance of the award, in whole or in part, to the tribunal for reconsideration; setting the award aside in whole or in part; or declaring the award to be of no effect, in whole or in part. 10.104

Before commenting briefly on some of the different types of 'serious irregularity' identified in this section, it is worth observing that the mere existence of such an irregularity is not sufficient. It needs to have caused, or be reasonably certain to cause, 'substantial injustice to the applicant'. The DAC Committee has described this legal standard in the following terms: 10.105

> The test of '*substantial injustice*' is intended to be applied by way of support for the arbitral process, not by way of interference with that process. Thus it is only in those cases where it can be said that what has happened is so far removed from what could reasonably be expected of the arbitral process that we would expect the Court to take action. The test is not what would have happened had the matter been litigated. To apply such a test would be to ignore the fact that the parties have agreed to arbitrate, not litigate. Having chosen arbitration, the parties cannot validly complain of substantial injustice unless what has happened simply cannot on any view be defended as an acceptable consequence of that choice.[161]

In other words, the requirement that there be a 'substantial injustice' prevents section 68 from becoming 'another bite at the apple' for losing parties, and renders it a very limited ground on which to lodge challenges against those rare awards that contain or are founded on fundamental breaches of due process and other types of non-feasance or misfeasance by arbitral tribunals.[162] 10.106

[161] DAC Report (n 7) para 280.

[162] *Lesotho Highlands Development Authority v Impregilo SpA* [2005] 2 Lloyd's Rep 310, finding that the threshold established by s 68 is very high and will admit only the most extreme cases; see also *CNH Global NV v PGN Logistics Ltd* [2009] EWHC 277 (Comm), finding, in a case the Court described as a 'howler', that the arbitral tribunal's failure to award interest as part of its overall disposition of the case, and its improper subsequent issuance of an addendum concerning the interest due was a serious irregularity which, however, did not

10.107 The instances of 'serious irregularity' listed under section 68(2) are not mutually exclusive, although their overlap with other sections of the Act, such as 67, is either explicitly disclaimed[163] or avoided via the interpretive presumption that no such overlap was intended among the Act's various sections. The most frequently evoked provision is section 68(2)(a), an allegation that the tribunal did not comply with the mandatory requirements under section 33, which lists the overriding obligations of arbitrators, such as according due process to the parties and treating them equally.[164] Similarly, section 68 establishes a cause of action when, for example, the tribunal has applied the wrong law to certain legal issues (section 68(2)(b)), when the tribunal has failed to deal with all the issues in the arbitration (section 68(2)(d)), or when a party prevails in an arbitration by deliberately abusing the arbitral process (section 68(2)(g)).

10.108 Notably, applications under section 68 have the same procedural prerequisites as those under section 67: exhaustion of arbitral remedies and lodging of the claim within 28 days from the relevant arbitral award.

10.5.2 Appeal on point of law

10.109 Section 69 of the Act introduces a limited (in terms of both substantive scope and procedural requirements) right to appeal against an award on a point of law.[165] Such an appeal can be lodged against partial or provisional awards as well, although the merits of such a petition may be affected adversely by the arbitrators' ability to address any contested point of law later in the proceedings. The parties are at liberty to contract out of this section:

> (1) Unless otherwise agreed by the parties, a party to arbitral proceedings may (upon notice to the other parties and to the tribunal) appeal to the court on a question of law arising out of an award made in the proceedings.
> An agreement to dispense with reasons for the tribunal's award shall be considered an agreement to exclude the court's jurisdiction under this section.
> (2) An appeal shall not be brought under this section except—
> (a) with the agreement of all the other parties to the proceedings, or
> (b) with the leave of the court.
> The right to appeal is also subject to the restrictions in section 70(2) and (3).
> (3) Leave to appeal shall be given only if the court is satisfied—
> (a) that the determination of the question will substantially affect the rights of one or more of the parties,
> (b) that the question is one which the tribunal was asked to determine,
> (c) that, on the basis of the findings of fact in the award—
> (i) the decision of the tribunal on the question is obviously wrong, or

---

constitute grounds for a s 68 petition because it did not result in substantial injustice to the party ordered to pay the interest.

163 See 1996 Act, s 68(2)(b).

164 Merkin and Flannery (n 10) 158, citing *Petroships Pte Ltd v Peter Trading and Investment Corp, the Petro Ranger* [2001] 2 Lloyd's Rep 348; for a very thorough overview of the various contours of s 68, see Merkin and Flannery at 156–63.

165 Repeatedly articulated concerns about the potential for abuse of this s 69 are not necessarily borne out in case statistics. In a 2009 study conducted by the London Maritime Arbitrators Association, it was found that of 151 s 69 applications to appeal were made between 2006 and 2008, 36 obtained leave to appeal, and only 14 resulted in the setting aside, variation, or remittal of an award. See Lord Mance's Advisory Committee on Section 69 of the Arbitration Act 1996, 'First Interim Report on the Workings of Section 69 of the 1996 Act in Regard to Maritime Arbitrations in London Before the Commercial and Admiralty Court' (2009) available at <http://www.lmaa.org.uk>.

(ii) the question is one of general public importance and the decision of the tribunal is at least open to serious doubt, and
(d) that, despite the agreement of the parties to resolve the matter by arbitration, it is just and proper in all the circumstances for the court to determine the question.
(4) An application for leave to appeal under this section shall identify the question of law to be determined and state the grounds on which it is alleged that leave to appeal should be granted.
(5) The court shall determine an application for leave to appeal under this section without a hearing unless it appears to the court that a hearing is required.
(6) The leave of the court is required for any appeal from a decision of the court under this section to grant or refuse leave to appeal.
(7) On an appeal under this section the court may by order—
(a) confirm the award,
(b) vary the award,
(c) remit the award to the tribunal, in whole or in part, for reconsideration in the light of the court's determination, or
(d) set aside the award in whole or in part.
The court shall not exercise its power to set aside an award, in whole or in part, unless it is satisfied that it would be inappropriate to remit the matters in question to the tribunal for reconsideration.
(8) The decision of the court on an appeal under this section shall be treated as a judgment of the court for the purposes of a further appeal.
But no such appeal lies without the leave of the court which shall not be given unless the court considers that the question is one of general importance or is one which for some other special reason should be considered by the Court of Appeal.

There are four main observations to make about this provision. First, the question of law at issue must affect substantially the 'rights of the parties' (section 69(3)(a)). This has been interpreted to exclude legal issues that did not constitute part of the underlying arbitral award's reasoning, or that pertain to matters of procedure, not substance. In this regard, the reference to the parties' 'rights' concerns rights that are at issue in the dispute, not those that may be collaterally affected by it (such as unrelated financial interests). **10.110**

Second, section 69(3)(b) imposes an estoppel on arguments that were not raised during the arbitration proceedings. Nevertheless, if the arbitrators have chosen to address a point of law that was never brought before them, that point may be appealed under section 69 if it bears significantly on the outcome of the arbitration.[166] By contrast, if the parties attempt to introduce new evidence, in the absence of serious irregularity, the courts are not allowed to remit the award or take an action that would allow the consideration of the new evidence after an award has been rendered. **10.111**

Third, the factual review mandated by section 69(3)(c) implies a level of deference to the arbitrators,[167] who had the benefit of interpreting specific facts in the light of the entire factual record—the presentation of which may not be possible in a section 69 proceeding, especially if it takes place solely on the papers under section 69(5). Importantly, the ultimate question presented should be one of law, and not purely of fact.[168] **10.112**

[166] Merkin and Flannery (n 10) 167, citing *Omnibridge Consulting Ltd v Clearsprings (Management) Ltd* (unreported).
[167] *Trustees of Edmond Stern Settlement v Levy* [2007] EWHC 1187 (TCC).
[168] *Mary Harvey v Motor Insurer's Bureau* QBD (Merc) (Manchester).

10.113 Finally, as with several other sections under the 1996 Act, the remedies under section 69 are circumscribed procedurally by section 70(2) to (3), so an application requires either leave from the tribunal or agreement by all parties. Moreover, the applicant must have exhausted the remedies available within the arbitration, and bring its claim 28 days from the date of the award.

10.5.3 Enforcement

10.114 Upon the rendering of an arbitral award the losing party may (and often does) comply voluntarily with the terms of the award. If it does not, however, enforcement via the courts is necessary. The enforcement of arbitral awards under the Act may be accomplished in two principal ways: first, by operation of the 'summary procedure' outlined in section 66; and second, by operation of international conventions to which the United Kingdom is a party, such as the New York Convention.

10.115 According to section 66 of the 1996 Act:

> (1) An award made by the tribunal pursuant to an arbitration agreement may, by leave of the court, be enforced in the same manner as a judgment or order of the court to the same effect.
> (2) Where leave is so given, judgment may be entered in terms of the award.
> (3) Leave to enforce an award shall not be given where, or to the extent that, the person against whom it is sought to be enforced shows that the tribunal lacked substantive jurisdiction to make the award.
> The right to raise such an objection may have been lost (see section 73).
> (4) Nothing in this section affects the recognition or enforcement of an award under any other enactment or rule of law, in particular under Part II of the Arbitration Act 1950 (enforcement of awards under Geneva Convention) or the provisions of Part III of this Act relating to the recognition and enforcement of awards under the New York Convention or by an action on the award.

10.116 Section 66 allows the enforcement of awards regardless of where the arbitration was seated[169] by requesting permission from the English courts. That permission, if granted, does not amount to a court order itself, so failure to comply does not entail the same remedies as violation of such an order (eg contempt of court). As mentioned previously, the time limitation for the enforcement of an arbitral award is six years from the time it was supposed to be complied with, regardless of whether enforcement is sought under section 66 or under the New York Convention, which the Act incorporates.

10.117 Enforcement is at the discretion of the courts and is rarely refused, usually only on grounds of serious deficiency with the underlying arbitral award, or if the award cannot be enforced because enforcement would be contrary to public policy in England and Wales.[170] A party may oppose an application for permission to enforce an award by evoking section 66(3). In practice, resistance of enforcement because of lack of substantive jurisdiction under section

---

[169] Arbitration Act 1996, s 2(2)(b).

[170] The public policy exception to enforcement is not explicitly mentioned in s 66, but the DAC Report considered it as being implicit in the courts' exercise of discretion: DAC Report (n 7) para 273. In addition, the DAC Report appears to recommend the less stringent application of the public policy exception where the governing law is not English law: 'it must always be borne in mind that the parties' rights and obligations may well be governed by a law other than our own, under which, for example, matters are arbitrable which would not be the case under our own law. In such cases it would not automatically follow that the Court would refuse to enforce the award, unless of course public policy dictated that course': DAC Report, para 376.

66(3) is technically possible but rare, as it can be asserted only by a non-participant in the arbitration proceedings, or a party that has lodged a timely jurisdictional objection that has not been resolved.

Even if those conditions are satisfied, the opposing party may not have the opportunity to file a timely application, as requests for enforcement do not require notice to the other party.[171] After the order of enforcement is issued, a party may still apply to have it set aside, not only under section 66(3), but also the other grounds available under the Act for setting aside awards discussed previously. **10.118**

The fact that a foreign court has refused enforcement does not prevent the English court from proceeding with enforcement according to section 66, although issue estoppel may apply with respect to the foreign court's factual and legal findings.[172] **10.119**

Awards may also be enforced summarily pursuant to section III of the 1996 Act if they are covered by the New York Convention, and under section II of the Arbitration Act 1950, which is incorporated into the 1996 Act via section 99, if they are covered by the Geneva Convention but not the New York Convention.[173] Such instances are rare, as the Geneva Convention has been eclipsed almost entirely by the New York Convention. **10.120**

Section III incorporates into English law the United Kingdom's undertaking under the New York Convention to enforce an award made pursuant to an arbitration agreement in the territory of a state (other than the United Kingdom) that is a party to the New York Convention.[174] Section 102 of the 1996 Act outlines the documentary requirements for summary enforcement of a New York Convention award—namely duly authenticated and if necessary translated copies of the award and the arbitration agreement. The party seeking enforcement need not demonstrate that the award is binding on the other party, although such evidence may be required as part of a challenge to enforcement under the New York Convention. **10.121**

The grounds on which a party can resist enforcement under the Convention are very narrow, a fact that is reflected in section 103 of the 1996 Act.[175] The English courts have refused **10.122**

---

[171] See St John Sutton, Gill, and Gearing (n 4) s 8-003.

[172] See Merkin and Flannery (n 10) 149.

[173] Convention on the Execution of Foreign Arbitral Awards (26 September 1927) <http://interarb.com/vl/g_co1927> ('Geneva Convention'). The Geneva Convention provides for the enforcement of arbitral awards done pursuant to the Protocol on Arbitration Clauses presented at a League of Nations Conference in 1923. That Protocol is appended as Sch I to the Arbitration Act 1950, s 35 of which provides, among others, for the enforcement of 'any award made after the twenty-eighth day of July, nineteen hundred and twenty-four—(a) in pursuance of an agreement for arbitration to which the protocol set out in the First Schedule to this Act applies . . .'

[174] The formalities under the New York Convention concerning the arbitration agreement, including the requirement that it be in writing, are not the same as under the 1996 Act.

[175] Arbitration Act 1996, s 103 provides in the relevant part:

(2) Recognition or enforcement of the award may be refused if the person against whom it is invoked proves—
  - (a) that a party to the arbitration agreement was (under the law applicable to him) under some incapacity;
  - (b) that the arbitration agreement was not valid under the law to which the parties subjected it or, failing any indication thereon, under the law of the country where the award was made;
  - (c) that he was not given proper notice of the appointment of the arbitrator or of the arbitration proceedings or was otherwise unable to present his case;

to apply a more (or less) stringent standard of scrutiny in evaluating set-aside applications based on the New York Convention versus the grounds provided under Part I of the 1996 Act.[176]

10.6 Conclusion

10.123 Our assessment of England and Wales as a venue for arbitration leads to two firm conclusions. First, England and Wales possesses a comprehensive and clearly articulated legal framework governing arbitration, and a sophisticated, impartial judiciary with ample experience in complex arbitral disputes and the collateral issues they raise under both English law and foreign laws and regulations. Second, the jurisdiction is distinctly arbitration-friendly, with a keen understanding of the benefits arbitration aims to confer on parties, and the policy considerations such benefits entail.

10.124 In this light, we hope our opening observation regarding the supremacy of London as a seat of arbitration involving parties from all over the world has become that much more justified.

(d) that the award deals with a difference not contemplated by or not falling within the terms of the submission to arbitration or contains decisions on matters beyond the scope of the submission to arbitration (but see subsection (4));
(e) that the composition of the arbitral tribunal or the arbitral procedure was not in accordance with the agreement of the parties or, failing such agreement with the law of the country in which the arbitration took place;
(f) that the award has not yet become binding on the parties, or has been set aside or suspended by a competent authority of the country in which, or under the law of which, it was made.

(3) Recognition or enforcement of the award may also be refused if the award is in respect of a matter which is not capable of settlement by arbitration, or if it would be contrary to public policy to recognise or enforce the award.
(4) An award which contains decisions on matters not submitted to arbitration may be recognised or enforced to the extent that it contains decisions on matters submitted to arbitration which can be separated from those on matters not so submitted.
(5) Where an application for the setting aside or suspension of the award has been made to such a competent authority as is mentioned in subsection (2)(f), the court before which the award is sought to be relied upon may, if it considers it proper, adjourn the decision on the recognition or enforcement of the award.

[176] See eg *R v V* [2008] EWHC 1531, rejecting the claimant's argument that the court was obliged to scrutinize the arbitral tribunal's findings more stringently because it was exercising 'supervisory jurisdiction' under s 68 of the Act, and not under the New York Convention.

11

MEXICO CITY

Claus von Wobeser

11.1 The History and Development of Arbitration in Mexico

11.1.1 Background

In Mexico, arbitration can be traced back to 1603 when Mexico (*Nueva España*) was under Spanish imperium and applied the *Siete Partidas* of Alfonso X. Under this statute, the legal concept of an arbitrator was a person who resolved disputes but whose decisions lacked authority.[1] **11.01**

The Cádiz Constitution of 1812 provided for arbitration to resolve civil matters.[2] However, it was not until the adoption of the 1854 Commercial Code that commercial arbitration **11.02**

[1] R Cruz Miramontes and O Cruz Barney, *El Arbitraje. Los Diversos Mecanismos de Solución de Controversias: Análisis y Práctica en México* (Porrúa, 2004) 63.
[2] Cruz Miramontes and Cruz Barney (n 1) 84.

was established as an alternative mechanism for solving disputes.[3] Later, in the 1872, 1880, and 1884 Federal Procedure Civil Codes, arbitration was made available for civil matters.[4]

11.03 In 1989 that the first formal legislative approach towards international and domestic arbitration occurred, and a section entitled 'Of the Arbitration Proceedings' was included in the Commercial Code.[5]

11.04 Further, in 1993, the Model Law on International Commercial Arbitration of the United Nations Commission on International Trade Law (UNCITRAL Model Law)[6] was adopted, with minor legal modifications, under Book V, Title IV of the Commercial Code, becoming a milestone for arbitration in Mexico.[7] With the adoption, and ongoing updating, of the Model Law, Mexican arbitration legislation has been evolving progressively.[8] Coupled with judicial support, these legislative initiatives have unified the law and practice of arbitration in Mexico.

11.05 On the international front, Mexico ratified the Convention on the Recognition and Enforcement of Foreign Arbitral Awards (the 'New York Convention') in 1971.[9] Additionally, in 1978, Mexico ratified the Inter-American Convention on International Commercial Arbitration (the 'Panama Convention'),[10] and in 1987, the Inter-American Convention on Extraterritorial Validity of Foreign Judgments and Arbitral Awards (the 'Montevideo Convention').[11] Mexico has also entered into numerous free trade agreements and bilateral investment treaties (BITs), establishing international arbitration as the primary means of resolving disputes.[12]

11.06 The North American Free Trade Agreement (NAFTA)[13] allows individual investors in a member state to arbitrate investment disputes directly with another member state, under the following rules: (a) the Convention on the Settlement of Investment Disputes between States and Nationals of Other States (the 'ICSID Convention'), (b) the Arbitration (Additional Facility) Rules of the International Centre for Settlement of Investment Disputes (the 'ICSID Additional Facility Rules'),[14] or (c) the Arbitration Rules of the United Nations Commission on International Trade Law ('UNCITRAL Arbitration Rules').

---

[3] Cruz Miramontes and Cruz Barney (n 1) 98.

[4] Cruz Miramontes and Cruz Barney (n 1) 88.

[5] J Luis Siqueiros, 'La ley mexicana en material de arbitraje comercial' (1999) 28 Boletín informativo del Capítulo Mexicano de la Cámara de Comercio 28.

[6] Text of the UNCITRAL Model Law, available at <http://www.uncitral.org/uncitral/en/uncitral_texts/arbitration/1985Model_arbitration.html> (accessed 25 February 2013).

[7] The Federal Code of Civil Procedure supplements any deficiency of the Commercial Code.

[8] Amendments published on 27 January 2011 and 6 June 2011 in the *Official Gazette* of Mexico ('DOF'), available at <http://www.diputados.gob.mx/LeyesBiblio/ref/ccom/CCom_ref43_27ene11.pdf> and <http://www.diputados.gob.mx/LeyesBiblio/ref/ccom/CCom_ref44_06jun11.pdf> (accessed 25 February 2013).

[9] Text of Convention on the Recognition and Enforcement of Foreign Arbitral Awards, available at <http://www.uncitral.org/uncitral/en/uncitral_texts/arbitration/NYConvention.html> (accessed 25 February 2013).

[10] Text of the Inter-American Convention on International Commercial Arbitration, available at <http://www.oas.org/juridico/english/treaties/b-35.html> (accessed 25 February 2013).

[11] Text of the Inter-American Convention on Extraterritorial Validity of Foreign Judgments and Arbitral Awards, available at <http://www.oas.org/juridico/english/treaties/b-41.html> (accessed 25 February 2013).

[12] To date, Mexico has executed bilateral investment treaties with Argentina, Australia, Austria, Belarus, China, Cuba, the Czech Republic, Denmark, the Economic Union of Belgium and Luxembourg, Finland, France, Germany, Greece, Iceland, India, Italy, the Netherlands, Panama, Portugal, Slovakia, South Korea, Spain, Sweden, Switzerland, Trinidad and Tobago, the United Kingdom, and Uruguay.

[13] Text of the North American Free Trade Agreement, available at <http://www.nafta-sec-alena.org/en/view.aspx?conID=590> (accessed 25 February 2013).

[14] On 27 September 1978 the ICSID Additional Facility Rules were approved by Mexico.

It is relevant to mention that Mexico is not a party to the ICSID Convention, and therefore is not able to resolve disputes before ICSID under such rules. However, Mexico frequently makes use of the ICSID Additional Facility Rules to resolve NAFTA and BIT disputes.[15] Mexico has also resolved disputes under the UNCITRAL Arbitration Rules.[16] **11.07**

Finally, due to the adoption of the UNCITRAL Model Law and the ratification of the New York Convention, the judicial approach towards the recognition and enforcement of arbitral awards is favourable. Mexican law is modern and supportive of arbitration and since Mexican courts have been receptive to international arbitration, Mexico has become one of the most attractive arbitration venues in Latin America. **11.08**

The flexible nature of arbitration, the extensive legislative infrastructure at the federal level, and the support of the judiciary have enabled Mexico to embrace international arbitration as the most effective alternative for the resolution of commercial disputes in Mexico. **11.09**

11.1.2 Involvement in international arbitration

In the year 2000, only 27 Mexican parties, both business entities and individuals, participated in International Chamber of Commerce (ICC) arbitrations, and Mexico City was selected as the seat of arbitration proceedings in four cases. A total of 23 Mexican arbitrators were either confirmed or appointed by the ICC Court.[17] **11.10**

These figures have evolved positively over the recent years. According to statistics published in 2010 by the International Chamber of Commerce, Mexico was one of the most frequent Latin-American nationalities present in ICC arbitration proceedings that year, together with the United States, Germany, France, the United Kingdom, Spain, Brazil, Turkey, and India.[18] **11.11**

According to the 2010 ICC Statistical Report, in 2010, there were a total of 62 Mexican parties involved in ICC arbitration proceedings in that year. Moreover, Mexico City was the selected seat of arbitration proceedings in 13 cases in 2010. Furthermore, a total of 24 Mexican arbitrators were either confirmed or appointed by the ICC Court, placing Mexico City among the top ten seats of arbitration chosen worldwide during 2010.[19] **11.12**

---

[15] *Metalclad Corp v Mexico* (Case No ARB/97/1); *Robert Azinian and ors v Mexico* (Case No ARB/97/2); *Waste Management, Inc v Mexico* (Case No ARB/98/2); *Marvin Roy Feldman Karpa v Mexico* (Case No ARB/99/1); *Técnicas Medioambientales Tecmed SA v México* (Case No ARB/00/2); *Waste Management, Inc v Mexico* (Case No ARB/00/3); *Fireman's Fund Insurance Co v Mexico* (Case No ARB/02/1); *Corn Products International, Inc v Mexico* (Case No ARB/04/1); *Archer Daniels Midland Co and Tate & Lyle Ingredients Americas, Inc v Mexico* (Case No ARB/04/5); *Gemplus SA, SLP SA, Gemplus Industrial SA de CV, and Talsud SA v Mexico* (Case Nos ARB/04/3 and ARB/04/4); *Bayview Irrigation District and ors v Mexico* (Case No ARB/05/1); *Cargill, Inc v Mexico* (Case No ARB/05/2), available at <http://www.economia.gob.mx/comunidad-negocios/comercio-exterior/solucion-controversias#inversionista-estado> (accessed 25 February 2013).

[16] *Gami Investments, Inc v México* (Award of 15 November 2004); *International Thunderbird Gaming Corp v Mexico* (Award of 26 January 2006) <http://www.economia.gob.mx/comunidad-negocios/comercio-exterior/solucion-controversias#inversionista-estado> (accessed 25 February 2013).

[17] 2000 Statistical Report of the International Chamber of Commerce (ICC), available at <http://iccwbo.org/court/arbitration/index.html?id>.

[18] 2010 Statistical Report of the International Chamber of Commerce (ICC), available at <http://iccwbo.org/court/arbitration/index.html?id>.

[19] Preceded by Paris, London, Geneva, Zurich, Singapore, New York, Hong Kong, and Vienna. 2010 Statistical Report of the International Chamber of Commerce (ICC), available at <http://iccwbo.org/court/arbitration/index.html?id>.

11.13 These statistics indicate that within ten years, the number of Mexicans parties that submitted their disputes to ICC arbitrations more than doubled. These figures, although limited to ICC arbitration, are useful in understanding recent trends in the development of commercial arbitration in Mexico.

11.1.3 Current arbitration legislation

11.14 In 2011, the arbitration chapter of the Commercial Code, articles 1464 to 1480, underwent a comprehensive reform in response to Mexico's growing role in international commercial arbitration. The main amendments were published on 27 January 2011,[20] and months later, on 6 June 2011, a second reform was implemented.[21]

11.15 The most noteworthy 2011 amendments include provisions for the enforcement of arbitration agreements, court referral to arbitration, judicial assistance in arbitration, provisional remedies, arbitrator liability, and recognition and enforcement of arbitral awards. The key changes were:

- The introduction of express regulation of the intervention or assistance of national courts. Previously, this intervention had not been regulated, and Mexican arbitration law was ambiguous on the subject.
- The creation of a presumption of arbitrability in support of arbitration. The intervention of national courts in arbitration proceedings is now framed in the Commercial Code as judicial assistance in support of arbitration, rather than as interference. Judicial assistance is available at the request of either party, in the limited circumstances expressly regulated by the Code.[22]
- The introduction of a brief special proceeding known as a 'special proceeding for commercial transactions and arbitration', applicable to the setting aside or annulment of arbitral awards. This special proceeding promotes the speed and efficiency of the arbitral process.
- The addition of a provision to article 1480, establishing that arbitrators are liable for any losses and damages arising from provisional remedies they order.

11.16 Although the 2011 amendments significantly advance the practice of arbitration, they are recent, and Mexican courts have yet to interpret these provisions or develop case law.

11.17 In addition to the modifications to the Commercial Code, the Public Works Law and the Public Acquisitions Law also underwent important modifications. Until May 2009, arbitration with the government was highly restricted, as the national framework allowed only two state-owned companies—the oil company, Petróleos Mexicanos (PEMEX), and the power company, Comisión Federal de Electricidad (CFE)—to submit disputes to commercial arbitration.[23]

---

[20] Amendments published on 27 January 2011 and 6 June 2011 in the DOF, available at <http://www.diputados.gob.mx/LeyesBiblio/ref/ccom/CCom_ref43_27ene11.pdf> (accessed 25 February 2013).

[21] Amendments published on 6 June 2011 in the DOF, available at <http://www.diputados.gob.mx/LeyesBiblio/ref/ccom/CCom_ref44_06jun11.pdf> (accessed 25 February 2013).

[22] These are: (a) referral to arbitration upon the existence of an arbitration agreement at the request of either party; (b) appointment of arbitrators; (c) production of evidence in arbitration; (d) consultation on arbitrator's fees; (e) challenge of arbitrators; (f) provisional relief; (g) recognition and enforcement of provisional relief ordered by the arbitral tribunal; and (h) jurisdiction of the arbitral tribunal.

[23] Art 24 of the Organic Law of Petróleos Mexicanos and its Subsidiaries (Ley Orgánica de Petróleos Mexicanos y Organismos Subsidiarios) expressly provided for arbitration. This article was replaced on 28 November 2008 by art 6, para 2 of the Regulatory Law of article 27 of the Constitution in the Petroleum Sector

In 2009, amendments to the Public Works Law and to the Public Acquisitions Law introduced international or domestic arbitration as a method of settling disputes arising from contracts between a private party (either Mexican or foreign) and a state entity, thereby increasing the number of arbitrations in which a Mexican state entity is a party.[24] There are exceptions in this legislation to the arbitrability of certain matters, including administrative rescission for non-performance. Despite these exceptions, the 2009 reforms to the Public Works Law and Public Acquisitions Law represent important progress with respect to the opening of federal government contracts to alternative dispute resolution and arbitration. 11.18

Finally, another legislative recent change is noteworthy. The Public-Private Associations Law was published in January 2012, regulating public-private projects that establish long-term contractual relationships between public and private entities in order to render public services, with the infrastructure provided totally or partially by the private sector.[25] Article 139 of this law provides for the arbitration of disputes arising under these types of agreements. 11.19

11.1.5 Comparison with other regional or national venues

Over the past few years, Mexico has played a significant role in international arbitration and has positioned itself as one of the most attractive venues in Latin America. Mexico is an arbitration-friendly venue: it offers a favourable legislative environment and a supportive judiciary. It has also been an important centre for institutions that administer domestic and international commercial arbitration, including the Mexican Chapter of the International Chamber of Commerce,[26] the Arbitration and Mediation Commission of the Mexico City Chamber of Commerce (CANACO),[27] and the Mexican Arbitration Center (CAM).[28] 11.20

(Ley Reglamentaria del artículo 27 Constitucional en el Ramo del Petróleo) <http://www.diputados.gob.mx/LeyesBiblio/pdf/206.pdf> (accessed 26 February 2013); and art 72 of the Law of Petróleos Mexicanos <http://www.diputados.gob.mx/LeyesBiblio/pdf/LPM.pdf> (accessed 26 February 2013).

See also Law of the Public Service of Electric Energy (Ley del Servicio Público de Energía Eléctrica) art 45 <http://www.diputados.gob.mx/LeyesBiblio/pdf/99.pdf> (accessed 26 February 2013).

24 Law on Public Works and Related Services (Ley de Obras Públicas y Servicios Relacionados con las Mismas), art 98, para 1: 'An arbitration may be entered into with respect to disputes between the parties for the interpretation of contractual clauses or questions derived from their execution, under terms of the Title Four of the Fifth Book of the Commercial Code. The administrative rescission and the anticipated termination of the contracts as any other matter reserved by the Regulations shall not be subject to arbitration' <http://www.diputados.gob.mx/LeyesBiblio/pdf/56.pdf> (accessed 26 February 2013). Law of Acquisitions, Leases, and Services of the Public Sector (Ley de Adquisiciones, Arrendamientos y Servicios del Sector Publico), art 80: 'An arbitration may be entered into with respect to disputes between the parties for the interpretation of contractual clauses or questions derived from their execution, under terms of the Title Four of the Fifth Book of the Commercial Code. The administrative rescission and the anticipated termination of the contracts as any other matter reserved by the Regulations shall not be subject to arbitration' <http://www.diputados.gob.mx/LeyesBiblio/pdf/14.pdf> (accessed 26 February 2013).

25 Public-Private Associations Law, art 2 <http://www.diputados.gob.mx/LeyesBiblio/pdf/LAPP.pdf> (accessed 26 February 2013).

26 The Mexican Chapter of the International Chamber of Commerce is a non-profit institution formally established in 1985, with offices located in Indiana 260, 5th level, office 508, Col Ciudad de los Deportes, CP 03810, Mexico City, Federal District <http://www.iccmex.org.mx>.

27 The Arbitration and Mediation Commission of the Mexico City Chamber of Commerce (CANACO) is a non-profit organization located at Paseo de la Reforma no 42, Delegación Cuauhtémoc, CP 06040, Mexico City, Federal District <http://www.arbitrajecanaco.com.mx>.

28 The CAM was created in 1997. The organization is located at Tecnológico de Monterrey, Campus Santa Fe, Av Carlos Lazo No 100, Edificio Aulas 1, Nivel 5, Col Santa Fe, México, Federal District, CP 01389 <http://www.camex.com.mx>.

11.21 Aside from these legislative and judicial advantages, Mexico presents additional advantages over other jurisdictions or venues in the region. Mexico is a desirable seat for both Spanish and English language arbitrations, with a geographical location that is conducive to international arbitration in the Americas.

11.22 While Mexico has worked to embrace international arbitration and create a pro arbitration legal milieu, other Latin American countries have not favoured the use of international arbitration. For example, in 2007, Bolivia withdrew from the ICSID Convention, followed by Ecuador in 2009 and Venezuela in 2012. In contrast, Mexico has executed over 20 BITs granting access to investment arbitration to foreign investors. As explained previously, Mexico has participated in various NAFTA and investment arbitrations under the ICSID Additional Facility Rules.[29] Similarly, Mexico embraces the ICSID Additional Facility forum for remedies under many of its bilateral investment treaties (eg the Mexico-France BIT).[30]

11.23 The continuing trend in Mexico is one of increased receptiveness towards international arbitration and increased recourse to various arbitral forums. Mexico's receptiveness to the reality of the increased necessity of international arbitration as a response to the increase in cross-border transactions and investment spawned by globalization has positioned it as a regional and global leader in this field.

11.2 Commencing the Arbitration

11.2.1 Legal requirements concerning the form and content of the arbitration agreement

11.24 The Commercial Code requires that the arbitration agreement be in writing and signed by the parties, which may include an exchange of letters, telexes, telegrams, or faxes, or any other means of telecommunication that properly records the parties' agreement. It may also be an exchange of a written complaint and a written answer from which the agreement can be asserted by one party without being denied by the other. Under Mexican law, reference in an agreement to a document that contains an arbitration clause constitutes an agreement to arbitrate, as long as the agreement is in writing and the clause incorporated by reference.[31]

11.25 Furthermore, to be enforceable, an arbitration agreement must also meet the basic requirements for any contract, which include (a) that is has a legal purpose; (b) that the parties' consent was not given in error, or obtained by fraud or under duress; and (c) that the parties had full legal capacity to enter into the agreement.[32]

[29] *Metalclad Corp v Mexico* (Case No ARB/97/1); *Robert Azinian and ors v Mexico* (Case No ARB/97/2); *Waste Management, Inc v Mexico* (Case No ARB/98/2); *Marvin Roy Feldman Karpa v Mexico* (Case No ARB/99/1); *Waste Management, Inc v Mexico* (Case No ARB/00/3); *Fireman's Fund Insurance Co v Mexico* (Case No ARB/02/1); *Corn Products International, Inc v Mexico* (Case No ARB/04/1); *Archer Daniels Midland Co and Tate & Lyle Ingredients Americas, Inc v Mexico* (Case No ARB/04/5); *Bayview Irrigation District and ors v Mexico* (Case No ARB/05/1); *Cargill, Inc v Mexico* (Case No ARB/05/2) <http://www.economia.gob.mx/comunidad-negocios/comercio-exterior/solucion-controversias#inversionista-estado> (accessed 25 February 2013).

[30] Agreement between the Government of the Republic of France and the Government of the United Mexican States on the Reciprocal Promotion and Protection of Investments (signed and entered into force 12 November 1998), art 9(3)(i) <http://unctad.org/sections/dite/iia/docs/bits/mexico_france.pdf> (accessed 25 February 2013).

[31] Commercial Code, art 1423.

[32] Federal Civil Code, art 1795.

Finally, it is also worth mentioning that an arbitration clause in a contract is deemed to be an agreement independent from the rest of the contract. In the event that the main contract is found to be null and void, this does not entail the nullity of the arbitration clause.[33] 11.26

11.2.2 The role of courts in enforcing arbitration agreements

The Commercial Code requires courts to enforce arbitration agreements unless they find that the agreement to arbitrate is null and void, ineffective, or impossible to enforce.[34] Accordingly, in the event that a court proceeding is initiated despite the existence of an arbitration agreement, the court before which the proceeding has been initiated must, at the request of either party, refer the parties to arbitration.[35] The commencement of court proceedings does not preclude arbitration from being initiated or continued.[36] 11.27

The 2011 amendments to the Commercial Code establish a special procedure for seeking judicial referral to arbitration when there is an agreement to arbitrate. The Commercial Code provides that the request must be made in the applicant's first written submission.[37] The procedure for referring the parties to arbitration requires an application by a party, and does not operate on an *ex officio* basis. Once a party requests that a dispute be referred to arbitration, the court must issue a decision immediately, after giving the other party the opportunity to respond. 11.28

In the event that the court enforces the arbitration agreement, as opposed to finding it null, void, ineffective, or impossible to enforce, and refers the parties to arbitration, it must order the suspension of the judicial proceedings. Consequently, referral to arbitration by the national courts must be immediate. Once the dispute has been finally settled in arbitration, the court must terminate the judicial proceedings upon the request of either party. There is no recourse against a decision referring the parties to arbitration and suspending the judicial proceedings.[38] 11.29

If the arbitration agreement is declared null and void, the arbitral tribunal found to lack jurisdiction, or if for any reason the dispute is not resolved in arbitration, the suspension will be lifted, upon the request of either party, provided that all parties involved are given the opportunity to be heard.[39] 11.30

In addition, it is worth mentioning that the parties to an arbitration seated in Mexico should make sure to grant proper powers of attorney to the lawyers representing them in the arbitration.[40] Notwithstanding that most arbitral tribunals do not formally require the parties to submit these documents, Mexican law may be interpreted as requiring the lawyers representing the parties in an arbitration to act under a valid power of attorney. 11.31

11.2.3 Court assistance in appointing arbitrators

The parties may freely agree on the number, procedure for appointment, and requirements applicable to arbitrators.[41] Consequently, there are no legal limitations as to who can act as 11.32

[33] Commercial Code, art 1432.
[34] Commercial Code, art 1424.
[35] Commercial Code, art 1424.
[36] Commercial Code, art 1424.
[37] Commercial Code, art 1464.
[38] Commercial Code, art 1464.
[39] Commercial Code, art 1464.
[40] Federal Civil Code, arts 2554 and 2587.
[41] Commercial Code, art 1427.

arbitrator and arbitrators are not required to be lawyers or members of a local bar. However, Mexican law is clear that arbitrators must be impartial and independent.

11.33 The Commercial Code also provides a default procedure for the constitution of an arbitral tribunal in the absence of agreement by the parties. According to the Commercial Code, in the absence of agreement by the parties the default number of arbitrators is a sole arbitrator.[42] In arbitrations in which the parties do not reach agreement on the appointment of a sole arbitrator, the competent court will, at the request of either party, make the appointment.[43]

11.34 In arbitrations with three arbitrators, each party appoints one arbitrator, and the party-appointed arbitrators select the third arbitrator. If a party fails to name an arbitrator within 30 days of a request to do so by the other party, or if the arbitrators named by the parties do not agree on the third arbitrator within 30 days from their designation, the appointment will be made by the court upon request of either party.

11.2.4 The role of courts in resolving jurisdictional questions

11.35 The Commercial Code provides that an arbitral tribunal has the authority to determine its own jurisdiction and rule on any challenges to the existence or validity of an arbitration agreement.[44] For this purpose, an arbitration clause in a contract is deemed an agreement independent of all other stipulations in the contract. A determination by an arbitral tribunal declaring a contract null and void does not void the arbitration clause.

11.36 A plea of lack of jurisdiction of the arbitral tribunal must be raised at the time of filing the answer, at the latest. The parties will not be barred from asserting this plea by virtue of having appointed an arbitrator or participated in the appointment. A plea that the tribunal exceeded its powers must be asserted as soon as the matter that allegedly exceeds the tribunal's powers is raised during the arbitration. The tribunal may, however, in either case, admit a plea made after these terms have expired, provided that the delay is justified.

11.37 The arbitral tribunal may deal with objections to jurisdiction *a priori* or in the final award on the merits. If prior to the issuance of its final award the tribunal declares itself competent, either party may, within 30 days, request the court to review this determination, and the court's decision is not subject to appeal. While such a petition is pending, the arbitral tribunal may continue to act and render an award.

11.2.5 The role of courts in enjoining arbitration

11.38 In Mexico, parties are nearly always free to forgo litigation by including an arbitration clause in their contracts. As just noted, unless there is a specific legal provision that prohibits arbitration in the specific context of the contract or the facts of the case, Mexican courts will always enforce a contractual arbitration agreement and refer the parties to arbitration immediately, unless the court finds that the arbitration agreement is null, void, ineffective, or impossible to enforce; or unless the party that opposes arbitration proves that the arbitration agreement has already been declared null and void in a previous ruling or award.[45]

[42] Commercial Code, art 1426.
[43] Commercial Code, art 1426.
[44] Commercial Code, art 1432.
[45] Commercial Code, art 1424.

Moreover, judicial assistance is triggered only by a party's request and is limited to situations specifically regulated by law, making it unlikely for national courts to enjoin, delay, or frustrate arbitrations. 11.39

11.2.6 Provisional measures

Perhaps the most innovative provisions of the 2011 amendments to the Commercial Code concern provisional remedies ordered in arbitration proceedings, both by the arbitral tribunal and by national courts. The recently amended legislation now fully guarantees the availability of provisional measures in support of arbitration. Specifically, courts are able to order provisional relief before or during the arbitration proceedings, and in aid of arbitrations seated both within and outside Mexico.[46] 11.40

The Commercial Code provides that, upon a party's request, courts are authorized and have complete discretion to order any interim measures that may be appropriate in aid of arbitration.[47] The provisional remedies available in arbitration are therefore subject to the court's discretion, and the specific nature of the dispute. As the Commercial Code does not contemplate any specific conditions or requirements for qualifying for provisional remedies, the court's discretion is limited only by Mexican public policy standards and due process requirements. 11.41

In order to obtain provisional relief from the courts, a request must be filed by means of a procedure known as a 'special proceeding for commercial transactions and arbitration'. Once the competent court has admitted the request for provisional remedies, it must summon the respondent and grant him 15 days to respond.[48] 11.42

Upon expiration of the 15-day period, if the parties did not submit any evidence (to prove the need and urgency of granting the measure or respondent to the contrary) and the court did not deem the production of evidence to be necessary, there will be an oral hearing within the next three days, which will proceed regardless of the parties' appearance.[49] If the parties have produced evidence or the court deems the production of evidence to be necessary, the court will grant ten days.[50] After the hearing, the court will summon the parties to hear its decision, which is not subject to appeal.[51] 11.43

Provisional remedies may also be ordered by the arbitral tribunal itself. The 2011 amendments provide that, upon the request of either party, the arbitral tribunal may order any provisional remedies that may be necessary in connection with the subject matter in dispute.[52] Interim measures ordered by an arbitral tribunal are recognized as binding by the courts. Unless otherwise determined by the tribunal, interim measures may be enforced by the courts, regardless of the stage at which they are ordered. A party that requested or obtained the enforcement of an arbitral interim measure must immediately inform the court in the event of revocation, suspension, or modification of the measure. The court may, if 11.44

46 Commercial Code, arts 1415 and 1425.
47 Commercial Code, art 1478.
48 Commercial Code, arts 1470-III, 1472, and 1473.
49 Commercial Code, art 1474.
50 Commercial Code, art 1475.
51 Commercial Code, art 1476.
52 Commercial Code, art 1433.

appropriate, order the applicant to provide security, if the arbitral tribunal has not done so or if this is necessary to protect third-party rights.[53]

11.3 During the Arbitration

11.3.1 The role of courts in deciding challenges to arbitrators

11.45 The Commercial Code requires persons who have been proposed as arbitrators to disclose all circumstances that may give rise to justifiable doubts regarding their impartiality and independence.[54] Prospective arbitrators must reveal to the parties, without delay, from the time of their appointment and during the time that they perform their arbitral functions, any circumstances that could raise doubts as to their impartiality.

11.46 Arbitrators can be challenged only if there are such circumstances, or if the arbitrator lacks specific qualities or qualifications agreed on by the parties. A party can challenge an arbitrator that it appointed, or in whose appointment it participated, only on grounds that come to the party's knowledge after the appointment is made.[55]

11.47 Mexican law gives the parties complete freedom to agree on the procedure for the challenge of arbitrators.[56] In the absence of agreement, the party launching the challenge must, within 15 days from the time that the arbitral tribunal is constituted, or 15 days from the time the party obtains knowledge of the relevant facts, submit to the tribunal in writing the alleged grounds. Unless the challenged arbitrator voluntarily resigns or the other party accepts the challenge, the arbitral tribunal will rule on the challenge.[57] If the challenge of an arbitrator succeeds, a substitute arbitrator will be appointed under the same procedure as that used for the appointment of the arbitrator sought to be replaced.[58]

11.48 If the challenge is rejected, the petitioner may, within 30 days of the notice of rejection, request judicial review. During this time, the arbitral tribunal, including the arbitrator being challenged, may continue with the proceedings and issue an award.[59]

11.3.2 The role of courts in fixing deposits for arbitration costs

11.49 After the arbitral tribunal has been constituted, it may request each party to deposit an equal amount in advance for the arbitral tribunal's fees, travel expenses, and any other expenses incurred by the arbitrators, as well as for costs of expert evidence.[60] During the course of the proceedings, the arbitral tribunal may request the parties to make additional deposits.

11.50 Upon the request of any of the parties, and provided that the judge agrees, the arbitral tribunal shall fix the amount of the deposits only after consulting with the court, which may provide any observations it deems appropriate.[61]

[53] Commercial Code, art 1479.
[54] Commercial Code, art 1428.
[55] Commercial Code, art 1428.
[56] Commercial Code, art 1429.
[57] Commercial Code, art 1429.
[58] Commercial Code, art 1431.
[59] Commercial Code, art 1429.
[60] Commercial Code, art 1456.
[61] Commercial Code, art 1456.

11.3.3 The role of courts in compelling testimony/evidence

The Commercial Code establishes that the parties may freely agree on the procedure to be followed by the arbitral tribunal. In the absence of agreement, the tribunal may conduct the proceedings as it deems appropriate. This power includes the discretion to determine the admissibility and relevance of evidence, and the tribunal therefore has the power to determine the procedural rules applicable to witness testimony.[62] **11.51**

The arbitral tribunal, or either party with prior authorization of the tribunal, may request the assistance of court in taking evidence.[63] The 2011 reforms added article 1466 to the Commercial Code, which provides that the procedure for obtaining judicial assistance in the taking of evidence[64] will be that for 'voluntary' or non-contentious jurisdiction, as regulated by the Federal Civil Procedure Code. One might conclude that the general rules of evidence set forth in the Civil Procedure Code would be applied by courts assisting in the taking of evidence in support of arbitration, but there has not yet been case law interpreting this provision in the arbitration context. **11.52**

11.3.4 Local requirements for the conduct of arbitration hearings

The parties are free to determine the place of arbitration. In the absence of such agreement, the arbitral tribunal will determine it, taking into consideration the circumstances of the case. Unless otherwise agreed by the parties, the arbitral tribunal may hold meetings, deliberate, hear the parties or experts, or inspect any goods, property, or documents in any place it sees fit.[65] **11.53**

Default procedural provisions in the absence of agreement of the parties

The parties are free to agree on the procedure to be followed by the arbitral tribunal. In the absence of agreement, the tribunal may conduct the proceedings as it deems appropriate, provided the parties are treated equally and given the opportunity to present their case.[66] In addition, the Commercial Code contains certain default rules for the conduct of the arbitration. **11.54**

Unless otherwise agreed by the parties, the proceedings commence on the date on which the respondent receives the request for arbitration.[67] The parties are free to determine the language or languages in which the proceedings are conducted. In the absence of agreement, the arbitral tribunal will make the determination.[68] **11.55**

Within the time agreed by the parties or established by the tribunal, and unless the parties have agreed otherwise, the claimant must submit the facts and circumstances on which the claim is based, the issues in dispute, and the relief sought, and the respondent must respond to all matters set forth in the claim. The parties may include in these submissions any documents they deem appropriate, or make reference to the documents or other evidence they will submit. Unless otherwise agreed, the parties may modify or supplement the claim or **11.56**

---

[62] Commercial Code, art 1435.
[63] Commercial Code, art 1444.
[64] Commercial Code, art 1466 also applies to the court appointment of arbitrators and consultation on the fees of the arbitral tribunal.
[65] Commercial Code, art 1436.
[66] Commercial Code, arts 1434 and 1435.
[67] Commercial Code, art 1437.
[68] Commercial Code, art 1438.

defence, unless the arbitral tribunal considers that such amendment is not appropriate in view of the delay involved.[69]

11.57 Unless otherwise agreed by the parties, the arbitral tribunal will decide whether to hold hearings for the presentation of evidence or oral argument, or to conduct the proceedings based solely on documentary and other materials. If the parties have not agreed to dispense with oral hearings, the arbitral tribunal must hold such hearings at an appropriate stage of the proceedings, upon request of either party.[70]

11.58 The parties must be given sufficient advance notice of the commencement of any hearings, as well as of any meetings to be held by the arbitral tribunal for the inspection of goods, other property, or documents. Any statements, documentary evidence, expert reports, or other information provided to the tribunal by one of the parties, must be communicated to the other party.[71]

11.59 Pursuant to the provisions of the Commercial Code, and unless otherwise agreed by the parties, if, without sufficient cause, the claimant does not file its statement of claim as just outlined, the tribunal must terminate the proceedings. If the respondent fails, without sufficient cause, to file its statement of defence, the tribunal must continue the proceedings, without treating such failure as an admission of the claimant's allegations. If either party fails to appear at a hearing or to produce documentary evidence, the arbitral tribunal may continue the proceedings and issue the award based on the evidence before it.[72]

11.60 Unless otherwise agreed by the parties, the arbitral tribunal has the power to appoint experts to report to it on specific issues, and may require the parties to provide such experts with any relevant documents, goods, or other property.[73]

11.61 Unless otherwise agreed by the parties, at the request of either party or if the arbitral tribunal deems it necessary, the expert must, after submitting his or her report, either orally or in writing, attend a hearing at which the parties are given the opportunity to ask any questions and present expert witnesses to testify about the points at issue.[74]

11.3.5 Foreign practitioners

11.62 Unless otherwise agreed by the parties, there are no restrictions regarding the nationality of counsel or arbitrators. The parties may freely agree on the number, appointment procedure, and requirements applicable to arbitrators.[75] Consequently, the only limitation is that arbitrators must be impartial and independent.

11.63 In connection with the payment of taxes and specifically regarding value added tax (VAT), both foreign and domestic arbitrators' fees are taxed in Mexico whenever the services of the arbitrators are performed within Mexican territory or have an effect on Mexican parties. In this regard, the VAT payable can and must be included in the costs of arbitration.

---

69 Commercial Code, art 1439.
70 Commercial Code, art 1440.
71 Commercial Code, art 1440.
72 Commercial Code, art 1441.
73 Commercial Code, art 1442.
74 Commercial Code, art 1443.
75 Commercial Code, art 1427.

Domestic arbitrators' fees are also subject to income tax in Mexico. Determining the rules applicable to foreign arbitrators is complex because Mexico is a party to several treaties for the avoidance of double taxation. The rules applicable to foreign arbitrators must therefore be determined in each particular case. Generally speaking, there are two basic criteria for the payment of taxes by foreign residents. According to the first criterion, the source of the income is considered: income will be taxed if it is related preponderantly to Mexican territory. The second criterion relates to the permanent establishment of the service provider and is contained in several taxation treaties and the Income Tax Law, which establishes that revenues from salaries and from the rendering of personal services by individuals or entities residing abroad and having no permanent establishment within Mexican territory (or having an establishment unrelated to the services), are exempt from the payment of income tax, provided the foreign arbitrators' stay, in the national territory, was less than 183 calendar days, consecutive or otherwise, in a 12-month period.[76] **11.64**

11.4 The Award

11.4.1 Mandatory rules as to form

Pursuant to the Commercial Code, the award must be in writing and signed by the arbitrators; if there is more than one arbitrator, the signatures of a majority will be sufficient, as long as the reasons why any remaining arbitrators failed to sign are set forth.[77] Although there are no specific provisions regarding dissenting opinions, it can be inferred from this that dissenting opinions are permitted. **11.65**

The award must be reasoned, unless the parties have agreed otherwise or have reached a settlement. Likewise, the award must set forth the date it was rendered and the place where it is deemed to have been made. After the award is made, the tribunal must give notice to the parties by delivering to them a signed copy of the award. **11.66**

The arbitral tribunal may correct any errors of computation, any clerical or typographical errors, or errors of a similar nature on its own initiative within 30 days from the date of the award. Unless the parties agree on a different time period, within 30 days after a final award is entered, either party may, upon due notice, request the tribunal to correct any such errors, or, if the parties have so agreed, to give an interpretation of an issue or a specific part of the award. If the tribunal considers this justified, it must make the correction or give the interpretation requested within 30 days from receipt of the request. Any such interpretation is deemed to form part of the award.[78] **11.67**

11.4.2 Mandatory rules as to substance

Costs

The costs of the arbitration include the fees of the arbitral tribunal, travel and other expenses incurred by the arbitrators, the fees for expert advice or any other assistance required by the tribunal, travel and other expenses incurred by witnesses if approved by the arbitral tribunal, the costs and legal fees of the prevailing party if they are claimed during the arbitration and **11.68**

[76] Income Tax Law, art 181.
[77] Commercial Code, art 1448.
[78] Commercial Code, art 1450.

only in an amount approved by the arbitral tribunal as reasonable, and the fees and expenses of the institution that designated the arbitrators.[79]

11.69 There are no legal limitations on the recovery of costs in arbitration, provided they are reasonable and take into consideration the amount in dispute, the complexity of the matter, the time spent by the arbitrators, and any other circumstances relevant to the case.

11.70 As a general rule, the costs of the arbitration are borne by the losing party. The arbitral tribunal has the discretion to apportion the costs on a pro rata basis between the parties, if appropriate and after considering the specific circumstances of the dispute.

11.71 Notwithstanding the foregoing, the parties are free to agree, either directly or through the adoption of institutional rules, on other provisions regarding the arbitration costs, and the tribunal will be bound by such agreement.[80]

11.72 The Commercial Code provides that if the parties have not agreed on any rules, the tribunal is entitled to decide on the arbitrators' fees, which must be reasonable, bearing in mind the amount in dispute, the complexity of the matter, and the time spent by the arbitrators. The fees of each arbitrator must be indicated separately and fixed by the arbitral tribunal.

11.73 Notwithstanding the foregoing, upon the request of a party, the arbitral tribunal will fix its fees after consulting with the court, which may intervene and make any observations and clarifications it deems appropriate.

11.74 Regarding the parties' costs of representation and legal assistance, the arbitral tribunal, taking into account the specific circumstances of the case, is empowered to decide which party will pay such costs or to apportion them between the parties if it considers this reasonable.[81]

11.75 When the tribunal issues any order for the termination of the arbitral proceedings, or an award pursuant to terms agreed by the parties, the tribunal must fix the arbitration costs in the order or award. In the event that any interpretation, correction, or completion of the award is needed, the arbitral tribunal may not charge additional fees.[82]

Damages and interest

11.76 Under Mexican law, only compensatory damages are available. Punitive damages cannot be awarded.[83]

11.77 Arbitrators may award interest, but only if it is requested during the proceedings. If parties have requested interest without specifying the applicable rate, the statutory interest rate of 6 per cent in commercial matters and 9 per cent in civil matters will apply.

11.5 After the Award

11.78 The 2011 amendments to the arbitration statute included new provisions on the recognition and enforcement of arbitral awards, pursuant to which awards are presumed to be valid and

[79] Commercial Code, art 1416(IV).
[80] Commercial Code, art 1452.
[81] Commercial Code, art 1455.
[82] Commercial Code, art 1455.
[83] Federal Civil Code, arts 2108 and 2110.

binding, and can be set aside upon request of a party only on the exceptional grounds specifically contemplated by the law.

11.5.1 Local standards for setting aside/annulment

Grounds

Under article 1457 of the Commercial Code, arbitral awards may be set aside by the competent court only if the party requesting the annulment proves: **11.79**

(1) that one of the parties to the arbitration agreement was subject to a legal incapacity, or the agreement is null and void pursuant to the laws chosen by the parties or pursuant to Mexican law if no other law was chosen by the parties;
(2) that the applicant was not given proper notice of the appointment of one of the arbitrators or of the arbitration proceedings, or was otherwise unable to present his case;
(3) that the award deals with a dispute not contemplated in the arbitration agreement, or contains decisions that exceed the scope of the arbitration agreement (if parts of the award that refer to matters falling under the arbitration agreement can be separated from those that do not, only the latter will be set aside); or
(4) that the constitution of the arbitral tribunal or the arbitration procedure were not in accordance with the agreement between the parties, unless such agreement contravenes any provision of the Commercial Code that the parties cannot waive, or, in the absence of any agreement, is not in accordance with the Code.

An arbitral award may also be set aside if the court finds, according to Mexican law, that the subject matter of the dispute is not arbitrable or the award is contrary to public policy.[84] **11.80**

Procedure

An application to set aside an award must be filed within three months from the date of notice of the award to the parties. However, in the event that either party requests the tribunal to correct any errors of the award, to give an interpretation of such award, or to render an additional award regarding claims presented in the proceedings but omitted from consideration in the award, the aforementioned three-month period begins on the date on which that request is disposed of by the arbitral tribunal.[85] **11.81**

One of the main advantages of the Mexican approach towards arbitration is that there is no right of appeal against arbitral awards under the Commercial Code. Consequently, when a party files a petition before the competent court to set aside the award, the court is not authorized to review the merits of the dispute or to set aside the award based on errors of law. The challenge of arbitral awards is limited to the restrictive grounds provided in article 1457 of the Commercial Code. The provisions of article 1457 are public-policy related and cannot be excluded by the parties. **11.82**

Timing

Pursuant to the Commercial Code, the setting aside or annulment of arbitral awards involves a special procedure applicable to commercial transactions and arbitration.[86] **11.83**

[84] Commercial Code, s II, art 1457.
[85] Commercial Code, art 1458.
[86] Commercial Code, art 1470(V).

11.84 Once the request has been filed, the court must summon the parties and provide the respondent with a period of 15 days in which to submit an answer. Upon the expiration of this period and if the parties do not offer any evidence and the court does not deem this necessary, the parties will be summoned to a hearing, to take place within the following three days, with or without the parties. If the parties produce evidence or if the court deems it necessary to hear evidence, an evidentiary period of ten days will be granted. Once that hearing is held, the judge will summon the parties to hear the final resolution.[87] Intermediate resolutions and the final resolution rendered in this special procedure are not subject to appeal.[88]

11.85 This special procedure promotes the speed and efficiency of the arbitral process. The final judicial resolution with respect to the award may be challenged through a constitutional procedure known as an *amparo* proceeding.[89] An *amparo* is an exceptional remedy that can be filed in the event the final judicial resolution (the decision enforcing the award, rejecting its enforcement, or setting it aside) infringed fundamental rights provided under the Federal Constitution.[90] Only in cases in which there was an infringement of fundamental rights should *amparo* relief be granted. This has not, however, entirely prevented its abuse as a dilatory tactic. The resolution of the *amparo* may take between six months and one year, depending on the complexity of the case and the courts' workload.

11.5.2 Recognition and enforcement of foreign awards

11.86 Regardless of the country in which an award was rendered, it is deemed to be valid and binding and will be enforced upon written request to the court. The party relying on an award or requesting its enforcement must file the duly authenticated original award or a certified copy of it, together with the original arbitration agreement or a certified copy. If the award or arbitration agreement is not in Spanish, the party must file a certified translation.[91]

11.87 It is relevant to note that no official confirmation procedure is needed for the recognition and enforcement of awards.[92] Pursuant to the Commercial Code, recognition and enforcement

---

[87] Commercial Code, art 1476.

[88] Commercial Code, art 1476.

[89] The Political Constitution of the United Mexican States, arts 103 and 107; the Law of Amparo, art 1.

[90] The Political Constitution of the United Mexican States, art 107(V); the Law of Amparo, art 1.

[91] Commercial Code, art 1461.

[92] According to the Federal Code of Civil Procedure, art 569, foreign judgments shall be effective and recognized in Mexico, except for those contrary to national public policy. Pursuant to the Federal Code of Civil Procedure, art 570, an official confirmation procedure must be followed in order for a foreign judgment, excluding awards, to be compulsorily enforced in the Mexican Republic.

Any foreign party should bear in mind that Mexican courts are willing to recognize and enforce a foreign judgment provided that:

- the formalities and conditions regarding rogatory letters have been met;
- the resolution did not result from the exercise of an action in rem;
- the foreign court had correctly assumed jurisdiction;
- the claim was properly served on the defendant;
- the foreign judgment is non-appealable and *res judicata* in the country in which it was rendered;
- the action that gave rise to the resolution is not a pending matter between the same parties in Mexican courts; and
- the judgment does not conflict with a mandatory law or Mexican public policy.

The court may deny the recognition and enforcement of a foreign judgment if the country in which the judgment was rendered, does not recognize or enforce foreign judgments in analogous cases.

According to Federal Code of Civil Procedure, art 572, the court that requests assistance to enforce a judgment must send a copy of the judgment duly authenticated and also a copy of the court file in order to prove that: (a) the claim was properly served on the defendant and (b) the foreign judgment is non-appealable and

of awards is obtained through the same special procedure for commercial transactions and arbitration that applies to annulment.[93]

The recognition or enforcement of an award will be denied only if the party opposing it proves that (a) one of the parties to the arbitration agreement was subject to a legal incapacity, (b) the agreement is null and void pursuant to the laws chosen by the parties or pursuant to the law of the country in which the award was issued; (c) the party opposing enforcement was not given proper notice of the appointment of an arbitrator or of the arbitration proceedings, or was otherwise unable to present his case; (d) the award deals with a dispute not contemplated by the arbitration agreement or contains decisions that exceed the scope of the arbitration agreement;[94] (e) the constitution of the arbitral tribunal or the arbitration proceedings was not in accordance with the agreement between the parties, or in the absence of such agreement, not in accordance with the law of the country in which the arbitration was conducted; or (f) the award is not yet binding upon the parties or was annulled or suspended by the courts of the country in which it was rendered or to whose laws it was subject.[95] **11.88**

Likewise, the recognition and enforcement of an arbitral award may be denied if the court finds that according to Mexican law, the subject matter of the dispute is not arbitrable, or the recognition and enforcement of the award is contrary to public policy. **11.89**

For all matters related to setting aside proceedings and recognition and enforcement of arbitral awards, the competent court is the court of first instance with jurisdiction in the place where the respondent is domiciled or where his assets are located. **11.90**

Due process

As noted previously, the internationally accepted standards provided by the New York Convention for the validity of arbitral awards have been recognized and adopted by Mexican law. In both the setting aside and recognition and enforcement of arbitral awards, due process is an indispensable requirement for the validity of an award. Under Mexican standards, due process is directly related to the opportunity of the parties to present their case and to assert a proper defense. **11.91**

In this regard, article 1434 of the Commercial Code provides that 'the parties shall be treated equally and be given a full opportunity to present their case'. This Model Law provision echoes the essential due process requirements established by article 14 of the Political Constitution of the United Mexican States, according to which due process formalities are those that allow and guarantee parties an accurate and appropriate defence before any act that deprives them of their life, freedom, properties, possessions, or rights. **11.92**

Mexican judicial precedent has established the following essential elements of due process: (a) that the parties are duly notified of the commencement of the proceeding and of its consequences; (b) that they are given the opportunity to submit and present any evidence on which their defence relies; (c) that they are given the opportunity to comment on the other party's defences; and (d) that a decision is issued in which all matters in dispute are resolved. **11.93**

---

res judicata in the country in which it was rendered. The necessary translations of the documents must also be provided. The requesting party must designate a domicile in the place of enforcement, for receiving notices.

93 Commercial Code, art 1471.

94 Provided, however, that if the provisions of the award which refer to matters subject to the arbitration can be separated from those which are not, only the latter will not be enforced.

95 Commercial Code, art 1462.

Failure to satisfy any of these requirements constitutes a violation of due process.[96] The Mexican concept of 'full opportunity to assert one's rights' is the same essential requirement of due process recognized in other jurisdictions, under concepts of 'natural justice', 'a reasonable opportunity of presenting a case', the 'right to be heard', the 'confrontation principle', the 'right to be treated equally', etc.[97]

11.94 The concept of 'full opportunity' in article 1434 of the Commercial Code has nevertheless led to some ambiguity. Some argue that a measure adopted or ordered by an arbitral tribunal will be deemed to violate due process if it obstructs in any way the parties' right to take any procedural steps. Others consider that the congruence between the actions taken by the tribunal and the principle of due process should be determined in each particular case, according to the procedural features selected by the parties. The rationale for the second view is that when parties chose arbitration to settle their disputes, it may be inferred that they intended to avoid the rigid formalities and unnecessary delays of judicial proceedings.[98]

11.6 Practical Information

11.95 In Mexico, hearings are usually held at hotel business centres, or at domestic arbitral institutions that have facilities for holding hearings, such as the Arbitration and Mediation Commission of the Mexico City Chamber of Commerce (CANACO)[99] and the Mexican Arbitration Center (CAM).[100]

11.96 If interpreters are needed, Mexico has many fluent English speakers who can provide services. Additionally, Mexico offers capable reporters for transcribing the hearings.

11.7 Conclusion

11.97 This chapter outlines the advantages, efficiency, and expediency of judicial proceedings involving arbitrations seated in Mexico. The arbitration community has turned its eyes to Mexico as an attractive venue in which to conduct arbitration, because of its complete and exhaustive legal framework, coupled with the availability of effective judicial assistance.

[96] Judicial Precedent entitled 'Essential Procedural Formalities are those that Guarantee the Accurate and Opportune Defense Prior to the Depriving Act' (May 1992) Register No 205, 679.

[97] F Gonzalez de Cossío, *Arbitraje* (1st edn, Porrúa, 2004) 218.

[98] Gonzalez de Cossío (n 97) 217.

[99] The Arbitration and Mediation Commission of the Mexico City Chamber of Commerce (CANACO) is a non-profit organization located at Paseo de la Reforma No 42, Delegación Cuauhtémoc, CP 06040, Mexico City, Federal District <http://www.arbitrajecanaco.com.mx>.

[100] The CAM was created in 1997. The organization is located at Tecnológico de Monterrey, Campus Santa Fe, Av Carlos Lazo No 100, Edificio Aulas 1, Nivel 5, Col Santa Fe, México, Federal District, CP 01389 <http://www.camex.com.mx>.

12

MOSCOW

Mikhail Ivanov and Inna Manassyan

12.1 Background

12.1.1 The history and development of arbitration in Russia

During Soviet times, arbitration was less widely used for settling commercial disputes than in European countries. In the 1920s, arbitral tribunals were able to consider only certain civil law disputes between and among private entities, and were subject to strict state control. Moreover, arbitration agreements with respect to future disputes were not recognized as valid.[1] **12.01**

Nevertheless, some forms of arbitration were in use in the Soviet Union. In the 1920s, arbitration commissions were established at commodity and stock exchanges that were competent to consider disputes between participants of those organizations. The state made **12.02**

[1] Arbitration Court Regulations, art 2, appended to ch 22 of the Civil Procedural Code (Civil Proc Code) Russian Soviet Federatove Socialist Republic (RSFSR), as amended on 16 October 1924, provided for the ability of any party in the event of the conclusion among them of an agreement on the consideration by an arbitration court of 'all disputes altogether or all disputes of a certain kind as may arise henceforth' to apply, nevertheless, to a state court for resolution of their dispute in accordance with the general rules of the applicable Civil Proc Code.

numerous attempts to regulate the activities of these arbitration commissions, including attempts by state judicial bodies to exercise control over them.

12.03 Soviet arbitration entered a new phase with the formation of the Foreign Trade Arbitration Commission (FTAC) of the All-Union Chamber of Commerce of the USSR in 1932.[2] The task of the FTAC was to provide for arbitration in the Soviet Union of disputes arising between Soviet foreign trade associations and their foreign partners in export-import transactions.

12.04 In this connection, amendments were made to article 3 of the Civil Procedure Code of the RSFSR of 10 January 1934, to provide that:

> . . . disputes arising from international trade transactions, in particular, disputes between foreign companies and Soviet economic organizations shall be considered by the foreign trade arbitration commission of the All Union Chamber of Commerce in international arbitration procedures in accordance with the special regulations on the same.[3]

This minimized the risk that an arbitration agreement in contracts between Soviet foreign trade organizations and foreign companies with respect to potential disputes would be deemed invalid.

12.05 Before the creation of the FTAC, neither USSR law nor the law of the Soviet Republics provided rules for the arbitration of foreign trade disputes using a permanent, non-state arbitration institution. The establishment of the FTAC as a permanent arbitration institution for the consideration of international commercial disputes was therefore of considerable significance for the development of foreign trade arbitration practice in the USSR, as it created a platform on which arbitration with a seat in the USSR could be proposed to foreign partners. FTAC arbitration clauses were included in a number of international trade agreements concluded by the Soviet Union during the pre-war period.

12.06 In the 1950s and 1960s, on the wave of a post-war economic resurgence, the use of arbitration in resolving economic disputes increased significantly. To that end, a number of laws were enacted with the aim of improving domestic arbitration procedure.[4] However, the sphere of arbitration remained over-regulated. This manifested itself, for example, in the fact that executive bodies of the state had the right to approve the rosters of arbitrators.[5] State courts could examine arbitral decisions at the time of enforcement, essentially intervening in the substance of the award on the basis of the 'principle of lawfulness' and verifying the merits of the arbitral tribunal's decision.[6] This was a reflection of the state's sceptical attitude to arbitration, whether domestic or foreign.

12.07 It therefore comes as no surprise that foreign entities were reluctant to agree on arbitration under the FTAC or MAC Rules, despite the insistence of their Soviet counterparties. In the 1970s, rapidly developing trade between the United States and the Soviet Union led to the

---

[2] VtsIK and SNK USSR Resolution on the Foreign Trade Arbitration Commission of the All-Union Chamber of Commerce, Collected Legislation of the USSR 1932 No 48, art 281 (17 June 1932).

[3] AS Komarov, 'Three quarters of a century in step with the times: 75 years of ICAC' in AS Komarov (ed), *International Commercial Arbitration: Compilation of Articles on the 75th Anniversary of the International Commercial Arbitration Court of the RF Chamber of Commerce and Industry* (Statut, 2007).

[4] OY Skvortsov, *Arbitration of Business Disputes in Russia: Problems, Tendencies, Perspectives* (Wolters Kluwer, 2005) para 1.2.

[5] Skvortsov (n 4) para 1.2.

[6] EV Tikhonova, *Litigation and Arbitration Procedures* (Izdatelstvo RV Pershina, 2011) s V(1).

search for mutually acceptable arbitration rules and venues that were not native to either party. For that purpose, the American Arbitration Association and the USSR Chamber of Commerce and Industry agreed on Sweden as a location that had the basic characteristics acceptable to both countries.[7] The Stockholm Chamber of Commerce (SCC) was recognized in the 1970s by the United States and the Soviet Union as a neutral centre for the resolution of East-West trade disputes.

In January 1977, a tailored model clause was drafted for use in contracts between US parties and Soviet foreign trade organizations. This model clause provided for arbitration in Sweden under the UNCITRAL Rules, with the SCC having the authority to appoint the presiding arbitrator.[8] The tradition of referring East-West disputes to the SCC continued after the fall of the Soviet Union in the early 1990s, when trade with the United States was revived. **12.08**

Following the collapse of the Soviet Union, the rise of private enterprise and the abandonment of the state's monopoly on foreign economic activities enabled numerous enterprises and companies of all kinds to enter into foreign trade. The increase in the number of Russian actors in international commerce led to a corresponding increase in the number of foreign trade disputes. In response to the changes taking place in society, the attitude towards international commercial arbitration also underwent a sea change: for the first time, a complete legislative framework was created for arbitration in international trade. In Russia, a number of important arbitration laws were adopted: **12.09**

- The Interim Regulations on the Arbitration Court for Economic Dispute Resolution, approved by the Russian Federation Supreme Soviet on 24 June 1992. These regulations, in particular, provided for the right to establish arbitration institutions for resolving domestic and international disputes at chambers of commerce, associations, exchanges, and other organizations. This broke the monopoly on international commercial dispute resolution previously held by two arbitration institutions (the Maritime Arbitration Commission of the All-Union Chamber of Commerce of the USSR and FTAC; now, respectively, the Maritime Arbitration Commission (MAC) and the International Commercial Arbitration Court (ICAC) of the Russian Federation Chamber of Commerce and Industry);
- The Russian Federation Law on International Commercial Arbitration of 7 July 1993 (ICA Law), in particular, approved new Regulations on the ICAC and MAC. The ICA Law itself is based on the 1985 UNCITRAL Model Law on International Commercial Arbitration (Model Law). The ICAC Regulations fix ICAC's status as an independent, permanent arbitration centre carrying out its activities in accordance with the ICA Law. The ICA Law grants the Chamber of Commerce and Industry of the Russian Federation (CCI) the power to approve the ICAC Rules, the procedure for calculating arbitration fees, arbitrator remuneration, and other expenses, and requires the Chamber to lend the institution assistance.

With respect to international treaties, Russia succeeded to all the multilateral and bilateral arbitration treaties of the USSR, including the 1958 New York Convention on the Recognition and Enforcement of Foreign Arbitral Awards (New York Convention).[9] **12.10**

---

[7] HM Holtzmann, 'Dispute Resolution Procedures in East-West Trade' (1979)13 Intl LJ 233, 242–3.

[8] Holtzmann (n 7) 242–3.

[9] The Soviet Union was party to a number of international treaties concluded with respect to international arbitration, both multilateral and bilateral, including the 1958 New York Convention on the Recognition

The Russian Federation signed the 1965 Washington Convention on the Settlement of International Investment Disputes in 1992, but it has not been ratified or entered into force.

12.11 At this stage of its development, Russia largely follows international standards regulating commercial arbitration. Today, in principle, the merits of an arbitral award cannot be reviewed by a state court, and state supervision of arbitration has been moved to the appeal and enforcement phase. The enforcement of international commercial arbitral awards may be denied, or awards set aside, on a number of limited grounds set by law.

12.12 At the same time, for Russian court practice, particularly in the lower courts, most of the issues encountered by a court when it applies international law or international instruments concerning international arbitration continue to be new and unfamiliar. Unfortunately, in many cases Russian courts tend to exercise an overcautious approach to these sources.

12.13 Another impediment to the wider use of arbitration in Russia is the tendency of state courts to review the arbitral tribunal's decision on the merits as part of the exercise of their lawful power to supervise the compliance of arbitration proceedings with mandatory provisions of law. In fact, Russian state courts tend to apply a broad interpretation to these mandatory rules, effectively circumventing the general rule that an arbitral tribunal's decision on the merits of the dispute is final.

12.14 Thus, judicial practice in Russia on matters relating to international commercial arbitration has yet to reach a point of stability. At the same time, it must be noted that the situation has begun to improve in recent times, undoubtedly assisted by the Russian Federation (RF) Supreme Commercial Court's[10] analysis and recommendations issued in the form of overviews of judicial practice.[11] Russian court practice is expected to become more predictable as international approaches to resolving matters in international commercial arbitration begin to find acceptance.

12.1.2 Recent developments

12.15 Certain Russian rules on arbitration introduced in the early 1990s no longer reflect current international standards. The groundwork is now in place for further modernization of Russian arbitration legislation and the elimination of some of the legal impediments to the normal functioning of arbitration proceedings.

---

and Enforcement of Foreign Arbitral Awards (New York Convention), the 1961 Geneva Convention, and the 1992 Agreement on the Procedure for Resolution of Disputes Relating to Economic Activities (Kyiv Treaty), concluded between some of the CIS member states.

[10] *Vysshiy Arbitrazhniy Sud* (Supreme Commercial Court of the Russian Federation). The Russian commercial courts are a system of state courts that have jurisdiction over most commercial disputes and many other cases involving business entities. Another frequently used English translation for the system of Russian commercial courts is '*arbitrazh* courts'. It is important to note that '*arbitrazh* courts' are not arbitral tribunals and do not conduct arbitration. In addition, as in the name 'International Commercial Arbitration Court', the word 'court' is often used to designate what is in fact an arbitral institution.

[11] eg Information Letter of the Presidium of the RF Supreme Commercial Court No 156 (26 February 2013); Information Letter of the Presidium of the RF Supreme Commercial Court No 58 (18 January 2001); Information Letter of the Presidium of the RF Supreme Commercial Court No 96 (22 December 2005). See also Decision of the Presidium of the RF Supreme Commercial Court No 5243/06 (19 September 2006); Decision of the Presidium of the RF Supreme Commercial Court No 10718/08 (20 January 2009); Decision of the Presidium of the RF Supreme Commercial Court No 9899/09 (13 September 2011); Decision of the Presidium of the RF Supreme Commercial Court No 6478/11 (18 October 2011).

In keeping with this objective, and in order to bring applicable Russian law into line with internationally recognized approaches to the regulation of arbitration, a federal bill on amendments to the ICA Law was introduced in the Russian Parliament in 2011.[12] The draft is based on amendments to the Model Law adopted by the United Nations Commission on International Trade Law in 2006. The bill was adopted by the State Duma (the lower chamber of the Russian Parliament) in its first reading on 25 January 2012, and the ICA Law is expected to be amended in 2013–14. **12.16**

The proposed amendments cover general issues such as the form of an arbitration agreement and provisions on interim measures. They also facilitate the procedure for the recognition and enforcement of an arbitral award by excluding the arbitration agreement from the list of documents that need to be provided to the court by the party seeking enforcement. The only document required by the amended ICA Law is the arbitral award. **12.17**

Other proposed amendments to the ICA Law pertain to the form of the arbitration agreement. The Model Law offers two ways of regulating the form of an arbitration agreement: the first consists of a detailed description of the options for satisfying the written form requirement, taking into consideration current practice in the conclusion of commercial agreements, while the second, 'alternative', option does not include formal requirements for the agreement. The proposal for amending the Russian ICA Law follows the first option. **12.18**

In line with the Model Law, the ICA Law is expected to provide that an arbitration agreement is considered to be in writing if it is set down in any form, including electronic communication. However, the bill supplements this Model Law definition by adding that the form should enable the recording of the information contained therein or make it accessible for subsequent use. **12.19**

The general provisions pertaining to the rights of the arbitral tribunal to order interim measures, both in the federal bill of amendments to the ICA Law and in the Model Law, remain unchanged. At the same time, the bill introduces additional provisions on the ability to grant interim measures in any form, on the conditions for the granting of interim measures, and on the temporary nature of such measures. In addition to these provisions, the bill provides for granting preliminary orders for interim measures on an *ex parte* application and the specific regime for obtaining this relief. In particular, the bill provides that such preliminary orders apply only to the parties, and do not constitute an arbitral award capable of judicial enforcement. **12.20**

Another proposed amendment is the new wording of article 34(1) of the ICA Law, in accordance with which the parties may provide in the arbitration agreement that the arbitral award is final. The law previously permitted agreements giving arbitral awards finality only in domestic arbitration cases.[13] An identical provision is now proposed for the ICA Law—eliminating the chance of the arbitral award being reviewed in judicial supervision—if the parties agree in their arbitration agreement that the arbitral award is to be deemed final. This **12.21**

---

[12] Draft amendments to the ICA Law, available at <http://base.consultant.ru/cons/cgi/online.cgi?req=doc;base=PRJ;n=88337;fld=134;dst=4294967295>.

[13] Federal Law No 102-FZ 'On Arbitration Courts in the Russian Federation' (24 July 2002), art 40.

means that the parties may exclude recourse for setting aside the award. However, this will not prevent a party from objecting to enforcement.

12.22 This amendment codifies existing practice. Although there is no analogous provision in the ICA Law allowing parties to exclude setting aside by providing for a 'final' award, the state commercial courts have begun to extend this rule to international arbitration. In *EuroPol Gaz v Gazprom Export*, the RF Supreme Commercial Court held that if the intent of the parties to the contract was that the ICAC's decisions be final and binding, a party would not have the option of applying to a state court to have the award set aside, and if such an application were made the proceedings should be dismissed.[14] The RF Supreme Commercial Court cited paragraph 44 of the ICAC Rules, pursuant to which ICAC decisions are final and binding as of the date they are handed down, are to be complied with by the parties voluntarily in the established timeframe, and, if not performed, are enforceable in accordance with the law and international treaties. The court noted that any violations of arbitral procedure that could serve as grounds for the setting aside of an award could be brought to light during court proceedings seeking enforcement.

12.23 As part of the general modernization of the arbitration process, on 23 June 2010, the CCI adopted amendments to the ICAC Rules, allowing, *inter alia*, the parties to take part in hearings via videoconference. As part of the same modernization of arbitration practice, on 27 August 2010, the CCI endorsed Rules on Impartiality and Independence of Arbitrators that are similar (although not identical) to the IBA Guidelines on Conflicts of Interest in International Arbitration. Like the IBA's Guidelines, the Rules on Impartiality and Independence are of an advisory nature, but are likely to apply in ICAC proceedings, as well as providing guidelines on conflicts of interest rules for the Russian state courts when seised with challenges to arbitrators.

12.1.3 Comparison with other regional or national venues

12.24 Historically, Moscow has been the main arbitration venue in Russia. This remains the case today. As discussed, two major arbitration institutions in Russia—the Maritime Arbitration Commission (MAC) and the ICAC—were established in Moscow in the 1930s. The ICAC is the leading arbitration institution in Russia and Eastern Europe that deals with the resolution of international disputes. In 2012 the ICAC received 241 claims with claimants from 47 countries.[15]

12.25 MAC was originally founded for the consideration of disputes arising out of the salvage of shipping and sea cargo, but now hears both traditional disputes arising from contracts of carriage, marine insurance, rescue, collision between seagoing vessels, fishing operations, and disputes incidental to broker and agency contracts, repair of vessels, vessel management, and others in the area of the maritime trade and traffic. Both ICAC and MAC are independent and permanent arbitration institutions operating in accordance with the ICA Law, and the respective rules and statutes of the ICAC and MAC are annexed to the ICA Law.

12.26 Other major arbitral venues within the Russian Federation and more globally in the Eastern European region include the arbitration institutes of the St Petersburg Chamber of

---

[14] *EuroPol Gaz v Gazprom Export* Ruling of the RF Supreme Commercial Court No VAS-15525/09 (29 December 2009).

[15] <http://www.tpprf-mkac.ru/ru/whatis/-2012->.

Commerce and Industry,[16] the Ukrainian Chamber of Commerce and Industry,[17] and the Chambers of Commerce and Industry of the Republic of Kazakhstan[18] and the Republic of Belarus.[19] As a general rule, arbitration institutions in the region started to function in their present capacity in the 1990s, following the collapse of the Soviet Union.

12.2 Commencing Arbitration

12.2.1 The arbitration agreement as a bar to court proceedings

According to the ICA Law if, despite the existence of an arbitration agreement, an action concerning a dispute is commenced in a state court, the court must, upon the timely request of a party, stay proceedings and refer the parties to arbitration, unless it determines that the agreement is null and void, inoperative, or incapable of being performed.[20] This provision of the ICA Law is similar to Article 8(1) of the Model Law, on which it is based. Apart from prohibiting state court interference in a dispute that is subject to an international arbitration agreement, this statutory provision gives Russian state courts the authority to conduct a *prima facie* examination of the existence and validity of the arbitration agreement before the commencement of arbitration.[21] **12.27**

This provision of the ICA Law is widely applied by Russian courts, which regularly decline jurisdiction[22] and direct the parties to arbitration. In one recent case, a Russian court had no difficulty referring the parties in a multi-contract dispute to arbitration when a main construction contract contained an arbitration agreement referring to the SCC arbitration all disputes arising from or in connection with the contract. At the same time, an assignment agreement concluded by one of the parties with a third party included a forum-selection clause providing that all disputes under that agreement were to be considered by the St Petersburg and Leningrad Oblast Commercial Court. The other party—the contractor—applied to the commercial court for invalidation of the assignment agreement, on the ground that it had not consented to the transfer of the debt under the construction contract. The court refused to hear the case, ruling that the contractor was not a party to the assignment agreement, and therefore the forum selection clause did not apply. The court also noted that the action was based on the contract, and was therefore to be considered in arbitration.[23] **12.28**

In another recent unreported case, the claimant brought an action in the Moscow Commercial Court, despite the fact that the contract on which it was based contained **12.29**

[16] See <http://www.spbcci.ru/engarbitaltribunal>.

[17] See <http://www.ucci.org.ua/arb/icac/en/icac.html>.

[18] See <http://www.cci.kz/index.php/ru/arbitrazh-pri-tpp-rk>.

[19] See <http://www.cci.by/en/node/158>.

[20] ICA Law, art 8(1); cf New York Convention, Art II. Further, ICA Law, art 8(2) repeats the Model Law provision (where an action has been brought to a court, arbitral proceedings may nevertheless be commenced or continued, and an award may be made, while the issue is pending before the court).

[21] NG Vilkova, AS Komarov, and AN Prisyazhnuk, *Statutory Regulation of the International Commercial Operations in the Russian Federation: Textbook* (2nd edn, GOU VPO VAVT of the Ministry of Economic Development of the Russian Federation, 2009) para 6.3.

[22] There are currently differences in terminology between the ICA Law, art 8 which prescribes dismissal of the case, and the RF Arbitral Procedure Code (APC), art 148.5(1) in accordance with which the case should be dismissed without prejudice. As a rule, Russian courts defer to the APC and dismiss the cases without prejudice.

[23] Ruling of the St Petersburg and Leningrad Oblast Commercial Court No A56-5264/2012 (6 April 2012).

an arbitration agreement referring all disputes to arbitration by the Moscow Chamber of Commerce. Notwithstanding the somewhat unclear reference to the arbitration body, the court dismissed the action. On the basis of the documents submitted by the respondent, the court found that the MCC had only one permanent court of arbitration, which was therefore the proper institution for the arbitration of disputes between the parties arising under the arbitration agreement, and directed the parties to arbitration.

12.30 However, court practice in interpreting and applying the criteria that make an arbitration agreement 'null and void, inoperative or incapable of being performed'[24] (thereby defining the limits of judicial control) has not been consistent.

12.31 In one illustrative case, the claimant brought an action in Novosibirsk Oblast Commercial Court, although there was an arbitration clause providing for the resolution of disputes by the International Arbitration Court of the Chamber of Commerce and Industry of the Republic of Kazakhstan in Astana. The court established that the only international arbitration court at the CCI in the Republic of Kazakhstan was located in Almaty, rather than Astana. On this basis, the court found that the parties had not concluded an arbitration agreement and that it therefore had jurisdiction.[25] The court reasoned that an arbitration agreement is deemed concluded if the parties have reached agreement on all essential terms of the agreement, which includes agreement to resolve disputes through arbitration, the precise name of the arbitration institution, the range of disputes subject to arbitration, and the applicable law. The absence or uncertainty of any of these terms would mean the arbitration agreement was not validly concluded.

12.32 Similarly, in a more recent case, the court refused to give effect to a bilingual arbitration clause that indicated the name of the arbitral institution differently in Russian and English ('Arbitration Court of the International Chamber of Commerce' as opposed to 'International Commercial Arbitration Court of the RF Chamber of Commerce').[26] These decisions are clearly not in line with the international trend of interpreting pathological clauses in such a way as to give effect to arbitration based on the expression of the parties' intent.

12.33 Another example of the Russian courts' approach to the issue of the validity of an arbitration agreement is the case of *CJSC Russian Telephone Co v LLC Sony Ericsson Mobile Communications Rus*.[27] In this case the seller, LLC Sony Ericsson, failed to perform its contractual obligations to supply mobile telephones. The purchaser initiated court action. The supply contract contained an arbitration clause providing, *inter alia*, that:

> Any dispute arising in connection with this Contract... shall be finally resolved in accordance with the Rules of Conciliation and Arbitration of the International Chamber of Commerce... This arbitration clause does not limit the right of Sony Ericsson to take action in a court of competent jurisdiction to recover sums owed for products supplied.

12.34 The Presidium of the RF Supreme Commercial Court called into question the validity of the arbitration agreement because of the alleged violation of the principle of equal

---

24 ICA Law, art 8(1).

25 Ruling of the West Siberian District Federal Commercial Court No A45-13290/2009 (4 June 2010).

26 Ruling of the Moscow District Federal Commercial Court No A40-72305/10-50-606 (25 May 2011).

27 *CJSC Russian Telephone Co v LLC Sony Ericsson Mobile Communications Rus* Decision of the Presidium of the RF Supreme Commercial Court No VAS-1831/12 (19 June 2012).

treatment of the parties. An asymmetrical arbitration clause, the Presidium held, violates the principle of equal procedural rights:

> ... the dispute resolution agreement [contains] a provision fixing the right of only one party to the contract... to submit disputes to a state court... this choice-of-forum clause places LLC Sony Ericsson at an advantage compared to the claimant, since it gives only to LLC Sony Ericsson the right to choose the means of dispute resolution (arbitration or state court), and therefore it violates the balance of interests of the parties.

The Presidium of the RF Supreme Commercial Court further held that any such 'asymmetrical' arbitration agreements should be considered invalid.

12.2.2 Interim measures

State courts may also support arbitration by granting interim measures in order to thwart attempts by a party to prevent the effective enforcement of an eventual arbitral award.[28] State courts may grant interim measures to secure the claimant's interests even before the claim is filed in arbitration. The Presidium of the RF Supreme Commercial Court has clarified that preliminary interim measures may be granted upon the application of a party to arbitration proceedings in accordance with the general rules of the APC,[29] in order to secure the enforcement of any arbitral award, provided the requirements of article 90(2) of the APC are satisfied.[30] These include a demonstration that preliminary interim measures would prevent significant harm to the applicant,[31] and failure to impose them would prejudice or render impossible the implementation of the ultimate judicial decision (even in cases in which enforcement might be sought abroad). **12.35**

The court's ruling granting the preliminary interim measures must set a deadline, which is not to exceed 15 days, for initiating the arbitration proceedings in connection with which the court has granted the interim measures. If the proceedings are not initiated by the specified date, the interim measures will be lifted.[32] **12.36**

The ICA Law expressly provides that it is not incompatible with an arbitration agreement for a party to request a court to order interim measures of protection, either before or during arbitral proceedings, and for a court to grant such measures.[33] The ICA Law also empowers the arbitral tribunal to order interim measures, and to require a party to provide security in connection with such measures.[34] Russian legislation has therefore adopted the internationally recognized principle of the concurrent jurisdiction of state courts and arbitral tribunals in matters relating to interim measures.[35] The advantage of applying to a state court for interim measures is the court's ability to compel third parties to comply.[36] **12.37**

---

28 ICA Law, art 9; APC, art 99.

29 Information Letter of the Presidium of the RF Supreme Commercial Court No 78 'Survey of Commercial Court Practice in Applying Preliminary Injunctive Relief' (7 July 2004), item 2. While the name 'Arbitral Procedure Code' might be misleading, it should be clarified that the APC establishes rules of procedure for the state *arbitrazh* (commercial) courts, not arbitration rules.

30 Information Letter No 78 (n 29) item 2.

31 APC, art 90(2).

32 Information Letter No 78 (n 29) item 16.

33 ICA Law, art 9; Model Law, Art 9.

34 ICA Law, art 17.

35 The principle of concurrent jurisdiction is limited to certain boundaries which are determined by the parties in the arbitration agreement, and also by laws setting forth the exclusive competence of state courts with respect to certain interim measures.

36 APC, art 91.

12.38 As a general note, the provision allowing a Russian state commercial court to grant interim measures in support of arbitration first appeared in the 2002 APC but was rarely used in practice until recently. It was unclear whether the state courts had the power to impose interim measures in relation to arbitration proceedings taking place outside the territory of the Russian Federation. This was a subject of debate in Russia until the 2010 decision of the Presidium of the RF Supreme Commercial Court in *Edimax Ltd v Chigirinsky*,[37] which confirmed that a Russian commercial court was competent to impose interim measures in international commercial arbitration taking place abroad.

12.39 *Edimax* concerned arbitration proceedings under the auspices of the LCIA. The claimant applied to the Moscow commercial court, seeking attachment of the respondent's Moscow apartment and a prohibition against the registration of any transfer of title to the property. The Presidium of the RF Supreme Commercial Court overruled lower court decisions refusing the requested interim measures, and held that Russian state courts could impose interim measures upon application of a party to arbitration in (a) the local court of the seat of the arbitral tribunal, (b) the local court of the debtor's place of residence, or (c) the local court of the debtor's property.

12.40 The proposed amendments to the ICA Law expressly grant the state courts power to impose interim relief in arbitration proceedings, whether seated in the Russian Federation or elsewhere. If adopted, these amendments would codify the decision in the *Edimax* case and establish guidelines on interim measures for the Russian judiciary.

12.2.3 Assistance in appointing arbitrators

12.41 If for some reason it is not possible to constitute an arbitral tribunal by agreement of the parties (eg if a party refuses to appoint an arbitrator), an independent person or body must become involved in order to avoid deadlock in the arbitration proceedings. That role may be played by an arbitration institution or, for ad hoc arbitration, by the person or entity designated in the arbitration agreement or determined in accordance with the rules to which the parties have submitted the arbitration. In contrast with many other jurisdictions, Russian law does not provide for recourse to the courts in constituting the arbitral tribunal.

12.42 As a general rule, the ICA Law allows the parties to agree on any procedure for the appointment of the arbitral tribunal (or sole arbitrator).[38] If a party does not comply with the agreed procedure for the appointment of arbitrators, or if the parties or two arbitrators are unable to reach agreement in accordance with that procedure, or a third party, including an institution, fails to perform any of the functions placed on it in accordance with the procedure, any party may ask the President of the CCI to make the appointment. This decision cannot be appealed.[39] While the parties could, in theory, authorize the state court to take the action to overcome difficulties in forming the arbitration tribunal, Russian procedural law does not regulate such proceedings and Russian courts do not have the authority to assist parties in this area. It is therefore unlikely that such an agreement would be given effect by state courts.

---

[37] *Edimax Ltd v Chigirinsky* Decision of the Presidium of the RF Supreme Commercial Court No 17095/09 (20 April 2010).

[38] ICA Law, art 11(2).

[39] ICA Law, art 11(4)–(5).

12.43 In Russian domestic arbitration, the law provides that if one party fails to select its arbitrator within 15 days of receiving a request to do so from another party, or if two arbitrators are unable to appoint a third within 15 days of appointment, consideration of the dispute in arbitration is ended and the dispute may be submitted to the competent state court.[40] Clearly, this rule, which is not found in the ICA Law, gives the respondent unlimited scope to avoid arbitration.

12.44 It should be noted that a number of commentators see the absence of judicial control over the formation of arbitration tribunals as relieving parties of the need to ask state courts to appoint arbitrators, thereby protecting them from unwanted judicial scrutiny of the validity of the arbitration agreement.[41]

12.2.4 The role of courts in resolving jurisdictional questions

12.45 One of the most important issues arising during arbitration proceedings is the scope of the arbitral tribunal's jurisdiction. In accordance with the ICA Law, which adopts, along with other provisions of the Model Law, the *competence-competence* principle, the arbitral tribunal itself determines whether it has jurisdiction to consider a dispute submitted to it for resolution, including in cases in which one of the parties contends that there is no arbitration agreement or the arbitration agreement is invalid.[42] One of the effects of the *competence-competence* principle is that state courts are precluded from considering the scope of the arbitrators' authority until the arbitral tribunal makes its own decision.

12.46 In compliance with the provisions of Article 16(3) of the Model Law, the ICA Law provides that if the arbitral tribunal rules as a preliminary question that it has jurisdiction, any party may, within 30 days after having received notice of that ruling, request the state court to decide the matter,[43] without having to wait until the termination of the arbitral proceedings and the issuance of the final award. If there is no such tribunal ruling on jurisdiction, the state courts may not entertain an interlocutory action challenging the jurisdiction of the arbitral tribunal. This position was developed more than a decade ago by the RF High Court as a recommendation for the practice of state courts.[44]

12.47 The procedure for opposing an arbitral tribunal's interim ruling that it has jurisdiction is set forth in article 235 of the APC and article 16 of the ICA Law.[45] A party to the arbitration has the right to apply to the court within 30 days of receiving the tribunal's ruling. An application opposing the ruling on jurisdiction is considered by a judge unilaterally within one month of filing with the state commercial court. The arbitral tribunal may continue the proceedings and issue an award while the state court considers the request.

12.48 Under article 16 of the ICA Law, the court's ruling cannot be appealed. However, as noted by one of the commentators, the provisions of article 235 of the APC are not in compliance

---

[40] Federal Law No 102-FZ (n 13) art 10(4).

[41] SA Kurochkin, *State Courts in Arbitration and International Commercial Arbitration* (Wolters Kluwer, 2008) para 23.

[42] ICA Law, art 16(1).

[43] ICA Law, art 16(3).

[44] Decision of the RF High Court No 5-G02-49 (7 May 2002).

[45] Like the legislature of other Model Law-based countries, the ICA Law does not envisage an appeal against an arbitral tribunal's ruling that it does not have jurisdiction. Therefore, Russian courts consistently refuse to consider such appeals.

with the ICA Law and do not stipulate that such court ruling cannot be appealed. Therefore, arguably, cassation appeal is possible under the general provisions of chapter 30 of the APC.[46] This position is supported by recent court practice.[47]

12.49 Despite these provisions of the ICA Law, the question whether state courts can consider actions aimed directly at attacking the existence or validity of an arbitration agreement has arisen in practice. As discussed, the provisions of articles 5 and 16(3) of the ICA Law limit the authority of state courts to intervene in the arbitration process, and provide for the arbitrators' competence in ruling on their jurisdiction. Also, article 27 of the APC does not refer disputes concerning the competence of arbitrators to the jurisdiction of state courts.

12.50 However, the provisions of Article VI(2) and (3) of the 1961 European Convention on International Commercial Arbitration (European Convention), to which Russia is a signatory, provide for a somewhat different treatment. Under Article VI(2):

> *In taking a decision concerning the existence or the validity of an arbitration agreement*, courts of Contracting States shall examine the validity of such agreement with reference to the capacity of the parties, under the law applicable to them, and with reference to other questions (emphasis added).

Under Article VI (3):

> Where either party to an arbitration agreement has initiated arbitration proceedings before any resort is had to a court, courts of Contracting States subsequently asked to deal with the same subject-matter between the same parties or with the question whether the arbitration agreement was non-existent or null and void or had lapsed, shall stay their ruling on the arbitrator's jurisdiction until the arbitral award is made, *unless they have good and substantial reasons to the contrary* (emphasis added).

12.51 The Federal Commercial Court for the Moscow District has interpreted these provisions of Article VI of the European Convention as granting the state courts the authority to consider actions directly challenging an arbitration agreement.[48] Commentators have, however, criticized this overly broad interpretation of Article VI[49] and, in a recent case challenging an arbitration agreement, the RF Supreme Commercial Court ruled that the arbitral tribunal has priority in deciding on its own jurisdiction.[50]

12.2.5 Role of courts in enjoining arbitration

12.52 Article 5 of the ICA Law limits court intervention in arbitration proceedings to matters expressly provided for in the Law. As previously described, the state courts are generally empowered to enjoin arbitration under the provisions of article 16(3) of the ICA Law

[46] BR Karabelnikov, *Enforcing and Challenging International Commercial Arbitral Awards: Commentary on the 1958 New York Convention and Chapters 30 and 31 of the 2002 APC RF* (3rd edn, Statut, 2008) ch 4, s 1. See Ruling of the Moscow District Federal Commercial Court No A40-65888/11-8-553 (24 January 2012).

[47] eg Ruling of the Moscow District Federal Commercial Court in case No A40-65888/11-8-553 (24 January 2012).

[48] Review of the court practice of the Federal Commercial Court for the Moscow District on Consideration of Cases with Participation of Foreign Parties (2000).

[49] MA Rozhkova, *Claims and Court Rulings: Collected Works* (Statut 2009) 80. See also Karabelnikov (n 46) ch 1, s 2(B).

[50] Ruling of the RF Supreme Commercial Court No VAS-3040/09 (1 April 2009). See also Ruling of the RF Supreme Commercial Court No VAS 838/10 (24 March 2010).

if the arbitral tribunal rules as a preliminary question that it has jurisdiction and a party to arbitration requests the court to decide the matter. Recent court practice holds in this respect that in the absence of the arbitral tribunal's ruling on jurisdiction, direct challenge of the arbitration agreement in court is not allowed.[51] Also, in practice, it is increasingly more common for these matters to come before the courts in the context of actions brought despite the existence of an arbitration agreement than as actions directly seeking to enjoin arbitration.

12.3 During the Arbitration

12.3.1 Role of courts in deciding challenges to arbitrators

Russian law does not authorize state courts to resolve issues concerning the removal of arbitrators during arbitration proceedings. Judicial control over the formation of the arbitral tribunal is exercised only at the stage of contesting the final award. **12.53**

In line with the Model Law, article 12 of the ICA Law sets out the grounds for challenges to arbitrators. In connection with a possible appointment as an arbitrator, a person must disclose any circumstances likely to give rise to justifiable doubts as to her/his impartiality or independence. From the time of the appointment and throughout the arbitral proceedings, the arbitrator must without delay disclose any such circumstances to the parties unless they have already been informed of them. An arbitrator may be challenged only if circumstances exist that give rise to justifiable doubts as to his impartiality or independence, or if she/he does not possess qualifications agreed to by the parties. A party may challenge an arbitrator it appointed, or in whose appointment that party has participated, only for reasons of which the party became aware after the appointment was made. **12.54**

Under article 13(1) and (2) of the ICA Law, which again replicates the Model Law provisions, the parties are generally free to agree on a procedure for challenging an arbitrator. Failing the parties' agreement, a party who intends to challenge an arbitrator shall, within 15 days after becoming aware of the constitution of the arbitral tribunal or after becoming aware of any circumstance referred to in article 12(2) of the Law, send a written statement of the reasons for the challenge to the arbitral tribunal. Unless the challenged arbitrator withdraws from office or the other party agrees to the challenge, the arbitral tribunal shall decide on the challenge. **12.55**

If a challenge under the envisaged procedure is not successful, the ICA Law authorizes the president of the RF CCI to rule on challenges to arbitrators. Under the ICA Law provisions, the President of the CCI is vested with authority that under the Model Law provisions rests with the state courts, which also includes the authority to appoint arbitrators as previously discussed. In accordance with the ICA Law, in the event that the parties are unable to agree on the challenge, or if the arbitrator does not withdraw from office, or if the challenge is rejected, the challenging party may, within 30 days after having received notice of the decision rejecting the challenge, request the President of the RF CCI to decide on the challenge, which decision is not subject to appeal.[52] **12.56**

[51] Ruling of the RF Supreme Commercial Court No VAS-3040/09 (1 April 2009).
[52] ICA Law, arts 13(3), 6(1).

12.57 Also in accordance with the Model Law, the ICA Law provides that while such a request is pending, the arbitral tribunal, including the challenged arbitrator, may continue the arbitral proceedings and make an award.[53] This rule is intended to form a safeguard against abusive parties attempting to delay the proceedings.

12.58 The Russian state courts exercise control over the formation of the arbitral tribunal in compliance with national law and the agreement of the parties in the capacity of a final instance, after the arbitral award has been made. Judicial practice has yet to develop a consistent approach to establishing uniform criteria for confirming irregularities in the composition of the arbitral tribunal.

12.59 For example, in *Novolipetsky Metallurgicheskii Kombinat v NV Maksimov*, the Russian courts considered the question of an arbitrator's failure to disclose circumstances that might give rise to reasonable doubts as to his impartiality and independence.[54] In this case, the claimant submitted two expert opinions during the arbitration proceedings. In the state court, the respondent claimed that the award should be set aside because the two arbitrators failed to disclose that they had worked at the same scientific institutions as the experts, who held positions superior to the arbitrators.

12.60 With reference to the provisions of the Rules on Impartiality and Independence of Arbitrators endorsed by the Chamber of Commerce and Industry in 2010, the courts found that arbitrators are obliged to disclose that they have employment relationships with the same organization as counsel to one of the parties or an expert giving evidence in the arbitration. The state courts further held that the respondent's failure to challenge the arbitrators or to object to the admissibility of the expert opinions during the arbitral proceedings did not prevent the courts from considering the respondent's application to set aside the award on the basis that the arbitrators had breached their duties. Failure to disclose, in the view of the Russian courts, violates the principles of an arbitrator's impartiality and independence and therefore amounts to a violation of public policy. This line of reasoning demonstrates once again the tendency of Russian courts towards a broad interpretation of the public policy standard. The inconsistent position of Russian courts on this issue is partly attributable to the fact that the term 'public policy' is not defined in Russian law and is left to the discretion of the courts.

12.3.2 Role of courts in compelling testimony/evidence

12.61 In the course of arbitral proceedings, the arbitral tribunal and the parties may find it necessary to obtain and examine evidence held by the other party or third party. In this situation, the powers available to the arbitrators may be insufficient to ensure the fullness and accuracy of the evidence, to obtain written evidence and testimony from third parties, or to secure evidence.

12.62 Russian law, following the Model Law, allows recourse to a court for assistance in obtaining evidence from persons who refuse to provide it to arbitrators. The application to the court may be made by the arbitral tribunal itself, or by one of the parties. In accordance with the ICA Law, an arbitral tribunal, or one of the parties with the tribunal's consent, may apply to

---

[53] ICA Law, art 13(3).

[54] *Novolipetsky Metallurgicheskii Kombinat v NV Maksimov* Ruling of the RF Supreme Commercial Court No VAS-15384/11 (30 January 2012).

a competent state court for assistance in obtaining evidence. The court may grant the request on the basis of the general rules on the preservation of evidence, including those on court orders.[55]

Article 27 of the ICA Law has been applied in ICAC practice. In one case, proceedings before the ICAC were adjourned to enable a party to exercise this right; in another, the arbitral tribunal consented to a claimant's request to apply to the state court for assistance in obtaining evidence.[56] **12.63**

Compelling a third party to take action in support of arbitral proceedings can be achieved only by seeking interim measures from the court as discussed. **12.64**

12.3.3 Ability of foreign practitioners to appear as counsel or arbitrator

Russian law does not impose any express restrictions on the participation of foreign practitioners in arbitration as either counsel or arbitrator. However, Russian law and legal practice do establish a number of general restrictions that should be noted by foreign practitioners involved in arbitration in the Russian Federation. **12.65**

For example, the position of the Presidium of the RF Supreme Commercial Court has been that state courts should deny enforcement of an arbitral award if the court finds that a person acting as arbitrator did not have the right to serve as an arbitrator under Russian Federation law. This view was taken by the Presidium in a case in which a foreign company applied to a commercial court seeking recognition and enforcement of an award issued in the Russian Federation. The other party opposed the enforcement, claiming that the composition of the arbitral tribunal that rendered the award violated Russian law because the arbitrator was an official in a judicial capacity. The arbitrator's place of work and title were indicated in the arbitral institution's list of arbitrators, and the parties did not deny that they were aware of his position. **12.66**

According to article 11 of the Federal Law on the Principles of State Service in the Russian Federation in effect at the time of the arbitration, public officials were not permitted to undertake paid activities other than of a pedagogical, scholarly, or creative nature. The Presidium thus found that the arbitrator was not entitled to be on the arbitration panel, agreed with the findings of the lower court that the composition of the arbitral tribunal did not comply with federal law, and, pursuant to article 239 of the APC, denied the enforcement application.[57] While the current RF Federal Law on State Civil Service does not include this prohibition,[58] it can still be found in the Federal Law on the Status of the Judges in the Russian Federation.[59] Therefore, the Russian judiciary remains excluded from the pool of potential arbitrators in the Russian Federation.[60] **12.67**

12.3.4 Hearings

The ICA Law contains the standard Model Law provision that, subject to the agreement of the parties, the arbitral tribunal decides whether to hold oral hearings, or to conduct proceedings solely on the basis of documents and other written materials. However, if requested by one of the parties, the arbitral tribunal must hold a hearing at the appropriate stage of the **12.68**

[55] ICA Law, art 27.
[56] ICAC arbitral awards No 244/2000 (27 February 2002), and No 100/2001 (21 March 2002).
[57] Information Letter No 96 (n 11).
[58] RF Federal Law No 79-FZ 'On State Civil Service in the Russian Federation' (27 July 2004).
[59] RF Federal Law No 3132-1 'On the Status of the Judges in the Russian Federation', art 3.3(5) (26 June 1992).
[60] Decision of the Presidium of the RF Supreme Commercial Court No 17412/08 (31 March 2009).

proceedings.[61] Hence, the right to choose the form of the proceedings belongs to the parties to the arbitration agreement; as a default rule, if the parties have agreed on this, or if one of the parties requests an oral hearing, the arbitral tribunal must hold a hearing.

12.69 As provided by the ICA Law, if the arbitral tribunal decides to hold oral hearings, it independently determines the optimal stage of the proceedings at which to do so. However, while indicating that there is a choice of stage of the proceedings, the ICA Law does not specify any procedural stages; moreover, the Law does not specify the scope of such oral hearings. Some guidance is provided by articles 32 and 33 of the Rules of the ICAC, specifying the nature and scope of oral hearings. Given that the majority of cases resolved by international commercial arbitration involve an element of commercial secrecy, the Rules provide that oral hearings are not public; a third party may participate in the hearings only by agreement of the parties and with the consent of the arbitral tribunal.

12.70 In respect of the language of the proceedings, the ICA Law provides that the parties may, at their discretion, agree on the language or languages to be used in the course of arbitration. In the absence of such an agreement, the arbitral tribunal will determine the language to be used in proceedings.[62] Hence, the ICA Law's default rule allows the parties the freedom to choose the language in which the proceedings will be conducted. At the same time, the ICAC Rules establish that by default, arbitral proceedings are to be conducted in Russian. Under the ICAC Rules, proceedings can be conducted in other languages by agreement of the parties.[63]

12.71 The ICA Law does not contain any particular provisions on witness examination. This can partly be attributed to the fact that, contrary to common law practice, evidence in the form of witness statements and further examination of witnesses at the hearings is not a customary feature of Russian court proceedings. Similarly, the ICAC Rules contain only one related provision: that the arbitrators have the right at their own discretion to call and hear witnesses.[64] It would appear therefore that, because there are no mandatory provisions applicable to the matter, the procedure for witness examination should be established on case-by-case basis by the arbitral tribunal.

12.4 The Award

12.4.1 Mandatory rules as to form

12.72 The ICA Law establishes the following mandatory requirements for the form of an arbitral award:

- the award must made be in writing;
- the award must be signed by the arbitrator or arbitrators (if the dispute is considered by several arbitrators, the signatures of the majority are sufficient, provided the reason why the other signatures are missing is stated);
- the award must state the date and place of issuance.[65]

---

[61] ICA Law, art 24.
[62] ICA Law, art 22.
[63] ICAC Rules, art 23(1).
[64] ICAC Rules, art 31.
[65] ICA Law, art 31.

The written form requirement is not merely a formal statutory requirement: a certified copy of a written award is necessary when applying for recognition and enforcement,[66] as well as when filing an application for setting aside.[67]

The ICA Law and international treaties establishing the grounds for the setting aside of arbitral awards do not deal expressly with the absence of arbitrators' signatures or of the indication of the place of issuance as grounds for setting aside. Nevertheless, as an arbitral award rendered in Russia needs to comply with the legal requirements as to its form, failure to indicate signatures and/or the date and place of the award could be regarded by Russian courts as a violation of article 34(2) of the ICA Law and Article V(1)(d) of the New York Convention[68] and therefore constitute grounds for setting aside or denial of enforcement. Another possible scenario in such a situation would be to return the matter to the arbitrators for rectification. For this purpose, a Russian state court may choose to apply article 34(4) of the ICA Law, providing for remand to the arbitral tribunal to cure grounds for setting aside, which mirrors the Model Law provision.[69] **12.73**

Depending on the grounds for terminating the proceedings, the arbitral tribunal may issue one of the following determinations: **12.74**

- an award that is the final judgment in consideration of the claim on its merits;
- an order—a determination indicating there are circumstances that by law prevent the issuance of an award on the merits of the dispute. This document does not settle the dispute on the merits, but merely states that there are legal obstacles to deciding the dispute.[70]

The ICA Law lists the cases in which arbitral tribunals seated in Russia are required to issue an order terminating proceedings. The law states that the issuance of the order is an obligation of the arbitral tribunal rather than a right, which indicates the rule's mandatory nature. This is also confirmed in the practice of Russian courts, which may treat the issuance of an award rather than an order terminating arbitration proceedings as a violation of imperative rules of law, and may serve as grounds for setting aside pursuant to article 34(2) of the ICA Law and Article V(1)(d) of the New York Convention as violating the law of the country where the arbitration took place.[71] **12.75**

12.4.2 Mandatory rules as to substance

Article 31 of the ICA Law lists three essential substantive elements of an arbitral award: first, the reasoning underlying the award; secondly, a conclusion on the satisfaction or denial of **12.76**

---

66 APC, ch 31.

67 APC, ch 30.

68 New York Convention, Art V.1(d) provides:

> Recognition and enforcement of the award may be refused...if...the composition of the arbitral authority or the arbitral procedure was not in accordance with the agreement of the parties, or, failing such agreement, *was not in accordance with the law of the country where the arbitration took place.* (emphasis added)

69 cf Model Law, art 34(4):

> The court, when asked to set aside an award, may, where appropriate and so requested by a party, suspend the setting aside proceedings for a period of time determined by it in order to give the arbitral tribunal an opportunity to resume the arbitral proceedings or to take such other action as in the arbitral tribunal's opinion will eliminate the grounds for setting aside.

70 ICA Law, art 32.

71 Ruling of the Moscow District Federal Commercial Court No KG-A40/8586-08 (18 September 2008).

the claims; and thirdly, the amount of the arbitration fees and costs, as allocated among the parties.

12.77 Additional details are provided by section 39 of the ICAC Rules, which specifies that the arbitral award must state, *inter alia*:

- the subject of the dispute and a brief description of the circumstances of the case;
- the reasoning behind the award;
- a conclusion on the satisfaction or denial of the claims;
- the arbitration fees and case expenses, and their allocation among the parties.

12.78 In Russian judicial practice, the absence of a conclusion on the satisfaction or denial of the claims in the reasoning or judgment of an award or in an order terminating proceedings may serve as grounds for setting aside the award as violating the law of the country where the arbitration took place.[72]

12.5 After the Award

12.5.1 Standards for setting aside/annulment

12.79 Russian law provides two opportunities for judicial control over arbitral awards: when the award is challenged in setting aside proceedings and when enforcement is sought. As a rule, actions for setting aside awards are brought by the losing party, while applications for enforcement are made by the successful party.

12.80 The recognition and enforcement of arbitral awards in the Russian Federation is carried out by means of the *exequatur* procedure, ie by applying to the court for enforcement by state authorities vis-à-vis the obligated entity or its property. Arbitral awards with a seat of arbitration in the Russian Federation are enforced in accordance with the enforcement rules established in chapter 30 of the APC, on the basis of a writ of execution issued by a competent state court.[73]

12.81 The ICA Law contains an exhaustive list of grounds on which an arbitral award may be set aside, which essentially reiterates the language of Article 5 of the 1958 New York Convention and Article 34 of the Model Law. Most of these grounds are based on procedural breaches during the course of the arbitral proceedings and must be proved by the applicant. An arbitral award may be set aside by the state commercial court if:

(1) the party making the application for setting aside furnishes proof that:
  (a) a party to the arbitration agreement was under some incapacity, or the agreement is not valid under the law to which the parties have subjected it, or, failing any indication thereof, under the law of the Russian Federation;
  (b) a party was not given proper notice of the appointment of an arbitrator or of the arbitral proceedings, or was otherwise unable to present its case;
  (c) the award was made regarding a dispute not contemplated by or not falling within the terms of the arbitration agreement, or contains decisions on matters beyond

[72] Ruling of the Moscow District Federal Commercial Court No KG-A40/8586-08 (18 September 2008). See also Ruling of the Moscow District Federal Commercial Court No KG-A40/9640-04 (20 October 2004).

[73] See also ICA Law, s VIII.

the scope of submission to arbitration, provided that if the decisions on matters submitted to arbitration can be separated from those on matters not so submitted, only that part of the award that contains decisions on matters not submitted to arbitration may be set aside; or

(d) the composition of the arbitral tribunal or the arbitral procedure was not in accordance with the agreement of the parties, unless such agreement was in conflict with a provision of the ICA Law from which the parties cannot derogate, or, failing such agreement, was not in accordance with the ICA Law; or

(2) the court finds that:

(a) the subject matter of the dispute is not capable of settlement by arbitration under the law of the Russian Federation; or

(b) the award is in conflict with the public policy of the Russian Federation.[74]

The grounds for refusing recognition or enforcement of an arbitral award are almost the same as for annulment of the award. Recognition or enforcement of an arbitral award, irrespective of the country in which it was made, may be refused only: **12.82**

(1) at the request of the party against whom it is invoked, if that party furnishes proof to the competent court where recognition or enforcement is sought that:

(a) a party to the arbitration agreement was under some incapacity, or the agreement is not valid under the law to which the parties have subjected it or, failing any indication thereof, under the law of the country where the award was made;

(b) the party against whom the award was made was not given proper notice of the appointment of an arbitrator or of the arbitral proceedings or was otherwise unable to present its case;

(c) the award was made regarding a dispute not contemplated by or not falling within the terms of the arbitration agreement, or it contains decisions on matters beyond the scope of submission to arbitration, provided that if the decisions on matters submitted to arbitration can be separated from those on matters not so submitted, that part of the award which contains decisions on matters submitted to arbitration may be recognized and enforced;

(d) the composition of the arbitral tribunal or the arbitral procedure was not in accordance with the agreement of the parties or, failing such agreement, was not in accordance with the law of the country in which the arbitration took place; or

(e) the award has not yet become binding on the parties or has been set aside or suspended by a court of the country in which or under the law of which that award was made; or

(2) if the court finds that:

(a) the subject matter of the dispute is not capable of settlement by arbitration under the law of the Russian Federation; or

(b) the recognition or enforcement of the award would be contrary to the public policy of the Russian Federation.[75]

Many of the grounds for setting aside and for refusing the recognition and enforcement of international commercial arbitral awards are identical. Additional grounds applicable to **12.83**

[74] ICA Law, s VIII, art 34.

[75] ICA Law, s VIII, art 36.

the enforcement of international commercial arbitral awards include the non-final (and therefore non-binding) nature of the award, and its annulment or suspension by a competent authority (court) of the state in which it was issued. The law also highlights differences in allocating the burden of proof, which have been repeatedly emphasized in Russian court enforcement practice.

Invalid arbitration agreement; incapacity of a party

12.84 The most frequent situations in which Russian courts find that an arbitration agreement is invalid or was not concluded are (a) when the parties failed to observe the mandatory written form of the arbitration agreement,[76] or (b) when the parties did not agree on the essential conditions of the arbitration agreement. As applied by Russian courts, essential conditions of the arbitration agreement include, in particular, the obligation of the parties to resolve disputes through arbitration; the indication of a permanent arbitration institution or the procedure for ad hoc arbitration; and the scope of disputes subject to arbitration.[77]

12.85 In *ESF Euroservices BV v Hyundai Merchant Marine*,[78] the lower courts denied recognition and enforcement of an award on several grounds, including that, in the absence of the signatures of the parties, a bill of lading cannot establish an arbitration agreement. The RF Supreme Commercial Court—supported by its Presidium—ordered enforcement of the award, finding that the parties' performance under the bill of lading affirmed their consent to arbitration. Following the Presidium's decision, Russian courts may be more inclined to accept that the written form requirement can be satisfied by an exchange of documents, whether or not signed, interpreted in the light of the parties' conduct.

12.86 A commonly alleged ground for invalidity is that one party exceeded its legal authority and therefore lacked capacity to enter into an arbitration agreement. As pointed out by the leading commentator on the application of the provisions of the New York Convention in the Russian Federation, defects in legal capacity are often argued by state authorities, which, after a dispute arises, wish to avoid arbitration.[79]

12.87 In the past, Russian courts systematically denied recognition and enforcement on these grounds. However, a different approach was taken in the recent decision of the Presidium of the RF Supreme Commercial Court in *Stena RoRo AB v Baltiyskii Zavod*.[80] In this case, the lower court denied recognition and enforcement of an arbitral award rendered in Sweden on several grounds, one of which was that the award pertained to a dispute not contemplated by the terms of arbitration agreement: it formed part of contracts that had not come into force,

[76] ICA Law, s VIII, art 7(2). See also Ruling of the Moscow District Federal Commercial Court No A40-89595/11-8-756 (22 February 2012).

[77] Ruling of the West Siberian District Federal Commercial Court No A45-13290/2009 (4 June 2010).

[78] *ESF Euroservices BV v Hyundai Merchant Marine* Decision of the Presidium of the RF Supreme Commercial Court No 16727/09 (30 March 2010).

[79] Karabelnikov (n 46) ch 3, s 1(B). Karabelnikov believes that for the state organizations of members of the 1961 European Convention, the ability to cite defects in their own legal capacity in connection with the conclusion of arbitration agreements is limited by Art II of the Convention. This article states that if the respective state did not make a special proviso at the signing or ratification of the European Convention, or accession to it, its organizations 'will be able to conclude arbitration agreements'. Therefore, Russian public legal entities cannot cite the restriction of their legal capacity to conclude arbitration agreements.

[80] *Stena RoRo AB v Baltiyskii Zavod* Decision of the Presidium of the RF Supreme Commercial Court No 9899/09 (13 September 2011).

because they lacked the approval of the contemplated transactions by the Stena RoRo AB Board of Directors in the form of a protocol.

12.88 The Presidium of the RF Supreme Commercial Court overturned the decision of the lower court and ruled that the arbitral award should be enforced, stating that the parties' performance under the contracts confirmed their consent to arbitrate. The Court held that formalization of the Board's agreement by way of a signed protocol was not mandatory. For purposes of proving that the transaction had been approved by the Board of the company, a letter issued by Stena RoRo, along with the parties' conduct under the contracts, was considered sufficient.

Violation of the right of parties to present their case

12.89 Violation of the parties' right to present their case is an independent ground for setting aside and denial of enforcement. Party equality is a fundamental premise of Russian arbitration procedure. Violation of these due process standards could take the form of a party being deprived of the ability to fully participate in the consideration of the arbitration case for reasons outside its control, including during the formation of the arbitral tribunal, or being unable to defend its position, submit evidence, or attend hearings. In this context law and practice recognize a failure to properly notify the parties of the arbitration, to appoint arbitrators, or to set the time and place of arbitration hearings, as well as *force majeure* preventing a party from taking part in the arbitration.[81]

12.90 In the past, foreign arbitral awards were systematically denied recognition and enforcement by the RF state courts on the grounds that the respondents were not duly notified of the proceedings or were otherwise unable to present their case. In *Belintertrans v TransEurope-Inform*, the North-West District Federal Commercial Court denied recognition and enforcement of the award because of improper notice to the respondent.[82] It is notable is that notice was sent to the address stipulated in the contract, but the respondent argued that the person who signed in confirmation of receipt of the notice was not the respondent's employee. It can therefore be concluded that sending notice to the address stipulated in a contract does not guarantee that proper notice has been given if it is received by an unauthorized person.

12.91 However, this formalistic approach may change in the light of a recent decision of the RF Supreme Commercial Court. In *Loral Space and Communications Holding Corporation v Globalstar*, the Russian state commercial courts denied recognition and enforcement of an LCIA award because of lack of proper notice to the respondent.[83] The Presidium of the RF Supreme Commercial Court overturned the decisions of the lower instances and concluded that proper notice does not necessarily require a single integrated document, but may include a number of complementary communications in accordance with the relevant arbitration rules. Similarly, in *Valars SA v Agro-Holding*, which also involved recognition and

[81] Ruling of the West-Siberian District Federal Commercial Court in case No A67-1438/2010 (27 October 2010); Ruling of the RF Supreme Commercial Court No VAS-4201/12 (18 April 2012); Ruling of the RF Supreme Commercial Court No VAS-3226/12 (29 March 2012); Decision of the Presidium of the RF Supreme Commercial Court No 3253/04 (22 June 2004).

[82] *Belintertrans v TransEurope-Inform* Ruling of the North-West District Federal Commercial Court No A21-8497/2008 (13 March 2009).

[83] *Loral Space and Communications Holding Corp v Globalstar* Decision of the Presidium of the RF Supreme Commercial Court No 10718/08 (20 January 2009).

enforcement of a foreign award, the RF Supreme Commercial Court concluded that the defendant's correspondence with the arbitral tribunal and the claimant was sufficient proof of proper notice.[84] This suggests that the same line of reasoning might be applied by the state courts in cases in which the Russian Federation is the seat of arbitration.

Ultra vires—*exceeding the scope of the arbitration agreement*

12.92 An illustrative case on the application of this ground for setting aside or denying enforcement is the recent case *Frener & Reifer Russia v Enka Insaat ve Sanayi AS*.[85] The RF Supreme Commercial Court found that an arbitral tribunal exceeded the scope of an arbitration agreement in a construction contract by ruling that the clause also covered disputes between the employer and the contractor over the employer's rights under a third-party bank guarantee to secure the contractor's obligations under the contract.

Improper composition of the arbitral tribunal; non-conformity of arbitration procedure to the law and the agreement of the parties

12.93 Violation of the rules applicable to the formation of arbitral tribunals and arbitration procedure, in particular as set forth in articles 11, 12, and 19 of the ICA Law, constitutes grounds for setting aside or denial of enforcement of an arbitral award. In particular, Russian state courts will set aside an arbitral award or deny enforcement, if the court determines that:

- the appointment of an arbitrator by an appointing authority was not in accordance with the parties' agreement, or a person appointed as arbitrator did not have the right to act as an arbitrator under RF law. For example, acting or retired judges are prohibited from serving as arbitrators, as discussed in more detail at paragraphs 12.65–12.67.[86]
- the principle of independence and impartiality of arbitrators was violated, and an arbitrator had a direct or indirect interest in the outcome of the case.

12.94 In one case, the RF Supreme Commercial Court held that where an arbitrator failed to disclose that he took part in seminars and international conferences arranged and paid for by counsel for a party, this raised doubts about the impartiality and independence of the arbitrator.[87]

12.95 As discussed at paragraph 12.85, in the recent *ESF Euroservices BV* case,[88] the Presidium of the Russian Supreme Commercial Court rejected the lower courts' conclusion that a member of the arbitral tribunal had had an interest in the outcome of the case because he (a) chaired the bar association to which counsel for the claimant belonged, and (b) the bar association sub-leased premises from the law firm representing the claimant.[89] Given the circumstances, the Presidium held that no evidence was provided to prove the arbitrator's interest in the

---

[84] *Valars SA v Agro-Holding* Ruling of the RF Supreme Commercial Court No 16894/08 (26 February 2009).

[85] *Frener & Reifer Russia v Enka Insaat ve Sanayi AS* Ruling of the RF Supreme Commercial Court No VAS-16822/10 (14 February 2011).

[86] Ruling of the North-West District Federal Commercial Court No A21-5758/2005 (3 May 2006); Clarifications by the RF High Judicial Qualification Panel (18 March 2004), item 15.

[87] Ruling of the RF Supreme Commercial Court No 14956/07 (10 December 2007). See also *Novolipetsky Metallurgicheskii Kombinat v NV Maksimov* Ruling of the RF Supreme Commercial Court No VAS-15384/11 (30 January 2012).

[88] *ESF Euroservices BV v Hyundai Merchant Marine* Decision of the Presidium of the RF Supreme Commercial Court No 16727/09 (30 March 2010).

[89] *ESF Euroservices BV* (n 88).

outcome of the case. It further stated that attorneys are not prevented by law from acting as arbitrators, as long as they are not bound by an advocate-client relationship with any party participating in proceedings, and in the absence of any other interest in the case.

Non-final nature of the award; setting aside or suspension by a court of the state in which it was made

12.96 The question of whether arbitral awards that have been set aside can be enforced is resolved in Russia in various ways. Under article 23(2)(5) of the APC, a state court may deny issuance of a writ of execution if the party against which the award was made submits evidence that the award has been set aside or enforcement suspended by a commercial court or other state court in the Russian Federation, a court of the state in which the award was issued, or the state of the applicable law.[90]

12.97 In relations among the member states of the 1961 European Convention on International Commercial Arbitration, to which the Russian Federation is a party, Article IX(2) limits the application of Article V(1)(e) of the New York Convention to the cases referred to in Article IX(1) of the 1961 European Convention. Thus, if an award has been set aside by a court of the state in which it was issued on the basis of a violation of national public policy, the annulment will not have extraterritorial effect and will not serve as grounds for opposing the recognition or enforcement of the award in the Russian Federation.[91]

12.98 This question was considered in *Ciments Français v Sibirskiy Cement Holding Co.*[92] On 20 July 2011, the first instance commercial court in the city of Kemerovo issued a decision recognizing an ICC award that had been set aside at the arbitral seat. The court examined the interrelationship between Article IX of the 1961 European Convention and Article V of the New York Convention. The award in question, a partial award, had been issued by an ICC arbitral tribunal seated in Istanbul, Turkey. The successful claimant, *Ciments Français*, sought to have the award recognized in the Russian Federation, and the respondent, the *Sibirskiy Cement Holding Company*, objected on several grounds.

12.99 In particular, the respondent argued that the award was not binding because it had been set aside in Turkey. It also suggested that the recognition of the award would violate the public policy of the Russian Federation, because a Russian court had previously invalidated an underlying share purchase agreement. The Kemerovo court rejected the respondent's arguments and ordered recognition of the award in the Russian Federation. The court ruled that the alleged non-compliance of the award with certain domestic laws of Turkey, which was the ground cited for annulment of the award before the Turkish court, did not preclude a Russian court from recognizing the award in Russia, since the ground for annulment applied by the Turkish court was not expressly contemplated in the 1961 European Convention.

---

[90] cf in accordance with the 1958 New York Convention, Art 1(e), recognition and enforcement of a foreign arbitral award may be denied at the request of the party against which it is directed only if that party provides the competent local authorities with evidence that the award was set aside or suspended by a competent authority in the country whose law is applicable.

[91] This refers to local and international standards of annulment of arbitral awards, where the first have only a territorial effect (legal significance only in one state), and the second have international significance.

[92] *Ciments Français v Sibirskiy Cement Holding Co* Ruling of the RF Supreme Commercial Court No VAS-17458/11 (27 August 2012).

12.100 The ruling of the Kemerovo court followed an interesting path. It was overturned on appeal, by virtue of the prior invalidation of the underlying share purchase agreement. This decision of the appellate court was later affirmed by the RF Supreme Commercial Court.[93] The Supreme Commercial Court held that recognition of the partial award rendered on the basis of the invalid agreement violated Russian public policy. The *Ciments Français* case demonstrates the implications of recognition and enforcement in Russia of an arbitral award when the underlying contract has been invalidated by a Russian commercial court. This is, regrettably, often asserted by respondents resisting the enforcement of an arbitral award. Under Russian corporate law any shareholder, public prosecutor, or other governmental official may initiate court proceedings seeking invalidation of a contract containing an arbitration clause. Such claimants can apply to the Russian state courts because they are not bound by the arbitration agreement.

Arbitrability

12.101 The ICA Law, in the most general terms, indicates the types of disputes that may be considered and resolved in international commercial arbitration. According to the Moscow District Federal Commercial Court, a court should find that a particular category of dispute is not arbitrable if the dispute displays evidence of having a public policy nature. This conclusion must be supported by reference to federal law excluding that category of disputes from the competence of arbitral tribunals.[94]

12.102 A commercial court will grant an application for setting aside an arbitral award if it establishes that the award concerns matters within the exclusive competence of the Russian Federation commercial courts.[95] While only a few federal laws expressly provide for the exclusive competence of the state courts as a means of dispute resolution,[96] it has traditionally been considered that matters involving state regulation in various areas in which arbitration is not expressly excluded (subsoil, insurance, the securities market, employment, etc) could have 'public law' elements, and would be regarded by state courts as non-arbitrable.

12.103 A recent precedent-setting case on the arbitrability of disputes pertaining to real property is the decision of the Constitutional Court of the Russian Federation in *LLC Commercial Bank of Economic Development Bank Kazan v LLC BulgarRegionSnab, LLC DataDotZakamye*, which finally resolved a long-disputed question as to whether arbitrators may rule on issues involving the transfer of title to real property.[97] In this case, the RF Constitutional Court had to decide whether the arbitral tribunal had the right to make an award on the forfeiture of mortgaged property. Traditionally, Russian state courts had held that arbitral tribunals are not state judicial bodies and therefore cannot resolve real property disputes involving a public law element. In this case, arguably the 'public law element' concerned the statutory provisions prescribing amendment of the RF Unified State Register of Rights to Real Property following the transfer of title to the property.

---

[93] *Ciments Français* (n 92).

[94] APC, art 233(3)(1). See also Decision of the RF Supreme Commercial Court No 207/04 (11 May 2005).

[95] Information Letter No 96 (n 11) item 28.

[96] eg Federal Law No 127-FZ 'On Insolvency (Bankruptcy)' (26 October 2002), art 33(3); Federal Law No 135-FZ 'On Protection of Competition' (26 July 2006) arts 39, 52; Civil Proc Code, art 1406. See also Resolution of the Plenum of the RF High Court No 5, Plenum of the RF Supreme Commercial Court No 29 (26 March 2009) item 48.

[97] *LLC Commercial Bank of Economic Development Bank Kazan v LLC BulgarRegionSnab, LLC DataDotZakamye* Decision of the RF Constitutional Court (26 May 2011).

The RF Constitutional Court held, however, that the state registration of the real estate title neither formed part of the dispute nor changed the nature of the legal relationship. Therefore, state registration of title should not preclude an arbitral tribunal from resolving disputes involving real property. In parallel with this, the Constitutional Court expressly differentiated between state courts and arbitral tribunals, implying that the latter lack the power of the state judiciary to make directly applicable decisions concerning the forfeiture of mortgaged property. The RF Constitutional Court particularly stressed that in such cases, the transfer of title to real property is not founded on the arbitral award, which serves only as grounds for obtaining an execution order. The transfer of title takes place by an agreement executed further to a public auction or sale. Although the RF Constitutional Court did not directly address the constitutional issue of whether arbitral tribunals are part of the Russian Federation judiciary system, this decision may have far-reaching effects for the development of arbitration practice in Russian courts. **12.104**

Recent judicial practice excludes corporate disputes from the domain of arbitration. This could be seen as a serious step backwards compared to worldwide trends. It is likely that in the long term this will result in arbitration involving Russian organizations tending to move abroad, with all the ensuing consequences. In a recent controversial decision, the Presidium of the RF Supreme Commercial Court upheld lower court decisions that disputes arising out of corporate matters are not arbitrable. In the aforementioned *Novolipetsky Metallurgicheskii Kombinat* case, a dispute arising out of a share sale and purchase agreement had been resolved by ICAC arbitration.[98] The first instance court set aside the arbitral tribunal's award. In its findings, supported by the higher courts, the court interpreted amendments introduced into the APC on 19 July 2009 as vesting commercial courts with exclusive powers to resolve corporate disputes. The state cassation court pointed out that the wording of the new section 28(1) of the APC not only confirmed the attribution of competence between the state courts (commercial courts as opposed to courts of general jurisdiction), but also confirmed that corporate disputes cannot be resolved by arbitration. **12.105**

Public policy

There is a widespread perception that parties opposing the enforcement of awards in Russia almost invariably raise alleged violations of Russian public policy, which are, as a rule, upheld by the Russian courts. The inconsistent findings of Russian courts on this issue are partly attributable to the fact that the term 'public policy' is not defined in Russian law and is left to the discretion of the courts. At the same time, recent years have seen Russian courts work towards a more uniform conception of what should be understood by the term 'infringement of public policy'. **12.106**

In its recent overview of the court practice on the implementation of the public policy defence as a ground for denial of recognition and enforcement of foreign arbitral awards, the Presidium of the RF Supreme Commercial Court considered 12 cases and provided its guidance on the application of this defence.[99] **12.107**

The overriding position of the Presidium is that the broad interpretation of the concept of the public policy once favoured by the Russian courts, yields its position to a narrower one. **12.108**

---

[98] *Novolipetsky Metallurgicheskii Kombinat v NV Maksimov* Ruling of the RF Supreme Commercial Court No VAS-15384/11 (30 January 2012).

[99] Information Letter No 156 (n 11).

The Presidium clearly favoured a definition of public policy that narrows the grounds for challenging an arbitral award to situations in which it violates 'the fundamental principles of law that are supra-mandatory, universal, have distinctive public value, and form the basis of the economic, political and legal system of a state'. The Presidium also stressed that public policy grounds for overturning an arbitral award could be raised by the court *ex officio*.

12.109 In its previous recommendations, the RF Supreme Commercial Court also indicated that violation of public policy should be cited in cases where foreign law is applied. Where an arbitral award is made on the basis of Russian law, reference should be made to the failure to observe the fundamental principles of Russian Federation law.[100]

12.110 The recommendations of the RF Supreme Commercial Court summarize the approach to the issue of public policy already applied by some state courts. In *Odfjell v Severnoye Mashinostroitelnoe Predpriyatie*, the North-West District Federal Commercial Court concluded that an international arbitral award may infringe the public policy of the Russian Federation if enforcement would result in actions that: (a) either directly violate the law or are detrimental to the sovereignty or security of the state; (b) affect the interests of large social groups; (c) are incompatible with the fundamental principles of the country's economic, political, or legal systems; (d) affect the constitutional rights and liberties of individuals; or (e) contradict basic principles of civil law, such as the equality of the parties, the inviolability of property, and freedom of contract.[101]

12.111 In relation to the reconsideration of the merits of an arbitral award by state courts, the courts typically hold that a party's objections to the arbitral tribunal's application of the substantive law, establishment of the facts of the case, or assessment of evidence, do not constitute public policy grounds for setting aside under Russian law.[102]

12.112 It remains at issue whether international arbitral awards imposing specific penalties conform to the fundamental principles of Russian law. The Moscow District Federal Commercial Court, for example, has held that the award of an ad hoc tribunal in Stockholm was contrary to Russian public policy because the penalty imposed by the tribunal was punitive.[103] The Presidium of the RF Supreme Commercial Court did not concur in this decision and

---

[100] Ruling of the RF Supreme Commercial Court No VAS-3436/09 (18 May 2009); Ruling of the RF Supreme Commercial Court No 13452/07 (6 December 2007).

[101] *Odfjell v Severnoye Mashinostroitelnoe Predpriyatie* Ruling of the North-West District Federal Commercial Court No A05-10560/2010 (10 March 2011). This ruling was upheld by the RF Supreme Commercial Court; Ruling No VAS-4369/11 (26 May 2011). Russian judicial practice consistently recognizes the basic principles of civil law set out in the Civil Proc Code, art 1 (eg equality of parties to civil law relations, inviolability of property, freedom of contract, commensurate civil liability for the party at fault) as part of Russian public policy. See Ruling of the RF Supreme Commercial Court No VAS-5156/12 (28 April 2012); Decision of the Presidium of the RF Supreme Commercial Court No 15421/06 (20 March 2007). The RF Supreme Commercial Court has also held that in cases where recognition of an arbitral award is sought on the basis of an underlying contract that has been held invalid by a Russian court, recognition of an arbitral award would lead to the coexistence of contradictory judicial acts on the territory of the Russian Federation. In such cases a Russian court judgment invalidating the contract would take precedence over recognition of an arbitral award as a matter of Russian public policy. See *Ciments Français v Sibirskiy Cement Holding Co* Ruling of the RF Supreme Commercial Court No VAS-17458/11 (27 August 2012).

[102] Ruling of the RF Supreme Commercial Court No VAS-2532/12 (27 February 2012); Ruling of the RF Supreme Commercial Court No VAS-2682/10 (19 April 2010); Ruling of the East Siberian District Federal Commercial Court No A58-2103/05-F02-2135/06-C2 (16 October 2006).

[103] Ruling of the Moscow District Federal Commercial Court No KG-A40/922-06 (21 March 2006).

overturned the ruling, stating that Russian civil law provides liability for default or improper performance of contractual obligations in the form of a penalty. Therefore, penalties are part of the Russian Federation legal system and cannot per se be contrary to public policy.[104] Clearly, in this case, the Federal Commercial Court had appraised the facts of the case on the basis of the commensurateness of civil law liability and the consequences of the breach, with consideration for fault, ie it had reviewed the merits of the case.

In *Odfjell*, the respondent alleged that the amount of damages awarded by the arbitral tribunal was unfairly high and the award therefore violated Russian public policy.[105] This was rejected by the Cassation Court. The Court reasoned that the arbitral tribunal had fixed the amount of damages on the basis of applicable Swedish law. The Court further held that the tribunal's decision was made in accordance with relevant procedural and substantive law. Hence, in this case, the Federal Commercial Court took the view that the respondent's allegations sought to revisit the merits of the case and therefore should not be considered by the state courts.[106] **12.113**

12.5.2 Local procedures for setting aside/annulment

According to the ICA Law, an arbitral award may be challenged by a party to the proceedings by filing an application for setting aside with a competent state court.[107] The procedure for cases involving challenges to international arbitration awards with a seat in the Russian Federation is found in section 1 of Chapter 30 of the APC. **12.114**

Awards may be challenged only by the parties to the arbitration proceedings.[108] Other parties have the right to dispute an arbitral award only if the award has infringed their rights and lawful interests, or if it concerns their rights and obligations.[109] For example, local state authorities in a dispute concerning the recognition of title to an unauthorized building could take court action to defend their rights and lawful interests by seeking the annulment of an arbitral award.[110] **12.115**

By its nature, the setting aside procedure applies to final arbitral awards. However, these provisions are also applied to challenges against partial awards. Furthermore, in accordance with the procedure set out in section 1 of chapter 30 of the APC, challenges can be **12.116**

[104] Decision of the Presidium of the RF Supreme Commercial Court No 5243/06 (19 September 2006). See also Decision of the Presidium of the RF Supreme Commercial Court No 15421/06 (20 March 2007).

[105] *Odfjell v Severnoye Mashinostroitelnoe Predpriyatie* Ruling of the North-West District Federal Commercial Court No A05-10560/2010 (10 March 2011).

[106] In relation to liquidated damages, the position supported by the RF Supreme Court is as follows. A liquidated damages provision agreed by the parties in a contract will not be considered punitive damages or infringe Russian public policy merely because amount of such damages exceeds the actual damages or lost profits incurred by a party. To the extent the amount of the agreed liquidated damages is reasonable, the punitive component in a party's liability is admissible. However, violation of public policy is present in cases where the amount of the liquidated damages is abnormally high and manifestly exceeds the amount that parties could have foreseen entering into the contract, or in cases of abuse of the principle of the freedom of contract (weak negotiating party, violation of public interests, etc). See Information Letter No 156 (n 11).

[107] ICA Law, art 34.

[108] APC, art 230(2).

[109] eg Ruling of the RF Supreme Commercial Court No VAS-5417/10 (17 May 2010); ruling of the Volga-Vyatka District Federal Commercial Court No A11-4389/2010 (13 January 2011). While the cited cases were considered under Russian domestic arbitration regulations, it would be justifiable to suggest that the same line of reasoning might be applied by Russian courts in international arbitration cases where the Russian Federation is the seat of arbitration.

[110] Ruling of the Urals District Federal Commercial Court No F09-910/07-C5 (21 February 2007).

made against arbitral awards on agreed terms and consent awards, which are provided for in article 30 of the ICA Law and have equivalent legal force to a final award.[111]

12.117 At present, international commercial arbitration rulings in the form of an order cannot be challenged in a state court. An arbitral order dismissing arbitration proceedings without a final award can also not be challenged.[112]

12.118 The categorical position of the RF Supreme Commercial Court is that separate arbitral awards—including arbitral awards on the recovery of arbitration costs, determination of jurisdiction, or interim measures—issued in the form of a separate award, cannot be recognized or enforced in the Russian Federation. The RF Supreme Commercial Court bases this conclusion on the fact that a separate arbitral award is an interim act, while in accordance with applicable Russian law and the New York Convention, only arbitral awards resolving the dispute on its merits and issued at the end of the arbitration procedures can be enforced.[113] Therefore, it is important that a partial award, in contrast to a separate award, be the arbitral tribunal's final decision on the issues it concerns.

Precondition for raising jurisdictional objections at the enforcement stage

12.119 Several recent decisions of the RF Supreme Commercial Court evidence its intention to formulate a specific requirement for challenges to enforcement in the Russian Federation of arbitral awards rendered outside Russia. In the view of the RF Supreme Commercial Court, a party that participated in the arbitration proceedings and did not object to jurisdiction at the courts of the seat of arbitration is not allowed to challenge the enforcement of an award on jurisdictional grounds before the Russian state courts. This reasoning has been applied in *Living Consulting Group AB v Sokotel*, where the RF Supreme Commercial Court held that challenges to the tribunal's jurisdiction should be raised at the state courts of the seat of arbitration (in this case, the Swedish courts).[114] Failure to challenge the tribunal's jurisdiction at the seat undermines further attempts of an unsuccessful party to prevent the enforcement of the award by challenging the arbitral tribunal's jurisdiction at the enforcement court. In the opinion of the RF Supreme Commercial Court, such belated objections cannot constitute grounds for refusing the enforcement.

12.6 Conclusion

12.120 In a recent Survey on Russia as a Place for Arbitration conducted by the Russian National Committee of the International Chamber of Commerce, most respondents indicated that

[111] IV Reshetnikova, *Practice in the Application of the Arbitral Procedure Code of the Russian Federation* (2nd edn, Yright, 2012) 157.

[112] In 1998, the RF High Commercial Court clarified that in accordance with the ICA Law, art 32.2(3) an arbitral tribunal issues an order dismissing arbitration proceedings if it determines that continuing proceedings would be unnecessary or impossible for some reason. Challenges to an arbitral tribunal's orders dismissing arbitration proceedings are not provided for in the said Law. See High Court RF Survey of Judicial Practice 'Certain Aspects of Judicial Practice in Civil Cases' (1998) item 34.

[113] Decision of the Presidium of the RF Supreme Commercial Court No 6547/10 (5 October 2010).

[114] *Living Consulting Group AB v Sokotel* Ruling of the RF Supreme Commercial Court No VAS-11800/2011 (12 December 2011). See also Decision of the Presidium of the RF Supreme Commercial Court No 1787/11 (14 June 2011); *Odfjell v Severnoye Mashinostroitelnoe Predpriyatie* Ruling of the North-West District Federal Commercial Court No A05-10560/2010 (10 March 2011).

they did not have any manifestly positive or negative attitude towards Russia as a place for arbitration. Respondents were prepared to opt for Russia primarily when the governing law in the transaction in dispute was Russian or if refusing to accept Russia as the seat would be a deal breaker. This wariness could be explained by the fact that only a few of the respondents perceived Russia as being arbitration-friendly; however, relatively few respondents definitely considered Russia to be arbitration-*un*friendly.

This absence of 'exceptionally positive' or 'exceptionally negative' views evidences that con- **12.121**
tinued efforts in providing greater support to arbitration are required in order to bring the status of Russia's current international arbitration practices into line with international trends. On a positive note, it is perhaps fair to conclude that the Russian Federation appears to be moving gradually towards improving the efficiency of its legislation on international arbitration and abandoning the historical, overly formalistic approach of state courts on matters related to arbitration.

13

PARIS

*Carole Malinvaud and Christian Camboulive**

13.1 Background

13.1.1 History and development of arbitration

13.01 The development of arbitration in the history of the French legal system finds its roots during the French Revolution. Among the multiple reforms brought to French society at the time, one was devoted to the judicial reorganization of the country through a law adopted in August 1790. One of the three distinct pillars of the new judicial organization was arbitration. Article 1 of this text stated: 'As arbitration is the most reasonable means to settle disputes between citizens, the legislators shall not take any measure which would result in diminishing the attractiveness or the efficiency of the *compromis* (arbitration agreement).'[1]

13.02 Arbitration was, however, to face a significant setback in the middle of the 19th century, with a ruling of the Cour de Cassation holding that arbitration clauses (ie agreements to arbitrate

* The authors would like to thank Bassam Mirza and Astrid Westphalen for their valuable assistance.

[1] Quoted in J-J Clère, 'L'arbitrage révolutionnaire: apologie et déclin d'une institution (1790–1806)' Rev arb 1981.3, 7.

future disputes) were void.[2] It was only by a law of 31 December 1925 that the validity of arbitration clauses was re-established, but then only in commercial matters.[3]

At around the same time, in 1923, the International Chamber of Commerce (ICC) established the International Court of Arbitration, which has been headquartered in Paris since its inception and has enjoyed a steady development. This institution is now widely recognized as one of the most important arbitration institutions around the world, and has contributed to the prominence of Paris as an international arbitration venue. **13.03**

The arbitration-friendly attitude of France was bolstered by a series of landmark judicial decisions in the 1960s and 1970s. French courts laid down a series of substantive rules reinforcing the effectiveness of international arbitration clauses. These included autonomy of arbitration agreements from the main contract,[4] validity of arbitration agreements concluded by state-owned entities,[5] and validity of international arbitration agreements.[6] **13.04**

The flexibility and liberalism of the French approach towards international arbitration was then embodied in the law in the early 1980s, which further contributed to making Paris a leading venue in international arbitration. French arbitration law was recently reformed to consolidate its rules and further improve its efficiency. **13.05**

The flexibility of French arbitration law

Since the early 1980s, France has had a legislative framework that encourages and facilitates arbitration. The enactment of this legislative framework preceded by a few years the adoption of the UNCITRAL Model Law in 1985, which may explain why France did not adopt the Model Law. Initially derived from Decree no 80-354 of 14 May 1980 (for domestic arbitration) and Decree no 81-500 of 12 May 1981 (for international arbitration), French arbitration law has been praised for its flexibility and pro-arbitration stance.[7] **13.06**

French courts have further enhanced this supportive legislative approach. One of the most salient illustrations of French judicial support can be found in relation to the validity of arbitration clauses. In the 1960s and 1970s, French courts pursued their identification of 'substantive rules' (*règles matérielles*) of international arbitration law. A well-known 1993 case held that 'pursuant to a substantive rule of international law of arbitration, the arbitration clause is legally independent from the main contract providing it[8] . . . and its existence and its validity must be examined . . . without the need to refer to any national law',[9] emphasizing French law's favourable stance towards arbitration. **13.07**

According to the French approach to international arbitration, an international arbitrator does not render an award under the aegis of a given state legal system. The arbitral award is rather an international ruling that is not anchored in any legal order.[10] **13.08**

[2] Cass Civ 10 July 1843, *Compagnie l'Alliance v Prunier*, S 1843 I 561, D 1843 I 343 (Court of Cassation).

[3] M de Boisséson, *Le droit français de l'arbitrage interne et international* (GLN Joly Editions, 1990) para 16.

[4] Cass Civ (1) 7 May 1963, *Société Gosset v Société Carapelli*, Rev arb 1963.60 (Court of Cassation).

[5] Cass Civ (1) 2 May 1966, *Trésor Public v Galakis*, RCDIP 1967.553 (Court of Cassation).

[6] Cass Civ (1) 4 July 1972, *Hecht v Société Buisman's*, Rev arb 1974.89 (Court of Cassation).

[7] J Rubellin-Devichi and E Loquin, 2012 Juris-Classeur Procédure Civile, fasc 1010, para 49.

[8] This principle of the separability of the arbitration agreement from the contract is now endorsed in the French Code of Civil Procedure (hereinafter 'CPC'), art 1447.

[9] Cass Civ (1) 20 December 1993, *Municipalité de Khoms El Mergeb v Société Dalico Contractors*, Rev arb 1994.116 (Court of Cassation).

[10] Cass Civ (1) 29 June 2007, *Société PT Putrabali Adyamulia v Société Rena Holding et autre*, Rev arb 2006.665 (Court of Cassation).

13.09 Another, more controversial, illustration of this principle concerns a case in which the setting aside of an award in the country in which it was rendered was held not to be an obstacle to its recognition in France.[11] This decision was based not on a lack of comity vis-à-vis a foreign court, but on the view that arbitral tribunals do not acquire authority from the state in which they are seated.

13.10 French courts, and especially the Paris courts, have long demonstrated a supportive approach to arbitration, devoid of undue interference in the arbitral process. This has now been codified by formalizing the function of *juge d'appui* or 'supporting judge', whose role is to assist the parties and the arbitrators and support arbitration proceedings, especially ad hoc proceedings. State courts have also adopted a restrictive approach to challenges aimed at setting aside international awards, thereby demonstrating an attitude that is protective of arbitration, applicable to all arbitrations seated in France, whether ad hoc or conducted under the rules of an arbitration institution.

13.11 Some 30 years after the 1980 reform, it was felt that the provisions of 1980 no longer reflected current French arbitration law as interpreted by its court decisions.

13.1.2 Modern and recent developments

The recent reform of the French law of arbitration

13.12 In 2010, the French public authorities expanded on and enhanced an initiative of the French *Comité de l'Arbitrage* to reform French arbitration law. Following broad consultation with all major stakeholders in the arbitration arena, the text eventually agreed entered into force through Decree no 2011-48 of 13 January 2011. The aim was to reform both domestic and international arbitration to consolidate existing case law, supplement the law, and introduce provisions inspired by other jurisdictions, in order to improve its efficiency.[12] The decree of 13 January 2011 entered into force on 1 May 2011. It was immediately applicable, with the exception of certain provisions that apply only to arbitration agreements concluded after 1 May 2011, and to arbitral tribunals constituted or awards rendered after that date.[13]

13.13 Preserving the approach of the 1980 legislation, the new decree maintains the distinction between domestic and international arbitration. An arbitration is considered to be international if it 'concerns international commercial interests'.[14] This definition has an economic rather than a geographical focus and does not depend on 'the nationality of the parties, the law applicable to the merits or to the arbitration, or the place of arbitration'.[15] An arbitration will generally be treated as international if it involves a cross-border flow

---

[11] Cass Civ (1) 23 March 1994, *Société Hilmarton v Société OTV*, Rev arb 1994.327 (Court of Cassation).

[12] Rapport au Premier ministre relatif au décret no 2011-48 du 13 janvier 2011 portant réforme de l'arbitrage, 2011 JO Rep fr 773.

[13] Decree No 2011-48 of 13 January 2011 regarding arbitration reform, 2011 JO Rep fr 777, art 3 (hereinafter 'Decree No 2011-48').

[14] CPC, art 1504.

[15] CA Paris 25 March 1999, *Consorts Häusler v Société européenne de Meunerie*, Rev arb 2003.123 (Regional Court of Appeal), a dispute arising out of various contracts concluded between two French companies, organizing the funding of foreign entities (Canada and Iran), and involving the guarantee of a company from Liechtenstein.

of funds,[16] goods,[17] or services.[18] The provisions on domestic arbitration are now codified in articles 1442 to 1503 of the CPC, and the provisions on international arbitration are in articles 1504 to 1527. Article 1506 CPC lists those domestic provisions that are also applicable to international arbitration unless the parties decide to opt out of them by agreement.[19] Article 1506 CPC is a beacon of French liberalism, as it allows parties to an international arbitration to derogate, directly or by reference to different rules, from provisions they consider ill-suited to their dispute.

As the focus of this chapter is on international arbitration, the French domestic rules will not be addressed unless they are relevant to international arbitral proceedings. **13.14**

13.2 Commencing the Arbitration

Under the principle of *competence-competence*, where there is an arbitration agreement that is not 'manifestly void or inapplicable', or once a dispute has been submitted to an arbitral tribunal, national courts must decline jurisdiction. However, despite the existence of an arbitration clause, national courts may play a significant role in supporting an arbitration. Indeed, French judges may order interim and conservatory measures despite the existence of an arbitration clause, and may resolve difficulties regarding the constitution of the arbitral tribunal. **13.15**

13.2.1 Stay of litigation

The principle of competence-competence

An arbitral tribunal can only decide matters that fall within its jurisdiction as defined by the arbitration agreement. When a party challenges the existence or scope of the arbitral tribunal's jurisdiction, the arbitral tribunal has priority in determining its own jurisdiction.[20] In effect, it is incumbent on an arbitral tribunal to decide upon the validity and scope of the arbitration agreement. While it does so under the ultimate control of the state courts, this control is to be exercised only after the award has been issued by the arbitral tribunal. **13.16**

---

[16] CA Paris 9 June 1983, *Société Iro-Holding v Société Sétilex*, Rev arb 1983.497 (Regional Court of Appeal), a dispute arising out of a contract concluded between a company from Liechtenstein and a German company, concerning the global broadcasting and distribution of a film).

[17] CA Paris 28 January 1988, *CCC Filmkunst v Société EDIF*, Rev arb 1988.565 (Regional Court of Appeal), a dispute arising out of a subcontract concluded between two French companies, closely linked to the main contract providing for the transfer of civil engineering outside France for the benefit of a foreign contracting authority.

[18] CA Paris 14 March 1989, *Société Murgue Seigle v Société Coflexip*, Rev arb 1991.355 (Regional Court of Appeal).

[19] CPC, art 1506 provides:

> Unless the parties have agreed otherwise, and subject to the provisions of the present Title, the following Articles shall apply to international arbitration: (1) 1446, 1447, 1448 (paras 1 and 2) and 1449 regarding the arbitration agreement; (2) 1452 through 1458 and 1460 regarding the constitution of the arbitral tribunal and the procedure governing application to the judge acting in support of the arbitration; (3) 1462, 1463 (para 2), 1464 (para 3), 1465 through 1470 and 1472 regarding arbitral proceedings; (4) 1479, 1481, 1482, 1484 (paras 1 and 2), 1485 (paras 1 and 2) and 1486 regarding arbitral awards; (5) 1502 (paras 1 and 2) and 1503 regarding means of recourse other than appeals or actions to set aside.

[20] Cass Civ (1) 5 January 1999, *M Zanzi v J de Coninck et autres*, Rev arb 1999.260 (Court of Cassation): 'according to the principle... under which the arbitrator must decide on his own jurisdiction'.

13.17 This principle of *competence-competence* has both a positive and negative effect. The positive effect is expressed in article 1465 CPC, according to which an arbitral tribunal has exclusive jurisdiction to rule on challenges to its jurisdiction. The negative effect, which was previously a combination of the old article 1458 CPC and case law,[21] is now embodied in article 1448 CPC. According to this provision, if the dispute has already been submitted to an arbitral tribunal, French courts are required to decline jurisdiction and refer the parties to arbitration. If the dispute has not yet been brought before an arbitral tribunal, French courts must decline jurisdiction unless the court finds that the arbitration agreement is manifestly void or manifestly inapplicable.

13.18 The concept of manifest nullity or manifest inapplicability is narrowly construed, and any uncertainty will be resolved in favour of arbitration.[22] The burden of proof is on the party seeking to avoid arbitration, who must establish that the arbitration agreement is manifestly void or manifestly inapplicable. The new regime confirms the previous presumption in favour of arbitration that applies from the moment an arbitration agreement is inserted into a contract.

13.19 The value that French courts give to the negative effect of the *competence-competence* principle can be illustrated by the following examples. Under certain circumstances, case law has accepted the extension of an arbitration clause to a party that was not signatory to, but was involved in the negotiation, performance or termination of, the contract containing the arbitration agreement, to the extent that that party is deemed to have accepted the arbitration clause. It is for the arbitrator to decide whether this third party should be a party to the arbitration;[23] the arbitrator will rule on his or her own jurisdiction to deal with the issue raised. Similarly, a party may claim that the wording of an arbitration agreement is broad enough to cover allegations of tort liability.[24] The French courts will not rule on the scope of the clause and will refer the parties to arbitration, leaving the arbitrators full jurisdiction to decide whether tort liability should fall under the ambit of a contractually agreed arbitration clause.

13.20 In the light of a recent decision of the Cour de Cassation, it is possible that French courts will not enforce agreements that confer on one party an unrestricted choice of forum while binding the other party. Although the Cour de Cassation had previously upheld an agreement that allowed one party to either submit a dispute to the Dutch courts or to arbitration,[25] it recently held that a clause requiring a bank's customer to litigate in the courts of Luxemburg while giving the bank the option to proceed in the courts of the customer's domicile or 'before any other competent court' was too discretionary ('*potestative*') and contravened the object and finality of prorogation

[21] Cass Civ (1) 16 October 2001, *Société Quarto Children Books Ltd v Société Editions du Seuil et Société Editions Phidal Inc*, Rev Arb 2002.919 (Court of Cassation).

[22] Cass Civ (1) 1 December 1999, *Société Exportles v Société Rusbois*, Rev arb 2000.96, note Fouchard (Court of Cassation).

[23] Cass Civ (1) 11 July 2006, *Société Roger Albert Distribution v Société British American Tobacco UK and Export Limited et autres*, Rev arb 2006.870 (Court of Cassation).

[24] Cass Civ (1) 25 April 2006, *Société DMN Machinefabriek BV v Société Tripette et Renaud*, Rev arb 2006.487 (Court of Cassation).

[25] CA Angers 25 September 1972, *S.A Sicaly v Société Grasso Stacon Koninklijke Machine Fabrieken NV et société Seffinco Engineering Company*, Rev arb 1973.164 (Regional Court of Appeal); Cass Civ (1) 15 May 1974, *Société d'intérêt Collectif Agricole (SICA), des Producteurs Agricoles du Centre Ouest (Sicaly) v Société Grasso Stacon NV et Société Grasso Stacon Koninklijke Machine Fabrieken NV*, Bull civ des arrêts Cass Civ (1) No 143 122 (Court of Cassation).

of jurisdiction under Article 23 of Regulation (EC) 44/2001.[26] While this case involved a clause providing for the selection of a judicial forum rather than arbitration, the same reasoning could apply to clauses giving only one party a choice between litigation and arbitration. It is as yet unclear, however, whether this reasoning will apply to all unilateral choice of jurisdiction clauses or only to clauses giving one party an unrestricted and therefore unpredictable unilateral choice.

13.2.2 Interim and conservatory measures

Obtaining interim and conservatory measures from state courts despite the existence of an arbitration agreement

When there is an arbitration agreement and the arbitral tribunal has not yet been constituted, parties may apply to the French *juge des référés* (the summary judge who is the president of the *Tribunal de grande instance* or the president of the *Tribunal de commerce*) in order to obtain interim or conservatory measures.[27] A party applying to the courts for provisional or protective measures does not waive its right to submit the merits of the dispute to an arbitral tribunal. In that context, a party may seek measures under article 145 CPC, under the classical *référé,* and under the *référé-provision.* **13.21**

Evidentiary measures pursuant to article 145 CPC Under French procedural law, article 145 CPC allows a party to apply for evidentiary measures prior to an action on the merits before state courts. This possibility may also be used in the context of arbitration, whether or not seated in France. The jurisdiction of the courts to order an evidentiary measure is defined on the basis of the domicile of the respondent or on the basis of the place of the performance of the measure sought. Indeed, despite the existence of an arbitration clause, a party may rely on article 145 CPC 'if there are legitimate grounds for preserving or establishing, prior to any legal proceedings, proof of facts which may determine the outcome of the dispute'. The urgency of the situation does not need to be proven,[28] however, no request can be made under article 145 CPC once the arbitral tribunal is constituted.[29] **13.22**

Interim and conservatory measures pursuant to article 1449 CPC Despite the existence of an arbitration agreement, the *juge des référés* may order any type of interim or conservatory measures to preserve the status quo.[30] In this situation, however, the party seeking such measures must prove the urgency of the situation. **13.23**

There has been scholarly debate over whether a measure can be granted in summary court proceedings once the arbitral tribunal has been constituted. Notwithstanding the lack of case law, leading scholars take the view that the *juge des référés* can order interim measures even after the constitution of the arbitral tribunal.[31] Indeed, the *juge des référés* should retain this **13.24**

[26] Cass Civ (1) 26 September 2012, *Mme X v Compagnie Financière Edmond de Rothschild et Banque Privée Edmond de Rothschild*, no 11-26.022 (Court of Cassation). Council Regulation (EC) 44/2001 on jurisdiction and the recognition and enforcement of judgments in civil and commercial matters [2001] OJ L012, known as the 'Brussels Regulation', governs the jurisdiction of the courts of the EU Member States over civil and commercial claims and takes precedence over national law.

[27] CPC, art 1449.

[28] Cass Civ (1) 20 December 1982, *SCI Le Panorama v Société immobilière et mobilière du Tertre (SIMT)*, Rev arb 1986.233 (Court of Cassation); Cass Ch mixte 7 May 1982, *BNP v SARL Fransucre*, RTD Civ 1982.786 (Court of Cassation).

[29] *SCI Le Panorama* (n 28).

[30] CPC, art 1449.

[31] C Jarrosson and J Pellerin, 'Le droit français de l'arbitrage après le décret du 13 janvier 2011' Rev arb 2011.5, para 18.

power, because the arbitral tribunal may lack the power to order certain types of measures (eg the attachment of assets; see also article 1468 CPC, which expressly provides that only courts may order conservatory attachments and judicial security).

13.25 **Interim measures through the *référé-provision*** Under French procedural law, a party may apply for an interim payment of sums allegedly due using the *référé-provision*. The *référé-provision* is an effective procedure that enables a creditor to enforce its rights before a ruling on the merits is made, provided these rights are not 'seriously disputable'.[32] As the *référé-provision* is a provisional measure, it is widely accepted that a party can use it despite the existence of an arbitration clause.[33] Whether the creditor's rights are seriously disputable or not may come close to being a substantive issue. It follows that the national courts' jurisdiction to grant a *référé-provision* and the arbitrators' jurisdiction over the merits may overlap. Thus, to limit the risk of a court's infringement of the arbitral tribunal's jurisdiction over the merits of the case, there are two additional cumulative conditions: (a) the arbitral tribunal has not been constituted and (b) the urgency of the situation can be established.[34] Therefore, as soon as the arbitral tribunal is constituted, the national courts can no longer order this provisional remedy and the arbitral tribunal will have the sole power to do so.

13.2.3 Judicial assistance in constituting the arbitral tribunal

13.26 Any difficulties in constituting of the arbitral tribunal will be resolved by the person or entity responsible for administering the arbitration, generally the arbitration institution chosen by the parties or, where there is no such person or entity, by the French *juge d'appui* (eg in the case of an ad hoc arbitration seated in France).[35]

13.27 Under French international arbitration law, unless the parties have agreed otherwise, the *juge d'appui* is the President of the *Tribunal de Grande Instance* of Paris.[36] The rationale for concentrating these cases in Paris, in the hands of a single specialized judge, is to increase the coherence of the decisions made in arbitration-related cases. The French *juge d'appui* has jurisdiction to assist the parties in the constitution of the arbitral tribunal in four situations.[37] The *juge d'appui* will assist the parties if (a) the arbitral seat is in France (geographical criterion), (b) the parties have agreed that the arbitration is to be governed by French procedural law (legal criterion), (c) the parties have introduced a jurisdiction clause permitting the French courts to rule on difficulties encountered in the arbitral proceedings (voluntary criterion), or (d) there is a risk of denial of justice if the court does not intervene. This last and newly introduced ground of jurisdiction was initially recognized in case law[38] before being codified by the decree of 13 January 2011. A denial of justice may arise when the parties cannot agree on the constitution of the arbitral tribunal and no other state court judge has jurisdiction or agrees to assist the parties with the constitution of the arbitral tribunal.

---

[32] CPC, art 809, para 2 and art 873, para 2.

[33] Cass Civ (3) 9 July 1979, *SCI La Lagune v SARL SERCIF*, Rev arb 1980.78 (Court of Cassation).

[34] Cass Civ (1) 6 March 1990, *Société Horeva v Société Sitas*, Rev arb 1990.633 (Court of Cassation); E Gaillard and J Savage (eds), *Fouchard, Gaillard, Goldman on International Commercial Arbitration* (Kluwer Law International, 1999) paras 1344–1345.

[35] CPC, arts 1452–1458.

[36] CPC, art 1505.

[37] CPC, art 1505.

[38] Cass Civ (1) 1 February 2005, *Etat d'Israel v Société NIOC*, Rev arb 2005 693 (Court of Cassation).

According to article 1460 CPC, the *juge d'appui* rules by way of an order. When the *juge d'appui* appoints an arbitrator, the order is not subject to appeal. Conversely, a ruling that no appointment need be made because the arbitration clause is manifestly void or manifestly inapplicable may be appealed.[39] **13.28**

In a 1989 case, the President of the *Tribunal de Grande Instance* of Paris ruled that the *juge d'appui's* scope of intervention is not limited to the constitution of the arbitral tribunal *ab initio*,[40] and that the *juge d'appui* also has the power to resolve any difficulty that arises from a later event affecting the constitution of the tribunal or preventing the arbitral tribunal from accomplishing its duties. For instance, the *juge d'appui* has jurisdiction to assist with the reconstitution of the arbitral tribunal after an arbitrator's default, resignation,[41] or death.[42] **13.29**

The decree of 13 January 2011 also introduced a new provision (article 1453 CPC), according to which, in a multi-party arbitration, the constitution of the arbitral tribunal must comply with the principle of equal treatment of the parties. This principle was drawn from a landmark multi-party case in which the claimant appointed the arbitrator of its choice but the two respondents, having diverging interests, could not reach an agreement as to the nomination of their joint arbitrator.[43] The ICC Court decided that the two respondents had to appoint an arbitrator jointly. The French courts subsequently annulled the award for inequality between the parties in the constitution of the arbitral tribunal, holding that 'the principle of equal treatment of the parties in the appointment of the arbitrators is part of public policy [and therefore, it could] only be waived after the dispute [had] arisen'. Therefore, the parties must be granted the same rights regarding the appointment of the arbitrators. **13.30**

Article 1453 CPC codified this principle and provides that: **13.31**

> If there are more than two parties to the dispute and they fail to agree on the procedure for constituting the arbitral tribunal, the person responsible for administering the arbitration or, where there is no such person, the judge acting in support of the arbitration (the *juge d'appui*), shall appoint the arbitrator(s).

Thus, in a multi-party arbitration where several respondents fail to appoint an arbitrator jointly, all arbitrators must be appointed by the juge d'appui or arbitral institution, irrespective of any prior appointment made. This new provision in article 1453 CPC mirrors similar changes made to a number of institutional arbitration rules.[44]

13.3 During the Arbitration

During the course of an arbitration, the parties can apply to the French courts when seeking to challenge an arbitrator or, under certain circumstances, when requesting an order for the production of evidence. There are no restraints on foreign practitioners acting as counsel or arbitrators, and the conduct of arbitration hearings in international arbitration is characterized by liberalism. **13.32**

39 CPC, arts 1455 and 1460.

40 TGI Paris 12 July 1989, *Société La Belle Créole SA v Société The Gemtel Partnership*, Rev arb 1990.176 (Superior Court).

41 TGI Paris 15 February 1995, *Société Industrialexport v K et autres*, Rev arb 1996.503 (Superior Court).

42 *Société La Belle* (n 40).

43 Cass Civ (1) 7 January 1992, *Sociétés BKMI et Siemens v Société Dutco*, Rev arb 1992.470 (Court of Cassation).

44 eg ICC Rules of Arbitration, art 12.8; LCIA Arbitration Rules, arts 8.1 and 8.2; HKIAC Administered Arbitration Rules, art 8.2.c; SIAC Rules, rr 9.1 and 9.2.

13.3.1 The role of the courts in deciding challenges of arbitrators

13.33 The confidence of the parties in the arbitral tribunal is crucial to arbitration. Arbitrators must therefore be and remain independent and impartial vis-à-vis the parties. If they are not, a party may raise a challenge before the administering institution, or, in ad hoc arbitration, before the *juge d'appui*.

Obligation to disclose any circumstances that may affect the arbitrator's independence or impartiality

13.34 French arbitration law requires arbitrators to be independent and impartial vis-à-vis the parties and to remain so during the entire arbitration process.[45] According to an old but still valid formulation of the Cour de Cassation, which applies to both domestic[46] and international[47] arbitration, 'an independent mind is indispensable to the exercise of judicial power, whatever the source of that power may be, [and it is] one of the essential qualities of an arbitrator'.

13.35 Independence is an objective notion, while impartiality is more subjective. Nonetheless, these concepts are intertwined and it is difficult to give a comprehensive definition of either. Guaranteeing the arbitrator's freedom of judgment, 'independence' refers to financial and material independence, and concrete evidence can be presented to prove or disprove it. On the other hand, 'impartiality' alludes to an abstract concept which is independence of mind, and therefore direct or positive proof of impartiality is harder to provide.

13.36 To ensure compliance with the obligations of independence and impartiality, article 1456 CPC requires an arbitrator to 'disclose any circumstances that may affect his or her independence or impartiality'. This is a continuous obligation applicable from the constitution of the arbitral tribunal until the award is rendered.[48]

13.37 The facts that must be revealed are restricted to those not publicly known (encouraging the parties to do their own homework), which may reasonably be expected to have an impact on the arbitrator's judgment.[49] The arbitrator must disclose 'all circumstances of a kind that may affect his or her judgment and that may provoke, in the eyes of the parties, a reasonable doubt concerning [his or her impartiality or independence]'.[50] This subjective standard of disclosure requires the arbitrator to take into account the parties' reasonable doubts, irrespective of whether he considers them justified or not. The Cour de Cassation has held that the obligation to disclose facts calling into question the independence and impartiality of an arbitrator is extensive.[51]

---

[45] CPC, art 1456, para 2.

[46] Cass Civ (2) 13 April 1972, *Consorts Ury v Galeries Lafayette*, JCP G II 1972.17 189; Rev arb 1975.235 (Court of Cassation).

[47] CA Paris 8 June 1972, *Woltz v SODIPAR*, Rev arb 1973.38 (Regional Court of Appeal); CA Paris 12 December 1996, *Société Commercial Agraria Hermanos Lucena v Société Transgrain France*, Rev arb 1998.699 (Regional Court of Appeal).

[48] CPC, art 1456, para 2.

[49] CA Paris 9 April 1992, *Société Annahold BV et D Frydman v L'Oréal et autres*, Rev arb 1996.483 (Regional Court of Appeal).

[50] Cass Civ (1) 16 March 1999, *Etat du Qatar v Société Creighton*, Rev arb 1999.308 (Court of Cassation).

[51] Cass Civ (1) 20 October 2010, *M Marcel Batard v Sté Prodim et autre*, Rev arb 2011.669 (Court of Cassation).

In *Batard v Prodim*, the arbitrator failed to disclose that he had already been appointed 34 times by the same party. The French Court set aside the award because of this lack of disclosure, reasoning that the arbitrator's disclosure obligation required him to disclose to the parties the full situation. According to recent case law, failure to disclose information, even if unknown to the arbitrator and therefore scarcely affecting his independence or impartiality, may suffice to disqualify the arbitrator or set aside the award.[52] Conversely, French courts refuse to set aside arbitration awards when the applicant does not demonstrate how the undisclosed circumstances would have created a 'reasonable' doubt as to the independence or impartiality of an arbitrator.[53] This issue has given rise to intense scholarly debate. It illustrates the difficult balance between the legitimate expectations of the parties concerning the independence of the arbitrator and the necessary confidence and peace of mind required by an arbitrator in deciding a dispute. **13.38**

The requirements for the challenge of an arbitrator

The parties may challenge an arbitrator who has failed to comply with his or her obligation of independence and impartiality. Article 1458 CPC provides that an arbitrator can be removed only 'with the unanimous consent of the parties'. If the parties cannot agree on the removal of an arbitrator, the person or entity responsible for administering the arbitration, or the *juge d'appui* in an ad hoc arbitration, will resolve the issue.[54] **13.39**

The decree of 13 January 2011 introduced article 1456 CPC, which provides that for tribunals constituted after 1 May 2011, a party may challenge an arbitrator before the *juge d'appui* within a period of one month after the disclosure or discovery of a fact casting doubt on the arbitrator's qualities. If a party fails to invoke the lack of independence or impartiality of the arbitrator in a timely fashion, it will be deemed to have waived the right to challenge the arbitrator before the *juge d'appui* during the arbitration. Each party must act in good faith and must not wait for the award stage to suddenly raise objections of which it had prior knowledge. However, as long as the party raises its concern before the arbitral tribunal during the arbitration process, it will be able to challenge the award when rendered. **13.40**

In the context of institutional arbitration, challenges against arbitrators are to be raised and dealt with in accordance with the applicable arbitration rules. The *juge d'appui* has no supervisory role over the decisions of the institution and the issue can be submitted to the French courts only in the context of a challenge to the award. **13.41**

13.3.2 Role of courts in compelling testimony and evidence

While arbitral tribunals have the power to order the parties to the arbitration to disclose evidence and are, more generally, responsible for deciding any evidentiary matters, French courts may, with leave of the arbitral tribunal, summon a third party to the arbitration to produce evidence. **13.42**

[52] CA Reims 2 November 2011, *SAJ & P Avax v Société Tecnimont SPA* (2012) ASA Bulletin 197, Rev arb 2012.112 (Regional Court of Appeal).
[53] Cass Civ (1) 10 October 2012, *EURL Tecso v SAS Neoelectra Group*, No 11-20.299 (Court of Cassation).
[54] CPC, art 1456, para 3.

The arbitral tribunal may order a party to the arbitration to disclose evidence

13.43 Article 1467 CPC provides that arbitral tribunals may order a party to the arbitration to disclose evidence in its possession, even attaching penalties for non-compliance. The arbitrator's new express power to order penalties in the event of non-compliance was previously recognized by case law.[55] According to certain scholars, as soon as the arbitral tribunal is constituted, the French courts lose jurisdiction to order a party to produce evidence.[56] The rationale is that the drafters of the decree considered the arbitral tribunal's power adequate and intervention from the French courts unnecessary once arbitrators are in place to take the necessary steps.[57]

The courts may order a third party to disclose evidence

13.44 The arbitral tribunal, lacking *imperium* over third parties to the arbitration, cannot order them to produce evidence. However, the French courts can assist the parties in obtaining documents held by third parties. Indeed, article 1469 CPC states that if a party:

> ... intends to rely on an official or private deed to which it was not a party or on evidence held by a third party, it may, with leave of the arbitral tribunal, have that third party summoned before the President of the Tribunal de Grande Instance for the purpose of obtaining a copy thereof or the production of the deed or item of evidence.[58]

Commentators have characterized this new provision as an 'ambitious and balanced' procedure under which a party requests the authorization of the arbitral tribunal to bring the matter before the president of the *Tribunal de Grande Instance.*[59] Then, if the arbitral tribunal agrees, the president of the *Tribunal de Grande Instance* will decide whether to summons the third party to produce the document in question.

13.45 The proceedings before the president of the *Tribunal de Grande Instance* take the form of summary proceedings (*référé*). However, and by contrast with orders issued in other summary proceedings, the order rendered is not immediately enforceable and a party can appeal against it within 15 days following service (*signification*). The mechanism of article 1469 CPC combines the concentration of powers in the hands of the arbitrator, who controls the arbitration, with the *imperium* of the court, which supports the arbitration process.

13.3.3 Ability of foreign practitioners to appear as counsel or arbitrator

13.46 Despite the silence of the CPC on this issue, it is commonly accepted that for an arbitration taking place in France, a party may appear in person or be represented by the person of its choice. Under French arbitration law, there is no requirement for specific diplomas or bar admission to assist a party to an arbitration[60] or to be an arbitrator. Foreign practitioners are therefore free to appear in Paris-venued arbitrations as counsel or arbitrators.

---

[55] CA Paris 7 October 2004, *Société Otor Participations et autres v Société Carlyle Holdings 1 et autre*, Rev arb 2005.737 (Regional Court of Appeal).

[56] E Gaillard and P de Lapasse, 'Le nouveau droit français de l'arbitrage interne et international' (January 2011) 3 Recueil Dalloz 175, para 14.

[57] Gaillard and de Lapasse (n 56) para 14.

[58] CPC, art 1469, para 1.

[59] T Clay, 'L'appui du juge à l'arbitrage' (2011) 2 Paris J Intl Arb 331, para 56.

[60] CA Paris 14 October 1977, D 1978.298 (Regional Court of Appeal); Cass Civ (1) 19 June 1979, *SARL Primor v Société d'exploitation industrielle de Betaigne, Association nationale des Avocats et autres*, Rev arb 1979.487 (Court of Cassation).

13.3.4 Local requirements for the conduct of arbitration hearings

The parties may, in their arbitration agreement, define 'the procedure to be followed in the arbitral proceedings, directly or by reference to arbitration rules or to procedural rules'.[61] Unless the arbitration agreement provides otherwise, arbitrators have the power to determine the procedure as they see fit, 'either directly or by reference to arbitration rules or to procedural rules'.[62] However, the arbitral tribunal must uphold the principle of due process and equal treatment of the parties.[63] The arbitrators must also act diligently and in good faith in the conduct of the proceedings.[64] This obligation is now expressly integrated in the new article 1464 CPC. However, failure to comply with such obligation is not, at this stage, subject to any sanction.[65] Moreover, this obligation was already implicitly recognized by French courts.[66] **13.47**

Aside from these fundamental principles, French arbitration law is flexible regarding the conduct of the hearings. The parties can choose the language applicable to the arbitration, and witnesses called to give evidence do not have to be sworn.[67] **13.48**

There has been a debate in France, as elsewhere, as to whether international arbitration proceedings should be confidential. While confidentiality is now expressly imposed in domestic arbitration,[68] there is no such requirement in the statutory provisions applicable to international arbitration. In 1986, a French court stated that confidentiality was inherent to the nature of arbitral proceedings.[69] In a 2004 decision, however, the Court of Appeal raised doubts by stating that in international arbitration the parties must prove the existence of an obligation of confidentiality.[70] Scholars consider that the absence of a general statutory provision for the confidentiality of international arbitration in the new regime results from a deliberate choice by the French legislator not to impose confidentiality on international investment arbitrations, in which it would not be appropriate.[71] There is a debate between scholars on whether or not confidentiality would still constitute a principle inherent to international arbitration.[72] In that context, parties wishing to provide for the confidentiality of an international arbitration to which French arbitration law will apply would be well advised to expressly stipulate it in their arbitration agreement. **13.49**

13.4 The Award

When rendering an award, the arbitrators must comply with mandatory rules as to form and substance. **13.50**

[61] CPC, art 1509, para 1.
[62] CPC, art 1509, para 2.
[63] CPC, arts 1509 and 1510.
[64] CPC, arts 1509 and 1464, para 3.
[65] Jarrosson (n 31) 2011.16, para 34.
[66] CA Paris 28 February 2008, *Liv Hidravlika DOO v SA Diebolt*, Rev arb 2008.712 (Regional Court of Appeal); CA Paris 22 January 2009, *SNF SAS v Chambre de Commerce Internationale*, RTD Com 2010.542 (Regional Court of Appeal).
[67] CPC, art 1467.
[68] CPC, art 1509 and art 1464, para 4.
[69] CA Paris 18 February 1986, *G Aïta v A Ojjeh*, Rev arb 1986.583 (Regional Court of Appeal).
[70] CA Paris 22 January 2004, *Société National Company For Fishing and Marketing 'NAFIMCO' v Société Foster Wheeler Trading Company AG*, Rev arb 2004.647 (Regional Court of Appeal).
[71] E Gaillard and P de Lapasse, 'Commentaire analytique du décret du 13 janvier 2011 portant réforme du droit français de l'arbitrage' (2011) 2 Paris J Intl Arb 371, para 106.
[72] Jarrosson (n 31) 2011.59 para 86; *contra* Gaillard and de Lapasse (n 71) para 106.

13.4.1 Mandatory rules as to form

13.51 French domestic arbitration law dictates rules as to the decision-making process and requires that the reasons for the award and other specific information be stated in the arbitral award. By contrast, in the context of international arbitration, these rules apply only to the extent that the parties have not agreed otherwise.

Rules applicable to the decision-making process

13.52 There are few mandatory rules applicable to the decision-making process in international arbitration. The method of deliberation is free but must allow for an actual discussion on the merits of the claims, the arguments, and the evidence exchanged during the proceedings. In French domestic and international arbitration, the arbitral tribunal's deliberations are confidential[73] and held exclusively among the arbitrators.

13.53 In international arbitration, unless the parties agree otherwise, the award must also be made by a majority and signed by all of the arbitrators.[74] However, if there is no majority, the chairman of the arbitral tribunal may rule alone.[75] If the other arbitrators refuse to sign, the chairman may so state in the award and sign it on his own.

The reasons for the award

13.54 Reasons for the award must be included in both domestic[76] and international[77] awards. In domestic arbitration, the award will be void if this requirement is not complied with. By contrast, this sanction does not apply to international awards. Indeed, the Cour de Cassation has held that in an international arbitration, failure to give reasons is not in itself contrary to the French understanding of international public policy[78] and thus should not lead to the setting aside of an award. However, international arbitration awards generally state the reasons for the decision. Moreover, the French Cour de Cassation has held that an award giving contradictory reasons need not be set aside, as the scope of review in setting aside proceedings is not sufficiently substantive to enable a court to review for consistency.[79]

Other information required in the award

13.55 Certain other information must also appear in the award. An award must state the name and the domicile of the parties, the name of the parties' attorneys if any, the name of the arbitrators, and the date and place where the award was rendered.[80] These provisions used to apply solely to domestic arbitration, but are now also applicable to international arbitration.[81] In domestic arbitration, the award will be void if these provisions are not complied with.[82] However, as with the requirement of a reasoned award, there is no specific provision as to the

[73] CPC, art 1479.
[74] CPC, art 1513, para 2.
[75] CPC, art 1513 para 3.
[76] CPC, art 1482.
[77] As a result of the reference to CPC, art 1482 in CPC, art 1506.
[78] CA Paris 17 April 2008, *Itani v Société générale de Banque au Liban*, Rev arb 2008.343 (Regional Court of Appeal).
[79] CA Paris 30 May 2006, *Société Paprec Réseau v SA Interseroh*, Rev arb 2007.837 (Regional Court of Appeal).
[80] CPC, art 1481.
[81] CPC, art 1506 specifies that art 1481 shall apply to international arbitration.
[82] CPC, art 1483.

sanction that would apply if this information were missing from an international arbitration award. Most scholars consider that the sanction should not be the nullity of the award.[83]

Finally, there is no provision applicable to international arbitration prescribing how an award is to be delivered by the arbitrators to the parties. Generally, the sole arbitrator or the arbitral tribunal sends a copy of the award to each party by registered mail to ensure delivery and fix the date thereof. **13.56**

13.4.2 Mandatory rules as to substance

In French international arbitration law, there are no requirements as to the substance of an award. However, the arbitrator, like any other judicial authority, is bound by international public policy rules, and an award rendered in France will be set aside if it results in a violation of a rule considered to be part of the French principles of international public order.[84] **13.57**

13.5 After the Award

A party to an international arbitration in France can seek recognition and enforcement of the award rendered by the arbitral tribunal or seek to challenge the award. An appeal of a recognition and enforcement decision with respect to an award has the same effect as a challenge action. Neither the challenge action nor the appeal of an enforcement decision is an appeal of the award, however, and the judge will not re-try the merits of the case. The French court will confine itself to verifying whether the award is subject to annulment on certain limited grounds. An action to set aside an international arbitration award rendered in France is brought before the Court of Appeal.[85] The recent reform also introduced a form of recourse against international awards aimed at reconsideration of the case. **13.58**

13.5.1 Local standards for the recognition and enforcement of awards

When the recognition and enforcement of the award are sought in France, the enforcing court, seised by way of an *ex parte* application, conducts a *prima facie* review of the award. This is the case whether or not the arbitral award was rendered in France. Article 1514 CPC provides that an international award will be recognized if (a) its existence is proven, and (b) its recognition and enforcement would not be manifestly contrary to international public policy. An enforcement order is requested from and issued by the *Tribunal de grande instance* of the place where the award was made for awards rendered in France, and by the *Tribunal de grande instance* of Paris for awards rendered abroad.[86] **13.59**

The order for enforcement can be affixed either to the original of the award or to duly authenticated copies of the award, as both comply with authenticity requirements.[87] Article 1517 CPC provides that the reasons for a decision denying enforcement must be stated. **13.60**

No appeal can be made against an order granting enforcement of an award rendered in France,[88] but an action to set aside an award rendered in France automatically entails appeal **13.61**

---

83 Gaillard and de Lapasse (n 56) para 33.
84 Gaillard and de Lapasse (n 56) paras 73–74.
85 CPC, art 1518.
86 CPC, art 1516.
87 CPC, art 1516, para 3 and art 1517, para 1.
88 CPC, art 1524, para 2.

against the order granting enforcement. As will be discussed in more detail later, even if the parties waive the right to bring annulment actions against French awards, they will be entitled to appeal against an enforcement order. Conversely, for awards rendered abroad, a party may, in any case, appeal against the order granting enforcement of an award and the Court of Appeal will examine the award in adversarial proceedings. The appeal against the enforcement order will be based on the same limited grounds as those applicable to an action to set aside an award[89] and must be brought within one month following service (*signification*) of the enforcement order.[90] One month will be added to the normal time limit for parties domiciled in the French overseas departments and territories and two months for parties domiciled abroad.[91]

13.62 The decree of 13 January 2011 introduced a significant change by providing that the appeal against an enforcement order no longer suspends enforcement of the award. The same also now applies to proceedings for the setting aside of the award. However, 'the first President of the Court of Appeal or the judge assigned to the matter [*le juge de la mise en l'état*] may stay or set conditions for enforcement of an award where enforcement could severely prejudice the rights of one of the parties'.[92] Accordingly, a party may specifically request suspension of enforcement where enforcement could be seriously detrimental to its rights. The judge will assess the circumstances of the case, but the mere fact that one party is foreign or domiciled abroad will not suffice.[93] Notwithstanding the silence of the CPC, scholars consider that such a request can be made only after the filing of an appeal against the enforcement order or of an action to set aside the award.[94]

13.5.2 Local standards for setting aside/annulment

13.63 An action to set aside an award rendered in France can be brought only before the Court of Appeal of the place where the award was made. Arbitral awards are the only type of arbitral decision that can be challenged. Actions to set aside an award can only be brought on specific grounds and within a specific time limit. A party cannot raise a ground that was not invoked before the arbitral tribunal. Another innovation of the 2011 reform is that the parties may now waive the right to challenge awards.

Decisions that may be challenged

13.64 An award is the only type of arbitral decision that can be challenged. It is therefore essential to distinguish awards from procedural orders or orders for provisional measures. Most instruments governing international arbitration do not contain the definition of an arbitral award. The characterization of a decision as an award is solely determined by the nature of the decision itself. French case law defines an arbitral award as a binding decision rendered by a sole arbitrator or an arbitral tribunal, resolving all or part of a given dispute, whether it

89 See para 13.58.
90 CPC, art 1525, para 2.
91 CPC, arts 643 and 645.
92 CPC, art 1526, para 2.
93 Gaillard and de Lapasse (n 71) para 109.
94 C Seraglini, 'L'efficacité et l'autorité renforcées des sentences arbitrales en France après le décret n° 2011-48 du 13 janvier 2011' (2011) 2 Paris J Intl Arb 375, para 20.

concerns the merits of the dispute, jurisdiction, or a procedural issue the resolution of which entails the end of the proceedings.[95]

Time limit for challenging and effect on enforcement

Previously, the time limit for challenging an award was one month from the date of notification of recognition of the award. This rule was criticized because the starting point of the time limit was uncertain and could be delayed for months or years (or indeed, it might never occur), especially when recognition and enforcement proceedings were first filed abroad. The decree of 13 January 2011 has tackled these difficulties, and article 1519 CPC now requires that an application to set aside an award be made within one month following notification of the award.[96] Unless otherwise agreed by the parties, the award will be notified by personal service (*signification*).[97] A question arises as to whether the reference to a set of arbitration rules which provide that the award will be notified to the parties will suffice to constitute an alternative agreement to the service of the award. This issue has not been decided by the Cour de Cassation yet, and scholars consider that the question is still open.[98] **13.65**

Under the former regime, an application to set aside an award would have suspended the enforcement of the award. Since the entry into force of the new decree, an award is immediately enforceable despite any action to set it aside before the Court of Appeal.[99] This provision is a major innovation and a step towards increasing the efficiency of international arbitration; however, article 3 of the decree specifies that the rule applies only to awards rendered after 1 May 2011. **13.66**

Under article 1526 CPC, the first president of the Court of Appeal or the judge assigned to the matter may stay the enforcement of an award against which an action to set aside has been brought where enforcement could be seriously detrimental to the rights of a party.[100] **13.67**

Grounds for challenge

Article 1520 CPC provides five exclusive grounds on which an international arbitration award rendered in France can be set aside.[101] These grounds are also applicable to an appeal of an order granting recognition or enforcement of an arbitral award rendered outside France,[102] and were not substantively changed by the recent reform. They are more restrictive than the grounds set out in Article V of the 1958 New York Convention and, accordingly, French arbitration law falls under the more favourable law provision of Article VII of the Convention.[103] These grounds focus on jurisdictional and procedural issues, and the defects must be fundamental. They are also restrictively construed by French courts. **13.68**

---

[95] CA Paris 25 March 1994, *Société Sardisud et autre v Société Technip et autre*, Rev arb 1994.391 (Regional Court of Appeal); Cass Civ (1) 12 October 2011, *Société Groupe Antoine Tabet v Republique du Congo*, Rev arb 2012.86 (Court of Cassation).

[96] CPC, art 1519, para 2.

[97] CPC, art 1519, para 3.

[98] C Jarrosson and J Pellerin, 'Le droit français de l'arbitrage après le décret du 13 janvier 2011' Rev arb 2012.403.

[99] CPC, art 1526, para 1.

[100] See para 13.62.

[101] J-F Poudret and S Besson, *Comparative Law of International Arbitration* (Thomson, Sweet & Maxwell, 2007) para 788; Cass Civ (1) 6 January 1987, *Southern Pacific Properties Ltd v République arabe d'Egypte*, Rev arb 1987.469 (Court of Cassation).

[102] CPC, art 1525, para 4.

[103] The New York Convention, Art VII provides: 'The provisions of the present Convention shall not affect the validity of multilateral or bilateral agreements concerning the recognition and enforcement of arbitral

13.69 The vast majority of actions to set aside an arbitration award are consequently denied by French courts.[104] An award may thus be set aside only when:

(1) the arbitral tribunal wrongly upheld or declined jurisdiction;
(2) the arbitral tribunal was irregularly constituted;
(3) the arbitral tribunal rendered its decision without complying with the mandate conferred upon it;
(4) the requirements of due process were not respected; or
(5) the recognition or enforcement of the award would be contrary to French international public policy.

13.70 Considered to be a matter of public policy, these statutorily limited grounds cannot be contractually modified. A challenge to an award on these grounds will never result in a review of the merits.

13.71 **The arbitral tribunal wrongly upheld or declined jurisdiction** Broadly speaking, this ground covers issues relating to the validity and scope of the arbitration clause and questions of jurisdiction.

13.72 An illustration of the issues addressed under this ground and of the approach adopted by the French courts can be found in the question of extension of the arbitration agreement to third parties. Ordinarily, an arbitral tribunal will not have jurisdiction over entities that are not signatories to the arbitration clause. French courts have, however, extended an arbitration clause to groups of companies where this was 'justifiable on the basis of parties' express or implied intention'.[105] A well-known award ruled that:

> ... the arbitration clause expressly accepted by certain of the companies of the group should bind the other companies which, by virtue of their role in the conclusion, performance or termination of the contracts containing said clauses, and in accordance with the mutual intention of all parties to the proceedings, appear to have been veritable parties to these contracts or to have been principally concerned by them and the disputes to which they may give rise.[106]
>
> ... Irrespective of the fact that companies in the same group did not sign the arbitration agreement, it will be extended to them where 'their respective situations and activities raise the presumption that they were aware of the existence and scope of the arbitration clause'.[107]

13.73 Similarly, the French courts have decided that under certain circumstances a state can be bound by an arbitration agreement to which one of its constituent parts is a party. In the *Pyramids* case,[108] the Court of Appeal held that the words 'approved, agreed and ratified' followed by the signature of the Egyptian minister for tourism did not imply an intention on the part of the Egyptian state to be bound by the arbitration agreement, as the minister signed the contract merely as a supervisory authority. Although the award extending the

awards entered into by the Contracting States nor deprive any interested party of any right he may have to avail himself of an arbitral award in the manner and to the extent allowed by the law or the treaties of the country where such award is sought to be relied upon.'

[104] S Crépin, *Les sentences arbitrales devant le juge français* (LGDJ, 1995).

[105] Gaillard and Savage (n 34) para 502.

[106] Gaillard and Savage (n 34) para 503, citing interim award in ICC case No 4131, 23 September 1982, *Isover-Saint-Gobain (France) v Dow Chemical France*, Rev arb 1984.37.

[107] Gaillard and Savage (n 34) para 505, translating CA Paris 30 November 1988, *Société Korsnas Marma v Société Durand-Auzias*, Rev arb 1989.691 (Regional Court of Appeal).

[108] CA Paris 12 July 1984, *République arabe d'Egypte v Southern Pacific Properties (Middle East) Ltd*, Rev arb 1986.75 (Regional Court of Appeal).

arbitration clause to the Egyptian state was set aside, scholars considered that it did not mean that the Court of Appeal was against the principle of extending the arbitration clause to non-signatory states.[109] The award in the *Pyramids* case was annulled because, in the light of its particular circumstances, it was determined that the Egyptian state did not express its intention to become a party to the arbitration clause.

This approach was recently confirmed in the *Dallah* case, in which the Paris Court of Appeal upheld the extension of an arbitration clause to the State of Pakistan on the basis that the particular facts of the case showed that the state had intensively participated in the negotiation and performance of the contract containing the arbitration clause.[110] **13.74**

The arbitral tribunal was irregularly constituted While this ground primarily concerns issues relating to the appointment of arbitrators, for example where the arbitral tribunal was constituted or the sole arbitrator appointed in breach of the law or of the agreement of the parties, it has increasingly been invoked to raise questions concerning the independence and impartiality of arbitrators. Over the past few years, challenges to awards on the basis of independence and impartiality have had more success than other grounds. **13.75**

French arbitration law is becoming increasingly rigorous with respect to the independence and impartiality requirement. The Reims Court of Appeal recently set aside an award on the grounds of a failure to disclose the extent of the relationship between the law firm of the chairman of the arbitral tribunal and members of the group of companies of one of the parties.[111] Even though the arbitrator was unaware of some of the links between his firm and the party, the Court found that he was under an obligation to investigate and provide the parties with a full picture of these connections. It was irrelevant that he was of counsel, rather than a partner in the firm, and that his degree of involvement in the management of the firm was limited. The Court concluded in this case that by failing to disclose the information in a timely fashion, the arbitrator demonstrated a lack of independence. This recent decision has been criticized by commentators,[112] not only because it appears to confuse the requirement for independence and the associated duty to disclose, but also because it was not clear in the instant case whether the undisclosed, or belatedly disclosed, information could reasonably cast doubt on the independence or impartiality of the arbitrator.[113] **13.76**

The arbitral tribunal rendered its decision without complying with the mandate conferred upon it Although rarely successful, this ground for setting aside an award has a wide scope and can be raised in various situations. Indeed, an objection can be raised where the arbitral tribunal has not respected procedures expressly chosen by the parties.[114] A tribunal also exceeds **13.77**

---

[109] Gaillard and Savage (n 34) para 508.

[110] CA Paris 17 February 2011, *Gouvernement du Pakistan—Ministère des affaires religieuses v Dallah Real Estate and Tourism Holding Company*, Rev arb 2011.286 (Regional Court of Appeal).

[111] CA Reims 2 November 2011, *SAJ & P Avax v Société Tecnimont SPA*, ASA Bulletin 2012.197, Rev arb 2012.112 (Regional Court of Appeal).

[112] M Thomas, 'L'obligation imposée aux arbitres d'investiguer sur les conflits d'intérêts induits par leur appartenance à un cabinet d'avocats' (2012) 1188 Option Finance 30; J Béguin, 'Rigueur de l' "obligation de révélation" des arbitres' (2012) 9 la semaine juridique—Entreprise et affaires 36; M Henry, 'L'obligation de révélation: de l'éclarage excessif au risque d'aveuglement' Rev arb, 2012.112.

[113] This decision is subject to a recourse before the French Cour de Cassation (Court of Cassation).

[114] Cass Civ (1) 8 March 1988, *Société Sofidif et autres v OIAETI et autre*, Rev arb 1989.481 (Court of Cassation).

the mandate conferred by the parties if it decides *ultra petita*, awarding damages in excess of the relief sought by a party.[115]

13.78 A party may also challenge an award on this ground where the arbitral tribunal has applied a completely different law from the one chosen by the parties. However, French courts have held that, as long as an arbitral tribunal applies the law chosen by the parties, it does not violate its mission by, for example, referring to the French law that had inspired the Egyptian law chosen by the parties.[116] In addition, the fact that the tribunal simply refers to equitable principles is not enough to show that it departed from the law chosen by the parties,[117] nor will an arbitral award be set aside because the arbitral tribunal incorrectly applied the chosen law.[118]

13.79 The parties may empower the arbitral tribunal to rule as *amiable compositeur*, enabling it to judge in accordance with the general fairness of the case.[119] In this case, the award may be set aside for non-compliance with the mandate conferred upon the arbitral tribunal only if the arbitral tribunal decided to apply a particular law without explaining how the solution given by the law it chose is consistent with fairness,[120] or more generally when the arbitral tribunal fails to explain why the solution adopted is consistent with fairness.[121] However, if the parties have agreed on the law to be applied to the dispute, the award will be set aside if the arbitral tribunal, of its own motion, decides to rule as *amiable compositeur*.[122] Finally, the award will not be set aside where the parties did not choose the law applicable to the dispute and the arbitral tribunal decided to apply the *lex mercatoria*, as this is not considered to constitute ruling as *amiable compositeur*.[123] More generally, choice of law decisions by the arbitral tribunal will not be reviewed where the parties simply did not choose an applicable law, as the arbitral tribunal is empowered in such cases by article 1511 of the CPC to apply the law it considers to be the most appropriate.

13.80 **The requirements of due process were not respected** This ground for setting aside an award can be raised in relation to various alleged procedural irregularities. Arbitrators must ensure that they respect the right of defence (also known as due process), which includes the right to a fair hearing,[124] and the principle of adversarial proceedings.[125] This last principle is broadly interpreted in France and is considered to be a 'superior principle… necessary for due process'.[126] This principle also prohibits an arbitrator from relying on documents or arguments that have not

[115] CA Paris 1 December 2011, *SA Victocor Technologies v Société Benteler Automobiltechnik*, GMBH No 10/19655 (Regional Court of Appeal).

[116] CA Paris 10 March 1988, *Société Crocodile Tourist Project Company (Egypte) v Aubert ès qual et autres*, Rev arb 1989.269 (Regional Court of Appeal).

[117] CA Paris 28 February 1980, *Compagnie Financière MOCUPIA v Société INVEKO France*, Rev arb 1980.538 (Regional Court of Appeal).

[118] CA Paris 25 May 1985, *Beernaert v CAT*, Rev arb 1989.228 (Regional Court of Appeal).

[119] CPC, art 1512.

[120] CA Paris 3 June 2004, *SA Exodis v SA Ricoh France*, Rev arb 2004.683 (Regional Court of Appeal); Cass Civ (2) 15 February 2001, *Halbout et société Matenec HG v Epoux Hanin*, Bull civ II No 26, 19 (Court of Cassation).

[121] Cass Civ (2) 15 February 2001, *Halbout et société Matenec HG v Epoux Hanin*, Rev arb 2001.135 (Court of Cassation).

[122] CA Paris 30 May 1996, *Société Arabian Construction v Société Saipem*, Rev arb 1996.645 (Regional Court of Appeal).

[123] Cass Civ (1) 22 October 1991, *Société Compania Valenciana de Cementos Portland v Société Primary Coal Inc*, Rev arb 1992.457 (Court of Cassation).

[124] Cass Civ (1) 5 February 1991, *Société Almira Films v Pierrel ès qualités*, Rev arb 1991.625 (Court of Cassation).

[125] CPC, art 1510.

[126] *Société Almira* (n 124).

been submitted in adversarial proceedings.[127] There has been a series of recent annulments on this basis.[128] However, failure to raise these irregularities in a timely fashion precludes the parties from raising them to challenge the award.

The award is contrary to French international public policy An award will be set aside where its recognition or enforcement would be contrary to French principles of international public policy. As the term international public policy suggests, this ground does not cover all of the rules that would be considered to be public policy under French law. Rather, it refers to a very narrow category of rules. International public policy rules have been defined as principles that are considered in France to reflect fundamental convictions, or to have an absolute value.[129] French international public policy rules can be defined as 'the set of values a breach of which could not be tolerated by the French legal order, even in international cases'.[130] **13.81**

International public policy comprises procedural rules as well as fundamental principles on the merits. For instance, an award may be set aside if the decision is based on religious or racial discrimination. An award that does not consider a contract obtained through corruption to be void will also be set aside.[131] As the appellate courts cannot review the merits of the case, their power of review is limited and the breach of international public policy must be 'clear, effective and concrete'.[132] **13.82**

A successful action to set aside an award will annul the disputed award in whole or in part. New proceedings will have to be initiated before a newly constituted tribunal (unless the award was set aside because the arbitration clause was invalid). **13.83**

Estoppel

The Cour de Cassation relatively recently adopted the principle of estoppel based on the requirement of consistency and procedural loyalty.[133] It prohibits one party from contradicting itself to the detriment of the other party. Accordingly, a party cannot change its legal line of argument, and a ground for annulment that was not raised before the arbitral tribunal cannot be raised for the first time as a ground to set aside an award before the Court of Appeal. This principle was codified by the decree of 13 January 2011 in article 1466 CPC, which is immediately applicable even if the arbitral tribunal was constituted or the award rendered before 1 May 2011. **13.84**

However, an exception to the principle of estoppel has been laid down by case law. The French courts have held that a party may make a claim for annulment on the grounds of **13.85**

[127] Cass Civ (1) 12 October 2011, *Société Groupe Antoine Tabet v République du Congo*, Rev arb 2012.91 (Court of Cassation).

[128] Cass Civ (1) 23 June 2010, *Société Malicorp v République arabe d'Egypte et autres*, Rev arb 2011.442 (Court of Cassation); Cass Civ (1) 29 June 2011, *Société Overseas Mining Investments Ltd v Société Commercial Carribean Niquel*, Rev arb 2011.678 (Court of Cassation).

[129] 'Cass Civ (1) 25 May 1948, *Lautour v Veuve Guiraut*' in B Ancel and Y Lequette, *Grands arrêts de la jurisprudence de Droit international privé* (5th edn, Dalloz, 2006) 165.

[130] Gaillard and Savage (n 34) para 1648.

[131] CA Paris 30 September 1993, *Société European Gas Turbines SA v Société Westman International Ltd*, Rev arb 1994.359 (Regional Court of Appeal).

[132] CA Paris 18 November 2004, *SA Thalès Air Défense v GIE Euromissile*, Rev arb 2005.751 (Regional Court of Appeal).

[133] Cass Civ (1) 6 July 2005, *Golshani v Gouvernement de la République islamique d'Iran*, Rev arb 2005.993 (Court of Cassation).

breach of international public policy before the Court of Appeal even if the argument was not raised before the arbitral tribunal.[134] The rationale for this is that the preservation of international public policy should prevail over any other considerations.[135] Indeed, it was held in a well-known case that the extent of judicial policing of international public policy should not be conditional on the parties' procedural conduct.[136]

Waiver of right to challenge

13.86 The right to bring an action to set aside an award was previously considered to be a matter of public policy that the parties could not waive, notwithstanding any provision in arbitration rules or the arbitration agreement purporting to waive it.[137] The decree of 13 January 2011 introduced a significant change by enabling the parties to an international arbitration to waive their right to challenge the award in the arbitration clause or in a subsequent agreement. The ability to waive the right to seek the annulment of the award is limited to arbitrations in which the arbitral tribunal was constituted after 1 May 2011.

13.87 Article 1522 CPC requires the parties to 'expressly waive their right to bring an action to set aside'. Contrary to Swiss and Belgian law, under French arbitration law, French parties or parties domiciled in France can also waive this right.[138] However, there are two requirements to effectively waive the right to bring an action to set aside an award. There must be (a) a specific agreement, and (b) an express waiver. This specific agreement need not comply with any formal requirements as long as the parties' intent is clear. However, it is doubtful whether wording such as that in article 34.6 of the ICC rules[139] would constitute a valid waiver of annulment proceedings. Some scholars have already argued that article 34.6 would not suffice to waive the right, nor would contractual provisions merely stating that the award to be issued shall be 'final'.[140] Scholars consider that a party can only waive its right if it expressly indicates that it is specifically doing so.[141]

13.88 Moreover, a party waiving its right to bring an action to set aside an award is not barred from appealing against an order granting recognition or enforcement.[142] According to commentators, the underlying idea is that the regularity of an international award should be assessed where the award will be executed.[143]

13.5.3 Procedure before the Court of Appeal

13.89 The ordinary rules of procedure applicable to litigation before the Court of Appeal apply to actions to set aside an award. The national court can refuse to annul the award and order the

134 CA Paris 14 June 2001, *Société Cargill France v SA Tradigrain France*, Rev arb 2001.773 (Regional Court of Appeal).

135 P Mayer, 'La sentence contraire à l'ordre public au fond' Rev arb 1994.615.

136 CA Paris 18 November 2004, *SA Thalès* (n 132) (Regional Court of Appeal).

137 CA Paris 16 February 1989, *Société Almira Films v Pierrel ès qual*, Rev arb 1989.711 (Regional Court of Appeal).

138 E Kleiman and J Spinelli, 'La réforme du droit de l'arbitrage, sous le double signe de la lisibilité et de l'efficacité' (2011) 27 Gazette du Palais 9.

139 The ICC Rules of Arbitration, art 34.6 provides: 'the parties undertake to carry out any award without delay and shall be deemed to have waived their right to any form of recourse insofar as such waiver can validly be made'.

140 Jarrosson (n 31) 2011.71, para 104.

141 Gaillard and de Lapasse (n 71) para 119.

142 CPC, art 1522, para 3.

143 Gaillard and de Lapasse (n 56) para 41.

losing party to pay the other party's legal fees. The only recourse available against the Court of Appeal's ruling is the Cour de Cassation.

Procedural requirements and timetable for actions to set aside an award

Article 1527 CPC states that: 'Appeals against orders granting or denying enforcement and actions to set aside awards shall be brought, heard and decided in accordance with the rules applicable to adversarial proceedings set forth in articles 900 through 930-1 [CPC].' The procedure applicable to the challenge of an award is therefore governed by the ordinary rules of procedure applicable to cases before the Court of Appeal. However, in the past decade, three decrees[144] and one law[145] have extensively amended the procedure before the Courts of Appeal. **13.90**

Previously, a party bringing an action to set aside an award had to be represented before the Court of Appeal by an *avoué*. The *avoué* is a lawyer specifically registered with the Court of Appeal and his or her intervention was mandatory. Although the intervention of a lawyer is still mandatory, a law issued on 25 January 2011 abolished the requirement for representation of parties before the Court of Appeal exclusively by an *avoué*. Since 1 January 2012, parties have been able to choose any lawyer within the district of the relevant Court of Appeal to represent them in their setting aside action. **13.91**

The party seeking annulment of an award must apply for it within a month following service of the award.[146] The application for annulment must contain mandatory information such as identification of the decision being challenged, details of the lawyer instructed, and the identity of the court ruling on the challenge.[147] A party challenging an award in part must indicate the parts of the award that are being challenged.[148] **13.92**

The applicant has three months starting from the application date to submit its full arguments together with appropriate evidence (in most cases, only documentary evidence), failing which the application for annulment will be invalid.[149] The respondent then has two months starting from the notification of the applicant's submissions to submit its response to the application together with the evidence relied upon (again, in most cases, only documentary evidence) and to serve any counter-application, otherwise its submission in response or counter application will be inadmissible.[150] The judge assigned to the matter (*juge de la mise en l'état*) may, on his or her own motion and depending on the nature of the dispute, order shorter deadlines.[151] One month will be added to the normal time limit for parties domiciled in the French overseas departments and territories, and two months for parties domiciled abroad.[152] **13.93**

Under article 912 CPC, the judge assigned to the matter then has 15 days to review the case and fix the procedural closing date and hearing date. However, if the judge assigned to the **13.94**

144 Decree No 2009-1524 of 9 December 2009; Decree No 2010-1647 of 28 December 2010; Decree No 2012-634 of 3 May 2012.
145 Law No 2011-94 of 25 January 2011.
146 CPC, art 1519; Decree No 2011-48 of 13 January 2011. See also para 13.65.
147 CPC, art 901; Decree No 2012-634 of 3 May 2012.
148 CPC, art 901; Decree No 2012-634 of 3 May 2012.
149 CPC, art 908; Decree No 2012-634 of 3 May 2012.
150 CPC, art 909; Decree No 2012-634 of 3 May 2012.
151 CPC, art 911; Decree No 2012-634 of 3 May 2012, para 1.
152 CPC, art 911; Decree No 2012-634 of 3 May 2012, para 2.

matter considers that the dispute is not ready to be heard, he will draw up a procedural calendar for the further exchange of written submissions by the parties.[153] In practice, hearings before the Court of Appeal are confined to argument by the parties and generally take no longer than a few hours.

13.95 The duration of an action to set aside an arbitral award before the Court of Appeal depends on the circumstances of the case. However, in general, the whole process takes between one and two years.

13.96 Finally, as previously explained, applications to set aside awards no longer suspend enforcement. Parties may, however, seek from the Court of Appeal a stay of enforcement, if they can demonstrate that immediate enforcement would be seriously detrimental to the rights of a party.

Costs

13.97 Previously, the losing party had to pay the fees of both his and the opposing party's *avoué*, calculated as a percentage of the dispute. As the law introduced on 25 January 2011 abolished the requirement of an *avoué*, as from 1 January 2012, the losing party no longer pays *avoué* fees.

13.98 French courts can order a party to pay an amount of money, corresponding to the other party's legal fees, on the basis of article 700 CPC. When deciding on the amount to be paid as attorneys' fees, the judge not only takes into account factors such as fairness, but also the losing party's economic situation. The judge may also, at his or her discretion, decide that the losing party should not be required to pay anything. In domestic litigation, the judge rarely orders the losing party to pay the actual legal fees incurred. In the context of challenges to arbitration awards, there is a growing tendency of the courts to award legal costs more generously when the challenge is considered frivolous, although the sum awarded rarely covers all legal fees actually incurred by the party.[154]

Challenge of the Court of Appeal's decision

13.99 There is recourse against a Court of Appeal's ruling on an action to set aside an award before the Cour de Cassation (the highest court in France). This '*pourvoi en cassation*' does not, however, constitute an appeal: the Cour de Cassation cannot review findings of fact and will focus only on the Court of Appeal's application of the law. The Cour de Cassation may either dismiss the application or overturn the decision (in whole or in part). If the decision is overturned, the matter is sent back to another Court of Appeal so that it can apply the correct principles of law. The second Court of Appeal need not adopt the Cour de Cassation's view, in which case another application may be brought before the Cour de Cassation. Ultimately,

---

[153] CPC, art 911; Decree No 2012-634 of 3 May 2012, para 2.

[154] Examples of costs awarded in accordance with CPC, art 700: CA Paris 19 June 2008, *Gouvernement de la République arabe d'Egypte v sté Malicorp Ltd*, RTD Com 2010.545 (Regional Court of Appeal); CA Paris 12 May 2011, *Société Maschinenfabrik Möllers GMBH v Société Al Khaleej Sugar Company LLC*, No 10/08745 (Regional Court of Appeal); CA Paris 17 February 2011, *Gouvernement du Pakistan —Ministère des affaires religieuses v Dallah Real Estate and Tourism Holding Company*, Rev arb 2011.286 (Regional Court of Appeal); CA Paris 21 January 2010, *Inversiones Errazuriz Ltda v Kreditanstalt fur Wiederaufbau*, 25 July 2010 GP, para 206 (Regional Court of Appeal); CA Reims 2 November 2011, *SAJ & P Avax v Société Tecnimont SPA*, ASA Bulletin 2012.197, Rev arb 2012.112 (Regional Court of Appeal); CA Paris 1 December 2011, *SA Victocor Technologies v Société Benteler Automobiltechnik*, GMBH No 10/19655 (Regional Court of Appeal).

the case will then be referred to another Court of Appeal, which must then abide by the decision of the Cour de Cassation.

13.5.4 Reconsideration of the case (*recours en revision*)

Another, albeit narrow and exceptional, form of recourse is available against an international award rendered in France. Known as a '*recours en revision*', this option, which already existed for domestic awards, is now available for international awards pursuant to article 1506 CPC, unless the parties have agreed otherwise. **13.100**

Reconsideration of the case can take place only in certain limited situations such as fraud or the discovery of new decisive evidence concealed by one party during the initial arbitration. **13.101**

Unlike in domestic cases, where reconsideration is carried out primarily by the arbitral tribunal that rendered the initial award or by the Court of Appeal if the arbitral tribunal cannot be reconstituted, the reconsideration in international cases is carried out by the initial arbitral tribunal, or if this is impossible, a newly appointed arbitral tribunal. **13.102**

13.6 Conclusion

As was the case for the 1980–81 legal reforms, the French arbitration regime resulting from the 13 January 2011 reform is, to a large extent, a codification of French case law. **13.103**

With this new legal framework, French arbitration law continues to distinguish itself from the UNCITRAL Model Law. This new regime confirms the longstanding supportive approach of France towards arbitration, as an appropriate and well-adapted means to resolve international commercial disputes in particular. **13.104**

Yet on certain issues, such as the possibility of waiving the right to challenge awards or the computation of the time limit to introduce such challenges, the innovative provisions of the new French regime have yet to be tested in the courts. **13.105**

14

SÃO PAULO

Fernando Eduardo Serec and Antonio Marzagão Barbuto Neto

14.1 Background

14.1.1 Overview of arbitration in Brazil

14.01 Over the last decade, the extent of foreign direct investment in Brazil has increased significantly, along with an increasing demand for arbitration and a change in mentality among legal practitioners and the judiciary.

14.02 While Brazil's Arbitration Act has been in effect since 1996, the New York Convention on the Recognition and Enforcement of Foreign Awards was not ratified until 2002. Prior to the ratification of the New York Convention, arbitral awards issued abroad were submitted to a 'double exequatur' by both foreign and Brazilian courts in order to enjoy recognition and enforceability within Brazil. The late ratification of the New York Convention in essence obliged parties involved in an arbitration proceeding to comply with the rules set out in the 1927 Geneva Convention on the Execution of Foreign Arbitral Awards. In effect, this meant that a party seeking to enforce an arbitral award in another country would have to prove that the award was 'final' in the country in which it was made, in addition to conforming to the burdensome requirement of obtaining an exequatur in the country where enforcement was sought. Currently, an arbitral award issued abroad is subject only to a single 'homologation' (ie recognition) by the Superior Court of Justice (STJ)[1] in order to be enforceable.

This may help to explain why for many years arbitration in Brazil was viewed as a dubious and inefficient method of international dispute resolution. This was not helped by the perceived willingness of the Brazilian courts to ignore contractual arbitration agreements. **14.03**

By the same token, however, it is now safe to say that arbitration would never have become a viable mechanism for the resolution of commercial disputes in Brazil if not for the decisive role played by the Brazilian courts and practitioners. **14.04**

Starting with the Supreme Court's 2001 landmark ruling on the constitutionality of the Arbitration Law in *MBV Commercial and Export Management Establishment ('MBV') v Resil*,[2] and continuing with subsequent pro-arbitration decisions rendered by the STJ on the recognition of foreign awards, the Brazilian judiciary has paved the way for the widespread use of arbitration clauses, particularly in commercial transactions. **14.05**

In another important case, the STJ reversed a decision rendered by the Rio de Janeiro Appellate Court preventing an award creditor from taking attachment measures (execution) directly before a court of first instance, even though the award had been rendered in Rio de Janeiro. The lower court, by a majority vote, dismissed enforcement proceedings (*execução*), citing the need for confirmation proceedings, because the arbitral award had been rendered by the ICC, an international institution headquartered in Paris.[3] Although this decision was viewed by many as a lapse in correctly interpreting what constitutes a domestic arbitral award as opposed to an international award, the reversal at the STJ level ultimately evinces the proper guidance and direction of the Brazilian judiciary in terms of arbitration. According to the STJ, an arbitral award is deemed domestic as long it is rendered within Brazilian territory, even when the arbitrators decide on a conflict that has arisen from international trade. In other words, confirmation is not required for domestic awards—instead, they can be directly enforced by the court that would have had original jurisdiction to hear the case. **14.06**

More recently, the STJ not only confirmed its pro-arbitration stance, but also strengthened the use of arbitration by public companies. One of the grounds used by the STJ to uphold an arbitral award rendered against a public company was that arbitration was closely connected to the constitutional principle of efficiency.[4] **14.07**

[1] The Brazilian Supreme Court (STF) and Superior Court of Justice (STJ) are the two highest courts in Brazil. In essence, the difference between the these courts is that the latter is competent to decide cases not related to constitutional matters, while the former solely decides issues pertaining to the Brazilian Federal Constitution. Prior to Constitutional Amendment no 45, of 8 December 2004 (the 'Reform of the Judiciary'), the recognition and enforceability of a foreign arbitral award was granted by the Brazilian Supreme Court. The Amendment in effect transferred such attribution exclusively to the Superior Court of Justice. As a practical result of this transition, the Superior Court of Justice is in a better condition to respond to the number of filed requests for recognition (or 'homologation'), as it is composed of 33 justices, whereas the Supreme Court only 11 justices.

[2] This case relates to a dispute between two private companies, in which the enforcement of a foreign award issued in Spain was sought in Brazil. The conflict arose out of a disagreement with respect to the terms of a commercial representation contract between the representative (Spanish party) and its principal (Brazilian party). Among the provisions in the commercial contract, the parties had agreed to arbitrate disputes arising out of the contract. The Supreme Court upheld the constitutionality of arbitration agreements.

[3] Interlocutory Appeal no 0062827-33.2009.8.19.0000 *Petromec Inc v Nuovo Pignone SPA*, Tribunal de Justiça do Estado do Rio de Janeiro (27 February 2010), available at <http://www.tjrj.jus.br>.

[4] Special Appeal no 904.813/PR, *Companhia Paranaense de Gás—Compagás v Consórcio Carioca—Passarelli*, Superior Court of Justice (20 October 2011).

14.08 In short, Brazilian judges no longer view arbitration as a threat to their constitutional mission, but rather as an effective way to deliver justice pursuant to the parties' autonomy to select their own decision-makers. Courts are increasingly aware of their importance to arbitration proceedings—before and after the appointment of arbitrators—in ensuring the proper enforcement of agreements to arbitrate.

14.09 Much of this progress can be attributed to the Brazilian arbitration community. The Brazilian Arbitration Committee (CBAr) has played a fundamental role in the development of arbitration in Brazil and continues to fulfil its mission to serve as a conduit between arbitration, the courts, and the business community. Quality scholarly works are being published by respected authors and rising stars, and law schools are finally offering courses specifically designed to train students in alternative means of dispute resolution.

14.1.2 Role of São Paulo

14.10 As the largest city and business hub in South America, São Paulo is where a great number of contracts are signed and therefore one of the leading regions for the settlement of disputes related to those contracts by international arbitration.[5]

14.11 Indeed, the city offers good logistical facilities for arbitration, as most of the major Brazilian arbitral institutions are located within the city's business district. In addition, as a natural response to the demand for specialized judicial cooperation (before, during, and after the arbitral proceedings), São Paulo courts have educated and developed themselves to properly assist arbitral tribunals in both domestic and international arbitration.

Arbitration centres in São Paulo

14.12 Among the most commonly chosen institutions in Brazil are the Arbitration and Mediation Center of the Chamber of Commerce Brazil-Canada (CCBC), the São Paulo Chamber for Mediation and Arbitration (FIESP/CIESP), Conciliation and Arbitration Chamber of the Fundação Getúlio Vargas (FGV), the Corporate Chamber of Commerce in Brazil (CAMARB), the Arbitration and Mediation Center of the American Chamber of Commerce in São Paulo (AMCHAM), the Mediation and Arbitration Center of the Portuguese Chamber of Commerce in Brazil, and the Market Arbitration Center established by BOVESPA/BMF, Câmara de Arbitragem do Mercado (CAM)—all of which are located in the city of São Paulo.

14.13 The number of cases administered by these arbitral institutions has soared in recent years, and Brazil currently holds a prominent spot in the annual statistics published by the ICC. In 2011, 10 per cent of all cases submitted to the ICC involved Brazilian parties. The large inventory of cases currently administered by the major local arbitral institutions has led them to invest in qualified personnel to ensure proper and efficient proceedings, as well as to expand their panels of arbitrators.

[5] Established in August 2007, the CBAr has developed extensive research consisting of an in-depth analysis of every judicial decision on issues pertaining to arbitral proceedings issued in Brazil since the enactment of the Arbitration Act; see D Monteiro and G Ettore Nanni, 'Second Stage of the Research on "Arbitration and the Judiciary" Theme Report: Validity, Efficiency and Existence of Arbitration Agreement'(2010) Academic-Scientific Institutional Partnership São Paulo Law School of Fundação Getulio Vargas (DIREITO GV) Brazilian Arbitration Committee (CBAr) Research Paper 54, available at <http://bibliotecadigital.fgv.br/dspace/bitstream/handle/10438/6576/working%20paper%2054.pdf?sequence=5>, also published in (2011) *Revista Brasileira de Arbitragem* (Special Edition) 1. According to the Committee's report, São Paulo attracts approximately 30% of all arbitration-related lawsuits in Brazil.

Certain institutions, such as the Brazil Arbitration and Mediation Center of the Chamber of the CCBC, and the FIESP/CIESP, have also recently changed and adapted their arbitration rules to reflect current international practice, contributing to turning São Paulo into one of the main arbitration and mediation venues in the world. 14.14

Additionally, arbitral centres, such as the Arbitration and Mediation Center of the CCBC, are currently going through a process of 'internationalization' by entering into partnerships and agreements with foreign arbitral institutions, such as the Centro de Arbitraje y Mediación of Santiago (Chile). 14.15

Foreign arbitral providers, such as the ICC, the ICDR, and the LCIA are also commonly chosen to administer arbitral proceedings in seats like São Paulo, although none currently have offices in the country. 14.16

Courts in São Paulo

Needless to say, the developments previously mentioned would be ineffective without the proper assistance of local courts. As mentioned earlier, the STJ's attitude to arbitration has evolved significantly during the last few years. In São Paulo, this positive attitude has produced a string of pro-arbitration decisions by first instance judges, appellate bodies, and superior courts. 14.17

The São Paulo Appellate Court has demonstrated readiness and expertise with respect to a wide range of arbitration related matters, including the following. 14.18

Non-signatories and the extension of arbitration agreements In *Trelleborg v Anel*,[6] the São Paulo State Appellate Court extended the effect of an arbitration agreement to a non-signatory. *Trelleborg* involves an action to compel arbitration under article 7 of the Brazilian Arbitration Act,[7] in which the Swedish parent company (Trelleborg Industri AB) claimed it was not a proper party to an arbitration involving an acquisition agreement executed by its Brazilian subsidiary. The Court upheld the court-supervised Terms of Reference (the by-product of any action to compel arbitration), which included Trelleborg Industri AB as a respondent in the arbitration, finding that the parent company's 'active participation', 'clear involvement', and 'interest in the outcome' of the acquisition negotiations required its participation in the arbitral proceedings. 14.19

Enforceability of arbitration agreements In *CAOA Comércio Importação e Exportação Ltda* v *Renault SA*,[8] the São Paulo Appellate Court upheld a first instance judgment dismissing a lawsuit filed by CAOA against Renault before a civil court in São Paulo seeking damages in connection with the termination of CAOA's distributorship of Renault vehicles in Brazil, because there was an arbitration agreement between the parties regarding the termination of their commercial relationship. 14.20

Production of evidence in aid of arbitration In *Motorola Industrial SP v Turner South America Ltda*,[9] the São Paulo Appellate Court granted a preliminary injunction for the 14.21

[6] *Trelleborg v Anel* Appeal no 267.450.4/6-00, 7th Private Chamber of São Paulo Court of Appeals (24 May 2006).

[7] Brazilian Arbitration Act 1996 (BAA 1996).

[8] *Comércio Importação e Exportação Ltda v Renault SA* Appeal no 1.117.830-0/7, 36 Civil Chamber of São Paulo, Court of Appeals (26 February 2008).

[9] *Motorola Industrial SP v Turner South America Ltda* Civil Appeal no 494.408-4/6, São Paulo,Court of Appeals (28 June 2007).

production of evidence. The lower court had relied on the existence of an arbitration agreement to refuse the injunction, but the appellate court held that although the parties were bound by an arbitration agreement, courts have a duty to act in support of arbitration, pursuant to article 22(4) of the Brazilian Arbitration Act.

14.22 There have on rare occasions been decisions of the São Paulo Appellate Court that have been considered controversial by the arbitration community in Brazil, including *Energia Sustentável do Brasil SA v SulAmerica Companhia Nacional de Seguros*[10] and *Companhia do Metropolitano de São Paulo ('Metro') v Consorcio Via Amarela.*[11]

14.23 In the first case, the São Paulo Appellate Court ordered a stay of an arbitration initiated in London under an insurance policy covering the construction of one of the world's largest hydroelectric facilities. The Court held that the insurance companies were precluded from commencing arbitral proceedings in London until the Brazilian courts decided the merits of the insureds' challenge to the validity of the arbitration clause.

14.24 In *Metro v Consorcio Via Amarela*—an interesting case involving the compelled production of evidence in the course of an arbitration—the same court ordered an ICC tribunal sitting in São Paulo to re-examine evidence for the purpose of determining the amount of compensation claimed by the plaintiff.

14.25 In spite of the drawbacks contained in the findings of the Court, these precedents seem to be in line with a pro-arbitration jurisprudence that is gradually being formed in Brazil, due in no small part to the fact that São Paulo tends to attract a greater caseload of complex disputes as compared to most venues in Brazil, and that these often involve international parties.

14.26 **Specialized chamber of the appellate court for arbitration-related matters** The quality of arbitration jurisprudence is likely to improve even more with the recent creation of a specialized chamber of the São Paulo Appellate Court with exclusive jurisdiction over commercial law disputes (involving corporation law, unlawful competition, intellectual property, and licensing/franchise agreements), including arbitration-related litigation. The rationale for the creation of a specialized chamber was to streamline and enhance the decision-making process for commercial law in general and arbitration in particular.

14.27 Thus, as of August 2011, the *Câmara Reservada de Direito Empresarial* is the court of last resort (at the state level, ie the final instance in São Paulo) for actions in aid of arbitral proceedings, such as actions to compel arbitration, pre-arbitration injunctions, discovery orders, etc as well as actions to set aside or annul domestic arbitral awards.

14.28 Although this specialized chamber has been in place for a relatively short time, a review of its arbitration-related decisions to date already reveals a pro-arbitration stance.

14.1.3 Comparison with other regional or national venues

14.29 São Paulo is the quintessential business city, so it is no wonder most arbitration proceedings are held within its limits. No one denies that other capitals, particularly Rio de Janeiro, can

[10] *Energia Sustentável do Brasil SA v SulAmerica Companhia Nacional de Seguros* Interlocutory Appeal no. 0304979-49.2011.8.26.0000, Tribunal de Justiça do Estado do São Paulo (19 April 2012).

[11] *Companhia do Metropolitano de São Paulo ('Metro') v Consorcio Via Amarela* Writ of Mandamus no 053.10.017261-2, São Paulo Court of Appeals (7 June 2010).

be equally suited to host arbitrations, but São Paulo will remain, at least within the foreseeable future, as the preferred seat for national proceedings.

This is true, not only because of the assistance of local courts (as discussed), but also for reasons of geography and convenience: São Paulo is still home to most prominent Brazilian companies (including almost the entire financial industry), as well as the subsidiaries of multinationals; it is the destination of most international flights to Brazil; and is prolific in services and infrastructure normally associated with arbitration (hotels, conference centres, arbitral institutions, law firms, and other service providers). **14.30**

14.2 Commencing the Arbitration

14.2.1 Notice and appointment of arbitrators

Most arbitral institutions[12] in Brazil have established standard rules for initiating arbitral proceedings, which usually require the interested party to notify the secretariat of the arbitral institution of its intention to arbitrate, stating the nature of the dispute,[13] the amount in dispute, and relevant information pertaining to the other party, and attaching a copy of the contract under which the parties agreed to arbitrate their dispute.[14] **14.31**

The secretariat will then notify the other party of the request for arbitration and ask the parties to appoint the arbitrator(s) within a certain period of time. In an ad hoc arbitration, the Arbitration Act provides that if the parties have not agreed ahead of time on the procedure for initiating arbitral proceedings, the interested party shall notify the other party, either by mail or through any other means of communication, with confirmation of receipt, of its intention to commence arbitral proceedings. **14.32**

Usually, unless the parties have agreed otherwise (for instance, by choosing to have a tribunal with a sole arbitrator), the arbitrators appointed by the parties will, in turn, choose a third arbitrator from the institution's roster of arbitrators, who will preside over the arbitral tribunal. This also reflects the default appointment process outlined in article 13 of the Brazilian Arbitration Act. **14.33**

Depending on the arbitral institution that the parties have chosen and its institutional rules, the appointment of arbitrators who are not listed in the institution's roster of arbitrators will be subject to approval by the president of the arbitral institution. However, provided that the appointed arbitrator is a person with full legal capacity, impartial, and independent and, ultimately, trusted by the parties, this does not constitute a major concern among legal practitioners and parties conducting arbitral proceedings in Brazil, particularly since the **14.34**

---

12 For instance, under the CCBC Rules of Arbitration, s 5.1:

> The party, in a separate document containing a compromise clause which establishes the Center's competence to decide on contractual disputes by means of arbitration, shall notify the Center of its intention to arbitrate, declaring forthwith upon, the nature of the dispute, the amount involved and the name and relevant data of the other party, attaching a counterpart of the relevant contract.

13 The BAA 1996 allows 'persons capable of contracting' to 'settle through arbitration disputes related to patrimonial rights over which they may dispose'. The act's broad scope of arbitrability, however, excludes from the scope of arbitration issues that cannot be contracted away, such as criminal, antitrust, and patent matters.

14 In order to be valid, the arbitration agreement must be in writing and must be contained in the contract itself or in a separate document.

practice of limiting appointments to the institution's roster is gradually being abolished by arbitral institutions in Brazil.[15] In addition, Brazilian law does not require arbitrators to be Brazilian nationals.

14.35 Pursuant to the Brazilian Arbitration Act,[16] the arbitral tribunal is deemed constituted upon acceptance by the arbitrator of his nomination, in the case of a sole arbitrator, or by all, if there are several. However, prior to this acceptance, parties often find themselves trapped in a 'jurisdictional limbo' between being able to rely on a arbitral tribunal that has not yet been officially constituted, and resorting to a local court for support. This is particularly true where interim relief becomes necessary or when one of the parties is resisting the initiation of the arbitration.

14.36 Fortunately Brazilian law, institutional rules, and courts throughout Brazil (particularly those more experienced in dealing with issues involving arbitration) have developed and routinely apply effective mechanisms to deal with these situations.

14.2.2 Court assistance in compelling arbitration

14.37 Brazilian civil procedure rules require courts to dismiss any lawsuit brought by a party in violation of an agreement to arbitrate.[17] In addition, the Brazilian Arbitration Act[18] provides for a specific remedy in such cases, by means of a 'motion to compel arbitration' against the recalcitrant party.

14.38 In addition to serving as an effective tool to compel specific performance of arbitration agreements, the 'motion to compel arbitration' may also be used to give effect to defective or incomplete arbitration clauses. Thus, an interested party may resort to a local court in order to correct or supplement a defective arbitration clause.

14.39 São Paulo has a favourable track record involving motions to compel in which the court either dismissed the lawsuit brought in violation of an existing arbitration agreement between the parties, or entertained a motion to compel arbitration filed against a recalcitrant party. When faced with the so-called 'full arbitration clause', even if in its simplest form (language containing a commitment to arbitrate pursuant to the rules of a particular arbitral institution), courts in São Paulo will normally relinquish jurisdiction to arbitrators without further ado.[19]

---

[15] Under the new arbitration rules of the CCBC, in effect as of 2012, the presiding arbitrator is no longer required to be listed in the institution's roster of arbitrators.

[16] BAA 1996, art 19.

[17] Brazilian Civil Procedure Code, art 267: 'A lawsuit shall be dismissed without examination of the merits: ... VII—when parties have agreed to arbitrate the dispute'.

[18] BAA 1996, art 7:

> Where there is an arbitration clause but one of the parties shows resistance as to the commencement of arbitration, the interested party may request the court to summon the other party to appear in court so that the submission agreement (*compromisso*) may be signed; the judge shall designate a special hearing for this purpose... § 7—The judge's decision granting the motion shall be considered as the submission agreement (*compromisso*) itself.

[19] See for instance Civil Appeal no 267.450.4/6-00 *Anel Empreendimentos v Trelleborg*, São Paulo Court of Appeals (24 May 2006); Civil Appeal no 208.671-4/2-00 *Das Luiz Mangieri v Dirceu Alves Da Silva*, São Paulo Court of Appeals (23 September 2004); Interlocutory Appeal no 505.721-4/7-00 *José De Souza Cintra v Cervejaria Petrópolis*, São Paulo Court of Appeal (24 May 2007); Civil Appeal no 263.009-4/5-00 *Air Products Gases Industriais v AGF Brazsil Seguros*, São Paulo Court of Appeals (12 December 2005).

14.40 Recent disputes involving derivatives agreements containing arbitration clauses also illustrate the effective approach taken by São Paulo courts in enforcing specific performance of arbitration agreements. Derivatives disputes were the most visible by-product of the global financial turmoil that swept the world in September 2008. Many Brazilian exporters have disclosed significant financial losses arising from derivatives operations allegedly used to hedge against currency fluctuations. Many of these exporters filed lawsuits in São Paulo challenging the arbitration clauses inserted in the underlying agreements. Courts in São Paulo, however, reaffirmed the arbitrators' exclusive jurisdiction to decide on the existence and validity of the derivatives agreement executed between the parties and the obligations thereunder (article 8 of the Brazilian Arbitration Act, which reflects the principle of *competence-competence*). As a result, in one case state judges enforced the arbitration clause and remitted the dispute to arbitration.[20]

14.41 It is worth noting that the action to compel arbitration under article 7 of the Brazilian Arbitration Act is only necessary in cases of 'defective arbitration clauses', ie where the parties themselves failed to agree on a self-executing procedure for triggering the arbitral process. In other words, a 'full arbitration clause' (providing for such mechanism, as it is the case in virtually all rules of administering organizations) allows for a party to initiate and pursue claims without seeking the assistance of a Brazilian court.

14.2.3 Pre-arbitration interim relief by courts

14.42 Brazilian arbitration law allows an arbitral tribunal to grant provisional remedies in certain situations and as it deems necessary to safeguard the effectiveness of a prospective award.[21] As a basic matter, however, it is important to establish whether or not an arbitral tribunal has been effectively constituted, as this will determine whether parties can still resort to local courts in Brazil in order to obtain provisional measures.

14.43 If the arbitral tribunal has not yet been constituted, an interested party may request a local court[22] to grant interim relief up to 30 days prior to and 'in preparation' of a main proceeding (in this case, an arbitral proceeding). The party seeking interim measures must prove that it has already taken the appropriate measures to commence arbitral proceedings, or do so within 30 days after filing the request. Should the interested party fail to initiate arbitration within that time any measures ordered will lose.

14.44 When filing a request for 'preparatory' interim relief, a party requests the judge that would otherwise have had original jurisdiction to hear the case in the absence of an arbitration agreement to grant an injunction (*liminar*) to order certain measures such as the production of evidence, the freezing of bank accounts, or restraining orders against the sale of property in dispute or even to prevent a shareholders' meeting from taking place, until the arbitrators are able to exercise jurisdiction over the merits of the dispute.

---

[20] See Interlocutory Appeal no 7.343.768-4, 13th Chamber of Private Law of São Paulo Court of Appeals (13 June 2009).

[21] BAA 1996, art 22:

> The arbitrator or the arbitral tribunal may take the parties' deposition, hear witnesses and determine the production of expert and other evidence deemed necessary, either ex officio or at the parties' request . . . § 4—With the exception of the provisions of Paragraph 2, if coercive or injunctive orders become necessary, the arbitrators may request them from the State Court originallycompetent to decide the case.

[22] Usually located in the venue in which the urgent measure is to be implemented.

14.45 The merits of a decision on urgent matters rendered by a local court may be reviewed and revoked later by the arbitral tribunal, once it is constituted, as the arbitrators ultimately have jurisdiction to examine the merits by virtue of the arbitration agreement. Thus, according to a prevailing view among scholars in Brazil, 'the majority Brazilian doctrine holds that after the institution of the arbitration, coercive or urgent measures may only be requested from the arbitral tribunal. Only if the party against which the decision is issued does not comply will the intervention of the state court be necessary'.[23]

14.46 The rationale behind this intertwining of functions is that, unlike a court, an arbitral tribunal lacks coercive powers, even though arbitrators in general enjoy equal footing with judicial courts in Brazil.[24]

14.47 Additionally, some arbitral institutions, such as the Arbitration Center of the BM&FBOVESPA (Brazilian Stock Exchange), have recently updated their rules[25] to allow interested parties to obtain injunctive relief through the institution prior to the constitution of the arbitral tribunal, similar to the 'emergency arbitrator' mechanism under the new ICC Rules of Arbitration.[26] Other arbitration entities, such as the Brazilian Center for Mediation and Arbitration, expressly provide for recourse to the courts in order to obtain interim relief prior to the constitution of the arbitral tribunal.[27]

14.48 In São Paulo, the courts are generally amenable to pre-arbitration injunctive relief (ie those precautionary measures that are designed to 'hold the fort' until the arbitral tribunal is constituted). Statistics published by the Brazilian Arbitration Committee (CBAr)[28] show that São Paulo not only attracts the greatest number of cases involving pre-arbitration interim relief by courts (of 57 examined decisions, 37 were issued by the São Paulo Appellate Court), but that the decisions overall evince a pro-arbitration stance and that judges in that venue are well-educated in this area (of the 37 decisions issued by the São Paulo Appellate Court, 33 granted the interim relief sought while preserving the arbitral the jurisdiction of the arbitrators once they were properly appointed).

---

[23] JTP Muniz and ATP Basilio, *Arbitration Law of Brazil: Practice and Procedure* (Juris Publishing, 2006) 127.

[24] In accordance with BAA 1996, art 18: 'An arbitrator acts as judge of fact and law and the award rendered shall not be subject to judicial review, appeal or ratification.'

[25] The new BM&FBOVESPA Rules of the Market Arbitration Chamber, s 5.1:

> *Urgent Interim or Conservatory Measures before the Arbitration Tribunal has been constituted.* If before the Arbitration Tribunal has been constituted a party deems urgent interim or conservatory measures necessary to prevent imminent harm or irreparable injury, the party shall submit a motion to this effect to the President of the Arbitration Chamber, who shall appoint a permanent member of the Arbitration Chamber to act as emergency arbitrator. The role of the emergency arbitrator is to take a decision regarding the motion for urgent interim or conservatory measures, which if granted shall remain in force until the Arbitration Tribunal decides upon the merits ('Emergency Arbitrator'). The Emergency Arbitrator shall be appointed in accordance with Law 9307 (September 23, 1996), article 13, paragraph 6.

[26] BAA 1996, art 29.

[27] Rules of Arbitration of the Brazilian Center of Mediation and Arbitration, s 11:

> *Provisional Remedies, Coercitive or Anticipatory Remedies*: 11.1—At the request of any of the parties or at its sole discretion, the Tribunal may take any provisional remedies, coercitive [*sic*] or anticipatory remedies, it deems necessary. 11.2—If it is urgent and the Tribunal has not yet been established, the parties can request provisional or coercitive [*sic*] remedies to the competent judicial authority. In this in case, the party shall immediately notify such request to the Center.

[28] Monteiro and Nanni (n 5) 1.

14.3 During the Arbitration

14.3.1 Courts and challenges to arbitrators

Upon being nominated to an arbitral tribunal, arbitrators are required by law and institutional rules to submit a statement of independence or equivalent document disclosing any circumstances that might give rise to concerns about the existence of a potential conflict of interest affecting the arbitration. As addressed later, unresolved conflicts of interest can lead to the annulment of the award. **14.49**

The grounds for challenging an arbitrator under the Brazilian Arbitration Act are essentially the same as 'impediments' and 'suspicions' for the disqualification of a judge under the Brazilian Code of Civil Procedure. Similarly to the disqualifying factors listed under the 'red list' of the IBA Guidelines on Conflicts of Interest,[29] an impediment is a clear sign that the arbitrator is biased and may not act in the proceeding with an objective interpretation of the circumstances. 'Suspicions', on the other hand, offer a subjective and tentative analysis of the decision-maker's state of mind and do not necessarily lead to the conclusion that an arbitrator is biased in favour of one of the parties or has an interest in the subject matter in dispute. **14.50**

While there are only a few court decisions rendered in Brazil specifically relating to conflicts of interest of arbitrators, recent precedents indicate judges' scepticism concerning challenges to the impartiality and independence of arbitrators, particularly when these issues are raised outside the framework established by the Arbitration Act[30] and the respective arbitration rules. **14.51**

The STJ recently held that challenges to the partiality/independence of arbitrators must be made within the timeline specified by the respective arbitration rules.[31] Likewise, the São Paulo Appellate Court rejected an attempt to stay the effects of an arbitral award based on allegations of impartiality regarding one of the arbitrators.[32] **14.52**

As far as institutional regulation is concerned, some of the major arbitration institutions in Brazil have prepared guidelines on arbitrators' conflicts of interest. For example, the Center of Arbitration of the CCBC adopted in 2008 its Code of Ethics for arbitrators, which addresses issues of conflicts of interest, among other matters. The National Council for Mediation and Arbitration Institutions (CONIMA) also has its own Code of Ethics for arbitrators. Many institutions (such as CONIMA and the CCBC, among others) have set up special commissions to adjudicate challenges against arbitrators, thereby increasing the degree of predictability and satisfaction of the parties. **14.53**

In Brazil, an arbitrator's duty to disclose potential conflicts of interest is therefore perceived as an indispensable requirement. Unless waived by the parties (at their own discretion), a well-founded challenge is likely to result in the withdrawal of the designated arbitrator. When in doubt, an **14.54**

---

[29] Available at <http://www.ibanet.org>.

[30] Pursuant to BAA 1996, art 20, those wishing to make challenges to the 'disqualification of the arbitrator or arbitrators, as well the nullity, invalidity or inefficacy of the arbitration agreement, must do so at the first opportunity, after the initiation of the arbitration'.

[31] SEC 4.837/EX *YPFB Andina S/A v Univen Petroquímica Ltda*, STJ Reporting Justice Francisco Falcão, Special Chamber (15 August 2012).

[32] Interlocutory Appeal no 0025150-66.2012.8.26.0000, Tribunal de Justica São Paulo, 12th Private Law Chamber, Reporting Judge Tasso Duarte de Mello (30 May 2012).

arbitrator is encouraged to disclose any facts capable of giving rise to a challenge. Similarly, parties should undertake reasonable investigation of any factors potentially compromising the arbitrator's fitness to decide the matter.

14.3.2 Production of evidence—standards and the role of the courts

14.55 Once the arbitrators have accepted their nominations, as a rule, assistance by local courts will be limited to the implementation of orders or decisions issued by the arbitral tribunal in the event that parties do not comply voluntarily, since arbitrators lack coercive powers. A judge will usually refrain from examining the merits of the arbitrator's deliberations and will only rarely, and on serious grounds (such as lack of an arbitration agreement or violation of public policy), refuse to give effectiveness to orders issued by the arbitral tribunal.

14.56 In effect, article 22 of the Brazilian Arbitration Act provides that 'the arbitrator or the arbitral tribunal, at the request of the parties or on its own motion, may take depositions of the parties, hear witnesses, order expert examinations and any other evidence it may deem appropriate', and further, that 'the arbitrators may request to the judicial body that would have originally been competent to hear the case, to grant interim measures of protection'.[33]

14.57 While litigation in Brazil is inherently characterized by the inquisitorial system, in which courts play a fundamental role in the investigation of the facts, the same may not be said with respect to arbitral proceedings in Brazil. Attorneys unfamiliar with arbitral proceedings are often surprised by the adversarial nature of arbitration in Brazil and their expected active role in the proceedings with respect to the production of evidence and conduct of hearings. Nonetheless, as a result of the influence of Brazilian procedural rules, most commentators maintain that once the arbitral tribunal is duly constituted, the arbitrators may order the production of evidence on their own initiative, which is consistent with the wording of article 22 of the Act.

14.58 Most types of evidence are admitted in court in Brazil, including the testimony of witnesses domiciled abroad and expert evidence. Regardless of whether the production of evidence is directly ordered by the arbitral tribunal or by means of judicial intervention (when needed), however, it is important to note that, as a general rule in Brazil,[34] parties will only be required to present evidence on which they intend to rely to prove their case and may introduce *any lawfully obtained* evidence during the evidentiary stage of the proceeding.

14.59 Thus, the standards of admissibility of evidence in Brazil are essentially two—the relevance of evidence to the facts, and the lawfulness of the means by which the evidence is obtained. With respect to the relevancy burden, evidence must be necessary and useful to the arbitrators in understanding and investigating the facts of the case. As for the lawfulness requirement, evidence will be admitted in the arbitral proceedings provided it is not considered contrary to Brazilian law.

14.60 These rules, which grant the decision-maker the authority and discretion to admit evidence, seem to be in line with the rules applied in other jurisdictions, as well with the IBA Rules on the Taking of Evidence ('The Arbitral Tribunal shall determine the admissibility, relevance,

[33] BAA 1996, art 22, s 4.

[34] Brazilian Civil Procedure Code, art 355 establishes that 'a judge may order a party to produce documents or present exhibits in its possession'. Nevertheless, in spite of the broad scope of this rule, as an important counterweight, a party will not be compelled to produce unfavourable evidence under Brazilian law, unless required by law or court order (eg by virtue of a court order to allocate the burden to produce evidence to the opposing party).

materiality and weight of evidence').[35] Among the existing institutional rules in Brazil, many national arbitration providers have adhered to this 'universal' standard as well, including the CCBC[36] and the FIESP/CIESP.[37]

There are a number of decisions by Brazilian courts confirming the autonomy of arbitrators and limiting judicial assistance to implementing the arbitral tribunal's orders. Illustratively, in an interesting matter involving a conflict between partners of a law firm, the São Paulo Appellate Court upheld the lower court's decision directing compliance with an arbitral tribunal's order to produce documents.[38] **14.61**

14.3.3 Referral to court—stay of arbitral proceedings

Article 25 of the Brazilian Arbitration Act requires arbitrators to defer to the courts whenever an issue involving non-disposable/negotiable rights arises in the course of arbitral proceedings. In other words, if the resolution of such a non-arbitrable issue is a condition precedent for the arbitral award, arbitrators must refer the matter to the respective court of competent jurisdiction, thereby suspending the entire arbitration. **14.62**

That is the case, for example, when the respondent challenges the enforceability of a particular contract by invoking his/her lack of civil capacity to enter into agreements, a matter subject to the exclusive jurisdiction of the courts. In this scenario, proceedings will be suspended until a final and unappealable court decision is rendered on such a 'prejudicial' issue. **14.63**

In practice, this type of stay of arbitral proceedings is rarely verified and courts, especially those located in São Paulo, are reluctant to interfere with the arbitrators' ability to decide on their own jurisdiction (the *competence-competence* principle, as stated in article 8 of the Brazilian Arbitration Act). **14.64**

14.3.4 Restrictions and requirements in arbitral proceedings

Arbitrability

As far as subjective arbitrability is concerned (the personal status of the parties involved in the arbitral proceedings and their standing to be parties), the Brazilian Arbitration Act expressly provides that parties must have full legal capacity in order to arbitrate a dispute. **14.65**

As for objective arbitrability (which pertains to the susceptibility of the disputed subject matter to arbitration) under the Brazilian Arbitration Act, arbitration is permitted only in cases involving so-called 'negotiable rights' (*direitos disponíveis*). This means that certain **14.66**

---

35 IBA Rules on the Taking of Evidence, art 9.

36 The Rules of Arbitration of the CCBC, art 9.5 (2012) provides as follows:

> The parties can submit all the evidences they deem convenient in order to instruct the proceedings and to enlighten the arbitrators. Yet, the parties shall present any other available evidences that any member of the Arbitration Tribunal may consider necessary for the understanding and settlement of the dispute. It is up [to] the Arbitration Tribunal to accept any evidence deemed as convenient, necessary or relevant.

37 The FIESP Rules of Arbitration, art 8.5 establishes that the:

> Parties may submit all evidence as they deem useful to the understanding of the facts by the arbitrators, as well as any other available evidence requested by the arbitral tribunal, as may be the case. The arbitral tribunal shall decide whether to admit evidence deemed useful, necessary and pertinent to the dispute.

38 Interlocutory Appeal no 0526704.47.2010.8.26.0000 São Paulo Court of Appeals (16 March 2011).

matters may not be arbitrated even if the parties agree to arbitrate them: family matters, certain public law matters, and possibly, according to a recent decision of the Superior Labor Court, individual employment-related matters. However, most commercial matters may be arbitrated, including many (though not all) involving the government or a government-controlled entity as a party.

14.67 Additionally, arbitration clauses in consumer contracts or adhesion contracts are considered valid and effective only when the consumer or adhering party initiates the arbitration, or if the arbitration provision is in bold type or appears in a separate signed document.

Procedural requirements

14.68 Provided that the subject matter in dispute is arbitrable under Brazilian law and that parties have full legal capacity in law, there are generally very few restrictions on undertaking arbitral proceedings in Brazil. Overall, parties can freely determine in the arbitration agreement the procedure that will be applied. They can choose the arbitration rules of an institution or entity, establish the rules that will govern the arbitration, or attribute to the arbitral tribunal the power to define the procedure.

14.69 Certain procedural rules and principles must nevertheless be observed throughout the proceedings, particularly ones that derive from the concept of due process, such as full defence and proper response, equal treatment of the parties, arbitrators' impartiality, and independence.

Foreign practitioners

14.70 An arbitrator may be an 'individual with legal capacity' and the law does not impose any citizenship requirement or special qualification (eg licensed to practice law in Brazil).[39] Therefore, arbitrators in both domestic and international proceedings may be foreigners and non-lawyers. Some arbitral institutions, such as the CCBC, have recently expanded their roster of arbitrators to include foreigners in the list.

14.71 As for attorneys, the Brazilian Arbitration Act does not prevent foreign practitioners from participating as counsel in arbitral proceedings. In fact, legal representation of parties in arbitral proceedings is not a requirement under the Brazilian Arbitration Act, although it would be a rare case in which the parties chose not to be represented by counsel.

Hearings and meetings abroad

14.72 Hearings and procedural meetings of arbitrations with their seat in Brazil may also take place outside Brazil. Brazilian law does not prevent the arbitrator from choosing the most convenient place to carry out the hearings and procedural meetings. This will not affect the choice of the seat of arbitration.

14.73 Only with respect to arbitral awards does the Brazilian Arbitration Law consider a foreign award as one rendered outside the national territory, as opposed to domestic awards, which are issued within Brazilian boundaries.

Language requirements

14.74 As a rule, arbitral proceedings may be conducted in any language, particularly since this falls within the autonomy of the parties, along with the choice of the institution, rules,

---

[39] BAA 1996, art 13.

deadlines, etc. In Brazil, language is not a mandatory requirement in arbitral proceedings. Similarly, none of the Brazilian arbitral institutions require parties to conduct proceedings in Portuguese or in any other language. In fact, the use of languages other than Portuguese is quite common in arbitrations taking place in Brazil, particularly when one of the parties comes from a non-Portuguese speaking country.

It must be noted, however, that the 2004 Public-Private Partnership Law and the 2005 Amendment to the Concessions Law, which authorize the arbitration of disputes between public entities and private parties arising from transactions executed with the federal government, require that the arbitration be conducted in Brazil and in Portuguese—which in practical terms would narrow the options of qualified foreign arbitrators.[40] **14.75**

Foreign arbitral institutions

Foreign arbitral providers are permitted to operate in Brazil. Brazilian law does not provide any specific rules on the establishment of arbitral institutions in Brazil.[41] As previously mentioned, institutions such as the ICC, ICDR, and LCIA are commonly chosen to administer arbitral proceedings in seats like São Paulo, although none currently have offices in Brazil. **14.76**

14.4 The Award

14.4.1 Definition and status of an arbitral award

Arbitral awards issued within Brazilian territory (regardless of the nationality of the arbitral institution) are enforceable in Brazil in the same manner as final and non-appealable decisions rendered by a judicial court, and may therefore be challenged under very limited circumstances only.[42] **14.77**

14.4.2 Mandatory formal requirements

For an arbitral award to be considered valid and effective, it must satisfy certain formal and substantive requirements. **14.78**

Under Article 26 of the Brazilian Arbitration Act, an arbitral award must contain (a) a summary of the dispute and procedural history; (b) the reasons for the decision; (c) a decision as to the claims and any counterclaims; (d) the date and place of issuance of the arbitral award (seat); and (e) the signature of all arbitrators. An arbitral award that does not fulfil these requirements may be set aside. **14.79**

Summary of the dispute and procedural history

The summary of the dispute must contain all claims of the parties, as well as the procedural steps that led to the decision. **14.80**

Although such a summary is usually not mandatory in other jurisdictions, it is crucial in the Brazilian system, as it demonstrates that all evidence and arguments presented and raised by the parties were taken into consideration by the tribunal in rendering a final decision. **14.81**

[40] Specific requirements as to the seat (Brazil) and language (Portuguese) are found in Law 11.079/2004, article 11(III) (PPP Law) and Law 9.987/1995, art 23A (Concessions Law).

[41] BAA 1996, art 5.

[42] Under BAA 1996, art 31, with reference to the parties and their successors, the arbitral award shall have the same effects as a judgment rendered by the court and, should it be condemnatory, it will constitute a valid document to commence an prosecution process.

The reasons for the decision

14.82 Brazilian arbitration law requires that all grounds and reasons that led the arbitrators to their conclusions be clearly and logically expressed in the award. The main reason for this requirement is that the grounds for a decision are considered to be a matter of public policy in the Brazilian legal system, particularly in order to demonstrate that the decision was not arbitrary or biased.

Decision as to claims and counterclaims

14.83 An arbitral award must also contain an operative section addressing the conclusions of the tribunal, also referred to by Brazilian procedural law as the '*dispositiv*', in which the arbitrators are required to indicate clearly whether they have granted or rejected the claimant's claims and any counterclaims.

14.84 All claims submitted by the parties must be ruled on by the Arbitral Tribunal. It may not rule on matters beyond the scope of the arbitration agreement.

Date and place of signature

14.85 The indication of the date of signature of the arbitral award is important for several reasons, particularly in order to establish when the decision becomes *res judicata* among the parties, as well as to verify whether or not the arbitral tribunal complied with any time limits for the issuance of the award.

14.86 The place of signature is by far one of the most important formalities, as it determines where an award was issued and therefore whether it is domestic or foreign. Brazil has adopted the *territorial criterion*, whereby the place of issuance of the arbitral award is considered the seat of arbitration. This is particularly relevant for the purpose of enforcement. An award rendered in foreign venue will be considered a foreign award and therefore subject to recognition by the STJ, whereas an award rendered within Brazil can be enforced directly. Additionally, as a matter of *lex arbitri*, when the seat of arbitration is in Brazil, Brazilian arbitration law will apply on a subsidiary basis to any institutional rules chosen by the parties.

14.87 In order to facilitate and expedite the enforcement of an arbitral award in Brazil, parties often choose Brazil as the place of signature, particularly as this will avoid the need to apply to the STJ for recognition.

Signature of all arbitrators

14.88 An arbitral award must contain the signatures of all members of the arbitral tribunal. If an arbitrator cannot or will not sign the award, the chairman of the arbitral tribunal must certify this in the award in order to prevent it from being invalid.[43] The arbitrator who dissents from the majority may, if he so wishes, state his vote separately.[44]

14.4.3 Mandatory substantive requirements

14.89 The Brazilian Arbitration Act establishes only one substantive requirement: that the arbitrators determine the responsibilities of the parties for the payment of costs and fees, as well as for any bad faith in litigation.[45]

---

[43] BAA 1996, art 26.

[44] BAA 1996, art 24, s 2.

[45] Under BAA, art 27 '*The arbitral award shall decide the responsibility of the parties regarding costs and expenses for the arbitration, as well as fees due to bad-faith conduct, as may be the case, following the provisions of the arbitration agreement, if any*' (emphasis added).

The costs incurred by the parties must be presented through documents to the arbitral tribunal prior to the issuance of the arbitral award. Most arbitral institutions in Brazil do not have specific rules regarding attorney's fees and the recovery of costs and expenses. This provision of the Brazilian Arbitration Act will therefore apply complementarily to the rules of any institution. **14.90**

It is important to note that there is a substantial difference between costs and attorney's fees under Brazilian arbitration law. While costs relate to the conduct of the arbitral proceedings (including the arbitrators' fees), legal representation is not an essential requirement under the Arbitration Act, and therefore the lack of a decision on attorneys' fees will not affect the validity of an award. **14.91**

When establishing the costs and expenses due in arbitrations under Brazilian law, arbitrators often fix legal fees as a percentage of the final award, ranging from 10 to 20 per cent, based on factors such as the nature of the subject in dispute and the amount of work involved. The rationale for establishing such a percentage range is greatly influenced by the Brazilian civil procedure rules on the payment of fees, which requires courts to apply a 10–20 per cent ratio over the amount attributed to the claim (ie the economic value of the dispute).[46] **14.92**

14.5 After the Award

14.5.1 Request for clarification

Within five days of the issuance of the arbitral award, either party may request the arbitral tribunal to correct any errors in the award, to clarify any obscurity or inconsistency, or to decide on any omitted issue that should have been decided. The other party must be given notice of the request, and the tribunal must render its decision, in the form of an addendum to the award, within ten days. **14.93**

14.5.2 Annulment/setting aside

Pursuant to the Brazilian Arbitration Act, an arbitral award rendered in Brazil[47] may be annulled on very limited grounds only, and the request must be made within 90 days **14.94**

[46] Brazilian Code of Civil Procedure, art 20. Two distinguished Brazilian authors state that:

> For such reasons, a distinction must be drawn between attorney's fees referred to in Article 27 of the Law 9.307/96—which are broadly recognized as indemnification in the international scenario,—and the recovery of expenses established as such under Art. 20 of the Brazilian Code of Civil Procedure. The former derives from the general principle of reimbursement of losses, covering expenses incurred by the prevailing party in pleas. In effect, these losses correspond to the expenses paid to cover the costs of legal representation in the dispute and, in international arbitration, are attributed to the prevailing party. In contrast, the recovery fees referred to in Art. 20 of the Brazilian Code of Civil Procedure arise out of the legislator's choice to allow a judge to establish a percentage over the amount attributed to the case, regardless of whether expenses were in effect incurred by a party or of the existence of an attorney's fee agreement.

See G Tepedino and JE Nunes Pinto, *Notas sobre o ressarcimento de despesas com honorários de advogado em procedimentos arbitrais* (Padma, 2008); and R Ferraz and J de Paiva Muniz, *Arbitragem doméstica e internacional: estudos em homenagem ao. Prof. Theóphilo de Azeredo Santos* (Forense, 2008) 194–5).

[47] By contrast, an international arbitral award (issued outside the Brazilian territory) will not be vacated on these grounds. The grounds for refusal of recognition and enforcement provided in the New York Convention have been essentially reproduced in the last part of BAA 1996 (arts 38 and 39), and as such will apply for the purpose of setting aside a foreign award.

following the receipt of the award by the parties. Usually, the interested party will file for annulment of the award at the local court that would have had jurisdiction in the absence of an arbitration agreement between the parties. In any event, it is important to emphasize that Brazilian courts tend to be reluctant to grant a motion to vacate an arbitral award.

14.95 Under article 32 of the Brazilian Arbitration Law, an award rendered in Brazil may be set aside only where (a) the arbitration agreement is null and void; (b) the award was rendered by someone who could not serve as an arbitrator; (c) the award does not satisfy the requirements of article 26 of the Brazilian Arbitration Act (mandatory formal requirements for an arbitral award); (d) the award deals with matters outside the scope of the arbitration agreement; (e) the award does not resolve the entire dispute submitted to arbitration; (f) the award was procured by corruption, fraud, or graft; (g) the arbitral award was rendered after the time limit for rendering it had expired; or (h) the principles of due process of law, equality of the parties, impartiality of the arbitrator, or the arbitrator's discretion to decide have been violated. With respect to the grounds set forth in points (b), (d), and (e), the dispute may be remitted to the same arbitral tribunal for the issuance of an amended award. As for the remaining grounds, the arbitration agreement will be deemed invalid and the parties are free to resort to the courts for resolution of the dispute.

14.96 The growth of arbitration in Brazil has also brought an increase in the number of motions to vacate (or annulment actions). While the courts in São Paulo exercise constraint in annulling arbitral awards, judgment debtors are relatively successful in obtaining injunctions to suspend the execution/enforcement of the award until a final decision is rendered on the merits of their motions to vacate.

14.97 A recent decision by the São Paulo Appellate Court illustrates this trend in annulment actions: arguing violation of due process and challenging the impartiality of an expert report, a construction company successfully enjoined the enforcement of a multi-million dollar arbitral award arising from an EPC[48] agreement to build a hydroelectric power plant.[49]

Arbitration agreement is null and void

14.98 An arbitral award may be null and void when (a) the subject matter is non-arbitrable under Brazilian law; (b) the mandatory requirements for arbitration agreements, as set forth in article 10 of the Brazilian Arbitration Act,[50] were not satisfied; (c) the parties lack legal capacity; and (d) there are defects in the parties' consent to arbitration.[51]

Award rendered by someone who could not serve as arbitrator

14.99 As mentioned previously, arbitrators are required by law and institutional rules to submit a statement of independence or an equivalent document disclosing any circumstances that

---

[48] 'Engineering, Procurement and Construction', a common form of contracting arrangement within the construction industry.

[49] Interlocutory Appeal no 01345527-69.2012.8.26.0000, 34th Chamber of Private Law São Paulo Court of Appeals, Reporter Cristina Zucchi (4 February 2013).

[50] BAA 1996, art 10:

> The arbitration agreement must mandatorily indicate: I—the name, profession, marital status and domicile of the parties; II—the name, profession and domicile of the arbitrator or arbitrators, or, if applicable, the institution to which parties have delegated the appointment of arbitrators; III—the subject matter of the arbitral proceedings; and IV—the place where the arbitral award shall be made.

[51] BAA 1996, art 32.

might give rise to concerns about the existence of a potential conflict of interest. Thus, an arbitral award issued by an arbitrator who failed to disclose any conflicts of interest may be annulled. Additionally, an award issued by a person who lacks specific qualifications agreed by the parties may also be set aside, but the Arbitration Act requires the party who intends to make this challenge to do so 'at the first opportunity, after the initiation of the arbitration'.[52]

Award does not satisfy formal requirements of article 26

Article 26 of the Brazilian Arbitration Act sets forth the mandatory formal requirements for an arbitral award: (a) summary of the dispute and procedural history; (b) the reasons for the decision; (c) decision as to all claims and counterclaims; (d) date and place of issuance (seat); and (e) signatures of all arbitrators. Arbitral awards that fail to meet formal requirements may be set aside. **14.100**

Award deals with matters outside the scope of the arbitration agreement

This ground refers to decisions rendered outside the scope of the arbitral tribunals' jurisdiction ('*ultra petita*' awards) or in excess of the parties' claims ('*extra petita*'). In the former situation, the court will vacate the award and remit the case to the arbitrators for re-adjudication. In the latter case, the court can simply 'trim off' the excess, without the need to reconstitute the arbitral panel. **14.101**

Award does not resolve the entire dispute submitted to arbitration

Similarly, an arbitral award that falls short of what the parties claimed in the arbitration may be subject to annulment. In this case, the arbitral tribunal will be ordered to supplement the award. **14.102**

Award procured by passive corruption, fraud, or graft

This ground refers to situations of criminal misconduct by the arbitrators in the exercise of their mandates as arbitrators. The criminal acts are set out in the Brazilian Criminal Code. **14.103**

Award rendered after time limit expired

In spite of this provision, the time limit for the issuance of an award will not usually constitute an issue capable of justifying the annulment of an award. Parties may, by agreement, fix a time limit within which the arbitrators must deliver the award. As a default rule, if no time limit is provided for by the parties, or in the applicable institutional rules, article 23 of the Brazilian Arbitration Act establishes a six-month period as of the commencement of the arbitration (ie the acceptance by the arbitrators of their appointment). **14.104**

Many authors maintain that a party seeking to annul an award on this ground must notify the arbitral tribunal of its intention upon the expiration of the time limit. In practical terms, however, many arbitral institutions allow arbitrators to extend time limits by means of a procedural order.[53] **14.105**

---

[52] BAA 1996, art 20.

[53] For instance, the CCBC Rules of Arbitration provide as follows:

> 10.1. The Arbitration Tribunal shall pronounce the award within a 20 (twenty) day period, which shall be counted: a) if no hearing occurred, from the end of the period mentioned in article 9.3; b) if an instruction hearing occurred, from the end of the period for the final allegations as set forth in article 9.16. 10.2. The period mentioned in the previous article can be extended up to 60 (sixty) days, at the discretion of the chairperson of the Arbitration Tribunal.

Violation of principles of due process, equality, impartiality, or arbitrator discretion

14.106 This ground refers to a clear and damaging violation of fundamental procedural principles, such as the denial of the right to respond to the opposing party's allegations, unequal treatment of the parties, or flagrant partiality on the part of the arbitrators.

14.107 Occasionally, however, this ground is invoked frivolously by parties seeking to set aside an award, although Brazilian case law has proved to be particularly demanding with respect to standards of the burden of proof for the violation of said procedural principles.

14.108 The São Paulo Appellate Court has recently held that 'courts should not interfere with the merits of the arbitral awards, but merely verify whether formal requirements have been properly observed by the arbitrators when deciding the case'.[54] In this precedent, the appellate judges unanimously held that the judgment debtor was actually 'dissatisfied with the [unfavorable] result of the arbitration', rather than properly challenging the award under Article 32 of the Brazilian Arbitration Act. As a result, the annulment action was denied.

Annulment procedure

14.109 Following the issuance of an arbitral award, any of the parties may file for annulment within 90 days of the date on which the parties received notice of the arbitral tribunal's decision.

14.110 At the outset of the annulment proceeding, a judge may give the parties the opportunity to settle the dispute, as is customary in any civil lawsuit. If a settlement is not reached (which is quite common), a request for annulment will follow the same procedure as for ordinary lawsuits, meaning that the lower court's decision may be appealed and make its way up to the Brazilian high courts (the STJ for federal law matters; the STF for constitutional law matters). This can, unfortunately, add a substantial amount of time to the resolution of a dispute that was initially expected to end with the issuance of the arbitral award. Nevertheless, it is important to note that a request to set aside an arbitral award alone will not prevent the enforcement of the arbitral tribunal's decision. This may be achieved only by seeking injunctive relief from the court to prevent the arbitral award from producing its effects, by demonstrating (a) the likelihood of success of the annulment request, and (b) that failure to suspend the effects of the arbitral award will lead to irreparable harm.[55]

Annulment statistics

14.111 According to a report prepared by the Brazilian Arbitration Committee,[56] in its survey regarding the annulment of arbitral awards in Brazil between 2001 and 2008, of a total of 33 cases examined, 14 awards were set aside by state courts (only one by the São Paulo Appellate Court) and 19 annulment requests were denied. More importantly, however, only one decision (of the Espírito Santo Appellate Court) was considered by the Committee to be technically incorrect, making a total of 93 per cent of the annulment rulings correct.

---

[54] Appeal no 0039341-36.2010.8.26.0114, 6th Chamber of Private Law, Reporter Paulo Alcides (7 March 2013).

[55] See Interlocutory Appeal no 0173883-71.2012.8.26.0000, Special Chamber of Business Law, Reporter Maia Cunha (30 October 2012), here, the São Paulo Appellate Court enjoined enforcement/execution of the arbitral award because the judgment-debtor made a compelling showing that he was denied basic procedural guarantees (due process) during the arbitration proceedings.

[56] Monteiro and Nanni (n 5) 1.

14.5.3 Opposing the enforcement of an arbitral award

Pursuant to Article 31 of the Brazilian Arbitration Act, an arbitral award will 'produce as to the parties and their successors, the same effects as a judgment rendered by the court and, should it be condemnatory, it will constitute a valid document to commence an execution process'. This means that an arbitral award rendered within Brazil is considered as a judgment debt and may therefore be enforced in the same manner as a judgment rendered by a state court. **14.112**

Article 475-N of the Brazilian Code of Civil Procedure lists the different types of judgment debts as follows: (a) judgments rendered by means of civil procedure recognizing the existence of an obligation to perform, not to perform, to deliver a thing, or to pay an amount; (b) criminal convictions no longer subject to appeals; (c) homologation judgments or conciliation or transactional agreements, irrespective of judicial examination of the subject matter; (d) arbitral awards; (e) extrajudicial agreements of any nature recognized by a court; (f) foreign judgments recognized by the Superior Court of Justice; and (g) deeds of distribution solely with respect to the administrator of an estate, heirs, and singular or universal successors. **14.113**

As a last resort, during enforcement proceedings against a debtor that fails to comply voluntarily with the terms of the arbitral award, the debtor may raise certain defences which are significantly more strict than the grounds for annulment and limited to specific matters. Thus, article 475-L of the Brazilian Code of Civil Procedure provides a narrow list of conditions under which a judgment debt (*impugnação*) may be challenged: **14.114**

- a lack or nullity of service, in a case of default judgment;
- unenforceability of the decision;
- wrongful seizure or wrongful evaluation;
- lack of standing;
- the enforcement request exceeds the amount set out in the award; and
- any impeditive, modifying, or extinctive cause of the obligation (eg payment, statute of limitations), provided such cause is subsequent to the relevant decision.

In any event, it is important to note that under Brazilian procedural law, a challenge by a party resisting enforcement will in no way stay or impede the successful party from taking measures to collect the amount awarded. **14.115**

Additionally, if the defendant fails to perform the obligation set out in the arbitral award within the specified period, the court may impose a penalty of 10 per cent over the total amount owed, and property may be attached to an extent sufficient to secure the performance of the obligation. The attached amount is then made available to the court. This 'obligation' corresponds to a liquidated judicial debt (ie what was officially awarded to the successful party by the court) and is fully enforceable as of the moment the judgment is rendered. **14.116**

14.6 Conclusion

São Paulo is regarded as Brazil's locomotive, and while other regions of the country have experienced significant development in the past decade, São Paulo maintains its status as Brazil's leading centre for business and financial transactions. **14.117**

14.118 This business-oriented culture continues to be the perfect breeding ground for arbitration; from the creation of Brazil's first arbitration center (the CCBC in 1979), to the consolidation of an 'arbitration culture' by the relentless work of the local arbitration community, São Paulo remains Brazil's preferred venue for arbitral proceedings.

14.119 Finally, there is the pivotal role played by the local courts, whose decisions represent the most compelling evidence that São Paulo is comparable to other major international arbitration venues.

15

SINGAPORE

*Minn Naing Oo**

15.1 Background

15.1.1 Singapore's emergence as a leading venue for international arbitration

Singapore is currently one of the world's leading arbitration destinations. In addition to having recently hosted the 21st Congress of the International Council for Commercial Arbitration (ICCA), the reputation of the Singapore International Arbitration Centre (SIAC) and Maxwell Chambers as being among the leading arbitration-related institutions in the world is testament to the growing significance of international arbitration in the Asia-Pacific region, as well as to the leading role that Singapore has played in contributing to the collective jurisprudence, expertise, activity, and interest in international arbitration. **15.01**

As a venue in the *literal* sense, the building of Maxwell Chambers as a central 'one-stop' centre for alternative dispute resolution, boasting world-class hearing facilities and support services, has been acknowledged as a 'masterstroke' that is now being emulated in other jurisdictions. The recognition of Maxwell Chambers' facilities, as well as Singapore's natural advantage in terms of its geographical location, is evidenced in the increasing number of arbitrations being conducted in Singapore. In addition to Singapore-seated SIAC-administered **15.02**

* The author wishes to thank Mr Samuel Leong, Counsel at SIAC, for his invaluable assistance in the preparation of this chapter. All errors are, however, mine.

and ad hoc arbitrations, Maxwell Chambers' calendar of hearings now also regularly includes arbitrations that are being conducted under the auspices of ICSID, the Permanent Court of Arbitration, the ICC Court of International Arbitration, and other major arbitral institutions.

15.03 As a *conceptual* venue, ie as a juridical seat for international arbitrations, recent developments demonstrate that Singapore's robust international arbitration regime provides a reliable, neutral, and responsive framework for the expeditious, efficient, and just resolution of commercial disputes. This framework is a result of the steadfast commitment shared by the relevant stakeholders in Singapore, including the legislature and the judiciary, to entrenching Singapore's status as a decidedly 'pro-arbitration' jurisdiction. An analysis of the recent amendments made to the Singapore International Arbitration Act (Cap 143A)[1] (IAA) and the judicial decisions on international arbitration emanating from the Singapore Supreme Court provides clear evidence not only of Singapore's compliance with accepted principles of international arbitration but also of Singapore's contribution to the discourse on current issues in international arbitration. Since the amendments to the Singapore Legal Profession Act in 2004, the 'international arbitration bar' in Singapore has been entirely liberalized in relation to arbitral proceedings conducted in Singapore. In recognition of the importance of upholding the right of parties to appoint counsel[2] of their own choosing, counsel and arbitrators may freely conduct arbitrations in Singapore, irrespective of the governing law of the contract or the seat of the arbitration.

15.04 This chapter will consider the provisions of Singapore's statutory regime and jurisprudence that have contributed to establishing Singapore as a pro-arbitration jurisdiction. The chapter therefore provides selected 'snapshots' of the current legislative framework as well as recent judicial decisions in the Singapore courts on issues relating to international arbitration.

15.1.2 Legislative and judicial framework

15.05 With the publication of the 1985 UNCITRAL Model Law on International Commercial Arbitration and its steadily increasing adoption by legislatures around the world, it has, as a corollary, become considerably more difficult for any country to 'set itself apart' or 'excel' with regard to the support for arbitration that its domestic legislative framework provides. Yet Singapore has succeeded in this, by virtue of the unparalleled level of responsiveness that its Parliament demonstrates in addressing the concerns and needs of the 'arbitration bar'. This is borne out in particular by the last two rounds of amendments to the IAA.

15.06 Singapore adopted the Model Law in relation to international arbitrations[3] in 1994 when it legislated extensive revisions to the IAA. As a result of the 1994 revision, the Model Law (with the exception of Part VIII on recognition and enforcement of awards) now carries 'the force of law in Singapore'.[4] The first of the two rounds of amendments to the IAA mentioned previously ('2010 Amendment') came into force on 1 January 2010. The 2010 Amendment made three key changes to the international arbitration regime in Singapore, to: (1) provide

[1] International Arbitration Act (Cap 143A) (2002 Revised edition).

[2] Or non-legal representation.

[3] The adoption of Model Law principles in Singapore's domestic arbitration statute, the Arbitration Act (Cap 10) (AA) took place in 2001. See Chan Leng Sun, SC, *Singapore Law on Arbitral Awards* (Academy Publishing, 2011) para 1.8.

[4] IAA, s 3(1); L Boo, 'The Law and Practice of Arbitration in Singapore', ICCA Supplement No 38 (2003).

for court-ordered interim measures in support of foreign arbitrations; (2) update the definition of an arbitration agreement; and (3) stipulate how arbitral awards may be authenticated in Singapore.

In 2012, Singapore again amended the IAA ('2012 Amendment') to specify: (a) that the definition of an 'arbitral tribunal' includes an emergency arbitrator;[5] (b) that an objection to a *negative* ruling by an arbitral tribunal on its own jurisdiction may be made in the courts; (c) that an arbitral tribunal is empowered to award post-award interest (up to the date of payment); and (d) that in relation to foreign arbitrations, the definition of an 'arbitral award' shall include, in addition to the definition of an award under the 1958 United Nations Convention on the Recognition and Enforcement of Foreign Arbitral Awards ('New York Convention'), certain interlocutory orders or directions made or given by an arbitral tribunal in the course of an arbitration.[6] Also, the 2012 Amendment further updated the definition of 'arbitration agreement' under the IAA, to incorporate option I of Article 7 of the Model Law (as amended by UNICTRAL on 7 July 2006).[7] **15.07**

On Singapore's judicial policy towards arbitration as a dispute resolution mechanism, the Singapore (apex) Court of Appeal said, in *Tjong Very Sumito v Antig Investments Pte Ltd*: **15.08**

> An unequivocal judicial policy of facilitating and promoting arbitration has firmly taken root in Singapore. It is now openly acknowledged that arbitration, and other forms of alternative dispute resolution such as mediation, help to effectively unclog the arteries of judicial administration as well as offer parties realistic choices on how they want to resolve their disputes at a pace they are comfortable with. More fundamentally, the need to respect party autonomy (manifested by their contractual bargain) in deciding both the method of dispute resolution (and the procedural rules to be applied) as well as the substantive law to govern the contract, has been accepted as the cornerstone underlying judicial non-intervention in arbitration. In essence, a court ought to give effect to the parties' contractual choice as to the manner of dispute resolution unless it offends the law.
>
> ... *Courts should therefore be slow to find reasons to assume jurisdiction over a matter that the parties have agreed to refer to arbitration. It must also be remembered that the whole thrust of the IAA is geared towards minimising court involvement in matters that the parties have agreed to submit to arbitration.*[8]

Concurrent arbitration and court proceedings are to be avoided unless it is for the purpose of lending curial assistance to the arbitral process. Jurisdictional challenges must be dealt with promptly and firmly. If the courts are seen to be ready to entertain frivolous jurisdictional challenges or exert a supervisory role over arbitration proceedings, this might encourage parties to stall arbitration proceedings. This would, in turn, slow down arbitrations and increase costs all round. In short, the role of the court is now to support, and not to displace, the arbitral process. **15.09**

15.1.3 Comparison with other regional venues

As may be observed from the following, the recent developments in Singapore's legislative and judicial landscape have cemented its status as one of the foremost arbitral venues **15.10**

[5] IAA, s 2(1).
[6] IAA, s 27(1).
[7] Explanatory Statement, International Arbitration (Amendment) Bill (2012) (hereinafter Bill No 10 of 2012).
[8] SGCA 41 [2009] 28, 29.

in the Asia-Pacific region. Nevertheless, it must be added that Singapore's increased prominence as an arbitration destination also coincides with a larger 'wave' of economic activity and arbitration-awareness among the various stakeholders in Asia. This can be seen in the measures taken by legislatures in various Asian jurisdictions that have recently sought to bring their legislative regimes into consistency with the UNICTRAL Model Law.[9] Another indication of the increasing significance to the region of international arbitration as a dispute resolution mechanism may be observed in the establishment (and expansion) of various arbitral institutions, each with its own set of institutional arbitral rules, such as the Hong Kong International Arbitration Centre (HKIAC), the Korean Commercial Arbitration Board (KCAB), the Kuala Lumpur Regional Centre for Arbitration (KLRCA), the Japan Commercial Arbitration Association (JCAA), the Australian Centre for International Commercial Arbitration (ACICA), LCIA (India), and the ICC Court's office in Hong Kong. The growing diversity of players in the 'marketplace' of arbitral institutions and the increasing convergence among national arbitration laws would naturally serve to enrich the *corpus* of jurisprudence available on the legal issues surrounding international arbitration through transnational discourse on every level. This increased activity and emphasis on international arbitration bodes well for the future of international arbitration in Asia.

15.2 Commencing Arbitration

15.2.1 Definition of 'arbitration agreement'

15.11 Section 2A of the IAA broadly incorporates option I of Article 7 of the Model Law (as amended in 2006) with regard to the definition of 'arbitration agreement'.[10] Section 2A of the IAA expressly clarifies, *inter alia*, that the requirement that an arbitration agreement be recorded in writing is satisfied 'by an electronic communication if the information contained therein is accessible so as to be usable for subsequent reference'.[11] Section 2A(10) further explains that an 'electronic communication' means communication 'by means of data messages', which includes any communication carried out via electronic data interchange (EDI), email, telegram, telex, or telecopy. It is, however, pertinent to note that, in relation to foreign awards, Part III of the IAA specifically (re)defines 'arbitration agreement' to mean 'an agreement in writing of the kind referred to in paragraph 1 of Article II of the [New York] Convention'.[12]

15.12 The IAA's treatment of the definition of 'arbitration agreement' is clearly aimed at updating the relevant legislative provisions governing arbitral proceedings in Singapore as far as possible without affecting or departing from the application of the now-entrenched terms found in the New York Convention. Consequently, a Singapore-seated arbitral tribunal may safely take guidance from the updated definition of an arbitration agreement (which takes a broad view on the 'in writing' requirement); while an enforcing party may still draw comfort from

---

[9] <http://www.uncitral.org/uncitral/en/uncitral_texts/arbitration/1985Model_arbitration_status.html> (accessed 30 August 2013).

[10] Model Law, Art 7 (as amended in 2006).

[11] IAA, s 2A(5).

[12] IAA, s 27(1).

the knowledge that the requirements for the successful enforcement of a foreign award in Singapore remain squarely within the four corners of the New York Convention.

15.2.2 *Competence-competence*

As a hallmark of arbitration jurisprudence, the principle of *competence-competence*: that the arbitral tribunal has the power to rule on its own jurisdiction, and the principle of separability of the arbitration agreement, carry the force of law in Singapore by virtue of the adoption of the Model Law in 1994. In particular, Article 16(1) of the Model Law expressly provides that: **15.13**

> The arbitral tribunal may rule on its own jurisdiction, including any objections with respect to the existence or validity of the arbitration agreement. For that purpose, an arbitration clause which forms part of a contract shall be treated as an agreement independent of the other terms of the contract. A decision by the arbitral tribunal that the contract is null and void shall not entail *ipso jure* the invalidity of the arbitration clause.

The commitment of Singapore's arbitration framework to the upholding of an arbitral tribunal's power to determine its own jurisdiction and the arbitral process in general was put to the test in 2009 in *Insigma Technology Co v Alstom Technology Ltd.*[13] The dispute in *Insigma* concerned the calculation of annual royalties under a licence agreement by which Alstom granted Insigma use of its 'wet flue gas desulfurization' technology. The underlying 'hybrid' arbitration agreement stipulated: 'Any and all such disputes shall be finally resolved by arbitration before the Singapore International Arbitration Centre in accordance with the Rules of Arbitration of the International Chamber of Commerce . . .'. **15.14**

Alstom had initially commenced proceedings at the International Court of Arbitration of the ICC. In response, Insigma objected that the arbitration agreement required that arbitration be administered by SIAC, and not the ICC. Alstom then withdrew the ICC proceedings and subsequently commenced arbitral proceedings at SIAC. SIAC appointed a three-member tribunal, which then heard the parties on the issue of its jurisdiction as a preliminary question. In the course of deciding the question of its jurisdiction, the tribunal wrote to SIAC to ask whether SIAC was 'prepared to administer the arbitration in accordance with the ICC Rules and, if so, which bodies within SIAC would perform the functions assigned to the Secretary-General, Secretariat and the International Court of Arbitration of the ICC ('ICC Court') under the ICC Rules'.[14] SIAC replied in the affirmative, indicating that the SIAC Secretariat would undertake the role of the ICC Secretariat, the SIAC Registrar that of the ICC Secretary-General, and the SIAC Board of Directors the role of the ICC Court. The tribunal then rendered its decision on jurisdiction, holding that the arbitration clause was valid and that it had jurisdiction to render an award in the arbitration. **15.15**

Insigma then filed an application before the High Court to set aside the Tribunal's decision on jurisdiction on the basis that, *inter alia*, the arbitration clause in the licence agreement was not a valid arbitration agreement as it was void for uncertainty. The High Court rejected Insigma's argument, holding that the arbitration agreement was valid and binding and that the parties had essentially bargained for ad hoc arbitration in Singapore, which was to be **15.16**

[13] *Insigma Technology Co v Alstom Technology Ltd* 1 SLR(R) [2009] 23, HC; SGHC 134 [2008] HC; 3 SLR(R) 936 [2009] CA; SGCA 24 [2009] CA.

[14] *Insigma*, HC, at para 11.

administered by SIAC under the ICC Rules. According to Judith Prakash J 'there should be no practical problem, as well as no objection in principle, to providing for such a hybrid *ad hoc* arbitration administered by one institution but governed by the rules (as adapted where necessary) of another'.

15.17 On appeal (Insigma having obtained leave from the High Court), the Court of Appeal agreed with the decision and reasoning of the lower-court judge that the arbitration agreement was not void for uncertainty, and dismissed the appeal. According to the Court of Appeal:

> ... where the parties have evinced a clear intention to settle any dispute by arbitration, the court should give effect to such intention, even if certain aspects of the agreement may be ambiguous, inconsistent, incomplete or lacking in certain particulars ... so long as the arbitration can be carried out without prejudice to the rights of either party and so long as giving effect to such intention does not result in an arbitration that is not within the contemplation of either party.
>
> This approach to the interpretation of an arbitration agreement is necessary to uphold the underlying and fundamental principle of party autonomy as far as possible in the selection of the kind of arbitration and the terms of the arbitration. Given the inherently private and consensual nature of arbitration, our courts will ordinarily respect the principle of party autonomy and give effect to (workable) agreed arbitration arrangements in international arbitration, subject only to any public policy considerations to the contrary.[15]

15.2.3 Judicial reference on negative jurisdictional ruling by tribunal

15.18 Singapore, by virtue of the 2012 Amendment to the IAA, has departed from and 'added to' the Model Law position in relation to the principle of *competence-competence*, specifically, with regard to the power of the High Court[16] to consider a decision by an arbitral tribunal on the issue of its jurisdiction. In addition to its power to decide on an objection to a *positive* jurisdictional holding, the IAA now expressly empowers the High Court to decide on an objection to a ruling by an arbitral tribunal that it lacks the necessary jurisdiction to make an award on the dispute. Under section 10(3) of the IAA (which applies notwithstanding Article 16(3) of the Model Law), any party that is dissatisfied with a tribunal's ruling on jurisdiction may apply, within 30 days of having notice of the ruling, to the High Court for a decision on the issue of jurisdiction. Further, a decision of the High Court on the question of a tribunal's jurisdiction may be appealed, with the leave of the High Court, to the Court of Appeal of Singapore.[17]

15.19 This departure from the previous Model Law-derived position on the power of an Article 6 court to decide on objections to only positive jurisdictional rulings by an arbitral tribunal[18] has been acknowledged as a response by the Singapore Parliament to calls by practitioners and academics for legislative reform on this issue. In his speech in Parliament at the second reading of the bill proposing the 2012 Amendment, the Singapore Minister of Law specifically cited the Singapore Academy of Law (SAL) Law Reform Committee's Report on the Right to Judicial Review of Negative Jurisdictional Rulings (January 2011)[19] as being

---

15 *Insigma*, CA, at paras 31 and 34.
16 As the court designated pursuant to the Model Law, Art 6 (under IAA, s 8(1)).
17 IAA, s 10(4).
18 *PT Asuransi Jasa Indonesia (Persero) v Dexia Bank SA* [2007] 1 SLR(R) 597, para 66.
19 *Persero* (n 18) para 28.

supportive of empowering the High Court to review *negative* jurisdictional rulings by a tribunal as well.[20]

From a practical standpoint, the 2012 Amendment version of the IAA expressly stipulates that where the High Court (or the Court of Appeal, on appeal) decides that a tribunal erred by holding that it did not have the requisite jurisdiction, it must continue to preside over the arbitral proceedings and proceed to make an award in the arbitration. However, should the tribunal be 'unable or unwilling to continue the arbitral proceedings, the mandate of that arbitrator shall terminate and a substitute arbitrator shall be appointed in accordance with Article 15 of the Model Law'.[21] **15.20**

It may also be pertinent to note that Singapore is not alone in its departure from the Model Law position on judicial references on negative jurisdictional ruling by arbitral tribunals. Other jurisdictions in which national courts are able to exercise this power include Belgium, England, France, Italy, New Zealand, and Sweden.[22] **15.21**

Further, the 2012 Amendment to section 10 of the IAA has resolved, by legislative pronouncement, a conundrum that had previously resulted from negative jurisdictional rulings by arbitral tribunals,[23] ie: 'If a tribunal finds that it has no jurisdiction, can it award costs against the claimant for wrongfully commencing an arbitration?'[24] This issue was raised by the SAL in its recommendations on the IAA. In its discussion, the SAL made reference to the unsatisfactory (pre-2012 Amendment) situation in which a respondent who had been successful in arguing that a tribunal had no jurisdiction over it would be left without an enforceable decision on costs. This was further illustrated by the decision of the English High Court in *Crest Nicholson (Eastern) Ltd v Mr and Mrs Western*,[25] that in considering an arbitral tribunal's decision on jurisdiction, a court's jurisdiction on the issue of costs was limited only to the proceedings that had been conducted before it, and did not extend to the proceedings before the tribunal. **15.22**

In the light of this, the IAA now expressly provides that a tribunal, despite its own ruling that it has no jurisdiction, has the power to make an enforceable award on costs. This power is similarly extended to the courts when considering the same issue of the tribunal's jurisdiction, including the power to award costs for prior proceedings conducted before the tribunal. Section 10(7) reads: **15.23**

> In making a ruling or decision under this section that the arbitral tribunal has no jurisdiction, the arbitral tribunal, the High Court or the Court of Appeal (as the case may be) may make an award or order of costs of the proceedings, including the arbitral proceedings (as the case may be), against any party.

15.2.4 Stays of court proceedings and arbitration

Singapore's legislative position on the important issue of staying court proceedings commenced in contravention of an arbitration agreement is consistent with Article 8 of the **15.24**

---

[20] <http://www.news.gov.sg/public/sgpc/en/media_releases/agencies/minlaw/press_release/P-20120409-1/AttachmentPar/0/file/IAA%20-%202R%20speech.pdf> (accessed 30 August 2013).

[21] IAA, s 10(6).

[22] SAL Law Reform Committee's Report on the Right to Judicial Review of Negative Jurisdictional Rulings (January 2011) Annex A.

[23] Chan Leng Sun (n 3) para 2.22.

[24] Chan Leng Sun (n 3) para 2.22.

[25] *Crest Nicholson (Eastern) Ltd v Mr and Mrs Western* [2008] EWHC 1325 (TCC).

Model Law. Subject to the party that is applying for a stay making an application prior to 'delivering any pleading or taking any other step in the proceedings',[26] the court to which the application is made 'shall make an order, upon such terms or conditions as it may think fit, staying the proceedings so far as the proceedings relate to the matter, unless it is satisfied that the arbitration agreement is null and void, inoperative or incapable of being performed'.[27]

15.25 Further, in making an order staying judicial proceedings, a court may, in the exercise of its discretion, penalize the plaintiff 'for costs incurred in the improperly commenced court proceeding'.[28] Where 'a party has breached an arbitration clause by commencing court proceedings without good cause'[29] or 'pursued [an] entirely unmeritorious appeal, causing the respondent to incur additional costs',[30] indemnity costs[31] may be ordered against the party that commenced litigation.

15.26 The applicability of section 6 of the IAA and the requirement that a court grant a stay order upon the satisfaction of the elements contained in the provision was also examined in *The 'Engedi'*.[32] The facts in *The 'Engedi'* revolved around the arrest of the named vessel in the light of pending arbitration proceedings in London between the plaintiff and the former owner of the vessel. The plaintiff subsequently applied for and obtained a stay of proceedings under section 6 of the IAA in view of said pending arbitration proceedings in London. The owner of the vessel, acting as an intervener in the court proceedings, thus appealed the stay order on the ground that, *inter alia*, the action pending at arbitration (*in personam* against the former owner) was not the same action that was before the court (*in rem* against the vessel itself). Setting aside the stay order, Judith Prakash J held that section 6 of the IAA did not apply where only the action *in personam*, but not the action *in rem*, was before an arbitral tribunal. This was in order to preserve the rights of the owner of the *res* to defend against the claim, given that the owner 'was not a party to any arbitration agreement with the plaintiff and could not therefore be forced to litigate in another forum'.[33]

15.27 In addition to the statutory requirements for a stay application under the IAA (and the Model Law), the courts in Singapore have, at times, gone beyond the plain wording of the statute in order to arrive at a just resolution of the dispute between the parties on the proper forum of the dispute. In *Mitsui OSK Lines Ltd v Samudera Shipping Line Ltd*,[34] the Singapore High Court, in deciding that section 6 of the IAA did not have direct application on the facts (as the plaintiff was allegedly not a party to the arbitration agreement), invoked its power

---

26 IAA, s 6(1).

27 IAA, s 6(2).

28 L Boo (gen ed), 'Arbitration' in *Halsbury's Laws of Singapore*, Vol 1(2) (2001 Reissue) para 20.029.

29 *Tjong Very Sumito and ors v Antig Investments Pte Ltd* [2009] 1 SLR(R) 861; [2008] SGHC 202, HC, para 10.

30 *Tjong Very Sumito and ors v Antig Investments Pte Ltd* [2009] 4 SLR(R) 732; [2009] SGCA 41, CA, para 71.

31 The purpose of indemnity costs is to provide a party with compensation to as full an extent as possible for the outlay and trouble of litigation. While indemnity costs are often penal in nature, as they can be ordered to compensate one party following another party's wrongful conduct of proceedings, the compensation must never offend the indemnity principle. The party recovering costs must never recover more than it has actually spent, and does not usually recover 100% of that.

32 *The 'Engedi'* [2010] 3 SLR 409; [2010] SGHC 95, HC.

33 *The 'Engedi'* [2010] 3 SLR 409; [2010] SGHC 95, HC, para 26.

34 *Mitsui OSK Lines Ltd v Samudera Shipping Line Ltd* [2007] SGHC 41, HC.

under the Supreme Court of Judicature Act (Cap 322) to stay the judicial proceedings 'by reason of a multiplicity of actions',[35] pending a determination by the tribunal of the issue of the existence of an arbitration agreement between the parties.

A similar line of reasoning was taken by the High Court in *Yokogawa Engineering Asia Pte Ltd v Transtel Engineering Pte Ltd*,[36] where the court applied the common law doctrine of estoppel in considering an application for a stay of arbitral proceedings in Singapore. The dispute between the parties in *Yokogawa* related to the applicable version of the arbitration agreement that had been incorporated by reference in 'General Conditions of Sub-Contract'. Transtel, in reliance on representations given by Yokogawa as to the applicable version of the General Conditions, had commenced arbitration proceedings in Singapore. Yokogawa then argued that the 'correct' version of the General Conditions stipulated that arbitration had to be commenced in Thailand, and applied to the High Court of Singapore for a stay of the arbitral proceedings commenced by Transtel. **15.28**

The High Court dismissed the application (which did not appear to rely on any provision of the IAA) on the basis of the doctrine of estoppel, holding that in the light of Yokogawa's representations to Transtel as to the applicable version of the General Conditions, 'the plaintiff was estopped from asserting that the proper dispute resolution procedure is not arbitration in Singapore . . .'.[37] The decision of the High Court in this matter was subsequently affirmed by the Court of Appeal. **15.29**

15.2.5 Arbitrability

The issue of the arbitrability of a dispute, or whether a matter is capable of settlement by arbitration, may be raised either at the stage of enforcing an arbitration agreement or at the post-award stage, ie in the context of a setting aside application (at the primary jurisdiction) or of an application for enforcement.[38] **15.30**

The IAA deals with the concept of arbitrability and public policy, *inter alia*, in section 11: **15.31**

> Public policy and arbitrability
>
> 11.—(1) Any dispute which the parties have agreed to submit to arbitration under an arbitration agreement may be determined by arbitration unless it is contrary to public policy to do so.
>
> (2) The fact that any written law confers jurisdiction in respect of any matter on any court of law but does not refer to the determination of that matter by arbitration shall not, of itself, indicate that a dispute about that matter is not capable of determination by arbitration.[39]

In *Larsen Oil and Gas Pte Ltd v Petroprod Ltd (in official liquidation in the Cayman Islands and in compulsory liquidation in Singapore)*,[40] the Court of Appeal held[41] that in deciding an application for a stay of judicial proceedings, 'arbitrability is an important factor that ought **15.32**

35 *Mitsui OSK Lines* (n 34).

36 *Yokogawa Engineering Asia Pte Ltd v Transtel Engineering Pte Ltd* [2009] 2 SLR(R) 532, HC.

37 *Yokogawa Engineering* (n 36).

38 Boo 'Arbitration' (n 28) para 20.149.

39 Arbitrability (and public policy) is also referred to under the IAA, s 31(4) and the Model Law, Art 34.

40 *Larsen Oil and Gas Pte Ltd v Petroprod Ltd (in official liquidation in the Cayman Islands and in compulsory liquidation in Singapore)* [2011] 3 SLR 414; [2011] SGCA 21, CA.

41 Albeit in the context of a domestic arbitration under the AA (and not the IAA).

to be taken into consideration when determining whether to grant a stay...'.[42] The court went on to note that in the light of the apparent statutory paucity when it came to explaining 'what disputes are arbitrable... It has been left to the courts to shape the contours of the arbitrability exception'.[43]

15.33 Elaborating on the scope of the arbitrability exception, the court said:

> The concept of non-arbitrability is a cornerstone of the process of arbitration. It allows the courts to refuse to enforce an otherwise valid arbitration agreement on policy grounds. That said, we accept that there is ordinarily a presumption of arbitrability where the words of an arbitration clause are wide enough to embrace a dispute, unless it is shown that parliament intended to preclude the use of arbitration for the particular type of dispute in question (as evidenced by the statute's text or legislative history), or that there is an inherent conflict between arbitration and the public policy considerations involved in that particular type of dispute.[44]

15.34 Further, Rajah JA explained that an 'early' analysis of the arbitrability of a dispute also makes sense from an efficiency standpoint, as:

> An arbitral award in respect of [a] non-arbitrable claim is a *brutum fulmen* as it can be set aside... even if the issue of arbitrability is not raised by the parties. It is an utter waste of time for parties to incur time and cost through arbitration, only to obtain an arbitral award that is later set aside for non-arbitrability, and to have the entire litigation process repeated again to have their dispute sorted out.[45]

15.35 On the facts, *Larsen* was a dispute about the proper forum for the settlement of an action to avoid certain payments that Larsen had caused Petroprod to make to it (ie Larsen), having gained control over the finances of Petroprod (and four of Petroprod's wholly owned subsidiaries) under a Management Agreement. Petroprod's liquidators had sought to avoid the payments in question under, *inter alia*, the Singapore Bankruptcy Act (Cap 20) on the grounds that these payments amounted to unfair preferences or transactions at an undervalue within the meaning of sections 98 and 99 of the Bankruptcy Act, and that some of the payments were made with the intent to defraud Petroprod as a creditor of its subsidiaries. Having had its application for a stay of judicial proceedings dismissed by the High Court, Larsen appealed.

15.36 In dismissing the appeal, the Court of Appeal held that:

> A distinction should be drawn between disputes involving an insolvent company that stem from its pre-insolvency rights and obligations, and those that arise only upon the onset of insolvency due to the operation of the insolvency regime. Many of the statutory provisions in the insolvency regime are in place to recoup for the benefit of the company's creditors losses caused by the misfeasance and/or malfeasance of its former management. This is especially true of the avoidance and wrongful trading provisions. This objective could be compromised if a company's pre-insolvency management had the ability to restrict the avenues by which the company's creditors could enforce the very statutory remedies which were meant to protect them against the company's management. It is a not unimportant consideration that some of these remedies may include claims against former management who would not be parties to any arbitration agreement. The need to avoid different findings by different adjudicators is another reason why a collective enforcement procedure is clearly in the wider public interest.

42 *Larsen*, CA (n 40) para 24.
43 *Larsen*, CA (n 40) para 24.
44 *Larsen*, CA (n 40) para 44.
45 *Larsen*, CA (n 40) para 26.

> We, therefore, are of the opinion that the insolvency regime's objective of facilitating claims by a company's creditors against the company and its pre-insolvency management overrides the freedom of the company's pre-insolvency management to choose the forum where such disputes are to be heard. The courts should treat disputes arising from the operation of the statutory provisions of the insolvency regime *per se* as non-arbitrable even if the parties expressly included them within the scope of the arbitration agreement.[46]

15.2.6 Interim Relief

On no other issue of arbitral jurisprudence is Singapore's 'legislative responsiveness' more clearly demonstrated than on interim relief in aid of arbitration. **15.37**

On 1 December 2006, the Singapore Court of Appeal delivered its decision in *Swift-Fortune Ltd v Magnifica Marine SA*,[47] which was an appeal from a decision by Judith Prakash J in the High Court.[48] Prakash J had earlier decided to set aside a Mareva (freezing) injunction against Magnifica (a Panamanian company), which had been obtained *ex parte* by Swift-Fortune (a Liberian company) in view of pending arbitration proceedings between the parties in London over a dispute involving the purchase of a ship. **15.38**

Dismissing the appeal, the Court of Appeal held that the Singapore courts had no power to 'grant a Mareva injunction against the assets of a defendant in Singapore in aid of a foreign-seated arbitration unless the plaintiff has an accrued cause of action against the defendant that is justiciable in a Singapore court'.[49] Even where there is an accrued cause of action that is justiciable in a Singapore court, the Court of Appeal held that the power to grant an injunction was derived from section 4(10) of the Civil Law Act, and not the IAA, as section 12 of the IAA did not apply to foreign arbitrations. **15.39**

The decision by the Court of Appeal was met with fear that Singapore's arbitration-friendly reputation would suffer as, with the *Swift-Fortune* decision, the Singapore position on the issue, 'cuts a different picture, viz, that Singapore is actually only "pro-Singapore arbitration" '.[50] This decision also resulted in Singapore being inconsistent with other international arbitration venues, such as England and Hong Kong.[51] **15.40**

Parliament's response to *Swift-Fortune* was prompt. By virtue of the 2010 Amendment, the IAA was amended to include section 12A, which expressly states that the High Court has the power to grant certain interim relief in support of arbitration, 'irrespective of whether the place of arbitration is in the territory of Singapore'.[52] It is nevertheless important to note that the 2010 Amendment to the IAA includes certain restrictions on the nature of interim relief that may be sought from the High Court. Section 12A(2) expressly excludes the power to order security for costs and discovery of documents and interrogatories. It is therefore clear that 'the scope of the court's power is limited to interim measures in support of arbitration, **15.41**

---

[46] *Larsen*, CA (n 40) paras 45–46.
[47] *Swift-Fortune Ltd v Magnifica Marine SA* [2007] 1 SLR(R) 629; [2006] SGCA 42, CA.
[48] *Swift-Fortune* [2006] 2 SLR(R) 323; [2006] SGHC 36, HC.
[49] *Swift-Fortune*, CA, para 96.
[50] MN Oo and R Foxton, 'Recent Developments in International Arbitration in Singapore' (2011) Austrian Yearbook on Intl Arbitration 197, 201.
[51] Oo and Foxton (n 50) 200.
[52] Section 12A(1)(b), IAA.

and does not extend to procedural or evidential matters dealing with the conduct of the arbitration'.[53]

Emergency arbitrator

15.42 On 1 July 2010, the fourth edition of the Arbitration Rules of the Singapore International Arbitration Centre (2010 SIAC Rules) came into effect. A notable addition to the 2010 SIAC Rules, which did not exist in previous editions of the SIAC Rules, was the inclusion of provisions for an application for emergency interim relief before an 'Emergency Arbitrator'.[54] As the 2010 SIAC Rules gained more widespread adoption, along with the Emergency Arbitrator provision, the question of the enforceability of an Interim Order of an Emergency Arbitrator became increasingly pertinent. In passing the 2012 Amendment, the Singapore Parliament decided to respond proactively to the discourse by expanding the definition of 'arbitral tribunal' under section 2(1) of the IAA to include 'an emergency arbitrator appointed pursuant to the rules of arbitration agreed to or adopted by the parties including the rules of arbitration of an institution or organization'.

15.43 By virtue of the seemingly minor adjustment to the definition of 'arbitral tribunal', Parliament has expressly provided for the direct enforcement of interim orders by a Singapore Emergency Arbitrator under section 12(6), and for the enforcement of interlocutory orders by a foreign tribunal (and arguably even a foreign emergency arbitrator) under section 29(1) of the IAA.[55]

15.44 Another interesting development that has arisen as a result of the 2012 Amendment in relation to Emergency Arbitrators and the definition of 'arbitral tribunal' is the effect that the amendment has on section 12A(6) of the IAA, which reads:

> In every case, the High Court or a Judge thereof shall make an order under subsection (2) only if or to the extent that the arbitral tribunal, and any arbitral or other institution or person vested by the parties with power in that regard, has no power or is unable for the time being to act effectively.

In the light of this, the question that presently remains to be answered is whether a court in receipt of an application for interim relief in a situation in which the parties have elected for administered arbitration under rules that include provisions for the appointment of an Emergency Arbitrator, is required, by virtue of section 12A(6), to remit that application for interim relief to the arbitral institution for its appointment of an Emergency Arbitrator.

15.45 Given that the timelines set out in most institutional rules for the appointment of an Emergency Arbitrator are very short, in practice it would be difficult to argue that the relevant institution, and the Emergency Arbitrator (upon his/her appointment), would not be able to act on the application 'effectively'. For instance, Schedule 1 to the 2010 SIAC Rules stipulates that the Chairman of SIAC shall, subject to his determination that SIAC should accept any particular Emergency Arbitrator application, 'seek to appoint an Emergency Arbitrator within one business day of receipt by the Registrar of such application'.[56] Clause 5 of the same

[53] Oo and Foxton (n 50) 202.

[54] 2010 SIAC Rules, r 26.2 and Sch 1. As at 31 October 2012, SIAC has received a total of ten Emergency Arbitrator applications.

[55] Read with IAA, ss 27(1) and 2(1).

[56] 2010 SIAC Rules, Sch 1, cl 2.

Schedule 1 further provides that: 'The Emergency Arbitrator shall, as soon as possible but in any event within two business days of appointment, establish a schedule for consideration of the application for emergency relief.' It would be a challenge therefore to imagine a factual scenario in which an arbitral institution under its Emergency Arbitrator provisions, for example SIAC under the 2010 SIAC Rules, could be said to be unable to act effectively.

15.3 During the Arbitration

15.3.1 Appointment of arbitrators

Section 8(2) of the IAA stipulates that the statutory appointing authority under the IAA and pursuant to Article 11(3) and (4) of the UNCITRAL Model Law is the Chairman of the Singapore International Arbitration Centre (SIAC). Further, section 8(3) of the IAA states that the chief justice of Singapore may appoint any other person to exercise the appointing powers of the Chairman of SIAC. Section 8(3) has previously been invoked to also provide the deputy chairman of SIAC with the same appointing powers under the Act.[57] Naturally, this additional designation of the power to appoint an arbitrator under the IAA becomes necessary and important where the chairman himself is nominated for appointment as an arbitrator in the course of an arbitration. **15.46**

As the appointing powers under the Model Law have been statutorily vested in the SIAC chairman, there is no judicial recourse for the appointment of arbitrators. **15.47**

15.3.2 Number of arbitrators

Another point of departure from the Model Law in Singapore's enactment of the IAA concerns the default number of arbitrators. Pursuant to section 9 of the IAA, the default number of arbitrators to be appointed in the event that the parties have not come to agreement on the matter is one.[58] **15.48**

This issue was addressed by the High Court in *NCC International AB v Land Transport Authority of Singapore*,[59] where the parties were in dispute over the number of arbitrators to be appointed in an arbitration that was being administered under the 2007 SIAC Rules. In dismissing the NCC's application for a declaration that the Registrar of SIAC was empowered under the arbitration agreement to appoint a tribunal comprising three arbitrators, Tay Yong Kwang J held that the arbitration agreement, which required any dispute arising to be referred to 'an Arbitrator', meant that the parties had expressly agreed to the appointment of a sole arbitrator. In the light of the this holding, Tay J further held that an incorporated rule that permitted the SIAC Registrar to determine whether or not the dispute warranted the appointment of three arbitrators could not override the express agreement of the parties.[60] **15.49**

When the number of arbitrators to be appointed is three, the IAA also departs from the Model Law position on the default method of appointing the third arbitrator. Under article 11(3) of the Model Law, unless otherwise agreed upon by the parties, the third arbitrator shall be **15.50**

---

[57] Singapore Gazette Notification No 2547 of 2011.

[58] The default number of arbitrators under the Model Law is three, as stipulated in the Model Law, Art 10(2).

[59] *NCC International AB v Land Transport Authority of Singapore* [2009] 1 SLR(R) 985; [2008] SGHC 186, HC.

[60] *NCC International* (n 59) para 45.

appointed by the two co-arbitrators appointed by the parties. However, Section 9A(1) of the IAA varies this position to stipulate that: 'Notwithstanding Article 11(3) of the Model Law, in an arbitration with 3 arbitrators, each party shall appoint one arbitrator, and the parties shall by agreement appoint the third arbitrator.'

15.3.3 Challenge of arbitrators

15.51 The IAA incorporates the Model Law provision on challenges to arbitrators. Article 12(2) of the Model Law provides:

> An arbitrator may be challenged only if circumstances exist that give rise to justifiable doubts as to his impartiality or independence, or if he does not possess qualifications agreed to by the parties. A party may challenge an arbitrator appointed by him, or in whose appointment he has participated, only for reasons of which he becomes aware after the appointment has been made.

15.52 In the event of an unsuccessful challenge to an arbitrator on the grounds specified in article 12(2), whether under a procedure agreed upon by the parties or under article 13(2) of the Model Law, the challenging party may, within 30 days of notice of the result of the initial challenge, have recourse to the High Court. Also, in the event that a challenge results in the withdrawal or removal of the arbitrator, it may be pertinent to note that the same appointment procedure as was previously applicable would apply to his replacement.[61] Therefore, in the event that an arbitrator withdraws or is removed, the role of the chairman of SIAC[62] as the statutory appointing authority would remain.

15.3.4 Evidence in arbitration proceedings

15.53 Under the IAA, the power to make directions to the parties on discovery of documents and interrogatories is expressly reserved for the arbitral tribunal.[63] This is observed in the carve-out in section 12A(3) of the IAA (which deals with the power of the court to order interim measures in aid of arbitration proceedings), wherein the power to order security for costs[64] and to make directions on discovery of documents and interrogatories[65] has been excluded. In other words, the High Court in Singapore is empowered under section 12A of the IAA to order any party to produce evidence by affidavit[66] or provide for the sampling or testing of property that forms the subject of the dispute,[67] but not to make orders pertaining to discovery of documents and interrogatories. It may also be pertinent to note that such power is granted to the High Court, irrespective of whether the relief sought is in relation to arbitral proceedings seated within or outside Singapore.[68]

15.54 Should it be required, section 13(1) of the IAA also provides that: 'Any party to an arbitration agreement may take out a subpoena to testify or a subpoena to produce documents.' The witness against whom the subpoena is taken out may then be compelled by the High Court to attend before the arbitral tribunal, 'wherever he may be within Singapore'.[69]

---

[61] Model Law, Art 15.
[62] Or any other person designated under the IAA, s 8(3).
[63] IAA, ss 12(1)(b) and 12A(2).
[64] IAA, s 12(1)(a).
[65] IAA, s 12(1)(b).
[66] IAA, s 12A(2) read with s 12(1)(c).
[67] IAA, s 12A(2) read with s 12(1)(e).
[68] IAA, s 12A(1)(b).
[69] IAA, s 13(2).

In *ALC v ALF*,[70] the issue before the Assistant Registrar of the High Court was whether a party to an arbitration agreement could issue a subpoena in contravention of the agreement between the parties and the tribunal on the applicable rules of evidence.[71] The defendant in this case had unilaterally issued a court subpoena against a witness without first applying for directions from the tribunal, in contravention of the wording of article 4 of the 1999 IBA Rules on the Taking of Evidence in International Commercial Arbitration (IBA Rules), which the parties had agreed would apply 'as a guideline on procedural matters, and despite the tribunal having previously rejected the Defendant's application for directions that the witness be ordered to produce sworn testimony'. Recognizing that, as the parties had 'contractually chosen to utilize arbitration as their means of dispute resolution, recourse should be had to the contractual arrangement first before knocking on the doors of the court and seeking curial intervention',[72] the subpoena was set aside by the court. **15.55**

15.3.5 Foreign representation in arbitral proceedings

Since the 2004 amendment to the Singapore Legal Profession Act (Cap 161) (LPA), the 'arbitration bar' in Singapore has been liberalized in its entirety. In providing for a carve-out from sections 32 and 33 (which deal with the definition of an 'unauthorized person' under the LPA and the relevant criminal sanctions), section 35 expressly exempts 'any arbitrator or umpire lawfully acting in any arbitration proceedings';[73] 'any person representing any party in arbitration proceedings';[74] and 'the giving of advice, preparation of documents and any other assistance in relation to or arising out of arbitration proceedings except for the right of audience in court proceedings'.[75] Section 35(2) of the LPA further clarifies that the exemption found in the preceding subsection applies similarly in international and domestic arbitrations in Singapore, as well as in relation to foreign-seated arbitrations. **15.56**

15.4 The Award

15.4.1 Definition

Under the IAA, an 'arbitral award' is defined as 'a decision of the arbitral tribunal on the substance of the dispute and includes any interim, interlocutory or partial award but excludes any orders or directions made under section 12'.[76] Article 31 of the Model Law sets outs the requirements of an award with regard to its form and contents: **15.57**

> *Article 31. Form and contents of award*
>
> (1) The award shall be made in writing and shall be signed by the arbitrator or arbitrators. In arbitral proceedings with more than one arbitrator, the signatures of the majority of all members of the arbitral tribunal shall suffice, provided that the reason for any omitted signature is stated.

---

70 *ALC v ALF* [2010] SGHC 231.

71 The tribunal, with the consent of the parties, had directed that the International Bar Association Rules on the Taking of Evidence in International Commercial Arbitration (1 June 1999 edn) would apply as a guideline on procedural matters.

72 *ALC v ALF* (n 70) para 56.

73 LPA, s 35(1)(a).

74 LPA, s 35(1)(b).

75 LPA, s 35(1)(c). See also *Re Joseph David QC* [2012] 1 SLR 791; [2011] SGHC 262, HC.

76 IAA, s 12 deals with the power of the tribunal to make interlocutory orders and directions.

(2) The award shall state the reasons upon which it is based, unless the parties have agreed that no reasons are to be given or the award is an award on agreed terms under article 30.

(3) The award shall state its date and the place of arbitration as determined in accordance with article 20(1). The award shall be deemed to have been made at that place.

(4) After the award is made, a copy signed by the arbitrators in accordance with paragraph (1) of this article shall be delivered to each party.

15.58 Section 19A of the IAA also expressly stipulates that an arbitral tribunal may make more than one award on different matters and at different times:[77]

> 19A.—(1) Unless otherwise agreed by the parties, the arbitral tribunal may make more than one award at different points in time during the arbitral proceedings on different aspects of the matters to be determined.
>
> (2) The arbitral tribunal may, in particular, make an award relating to—
>
> (a) an issue affecting the whole claim; or
>
> (b) a part only of the claim, counter-claim or cross-claim, which is submitted to it for decision.
>
> (3) If the arbitral tribunal makes an award under this section, it shall specify in its award, the issue, or claim or part of a claim, which is the subject-matter of the award.

15.4.2 Post-award interest

15.59 An issue that was comprehensively clarified by the 2012 Amendment to the IAA is the matter of an arbitral tribunal's power to award post-award interest. Before the 2012 Amendment, the IAA expressly empowered tribunals to award interest 'for the whole or any part of the period up to the date of the award'. Thus, it was unclear whether a tribunal constituted under the IAA was able to award interest (as well as to stipulate the applicable rate to apply) for the period of time subsequent to the date of the award.

15.60 Under the 2012 Amendment, section 20 of the IAA was amended to expressly provide for the power of an arbitral tribunal to 'award simple or compound interest from such date, at such rate and with such rest as the arbitral tribunal considers appropriate, for any period ending not later than the date of payment'.[78]

15.5 After the Award

15.5.1 Setting aside application

15.61 In Singapore, section 24 of the IAA and Article 34 of the Model Law exclusively govern the procedure for setting aside an arbitral award made pursuant to the IAA.[79] As prescribed in Article 34(3), any party seeking to set aside an award[80] must make an application within

[77] Interestingly, it has been judicially noted that IAA, s 19A was 'a legislative response to the decision of [the Court of Appeal] in *Tang Boon Jek Jeffrey v Tan Poh Leng Stanley* [2001] 2 SLR(R) 273 in which it was clarified that an arbitral tribunal should have the power to make awards at different times in the course of arbitration'. See *PT Asuransi Jasa Indonesia (Persero) v Dexia Bank SA* [2007] 1 SLR(R) 597; [2006] SGCA 41, CA, para 69.

[78] IAA, s 20(1).

[79] See *Sui Southern Gas Co Ltd v Habibullah Coastal Power Co (Pte) Ltd* [2010] 3 SLR 1; [2010] SGHC 62, HC, para 21.

[80] In *Astro Nusantara International BV and ors v PT Ayunda Prima Mitra and ors* [2012] SGHC 212, HC, the High Court held (at paras 118–120) that the 3-month time limit for an application to set aside found in Model Law, Art 16(3) did not apply to an application under the IAA, s 24.

three months of having received the award, or of the tribunal's disposal of a request made under Article 33 of the Model Law.[81]

Article 34(2) provides that an arbitral award may be set aside only if: 15.62

(a) the party making the application furnishes proof that:
  (i) a party to the arbitration agreement referred to in Article 7 was under some incapacity; or the said agreement is not valid under the law to which the parties have subjected it or, failing any indication thereon, under the law of this State; or
  (ii) the party making the application was not given proper notice of the appointment of an arbitrator or of the arbitral proceedings or was otherwise unable to present his case; or
  (iii) the award deals with a dispute not contemplated by or not falling within the terms of the submission to arbitration, or contains decisions on matters beyond the scope of the submission to arbitration, provided that, if the decisions on matters submitted to arbitration can be separated from those not so submitted, only that part of the award which contains decisions on matters not submitted to arbitration may be set aside; or
  (iv) the composition of the arbitral tribunal or the arbitral procedure was not in accordance with the agreement of the parties, unless such agreement was in conflict with a provision of this Law from which the parties cannot derogate, or, failing such agreement, was not in accordance with this Law; or
(b) the court finds that:
  (i) the subject-matter of the dispute is not capable of settlement by arbitration under the law of this State; or
  (ii) the award is in conflict with the public policy of this State.

Further, section 24 of the IAA provides that, in addition to the grounds laid out in Article 34(2) of the Model Law, the High Court of Singapore may set aside an arbitral award if it finds that '(a) the making of the award was induced or affected by fraud or corruption; or (b) a breach of the rules of natural justice occurred in connection with the making of the award by which the rights of any party have been prejudiced'. 15.63

In *Sui Southern Gas Co Ltd v Habibullah Coastal Power Co (Pte) Ltd*,[82] the High Court upheld the exclusive application of the grounds set out in the IAA with regard to any application to set aside an arbitral award. Dismissing an application in which the plaintiff had relied on the argument that the award was 'perverse, manifestly unreasonable and irrational', Judith Prakash J held: 'As the Model Law has the force of law in Singapore, it was not open to me to set aside the Award on the freestanding ground that its substantive decision on the merits was outrageous or irrational.'[83] 15.64

Further, the court in *Sui Southern Gas* also held, in relation to the plaintiff's argument under Article 34(2)(b)(ii) of the Model Law, that an 'ambiguous contention that the Award was "perverse" or "irrational" could not, of itself, amount to a breach of public policy.'[84] 15.65

[81] Model Law, Art 33 deals with requests for the correction and interpretation of awards rendered and additional awards.

[82] *Sui Southern Gas Co Ltd v Habibullah Coastal Power Co (Pte) Ltd* [2010] 3 SLR 1; [2010] SGHC 62, HC.

[83] *Sui Southern Gas* (n 82) para 21.

[84] *Sui Southern Gas* (n 82) para 48.

15.66 The Court of Appeal in *CRW Joint Operation v PT Perusahaan Gas Negara (Persero) TBK*[85] summarized the 'limited' grounds provided under the IAA for the setting aside of an arbitral award:

> The relevant grounds in this regard can be classified into three broad categories... First, an award may be challenged on jurisdictional grounds (*ie*, the non-existence of a valid and binding arbitration clause, or other grounds that go to the adjudicability of the claim determined by the arbitral tribunal). Second, an award may be challenged on procedural grounds (*eg*, failure to give proper notice of the appointment of an arbitrator), and, third, the award may be challenged on substantive grounds (*eg*, breach of the public policy of the place of arbitration).[86]

15.67 The issue of the scope of application of Article 34 of the Model Law in relation to an application to set aside a decision on jurisdiction by an arbitral tribunal was considered as a 'serious issue' that merited 'full consideration' by the Court of Appeal in *PT Asuransi Jasa Indonesia (Persero) v Dexia Bank SA*.[87] In the light of the fundamental nature of the issue, the Court of Appeal appointed the then Deputy Chairman of SIAC, Professor Lawrence Boo, as *amicus curiae* to address the court on the question:

> Whether or not the decision of an arbitral tribunal convened under the auspices of the [IAA] that it has no jurisdiction to determine an issue referred to it under an arbitration agreement constitutes an award for the purposes of Section 2(1) of the Act such that it may be set aside by the Court in exercise of its jurisdiction under any of the provisions of the Act, if the circumstances of the case justify.[88]

15.68 The *amicus curiae* submitted, and the Court of Appeal agreed, that in the light of the reference to 'the substance of the dispute' in the definition of 'award' in section 2 of the IAA, the correct answer was that it did not constitute an award capable of being set aside, irrespective of how the jurisdictional ruling was titled by the tribunal.[89] However, it may be pertinent to point out that the distinction between a *negative* jurisdictional ruling and an 'award' under the IAA may effectively be moot, as the 2012 Amendment now specifically provides for the power of the High Court to 'review' a *negative* jurisdictional ruling by a tribunal under Section 10(3)(b) of the IAA.

15.69 Following the holding in *PT Asuransi*, the High Court in *PT Pukuafu Indah and ors v Newmont Indonesia Ltd and anor*[90] held, on an application under section 24(b) of the IAA and Article 34(2)(b)(ii) of the Model Law, that an interlocutory order made by an arbitral tribunal under section 12 of the IAA is not an 'award' under section 2 of the IAA.[91] Consequently, Lee Seiu Kin J held that the Court therefore did not have the jurisdiction to consider an application for the setting aside of the order under section 24 of the IAA and Article 34 of the Model Law, as those powers extend only to an 'award'.[92]

Award beyond scope of submission

15.70 A two-stage test for the application of Article 34(2)(a)(iii) of the Model Law as a ground for the setting aside of an arbitral award was laid down by the Court of Appeal in *PT Asuransi*

---

85 *CRW Joint Operation v PT Perusahaan Gas Negara (Persero) TBK* [2011] 4 SLR 305; [2011] SGCA 33, CA.
86 *CRW Joint Operation* (n 85) para 27.
87 *PT Asuransi Jasa Indonesia (Persero) v Dexia Bank SA* [2007] 1 SLR(R) 597; [2006] SGCA 41, CA.
88 *PT Asuransi* (n 87) para 61.
89 *PT Asuransi* (n 87) paras 66 and 70.
90 *PT Pukuafu Indah and ors v Newmont Indonesia Ltd and anor* [2012] SGHC 187, HC.
91 *PT Pukuafu* (n 90) para 19.
92 *PT Pukuafu* (n 90) para 19.

Jasa Indonesia (Persero) v Dexia Bank SA.[93] First, the Court had to ascertain the matters that were within the scope of submission to the tribunal; and second, whether a 'new difference' that was not within the scope of submission to arbitration had arisen and 'accordingly would have been irrelevant to the issues requiring determination'.[94] The Court of Appeal in *CRW*[95] subsequently built on this test by setting out some of the legal principles underlying the application of Article 34(2)(a)(iii) of the Model Law:

> Article 34(2)(a)(iii) addresses the situation where the arbitral tribunal exceeded (or failed to exercise) the substantive jurisdiction that the parties granted to it[96]...
>
> A failure by an arbitral tribunal to deal with *every* issue referred to it will *not* ordinarily render its arbitral award liable to be set aside. The crucial question in every case is whether there has been real or actual prejudice to either (or both) of the parties to the dispute.[97]

Mere errors of law or even fact are not sufficient to warrant setting aside an arbitral award under Article 34(2)(a)(iii) of the Model Law.[98]

The facts in *CRW* concerned an arbitration agreement that incorporated the *Conditions of Contract for Construction: For Building and Engineering Works Designed by the Employer* (1st edn, 1999) ('the 1999 FIDIC Red Book') published by the Fédération Internationale des Ingénieurs-Conseils ('FIDIC'), which provided for reference of a dispute to a Dispute Adjudication Board (DAB). The DAB found in favour of CRW and awarded US$17,298,834.57 to CRW. Dissatisfied with the holding of the DAB, PGN commenced arbitration proceedings in Singapore before the ICC International Court of Arbitration. A preliminary issue that then arose before the three-member arbitral tribunal appointed was whether CRW was entitled to immediate payment of the US$17,298,834.57 awarded by the DAB. After a preliminary hearing, a majority of the tribunal issued a final award against PGN for the immediate payment of the aforementioned sum. PGN proceeded to apply to the Singapore High Court to set aside the award on, *inter alia*, the ground that the tribunal had neither heard the parties nor determined the merits of the underlying dispute between the parties, before making the DAB's award 'final'. The High Court granted PGN's application and set aside the majority's final award. **15.71**

In dismissing the appeal filed by CRW, VK Rajah, JA held that: **15.72**

> The failure of the Majority Members to consider the merits of the Adjudicator's decision before making the Final Award meant that they exceeded their jurisdiction in making that award. Further, it meant that [the Respondent] had to pay the sum awarded by the Adjudicator whilst being deprived of its contractual right to have the Adjudicator's decision reviewed unless it incurred additional time and costs in commencing fresh arbitration proceedings (assuming such an option were legally feasible). In our view, [the Respondent] suffered real prejudice as a result of the decision of the Majority Members.[99]

---

93 *PT Asuransi Jasa Indonesia (Persero) v Dexia Bank SA* [2007] 1 SLR(R) 597; [2006] SGCA 41, CA.

94 *PT Asuransi* (n 93) paras 40 and 44. See also *CRW Joint Operation v PT Perusahaan Gas Negara (Persero) TBK* [2011] 4 SLR 305; [2011] SGCA 33, CA, para 30.

95 *CRW Joint Operation* (n 94).

96 *CRW Joint Operation* (n 94) para 31.

97 *CRW Joint Operation* (n 94) para 32.

98 *CRW Joint Operation* (n 94) para 33.

99 *CRW Joint Operation* (n 94) para 85.

The Court also ruled, on the these facts, that the respondent also suffered 'real prejudice' as it was not accorded a proper opportunity to comprehensively present its case and thus held that there was also a breach of natural justice under section 24(b) of the IAA.[100]

15.73 The Court of Appeal, in *PT Prima International Development v Kempinski Hotels SA and other appeals*,[101] further expounded on the scope of an application made under Article 34(2)(a)(iii) of the Model Law, contrasting the 'scope of the submission to arbitration' and the 'scope of an arbitration agreement'. Chan Sek Keong CJ, explained that:

> An arbitration agreement is merely an agreement between parties to submit their disputes for arbitration. The disputes submitted for arbitration determine the scope of the arbitration. It is plain that the scope of an arbitration agreement in the broad sense is not the same as the scope of the submission to arbitration. The former must encompass the latter, but the converse does not necessarily apply, in that the particular matters submitted for arbitration may not be all the matters covered by the arbitration agreement. The parties to an arbitration agreement are not obliged to submit whatever disputes they may have for arbitration. Those disputes which they choose to submit for arbitration will demarcate the jurisdiction of the arbitral tribunal in the arbitral proceedings between them. An arbitral tribunal has no jurisdiction to resolve disputes which have not been referred to it in the submission to arbitration. Simply put, a party cannot raise a new dispute in an arbitration without the consent of the other party. These propositions flow inexorably from the consensual nature of arbitration.[102]

15.74 Relying on the reasoning of the Court of Appeal in *PT Asuransi* and *CRW*, the High Court in *Quarella SpA v Scelta Marble Australia Pty Ltd*,[103] held that an application for the setting aside of an award on the basis of a 'purportedly wrong interpretation of the choice of law clause (chosen by the parties to govern their distributorship agreement) by a tribunal' did not come within the ambit of Article 34(2)(a)(iii) of the Model Law.[104]

Violation of public policy

15.75 The Court of Appeal in *AJU v AJT*[105] considered the question of the scope of argument that is available to a party making an application to set aside an arbitral award under the public policy ground in Article 34(2)(b)(ii) of the Model Law. Chan Sek Keong CJ clarified many pertinent and important issues relating to the application of the provisions of the IAA on public policy. First, that the 'concept of public policy' that arises in a setting aside application[106] and in an application for (or objection to) enforcement of a foreign award, is the same. Chan CJ explained that: 'In our view, there is no difference between these two regimes as far as the concept of public policy is concerned because the legislative purpose of the IAA is to treat all IAA awards as having an international focus'.[107]

15.76 Second, the Court of Appeal also clarified Singapore's position 'vis-à-vis the circumstances in which the court may reopen an arbitral tribunal's decision that an underlying contract

---

[100] *CRW Joint Operation* (n 94) para 96.
[101] *PT Prima International Development v Kempinski Hotels SA and other appeals* [2012] 4 SLR 98; [2012] SGCA 35, CA.
[102] *PT Prima* (n 101) para 32.
[103] *Quarella SpA v Scelta Marble Australia Pty Ltd* [2012] SGHC 166, HC.
[104] *Quarella* (n 103) para 55.
[105] *AJU v AJT* [2011] 4 SLR 739; [2011] SGCA 41.
[106] Model Law, art 34(2)(b)(ii).
[107] *AJU v AJT* (n 105) para 37.

is legal'.[108] Preferring the approach taken by the Colman J in *Westacre Investments Inc v Jugoimport-SPDR Holding Co Ltd*[109] in the English High Court as well as that of the majority of the English Court of Appeal in the appeal of that decision[110] over the reasoning of the court in *Soleimany v Soleimany*,[111] the Singapore Court of Appeal held:

> With respect, we do not agree with the approach taken in *Soleimany* and by Waller LJ in *Westacre (CA)*. In our view, it is the majority's approach in the latter case (which endorses Colman J's approach in *Westacre (HC)*) which is consonant with the legislative policy of the IAA of giving primacy to the autonomy of arbitral proceedings and upholding the finality of arbitral awards (whether foreign arbitral awards or IAA awards).[112]

Third, the Court of Appeal also clarified that, as a matter of Singapore law, should a Singapore court find itself in disagreement with an arbitral tribunal on the issue of illegality under Singapore law: **15.77**

> ... the court's supervisory power extends to correcting the Tribunal's decision on this issue of illegality. In our view, the answer to this question must be in the affirmative as the court cannot abrogate its judicial power to the Tribunal to decide what the public policy of Singapore is and, in turn, whether or not the Concluding Agreement is illegal (illegality and public policy being, as pointed out at [19] above, mirror concepts in this regard) ...

However, the decision in *AJU v AJT*[113] ultimately turned on the question of whether, on the facts, the court was 'entitled to reopen the arbitral tribunal's finding that the underlying contract is not illegal'.[114] Considering that the 'Tribunal did not ignore palpable and indisputable illegality',[115] the contract in question did not 'suggest, much less require, the doing of any illegal act by either the Appellant or the Respondent to trigger each other's obligations',[116] as well as that 'this case is not a *Soleimany*-type case involving an underlying contract clearly tainted by illegality',[117] the Court of Appeal ultimately found that 'this was not an appropriate case for the Judge to reopen the Tribunal's finding'.[118] Relying on section 19B(1), the court further explained that 'findings of fact made in an IAA award are binding on the parties and cannot be reopened except where there is fraud, breach of natural justice or some other recognised vitiating factor'.[119] Subject to these exceptions, the court held that the public policy objection in Article 34(2)(b)(ii) was therefore generally limited to 'findings of law by an arbitral tribunal', and that 'such an approach would also be fair to both the successful party and the losing party in an arbitration'.[120] **15.78**

108 *AJU v AJT* (n 105) para 58.
109 *Westacre Investments Inc v Jugoimport-SPDR Holding Co Ltd* [1999] QB 740, HC.
110 *Westacre Investments Inc v Jugoimport-SPDR Holding Co Ltd* [2000] QB 288, CA.
111 *Soleimany v Soleimany* [1999] QB 785. See also, the dissent by Waller LJ in *Westacre* (CA).
112 *AJU v AJT* [2011] 4 SLR 739; [2011] SGCA 41, para 60.
113 *AJU v AJT* (n 112).
114 *AJU v AJT* (n 112) para 63.
115 *AJU v AJT* (n 112) para 64.
116 *AJU v AJT* (n 112) para 64.
117 *AJU v AJT* (n 112) para 64.
118 *AJU v AJT* (n 112) para 64.
119 *AJU v AJT* (n 112) para 64.
120 *AJU v AJT* (n 112) para 69. See also *PT Asuransi Jasa Indonesia (Persero) v Dexia Bank SA* [2007] 1 SLR(R) 597; [2006] SGCA 41, CA, paras 57–59.

Breach of natural justice

15.79 The requisite elements of an application to set aside an award on the basis of a breach of natural justice were laid out by the Court of Appeal in *Soh Beng Tee & Co Pte Ltd v Fairmount Development Pte Ltd*.[121] While the arbitration from which the appeal in *Soh Beng Tee* arose came under the domestic Arbitration Act (Cap 10) (AA), the reasoning of the court is instructive, as the relevant provision in the AA is *in pari materia* with section 24(b) of the IAA. In the judgment, VK Rajah JA held:

> ... that a party challenging an arbitration award as having contravened the rules of natural justice must establish:
> (a) which rule of natural justice was breached;
> (b) how it was breached;
> (c) in what way the breach was connected to the making of the award; and
> (d) how the breach prejudiced its rights.[122]

15.80 Summarizing the relevant case law on this, Rajah JA said:

> (a) Parties to arbitration have, in general, a right to be heard effectively on every issue that may be relevant to the resolution of a dispute. The overriding concern ... is fairness. The best rule of thumb to adopt is to treat the parties equally and allow them reasonable opportunities to present their cases as well as to respond. An arbitrator should not base his decision(s) on matters not submitted or argued before him.
>
> (b) Fairness, however, is a multidimensional concept and it would also be unfair to the successful party if it were deprived of the fruits of its labour as a result of a dissatisfied party raising a multitude of arid technical challenges after an arbitral award has been made. The courts are not a stage where a dissatisfied party can have a second bite of the cherry.
>
> (c) Indeed, the latter conception of fairness justifies a policy of minimal curial intervention, which has become common as a matter of international practice ... Generally speaking, a court will not intervene merely because it might have resolved the various controversies in play differently.
>
> (d) The delicate balance between ensuring the integrity of the arbitral process and ensuring that the rules of natural justice are complied with in the arbitral process is preserved by strictly adhering to only the narrow scope and basis for challenging an arbitral award that has been expressly acknowledged under the Act and the IAA. In so far as the right to be heard is concerned, the failure of an arbitrator to refer every point for decision to the parties for submissions is not invariably a valid ground for challenge ...
>
> ...
>
> (f) Each case should be decided within its own factual matrix. It must always be borne in mind that it is not the function of the court to assiduously comb an arbitral award microscopically in attempting to determine if there was any blame or fault in the arbitral process; rather, an award should be read generously such that only meaningful breaches of the rules of natural justice that have actually caused prejudice are ultimately remedied.[123]

Setting aside an award on costs

15.81 In *VV v WW*,[124] the High Court of Singapore dismissed an application for an award on costs to be set aside. The grounds of the application were (a) that the alleged disproportionality of

---

[121] *Soh Beng Tee & Co Pte Ltd v Fairmount Development Pte Ltd* [2007] 3 SLR(R) 86; [2007] SGCA 28, CA.

[122] *Soh Beng Tee* (n 121).

[123] *Soh Beng Tee* (n 121) para 65. The Court of Appeal also relied on the same principles in coming to its decision in *LW Infrastructure Pte Ltd v Lim Chin San Contractors Pte Ltd* [2012] SGCA 57, CA.

[124] *VV v WW* [2008] 2 SLR(R) 929; [2008] SGHC 11.

the costs award in relation to the amount in dispute contravened Singapore public policy; (b) that the arbitrator did not have jurisdiction to award costs on a counterclaim over which he did not take jurisdiction; and (c) that the arbitrator breached the principles of natural justice by relying on his own knowledge of fees charged by eminent leading counsel in international commercial arbitrations in Singapore. In dismissing the setting aside application, Judith Prakash J held that:

> ... it is not part of the public policy of Singapore to ensure that the costs incurred by parties to private litigation outside the court system, *eg*, arbitration, whether the same is domestic or international, are assessed on the basis of any particular principle including the proportionality principle... There is no public interest involved in the legal costs of parties to one-off and private litigation. Such litigation sets no precedents and binds no one apart from the immediate parties.[125]

15.5.2 Seeking and resisting enforcement

Part III of the IAA incorporates the provisions and effect of the New York Convention into Singapore legislation and deals exclusively with the recognition and enforcement of foreign arbitral awards. Section 27(1) of the IAA defines 'foreign award' as 'an arbitral award made in pursuance of an arbitration agreement in the territory of a Convention country other than Singapore'. **15.82**

Section 31 of the IAA exhaustively sets out the grounds on which an application to the High Court to refuse to enforce a foreign arbitral award may rely. These grounds, as set out in section 31(2) and (4), correspond to the provisions of Article V of the New York Convention. It is pertinent to note that while a court has no residual discretion to refuse enforcement on other grounds, refusal of enforcement is not mandatory, even when a party is able to satisfy one or more of the grounds set out in section 31 of the IAA.[126] **15.83**

In *Aloe Vera of America, Inc v Asianic Food (S) Pte Ltd and anor*,[127] the High Court interpreted the effect of section 30 of the IAA to mean that its provisions on the production of evidence of an enforceable foreign arbitral award under Part III of the IAA called for a 'mechanistic' enforcement process, 'which does not require judicial investigation by the court of the jurisdiction in which enforcement is sought'.[128] Accordingly, at the enforcement stage, the burden on the party seeking to resist such enforcement is to prove that one or more of the 'exhaustive' grounds in section 31 of the IAA is satisfied, as 'the court has no residual discretion to refuse enforcement if one of those grounds is not established'.[129] **15.84**

Examining the specific grounds in section 31 of the IAA relied upon by the party resisting enforcement, Judith Prakash J applied the following principles. Where a resisting party is alleging that no valid arbitration agreement exists under section 31(2)(b) of the IAA, that party must provide evidence that there was no valid arbitration agreement under the applicable *foreign law*, failing which, 'the approach towards the decisions of foreign arbitral tribunals in Convention countries is to recognise the validity of the same and give effect to **15.85**

125 *VV v WW* (n 124) para 31.
126 Boo 'Arbitration' (n 28) para 20.140.
127 *Aloe Vera of America, Inc v Asianic Food (S) Pte Ltd and anor* [2006] 3 SLR(R) 174; [2006] SGHC 78, HC.
128 *Aloe Vera* (n 127) para 42.
129 *Aloe Vera* (n 127) para 46.

them subject to basic notions of morality and justice'.[130] On section 31(4)(a) of the IAA, the learned judge held that the resisting party had to show, as required by the relevant provisions, that the dispute in question was not arbitrable under Singapore law[131] or that enforcement of the award would be against Singapore public policy. Otherwise, and in general, 'the principle of comity of nations requires that the awards of foreign arbitration tribunals be given due deference and be enforced unless exceptional circumstances exist'.[132]

Challenging jurisdiction at enforcement of domestic international awards

15.86 In *Astro Nusantara International BV and ors v PT Ayunda Prima Mitra and ors*,[133] the High Court of Singapore was faced with a novel application[134] at the enforcement stage of a 'domestic international award', ie a Singapore award rendered under the IAA. The argument proffered by the party resisting enforcement (FM) was that it was entitled under the IAA, having raised a jurisdictional objection before the tribunal, to challenge the jurisdiction of the arbitral tribunal before the High Court at the enforcement stage, notwithstanding its failure to apply to the High Court for a ruling on the tribunal's jurisdiction under article 16 of the Model Law, or for a setting aside order under Article 34 of the Model Law.

15.87 On the important threshold question of whether there was a statutory basis for FM to invoke lack of jurisdiction as a ground to resist or refuse enforcement, which formed the crux of the matter before the court,[135] Belinda Ang J held in the negative, stating that 'there are no remaining grounds for this court to refuse recognition and enforcement of the Singapore Awards'.[136] Relying on sections 19 and 19B of the IAA, Ang J held that a domestic international award is recognized as final and binding, unless, and exclusively so, it is set aside under the grounds stipulated under the IAA.[137] 'Refusal of recognition and enforcement cannot be divorced from setting aside—a domestic international award is either recognised and *not* set aside, or it is not recognised and is set aside.'[138]

15.88 Ang J distinguished the 'English position of *increasing* judicial intervention'[139] as being 'out of line with the rest of the Model Law countries' and moving away from Singapore's chosen path of '*less* curial intervention, in line with the objectives of the Model Law'.[140] The learned judge said: 'The Model Law is not a creature typical of the statutes emanating from common law jurisdictions' but 'more properly resembles civil law drafting'.[141] Thus, 'any sensible discussion of the Model Law must draw from arbitration law in civil law jurisdictions'.[142]

130 *Aloe Vera* (n 127) paras 61 and 62. See also, *Denmark Skibstekniske Konsulenter A/S I Likvidation (formerly known as Knud E Hansen A/S) v Ultrapolis 3000 Investments Ltd (formerly known as Ultrapolis 3000 Theme Park Investments Ltd)* [2010] 3 SLR 661; [2010] SGHC 108, HC, para 43 (subsequently affirmed by the Court of Appeal).

131 *Aloe Vera* (n 127) para 70.

132 *Aloe Vera* (n 127) para 75.

133 *Astro Nusantara International BV and ors v PT Ayunda Prima Mitra and ors* [2012] SGHC 212, HC.

134 Two Queen's Counsel from the English Bar were granted ad hoc admission to the Singapore bar in order to address the court on this matter. See *Re Joseph David QC* [2012] 1 SLR 791; [2011] SGHC 262, HC.

135 *Astro* (n 133) paras 12, 67.

136 *Astro* (n 133) para 73.

137 *Astro* (n 133) paras 74, 79, 82, and 93.

138 *Astro* (n 133) para 82.

139 *Astro* (n 133) para 112.

140 *Astro* (n 133) para 84.

141 *Astro* (n 133) para 84.

142 *Astro* (n 133) para 85.

Further, the court distinguished between the IAA (which deals with domestic and foreign international awards separately) and the Model Law position as set out in Article 36 (which is intended to apply irrespective of the country in which the award was made). The learned judge held that the IAA position was in fact: 15.89

> ... much more consistent with the rest of the Model Law, and in particular, Arts 16(3) and 34 of the Model Law, which limit a party's right to seek recourse from the Art 6 court (ie, the High Court in Singapore) by prescribing *both* limited grounds for curial intervention *and* strict timelines. By privileging party autonomy over judicial control of arbitrations, the IAA was thus intended to reduce the amount of curial intervention, whether at the setting-aside or the recognition stage. 'Double control' via the introduction of Art 36 would have the contrary effect of decreasing party autonomy and increasing curial intervention.[143]

The learned judge also clarified that under the IAA, a party that objects to the jurisdiction of the tribunal when a positive preliminary jurisdictional ruling is rendered by the tribunal, has the onus of taking action on the objection: '—There are no passive remedies when it comes to challenging jurisdiction under the IAA—a party wishing to oppose a jurisdictional award must act.'[144] According to Ang J, this proposition is supported by the principle that: 15.90

> ... it should not be open to a party to hold off bringing a jurisdictional challenge and, at the same time, participate in the arbitration on the merits in the expectation that it can revive its jurisdictional challenge at a later stage should it prove to be unsuccessful in the arbitration. Such behaviour is bound to make a mockery of the finality and effectiveness of arbitral awards on jurisdiction.[145]

On the applicable time limits for a submission to the courts of an objection to a tribunal's jurisdiction under Article 16 of the Model Law, Ang J held: 15.91

> The time limits under Arts 16(2) and 16(3) are intended to promote the finality of a decision on jurisdiction at an early stage. As stated, should a party elect to remain within the Model Law system, it must lodge an appeal on jurisdiction under Art 16(3) within the 30-day time limit set out; otherwise, the tribunal's award on jurisdiction will become final and binding on the parties and be taken as accepted by the parties, after which there is no possibility of further recourse at the post-award stage to challenge jurisdiction.[146]

Interim orders and directions by foreign tribunals enforceable

Another notable change that was brought about in Singapore by the 2012 Amendment is the addition of 'an order or a direction made or given by an arbitral tribunal in the course of an arbitration in respect of any of the matters set out in section 12(1)(c) to (i)', ie interlocutory orders, to the definition of 'arbitral award' under section 27(1) in Part III of the IAA. 15.92

By way of background, Part III of the IAA specifically deals with foreign awards and gives effect to the New York Convention in Singapore, ie the recognition and enforcement of foreign arbitral awards in Singapore. As discussed earlier, section 12(1)(c) to (i) expressly provides for the power of an arbitral tribunal to make interlocutory orders or directions, including ordering 'an interim injunction or any other interim measure'.[147] The Explanatory 15.93

143 *Astro* (n 133) para 111.
144 *Astro* (n 133) para 151.
145 *Astro* (n 133) para 146.
146 *Astro* (n 133) para 162.
147 IAA, s 12(1)(i).

Statement appended to the 2012 Amendment Bill clarifies the legislative intent behind the amendment as being 'to clarify that orders and directions of interim measures set out in section 12(1)(*c*) to (*i*) made by arbitral tribunals in arbitrations outside Singapore are enforceable by the High Court.'[148]

15.94 In the light of this, under the IAA, an interim order of an arbitral tribunal (or perhaps even an emergency arbitrator) may be enforced as a foreign arbitral award under section 29(1) of the IAA. While this has not yet been judicially tested, it would appear that Singapore has sought to provide for the enforcement of interlocutory directions and orders made by tribunals. In this respect, Singapore has gone beyond its strict obligations under the New York Convention, which only concerns the enforcement of arbitral awards (as was the case under the IAA according to the pre-2012 Amendment definition). It may also be pertinent to note that this approach to the enforcement of interim measures or orders by foreign arbitral tribunals is consistent with Article 17H of the Model Law (as amended in 2006).

Authentication and certification of arbitral awards and arbitration agreements

15.95 The 2012 Amendment also addressed a practical consideration facing parties seeking to enforce an arbitral award, ie the authentication and certification of arbitral awards and arbitration agreements. Section 19C of the IAA expressly empowers the Minister to appoint persons to authenticate and certify arbitral awards 'for the purposes of the enforcement of an award in any [New York] Convention country'. Until the 2012 Amendment, there had been no public body in Singapore expressly designated to perform this function.[149] The Minister for Law of Singapore has since appointed the Registrar and Deputy Registrar of SIAC and the Chief Executive and Deputy Chief Executive of Maxwell Chambers Private Limited to 'authenticate the original award and certify copies thereof and to certify copies of the original arbitration agreement'.[150]

15.6 Conclusion

15.96 From this discussion, it is clear that as an arbitral venue, both the legislative and judicial philosophy towards international arbitration in Singapore can be described as resolutely non-interventionist and progressively pro-arbitration. This is particularly evident in the creative balance struck, in the current provisions of the IAA, and in Singapore arbitration jurisprudence, between the need to provide up-to-date legislative and judicial support for arbitral proceedings internationally without compromising on the *sui generis* certainty of enforceability that stems from the New York Convention.

---

[148] Explanatory Statement, International Arbitration (Amendment) Bill (2012) para (f) (Bill No 10 of 2012).

[149] Singapore Parliamentary Debates, Official Reports, 11th Parliament 86 (2009), Statement of Mr K Shanmugam, the Minister for Law.

[150] International Arbitration (Appointed Persons under Section 19C) Order 2009.

16

STOCKHOLM

*Fredrik Andersson and Kristoffer Löf**

16.1 Background

16.1.1 History and development of arbitration in Stockholm

Legislative background

Arbitration as a means of resolving disputes has been accepted by the Swedish legislator since the very first written laws. There are specific statutes on arbitration in the regional land laws, dating back to the Middle Ages.[1] The first national statute on arbitration, the Act on Arbitrators, was adopted in 1887. This Act included provisions on the kinds of disputes that could be submitted to arbitration, the effect of an arbitration agreement as a bar to court proceedings, and restrictions on appeal of arbitral awards. **16.01**

The 1887 Act was replaced by a new Act on Arbitrators in 1929. At the same time, the Act Concerning Foreign Arbitration Agreements and Awards was adopted, **16.02**

* The authors are indebted to David Sandberg, associate at Mannheimer Swartling, for his assistance with the research for this contribution.

[1] K Hobér, *International Commercial Arbitration in Sweden* (1st edn, OUP, 2011) 1.

incorporating into Swedish law the Geneva Protocol on Arbitration Clauses[2] and the Geneva Convention on Enforcement of Foreign Arbitral Awards.[3] The main purpose of the 1929 Act was to make the arbitral procedure more efficient. When enacted, the 1929 Act on Arbitrators was a modern piece of legislation. It provided the legal framework for conducting arbitrations in Sweden for 70 years. However, in the early 1990s, the Arbitration Institute of the Stockholm Chamber of Commerce (SCC) took the view that the 1929 Act needed to be revised and updated in the light of increased commercial activity, both internationally and in Sweden, since its adoption.[4] In addition, Stockholm, and the SCC, had, since the 1970s, established a strong position as a venue for resolving international disputes, which the SCC's proposed modernization sought to maintain.[5]

16.03 In April 1999, the Swedish Arbitration Act of 1999, (the 'Act') entered into force, replacing the 1929 Act on Arbitrators as well as the 1929 Act Concerning Foreign Arbitration Agreements and Awards. According to the legislative history, the overriding purpose of the Act was to implement modern legislation that could meet the need for speed and due process in arbitral proceedings and maintain Sweden's strong position as a preferred venue for resolving international commercial disputes.[6]

16.04 In the course of drafting the Act, the UNCITRAL Model Law[7] was carefully considered. Although the Act does not fully incorporate the Model Law, it is based on, and incorporates, the Model Law's main principles. As will be seen here, however, there are a few instances in which the Act deviates from the Model Law.

Attitude of courts, institutions, and members of the local bar

16.05 The fact that the 1929 Act could work satisfactory for 70 years is in all likelihood due to the autonomy that the arbitral process has always enjoyed in Sweden.[8] Swedish courts have been arbitration friendly by tradition and do not interfere unduly in arbitral proceedings. As does the Act, the courts generally take a restrictive approach to setting aside arbitral awards.

16.06 The rules for enforcing foreign awards laid down in the Act mirror those of the New York Convention. Enforcement of a foreign arbitral award has, to the authors' knowledge, been denied in only two cases since the 1999 Act came into force.[9]

16.07 Foreign parties should be aware that Swedish courts, when assessing a challenge to an arbitral award, are, in some respects, influenced by Swedish procedural law principles, and may apply these principles as a starting point in their assessment (although less so with respect to

---

[2] Geneva Protocol on Arbitration Clauses (Geneva, 24 September 1923, 27 LNTS 158).

[3] Geneva Convention on the Execution of Foreign Arbitral Awards (Geneva, 26 September 1927, 92 LNTS 302).

[4] K Hobér, 'Arbitration Reform in Sweden' (2001) 17(4) Arb Intl 351, 352.

[5] On the SCC's and Stockholm's role as an important venue for East-West disputes, see further para 16.13.

[6] Govt Bill 1994:81, p 71; F Madsen, *Commercial Arbitration in Sweden* (3rd edn, OUP 2007) 39.

[7] UNCITRAL Model Law on International Commercial Arbitration (the UNCITRAL Model Law) (1985) 24 ILM 1302.

[8] Hobér (n 4) 388.

[9] The Supreme Court denied enforcement in *Robert G v Johnny L*, NJA 2002, p 45 n C, having found that the award was a sham, see para 16.70. In the Supreme Court ruling in *Lenmorniiproekt OAO v Arne Larsson & Partner AB*, NJA 2010, p 219, the Supreme Court denied enforcement on due process grounds, finding that the respondent in the arbitration had proved that it had not been notified of the arbitral proceedings.

international arbitrations).[10] For instance, Swedish procedural law provides that a prayer for relief must be specific enough so as to be directly enforceable. In other words, a request for 'appropriate relief' or 'just and fair relief' cannot be granted. The reason is that it must be possible for the respondent to know exactly what claims to respond to. The prayers for relief also determine the scope of the arbitral tribunal's mandate.

Swedish procedural law is also rather strict on the requirement that the tribunal not base its award on factual allegations not relied upon by any of the parties. Again, the rationale for this principle is that the respondent must be able to know exactly what to respond to. The principle is not expressed in the Act but has been referred to by courts in challenge proceedings.[11] Parties are therefore well advised to highlight in their pleadings the facts they rely on to support the granting of the relief requested. Similarly, tribunals should take care not to base the outcome of the case on facts other than those advanced by the parties as entitling a party to the relief sought. **16.08**

The SCC is the dominant arbitral institution in Sweden. Founded in 1917, it has a modern set of arbitration rules, which were revised in 2010. The caseload at the SCC is around 200 cases per year, of which approximately 46 per cent are international arbitrations, including investment arbitrations under bilateral investment treaties or the Energy Charter Treaty,[12] in which the SCC is one of three designated arbitration options.[13] The SCC also acts as an appointing authority under the UNCITRAL Rules. In addition to arbitrations taking place at the SCC, an unknown but considerable number of ICC, UNCITRAL, and ad hoc arbitrations take place in Sweden each year. **16.09**

For decades, the vast majority of contractual disputes between Swedish commercial parties have been resolved by arbitration, whereas disputes involving non-commercial parties and non-contractual disputes are handled by the courts. In general, Swedish commercial lawyers are familiar with the general principles of arbitration and have confidence in the system. In recent years, a number of initiatives have been taken by the arbitration community to further enhance the knowledge and experience of Swedish arbitration practitioners. Since 2006, the Swedish Arbitration Association has held arbitration courses for younger practitioners. A number of new arbitration associations have been created, and interest in arbitration among Swedish lawyers is increasing. A number of new books and writings on arbitration have been published, with more anticipated.[14] **16.10**

---

[10] See n 11.

[11] Svea Court of Appeal ruling in *Systembolaget AB v Vin & Sprit AB*, RH 1 December 2009, case no T 4548-08. The Svea Court of Appeal's ruling was largely based on an expert opinion submitted by Professor Lars Heuman. In the expert opinion, Professor Heuman emphasizes that the procedural principle that allegations must be specifically relied upon by the parties, in order for the arbitral tribunal to base the award on them, ought to be upheld in domestic Swedish arbitration, but that other considerations must be made in international disputes. The relevance of the case—and of the principle—in international cases may therefore be questioned.

[12] Energy Charter Treaty (Lisbon, 17 December 1994, 2080 UNTS 95).

[13] 'The SCC in numbers', SCC Institute (2012), available at <http://www.sccinstitute.com/hem-3/statistik-2.aspx> (accessed 7 March 2013).

[14] The main English language works on Swedish arbitration are: L Heuman, *Arbitration Law of Sweden—Practice and Procedure* (JurisNet, 2003); K Hobér, *International Commercial Arbitration in Sweden* (1st edn, OUP, 2011); F Madsen, *Commercial Arbitration in Sweden* (3rd edn, OUP, 2007); F Andersson et al, *Arbitration in Sweden* (Jure, 2011); and U Franke et al (eds), *International Arbitration in Sweden: A Practitioner's Guide* (Kluwer, 2013). In addition, there are a number of Swedish language works, most notably Swedish Supreme Court Justice Stefan Lindskog's book *Skiljeförfarande—En kommentar* (2nd edn, Collins Law, 2012).

Important developments

16.11 There have been no major changes to the Act since it came into force in 1999. There is, however, an ongoing discussion within the arbitration community on whether the Act should be amended so as to incorporate the Model Law fully and make Sweden a Model Law jurisdiction. To date, this discussion has not resulted in any concrete proposal and no changes to the Act are anticipated in the near future.

16.12 An increased use of arbitration in the financial sector, which traditionally has preferred to bring its disputes to court, can be noted. Another trend in recent years is a continued increase in the number of fast-track arbitrations under the SCC's Expedited Arbitration Rules.[15]

16.1.2 Comparison with other regional or national venues

16.13 Arbitration in Stockholm under the SCC Rules is a globally recognized way of resolving international disputes. There is no comparable regional or national venue. Although the other Scandinavian countries have adopted modern arbitration acts, the international arbitration centre of the Nordic region is undoubtedly the SCC and Stockholm. One explanation for this is the historical choice of Stockholm as a preferred venue for East-West dispute resolution. In 1977, the SCC became a signatory to a dispute resolution agreement between the Soviet Union and the United States that recommended that all trade contracts between them should include an arbitration agreement under the UNCITRAL rules with Stockholm as the arbitral seat and the SCC as appointing authority.[16] Starting in 1978, when the first exchange of delegations from China and Sweden took place, China also started to recommend SCC arbitration in its international trade agreements. Many have since followed in Russia's and China's footsteps. The 1977 agreement was updated in 1992, with the Russian Federation replacing the Soviet Union as a contracting party.[17] The disputes emanating from these arrangements gave Stockholm, the SCC, Swedish lawyers, and Swedish courts experience in handling international disputes that other countries in the region lacked. Stockholm and the SCC are still the only internationally recognized options in the Nordic region.

16.2 Commencing the Arbitration

16.2.1 The arbitration agreement as a bar to court proceedings

16.14 Under section 4 of the Act, a valid arbitration agreement constitutes a bar to court proceedings relating to the subject matters covered by the arbitration agreement, provided such matters are arbitrable. If a party invokes the arbitration agreement in its first submission on the merits in the court proceedings, the court must dismiss, or in some situations stay, the

[15] J Ragnwaldh, 'Need for Speed—Expert View: Fast Track Arbitration', Commercial Dispute Resolution, 2 March 2012, available at <http://www.cdr-news.co.uk/categories/arbitration-and-adr/need-for-speed-fast-track-arbitration> (accessed 7 March 2013).

[16] 1977 US-USSR Optional Clause Agreement between the American Arbitration Association and the USSR Chamber of Commerce and Industry (12 January 1977). The full text of the US-USSR Optional Clause Agreement is reproduced as appendix 5 in *Arbitration in Sweden* (2nd edn, Stockholm Chamber of Commerce, 1984).

[17] A Magnusson, 'International Dispute Resolution—A Modern Success Story of Legal Integration', Ekaterinburg, 7 June 2012, available at <http://www.sccinstitute.com/filearchive/4/43740/Magnusson%207%20June%202012%20Ekaterinburg.pdf> (accessed 7 March 2013).

proceedings. However, if a party fails to invoke the arbitration agreement in its first submission, it is deemed to have waived its right to object to the court's jurisdiction over the dispute. Pursuant to section 49 of the Act, the provision in section 4 applies irrespective of whether the arbitration agreement is governed by Swedish or foreign law, and irrespective of whether it provides for arbitration in Sweden or elsewhere.[18]

If the respondent invokes the arbitration agreement as a bar to court proceedings and the claimant, in response, contests the validity or applicability of the arbitration agreement, it is for the court to assess whether to dismiss, stay, or proceed with the case. As part of the assessment, the court will, on its own motion, consider whether the dispute is arbitrable. If it is not, the arbitration agreement does not prevent the court from trying the case on the merits.[19] **16.15**

It is for the party invoking the arbitration agreement to prove that there is an effective arbitration agreement between the parties. If Swedish law applies to the arbitration agreement, ordinary Swedish rules on formation, invalidity, and interpretation of contracts apply. Thus, there are no specific formal requirements as to the formation of arbitration agreements, which can be entered into orally, by conduct, through reference in other contracts, by usage, or which can even be considered as implied terms. The issue of whether there is an arbitration agreement between the parties will ultimately be a matter of the substantive law applicable to the arbitration agreement, and of evidence. **16.16**

If the existence of the arbitration agreement as such is not contested, but the applicability of the agreement to the case at hand is challenged, the court will have to assess whether the scope of the arbitration agreement covers the claims made in the case. However, the court need not assess whether the claimant's assertions as to the factual basis of the claim have any merit. For the purpose of the court's assessment of jurisdiction, the facts asserted by the claimant are to be accepted at face value, as long as the claim is not manifestly unfounded. This test has been described in Swedish case law as the 'Doctrine of Assertions'.[20] **16.17**

As mentioned previously, a Swedish court will dismiss an action covered by an arbitration agreement, if the arbitration agreement is duly invoked by a party. Sometimes a dispute encompasses several interdependent claims and objections. The determination of a claim or objection may decide the outcome of other issues in dispute. If some of these issues fall within the scope of an arbitration agreement, while others do not, a situation may arise in which the court will have only partial jurisdiction. One solution provided by the Supreme Court in this situation has been to stay the court proceedings and to instruct the initiating party to commence arbitration in order to have the issues falling under the arbitration agreement decided first.[21] In other cases, for example where declaratory relief is sought, the court may be able to try the part of the case falling outside the scope of the arbitration agreement, and render a judgment that is conditional upon the outcome of the arbitration with respect to the remaining issues.[22] **16.18**

---

[18] The provision is based on the Convention on the Recognition of Foreign Arbitral Awards, Art II(3) (the New York Convention) (New York, 10 June 1958, 330 UNTS 38) and corresponds to the Model Law, Art 8.

[19] For the concept of arbitrability under Swedish law, see paras 16.67–16.69.

[20] Hobér (n 1) 103.

[21] See Supreme Court ruling in *Nykvarns Skyltaktiebolag v Esselte Dymo AB*, NJA 1982, p 738.

[22] See Supreme Court ruling in *O Forsman v A Inovius*, NJA 1973, p 480, where the Supreme Court upheld a judgment that provided for two alternative declarations, one declaration to be effective if the outcome of a parallel arbitration was that one of the parties had acquired title to a certain asset through an agreement that was subject to arbitration, and one declaration to be effective if the arbitration resulted in another outcome.

16.19 Although Swedish courts fully respect the arbitration agreement as a bar to judicial proceedings, this does not necessarily mean that foreign courts have the same respect for arbitration agreements that provide for arbitration in Sweden. The question is therefore sometimes raised (mostly by common law lawyers) of whether Swedish law allows courts to issue anti-suit injunctions. With respect to court proceedings initiated in breach of a Swedish arbitration agreement in another European Union country, the answer to that question is clearly 'no', following the ECJ's ruling in *West Tankers*.[23] With respect to court proceedings in non-EU jurisdictions, however, it is possible that Swedish courts would grant an injunction, under Chapter 15, section 3 of the Swedish Code of Judicial Procedure, protecting a party's substantive rights under an arbitration agreement. Under this provision, the Swedish courts have wide discretionary powers to order appropriate interim measures necessary to safeguard and protect the applicant's substantive rights. It should be emphasized that this has not been tested in the Swedish courts, for the simple reason that such an anti-suit injunction has never been applied for. If a court were to agree to grant an anti-suit injunction, it would take the form of an order prohibiting the party to the arbitration agreement from taking actions in foreign courts that would risk diminishing the rights of the applicant under the arbitration agreement. Such an order may be made under the penalty of a fine.

16.2.2 The role of courts in appointing arbitrators

16.20 Under section 13 of the Act, the default rule is that the arbitral tribunal is composed of three arbitrators, with the parties each appointing one arbitrator, and the arbitrators so appointed appointing the chairperson. The parties may decide to deviate from this rule, for example by providing for a sole arbitrator or for one or all arbitrators to be appointed by a third party (most often an arbitral institution). If any of these mechanisms fail, the competent district court is available to assist in appointing arbitrators.

16.21 The courts of competent jurisdiction with respect to the appointment and removal of arbitrators are: (a) the district court(s) at the place(s) where either of the parties is domiciled, provided that such domicile is in Sweden; (b) the district court at the place of arbitration; and (c) the Stockholm District Court. The reason for giving jurisdiction to the Stockholm District Court in addition to the courts that follow from the parties' domicile and the place of arbitration, is to make sure that there is always a competent court, even in cases in which none of the parties is domiciled in Sweden, or when the place of arbitration is, for whatever reason, not clear. If possible, the opposing party must be afforded the opportunity to comment on an appointment application before it is granted.

16.22 Upon application by a party, the competent district court will assist in appointing arbitrators in the following situations:

- where the default rule applies, the claimant has named its arbitrator, and the respondent has failed to name its arbitrator within 30 days of receipt of notice of the claimant's choice of arbitrator;[24]

In Supreme Court ruling in *Lars S v Försäkringsaktiebolaget Skandia*, NJA 1984, p 229, the arbitration clause was narrowly drafted and only covered the issue of valuation of damaged property. A claim for compensation brought before the Court by an insured party under an insurance policy was therefore deemed by the Court not to be covered by the arbitration agreement. Thus, the lower courts entertained the action. The Supreme Court held, however, that the courts were barred from examining quantum issues and that the case should be stayed until such issues had been decided in an arbitral award.

[23] Case 185/07 *Allianz SpA and Generali Assicurazioni Generali SpA v West Tankers Inc* [2009] ECR I-00663.

[24] Arbitration Act 1999, s 14.

- where the default rule applies, and the two party-appointed arbitrators have failed to appoint a third arbitrator within 30 days, counting from the date of appointment of the second arbitrator;[25]
- if an arbitrator, pursuant to parties' agreement, is to be appointed by the parties jointly and the parties fail to agree on an arbitrator within 30 days from the date on which the question was raised through proper notice by one of the parties; and[26]
- where an arbitrator, pursuant to the parties' agreement, is to be appointed by someone other than a party or the arbitrators, and such appointment has not been made within 30 days of the date on which a party desiring the appointment of an arbitrator requested that the appointment be made.[27]

In addition, under section 16 of the Act, the competent district court will assist in the appointment of a replacement arbitrator in situations in which an arbitrator resigns or is discharged. However, if the arbitrator's resignation or discharge is due to circumstances that arise after his appointment, the appointment of the replacing arbitrator is to follow the procedures of the original appointment. Accordingly, if the resigning arbitrator was appointed by a party, that party will appoint the new arbitrator, and if the resigning arbitrator was appointed by an appointing authority, that entity will appoint the new arbitrator. Sections 14 and 15 of the Act also apply with respect to the replacement of an arbitrator. Consequently, the new arbitrator must be appointed within 30 days from the date on which the appointing party or entity became aware of its duty. **16.23**

If a party objects before a court that there is no valid or applicable arbitration agreement, section 18 of the Act provides that an application for the appointment of an arbitrator may be rejected only if it is *manifest* that the arbitration is not legally permissible. Accordingly, if there are arguments both for and against the existence of an arbitration agreement, a court will normally proceed with the appointment of the arbitrator without going into an assessment of the merits of the objection. **16.24**

An application for the appointment (or removal) of an arbitrator is generally handled swiftly, by a single judge and without any oral hearing. A decision by a district court granting a request to appoint or remove an arbitrator is final and may not be appealed. **16.25**

16.2.3 The role of courts in resolving jurisdictional questions

Section 2 of the Act states that when arbitration has commenced, the starting point is that the tribunal is competent to rule on its own jurisdiction. A finding by the arbitral tribunal that it has jurisdiction over the dispute is, however, not final, but can be revisited at any stage during the arbitral proceedings. If the tribunal finds that it lacks jurisdiction, it must issue an award terminating the arbitration. As explained in paragraph 16.63, such an award may be appealed in court pursuant to section 36 of the Act. **16.26**

The *competence-competence* of the arbitral tribunal does not exclude the jurisdiction of Swedish courts to rule on an arbitral tribunal's jurisdiction. Such a determination by the court may be made in two instances: (1) after the arbitral award has been made, as part of a challenge action or an action to set aside the award (see further paragraphs 16.74–16.76); **16.27**

[25] Arbitration Act 1999, s 15.
[26] Arbitration Act 1999, s 15.
[27] Arbitration Act 1999, s 15.

and (2) during an ongoing arbitration, either before or after the tribunal has made its own assessment, as part of determining the arbitral tribunal's jurisdiction under section 2 of the Act. Section 2 of the Act provides that, although the arbitral tribunal may rule on its own jurisdiction to decide a dispute, this does not prevent a court from ruling on the arbitral tribunal's jurisdiction at the request of a party. The arbitral tribunal may, however, continue the arbitral proceedings pending the determination by the court.

16.28 A court action pursuant to section 2 will take the form of a request for declaratory relief. Thus, the claimant will ask the court to declare that the arbitral tribunal lacks jurisdiction (or 'authority' in the terminology of the Act) over the dispute in question. The legal basis for the arbitral tribunal's lack of jurisdiction may relate to the validity, scope, or existence of the arbitration agreement, as well as to formal irregularities relating to the constitution of the arbitral tribunal or the initiation of the arbitration.

16.29 In order for the court to entertain an action under section 2 of the Act, it must be satisfied that the action meets the general requirement with respect to declaratory actions under Chapter 13, section 2 of the Code of Judicial Procedure. An action for declaratory relief may be admitted only if there is uncertainty as to the existence of the legal relationship subject to the declaratory claim (ie the issue of whether the arbitral tribunal has jurisdiction must be contentious). This uncertainty must also be to the detriment of the party seeking the declaration, ie the claimant in the court action.

16.30 Normally, 'uncertainty' is easily determined with reference to the fact that one party asserts that the arbitral tribunal has jurisdiction and the other party contests this. Since this uncertainty entails a risk that the future arbitral award will not be enforceable or upheld in a challenge action, the 'detriment' will usually be obvious from the risk of having to participate in arbitral proceedings which might not lead to an enforceable, or even valid, award.

16.31 However, for a declaratory judgment to be an effective way to offset this detriment, it must finally resolve the matter of the arbitral tribunal's jurisdiction before the arbitral award is rendered. Since an action for declaratory relief is subject to appeal (with leave), to both the courts of appeal and the Supreme Court, it will in some situations be likely that the arbitration will be concluded before the declaratory judgment is rendered. In such a situation, the declaratory relief will not serve to remove the detriment. If a party to the arbitration wishes to challenge the arbitral tribunal's jurisdiction, it might therefore be a faster solution to seek to set aside the award after it has been made. As explained in paragraph 16.94, an action to set aside an award is brought before a court of appeal as the court of first, and in most cases only, instance. In an action to set aside an award, exactly the same grounds may be invoked as in an action for declaratory relief under section 2 of the Act.

16.32 For these reasons, the Supreme Court has held, in *RosInvestCo UK Ltd v The Russian Federation*, that an action for declaratory relief should not be accepted by a district court if it may reasonably be expected that the arbitral award will soon be rendered.[28] In the same case, the Supreme Court clarified that if an action for declaratory relief is still pending when the award is being challenged, the challenge proceedings are to be stayed in order to await the outcome of the declaratory judgment, so as not to have two courts determining the same

[28] Supreme Court Ruling in *RosInvestCo UK Ltd v The Russian Federation*, NJA 2010, p 508.

issues. The final outcome of the action for declaratory relief will then be decisive for the assessment of the same issues in the challenge proceedings.

16.2.4 The role of courts in enjoining arbitration

As previously explained, under section 2 of the Act, Swedish courts have the power to issue declaratory relief to the effect that an arbitral tribunal lacks jurisdiction. Such a final declaratory judgment is binding for the arbitral tribunal's assessment of jurisdiction and means that the arbitral tribunal thereafter lacks jurisdiction to proceed with the arbitration.[29] If the arbitral tribunal is declared to lack jurisdiction, the arbitrators must terminate the proceedings. If the arbitral tribunal nevertheless continues the proceedings, this may constitute grounds to challenge the future award. **16.33**

Apart from the effect of a declaratory judgment regarding the arbitral tribunal's jurisdiction, Swedish courts have no power to enjoin arbitration. The courts have no power to issue temporary injunction orders forcing an arbitration stay pending the determination of another issue. On the contrary, the Act expressly provides that the arbitral tribunal may proceed with the arbitration pending the outcome of an action under section 2, as well as an action under section 10 challenging an arbitrator for lack of independence or impartiality. **16.34**

Swedish courts have no power to order parties to commence arbitration or to participate in an arbitration. As explained in paragraphs 16.14–16.18, however, a Swedish court may suspend court proceedings pending the outcome of arbitral proceedings, which, in a sense, ought to at least indirectly compel the parties to commence arbitration. **16.35**

16.3 During the Arbitration

16.3.1 The role of courts in challenges to arbitrators

If a party so requests, an arbitrator may be removed if any circumstance exists that objectively might diminish confidence in the arbitrator's impartiality. Under sections 8 and 10 of the Act, a challenge against an arbitrator must be made within 15 days from the date on which the party became aware both of the appointment of the arbitrator and of the existence of the circumstance.[30] **16.36**

Unless the parties have agreed otherwise by reference to institutional rules, the arbitral tribunal will itself rule on the challenge of an arbitrator. If the challenge is successful, the arbitral tribunal's decision is not subject to appeal. However, if the challenge is denied, a dissatisfied party may file an application with the competent district court, requesting that the arbitrator be removed, in accordance with section 10(1) of the Act. Under section 10(3), this application must be submitted within 30 days from the date on which a party has received the arbitral tribunal's decision. The arbitral tribunal may continue with the arbitral proceedings pending the determination of the district court. The forum rules in section 44 of the Act just **16.37**

[29] However, the arbitrators are still authorized to issue an award terminating the proceedings, including decisions on the cost of the arbitration.

[30] The Act mentions only 'impartiality', as opposed the Model Law, which mentions 'impartiality and independence' (Model Law, Art 12). However, no deviation from the Model Law was intended by the legislator, which concluded that the Swedish word for impartiality also includes a requirement of independence. See Govt Bill 1998/99:35, p 82; see also Hobér (n 1) 162.

described with respect to the appointment of arbitrators also apply with respect to identifying the court of competent jurisdiction to hear a challenge against an arbitrator.

16.38 Under section 11 of the Act, the parties may agree that the challenge of an arbitrator shall be conclusively determined by an arbitral institution. In order for an agreement referring challenge decisions to an arbitral institution to exclude court jurisdiction, either the arbitration agreement or the rules to which the arbitration agreement refer, must unambiguously provide that the arbitral institution's decision shall be final.[31]

16.39 Section 44 of the Act requires the court to communicate the challenge application for removal of an arbitrator to the other party, or parties, and to the arbitrator concerned, inviting them to comment. Once a challenge application has been filed, it will be processed by the court in accordance with the Judicial Matters Act, which provides for a simpler procedure than the Code of Judicial Procedure. Thus, the application may be determined swiftly by a sole judge and without any oral hearing.

16.3.2 The role of courts in compelling testimony/evidence

16.40 The Act allows Swedish courts to provide assistance with the taking of evidence—both documentary as well as testimonial. Section 26 of the Act provides for a procedure involving two steps.

16.41 First, a party who wishes to receive court assistance must request permission from the arbitral tribunal,[32] which is to approve the request if it considers the measure to be 'justified having regard to the evidence in the case'. The evidence must, *prima facie*, be of relevance to a factual allegation that, if proven, would be capable of affecting the outcome of the case.

16.42 As to examinations of a witness, expert, or party, an arbitral tribunal sitting in Sweden is not empowered to administer oaths. Should a party deem it essential to hear a witness under oath, the examination will therefore have to take place with the assistance of a district court judge. In such a situation, the party seeking court assistance must also satisfy the arbitral tribunal of the reasons for granting permission to hear the witness under oath, and not just before the arbitrators at an evidentiary hearing in the arbitration. By virtue of section 25(2) of the Act, the arbitral tribunal may also refuse to give its consent if the request is deemed to have been made too late in the proceedings. There is no recourse during the arbitration should the arbitral tribunal refuse to consent to the taking of evidence in court, whether this is because the request is made too late or because the arbitral tribunal does not see a need for such assistance. A non-justified decision refusing this permission may constitute a procedural error that could be relevant in a future challenge of the award.

16.43 Second, once the arbitral tribunal has approved the request, the party may submit an application to the district court. The approval of the arbitral tribunal must accompany the application to the court. Unless the arbitral tribunal has designated a different court, the application is to be considered by the Stockholm District Court by virtue of sections 26 and 44(2) of the Act.

[31] See Govt Bill 1998/99:35, p 88.

[32] There is some uncertainty as to whether the parties can agree that the District Court is to assist with the taking of evidence at a party's request without the arbitrators' consent being required (see Heuman (n 14) 458).

The district court will grant the application if 'the measure may lawfully be taken'. This means that the court will assess whether Swedish procedural law allows the court to order the measure in question. For instance, a requested document must be sufficiently identified for an order to be able to be enforced.[33] Moreover, the rules on privilege in the Code of Judicial Procedure may prevent the court from ordering a witness to testify or a document to be disclosed. It is not uncommon for the other party to object that the requested documents contain trade secrets.[34] A measure ordering the disclosure of documents that include trade secrets may be lawfully taken only if there are extraordinary reasons for such disclosure.[35] The district court's examination is limited to issues of legality, and the court must accept the arbitral tribunal's assessment of evidentiary relevance.[36] **16.44**

If the documents contain trade secrets, the situation is somewhat more complex. As just mentioned, an order to disclose trade secrets is lawful only if there are 'extraordinary reasons' for such disclosure. In order to determine whether such reasons exist, the court's legality test must establish whether the evidentiary value of the document in question may be expected to be so high so as to outweigh the interest of a party not to have its trade secrets disclosed. The Supreme Court has made clear in *Euroflon Tekniska Produkter AB v Flexiboys i Motala AB* (the 'Flexiboys case')[37] that, where the documents in question contain trade secrets, the starting point remains for the court to accept the assessment of the evidentiary value made by the arbitral tribunal.[38] However, if the arbitral tribunal has not provided any details with respect to the evidentiary value of the documents in question, the court will not be able to weigh the interest of the evidence being disclosed against the interest of the protection of trade secrets, and will therefore be required to make its own assessment of the evidentiary value of the documents in question. This is thus an exception to the rule that it is ordinarily for the arbitral tribunal to assess whether the measure is justified. **16.45**

An application under section 26 of the Act may be directed against a foreign party. In *RosInvestCo v Russian Federation*,[39] which concerned a dispute as to whether the arbitral tribunal had jurisdiction, the Supreme Court concluded that, for Swedish courts to have jurisdiction, it is sufficient that the parties have agreed that the arbitral proceedings shall take **16.46**

---

[33] See eg the Supreme Court ruling in *Karin F v Sparbanken Sverige AB*, NJA 1998, p 590 (II), where the respondent requested that the claimant be ordered to disclose 'all written documentation' in relation to certain credits that were relevant in the case. The Supreme Court found that the documents were not sufficiently specified, nor were they identifiable in the sense that the party had explained which factual allegation the documents were intended to prove.

[34] Trade secrets are defined in the Swedish Trade Secrets Act, s 1. In the Swedish Code of Judicial Procedure, the term 'professional secrets' is used. However, the Supreme Court has concluded that the two terms have essentially the same meaning; see Supreme Court ruling in *Sparbanken Sverige AB v Marcus A et al*, NJA 1995, p 347.

[35] When assessing whether there is extraordinary reason for disclosure, the court must weigh the interests between the evidentiary value of the trade secret and its economic value and consider the likelihood of damages in case of disclosure; see P Fitger, *Rättegångsbalken III* (Norstedts Juridik) ch 36, s 6 (Commentary on the Swedish Code of Judicial Procedure).

[36] See Govt Bill 1998/99:35, p 229.

[37] Supreme Court Ruling in *Euroflon Tekniska Produkter AB v Flexiboys i Motala AB*, NJA 10 May 2012, case no 1590-11.

[38] Supreme Court Ruling in *Euroflon Tekniska Produkter AB v Flexiboys i Motala AB*, NJA 10 May 2012, case no 1590-17.

[39] Supreme Court Ruling in *RosInvestCo UK Ltd v The Russian Federation*, NJA 2010, p 508.

place in Sweden. This ruling of the Supreme Court has been relied on by the Swedish courts in evidentiary proceedings initiated under section 26 of the Act.[40]

16.47 In addition, in many international arbitrations in Sweden, the requested documents are located abroad and the witnesses are domiciled in other countries. Even in such situations, Swedish courts may assist in ordering the measures in question.[41] An order by a court to produce certain evidence can be made under the penalty of a fine, which may be substantial.

16.3.3 Restrictions/requirements regarding ability of foreign practitioners to appear in arbitration as counsel or arbitrators

16.48 Under section 7 of the Act, any person with full legal capacity may act as an arbitrator. Whether or not a person possesses full legal capacity in regard to his actions and property is determined under the personal law of that person. Under Swedish law, persons under 18 years of age or subject to legal guardianship or in bankruptcy lack full legal capacity. Foreign law will apply to persons not residing in Sweden. There are no restrictions to act as arbitrator with respect to profession, education, nationality, etc. However, the parties' arbitration agreement may set out requirements in this respect.

16.49 There are no restrictions or requirements with respect to acting as counsel in arbitration. Anyone who has been duly authorized by the parties may thus act as counsel. There are, in fact, no such restrictions in Swedish courts apart from the requirement that proceedings be conducted in Swedish, a requirement that, admittedly, significantly limits the pool of available counsel.

16.3.4 Local requirements for the conduct of arbitration hearings

16.50 Section 24 of the Act provides that if a party so requests, and provided that the parties have not agreed otherwise, an oral hearing must be held prior to the rendering of an award on the merits.[42] There is no provision in the Act that regulates the conduct of a hearing, leaving considerable leeway for the arbitral tribunal and the parties to set up a tailor-made schedule for the merits hearing. Although a party's right to argue its case orally is absolute, there is no right for a party to do so for an indefinite period of time. Within the confines provided by the principles of procedural equality and the parties' right to a reasonable opportunity to present their cases, the arbitral tribunal may, for example, impose time limits for oral arguments.

16.51 There is no requirement that a document must be submitted or referred to at the hearing in order for it to be relied upon as evidence. It suffices that the document has been filed and referred to in the written submissions.

16.52 There are no restrictions with respect to language under the Act. If the parties have not agreed on the language of the arbitration, it is for the arbitral tribunal to decide the language that is to apply to the proceedings. However, under section 24, a party must be given an

[40] See eg Svea Court of Appeal ruling in *Yara International ASA v Joint Stock Company Acron*, RH 9 March 2011, case no Ö 8181-10.

[41] See *Yara International* (n 40).

[42] It should be noted that the right to a hearing relates to the merits of the case. There is no corresponding right with respect to procedural or jurisdictional issues. Accordingly, although hearings are often organized to deal with such issues as well, the arbitral tribunal may decide them on the documents only, despite a request by one of the parties for a hearing to be held.

opportunity to review all documents and all other materials pertaining to the dispute that have been submitted to the arbitral tribunal. In this requirement lies an implied requirement that a party must be able to understand the submissions made by the other party. Accordingly, if a language other than the language of the arbitration is used at the hearing—by counsel, witnesses, or experts—the arbitral tribunal must ascertain that both parties (through their counsel) are provided with a translation.

Under section 25 of the Act, the arbitral tribunal may not administer oaths. This means that it is not an act of perjury under criminal law for a witness not to tell the truth at an arbitration hearing. Irrespective of this, arbitrators in Sweden often introduce the examination of a witness by reminding the witness that he is expected to tell the truth. And indeed, although not an act of perjury, there may be instances in which a witness may be held liable on other legal bases, civil as well as criminal, for false statements made in the course of an arbitration. In addition, as explained earlier, the arbitral tribunal may consent to a party seeking court assistance in order to have a witness testify under oath before the district court, although this possibility is rarely used. **16.53**

16.4 The Award

16.4.1 Definition

The Act distinguishes between 'awards' and 'decisions' (or 'orders'). Pursuant to section 27(1) of the Act, a determination, in whole or in part, of the substantive issues in an arbitration—ie the merits of the case—is to be made in an 'award'. Section 27(1) of the Act further provides that a decision by which the arbitral tribunal terminates the proceedings without ruling on the merits, is also to be made in the form an award. It does not matter how the arbitral tribunal characterizes its decision. If the decision is, in fact, an award, because (a) it includes a determination on the merits, or (b) it terminates the proceedings, it will be treated as an award by Swedish courts. Similarly, it does not matter whether a finding that the arbitral tribunal has jurisdiction is designated, for example, as a 'partial award on jurisdiction', since such a finding does not dispose of the merits of the case and since it does not result in the termination of the proceedings, it is, as a matter of Swedish law, a decision rather than an award.[43] **16.54**

16.4.2 Mandatory rules as to form

In accordance with the principle of party autonomy, the parties to an arbitration agreement are in essence at liberty to agree on the formal requirements of the award to be rendered by the arbitral tribunal. This freedom is limited only by certain statutory minimum requirements, laid down in section 31 of the Act: **16.55**

(a) The award must be made in writing.

[43] See S Brocker and K Löf, 'The Proceedings' in U. Franke et al (eds), *International Arbitration in Sweden: A Practitioner's Guide* (Kluwer, 2013) 153, 212, with references to eg Svea Court of Appeal ruling in *Joint Stock Company Acron v Yara International ASA*, RH 2010, p 75. In the case, the arbitral tribunal found, after a jurisdictional hearing, that it had jurisdiction. To this effect, the arbitral tribunal rendered a 'Partial Award on Jurisdiction'. The respondent in the arbitration brought a challenge against the partial award. The Court explained that, although styled 'Partial Award on Jurisdiction', it was in fact a procedural decision. As such, it could not be challenged.

(b) The award must be signed by the arbitrators.[44] It is sufficient, however, that a majority of the arbitrators sign the award, provided that the reason(s) why not all of the arbitrators have signed the award are stated in the award.[45] Moreover, the parties may agree that the chairperson alone sign the award.[46]
(c) The award must state the place of arbitration.
(d) The award must state the date upon which the award is made.
(e) If an award does not fulfil the statutory requirements with regard to written form and signature, ie items (a)–(b), the award will be invalid.[47] However, these deficiencies may be rectified by way of amendment of the award in accordance with section 35 of the Act, thus validating the award. The requirements concerning the place of arbitration and the date when the award was made, ie items (c)–(d), are not sanctioned; failure to observe these requirements would not lead to the invalidity of the award.[48]
(f) The award must contain a dispositive ruling on each prayer for relief, clearly indicating whether the arbitral tribunal has granted or denied the prayer for relief or granted it in part.

16.4.3 Mandatory rules as to substance

16.56 In addition, some types of awards must contain instructions with respect to seeking recourse against them:

(a) An award whereby the arbitrators have concluded the proceedings without ruling on the issues submitted to them—ie a final award without any ruling on the merits—must contain clear instructions to the parties as to how to appeal against the award,[49] (as explained, these awards can thus be 'appealed' instead of challenged, see paragraph 16.63).
(b) An award that includes an order to the parties to pay compensation to the arbitrators must instruct the parties how to bring an action against that part of the award, ie how to challenge the costs separately.[50]

16.57 Failure to include this information does not render the award invalid, but the time limit within which a party must bring an action against the award regarding the arbitrators' compensation will probably not begin to run until the award has been corrected or supplemented.[51] If the information on how to appeal is incorrect or missing in an award rendered in the situation described in point (a), a party who has failed to appeal in time may, with reference to the fact that the award was incomplete, be able to regain the time lost upon application to the relevant court.

16.58 There are no mandatory rules regarding the allocation of costs. Under section 42 of the Act, the arbitral tribunal may, upon request by a party, allocate the costs of arbitration between

---

[44] It is sufficient that the arbitrators sign the last page of the award. There is no obligation for the arbitrators to indicate the place and date of signing. It should also be noted that the award does not have to be signed at the place of arbitration. Govt Bill 1998/99:35, pp 232 and 242.

[45] Arbitration Act 1999, s 31(3).

[46] Govt Bill 1998/99:35, p 232. In this connection, it is noteworthy that s 31(1) of the Act does not authorize the parties to instruct any arbitrator other than the chairperson to sign the award alone.

[47] Arbitration Act 1999, s 33(1), item 3.

[48] Govt Bill 1998/99:35, p 232.

[49] Arbitration Act 1999, s 36(1).

[50] Arbitration Act 1999, s 41(1).

[51] Andersson (n 14) 139. However, the fact that the time for initiating court proceedings in respect of the arbitrators' compensation may not start to run does not mean that substantive rules on notification of claims (within a reasonable time) and statute of limitations rules cease to apply.

the parties at its discretion, unless the parties have agreed otherwise. Although not mandatory, the main rule applied by Swedish arbitrators is that the 'costs follow the event'.[52]

Parties are free to request pre- and post-award interest and there are no mandatory restrictions in that respect, provided that the award of interest does not exceed what the parties have requested. Accordingly, interest must be claimed in order to be ordered. Whether, and to what extent, interest is awarded depends on the substantive law applicable to the interest claim. With respect to interest on arbitration costs, the substantive right for a party to receive interest is provided in section 42 of the Act. Thus, Swedish law on interest, as set out in the Swedish Interest Act, applies to this kind of interest claim. **16.59**

16.5 After the Award

16.5.1 Local standards for setting aside/annulment

Introduction

A Swedish arbitral award is final and binding as of the day it is rendered. It is not possible to challenge an award on the merits. An award can neither be challenged due to an incorrect assessment of the evidence, nor on a point of law. As in most jurisdictions, however, an arbitral award may be attacked on certain narrowly defined procedural grounds. The standards for setting aside, or declaring invalid, an award will be described. However, in order to understand the Swedish system in this respect it is important first to describe certain basic features as regards challenge actions under the Act. **16.60**

As noted in paragraph 16.54, the Act distinguishes 'awards' and 'decisions'. Only awards are binding and may be challenged in court by the parties. Decisions are not binding and cannot be challenged separately by the parties.[53] **16.61**

The Act distinguishes between two different types of action in which an arbitral award may be attacked: an action to declare the award invalid pursuant to section 33, and an action to set aside the award under section 34. **16.62**

In addition to actions brought under sections 33 and 34, certain awards can be subject to appeal under section 36 of the Act. However, this provision is applicable only to awards through which the arbitrators have terminated the proceedings without ruling on the merits. Section 36 would thus be applicable to an award terminating the arbitration due to lack of jurisdiction. Section 36 also applies to awards terminating the proceedings as a result of the parties withdrawing their claims. **16.63**

Section 51 of the Act provides that non-Swedish commercial parties may enter into an exclusion agreement pursuant to which they waive, in advance, the right to challenge an award under **16.64**

[52] This rule is expressly provided for in the Rules of the Arbitration Institute of the Stockholm Chamber of Commerce (1999), art 43, under which the allocation of costs is to be made with 'regard to the outcome of the case and other relevant circumstances'. Although not expressly provided for under the Act, the principle that costs follow the event is the general rule under Swedish law, codified in the Swedish Code of Judicial Procedure, ch 1, s 1. The principle is therefore usually also applied in ad hoc arbitrations in Sweden, unless the parties have agreed otherwise. See Brocker and Löf (n 43) ch 8:VII. In other words, if the outcome is such that one party succeeds with all its claims, the other party will be ordered to compensate the winning party's legal costs and to bear alone the fees of the arbitral tribunal and any arbitral institution (in addition to its own costs).

[53] Andersson (n 14) 133.

section 34 of the Act. In order to be effective, the exclusion agreement must be made in writing and state explicitly that the right to challenge an award pursuant to section 34 has been waived.

Standards for declaring an award invalid

16.65 Section 33 of the Act sets forth an exhaustive list of the grounds rendering an award wholly or partially invalid. If there is ground for invalidity, the award is invalid *ab inito*. There is consequently no need to take legal action to annul or invalidate the award.

16.66 Under section 33(1) of the Act, an award is invalid if it includes the determination of an issue that, in accordance with Swedish law, may not be decided by arbitrators. Under section 1 of the Act, disputes concerning matters in respect of which the parties may enter into a settlement agreement are arbitrable. The rationale is that the parties should not be able to obtain a result through arbitration that they would not have been able to achieve by concluding a contract.[54]

16.67 Under Swedish law, the main rule is that the law applicable to the disputed issue determines whether a dispute may be settled by way of an agreement, and accordingly, whether the dispute is arbitrable. However, if the restriction on settling a particular dispute by way of agreement under the applicable foreign law is contrary to Swedish public policy, the dispute will still be arbitrable under Swedish law. Likewise, even if certain issues may be subject to settlement under a foreign legal system, a dispute concerning such issues will not be arbitrable under Swedish law, as deciding such issues by arbitration would be contrary to Swedish public policy.[55]

16.68 Generally, disputes that affect third-party interests are not arbitrable under Swedish law. It follows that disputes regarding tax matters, declarations of bankruptcy, the personal status of individuals and companies, and the validity of patents (except as between the parties) are not arbitrable. As to competition law issues, section 1 of the Act provides that the civil law effects of competition law, ie exclusively the effects between the parties, may be determined by arbitration.

16.69 Swedish case law in which an award has been declared invalid due to lack of arbitrability is scarce. The parties are generally entitled to settle all types of commercial disputes by way of agreement, and arbitrability is therefore rarely an issue in commercial arbitration. There are, however, a few exceptions in which the dispute has involved a public interest, or interests of third parties. For example, a claim that a party should be ordered to pay a penalty to the state (as opposed to a contractual penalty) has been held to be non-arbitrable.[56] Similarly, a dispute over the appointment of a liquidator of a partnership has also been declared non-arbitrable.[57] As to claims in bankruptcy, it follows from the *Svenska Kredit* case that,[58] if a claim affects third-party creditors, all affected creditors must consent to arbitration in order for a dispute regarding the claim to be arbitrable.

16.70 Under section 33(2) of the Act, an award is invalid if it, or the manner in which it arose, is manifestly incompatible with fundamental principles of Swedish law, ie Swedish public policy. This ground for invalidity is intended to be applied very restrictively by the courts.

[54] Andersson (n 14) 60.
[55] Andersson (n 14) 58–64.
[56] Supreme Court ruling in *Kanal 5 AB v TV3 Broadcasting Group Ltd*, NJA 2000, p 435.
[57] Supreme Court ruling in *G Wrande and I Wrande v S Wrande*, NJA 2005, p 276.
[58] Supreme Court ruling in *The Bankruptcy Estate of Svenska Kreditförsäkringsaktiebolaget v Certain Reinsurers*, NJA 2003, p 3.

It includes, for example, awards ordering a party to perform a criminal, or otherwise illegal, act. According to the preparatory works, another possible violation of public policy might be that an award disregards mandatory rules that safeguard a public or third-party interest. It can also be assumed that Swedish courts will follow the principles laid down in the *Eco Swiss case*,[59] ie that a violation of EU competition law may amount to a violation of Swedish public policy. There are few examples in case law where an award has been held to be contrary to Swedish public policy. In *Robert G v Johnny L*,[60] which concerned an application for the recognition and enforcement of a foreign award, the Supreme Court refused to recognize an award on grounds of a violation of Swedish public policy. However, it was apparent in that case that the award was a sham that had been made for the sole purpose of deceiving the bankruptcy estate of one of the parties.

Under section 33(3) of the Act, an award is invalid if it does not fulfil the mandatory requirements with regard to written form and signature, which follow from section 31 (see paragraph 16.55). If these requirements are not met, and the deficiencies not remedied pursuant to section 35 of the Act, the award is invalid.[61] **16.71**

Standards for setting aside an award after challenge

Section 34 of the Act contains the grounds for having an award, wholly or partially, set aside after challenge. Whereas the provisions regarding invalidity in section 33 of the Act are intended to protect the public interest and the interests of third parties, section 34 is designed to protect the parties to the arbitration. **16.72**

Section 34(2) sets forth a waiver rule pursuant to which a party may not invoke any circumstance of which it has been aware as grounds for challenge, if that party, by participating in the arbitral proceedings without objecting, or in any other way, can be considered to have waived the right to rely on that circumstance. Under section 34(3), there is also a time limit, which limits a party's right to bring a challenge action against an arbitral award to three months from the date on which the party received the complete award. **16.73**

Under section 34(1) an award may be set aside: **16.74**

(1) if it is not covered by a valid arbitration agreement between the parties;
(2) if the arbitrators have rendered the award after the expiration of the period decided by the parties or where the arbitrators have otherwise exceeded their mandate;
(3) if arbitral proceedings, under section 47, should not have been conducted in Sweden;[62]
(4) if an arbitrator has been appointed contrary to the parties' agreement or the Act;
(5) if an arbitrator was unauthorized due to any circumstance set out in sections 7 or 8; or
(6) if, without fault of the party, there otherwise occurred an irregularity in the course of the proceedings that probably influenced the outcome of the case.

No valid or applicable arbitration agreement The issue of whether there is a valid arbitration agreement covering the dispute is decided in accordance with the law applicable to the **16.75**

[59] Case 126/97 *Eco Swiss China Time Ltd v Benetton International NV* [1999] ECR I-03055.
[60] *Robert G v Johnny L*, NJA 2002 (n 9).
[61] In the Svea Court of Appeal ruling in *Wirgin Advokatbyrå Handelsbolag v If Skadeförsäkringar AB*, RH 12 September 2012, case no T 4390-04, an award that had been amended was held partially invalid on this ground. The amendment, which was found invalid, had been signed by the chairman of the arbitral tribunal, but not by the other arbitrators.
[62] The scope of application of this provision is very limited and will not be further commented upon.

arbitration agreement. In accordance with section 48 of the Act, the main rule is that the law agreed by the parties shall be applied to the arbitration agreement. If the parties have not designated any applicable law as regards the arbitration agreement (which is often the case), section 48 of the Act provides that the law at the seat of the arbitration shall apply. Accordingly, in the absence of any choice of law by the parties, and provided the seat of the arbitration is located in Sweden, Swedish courts will rely on Swedish contract and arbitration law to assess whether a dispute is covered by a valid arbitration agreement.

16.76 The conflict rules of Swedish international private law might designate a foreign law as applicable to determine a certain issue regarding the validity of an arbitration agreement, for example whether a proxy has had the authority to bind its principal. In such a case, Swedish courts will apply the applicable foreign law to decide the issue.[63]

16.77 **Exceeding scope of mandate** In order to succeed with a challenge of an award on the ground that the arbitral tribunal has exceeded its mandate, a party will have to prove that the arbitral tribunal failed to adhere to an agreed time limit for rendering of the award, or that it went beyond its procedural mandate as defined by the parties' pleadings or joint instructions.

16.78 An award can be set aside on this ground if it goes beyond the procedural frame defined by the parties' prayers for relief and the factual allegations relied on in direct support of the relief sought. The arbitral tribunal is bound by the parties' prayers for relief. Consequently, the prayers for relief are to be denied or granted in accordance with their wording and must not be changed or amended by the arbitral tribunal on its own motion. The arbitral tribunal may grant relief that is quantitatively less than requested (in accordance with the principle *major includit minor*), but it cannot award greater relief than requested, nor relief that is qualitatively different from that sought. Similarly, the arbitral tribunal cannot grant declaratory relief when an order for performance was sought, or vice versa.[64] Thus, if the arbitral tribunal has ordered relief in excess of the relief requested, this would be considered an excess of mandate.[65] If the arbitral tribunal bases its award on facts not relied on by a party this would, as a general rule, also amount to a challengeable excess of mandate.[66]

16.79 An award can never be set aside on the ground that the arbitrators failed to apply the applicable substantive law in a correct manner. However, according to the preparatory works to the Act, a failure to apply the substantive law agreed by the parties may amount to an excess of mandate.[67] This ground has never resulted in an award being set aside. The Svea Court of Appeal has laid down that, in order for an award to be set aside on this ground, the claimant in the challenge proceedings must prove that the arbitral tribunal deliberately disregarded the parties' choice of law.[68]

16.80 **Irregularities in the appointment of arbitrators** An award can be set aside if the arbitrators have not been appointed in accordance with the parties' arbitration agreement or the Act.

[63] Svea Court of Appeal ruling in *Ukraine v Norsk Hydro ASA*, RH 17 December 2007, case no T 3108-06.

[64] Andersson (n 14) 169–71.

[65] Svea Court of Appeal ruling in *If Skadeförsäkringar AB v Securitas* et al, RH 3 November 2005, case no T 8016-04.

[66] Svea Court of Appeal ruling in *Systembolaget AB v Vin & Sprit AB*, RH 1 December 2009, case no T 4548-08 (see n 11).

[67] Govt Bill 1998/99:35, p 123.

[68] Svea Court of Appeal ruling in *Czech Republic v CME Czech Republic BV*, RH 14 March 2003, p 55. The award was upheld in this case.

This challenge ground applies also if the arbitrators fail to fulfil qualifications set forth in the parties' arbitration agreement.

Non-authorized arbitrators An award can be set aside if an arbitrator who participated in making the award was unauthorized to act as an arbitrator pursuant to section 7 of the Act. Likewise, if an arbitrator is not impartial and independent, as required by section 8, the award may be set aside. In this respect, it is sufficient that there exist circumstances that objectively could diminish confidence in the impartiality or independence of an arbitrator. Whether an arbitrator actually is biased towards one of the parties is irrelevant. In assessing challenges based on allegations of impartiality, the Supreme Court has, among other authoritative sources, referred to the IBA Guidelines on Conflict of Interest in International Arbitration.[69] **16.81**

If a party is aware of a circumstance that it considers diminishes the confidence in an arbitrator's impartiality, the arbitrator will usually be challenged in the course of the arbitral proceedings, as described in paragraphs 16.36–16.39. Since participating in the arbitral proceedings without objecting to circumstances that might compromise an arbitrator's impartiality or independence will be deemed a waiver of the right to invoke such circumstances, there is no room for a party to quietly await the outcome of the arbitration before deciding whether to challenge the award on this ground. **16.82**

Other procedural errors In addition to the grounds just described, an award can be set aside if, without the fault of a party, an irregularity that is likely to have influenced the outcome of the case has occurred in the course of the proceedings. The purpose of this provision is to provide the parties with a remedy in the event that the arbitral tribunal fails to uphold due process. **16.83**

Under section 24 of the Act, the arbitrators are obliged to afford each party an opportunity to present its case in writing or orally, to the extent necessary. A failure to comply with this provision constitutes a procedural error. The assessment of whether there has been a violation of section 24 is, however, difficult, when balanced against the general obligation of the arbitral tribunal under section 21 of the Act to carry out the proceedings in a practical and speedy manner. The authors know of no example where an award has been set aside on this ground. It may be assumed that only a clear limitation of a party's right to present its case, which in the overall context would be considered unreasonable, would amount to a failure of the arbitral tribunal to afford the party an opportunity to present its case. **16.84**

According to section 21, the arbitral tribunal must act in accordance with the parties' instructions, to the extent that there is no impediment to doing so. A failure to comply with the parties' joint instructions would amount to a procedural error. For example, the SCC Rules and many other institutional rules require the tribunal to provide reasons for the award. Thus, if the tribunal in an SCC arbitration fails completely to provide reasons, or provides reasons that are so incomplete as to amount to a complete lack of reasons, this would constitute a challengeable procedural error under section 34 of the Act.[70] **16.85**

If the arbitral tribunal fails to examine all of the parties' claims and objections, this could also amount to a challengeable error. However, it is generally difficult for the challenging party to **16.86**

[69] Supreme Court ruling in *Jilkén v Ericsson AB*, NJA 2007, p 841 and Supreme Court ruling in *Korsnäs AB v AB Fortum Värme*, NJA 2010, p 317.

[70] Supreme Court ruling in *Soyak International Construction & Investment Inc v Hochtief AG*, NJA 2009, p 128; see also Andersson (n 14) 138.

prove that a claim or objection has not been considered by the arbitrators. The absence of a detailed account of every claim and objection in the award has not been accepted by Swedish courts as conclusive proof that a certain objection or claim was not considered.

16.87 Another potential area of procedural irregularity and ground for challenge could be that the arbitral tribunal, in an international arbitration, bases its award on a legal rule that none of the parties has put forward, and which has not been included in any material submitted by the parties in the course of the proceedings. Likewise, a failure to recognize the principles of *res judicata* or *lis pendens* may amount to a procedural error, challengeable under section 34.[71]

16.88 Section 34 requires that the procedural irregularity must have influenced the outcome of the case in order for an award to be set aside. It is the challenging party who bears the burden of proving that the error has affected the outcome,[72] which generally makes it very difficult to succeed with a challenge action on grounds of procedural irregularity.

16.89 It may be noted in this context that although an arbitrator owes a duty of confidentiality by virtue of his assignment, he or she may be summoned to appear as a witness in challenge proceedings. An arbitrator who is called as a witness may not refuse to answer questions about the proceedings or the deliberations of the tribunal if such information, according to the court's assessment, may be relevant to the outcome of the case.[73]

Appeal of awards under section 36 of the Act

16.90 As mentioned previously, if the arbitral tribunal terminates the proceedings without ruling on the issues submitted to it, the termination must be made through an award. A party may appeal against such an award under section 36 of the Act (see paragraph 16.63).

Challenge of the arbitrators' compensation

16.91 Under section 41 of the Act, a party or an arbitrator may initiate a separate action in the district court regarding the arbitrators' compensation as determined in the final award. Such an action must be initiated within three months from receipt of the award in its final form.

16.92 In *Soyak International Construction & Investment Inc v Hochtief AG*,[74] the issue arose of whether the right to initiate a court action regarding the arbitrators' compensation also applied when the compensation was determined by the SCC and included in the final award. The Supreme Court found that the fact that the compensation had been determined by an arbitral institution did not mean that the applicant had waived the right to initiate a court action pursuant to section 41. Although this Supreme Court ruling has been criticized for interfering with the autonomy of the institutional arbitral process, any other outcome would have been surprising, as section 41 does not provide any exception for institutional arbitrations. Further, it should be emphasized that the Supreme Court's decision merely confirmed that a party has procedural standing to challenge a cost decision by an arbitral institution in court if the decision is included in a final award. The Court did not assess the merits of the challenge.

16.93 The case was remitted to the district court and the dispute was subsequently settled. Had the case been heard, the Court would most likely have found that the parties and the

[71] Govt Bill 1998/99:35, p 236.
[72] However, if the irregularity is serious, this may create a presumption that the outcome has been affected.
[73] Andersson (n 14) 107.
[74] Supreme Court ruling in *WM et al v Soyak International Contruction & Investment Inc*, NJA 2008, p 1118.

arbitrators were bound by the fee structure laid down in the SCC Rules and incorporated into the arbitration agreement and, as a consequence, that the SCC's decision on arbitrator compensation was binding.

16.5.2 Local procedures for setting aside/annulment

Procedure, forum and time limits

A challenge against a Swedish arbitral award must be initiated before the court of appeal that has jurisdiction over the place where the seat of arbitration is located. If the seat of arbitration is Stockholm, the award may be challenged before the Svea Court of Appeal in Stockholm. A Swedish award that does not state the seat of arbitration may also be challenged before the Svea Court of Appeal in Stockholm. **16.94**

A challenge under section 34, or an appeal under section 36, must be initiated within three months from the date when the party received the award in its final form. It is not possible to introduce new grounds in support of an ongoing challenge action after the expiry of the three month time limit. Under section 43 of the Act, the ruling (or decision) of the court of appeal may not be appealed. However, the court of appeal may, at its discretion, grant leave to appeal where it is of importance as a matter of precedent that the appeal be considered by the Supreme Court. **16.95**

Time and cost

In the period 1 January 2009 to 25 June 2012, 50 new challenges of arbitral awards were brought before the Svea Court of Appeal. As of July 2012, 29 of these cases had been concluded. Out of those 29, only three cases resulted in the award being set aside. In two of these three, the award was set aside following a settlement between the parties, without the challenge being assessed by the court. In the third case, the award was set aside on grounds of an arbitrator's lack of impartiality.[75] **16.96**

The average time in the Svea Court of Appeal for deciding a challenge action, calculated on the basis of the 29 cases decided between 1 January 2009 and 25 June 2012, is 240 days. **16.97**

The main cost component for challenge proceedings in Sweden is the cost of legal counsel. The courts charge only a registration fee of approximately €50, irrespective of the nature or the size of the dispute. In challenge proceedings, the main principle that the losing side pays, laid down in the Code of Judicial Procedure, applies.[76] The compensation for litigation costs may cover reasonable costs and expenses, including counsel's fees incurred by a party in preparing and conducting the proceedings before the court.[77] **16.98**

16.6 Conclusion

Stockholm and the SCC have for many years maintained a position as a preferred venue for resolving international disputes in general and disputes with an East-West dimension in particular. The Swedish Arbitration Act is to a large extent based on the UNCITRAL Model law but contains a few solutions that are particular to Sweden. The long tradition of **16.99**

[75] Svea Court of Appeal ruling in *KPMG AB v Profilgruppen AB*, RH 29 September 2011, case no T 1085-11.
[76] Swedish Code of Judicial Procedure, ch 18.
[77] Swedish Code of Judicial Procedure, ch 18.

arbitration in Sweden has resulted in a rich body of case law relating to arbitration, providing for a predictable procedure. The Swedish courts respect and enforce arbitration agreements and do not interfere unduly in arbitration proceedings. It is not possible to challenge awards on the merits, and awards can be set aside only on the basis of serious procedural irregularities or narrowly defined issues of non-arbitrability or public policy. The legal framework, the practice of the courts, and the experience of Swedish arbitration practitioners, all ensure an arbitration-friendly environment at the highest international standards.

17

SWITZERLAND

*Dominique Brown-Berset and Diane Grisel**

17.1 Background

17.1.1 History and development

Geneva and Switzerland have a long history as a favoured neutral venue for international arbitration, as illustrated by the well-known *Alabama* arbitration. That case opposed the United States to Great Britain, and the proceedings took place in 1871–72 at a venue that has ever since been known as 'the Alabama Room' at Geneva's 'Hôtel de Ville'.[1] The question at issue was whether England had infringed its neutrality obligations by allowing the warship *Alabama* and several others to be built and fitted out there knowing that they would be sold to the Confederate States of America and, if so, whether the United States was entitled to damages for the US ships sunk by those warships.[2] The arbitral tribunal derived **17.01**

* The authors wish to thank James Boyce for his assistance in the finalization of this chapter and for his critical comments.

[1] Chancellerie de l'Etat de Genève, *Arbitrage Alabama Genève*, 1872, 2004; TW Balch, *The Alabama Arbitration* (Allen Lane & Scott, 1900); FW Hackett, *Reminiscences of the Geneva Tribunal of Arbitration, 1872, the Alabama Claims* (Bibliolife, 2009).

[2] G von Segesser and F Helgenstein, 'Switzerland: The birth of modern arbitration', IFLR, 1 May 2011; M Blessing, *Introduction to Arbitration, Swiss and International Perspectives* (Helbing & Lichtenhahn, 1999), No 10, available at <http://barkarrer.eu/upload/publications/4_3_10.pdf>.

its jurisdiction from the arbitration agreement contained in the 8 May 1871 Washington Treaty, which set out the detailed rules pursuant to which the arbitration was to be conducted. The Tribunal, which was composed of five arbitrators assisted by a secretary, issued its award on 14 September 1872. It held by a majority of four that Great Britain had been in breach of its obligations to remain neutral during the American Civil War and awarded damages of US$15.5 million in gold to the United States.[3] The case is considered both to have given birth to modern international public law arbitration and to have been the inspiration for the development of international commercial arbitration as the favorite means of resolving international trade disputes from the 1930s onwards.[4]

17.02 Switzerland's reputation as one of the preferred venues for international arbitration is attributable to several key political, legal, and organizational features.[5] On the political level, Switzerland is attractive for its neutrality and stability. On the legal level, Switzerland offers a predictable legal framework with modern rules, courts that are supportive of arbitration, and a skilled cosmopolitan bar, whose members are generally fluent in at least two national languages (ie German, French, Italian, or Romanche), as well as English, and are familiar with comparative law issues and international disputes. On a more practical level, Switzerland is situated at a crossroads in the heart of Europe and provides an extended infrastructure that facilitates the organization of arbitral procedures (hearing facilities, means of communication, transport, etc).

17.03 Given these advantages, which had already been instrumental in the selection of Geneva as the seat for the *Alabama* arbitration in 1871,[6] it is hardly surprising that Switzerland

---

[3] Balch (n 1) 143; von Segesser and Helgenstein (n 2) 5.

[4] Blessing (n 2) Nos 12–13.

[5] Among many others, see S Michelle, 'Arbitration of Asian Disputes: The Swiss Alternative' (2007) Asian Dispute Resolution 98.

[6] According to a contemporaneous author:

> It was most fit and proper to select Switzerland as the country, and Geneva as the city, in which to hold the session of the Tribunal.
>
> In fact, Switzerland, at the same time that it is the land of hospitality, inviting the frequentation of all the world by its picturesque scenery, the beauty and sublimity of its lakes and mountains, is also the land of neutrality par excellence. No other country possesses in the same degree these qualities conjoined. In no other country was it possible to avoid all invidious local suspicion, and to be exempt from any possible political influence foreign to the objects of the Arbitration.
>
> The selection was peculiarly agreeable to the United States, by reason of the striking similarity between our institutions and those of Switzerland. Both Governments cultivate a policy of international neutrality: the one, by reason of its isolation and remoteness from the Old World, and the other because of its geographical position in the midst of the great military Powers of Europe... In both countries the force of public life pervades society like the blood in the human system, so that every citizen is an active member of the Republic. Hence it is impossible to an intelligent American to avoid entertaining warm sympathy for the Swiss Confederation.
>
> Geneva is a cosmopolitan city,—situated in the very heart of Europe,—distinguished for the intelligence of its inhabitants and their love of liberty. It is city, in respect of the commodities of life; it is country, in so far as regards the locality and the surrounding natural objects, Lake Leman, the Jura, and the Alps.
>
> The Federal Government, as well as that of the Canton of Geneva, appreciated the honour of being the seat of this great international Tribunal, and did not fail to welcome most cordially the two Governments, their Agents and their Counsel, by conspicuous manifestations of political as well as of personal consideration.

(C Cushing, *The Treaty of Washington: Its Negotiation, Execution and the Discussions Relating Thereto* (Harper & Bros, 1873) 74–5; also cited by von Segesser and Helgenstein (n 2) 5; see also Chancellerie de l'Etat de Genève, *Arbitrage Alabama Genève*, 1872 (2004) 30).

has developed into one of the most frequently chosen venues for international commercial arbitration.[7] According to recent statistics, Switzerland was the second most often chosen country for arbitrations administered by the ICC in 2011, with 97 cases, behind France (112 cases), and ahead of the United Kingdom (62 cases).[8] It is also the only country that can claim two venues in the top ten most popular cities selected: Geneva and Zurich, which are ranked third and fourth, with 53 and 40 cases respectively.[9] Swiss law was chosen as the law governing the parties' contract in 11.9 per cent of all ICC cases in 2011 in which parties had made a choice of law, making it the most popular choice; English law came second (10.7%), followed by US laws (10.6%).[10] The 2010 White & Case/Queen Mary London International Arbitration Survey indicates that interviewed users most frequently refer to English law, followed by New York law and Swiss law, when they cannot impose their own law, because these are all perceived as well established and well known.[11] The survey also states that Geneva was the second preferred seat of the corporations interviewed, London being their first choice.[12] The venues most frequently used by the interviewees in the past five years were London, Paris, New York, and Geneva, all of which they described as either excellent or very good.[13]

There are also numerous ad hoc cases regularly arbitrated in Switzerland, in particular in Geneva, pursuant to tailor-made rules that either the parties or the arbitrators devise and adopt for their particular cases. Ad hoc arbitration has proven to meet the needs and requirements of the international business community and global business, and does not give rise to any procedural difficulties. Ad hoc arbitration also affords better confidentiality to parties because cases are not reported and generally not disclosed (unless this is required by law). When Swiss counsel are involved, confidentiality is enhanced as a result of the mandatory duty of secrecy imposed by law on Swiss attorneys, pursuant to which they must keep all matters relating to client work and the client strictly confidential.[14] This is particularly appreciated by states or state-owned parties, or by parties in sensitive high tech, IT or IP cases. **17.04**

Geneva and Zurich are the two preferred cities for arbitrations administered by the Swiss Chambers' Arbitration Institution, which since 2004 has administered arbitrations carried out under the Swiss Rules of International Arbitration (Swiss Rules) under the auspices of the **17.05**

---

[7] F Kellerhals and S Pfisterer, 'The Swiss Rules of International Arbitration: A Glimpse into Five Years of Experience', in *The European and Middle Eastern Arbitration Review 2010*, 3–5, who report that, besides the fact that Switzerland was the second most frequently chosen place of arbitration in ICC arbitrations in 2007, there were also a very high number of Swiss arbitrators in ICC cases (13.47% of the total number of arbitrators confirmed and appointed in ICC arbitrations in 2007 came from Switzerland). The latest statistics published by the ICC indicate that 12.6% of all appointment confirmations concerned Swiss arbitrators (169 arbitrators), putting Switzerland first along with the UK (169 arbitrators as well).

[8] (2012) 23(1) ICC International Court of Arbitration Bulletin 13; and (2011) 22(1) ICC International Court of Arbitration Bulletin 13.

[9] See n 8; London was ranked second in 2011, with 62 cases, and Paris, which the ICC predominantly selects when no specific choice of venue is made by the parties, topped the list with 111 cases.

[10] (2012) 23(1) ICC International Court of Arbitration Bulletin 14.

[11] Queen Mary University of London and White & Case LLP, '2010 International Arbitration Survey: Choices in International Arbitration' (2010) 9–14, in particular at 9 and 14, available at <http://www.whitecase.com/files/upload/fileRepository/2010-International-Arbitration-Survey-Choices-International-Arbitration.PDF>.

[12] Queen Mary/White & Case (n 11) 19.

[13] Queen Mary/White & Case (n 11) 17–19.

[14] In addition to bar sanctions, any breach of this duty may trigger criminal law sanctions (fines and even jail sentences; see paragraph 17.55).

country's main Chambers of Commerce.[15] The Swiss Rules, which are based on the UNCITRAL Arbitration Rules, have been revised twice since their introduction: in 2010 and in 2011.[16]

17.06 Switzerland is host to the Court of Arbitration for Sport (CAS) in Lausanne, on the shore of Lac Léman, some 60km from Geneva. Since its creation in 1983, the CAS has delivered an increasing number of awards. It received 374 requests for arbitration in 2012.[17] Since 1996, CAS has had ad hoc divisions for each of the Winter and Summer Olympic Games to resolve all disputes between participants, federations, organisers, and officials within 24 hours. The seat of the panels is always Lausanne, regardless of where the Olympics take place. Consequently, all Olympic arbitration cases are subject to Swiss arbitration law (ie Chapter 12 PIL Act, see paragraphs 17.08–17.12, in particular paragraph 17.11). Applications to set aside awards issued by CAS panels must therefore be raised before the Federal Tribunal, Switzerland's highest court (see paragraphs 17.85–17.86).

17.07 A UN and international organization hub, Geneva also hosts, *inter alia*, the Arbitration and Mediation Centre of the World Intellectual Property Organization (WIPO), which has its own rules of arbitration that are tailor-made for sensitive IP cases and contain specific provisions dealing with confidentiality and specialized experts, and which is also a leading provider of domain name dispute resolution services;[18] the United Nations Compensation Commission (UNCC);[19] as well as the World Trade Organization (WTO) and its Dispute Settlement Body.[20]

17.1.2 Arbitration friendly with liberal arbitration statutes

17.08 International arbitration is governed by Chapter 12 (articles 176 to 194) of the Private International Law Act (PIL Act),[21] which came into force in 1989.[22] An arbitration is international whenever at least one of the parties was neither domiciled nor habitually resident in Switzerland at the time the arbitration agreement was entered into (article 176(1) PIL Act). The parties' nationality has no effect on this definition.

17.09 Chapter 12 PIL Act contains only 19 provisions and is one of the few modern arbitration statutes which are not based on the UNCITRAL Model Law. Its conciseness is a reflection of a liberal conception of arbitration intended to favour party autonomy.[23] It limits regulation to the minimum necessary to ensure the proper functioning of the arbitration process, while safeguarding constitutional guarantees, in particular due process (ie the right to be heard in fair adversarial proceedings and the equal treatment of the parties).[24] Parties are entirely free

[15] Swiss Chambers' Arbitration Institution, Arbitration Statistics 2012, available at <https://www.swissarbitration.org/sa/download/statistics_2012.pdf>.

[16] P Habegger, 'The revised Swiss Rules of International Arbitration—an overview of the major changes' (2012) 2 ASA Bulletin 269.

[17] Court of Arbitration for Sport, Statistics 2012, available at <http://www.tas-cas.org/d2wfiles/document/437/5048/0/stat2012.pdf>.

[18] <http://www.wipo.int/amc/en/arbitration>.

[19] <http://www.uncc.ch>.

[20] <http://www.wto.org/english/tratop_e/dispu_e/dispu_e.htm>.

[21] RS 291 (Official Compilation of Federal Legislation).

[22] Domestic arbitration is governed by the Civil Procedure Code (CPC), arts 353–399, which came into force on 1 January 2011.

[23] J-F Poudret and S Besson, *Comparative law of International Arbitration* (2nd edn, Sweet & Maxwell/Schulthess, 2007) 49, No 64.

[24] Art 182(3) PIL Act; see paras 17.43–17.48.

to determine, directly or by reference to specific arbitration rules, the procedural rules that will govern the arbitration.[25]

When none of the parties has its domicile, habitual residence, or a business establishment in Switzerland, article 192 PIL Act also enables them to waive their right to bring an action to set aside the award through an express waiver or the exclusion of all possible challenges (also referred to as the 'exclusion provision'). The Federal Tribunal has confirmed the validity of such clauses on condition that the waiver is clearly and specifically expressed in the arbitration agreement.[26] **17.10**

The definition of arbitrability is extremely broad. Article 177(1) PIL Act provides that any dispute of a pecuniary nature may be the subject matter of arbitration.[27] Article 177(1) PIL Act is a substantive private international law rule that applies to all arbitrations with their seat in Switzerland, regardless of the parties' national laws or of the law governing their contract or the dispute. Article 177(2) further states that, a state or an entity controlled by a state cannot rely on its own law to challenge its capacity to be a party to an arbitration or the arbitrability of the dispute. **17.11**

The pro-arbitration character of the PIL Act is also reflected in the fact that there are limited grounds pursuant to which an award may be set aside, as is addressed in more detail at paragraphs 17.85–17.114. Setting-aside proceedings are within the exclusive jurisdiction of the Federal Tribunal,[28] which has been quite restrictive regarding the admissibility and acceptance of applications to set aside awards. Since 1989, only 7 per cent of the applications have been successful.[29] This has given rise to interesting debates as to whether the Federal Tribunal's reluctance to set aside awards may have an indirect effect on the quality of some of the awards issued in Switzerland by less conscientious arbitrators.[30] While the discussion may be heated at times, there is of course no way to verify the criticism expressed by those scholars who argue that there is insufficient control by the Federal Tribunal. Many prominent practitioners do not share this concern.[31] Practitioners do not report any meaningful difference in the quality of awards issued in Switzerland and those rendered in other leading arbitration venues. Ultimately, it is the quality of the arbitrators that matters most, not the place where they sit or the jurisprudence of the competent courts regarding challenges of awards, as long as the governing law is arbitration friendly. **17.12**

17.1.3 Recent developments

The PIL Act was amended in 2007 to enhance the efficacy of the process. Article 186(1) PIL Act, which embodies the *competence-competence* principle, pursuant to which it is for the arbitrators to rule on their jurisdiction (see paragraphs17.19–17.27), was amended to **17.13**

[25] Art 182(1) PIL Act; see section 17.3.

[26] Decision of the Swiss Federal Tribunal of 4 January 2012, ref 4A_238/2011 (reported in JdT 2013 II 138, 148); ATF 133 III 235; N Krausz, 'Waiver of Appeal to the Swiss Federal Tribunal: recent Evolution of the case law and compatibility with ECHR, Article 6' (2011) 2 J Intl Arb 137; C Brunner, 'Rechtsmittelverzicht in der internationalen Schiedsgerichtsbarkeit: eine Standortbestimmung nach dem Cañas—Urteil (BGE 133 III 235)' (2008) AJP 738–51.

[27] The definition is narrower for domestic arbitration; pursuant to art 354 CPC, all claims which the parties can freely dispose of are arbitrable.

[28] Art 191 PIL Act.

[29] Recent cases show that CAS awards are more often set aside than other awards.

[30] See eg P Lalive, 'L'article 190 al. 2 LDIP a-t-il une utilité?' (2010) 4 ASA Bulletin 726.

[31] P Schweizer, 'Quelques lignes en réponse à l'article du Professeur Lalive' (2011) 1 ASA Bulletin 66; PA Karrer, 'Une attaque de nostalgie?' (2011) 1 ASA Bulletin 70.

include a new paragraph, article 186(1*bis*), aimed at preventing parties from avoiding arbitration by initiating proceedings before foreign courts. Prior to the enactment of this new provision, it was unclear whether an arbitral tribunal sitting in Switzerland could assert jurisdiction when a party had already brought proceedings with regard to the same dispute before a foreign court. Article 186(1*bis*) PIL Act now clearly states that the arbitral tribunal 'shall decide on its jurisdiction without regard to an action having the same subject matter already pending between the same parties before a state court or another arbitral tribunal, unless serious reasons require to stay the proceedings'.

17.14 Apart from this modification, Chapter 12 of the PIL Act has not been amended since 1989. In the light of recent changes in a number of arbitration statutes in neighbouring countries and in some sets of arbitration rules,[32] consultations between the Federal Department of Justice, arbitration bodies, institutions, and practitioners have been under way to decide whether articles 176–194 PIL Act should be 'cleaned up' and possibly amended to be even more arbitration friendly.[33] The aim is mainly to reflect the Federal Tribunal's landmark jurisprudence and to further strengthen Switzerland's position as a preferred venue for international arbitration. If the issues under discussion give rise to an amendment of the PIL Act, they will not bring any major changes and will not affect the basic thrust and philosophy of Chapter 12 of the Act.

17.2 Commencing the Arbitration

17.2.1 Initiating arbitration

17.15 Arbitral proceedings are commenced by a notice or a request for arbitration addressed by the claimant to the respondent or to the arbitral institution chosen by the parties to administer the case. There are no mandatory rules as to the form or content of the request for arbitration under the PIL Act; the specific procedure is generally defined in the arbitration rules selected by the parties in administered arbitration and is left entirely to the parties in ad hoc cases.

17.16 Article 181 PIL Act provides that an arbitration is pending from the moment the arbitrators designated in the arbitration agreement are seised with the claim or when one of the parties initiates the procedure for appointing the arbitral tribunal, often by designating an arbitrator in the request for arbitration.

17.17 The principle of *competence-competence* embodied in article 186(1) PIL Act is closely linked with, and dependent on, the principle of the autonomy of the arbitration agreement.[34] The

[32] See eg French Decree No 2011-48 of 13 January 2011, the 2012 ICC Rules of Arbitration, the revision of the UNCITRAL rules, and that under consideration for other rules; A Furrer, 'Arbitration on the move' (2011) RSDIE/SZIER 579–82.

[33] Proposal No 12.3012, submitted to the National Council by the Legal Committee of the National Council on 3 February 2012; see also Proposal No 08.417, submitted to the National Council by National Councilor Christian Lüscher on 20 March 2008, which seeks to introduce the negative effect of the *competence-competence* principle into the PIL Act to ensure that courts decline their jurisdiction over matters in relation to which there is a *prima facie* valid arbitration clause so long as the dispute has not been brought to arbitration.

[34] B Berger and F Kellerhals, *International and Domestic Arbitration in Switzerland*, (2nd edn, Stämpfli, 2010) 174–5, No 606. It has been said that the principle of *competence-competence* is the 'procedural corollary' ('pendant procédural') of the principle of the autonomy of the arbitration agreement; G Kaufmann-Kohler and A Rigozzi, *Arbitrage international: droit et pratique à la lumière de la LDIP* (2nd edn, Weblaw, 2010) 236, No 421.

arbitrators are empowered to decide on their own jurisdiction themselves, without the intervention of state courts. The concept of *competence-competence* and the validity of an arbitration clause cannot be disputed on the ground that the main contract is invalid or illegal (see paragraphs 17.19–17.27).

It is essentially at the start of an arbitration that the supporting courts may be called upon to assist the process, with regard to either the constitution of the arbitral tribunal if the arbitration agreement is silent on the subject (see paragraphs 17.29–17.32), or with provisional measures (see paragraphs 17.33–17.38). **17.18**

17.2.2 *Competence-competence* and the autonomy of the arbitration agreement

Article 186(1) PIL Act affirms the *competence-competence* principle by providing that the arbitral tribunal has priority over state courts to decide on its own jurisdiction.[35] Consequently, a party cannot ask a national court to decide, by way of a declaratory action, on the validity of the arbitration agreement or on the competence of the arbitral tribunal.[36] **17.19**

Article 186(1) PIL Act is a mandatory provision. The arbitrators cannot be deprived of the power to decide on their jurisdiction, and any agreement to this effect would be void.[37] The arbitral tribunal may decide on its jurisdiction notwithstanding the fact that an action relating to the same dispute is already pending between the same parties before a state court or another arbitral tribunal, 'unless there are serious reasons to stay the proceedings' (article 186 (1)*bis* PIL Act). **17.20**

Any objection to the arbitral tribunal's jurisdiction must be raised prior to any defence on the merits, failing which the objection is considered to have been waived.[38] The arbitral tribunal usually decides on jurisdiction by a preliminary decision,[39] which may be challenged before the Federal Tribunal.[40] The arbitration may proceed while the challenge proceedings are conducted. **17.21**

The separability of the arbitration clause has been codified in Swiss law, and article 178(3) PIL Act specifically states that the arbitration agreement constitutes a contract separate from the contract that contains it. An arbitration clause may, therefore, be governed by a law different from that governing the main contract.[41] **17.22**

When the seat of the arbitral tribunal is in Switzerland, article 178(1) PIL Act provides that the arbitration agreement is valid with regard to its form if it is made by any means that permits it to be evidenced by a text. Article 178(2) PIL Act further states that the arbitration agreement is valid as to its substance if it conforms to either the law chosen by the parties, the law governing the subject matter of the dispute, or Swiss law. Article 178(2) PIL Act is a conflict-of-laws provision in favour of the validity of an arbitration clause or agreement, **17.23**

35 Poudret and Besson (n 23) 389, No 462; W Wenger, '*ad* Article 186', in SV Berti (ed), *International Arbitration in Switzerland* (Helbing & Lichtenhahn, 2000) 461, No 2.

36 P Lalive, J-F Poudret, and C Reymond, '*ad* Article 186' in *Le droit de l'arbitrage interne et international en Suisse: édition annotée et commentée du Concordat sur l'arbitrage du 27 mars 1969 et des dispositions sur l'arbitrage international de la Loi fédérale du 18 décembre 1987 sur le droit international privé* (Payot, 1989) 385–6, No 16.

37 Poudret and Besson (n 23) 389, No 462.

38 Art 186(2) PIL Act.

39 Art 186(3) PIL Act.

40 Unless there is a valid general exclusion agreement pursuant to art 192(1) PIL Act, or a waiver specifically concerning jurisdiction.

41 This is explicitly stated in art 178(2) PIL Act.

which means that the reference to Swiss law ensures the validity of the arbitration agreement as a matter of principle, given the arbitration-friendly nature of Swiss law on these issues.

17.24 Article 178(3) PIL Act expressly provides that the validity of the arbitration agreement 'cannot be contested on the ground that the main contract may not be valid or that the arbitration agreement concerns disputes that have not yet arisen'.

17.25 If a Swiss court is seised of a dispute relating to a contract containing an arbitration clause, it will refer the matter to arbitration if it is satisfied that there is a valid arbitration agreement pursuant to article 7 PIL Act[42] and Article II(3)[43] of the 1958 New York Convention on the Recognition and Enforcement of Foreign Arbitral Awards (New York Convention). According to current case law, whenever the arbitration clause provides for an arbitration with its seat in Switzerland, pursuant to article 7 PIL Act the courts must only examine the existence and validity of the arbitration agreement in a summary fashion, essentially on the ground that the issue may be raised again before the Federal Tribunal if any eventual arbitral award is challenged.[44]

17.26 If the seat of the arbitration is outside Switzerland, the Federal Tribunal has held that when a Swiss court is seised of a matter in relation to which the respondent objects to jurisdiction on the basis of an arbitration clause, that court's power to ascertain the validity of such clause is not limited to a *prima facie* assessment under Article II(3) of the New York Convention. The court has unlimited power to make such an assessment.[45]

17.27 This difference in standards has been construed by some as an indication that the PIL Act does not fully acknowledge the negative effect of the *competence-competence* principle in the same way as French law does, for instance, and this, they fear, might adversely affect Switzerland's popularity as a venue for international arbitration.[46] A bill is pending in the lower house of the Federal Parliament to amend article 7 PIL Act to remedy what the supporters of the bill perceive as a competitive handicap by extending statutorily the *prima facie* test developed by the Federal Tribunal for arbitration agreements with a Swiss seat to all

---

42 Art 7 PIL Act states as follows:

If the parties have entered into an arbitration agreement with respect to an arbitrable dispute, the Swiss court before which such dispute is brought shall decline its jurisdiction, unless:
(a) The defendant has proceeded to the merits without contesting jurisdiction;
(b) The court finds that the arbitration agreement is null and void, inoperative or incapable of being performed; or
(c) The arbitral tribunal cannot be constituted for reasons that are obviously attributable to the defendant in the arbitration.

43 Pursuant to Art II(3) New York Convention:

The court of a Contracting State, when seized of an action in a matter in respect of which the parties have made an agreement within the meaning of this article, shall, at the request of one of the parties, refer the parties to arbitration, unless it finds that the said agreement is null and void, inoperative or incapable of being performed.

44 This jurisprudence, while criticized (see, among others, J-F Poudret, 'Exception d'arbitrage et litispendance en droit Suisse, comment départager le juge et l'arbitre?' (2007) 2 ASA Bulletin 230), was recently upheld in ATF 138 III 681, cons 3.2; for the setting aside proceedings before the Federal Tribunal, see paras 17.85–17.114.

45 Decision of the Swiss Federal Tribunal of 25 October 2010, ref 4A_279/2010, cons 2.

46 E Gaillard, 'L'effet négatif de la compétence-compétence', in J Haldy, J-M Rapp, and P Ferrari (eds), *Études de procédures et d'arbitrage en l'honneur de Jean-François Poudret* (Faculté de droit de l'Université de Lausanne, 1999) 387-402, in particular at 390.

arbitration agreements.[47] The outcome of the bill is uncertain at the moment. A number of leading arbitration specialists consider that rather than increasing the popularity of international arbitrations carried out in Switzerland, as is intended by its supporters, the bill may simply favour arbitration abroad.[48]

17.2.3 Supporting role of state courts

At the commencement of an arbitration, parties may need the assistance of state courts with regard to the constitution of the arbitral tribunal, or, in certain circumstances, when they need to ensure the effective administration of justice through urgent or preliminary measures. **17.28**

Constitution of the arbitral tribunal

The composition of the arbitral tribunal and the designation of the arbitrators are, first and foremost, a matter for the parties to decide and agree, either in the arbitration clause itself, by reference to a set of arbitration rules, or by subsequent agreement.[49] Under the PIL Act, 'anyone may be an arbitrator'[50] so long as they are independent from the parties (lack of independence is a ground for challenge pursuant to article 180(1)(c) PIL Act as addressed in paragraphs 17.58–17.60). **17.29**

Parties may agree, directly or by reference to the application of arbitration rules, to assign to a third-party individual or institution, their right to designate arbitrators or the president of the arbitral tribunal (eg the Secretary General of the ICC or the President of the Swiss Arbitration Association (ASA)). The parties can also refer to the same third parties to appoint an arbitrator in case one of them fails to do so in breach of the arbitration agreement or when the party-appointed arbitrators cannot agree on a president of the arbitral tribunal. As a matter of principle, these third-party decisions cannot be challenged under Swiss law. Should a party oppose the choice of any of the appointed arbitrators, it will first have to raise the issue before the arbitral tribunal, whose preliminary decision on the constitution of the arbitral tribunal or its jurisdiction (depending on the grounds raised to oppose the arbitral tribunal's decision) may be subject to setting aside proceedings before the Federal Tribunal.[51] Where the appointing authority or third party refuses to appoint or otherwise rejects the request for an appointment, the matter may be referred to the competent court at the seat of the arbitral tribunal.[52] The court will make the appointment unless a summary examination of the matter shows that no arbitration agreement exists between the parties.[53] **17.30**

---

[47] Proposal No 08.417, submitted to the National Council by National Councilor Christian Lüscher on 3 March 2008, which proposes a new article 7(2) PIL Act stating that: 'In international matters, the Swiss court shall stay proceedings until the arbitral tribunal has ruled on its jurisdiction regardless of where the seat of the arbitral tribunal is located, unless a summary review of the case shows that there is no arbitration agreement between the parties' (free translation).

[48] See in particular S Besson, 'Réflexions sur le projet de modification de l'article 7 LDIP (initiative Lüscher)' (2011) 3 ASA Bulletin 574, who argues that such an amendment would not benefit arbitrations conducted in Switzerland but, rather, would be to the benefit of arbitrations conducted abroad.

[49] Art 179(1) PIL Act.

[50] B Berger and F Kellerhals (n 34) 207, No 721.

[51] Decision of the Swiss Federal Tribunal of 10 January 2013, ref 4A_146/2012, cons 3.3.2.

[52] P-Y Tschanz, '*ad* Article 179', in A Bucher (ed), *Commentaire romand de la Loi sur le droit international privé et sur la Convention de Lugano* (Helbing Lichtenhahn, 2011) 1567, Nos 37–38; Berger and Kellerhals (n 34) 225, Nos 784–785.

[53] Art 179(3) PIL Act.

17.31 When the seat of the arbitration is Geneva, the court competent to appoint an arbitrator in such cases is the Geneva Court of First Instance.[54] Like the other competent courts, the Geneva Court of First Instance generally provides swift and efficient support to the parties in the appointing of arbitrators, as illustrated, *inter alia*, by a decision it rendered in 2002.[55] In that case, the claimant in the arbitration applied for the court to designate an arbitrator for the respondent because the latter had refused to do so. Shortly before the hearing fixed by the court to entertain the claimant's application, the respondent informed the court and the claimant that it had designated an arbitrator and that the latter had accepted his appointment. The claimant applied for the court to proceed to appoint the arbitrator in question, in order to prevent the respondent from subsequently withdrawing its nomination. The court ruled that the claimant's application had become pointless under the circumstances and dismissed it. However, it ordered the respondent to pay all costs, including those incurred by the claimant, attributable to the respondent's dilatory attitude.

17.32 A supporting court's decisions to designate, nominate, or appoint, as the case may be, is not subject to appeal.[56] Pursuant to case law, the court's decisions are issued in a non-contentious procedure (*procédure non contentieuse*). Such decisions have no *res judicata* effect. This means that the arbitral tribunal retains the ability to freely review its jurisdiction and the regularity of its composition.[57] The arbitrators' interim award on the subject may be immediately challenged before the Federal Tribunal pursuant to article 190(3) PIL Act, on the grounds stated in article 190(2)(a) and (b) PIL Act.[58] In contrast, a decision by the competent supporting court at the seat not to nominate or appoint an arbitrator may immediately be brought before the Federal Tribunal.[59]

Provisional measures

17.33 Pursuant to article 183(1) PIL Act, the arbitral tribunal may, upon the application of a party and unless agreed otherwise by the parties,[60] 'order provisional or protective measures'. Its competence to do so is concurrent with that of the courts.[61] While article 183(1) PIL Act expressly allows agreements to exclude the jurisdiction of arbitral tribunals to order interim measures, the exclusion of the concurrent jurisdiction of ordinary courts gives rise to some debate. There seems to be a consensus at the moment that such an exclusion is valid under Swiss law whenever there is a properly constituted arbitral tribunal or an emergency arbitrator in place.[62] The issue is discussed in particular with regard to article R37 of CAS's Code of Sports-related Arbitration, which states in the last sentence of the third paragraph, that by

---

[54] Art 86 of the Judicial Organization Act of the Canton of Geneva (E 2 05), and art 179(2) PIL Act.

[55] B Ehle, 'Belated nomination of arbitrator before the Swiss *juge d'appui:* three recent decisions' (2008) 2 ASA Bulletin 392, 393.

[56] Tschanz (n 52) 1568, No 45.

[57] Decision of the Swiss Federal Tribunal of 10 January 2013, ref 4A_146/2012, cons 3.3.2; see also ATF 115 II 294 cons 2a and ATF 110 Ia 59 cons 2b.

[58] Decision of the Swiss Federal Tribunal of 10 January 2013 (n 57), cons 3.3.2; see also decision ref 4A_146/2012, ATF 110 Ia 59, cons 2b; P-Y Tschanz, '*ad* Article 190' in A Bucher (ed), *Commentaire romand de la Loi sur le droit international privé et sur la Convention de Lugano* (Helbing Lichtenhahn, 2011) 1684 No 47.

[59] Decision of the Swiss Federal Tribunal of 23 September 2008, ref 4A_215/2008, cons 1.1.

[60] Berger and Kellerhals (n 34) 321, Nos 1136–1138.

[61] A Bucher, '*ad* Article 183' in A Bucher (ed), *Commentaire romand de la Loi sur le droit international privé et sur la Convention de Lugano* (Helbing Lichtenhahn, 2011) 1611, No 6; M Wirth, 'Interim or preventive measures in support of international arbitration in Switzerland' (2011) 1 ASA Bulletin 31, 42.

[62] G von Segesser and C Boog, 'Interim measures' in E Geisinger and N Voser (eds), *International Arbitration in Switzerland, A Handbook for Practitioners* (2nd edn, Kluwer Law International, 2013) 125–6.

agreeing to submit to CAS arbitration 'the parties expressly waive their rights to request any such [interim] measures from state authorities or tribunals'.[63]

The arbitral tribunal has broad discretion as to the type of measures it may order. Three main categories of provisional measures are generally sought: conservatory measures that aim at maintaining the status quo between the parties during the arbitration and thus not aggravating the dispute; temporary measures regulating a legal relationship until a decision is issued by the arbitrators; and specific performance measures aimed at ensuring the temporary enforcement of disputed claims.[64] The arbitral tribunal may order any types of measures it finds appropriate, including measures unknown to Swiss law. **17.34**

To be successful, the petitioner must establish, with a reasonable degree of probability (a) the existence of an impending harm to its legal entitlement; (b) that it holds the entitlement which the interim measure sought is intended to protect and (c) that the harm it will suffer if no relief is granted could not easily be remedied.[65] **17.35**

Arbitral tribunals do not have the authority to enforce their own provisional measures. Article 183(2) PIL Act expressly states that if the party against which a provisional measure is granted by an arbitral tribunal does not voluntarily comply with the order, the tribunal may request the assistance of the competent court to enforce the measures it has ordered whenever such court has jurisdiction to do so. Article 183(2) specifies that such court 'shall apply its own law'. **17.36**

The competent court pursuant to article 183(2) PIL Act is not necessarily that of the seat of the arbitral tribunal but rather the court which has *ratione loci* and *ratione materiae* jurisdiction to order provisional measures.[66] The Federal Tribunal has held that decisions by arbitrators granting or denying provisional measures cannot be challenged.[67] **17.37**

Swiss courts do not grant anti-suit injunctions when proceedings are brought elsewhere in breach of an arbitration agreement.[68] As explained in the discussion of *competence-competence* in paragraphs 17.19–17.21, the determination of the existence and validity of the arbitration agreements is first for the arbitrators to make. **17.38**

17.3 During the Arbitration

Parties have unrestricted freedom to appoint counsel of their choice and to agree on the procedure to govern the arbitration, either directly, or by reference to, a set of arbitration rules, such as those of the ICC, the LCIA, the Swiss Rules, etc. **17.39**

Once the arbitral tribunal is constituted, the competent court at the seat of the arbitral tribunal may be seised in relation to the arbitration in the event of the challenge of an arbitrator **17.40**

63 The validity of such a waiver agreed by athletes by reference when adhering to various sport federations' statutes has been questioned. Sport arbitration specialists consider, however, that art R37(3) of the CAS Code is generally valid on the same conditions as those already mentioned and on condition that CAS is (a) as independent and impartial, and (b) as effective, as ordinary courts; see A Rigozzi and F Robert-Tissot, 'La pertinence du "consentement" dans l'arbitrage du Tribunal Arbitral du Sport', Jusletter, 16 July 2012, 5, 8.

64 ATF 136 III 200, cons 2.3.

65 Wirth (n 61) 37–8.

66 Lalive, Poudret, and Reymond (n 36) 365, No 8.

67 ATF 136 III 200, cons 2.3.5.

68 ATF 138 III 304, cons 5.3.1.

or to assist with the taking of evidence. The same court also has jurisdiction 'for any further judicial assistance' that may be required during the proceedings.[69]

17.3.1 Free choice of counsel

17.41 As is the case in most of the leading international arbitration venues, there is no legal restriction to the parties' choice of counsel in international arbitrations conducted in Switzerland. In fact, parties do not have to be represented by counsel if they do not so wish. Chapter 12 of the PIL Act is silent on the subject.[70] According to the Federal Tribunal, the right to be assisted by counsel in international arbitration derives from the right to be heard, which must be respected whatever type of procedure is chosen to govern the proceedings.[71] Unlike in court proceedings, there is no monopoly for lawyers admitted and registered with a Swiss bar,[72] since arbitration is a creature of contract, and counsel in arbitral proceedings do not act as an auxiliary of justice. Conversely, only lawyers who are authorized to practice pursuant to Swiss law,[73] or by virtue of an international treaty, may act as counsel before the Federal Tribunal, in accordance with article 40 of the Federal Act on the Swiss Federal Tribunal (FT Act).[74] Consequently, trainee lawyers or articled clerks (whether Swiss or not), as well as lawyers (Swiss and foreigners) who are not registered with a cantonal bar registry, are not authorized to act in setting aside proceedings before the Swiss Federal Tribunal,[75] with the exception of counsel from an EU or EFTA country.[76] A similar restriction applies to appearances before the competent supporting courts at the seat of the arbitration.[77]

17.3.2 Conduct of the arbitral hearings

17.42 The parties enjoy total freedom to choose the procedure or procedural rules governing the arbitration, either directly or by reference to specific arbitration rules.[78] In the absence of any agreement on the subject, the arbitral tribunal shall determine the procedure 'to the extent necessary'.[79] The arbitral tribunal must in all cases ensure equal treatment of the parties and their right to be heard in an adversarial procedure.[80]

Right to be heard in fair adversarial proceedings

17.43 The right to equal treatment and to be heard in a fair adversarial procedure is embodied in article 182(3) PIL Act and constitutes a minimum procedural standard for arbitral tribunals

---

[69] Art 185 PIL Act.

[70] In domestic arbitration, art 373(5) CPC merely states that the parties 'may act through a representative'.

[71] ATF 117 II 346, cons 1.

[72] F Bohnet and V Martenet, *Droit de la profession d'avocat* (Schulthess, 2009) 1343, No 3424.

[73] Federal Act on the free movement of lawyers, RS 935.61.

[74] Federal Act on the Swiss Federal Tribunal, RS 173.110.

[75] Kaufmann-Kohler and Rigozzi (n 34) 491, No 784.

[76] According to art 21 of the Swiss Federal Act on the free movement of lawyers, counsel from EU or EFTA countries may act before Swiss courts as service providers without having to be registered on a cantonal bar roll. This provision was adopted to implement the Bilateral Agreement on free movement of persons concluded between Switzerland and the EU (RS 0.142.112.681).

[77] Art 68(2)(a) CPC provides that only lawyers authorized to practise pursuant to the Federal Act on lawyers can act as professional representatives before Swiss courts.

[78] Art 182(1) PIL Act.

[79] Art 182(2) PIL Act.

[80] Art 182(3) PIL Act.

and state courts (due process).[81] Article 182(3) combines two notions, namely the right to be heard in the proper sense and the principle of contradiction.[82]

The right to be heard aims at ensuring that each party can express itself on all facts relevant to the outcome of the case, adduce evidence to support its factual allegations, develop its legal arguments, participate in the hearings, and be assisted or represented by counsel if it so wishes. The principle of contradiction guarantees each party the right to express itself on any factual and legal consideration brought up by the opposing party, to consider and address the evidence adduced by the latter, and to rebut it with its own evidence.[83] **17.44**

Equal treatment and the right to be heard in an adversarial procedure form part of the broader concept of procedural public policy,[84] which also includes, for example, the right to a fair trial[85] and the prohibition of the abuse of rights.[86] These procedural rights and guarantees must be respected, no matter what rules of procedure are chosen for the arbitration. They cannot be waived.[87] **17.45**

Breach of the procedural rights embodied in article 182(3) PIL Act

In the case of a breach of the rights guaranteed under article 182(3) PIL Act, the award may be set aside pursuant to article 190(2)(d) PIL Act. The Federal Tribunal has held, for instance, that CAS[88] breached an athlete's right to be heard by issuing an award against him without addressing at all the subsidiary arguments he had invoked during the arbitration.[89] This does not mean, however, that an arbitral tribunal must specifically address all arguments raised by the parties in its award, or that parties have a right to a reasoned award on all aspects of the dispute.[90] Accordingly, an arbitral tribunal does not have to rebut, even implicitly, considerations that objectively are completely irrelevant.[91] This being said, the arbitral tribunal must properly address the parties' relevant allegations of fact or legal submissions, or else there would be a risk of 'formal denial of justice' that might trigger the setting aside of the award.[92] **17.46**

The Federal Tribunal has also held that the application of legal principles different from those raised by the parties does not, per se, constitute a formal denial of justice. The arbitrators are entitled to consider legal principles that were not invoked by the parties because the *jura novit curia* principle applies to arbitrators and courts alike.[93] The Federal Tribunal has **17.47**

---

81 ME Schneider, '*ad* Article 182' in SV Berti (ed), *International Arbitration in Switzerland* (Helbing & Lichtenhahn, 2000) 411, No 50. Under Swiss domestic arbitration rules, these rights are grounded in art 373(4) CPC; they are also guaranteed under art 29(1) and (2) of the Swiss Federal Constitution.

82 ATF 117 II 346, cons 1a.

83 ATF 133 III 139, cons 6.1.

84 '*Ordre public procédural*', see decision of the Swiss Federal Tribunal of 11 June 2001, ref 4P_64/2001, cons 2d; see also Schneider (n 81) 411, No 51.

85 Decision of the Swiss Federal Tribunal of 11 June 2001, ref 4P_64/2001, cons 2d.

86 Lalive, Poudret, and Reymond (n 36) 430, No 6.

87 ATF 133 III 139, cons 6.1.

88 Court of Arbitration for Sport (see paragraph 17.06).

89 ATF 133 III 235, cons 5.3.

90 Decision of the Swiss Federal Tribunal of 9 October 2012, ref 4A_110/2012, cons 3.1.2.

91 Decision of the Swiss Federal Tribunal of 9 October 2012, cons 3.1.2.

92 See, *inter alia*, decision of the Swiss Federal Tribunal of 31 January 2011, ref 4A_360/2011, cons 5.1, and cited references.

93 See, *inter alia*, decision of the Swiss Federal Tribunal of 15 February 2010, ref 4A_464/2009, cons 4.1; decision of the Federal Tribunal of 3 August 2010, ref 4A_254/2010, cons 3.1.

further ruled that the limit to the application of this principle in arbitration pursuant to article 182(3) PIL Act is that an arbitral tribunal cannot take the parties by surprise and base its decision on legal grounds that were never addressed before it, or that the parties could not anticipate or had not considered relevant to the dispute.[94] If the tribunal considers that the parties overlooked a point, or did not address a relevant legal argument, it must draw their attention to it and ask them questions before finalizing its decision.[95]

17.48 Pursuant to the duty to act in good faith in arbitration proceedings, a party that considers that its procedural rights have been breached must protest immediately so that the arbitral tribunal may remedy the situation, if still possible.[96] Should it fail to do so, the party will be deemed to have waived its right to raise such grounds to challenge the final award.[97]

Testimonial evidence

17.49 In the absence of a specific agreement or an agreement by reference to arbitration rules, the arbitral tribunal determines how the testimonial evidence proceedings will be conducted,[98] within the limits laid down by article 182(3) PIL Act.[99] Party-representatives and third parties may be heard as witnesses, and it is for the tribunal to assess their testimony in the light of their position within the parties' organizations. Witness statements are usually filed during the pre-hearing proceedings, together with the parties' written submissions.

17.50 It has long been accepted in Switzerland that counsel may be in contact with potential witnesses to prepare their statements, contrary to the situation before the courts, where counsel may not address or be in touch with witnesses before the hearing. The specificity of counsel's role in international arbitration has been formally acknowledged in article 7(1) of the Swiss Code of Ethics for Lawyers,[100] which is not legally binding but is compulsory for all members of the Swiss Bar Association.

17.51 In practice, article 4 of the IBA Rules on the Taking of Evidence in International Arbitration[101] is often used as a guideline for witness interviews and the taking of testimonial evidence.

17.52 There is no obligation under Swiss law for witnesses to take an oath. They are invited to tell the truth and usually reminded that they may be subject to criminal sanctions in the case of false testimony. Some arbitrators read out the relevant provisions of the Swiss Criminal Code on the subject before each witness is heard.[102]

Confidentiality

17.53 Arbitration is not confidential by law. The PIL Act and the CPC are silent on the subject. However, it is considered to be private and should not be made public,[103] something that article 44 of the Swiss Rules specifically acknowledges.[104]

---

94 ATF 130 III 35, cons 6.

95 Decision of the Swiss Federal Tribunal of 3 August 2010, ref 4A_254/2010, cons 3.1.

96 ATF 119 II 386, cons 1a.

97 See n 96.

98 Art 182(2) PIL Act.

99 Berger and Kellerhals (n 34) 347, No 1219, and 348, No 1221.

100 Available at <http://www.bgfa.ch/scripts/getfile?id=1054>.

101 Available at <http://www.ibanet.org/Publications/publications_IBA_guides_and_free_materials.aspx#takingevidence>.

102 Art 307 Swiss Criminal Code (RS 311.0).

103 Poudret and Besson (n 23) 317, No 369.

104 Art 44 of the Swiss Rules states as follows:

Because arbitration is of a purely consensual nature, arbitral proceedings are deemed to remain within the private domain of the parties and are not public. Under Swiss law, this triggers a fiduciary duty of confidentiality for the arbitrators that extends to all their assistants.[105] This does not, however, apply to the parties themselves or to third parties involved in the arbitration (witnesses or expert witnesses). It is up to the parties themselves to provide for confidentiality in their agreement with third parties, or to agree on the general confidentiality of the arbitration, either expressly or by reference to arbitration rules that impose confidentiality obligations. **17.54**

Professional confidentiality (or even secrecy) is imposed by law or bar rules on Swiss counsel, as is the case in most civil law jurisdictions. The breach of this obligation constitutes a criminal offence, which may bear severe sanctions.[106] **17.55**

Unless the parties have validly excluded setting aside proceedings,[107] they cannot prevent the disclosure of the award in such proceedings, even if they have agreed not to publish it for reasons of confidentiality.[108] The Federal Tribunal's decisions regarding applications to set aside arbitration awards are published on its website,[109] which may affect the agreed confidentiality of an arbitration, even though the parties' names are not published as a matter of principle.[110] The Federal Tribunal has observed, in a case related to the validity of an agreement waiving the right to challenge an award under article 192 PIL Act, that such a waiver, when duly complied with, effectively enables the parties to guarantee the confidentiality of their arbitration.[111] **17.56**

17.3.3 Role of the supporting court in deciding challenges to arbitrators

The competent court at the seat of the arbitration has jurisdiction to decide upon challenges to arbitrators in the event of a dispute and to the extent the parties have not determined the procedure for the challenge.[112] Its decision is final. **17.57**

---

1. Unless the parties expressly agree in writing to the contrary, the parties undertake to keep confidential all awards and orders as well as all materials submitted by another party in the framework of the arbitral proceedings not already in the public domain, except and to the extent that a disclosure may be required of a party by a legal duty, to protect or pursue a legal right, or to enforce or challenge an award in legal proceedings before a judicial authority. This undertaking also applies to the arbitrators, the tribunal-appointed experts, the secretary of the arbitral tribunal, the members of the board of directors of the Swiss Chambers' Arbitration Institution, the members of the Court and the Secretariat, and the staff of the individual Chambers.
2. The deliberations of the arbitral tribunal are confidential.
3. An award or order may be published, whether in its entirety or in the form of excerpts or a summary, only under the following conditions: (a) A request for publication is addressed to the Secretariat; (b) All references to the parties' names are deleted; and (c) No party objects to such publication within the time-limit fixed for that purpose by the Secretariat.

[105] Berger and Kellerhals (n 34) 319, No 1120.

[106] Art 321 Swiss Criminal Code; see also para 17.04.

[107] See paras 17.115–17.117.

[108] Poudret and Besson (n 23) 319, No 372.

[109] Requests not to have the decision of the Swiss Federal Tribunal published are usually rejected; see decision of 6 June 2006, ref 4P.74/2006, cons 8.

[110] Federal Act on the Federal Tribunal (RS 173.110), art 27(2), which states that 'decisions are in principle published in an anonymous version'.

[111] Decision of the Swiss Federal Tribunal of 4 January 2012, ref 4A_238/2011, cons 3.2.

[112] Art 180(3) PIL Act.

Grounds for challenge

17.58 According to article 180(1) PIL Act, an arbitrator may be challenged on three different grounds: (1) failure to meet the requirements agreed by the parties; (2) grounds provided in the rules agreed by the parties; or (3) when circumstances exist that give rise to justifiable doubts as to the arbitrator's independence. The first two grounds relate to the particulars of the parties' agreement as to the background and requirements expected from the arbitrator and his or her actual factual situation. The third is conversely a legal ground, which the Federal Tribunal has held to be understood as comprising both 'independence' and 'impartiality' even though article 180(1) PIL Act only mentions independence.[113]

17.59 To determine whether an arbitrator is independent and impartial, reference must be made to the constitutional principles developed for judges in application of article 30(1) of the Swiss Federal Constitution[114] and Article 6(1) of the European Convention on Human Rights (ECHR), with consideration of the special characteristics of international arbitration.[115] Both provisions specifically afford parties the right to challenge a judge whose situation or behaviour is such as to give rise to doubts about his or her impartiality; they are intended to avoid a situation in which external circumstances not related to the case might influence the judgment.[116] This does not mean that the partiality of the judge must be established, and purely subjective or individual impressions are not decisive.[117] The 'justifiable doubts' of article 180(1)(c) PIL Act rather imply the existence of 'concrete facts that may objectively and reasonably be considered to give rise to suspicions as to the independence of the arbitrator'.[118] The same standards apply to all members of an arbitral tribunal.[119]

17.60 It is firmly established that the fact that an award has been set aside does not, in itself, give rise to justifiable doubts as to the arbitrator's independence and impartiality.[120] Similarly, the fact that an arbitrator participated on the same panel as counsel or a member of counsel's firm at a conference is not sufficient to establish such doubts, given the small circle of practitioners in international arbitration.[121]

Challenge procedure

17.61 Article 180(2) PIL Act limits challenges by providing that a party may not challenge an arbitrator it has appointed, or in whose appointment it was instrumental except on grounds that came to its attention after such appointment. In such an event, the ground for challenge 'must be notified to the arbitral tribunal and to the other party without delay'. This requirement derives from the duty to act in good faith imposed on all parties to an international

[113] ATF 136 III 605, cons 3.3.1.

[114] Art 30(1) Swiss Federal Constitution states: 'Anyone whose case fails to be judicially decided has the right to have their case heard by a legally constituted, competent, independent and impartial court. Ad hoc courts are prohibited'.

[115] ATF 129 III 445, cons 3.3.3; decision of the Swiss Federal Tribunal of 27 June 2012, ref 4A_54/2012, cons 2.2.1.

[116] ATF 128 V 82, cons 2a.

[117] ATF 136 III 605, cons 3.2.1.

[118] ATF 118 II 359, cons 3c. See Berger and Kellerhals (n 34) 228, No 795.

[119] ATF 136 III 605, cons 3.3.1.

[120] ATF 113 Ia 407, cons 2b.

[121] For a list of examples, see, *inter alia*, E Geisinger and N Voser, 'The Arbitral Tribunal' in E Geisinger and N Voser (eds), *International Arbitration in Switzerland, A Handbook for Practitioners* (2nd edn, Kluwer Law International, 2013) 64–6.

arbitration with its seat in Switzerland.[122] A party cannot, therefore, keep grounds for challenge in reserve in order to invoke them only at a later stage if the outcome of the arbitration has turned against it.[123]

The Federal Tribunal has held that a party cannot rely on facts that were available on the internet at the start of the proceedings or during the arbitration to raise allegations of bias against an arbitrator after the award has been issued.[124] It has also confirmed that the decision of the supporting court is final, as stated in article 180(3) PIL Act, and cannot be appealed.[125] **17.62**

17.3.4 Role of the supporting court at the seat regarding the taking of evidence

According to article 184(1) PIL Act, the arbitral tribunal itself takes evidence. As arbitral tribunals lack coercive powers, article 184(2) PIL Act specifies that where the assistance of state authorities is needed in relation to the taking of evidence, 'the arbitral tribunal or a party with the consent of the arbitral tribunal may request the assistance of the court at the seat of the arbitral tribunal; such court shall apply its own law'. **17.63**

Consequently, should the parties, witnesses, expert witnesses, etc. fail to cooperate as directed by the arbitral tribunal in the taking of evidence, the tribunal cannot impose its own sanctions, but must seek the assistance of the competent court at its seat.[126] In Swiss law, when a party refuses to produce a document, the arbitrators may draw inferences from the obstructive behaviour without having to apply for judicial assistance.[127] **17.64**

Procedure before the court

When seised with an application pursuant to article 184(2) PIL Act, the supporting court acts as an assistant to the arbitral tribunal.[128] It does not have to examine whether the arbitral tribunal has jurisdiction or undertake to determine whether the evidence sought is relevant unless the lack of jurisdiction or of relevance is manifest.[129] **17.65**

As the court applies 'its own law',[130] the applicable rules of the CPC will apply to the proceedings. The court is, however, entitled to apply foreign rules of procedure if that is justified by the circumstances of the case.[131] If the court decides to take the requested evidence itself, which is rare, given that usually the concerned witnesses or experts are not domiciled at the seat of the arbitration, it must respect the parties' right to be heard in an adversarial procedure.[132] **17.66**

The arbitral tribunal may seise the court at the seat or authorize a party to do so under article 184(2) PIL Act as a first step to obtaining legal assistance abroad pursuant to the 1970 **17.67**

---

[122] ATF 136 III 605, cons 3.2.2.
[123] See n 122.
[124] ATF 129 III 445, cons 4.2.2.1.
[125] ATF 138 III 270, cons 2.2.2.
[126] Some examples of applications for assistance from arbitral tribunals sitting in Geneva may be found in J Revaclier, 'Arbitrages et instances judiciaires du canton de Genève' (1994) 2 ASA Bulletin 303.
[127] ME Schneider, '*ad* Article 184', in SV Berti (ed), *International Arbitration in Switzerland* (Helbing & Lichtenhahn, 2000) 451, No 57.
[128] Berger and Kellerhals (n 34) 355, No 1242.
[129] A Bucher, '*ad* Article 184', in A Bucher (ed), *Commentaire romand de la Loi sur le droit international privé et sur la Convention de Lugano* (Helbing Lichtenhahn, 2011) 1619, No 13.
[130] Art 184(2) PIL Act.
[131] Poudret and Besson (n 23) 565, No 671; Bucher (n 129) 1619, No 15.
[132] Art 182(3) PIL Act; see also paras 17.43–17.45.

Hague Convention on the Taking of Evidence Abroad on Civil or Commercial Matters.[133] Although there are a number of precedents for such requests made to neighbouring countries, in practice this approach is not often pursued because it is slow and cumbersome.

17.4 The Award

17.68 All categories of awards (preliminary awards[134] on jurisdiction[135] or liability, final awards, etc.) are governed by the same rules regarding their making, form, content, and notification to the parties.[136]

17.69 As a rule, the award must be made in conformity with the procedure and the form agreed by the parties.[137] In the absence of such an agreement, 'the award shall be made by a majority decision, or, in the absence of a majority, by the presiding arbitrator alone. It shall be in writing, reasoned, dated and signed. The signature of the presiding arbitrator shall suffice'.[138]

17.4.1 Decision-making process

17.70 The deliberations of the arbitral tribunal are confidential and should not be disclosed or carried out in the presence of the parties. The Federal Tribunal has held that this duty of confidentiality applies to 'all opinions expressed in the course of the discussion, that is to say, ultimately, the way in which a majority decision was reached'.[139] It has further held that for an arbitrator to communicate the result (as opposed to the content) of deliberations to the party who appointed him was not a breach of his duty to keep deliberations confidential.[140] Nor does the act of the chairman informing parties of the outcome of an arbitral tribunal's deliberations regarding an application for the correction of an award constitute a breach of the arbitrator's duty to keep deliberations confidential.[141]

17.4.2 Form and content

17.71 The freedom afforded to the parties by article 189(1) PIL Act as to the form of the award implies that they could validly choose to waive their right to an award drawn up in writing. This could, however, be construed as tantamount to a waiver of the parties' right to challenge the award, and some authors have expressed the view that such a waiver would only be valid if the conditions in article 192 PIL Act were respected (ie neither party is domiciled or has its habitual residence in Switzerland and their agreement expressly excludes in writing all setting aside proceedings).[142] Other commentators disagree on the ground that the

---

133 RS 0.274.132.

134 According to art 188 PIL Act: 'unless the parties have agreed otherwise, the arbitral tribunal may make partial awards'.

135 Art 186(3) PIL Act states: 'The arbitral tribunal shall, in general, decide on its jurisdiction by a preliminary decision'.

136 Berger and Kellerhals (n 34) 382, No 1332.

137 Art 189(1) PIL Act.

138 Art 189(2) PIL Act.

139 Decision of the Swiss Federal Tribunal of 12 November 1991, ref 4P_61/1991, cons 1b/bb, published in (1992) 2 ASA Bulletin 264; free translation.

140 Decision of the Swiss Federal Tribunal of 12 November (n 139).

141 Decision of the Swiss Federal Tribunal of 10 November 2005, ref 4P_154/2005, cons 6.2.

142 A Heini, '*ad* Article 189', in D Girsberger et al (eds), *Zürcher Kommentar zum IPRG: Kommentar zum Bundesgesetz über das Internationale Privatrecht (IPRG) vom 18. Dezember 1987* (Schulthess, 2004) 2059, No 15.

autonomy of the parties as specifically set out in article 189(1) PIL Act should prevail.[143] In addition, for the parties to waive the requirement of an award in writing means that they would effectively also waive their right to an enforceable award in the event the award is not voluntarily complied with.

In the absence of an agreement between the parties, the award must be rendered in writing, reasoned, dated, and signed.[144] The Federal Tribunal has ruled, regarding the second requirement, that the absence of reasons in an award does not per se amount to a breach of the parties' right to be heard and does not therefore constitute a ground for the setting aside of the award.[145] The right to be heard implies, however, a minimum obligation upon the arbitral tribunal to examine and address all relevant issues.[146] **17.72**

The date of the award is not decisive in determining the deadline by which the award must be challenged. The deadline starts running from the day after the award has been received by the parties or their counsel.[147] **17.73**

Article 189(2) PIL Act specifies that the signature of the chairman alone is sufficient. **17.74**

17.4.3 Notification of award

The way in which an award is to be communicated may be agreed upon by the parties or determined by the arbitral tribunal. The PIL Act is silent on the subject. **17.75**

In practice, awards are notified in a way that may prove proper delivery, such as by registered mail or courier with acknowledgement of receipt. The date of notification triggers the time limit for the filing of an application to set aside the award. **17.76**

17.4.4 *Jura novit arbiter*

Arbitrators sitting in Switzerland are considered to know the applicable law in the same way as judges: *jura novit curia* or *jura novit arbiter*. The arbitral tribunal may accordingly apply the law *ex officio*;[148] it may freely assess the legal scope of the facts and apply legal rules other than those that have been invoked by the parties.[149] The Swiss Federal Tribunal has held that such freedom should not be construed as a blank cheque for arbitrators to base their decision on legal provisions or arguments that have never been raised or addressed by the parties or the relevance of which the parties could not have anticipated.[150] **17.77**

17.5 After the Award

17.5.1 Recognition and enforcement of arbitral awards

The award is enforceable as soon as it is communicated.[151] **17.78**

---

[143] Berger and Kellerhals (n 34) 387, fn 20 and 388, No 1361.
[144] Art 189(2) PIL Act.
[145] ATF 130 III 125, cons 2.2.
[146] ATF 133 III 235, cons 5.2.
[147] Art 44 Federal Act on the Swiss Federal Tribunal.
[148] ATF 120 II 172, cons 3a; decision of the Swiss Federal Tribunal of 7 January 2011, ref 4A_440/2010, cons 3.1.
[149] Decision of the Swiss Federal Tribunal of 19 February 2007, ref 4P_168/2006, cons 7.1.
[150] See paras 17.46–17.48; see also ATF 130 III 35, cons 6.
[151] Art 190(1) PIL Act.

17.79 Pursuant to article 190(1), the PIL Act states that the award is 'final' from the time it is communicated, which means it has *res judicata* effect and is immediately enforceable. There is no need in Switzerland, therefore, for an *exequatur* decision prior to enforcement, as may be the case in other jurisdictions. From the point of view of Swiss law, the award is binding in the sense of Article V(1)(e) of the New York Convention from the moment it is issued and communicated, regardless of the deadline within which setting aside proceedings may be raised.[152] Consequently, an award issued in an arbitration with its seat in Switzerland may be immediately enforced in Switzerland and in the countries party to the New York Convention, unless an application to set it aside has been filed and an order suspending enforcement has been issued, which is relatively uncommon.

Enforcement of monetary awards

17.80 Monetary awards issued under the PIL Act are enforced pursuant to the applicable provisions of the Debt Collection and Bankruptcy Act (DCBA).[153] When the parties have waived their right to challenge the award pursuant to article 192(1) PIL Act and enforcement is sought in Switzerland,[154] article 192(2) PIL Act provides that the New York Convention 'shall apply by analogy'.

17.81 The enforcement of foreign awards is also carried out through debt collection proceedings. Proceedings usually start by way of a preliminary attachment application to obtain an order freezing the debtors' assets.[155] Attachment orders are issued in *ex parte* proceedings, followed by ordinary debt collection proceedings. The foreign award is recognized during the course of the attachment proceedings and addressed as a preliminary issue.[156] The creditor need only establish *prima facie* the existence of an enforceable award[157] and that the debtor holds assets in Switzerland. A more detailed examination of the conditions set out in Article V of the New York Convention, which applies to the enforcement of all foreign awards in Switzerland by virtue of article 194 PIL Act,[158] takes place during the proceedings that are usually triggered by the debtor's objection to the attachment order or its objection to a payment order served upon it by the creditor.[159]

Enforcement of non-monetary awards

17.82 If the foreign award concerns a non-monetary claim (eg the obligation to register real estate in the name of the successful party), the procedure for its recognition and enforcement is subject to the provisions of the CPC.[160]

---

[152] Art 191 PIL Act.

[153] RS 281.1.

[154] See paras 17.115–17.117.

[155] Arts 271(1) and (6) DCBA.

[156] Decision of the Swiss Federal Tribunal of 21 December 2012, ref 5A_355/2012 (ATF 139 III 135), cons 4.5.2.

[157] See n 156.

[158] According to art 194 PIL Act, entitled 'Foreign Arbitral Awards': 'recognition and enforcement of a foreign arbitral award is governed by the New York Convention of June 10, 1958 on the Recognition and Enforcement of Foreign Arbitral Awards'.

[159] Arts 271(1)(6), 278 and 74 DCBA. When a similar order is sought prior to the issuance of the award against a debtor which is not domiciled or established in Switzerland, the applicant must also demonstrate that there is a sufficient connection between the act or transaction out of which the claim against the debtor arises and Switzerland (article 271(1)(4) DCBA). This link, referred to as '*Binnenbeziehung*', is not considered as given, under current case law, when the link between the claim and Switzerland consists solely in the location of the debtor's assets in Switzerland (SJ 2013 I 361, cons 4.1.2).

[160] Berger and Kellerhals (n 34) 535, No 1864.

Pro-enforcement and arbitration-friendly case law

Swiss case law has long established a strong pro-arbitration and pro-enforcement policy and enforcement is rarely refused on the ground of Article V of the New York Convention.[161] This policy is evidenced by three main characteristics: **17.83**

(1) Swiss courts generally consider that the list of grounds set out in article V of the Convention for denying recognition and enforcement is exhaustive and cannot be extended;
(2) they interpret these grounds narrowly;
(3) they do not hesitate to do away with the literal meaning of article V to favour a liberal interpretation and application of the Convention in support of international arbitration.[162]

The Federal Tribunal has further held that the mere fact that an action to set aside an arbitral award is pending in the country where the award was rendered does not affect its binding character, and therefore cannot prevent enforcement under Article V(1)(e) of the New York Convention.[163] It further held that the fact that enforcement of the award may be suspended in the country where an action to set it aside has been introduced may only constitute a ground for denying enforcement in Switzerland pursuant to Article V(1)(e) of the Convention when suspension results from a judiciary decision and not when suspension automatically arises under the procedural rules governing the setting aside proceedings.[164] **17.84**

17.5.2 Setting aside an award

Awards issued by an arbitral tribunal with its seat in Switzerland may only be challenged on restricted grounds.[165] Applications must be filed directly with Switzerland's highest court, the Federal Tribunal.[166] They are generally handled quickly and are unlikely to succeed. Indeed, during the period from the entry into force of the PIL Act in 1989 up until 2009, only 6.5 per cent of setting-aside applications were successful;[167] the duration of the proceedings generally averaged between four and six months. **17.85**

A rather high number of the few awards that have been set aside are CAS awards. While these awards accounted for less than 15 per cent of all applications for setting aside awards filed up until 2006, their number has increased strikingly to approximately 55 per cent of total applications in recent years, which may explain the relatively high number of CAS decisions that have been set aside when compared with the extremely low percentage of set aside awards in commercial cases.[168] **17.86**

---

[161] E Geisinger, 'Implementing the New York Convention in Switzerland' (2008) 6 J Intl Arb 691.
[162] Geisinger (n 161) 695.
[163] ATF 135 III 136, cons 2.2.
[164] ATF 135 III 136, cons 3.
[165] Arts 190(2) and (3) PIL Act.
[166] Art 191 PIL Act.
[167] F Dasser, 'International Arbitration and setting aside proceedings in Switzerland—an updated statistical analysis' (2010) 1 ASA Bulletin 82, 85; for a review of the criticism voiced in some circles against the Federal Tribunal's restrictive case law on the subject, see para 17.12.
[168] C Jermini and N Bernardo, 'Suspensive Effect of Challenges Against International Arbitral Awards in Switzerland: A Trend Towards More Frequent Grants?' in C Müller and A Rigozzi (eds), *New Developments in International Commercial Arbitration 2011* (Schulthess, 2011) 79, 94.

Decisions subject to challenge

17.87 Four types of decisions rendered by an arbitral tribunal may be challenged under article 190 PIL Act:

(1) final awards (*sentences finales, Endentscheide*) that accept, deny or dismiss claims in full or in part;
(2) partial awards (*sentences partielles, Teilentscheide*) in the meaning of article 188 PIL Act, which rule on certain aspects of the claims definitely, without bringing the proceedings to a close;
(3) preliminary, interim, or interlocutory awards (*sentences préjudicielles ou incidentes, vor- oder Zwischenentscheide*) that dispose of preliminary questions of a procedural or substantive nature as a step towards the final award, but do not bring the proceedings to an end, such as decisions on liability, jurisdiction, time-bar, or *res judicata*.[169] Pursuant to article 190(3) PIL Act, the only such decisions that may be immediately challenged are those relating to the appointment of a sole arbitrator, the composition of the arbitral tribunal, or jurisdiction,[170] with other decisions capable of being challenged only with the final award; and
(4) corrective[171] or additional[172] awards which, according to case law, form integral parts of the initial awards to which they relate.

17.88 Only decisions that dispose of a claim are binding on the arbitral tribunal and may have *res judicata* effect. Procedural orders or decisions that do not definitively dispose of a claim are not binding upon the arbitrators, who can review or amend them during the course of the proceedings. These types of decisions are not subject to challenge.[173] When determining whether a challenge is admissible, the decisive factor for the Federal Tribunal is the content of the challenged decision, rather than its title.[174]

Grounds for challenge

17.89 Article 190(2) PIL Act sets out the five limited grounds pursuant to which an award may be set aside, namely: (a) irregular appointment of a sole arbitrator or irregular composition of an arbitral tribunal; (b) an incorrect decision on jurisdiction; (c) a decision that goes beyond the parties' claims (*ultra petita*) or which fails to answer those claims (*infra petita*); (d) violation of equal treatment or of the parties' right to be heard; and (e) incompatibility with public policy.

17.90 **Incorrect appointment of a sole arbitrator or irregular composition of the arbitral tribunal** Article 190(2)(a) PIL Act aims at ensuring the parties' right to fair adversarial proceedings before impartial and independent arbitrators. This right derives from article 30(1) of the Swiss Federal Constitution and Article 6 ECHR.[175] The Federal Tribunal will not, therefore, merely verify whether the constitution of the arbitral tribunal complies with the parties' agreement or the applicable arbitration rules but whether, under the circumstances, a party's right to an independent and unbiased arbitral tribunal has been violated.[176]

---

[169] ATF 130 III 76, cons 3.1; ATF 136 III 597, cons 4.1.
[170] Art 190(2)(a) and (b) PIL Act.
[171] ATF 131 III 164, cons 1.2.
[172] ATF 137 III 85, cons 1.2.
[173] ATF 136 III 200, cons 2.3.1.
[174] ATF 136 III 200, cons 2.3.3.
[175] ATF 129 III 445, cons 3.3.3.
[176] ATF 136 III 605, cons 3; see also decision of the Swiss Federal Tribunal of 20 March 2008, ref 4A_506/2007, cons 3.1.1.

In addition, the Federal Tribunal has held that when a party has challenged the independence or impartiality of an arbitrator before the competent court at the seat, pursuant to article 180(1)(c) PIL Act,[177] it is precluded from later challenging the final award on the same grounds.[178] **17.91**

As already discussed, interim or preliminary decisions, such as those addressed in article 190(2)(a) PIL Act, must be challenged immediately after they are issued,[179] failing which the parties are considered to have forfeited their right to challenge the final award on these grounds. **17.92**

Incorrect decision on jurisdiction An incorrect decision on jurisdiction may be the result of the incorrect interpretation of the *ratione materiae* or *ratione personae* scope of the arbitration agreement or of the parties' common intent in relation to the agreement,[180] a refusal to suspend proceedings in case of *lis pendens*,[181] or the incorrect disregard of the applicable contractual mechanism pursuant to which arbitration may be initiated, for instance when the parties have agreed to engage in mediation as a necessary step prior to arbitration.[182] **17.93**

Decisions on jurisdiction may be (a) final awards pursuant to which the arbitral tribunal declines jurisdiction, or (b) interim awards pursuant to which the arbitral tribunal affirms jurisdiction. Both types of award may be set aside pursuant to article 190(3) PIL Act, and the parties' right to raise this ground against the final award is deemed to have been waived if no application to set aside is filed immediately against these decisions. When assessing whether an arbitral tribunal has correctly affirmed or declined jurisdiction, the Federal Tribunal freely reviews the arbitrators' decision, including the preliminary issues they might have to consider to establish or deny jurisdiction.[183] **17.94**

Challenges based on article 190(2)(b) PIL Act have the highest rate of success (about 10 per cent), probably because of the broad scope of review of the legal issues related to jurisdiction, which does not exist for the other grounds.[184] **17.95**

***Ultra* or *infra petita* awards** An award may be set aside if the arbitral tribunal grants more than the relief sought by the parties (*ultra petita*) or fails to rule on a claim put to it (*infra petita).* Article 190(2)(c) PIL Act is one of the least-often raised grounds for challenging an award.[185] **17.96**

The prohibition against the arbitral tribunal deciding *ultra petita* is intended to protect the parties from the risk of an award being decided on an unexpected point that has not been addressed.[186] The arbitrators must rule on the parties' claims as they are expressed in their **17.97**

[177] See paras 17.57–17.62.
[178] ATF 138 III 270, cons 2.2.2.
[179] Art 190(3) PIL Act.
[180] Decision of the Swiss Federal Tribunal of 20 September 2011, ref 4A_103/2011, cons 3.1.1 and 3.1.2.
[181] Decision of the Swiss Federal Tribunal of 20 January 2010, ref 4A_548/2009, cons 2.2.
[182] Decision of the Swiss Federal Tribunal of 16 May 2011, ref 4A_46/2011, cons 3.
[183] Decision of the Swiss Federal Tribunal of 20 January 2010 (n 182), cons 3.1; decision of the the Swiss Federal Tribunal of 20 September 2011, ref 4A_103/2011, cons 3.1.1.
[184] Dasser (n 167) 88.
[185] Dasser (n 167) 87.
[186] Decision of the Swiss Federal Tribunal of 10 November 2005, ref 4P_154/2005, cons 5.

respective prayers for relief. Whenever the dispositive section of an award states that 'all other claims and counterclaims are dismissed', the award cannot be challenged pursuant to article 190(2)(c) PIL Act for being *infra petita*.[187]

17.98 **Violation of equal treatment or of a party's right to be heard** The fourth ground for setting aside an award provided by article 190(2)(d) PIL Act is the violation of equal treatment or of a party's right to be heard by the arbitral tribunal. Along with the 'incompatibility with public policy' ground of article 190(2)(e) PIL Act, this is the most often invoked ground to apply for the setting aside of awards.[188] As explained in paragraphs 17.42–17.56, the right to be heard guarantees each party the right to express itself on all relevant facts, to put forward its legal arguments, to request the taking of pertinent and material evidence, and to participate in evidence proceedings and evidentiary hearings. It does not include the right to present oral pleadings.[189] According to Swiss case law, the right to adduce evidence is not unlimited, and the arbitral tribunal is free to refuse evidence that is not relevant and topical to the parties' case or which is submitted after a deadline set by the tribunal.[190]

17.99 **Incompatibility with public policy** The fifth and last setting-aside ground that may be raised pursuant to article 190(2)(e) PIL Act is violation of public policy. According to this provision, public policy includes both procedural and substantive public policy.[191]

17.100 Procedural public policy guarantees the parties the right to an independent decision on their respective prayers for relief on the basis of the established facts. An award is incompatible with procedural public policy when fundamental and generally acknowledged principles of justice are violated so that the award appears absolutely incompatible with the basic values of due process and the rule of law as those are perceived in Switzerland.[192] Not all breaches of procedural rules may constitute a breach of procedural public policy. Only the violation of essential due process rules guaranteeing the fairness of proceedings may be invoked pursuant to article 190(2)(e) PIL Act.[193] In that sense, procedural public policy is a subsidiary ground for setting aside an award. It can only be raised if no other ground may be invoked under article 190(2) PIL Act.[194]

17.101 The Federal Tribunal held in a 2006 landmark decision that the concept of substantive public policy referred to in article 190(2)(e) PIL Act corresponds to that of 'international public policy', which is generally similar to the Swiss concept of public policy and includes fundamental and widely recognized values that constitute the basis of any legal system, according to the conceptions prevailing in Switzerland.[195] These principles include, in particular, *pacta sunt servanda*; the principle of good faith and its corollary, the prohibition of

[187] Decision of the Swiss Federal Tribunal of 7 March 2012, ref 4A_652/2011, cons 3.2.
[188] Dasser (n 167) 87.
[189] ATF 117 II 346, cons 1b.
[190] ATF 119 II 386, cons 1; decision of the Swiss Federal Tribunal of 18 October 2011, ref 4A_214/2011, cons 5.
[191] ATF 126 III 249, cons 3a.
[192] ATF 132 III 389, cons 2.2.1.
[193] ATF 129 III 445, cons 4.2.1; decision of the Swiss Federal Tribunal of 7 January 2011, ref 4A_440/2010, cons 5.1.1.
[194] ATF 138 III 270, cons 2.3; decision of the Swiss Federal Tribunal of 17 March 2011, ref 4A_600/2010, cons 4.3.
[195] ATF 132 III 389, cons 2.2.2.

abuse of right; the prohibition of spoliation and of expropriation without fair compensation; the protection of individuals who do not have legal capacity to act; the prohibition of bribery and corrupt practices; the prohibition of discriminatory measures; and the protection of individual rights.[196] It would be dangerous, observed the Federal Tribunal, to attempt to draw up an exhaustive list of all fundamental principles falling within the ambit of the definition of substantive public policy because of its ambivalent nature.[197] By way of example, it further observed that an award contrary to human dignity would be considered to be incompatible with substantive public policy.[198] On the other hand, the fact that the reasons given for an award are intrinsically incoherent does not mean that the award is contrary to public policy, as long as its dispositive section itself does not give rise to a violation of public policy.[199] In other words, it is the result of the decision that matters in such a case, not the supporting reasons.

Given this jurisprudence, very few awards have been set aside on procedural public policy grounds and even fewer for violation of substantive public policy. The first time an award was ever set aside on the latter ground was in 2012, some 23 years after the PIL Act came into force.[200] In the case in point, involving a CAS award, a Brazilian soccer player was unable to pay damages in excess of €12 million (pursuant to an earlier award upheld by the Federal Tribunal)[201] for the premature termination of his contract with a Ukrainian club. In disciplinary proceedings, the Federation of International Football Associations (FIFA) ordered the player, and the Spanish soccer club to which he had moved, to make payment within 90 days or face a worldwide and unlimited ban from the sport. The player and the Spanish team filed an appeal with CAS, which issued an award upholding the FIFA decision. The player then challenged the CAS decision before the Federal Tribunal, arguing that the FIFA disciplinary sanctions in this particular case were incompatible with substantive public policy within the meaning of article 190(2)(e) PIL Act. **17.102**

The Federal Tribunal held that the protection against excessive restrictions on an individual's personal freedom (as protected in Swiss law under article 27(2) of the Swiss Civil Code) is a fundamental and generally recognized value that forms the foundation of any legal order.[202] The fact that the ban imposed on the player was worldwide and unlimited in time constituted a serious violation of his individual personal rights to continue to earn a living as well as an excessive restriction on his personal freedom. The Tribunal noted that the ban, rather than encouraging the enforcement of the compensation due to the first club, made it impossible for this professional football player to make enough money to ever pay it. Weighing FIFA's interest against the player's personal freedom, the Federal Tribunal concluded that the CAS decision was incompatible with public policy and set the award aside.[203] **17.103**

---

[196] ATF 132 III 389, cons 2.2.1; decision of the Swiss Federal Tribunal of 18 June 2012, ref 4A_488/2011, cons 6.1; decision of the Swiss Federal Tribunal of 2 May 2012, ref 4A_16/2012, cons 4.1.

[197] Decision of the Swiss Federal Tribunal of 10 June 2010, ref 4A_458/2009, cons 4.1.

[198] See n 197.

[199] Decision of the Swiss Federal Tribunal of 15 February 2010, ref 4A_464/2009, cons 5.1; decision of the Swiss Federal Tribunal of 3 January 2011, ref 4A_386/2010, cons 8.3.

[200] ATF 138 III 322.

[201] Decision of the Swiss Federal Tribunal of 2 June 2010, ref 4A_320/2009.

[202] ATF 138 III 322, cons 4.3.1.

[203] ATF 138 III 322, cons 4.3.2–4.3.5.

Time limit for filing a setting-aside application

17.104 The time limit for filing an application to set aside an award is 30 days from the date the notified award is received by the parties or their counsel.[204] The deadline starts running the day following receipt of the award and cannot be extended.[205]

17.105 The application for setting aside the award must be submitted in one of the official Swiss languages and set out the applicant's prayer for relief (ie that the award be set aside),[206] a summary of the relevant facts, and the evidence supporting the application. It must be signed and the challenged award attached to it, together with a copy of the power of attorney granted to the applicant's representative in the proceedings. Awards issued in English do not need to be translated.[207]

17.106 The appellant must specify which of the grounds set out in article 190(2) PIL Act is relevant to the case and demonstrate in detail to what extent the challenged award violates the principles invoked.[208] The Federal Tribunal considers only those grounds raised by the parties and does not substitute its own grounds for those submitted. Failure to comply strictly with the requirements regarding the specific grounds for the application may well lead to dismissal.

17.107 Two sets of briefs are usually filed, and the proceedings are usually carried out entirely in writing. The Federal Tribunal hands down its decision within four to six months, either confirming or setting aside the challenged award. If it sets the award aside, the dispositive section declares that the award is set aside and the case remitted back to the arbitral tribunal for it to issue a new award. The arbitral tribunal may reopen proceedings only relating to those grounds which led to the setting aside of the first award.

Suspensive effect

17.108 As indicated, an application to set aside an arbitral award cannot per se suspend enforcement,[209] unless the Federal Tribunal decides otherwise upon a specific application by the applicant or on its own initiative.[210]

17.109 A stay of enforcement can only be issued as a provisional measure[211] and on condition that (a) the application is *prima facie* most likely to succeed; (b) the applicant can demonstrate that it would suffer irreparable harm in its 'legitimate interests' if the award were to be enforced immediately; and (c) the interests of the party applying for the suspension of enforcement prevail over those of the party opposing the request.[212]

---

[204] Art 100(1) FT Act.

[205] Arts 44 and 47(1) FT Act; see, para 17.73.

[206] Decision of the Swiss Federal Tribunal of 13 February 2012, ref 4A_428/2011, cons 1.4. There is no appeal *stricto sensu* against arbitral awards in Swiss law because the Federal Tribunal does not re-examine the dispute put to the arbitrators.

[207] ATF 138 III 520, cons 5.5; see also decision of the Swiss Federal Tribunal of 23 September 2008, ref 4A_176/2008, cons 1.2; decision of the Swiss Federal Tribunal of 7 March 2003, ref 4P.250/2002, cons 1.3.

[208] Arts 42(2) and 77(3) FT Act; ATF 128 III 50, cons 1c.

[209] See para 17.79.

[210] Art 103(3) FT Act.

[211] Art 104 FT Act.

[212] E Geisinger and A Mazuranic, 'Challenge and Revision of the Award' in E Geisinger and N Voser (eds), *International Arbitration in Switzerland, A Handbook for Practitioners* (2nd edn, Kluwer Law International, 2013) 234–5, and cited commentators.

Costs and security for costs

The court and parties' costs are fixed by reference to statutory tariffs based on the total amount in dispute and the circumstances of the case.[213] **17.110**

The court costs must be advanced by the appellant.[214] The maximum amount is CHF100,000, which can be doubled depending on the scope and complexity of the case, the conduct of the proceedings, and the financial situation of the parties.[215] The unsuccessful appellant must bear the court costs,[216] as finally fixed in the judgment, which generally correspond to the total advance made.[217] Unless specific circumstances call for a different decision, the Federal Tribunal tends to fix the amount of the advance on costs at the maximum possible (CHF200,000) when the value at stake is higher than CHF40 to 50 million.[218] **17.111**

The determination of the costs to be paid by the unsuccessful party to the other party is also within the discretion of the Federal Tribunal. The Federal Tribunal may take into account the importance and complexity of the case and the level of attorney's fees. There are no costs submissions by the parties, and attorney's fees are not assessed based on actual time spent but, rather, pursuant to a specific schedule for the determination of the legal costs in proceedings before the Federal Tribunal.[219] The final amount is eventually fixed in the judgment and must be paid by the unsuccessful party to the opposing party.[220] **17.112**

The party opposing the application may apply for an order requesting the applicant to provide security for costs. The Federal Tribunal may grant the order if the applicant is insolvent or is domiciled in a country with which there is no treaty or convention to which Switzerland is a party, facilitating the enforcement of judicial decisions on costs.[221] **17.113**

There seems to be a trend in recent cases for the Federal Tribunal to fix party costs at levels so high that they can have no relation to the expenses that may possibly be incurred by the party opposing the setting aside application or to the work carried out by its counsel.[222] This trend, coupled with the extremely narrow interpretation given by the Federal Tribunal in establishing the grounds listed in article 190(2) PIL Act, has given rise to concern among practitioners that the party costs awarded in some cases are punitive rather than reflective of the actual expenses and legal costs likely to have been incurred by the party resisting the application. This trend appears to go beyond the scope of the Federal Tribunal's discretion to fix parties' costs, and is certainly contrary to the spirit and letter of the law. Unless an application to set aside an award is frivolous, which may be specifically sanctioned, a party **17.114**

---

213 Arts 62–68 FT Act; see the Federal Regulation on court costs in proceedings before the Federal Tribunal (RS 173.110.210.1) and the Federal Regulation on parties' costs in proceedings before the Federal Tribunal (RS 173.110.210.3).

214 Art 62(1) FT Act.

215 Art 65(5) FT Act.

216 Art 66(1) FT Act.

217 Dasser (n 167) 92–3. Dasser has estimated, based on cases involving a dispute with claims between CHF1,000,000 and CHF2,000,000 decided between 2000 and 2009, that the total costs averaged 2.5% of the value at stake.

218 Arts 65(3)(b) and (5) FT Act. See Geisinger and Mazuranic (n 212) 237.

219 RS 173.110.210.3.

220 Art 68(2) FT Act.

221 Art 62(2) FT Act; Geisinger and Mazuranic (n 212) 237–8.

222 For a recent example of this trend, see decision of the Swiss Federal Tribunal of 10 January 2013, ref 4A_146/2012, cons 6.

to an international arbitration with its seat in Switzerland should be entitled to exercise the limited right that it enjoys under article 190(2) PIL Act as construed by the Federal Tribunal to challenge an award without being penalized for doing so.

17.5.3 Waiver of the right to challenge an award

17.115 Pursuant to article 192(1) PIL Act, the parties may waive their right to challenge an award on two cumulative conditions: (a) none of the parties is domiciled or has its habitual residence or place of business in Switzerland, and (b) the waiver is express and in writing. The mere reference to arbitration rules providing that the award is final and that the parties undertake to enforce it is not sufficient to constitute a valid waiver.[223] The waiver may be general or only relate to certain of the grounds for setting aside an award listed in article 190(2) PIL Act.[224]

17.116 In a 2012 decision, the Federal Tribunal held that Article 6 ECHR does not prevent an individual from waiving fundamental procedural rights on condition that the agreement to waive such rights is freely entered into, is not equivocal, and does not violate fundamental public interests.[225] Article 192(1) PIL Act meets all these requirements because it requires an express waiver agreement. The Federal Tribunal has also held that a waiver inserted in the rules of a sport association or federation cannot be held as valid for athletes because they have no choice but to agree to these rules in order to be allowed to compete.[226] As already discussed, the same type of concern has been raised regarding the advance waiver of interim measures before state courts contained in article R37(3) of the CAS Code.[227]

17.117 Article 192(2) PIL Act provides that the New York Convention applies by analogy to the enforcement in Switzerland of an award issued in a case in which a valid waiver was agreed.

17.5.4 Revision

17.118 Chapter 12 of the PIL Act does not address revision. The Federal Tribunal held in a 1992 landmark case that this silence constituted a gap (*lacuna*) that had to be filled by the judiciary.[228] It further held, in line with the legislator's approach in Chapter 12 of the PIL Act, that it had jurisdiction over applications for revision.[229]

17.119 Pursuant to article 123 FT Act,[230] an application for the revision of an award may be successful only when either of two grounds is established: (a) subsequent criminal proceedings have revealed that the award had been affected by misdemeanour or other criminal offences to the detriment of the party applying for revision;[231] or (b) new material facts or decisive evidence

---

[223] ATF 131 III 173, cons 4.2.1 and cited references; decision of the Swiss Federal Tribunal of 15 February 2010, ref 4A_464/2009, cons 3.1.1.

[224] ATF 131 III 173, cons 4.2.3.1. For a valid waiver, see also decision of the Swiss Federal Tribunal of 1 March 2011, ref 4A_514/2010, cons 4.1.2; decision of the Swiss Federal Tribunal of 21 March 2011, ref 4A_486/2010, cons 2.2.

[225] Decision of the Swiss Federal Tribunal of 4 January 2012, ref 4A_238/2011, cons 3.2.

[226] ATF 133 III 235, cons 4.3.2.2; Brunner (n 26).

[227] See para 17.33; Rigozzi and Robert-Tissot (n 63) 5ff.

[228] ATF 118 II 199, cons 2.

[229] ATF 118 II 199, cons 3.

[230] This provision corresponds to the former art 137 of the Federal Act on Judiciary Organization, which was applicable in 1992 and was cited in ATF 118 II 199, cons 4.

[231] Art 123(1) FT Act.

have been subsequently discovered which the requesting party was unable to invoke during the arbitration and which did not arise after the award was issued.[232]

The two grounds are interpreted narrowly, and the applicant must demonstrate not only their existence, but also how the criminal act or the newly found material facts would have affected the outcome of the award.[233] An application for revision will not be admissible if it is raised later than 90 days from the discovery of the relevant ground.[234] **17.120**

Only two cases of revision have been successful. One was based on a criminal offence established in foreign criminal proceedings ten years after the award was issued,[235] and the other on new material facts (false testimony, which was raised as a ground for revision before the related criminal investigations were over).[236] In both cases, the award was annulled and the case referred back to the arbitrators. **17.121**

17.6 Conclusion

Chapter 12 of the PIL Act establishes a concise and efficient legal regime that addresses all key aspects of the arbitral process. The Swiss Federal Tribunal is among the most experienced courts in the world in terms of deciding arbitration-related questions. The combination of Chapter 12 PIL Act, experienced courts and practitioners, as well as Switzerland's historical reputation as a major centre for international arbitration, renders Switzerland one of the most sought after and arbitration-friendly venues in the world. **17.122**

Switzerland's neutrality, central location in Europe, multi-lingual and multi-cultural environment, established infrastructure, experienced bar with a long tradition of comparative law, prominent scholars who contribute to the development of international arbitration theory and practice, and the dynamic Swiss arbitration association (ASA) have all contributed to the success of international arbitration seated in Switzerland. As a tribute to this contribution, suffice it to cite Bernard Hanotiau, a Belgian law professor and one of the world's most prominent arbitrators. When asked by a television journalist what could effectively be done for Singapore to be an even more successful arbitration venue, he replied: **17.123**

> And my final comment to the journalist—which I reiterated a few hours later to the Minister of Justice who had invited a few arbitrators to discuss the same issue—was that the best example I could give was Switzerland. And I would add that one of the main engines behind Switzerland's success story is the dynamic and innovative Swiss Arbitration Association which, year after year, under the guidance of very dynamic presidents, has been able to profile itself as the most active, creative, imaginative, arbitration association, a breeding ground for new ideas and new talents.[237]

---

[232] Art 123(2)(a) FT Act.

[233] For an example where those conditions were met, see decision of the Swiss Federal Tribunal of 29 August 2006, ref 4P.102/2006.

[234] Art 124(1)(d) FT Act. See decision of the Swiss Federal Tribunal of 22 August 2011, ref 4A_222/2011, cons 2.

[235] Decision of the Swiss Federal Tribunal of 6 October 2009, ref 4A_596/2008, cons 4.

[236] Decision of the Swiss Federal Tribunal of 29 August 2006, ref 4P.102/2006, cons 2–4.

[237] B Hanotiau, '*Laudatio* of Franz Schwarz, Recipient of the Inaugural ASA Prize for Advocacy in International Commercial Arbitration' in E Geisinger and G Tattevin (eds), *Advocacy in International Commercial Arbitration*, ASA Special Series No 36, 23–4.

17.124 Given this thriving environment and its combined tradition and history of arbitration, Switzerland will continue to foster and contribute to the development of international arbitration as the preferred means of dispute resolution in commercial matters. It will do so with a critical eye. This should ensure that not only Geneva and Zurich, but also Lausanne and Lugano, firmly remain in the league of the most favoured international arbitration venues.

18

SYDNEY

Doug Jones AO

18.1 Background

18.1.1 Domestic arbitration in Sydney

Australia has a long history of arbitration that pre-dates Western civilization. There is evidence to suggest that when differences arose between members of a community, Aboriginal peoples implemented dispute resolution systems that closely resembled the practice of arbitration, with Aboriginal elders acting as arbitrators.[1] Upon English settlement and colonization, Australia, like most Commonwealth states, derived many of its initial laws from those enacted in England, including the law relating to arbitration. These laws have, however, changed dramatically over the centuries as commercial disputes have become more complicated and the needs of industry have evolved. In modern times, Australia has enjoyed a steady growth in the use of arbitration as a means of successful dispute resolution. Evidence of this is found in the number of court-annexed arbitrations (matters referred to arbitration by the court with permission from the parties) and mandatory arbitrations prescribed for particular disputes. Discussions with commercial parties **18.01**

[1] Australian Law Reform Commission, 'Traditional Aboriginal Society and Its Law' in H Astor and C Chinkin, *Dispute Resolution in Australia* (2nd edn, LexisNexis Butterworths, 2002) 11.

in recent years indicate that arbitration is increasingly becoming the preferred means of dispute resolution.[2]

18.02 The current form of arbitration used in Australia has its roots in the laws that were brought by the English upon settlement in Sydney in 1788. Arbitration quickly became one of the most commonly used methods of dispute resolution among the newly formed colonies of Australia as a result of its centuries-long success in England. The arbitration law that English settlers brought with them stemmed from the English Act for Determining Differences by Arbitration 1698,[3] which is commonly believed to be the first ever arbitration act and the only source of formalized arbitration at the time. Some 135 years later, the Civil Procedure Act 1833 (UK) was enacted in England, which brought changes to the 1698 Act in the extent of court involvement in arbitration. Later, the Common Law Procedure Act 1854 (UK) and Arbitration Act 1889 (UK) strongly influenced the development of arbitration legislation in Australia.

18.03 Sydney, the capital of New South Wales, had inherited and applied England's arbitration legislation until the New South Wales Parliament enacted an arbitration statute of its own in 1867. As New South Wales is a state of Australia, its parliament has the exclusive power to legislate with respect to domestic arbitration within its state jurisdiction. All Australian states and territories have exclusive power over their respective state or territory jurisdictions. The Federal Government (also known as the Commonwealth Government), however, has the power to legislate with respect to international arbitration. Thus, Australia's arbitration regime is bifurcated, with domestic arbitration a product of state and territory legislation, and international arbitration a product of Commonwealth legislation.

18.04 New South Wales' first arbitration statute, the Arbitration Act 1867 (NSW), was based primarily on the inherited English legislation, however, it included some provisions that limited the court's power in relation to awards and arbitral tribunals, and others that contributed to the rules of tendering evidence. The subsequent Arbitration Act 1892 (NSW) was substantially the same as England's Arbitration Act 1889 (UK), however, it was repealed after only a short time and replaced by the Arbitration Act 1902 (NSW), which also applied in the Australian Capital Territory. This newer 1902 Act was also similar in substance to England's 1889 Act, however, it introduced amendments to the ways in which evidence could be taken and the available means to enforce an arbitral award.

18.05 At this point, each state and territory in Australia (including New South Wales) had moved independently of each other in terms of arbitration and had its own unique processes and procedures, and the practice of arbitration varied significantly from jurisdiction to jurisdiction. For arbitration to develop as an option for successful dispute resolution in Australia, there was a need for unification.

18.06 There was much debate as to possible changes in Australian arbitration law in the 1960s and 1970s. In 1974, the Standing Committee of Attorneys-General (the SCAG Committee), a federal government council comprising the Attorneys-General of Australia and its states and territories, reviewed the existing local arbitration legislation with a view to unifying

[2] Queen Mary University of London and White & Case LLP, '2010 International Arbitration Survey: Choices in International Arbitration' (2010).

[3] 9 & 10 Wm 3, c 15.

it. Following similar discussions with the arbitration community in New South Wales, in 1976 the New South Wales Law Reform Commission issued a report on the existing arbitration legislation and made recommendations for legislative reform aimed at unification. The report recommended that a new arbitration act be enacted in New South Wales and attached to its final version the draft Arbitration Bill 1976 (NSW).

This bill formed the basis for the unification of arbitration legislation across Australian jurisdictions, and after several years of negotiation and public consultation, between 1984 and 1990 all Australian states and territories introduced standardized domestic arbitration legislation (Uniform Acts). In New South Wales, the Uniform Act was known as the Commercial Arbitration Act 1984 (NSW). **18.07**

The Uniform Acts ensured that the rules, procedures, and laws relevant to arbitration were applied consistently throughout Australia in all its state and territory jurisdictions. While the Uniform Acts were intended to minimize procedural formalities and afford parties greater autonomy in the dispute resolution process, it soon transpired that they suffered from certain practical problems, including the inclination of arbitrators to import court procedures into the arbitration process, and the scope of court intervention in the arbitration process, most notably in relation to the review of arbitral awards. **18.08**

As a result of the inefficiencies of the Uniform Acts and associated problems, in 2009 the New South Wales Supreme Court encouraged changes to the arbitration landscape in Australia, calling for the adoption of the United Nations Commission on International Trade Law (UNCITRAL) Model Law on International Commercial Arbitration 1985 with its 2006 amendments (Model Law). This proposed change had a two-fold purpose: to improve the quality of domestic arbitration in Australia by bringing it into step with international best practices and to position Australia as a competitive destination on the map of potential international commercial arbitration seats. Following a meeting of the SCAG Committee in 2009, the Commonwealth Attorney-General's Department made an announcement that a new domestic arbitration act would be drafted to this effect, based on the Model Law. **18.09**

The federal Commercial Arbitration Bill 2009 proposed that the Model Law be used as the basis for the new uniform commercial arbitration acts, with amendments as necessary and appropriate. While the Model Law was not initially intended by UNCITRAL for use in domestic arbitration, it was felt that its application would result in uniformity, encourage consistency, and streamline the arbitration process. Furthermore, the adoption of the Model Law was expected to help restore arbitration as the preferred form of binding non-curial dispute resolution on an international front in Australia. It was suggested that the familiarity with the Model Law that would be gained by Australian arbitrators and counsel as a result of practicing in a domestic setting would provide them the opportunity to compete more effectively for international arbitration work internationally and locally. **18.10**

Supporting this legislative reform were several of Australia's major arbitration bodies, including the Australian Commercial Dispute Centre (ACDC), the Institute of Arbitrators and Mediators Australia (IAMA), the Chartered Institute of Arbitrators (Australia) (CIArb) (Australia), the National Alternative Dispute Resolution Advisory Council (NADRAC), and Australia's premier international arbitration institution, the Australian Centre for International Commercial Arbitration (ACICA). These organizations played, and continue to play, a crucial role in assessing and promoting the need for reform in Australian arbitration **18.11** law, with many actually contributing to the legislative reform by making submissions to the SCAG Committee.

18.12 The SCAG Committee finalized the Commercial Arbitration Bill 2010 in April 2010. This Commonwealth Bill was intended to be enacted in each jurisdiction so as to repeal the old Uniform Acts and establish a new national law.

18.13 New South Wales was the first Australian jurisdiction to enact the new law, which it did with the passage of the Commercial Arbitration Act 2010 (NSW) in June 2010. This new Act entered into force in October 2010 and contained a number of significant reforms that aimed to overcome the problems that existed under the old Commercial Arbitration Act 1984 (NSW). Consistent with generally accepted principles of arbitration, specific areas of reform included the obligation of confidentiality in arbitral proceedings, the powers of an arbitral tribunal to order interim measures of protection, the procedural requirements for the conduct of domestic arbitrations and the grounds for challenging the appointment of an arbitrator or an arbitral award.

18.14 As of 26 February 2013, New South Wales, Victoria, South Australia, Tasmania, and the Northern Territory are the Australian jurisdictions in which the new Commercial Arbitration Act is in force, while the remaining jurisdictions of Western Australia, Queensland, and the Australian Capital Territory are expected to adopt it in due course.

18.1.2 International arbitration in Sydney

18.15 At the same time that changes were being made to domestic arbitration in the early 1970s, the federal legislature of Australia enacted the International Arbitration Act 1974 (Cth) (IAA), which continues to govern international arbitration in Australia. The IAA is a Commonwealth Act, as international arbitration in Australia is governed by federal law.

18.16 Upon its enactment, the IAA incorporated the 1958 New York Convention on the Recognition and Enforcement of Foreign Arbitral Awards (New York Convention) and the 1965 Washington Convention on the Settlement of Investment Disputes between States and Nationals of other States (ICSID Convention). In 1989, the IAA was amended to incorporate the Model Law (1985 edition) as a Schedule to the Act. By section 16 of the IAA, the Model Law has the force of law in Australia. The IAA also supplemented these instruments by including provisions relating to subpoenas, confidentiality, and the consolidation of proceedings.

18.17 The IAA underwent significant reform in July 2010, with the enactment of the International Arbitration Amendment Act 2010 (Cth) (Amendment Act). The most important amendments were the incorporation of the 2006 UNCITRAL amendments to the Model Law and the repeal of provisions that allowed parties to opt out of the Model Law.

18.18 These amendments ensured that Australian arbitration law remained in line with international best practice, and assisted in further advancing Australia as a centre, and attractive venue, for international arbitration. These legislative changes also sought to improve consistency and certainty in the application of Australian international arbitration law, especially by mitigating the confusion caused by parties opting out of the Model Law. Prior to the amendment, the Queensland Court of Appeal held, in the 2001 *Eisenwerk* case,[4]

[4] *Eisenwerk Hensel Bayreuth Dipl-Ing Burkhardt GmbH v Australian Granites Ltd* [2001] 1 Qd R 461.

that when parties selected the ICC Arbitration Rules in their arbitration agreement, they opted out of the Model Law and into the state-based commercial arbitration acts. Despite subsequent decisions distinguishing *Eisenwerk*, and consensus in the arbitration community that it had been wrongly decided, it remained good law in Australia until the 2010 amendments.

The Supreme Court of New South Wales has jurisdiction to deal with arbitration matters in relation to any arbitration that takes place in New South Wales, domestic or international.[5] The Supreme Court of New South Wales has, for several years, operated a Commercial Arbitration List in its Equity Division. This specialist list ensures that commercial arbitration matters are dealt with efficiently and fairly by a judge with commercial arbitration experience. **18.19**

Additionally, parties to international arbitrations seated in Sydney have the option of applying to the Federal Court of Australia in arbitration matters. The Federal Court is a superior court that has jurisdiction to deal with most civil disputes governed by federal law and matters arising under the Constitution. **18.20**

The Federal Court has had considerable involvement in the promotion and support of arbitration. It has encouraged the inclusion in contracts of 'pre-litigation protocols' regarding arbitration and various other forms of alternative dispute resolution. Further, the court has assigned an 'Arbitration Coordinating Judge' in each state and territory, who has general responsibility for the management of arbitration matters in their state under the IAA. The Federal Court and its justices often highlight the level of judicial support for arbitration in Australia.[6] **18.21**

18.1.3 Comparison of arbitration in Sydney with other regional/national venues

Sydney is often regarded as the commercial centre of Australia and is home to the majority of Australia's domestic and international arbitration bodies, including the ACICA, ACDC, CIArb (Australia), and IAMA. As a global business hub, it boasts many characteristics that make it an ideal venue for international dispute resolution, including a stable economy and political atmosphere, supportive legal structures, and an independent judiciary. Sydney also offers a host of first class accommodation and restaurant options. **18.22**

Sydney has existed as a competitive venue for international arbitrations for several years and has become more attractive to disputing parties following Australia's recent domestic and international arbitration legislation reform. Melbourne (in Australia's State of Victoria) is also a beneficiary of these reforms and offers similar services and resources, rendering it, too, an excellent seat for international arbitrations. **18.23**

The two most relevant regional arbitration venues are Singapore and Hong Kong. Singapore has incorporated the Model Law into its international arbitration legislation, which it did in **18.24**

---

[5] IAA 1974 (Cth), s 18; CAA 2010 (NSW), s 6.

[6] See egThe Honourable Chief Justice of The Federal Court of Australia Patrick Anthony Keane, 'Judicial support for arbitration in Australia', 'Opening Address', Financial Review International Dispute Resolution Conference, Sydney, 15 October 2010; The Honourable Justice of the Federal Court of Australia John Middleton, 'International Commercial Arbitration—the role of the Courts; the enforcement of arbitration awards and anti-arbitration injunctions', International Commercial Litigation and Dispute Resolution Conference, Sydney, 27–28 November 2009.

1994. Singapore, like Australia (and Sydney), maintains separate systems for international and domestic arbitration; Singapore's International Arbitration Act governs international arbitration, while its 2001 Arbitration Act governs domestic arbitration. The law applied to arbitration in Singapore differs substantially between international and domestic arbitrations as there is a greater emphasis on judicial supervision in domestic arbitration. This is not necessarily the case with arbitration in Sydney, despite the fact that the legislation governing Sydney's domestic arbitrations has supplemented the Model Law by allowing parties to 'opt-in' to further judicial review of arbitral awards.[7] Singapore's main international arbitration body, the Singapore International Arbitration Centre (SIAC), was established in 1991. Hong Kong, much like Australia, recently underwent a major review of its domestic arbitration framework. In 2007, the Hong Kong Department of Justice issued an Arbitration Bill proposing that the legislation governing domestic arbitrations in Hong Kong be based on the Model Law. This resulted in the enactment of Hong Kong's Arbitration Ordinance in November 2010, replacing the Arbitration Ordinance 1996 which had been based primarily on England's Arbitration Act 1996. Hong Kong's primary international arbitration organization, the Hong Kong International Arbitration Centre (HKIAC) was established in 1985 and performs similar functions to those of SIAC and ACICA.

18.25 Cost is an important factor in selecting the venue of an international arbitration, and Sydney's lower living costs[8] and extensive range of accommodation and facilities can deliver significant cost savings in comparison to Singapore and Hong Kong.

18.2 Commencing the Arbitration

18.2.1 Court assistance in the commencement of arbitration

18.26 As arbitration is a creature of agreement, the commencement of an arbitration is contingent on the existence of a binding and valid arbitration agreement between the parties, and an arbitrable subject matter.

18.27 As discussed earlier, the Commercial Arbitration Act 2010 (NSW) governs domestic arbitration in Sydney and incorporates the Model Law. Part 2 of the 2010 Act dictates the statutory requirements for an arbitration agreement between the parties. The formal requirements that an arbitration agreement must satisfy are set out in section 7 of the 2010 Act. This section is substantially the same as option I of article 7 of the Model Law (as amended in 2006), which is the provision that governs the definition of arbitration agreement in international arbitrations under the IAA.[9]

18.28 The main requirement is that an arbitration agreement must be in writing.[10] This requirement is satisfied if the agreement is recorded in any form, whether concluded orally, by conduct, or by other means.[11] Two provisions added as part of the 2006 amendments to the Model Law make clear that the writing requirement is satisfied when the arbitration

---

7 CAA 2010 (NSW), s 34A.

8 Mercer Worldwide Cost of Living Survey—City Ranking (June 2012).

9 IAA 1974 (Cth), s 16(2).

10 CAA 2010 (NSW), s 7(3); Model Law, Art 7(2) as reproduced in IAA 1974 (Cth), Sch 2.

11 CAA 2010 (NSW), s 7(4); Model Law, Art 7(3) as reproduced in IAA 1974 (Cth), Sch 2.

agreement is incorporated by reference or its existence is alleged by one party in a statement of claim and not denied by the other in its defence.[12]

The second requirement is that the parties undertake to submit to arbitration all, or any, differences that have arisen, or that may arise between them in respect of a defined legal relationship, whether contractual or not.[13] In this regard, parties should also be wary of the use of the permissive 'may' rather than the mandatory 'must' or 'shall' in their agreement, as an agreement that intends to send disputes to arbitration should not convey only an option to do so. Australian courts will nevertheless enforce arbitration agreements containing the word 'may' where a proper interpretation of the clause demonstrates the parties' intent that arbitration be mandatory.[14] **18.29**

The final requirement is that the subject matter of the dispute be capable of settlement by arbitration.[15] The starting point for analysing whether a dispute is arbitrable is the principle that 'any claim for relief of a kind proper for determination in a court'[16] is arbitrable, reflecting an increasingly liberal attitude to arbitrability. In an international arbitration context at least, the general approach is to treat most commercial matters as arbitrable. **18.30**

As a matter of principle, Australian courts have held that some commercial matters warrant the kind of close public scrutiny that only courts can provide.[17] Broadly speaking, those matters may include intellectual property, antitrust and competition disputes, securities transactions,[18] insolvency, taxation,[19] disputes under the Corporations Act,[20] as well as insurance,[21] workplace,[22] and domestic building disputes.[23] **18.31**

However, even in these situations, disputes arising from private contractual interaction between two commercial entities are more likely to be considered arbitrable[24] than those involving the interaction of the state with a commercial entity, where rights are more likely to be 'required to be determined exclusively by a judicial power'.[25] **18.32**

An arbitration agreement that does not satisfy these criteria may render the IAA and the 2010 Act inapplicable to the arbitration in question, without necessarily invalidating the arbitration agreement. Arbitrations that are beyond the scope of the relevant Act will be governed by common law (as opposed to statutory) principles. **18.33**

---

12 Model Law, Art 7(5), as reproduced in IAA 1974 (Cth), Sch 2.

13 CAA 2010 (NSW), s 7(1); IAA 1974 (Cth), s 3(1).

14 *PMT Partners Pty Ltd (in liquidation) v Australian National Parks and Wildlife Service* [1995] 184 CLR 301.

15 IAA 1974 (Cth), s 3(1).

16 *Flakt (Aust) Ltd v Wilkins and Davies Construction Co Ltd* [1979] 25 ALR 605.

17 *Siemens Ltd v Origin Energy Uranquinty Power Pty Ltd* [2011] 279 ALR 759; MJ Mustill and SC Boyd, *Commercial Arbitration* (2nd edn, Butterworths, 1989) 149.

18 *Comandate Marine Corp v Pan Australia Shipping Pty Ltd* [2006] 157 FCR 45, 97–8, concerning an international commercial arbitration governed by the Model Law; *Nicola v Ideal Image Development Corp Inc* [2009] 261 ALR 1.

19 *AED Oil v Puffin FPSO Ltd* [2009] VSC 534, para 45.

20 *A Best Floor Sanding Pty Ltd v Skyer Australia Pty Ltd* [1999] VSC 170.

21 Statute-barred; see Insurance Contracts Act 1984 (Cth), s 43(1).

22 *Metrocall Inc (Successor by Merger to Pronet In) v Electronic Tracking Systems Pty Ltd* (2000) 52 NSWLR 1.

23 Some domestic building disputes are barred from arbitration by statute. See eg Home Building Act 1989 (NSW), s 7C. See generally D Jones, *Commercial Arbitration in Australia* (Lawbook Co, 2011) 152–61.

24 See, *inter alia*, *Comandate Marine Corp* [2006] 157 FCR 45, *Nicola* (2009) 261 ALR 1; *ACD Tridon Inc v Tridon Australia Pty Ltd* [2002] NSWSC 896; *IBM Australia Ltd v National Distribution Services Ltd* [1991] 22 NSWLR 466; *Rinehart v Welker* [2012] NSWCA 95.

25 *Tanning Research Laboratories Inc v O'Brien* [1990] 169 CLR 332, 351 (Dean J).

18.34 Furthermore, an arbitration agreement may be rendered 'null and void' when the agreement is affected by 'misrepresentation, duress, fraud or undue influence'.[26] Arbitration agreements that are contrary to the public policy of New South Wales or Australia (depending on whether the arbitration is domestic or international) will also be deemed null and void.[27]

18.35 An arbitration agreement is usually held 'inoperative' when the arbitral tribunal declines to proceed with the reference to arbitration, the court has declared that the agreement has ceased to have effect, or the right to arbitrate has been waived. Other situations in which an agreement will be inoperative include when it has been repudiated or abandoned, when it contains such inherent contradictions that it must cease to have effect, or when the parties have by their conduct implicitly revoked the agreement.[28] In any case, it is a question of fact and degree whether the conduct of the parties or the deficiencies in an arbitration agreement render it inoperative.

18.36 For an arbitration agreement to be deemed 'incapable of being performed', it must be shown that there is some obstacle preventing parties who are ready and willing to perform the agreement from actually doing so. These obstacles are usually associated with the carrying out of the arbitral proceedings in practice; an example of this is found in *Aminoil v Government of Kuwait*, where it was impossible to establish an arbitral tribunal, and so the agreement was held to be incapable of being performed.[29] While the issue has not been determined by Australian courts, other Commonwealth jurisdictions have concluded that constrained financial circumstances of the parties are not sufficient to render an agreement incapable of being performed.[30]

18.37 If the requirements of a valid arbitration agreement are met and the dispute in question is arbitrable, a claimant is entitled to begin arbitration proceedings. In the event that a party attempts to litigate the dispute instead of participating in the arbitration and commences court proceedings, the party intending to arbitrate may apply for a stay of the court proceedings. If the arbitration agreement satisfies the requirements set out here, the court must grant the stay, unless it finds that the arbitration agreement is 'null and void, inoperative or incapable of being performed'.[31]

18.38 The Supreme Court of Norfolk Island, in *Administration of Norfolk Island v SMEC Australia Pty Ltd*,[32] concluded that the onus of showing that an arbitration agreement is 'null and void, inoperative or incapable of being performed' lies with the party resisting the stay of curial proceedings.[33] The court explained that an arbitration agreement may be shown to be 'null and void, inoperative or incapable of being performed' by proving that the agreement is illegal or otherwise void *ab initio*, or has become void *ab initio* by operation of law or court order.[34]

---

26 *Comandate Marine Corp* [2006] 157 FCR 45.

27 For discussion regarding the meaning of 'public policy', see paras 18.116 and 18.117 in the section on the Setting Aside of Awards.

28 N Blackaby, C Partasides, A Redfern, and M Hunter, *Redfern and Hunter on International Arbitration* (5th edn, OUP, 2009).

29 *Aminoil v Government of Kuwait* [1982] XXI ILM 976.

30 *Janoz Paczy v Haendler & Natermann GmbH* [1981] 1 Lloyd's Rep 302 CA.

31 CAA 2010 (NSW), s 8(1).

32 *Administration of Norfolk Island v SMEC Australia Pty Ltd* [2004] NFSC 1.

33 *Norfolk Island* (n 32).

34 *Norfolk Island* (n 32).

If court proceedings are brought in respect of a dispute that is covered by an arbitration agreement, an arbitral tribunal can commence or continue the arbitral proceedings, or issue an award, even while the issue of whether a stay of court proceedings should be ordered is pending before the court.[35] **18.39**

This regime for mandatory stays in favour of arbitration (upon the application of one of the parties) demonstrates the Australian and New South Wales legislatures' intention to hold parties to their agreements to arbitrate. **18.40**

18.2.2 The appointment of arbitrators and their jurisdiction

Parties to an arbitration in Sydney are free to determine the arbitrators who will decide their dispute or the process by which those arbitrators are to be appointed. **18.41**

As discussed previously, Australia's IAA, which incorporates the Model Law as a schedule, governs international arbitration in Australia. Article 10 of the Model Law allows parties the freedom to determine the number of arbitrators, failure of which will result in the appointment of three arbitrators.[36] Article 11(2) allows parties the freedom to agree on the procedure for appointing arbitrators.[37] This may involve the use of an appointing authority such as an arbitral institution. In international arbitration in Sydney, Australia's chief international arbitration institution, the ACICA, is often entrusted with the authority to appoint arbitrators. **18.42**

Similar to the provisions governing domestic arbitration in Sydney, Articles 6(1), 11(3), and 11(4) of the Model Law give Australian courts the power to assist with the appointment of arbitrators. These powers are also conferred upon the ACICA,[38] to be exercised if the parties fail to appoint arbitrators, fail to act as required by an agreed appointment procedure, or, if an appointing authority other than ACICA fails to perform any of its duties in the appointment procedure.[39] Parties who find themselves in this situation can elect whether to have ACICA or the courts assist with the appointment.[40] The court's or ACICA's decision with respect to any of these matters is final. Both authorities are required to consider any arbitrator qualifications the parties have agreed on.[41] **18.43**

Both the 2010 Act and the IAA recognize the principle of *competence-competence*, and empower the tribunal to rule on its own jurisdiction, but limit this power by giving the decision a provisional status that is open to review by the court.[42] The tribunal's power to make this provisional ruling on its own jurisdiction arises from section 16(1) of the 2010 Act and Article 16 of the Model Law.[43] It is worthwhile noting that neither of these provisions prescribes the specific conditions or subject matter of a dispute that will affect a tribunal's jurisdiction: this is wholly dependent on the terms of the arbitration agreement between the parties and the limitations on the arbitrability of disputes as determined by New South Wales and Australian law. **18.44**

---

35 CAA 2010 (NSW), s 8(2); Model Law, Art 8(2), as reproduced in IAA 1974 (Cth), Sch 2.
36 Model Law, Art 10, as reproduced in IAA 1974 (Cth), Sch 2.
37 Model Law, Art 11(2), as reproduced in IAA 1974 (Cth), Sch 2.
38 International Arbitration Regulations 2011 (Cth), reg 4.
39 Model Law, Art 11(3) and (4) as reproduced in IAA 1974 (Cth), Sch 2.
40 Model Law, Art 11(3) and (4) as reproduced in IAA 1974 (Cth), Sch 2.
41 Model Law, Art 11(5), as reproduced in IAA 1974 (Cth), Sch 2.
42 *teleMates (previously Better Telecom) Pty Ltd v Standard SoftTel Solutions Pvt Ltd* [2011] NSWSC 1365.
43 CAA 2010 (NSW), s 16(1); Model Law, Art 16(1), as reproduced in IAA 1974 (Cth), Sch 2.

18.2.3 Court power to enjoin arbitration

18.45 The domestic arbitration legislation in force in New South Wales prior to the enactment of the 2010 Act did not limit the inherent jurisdiction of the courts to issue an injunction to permanently stay arbitral proceedings, whether commenced or not. There has been much debate as to whether this power is retained by Australian courts in domestic or international arbitrations after the 2010 reforms, given that Article 5 of the Model Law provides that 'in matters governed by this law, no court shall intervene except where so provided in this law',[44] and there is no provision in either the 2010 Act or the IAA enabling an Australian court to stay an arbitration.

18.46 There are conflicting views on this point in other Commonwealth jurisdictions. In Canada, the Court of Queen's Bench of Alberta, in *Western Oil Sands Inc v Allianz Insurance Company of Canada*,[45] held that the court's intervention should be limited only to that for which the Model Law provides, and given the lack of an express power in the Model Law to enjoin (stay) arbitral proceedings, the Court was unable to do so.[46] The High Court of New Zealand, however, held in *Carter Holt Harvey Ltd v Genesis Power Ltd (No 2)*[47] that the court retains inherent jurisdiction to stay arbitration despite the provisions of the Model Law.[48] This issue has yet to come before an Australian court, but given the strong pro-arbitration stance of the Australian judiciary, it is unlikely that the court will be found to retain jurisdiction to interfere with arbitral proceedings without an express statutory grant.

18.3 During the Arbitration

18.3.1 The courts' role in deciding challenges to arbitrators

18.47 Challenges to arbitrators in both domestic and international arbitrations are limited to the grounds set forth in section 12(3) of the 2010 Act and Article 12(2) of the Model Law as incorporated by the IAA: 'An arbitrator may be challenged only if circumstances exist that give rise to justifiable doubts as to the arbitrator's impartiality or independence, or if the arbitrator does not possess qualifications agreed to by the parties'. The use of the word 'only' in these provisions strictly limits these sections as the exclusive grounds for challenging an arbitrator.

18.48 Section 13 of the 2010 Act and Article 13 of the Model Law govern the procedure by which parties may challenge an arbitrator. Section 13(1) allows for autonomy of the parties in deciding on a procedure for challenging an arbitrator, while section 13(3) and Article 13(2) stipulate that any challenge is to be directed to and decided by the arbitral tribunal. While this may be the default situation in ad hoc arbitration, when the parties elect to participate in institutional arbitration and use institutional rules, the challenge procedure in those rules will apply.

18.49 The freedom afforded to the parties to agree on a procedure for challenge is constrained by section 13(4) of the 2010 Act and Article 13(3) of the Model Law, which instruct that the

---

44 Model Law, Art 5, as reproduced in IAA 1974 (Cth), Sch 2.
45 *Western Oil Sands Inc v Allianz Insurance Co of Canada* [2004] ABQB 79.
46 *Western Oil Sands* (n 45).
47 *Carter Holt Harvey Ltd v Genesis Power Ltd (No 2)* [2006] 3 NZLR 794.
48 *Carter Holt Harvey* (n 47).

arbitrators' decision on a challenge is subject to judicial review upon request by the challenging party. Further, section 13(5) of the 2010 Act and Article 13(3) of the Model Law dictate that a decision made by the court in its review of the tribunal's decision is final. Section 13(5) amends the wording of the Model Law to ensure that judicial decisions made 'within the limits of the authority of the Court' are final; in contrast, the Model Law does not consider the boundaries of the court's powers and specifies only that a court's decision 'shall be subject to no appeal'. Closely related to these provisions are section 14(2) of the 2010 Act and Article 14(1) of the Model Law as incorporated by the IAA, which confer power on the court to terminate the mandate of an arbitrator who becomes unable—in law or in fact—to perform. For domestic arbitration, the Supreme Court of New South Wales is the court that hears challenge applications.[49] For international arbitration, the applicant has the choice of having the matter heard in the Supreme Court of New South Wales or the Federal Court of Australia.[50]

Interestingly, the ACICA Rules provide a similar procedure for making decisions in relation to a challenge, with ACICA acting in the position of the court. Unlike the 2010 Act and the Model Law as incorporated by the IAA, however, article 14.2 of the ACICA Rules requires that a challenge to an arbitrator be made in writing to ACICA at the same time that the challenge is notified to the opposing party and to the arbitral tribunal. This differs from the approach taken by the legislation, which invites the court's involvement only once the initial deciding body (the arbitral tribunal) has made a decision on a challenge. Furthermore, article 14.4 of the ACICA Rules specifies that ACICA is to decide on the outcome of a challenge should the opposing party disagree with the challenge or if the challenged arbitrator refuses to resign; there is no provision for a decision by the arbitral tribunal. If ACICA rejects a challenge, the challenging party has the option of applying for court review within 30 days of receiving notice of the decision.[51] **18.50**

18.3.2 The courts' role in compelling testimony/evidence

Tribunals in domestic and international arbitral proceedings in Sydney are not bound by the evidence law applicable to court proceedings in New South Wales. Instead, arbitral tribunals are empowered to 'determine the admissibility, relevance, materiality and weight of any evidence'.[52] If no particular procedure for producing evidence has been previously agreed upon by the parties, section 24(1) of the 2010 Act and Article 24(1) of the Model Law allow the arbitral tribunal to decide whether evidence is to be produced in written or oral form. Arbitrators are thus afforded great freedom in deciding how to take evidence. Despite this, the practice in international arbitration in Sydney is often to refer to the International Bar Association (IBA) Rules on the Taking of Evidence to govern the evidence phase of the proceedings. For instance, article 27.2 of the ACICA Rules provides that the tribunal shall have regard to, but is not bound to apply, the IBA Rules. **18.51**

For international arbitrations, section 23J of the IAA empowers arbitrators to order parties to the arbitration proceedings to produce evidence relevant to those proceedings. Sections 27A and 23 of the 2010 Act and the IAA, respectively, allow parties to obtain subpoenas **18.52**

49 CAA 2010 (NSW), s 2.
50 IAA 1974 (Cth), s 18(3).
51 CAA 2010 (NSW), s 13(4); Model Law, Art 13(3) as reproduced in IAA 1974 (Cth), Sch 2.
52 CAA 2010 (NSW), s 19(3); Model Law, Art 19(2), as reproduced in IAA 1974 (Cth), Sch 2.

from the court ordering any person to appear for examination before an arbitral tribunal or to produce documents specified in the subpoena.[53] These provisions are intended to ensure the quality of evidence and procedural integrity in arbitrations in Sydney. In addition, section 27 of the 2010 Act and Article 27 of the Model Law allow an arbitral tribunal, or parties with the permission of an arbitral tribunal, to make a request to the court for assistance in taking evidence.

18.53 It is important to note that any subpoenas obtained by parties or orders made by a tribunal are likely to be enforceable only in Australia, thus limiting their utility in international disputes. However, as Australia is a signatory to The Hague Convention on the Taking of Evidence Abroad in Civil or Commercial Matters, one way around this is the use of letters rogatory, which are an example of the court assistance made available to parties by section 27 of the 2010 Act and Article 27 of the Model Law. Letters rogatory take the form of a 'letter of request' by the court, as provided by rule 24.5 of the Uniform Civil Procedure Rules 2005 (NSW), and can be used to invite the assistance of a foreign court in obtaining evidence. Such letters would be appropriate when the evidence of a witness beyond the jurisdiction of the court is required. In deciding applications for letters rogatory, an Australian court will consider section 6(3) of the Evidence on Commission Act 1995 (NSW), which lists factors such as the materiality of the evidence and whether justice will be better served by sending or refusing to send the letter. Letters rogatory are not used frequently in Australian arbitrations. From the parties' perspectives, this process can require extensive costs and lengthy amounts of time, and even if an Australian court issues a letter, it is at the discretion of the foreign court whether to honour the request.

18.3.3 Interim measures

18.54 Tribunals seated in Sydney are empowered to grant a wide range of interim measures. Article 17(2) of the Model Law defines an interim measure as:[54]

> ... any temporary measure, whether in the form of an award or in another form, by which, at any time prior to the issuance of the award by which the dispute is finally decided, the arbitral tribunal orders a party to:
> (a) Maintain or restore the status quo pending determination of the dispute;
> (b) Take action that would prevent, or refrain from taking action that is likely to cause, current or imminent harm or prejudice to the arbitral process itself;
> (c) Provide a means of preserving assets out of which a subsequent award may be satisfied; or
> (d) Preserve evidence that may be relevant and material to the resolution of the dispute.

18.55 The parties may opt out of the interim measures regime in the Model Law. Should the parties to an arbitration choose to opt out, they may come to their own agreement as to how interim measures should be handled by the arbitral tribunal.

18.56 The 2010 Act defines interim measures in the same terms as the Model Law, but further provides a non-exhaustive list of the types of orders that a tribunal might make, for example, orders with respect to the giving of evidence by affidavit or the inspection of property that is the subject matter of the dispute.[55]

---

53 CAA 2010 (NSW), s 27A; IAA 1974 (Cth), s 23.
54 CAA 2010 (NSW), s 17(2); Model Law, Art 17(2) as reproduced in IAA 1974 (Cth), Sch 2.
55 CAA 2010 (NSW), s 17.

The IAA does not contain specific examples of interim measures that the tribunal is empowered to order. However, sections 23J and 23K of the IAA detail specific interim relief available with regard to evidence and security for costs. The parties may opt out of these provisions. **18.57**

Section 23J of the IAA empowers the tribunal to inspect, photograph, observe, or conduct experiments on evidence in the possession of a party, and to take samples of such evidence. **18.58**

Section 23K of the IAA allows the tribunal to order a party to the arbitral proceedings to pay security for costs, which helps to prevent frivolous or vexatious actions and is particularly important where the ability of a party taking a matter to arbitration to pay for the costs of the other party is in doubt. **18.59**

Finally, it is important to note that the power to make *ex parte* preliminary orders under Articles 17B and 17C of the Model Law has not been incorporated into the IAA or the 2010 Act. However, Australian courts have parallel jurisdiction to grant interim orders in relation to arbitral proceedings.[56] The Model Law states that the court has the same power to issue interim orders in relation to arbitral proceedings as it has in relation to proceedings in courts. As a result, parties may apply to the courts for interim measures on an *ex parte* basis. **18.60**

If a foreign jurisdiction has adopted the 2006 amendments to the Model Law, Australian courts will enforce interim orders made in that jurisdiction pursuant to Articles 17H and 17I of the Model Law, unless the parties have opted out of Article 17.[57] **18.61**

18.3.4 Appearing as counsel or arbitrator in Sydney arbitrations

There are no formal requirements for appearing as counsel in either domestic or international arbitration in Sydney. Pursuant to sections 24A and 29 of the 2010 Act and the IAA, respectively, parties are free to be represented by any person of their choosing, which may include qualified legal practitioners from any jurisdiction (including foreign legal practitioners), experts in a field related to the subject matter of the dispute, or lay people. From a practical perspective, however, parties may prefer to engage counsel qualified to practice law in New South Wales, in case court action ensues. There are no formal requirements for serving as an arbitrator in Sydney. **18.62**

18.3.5 Conduct of arbitration hearings in Sydney

Both the IAA and the 2010 Act contain a number of provisions that affect the conduct of arbitrations in Sydney. These include provisions relating to the place of arbitration, the language of the arbitration, and the taking of oral evidence at hearings. Further, the IAA contains a number of optional provisions, some of which apply if the parties agree ('opt-in' provisions) and others that apply, unless the parties agree otherwise ('opt-out' provisions). **18.63**

Place of arbitration

In both domestic and international arbitrations in Sydney, unless the parties agree otherwise, the tribunal may convene, hold hearings, and inspect evidence at any place it considers appropriate.[58] **18.64**

56 CAA 2010 (NSW), s 17J; Model Law, Art 17J as reproduced in IAA 1974 (Cth), Sch 2.
57 IAA 1974 (Cth), s 23J(3).
58 CAA 2010 (NSW), s 20(3); Model Law, Art 20(2) as reproduced in IAA 1974 (Cth), Sch 2.

Language of arbitration

18.65 Section 22 of the 2010 Act and Article 22 of the Model Law allow the parties the freedom to agree on the language to be used in all arbitral proceedings, including hearings. Should the parties fail to agree on the language, the arbitral tribunal is empowered to decide upon the language to be used in the proceedings.[59]

Taking of oral evidence at hearing

18.66 As prevously discussed, section 24(1) of the 2010 Act and Article 24(1) of the Model Law allow an arbitral tribunal to decide whether oral hearings should be held or whether the proceedings should be conducted on the basis of written materials alone. Where an oral hearing is held, the usual practice in both domestic and international arbitration in Sydney is for evidence in chief to be provided in written form and for oral evidence to be given on cross-examination and re-examination only.

18.67 The IAA and the Model Law do not contain any provisions requiring the use of oaths or affirmations in the taking of oral evidence at hearings, so unless the parties have expressly agreed to that, the tribunal may order oral evidence to be taken in whatever manner it sees fit. This power stems from section 19(2) of the 2010 Act and Article 19(2) of the Model Law, which empower the arbitral tribunal to 'conduct the arbitration in such manner as it considers appropriate' in the absence of agreement by the parties. In the domestic context, section 19(4) of the 2010 Act makes clear that the tribunal's power in relation to the conduct of the hearing includes the power to determine whether oral evidence must be given by oath or affirmation. Section 19(5) of the 2010 Act empowers the tribunal to administer oaths and take affirmations where required.

'Opt in/opt out' provisions in international arbitrations

18.68 As previously stated, the IAA contains a number of optional provisions, some of which apply unless the parties agree otherwise ('opt-out' provisions) and others that apply if the parties agree ('opt-in' provisions).[60]

18.69 **The 'opt out' provisions** The first set of provisions (the 'opt out' provisions) *will* apply to an arbitration *unless* parties agree that they should not, and include rules relating to:[61]

(a) the right of parties to obtain subpoenas from the court;[62]
(b) the right of parties to apply to the court for orders compelling persons to provide evidence in the arbitration;[63]
(c) the power of an arbitral tribunal to continue with proceedings and make an award where a party to the arbitration agreement fails to provide evidence or otherwise assist the tribunal after being ordered to do so;[64]

---

[59] CAA 2010 (NSW), s 22; Model Law, Art 22 as reproduced in IAA 1974 (Cth), Sch 2.
[60] Pursuant to IAA 1974 (Cth), s 30 these provisions do not apply to arbitration agreements that were concluded before the commencement of IAA 1974 (Cth), Pt III (ie before 12 June 1989) unless otherwise agreed by the parties.
[61] IAA 1974 (Cth), ss 22(2)(a)–(h).
[62] IAA 1974 (Cth), s 23.
[63] IAA 1974 (Cth), s 23A.
[64] IAA 1974 (Cth), s 23B.

(d) the power of an arbitral tribunal to issue an order allowing the tribunal, a party or an expert to inspect, photograph, observe, conduct experiments on, or sample evidence in the possession of a party to the proceedings;[65]
(e) the power of an arbitral tribunal to order a party to provide security for costs;[66]
(f) the power of an arbitral tribunal to award interest up to the making of an award;[67]
(g) the power of an arbitral tribunal to award interest on the award debt;[68] and
(h) the power of an arbitral tribunal to award costs and to make orders in respect of their taxation.[69] The provisions relating to (a), (b), (d), (f), (g), and (h) are discussed elsewhere in this chapter.

In circumstances in which a person involved in arbitral proceedings refuses or fails to: **18.70**

(a) appear for examination before an arbitral tribunal when required by subpoena or when required by the tribunal;[70]
(b) produce documents required by subpoena or required by the tribunal;[71]
(c) take an oath, make an affirmation or answer a question that the person is required to answer by a tribunal;[72] or
(d) do any other thing which a tribunal may require to assist it in its functions,[73]

the IAA allows parties to apply to the court to issue an order compelling that person to comply with a subpoena or a requirement of the tribunal,[74] as long as that person would have been required to do the same in a proceeding before the court.[75] The court may also make orders for the transmission of evidence or other documents to the tribunal.[76]

If the person to whom the order is made is not a party to the arbitral proceedings, the court must first ensure that the person is provided an opportunity to make representations to the court before the order is made, and that the making of the order is 'reasonable in all the circumstances'.[77] As with all other court orders, a person who refuses to comply is likely to be in contempt of court. **18.71**

In the event that a party defaults by refusing or failing to comply with a subpoena or requirement of the tribunal,[78] regardless of whether applications for any court orders seeking that party's compliance are made, the IAA allows the arbitral tribunal to continue with the proceedings and make an award on the evidence before it.[79] **18.72**

---

65 IAA 1974 (Cth), s 23J.
66 IAA 1974 (Cth), s 23K.
67 IAA 1974 (Cth), s 25.
68 IAA 1974 (Cth), s 26.
69 IAA 1974 (Cth), s 27. For a discussion of subpoenas and evidence, see para 18.51–18.53. For a discussion of interest and costs, see paras 18.101–18.108.
70 IAA 1974 (Cth), s 23A(1)(a) and (b).
71 IAA 1974 (Cth), s 23A(1)(c) and (d).
72 IAA 1974 (Cth), s 23A(1)(e).
73 IAA 1974 (Cth), s 23A(1)(f).
74 IAA 1974 (Cth), s 23A(3)(a).
75 IAA 1974 (Cth), s 23A(4).
76 IAA 1974 (Cth), s 23A(3)(b).
77 IAA 1974 (Cth), s 23A(5).
78 IAA 1974 (Cth), s 23B(1).
79 IAA 1974 (Cth), s 23B(2).

18.73 Substantively similar provisions applicable in domestic arbitration are found in the 2010 Act.[80] However, in domestic arbitration, the tribunal itself may also make an application to the court for an order of this kind,[81] whereas the IAA permits applications for such orders to be made by the parties only.[82]

18.74 The IAA permits arbitral tribunals to order a party to the proceedings to pay security for costs at any point between the commencement of the arbitration and the issuance of a final award.[83] While the tribunal's discretion is quite broad in this regard, it cannot base its decision purely on the fact that that party is not ordinarily resident in Australia, is a corporation incorporated or an association formed under the laws of a foreign nation, or of which the central management or control takes place in a foreign nation.[84]

18.75 **The 'opt in' provisions** The second set of provisions (the 'opt in' provisions) *will not* apply to an arbitration *unless* parties agree that they should, and include rules relating to:[85]

(a) circumstances where the disclosure of confidential information relating to arbitral proceedings may or may not be allowed by either a tribunal or the court;[86] and
(b) the consolidation of arbitral proceedings.[87]

18.76 One of the hallmarks of arbitration is that it provides a level of confidentiality not generally available in litigation. This concept has had a tumultuous existence in Australia in the past two decades.

18.77 Prior to the High Court of Australia's decision in *Esso Australia Resources Ltd v Plowman*[88] in 1995, Australia had followed English jurisprudence and adopted the principle that the arbitral process was confidential. However, the High Court's decision in *Esso* concluded that arbitration is private, but not confidential unless the parties so agree, and that privacy does not equate to confidentiality. The corollary of this was that documents produced in the course of an arbitration would not be confidential purely because they were produced in arbitral proceedings. This sent a shockwave through the international arbitration community, and it was not until the enactment of the 2010 Act and the amendments to the IAA in 2010 that the Australian legislature responded to the concerns generated by *Esso*.

18.78 While the Model Law is silent on the subject of confidentiality, the IAA contains provisions that regulate the disclosure of confidential information.[89] However, these provisions apply to international arbitration only if the parties *agree* that they will apply.[90] The provisions relating to confidentiality in the IAA are thus 'opt in' provisions. Should the parties choose

---

80 CAA 2010 (NSW), s 27B.
81 CAA 2010 (NSW), s 27B(2).
82 IAA 1974 (Cth), s 23A(1).
83 IAA 1974 (Cth), s 23K(1).
84 IAA 1974 (Cth) s 23K(2).
85 IAA 1974 (Cth), s 22(3)(a)–(e) and (5).
86 IAA 1974 (Cth), ss 23C, 23D, 23E, 23F, and 23G.
87 IAA 1974 (Cth), s 24.
88 *Esso Australia Resources Ltd v Plowman* [1995] 183 CLR 10.
89 IAA 1974 (Cth), ss 23C–23G.
90 IAA 1974 (Cth), ss 22(3) and 23C.

not to opt in, they retain the freedom to agree on how confidentiality will be handled in their arbitration.

The IAA provides two exceptions to the rules of non-disclosure: general circumstances in which information may be disclosed and specific circumstances in which information may be disclosed with the authority of the tribunal or the court. **18.79**

The general circumstances in which confidential information may be disclosed include those where the disclosure is:[91] **18.80**

(1) consented to by all the parties to the arbitral proceedings;
(2) to be made to a professional or other adviser of any of the parties;
(3) necessary to ensure that a party has a full opportunity to present its case;
(4) necessary for the establishment or protection of the legal rights of a party;
(5) necessary for the purpose of enforcing an arbitral award;
(6) necessary for the purposes of the IAA (and the Model Law), depending on whether the arbitration is domestic or international;
(7) in accordance with an order made or a subpoena issued by the court; or
(8) authorized or required by another State or Territory law, Commonwealth law, or law of a foreign country (in the case of international arbitration), or is required by a competent regulatory body.

The tribunal has discretion to permit the disclosure of confidential information in circumstances beyond those listed in paragraph 18.80.[92] This is important, as it allows the tribunal to approach the matter with a degree of flexibility and to give consideration to the circumstances of the arbitration and the position of the parties. **18.81**

In the event that the tribunal permits the disclosure and another party to the proceedings is unhappy with the ruling, that party may apply to the court for an order preventing disclosure.[93] It is critical that the tribunal should first rule upon the issue before the court can intervene and order non-disclosure.[94] In addition, the court may order that the confidential information not be disclosed pending the outcome of the application.[95] **18.82**

In making a decision, the court must balance the public interest in preserving the confidentiality of the information with the public interest in favour of disclosure.[96] The High Court's decision in *Esso* considered the issue of public interest in refusing disclosure when governmental institutions are involved, favouring disclosure in this context. The decision concluded that 'the courts have consistently viewed governmental secrets differently from personal and commercial secrets'[97] and that this involved a reversal of the onus of proof, as 'the government must prove that the public interest demands non-disclosure'.[98] **18.83**

The court may also, upon application by a party, allow for disclosure of confidential information where it has been prohibited by the tribunal or the tribunal's mandate has **18.84**

91 IAA 1974 (Cth), s 23D(2)–(9).
92 IAA 1974 (Cth), s 23E.
93 IAA 1974 (Cth), s 23F(3).
94 IAA 1974 (Cth), s 23F(3).
95 IAA 1974 (Cth), s 23F(4).
96 IAA 1974 (Cth), s 23F(1).
97 *Esso Australia Resources Ltd v Plowman* [1995] 183 CLR 10.
98 *Esso* (n 97).

terminated.[99] The court is again required to weigh the public interest in disclosure against that in non-disclosure.[100]

18.85 An order made by the court in relation to these matters is final.[101]

18.86 The IAA provides for a tribunal to consolidate two or more separate arbitration proceedings upon application by a party to any of those proceedings if:

(1) a common question of law or fact arises in all those proceedings;
(2) the rights to relief claimed in all those proceedings are in respect of, or arise out of, the same transaction or series of transactions; or
(3) there is some other desirable reason specified in the party's application.[102]

18.87 In addition to allowing consolidation, the IAA also allows for the joint hearing of any of the related proceedings and the staying of any of the related proceedings pending the determination of any of the other related proceedings.[103] Given the undesirability noted in other Commonwealth jurisdictions of related proceedings being conducted separately and in parallel,[104] as well as the benefit of avoiding inconsistent decisions through consolidation,[105] the IAA confers a wide range of procedural powers on tribunals to optimize the handling of multiple related proceedings.

18.88 Consolidation does not necessarily rely on the approval of an application by a tribunal, as parties to related proceedings can agree to consolidate them and take such steps as are necessary to effect that consolidation.[106]

18.4 The Award

18.4.1 Mandatory rules as to form

18.89 Section 31 of the 2010 Act and Article 31 of the Model Law as incorporated by the IAA dictate the formal requirements for an award in domestic and international arbitration awards respectively.

18.90 Pursuant to sections 31(1) and 31(2) of the 2010 Act and Article 31(1) of the Model Law, awards in both domestic and international arbitration must be made in writing and signed by at least the majority of the arbitral tribunal. In an arbitration with a sole arbitrator, that arbitrator's signature is required for the award to be enforceable. By section 31(6) of the 2010 Act and Article 31(4) of the Model Law, a copy of the written award signed by the arbitrators is to be distributed to each of the parties to the proceedings.

---

[99] IAA 1974 (Cth), s 23G(3).
[100] IAA 1974 (Cth), s 23G(1).
[101] IAA 1974 (Cth), ss 23F(5) and 23G(4).
[102] IAA 1974 (Cth), s 24(1).
[103] IAA 1974 (Cth), s 24(2).
[104] *Taunton-Collins v Cromie* [1964] 1 WLR 633; *Abu Dhabi Gas Liquefaction Co Ltd v Eastern Bechtel Corp* [1982] 2 Lloyd's Rep 425.
[105] UNCITRAL, Note by the Secretariat: 'Possible Future Work in the Area of International Commercial Arbitration', UN Doc A/CN.9/460 (6 April 1999).
[106] IAA 1974 (Cth), s 24(8).

Section 31(4) of the 2010 Act and Article 31(3) of the Model Law require the award to state the date on which it was issued to the parties, as well as the place of arbitration. The date of issue is of great importance to parties as it is used to determine the length of time allowed for recourse against the award. The award is deemed to have been made at the place of arbitration.[107] **18.91**

Standard of reasons required in award

Section 31(3) of the 2010 Act and Article 31(2) of the Model Law govern the most important form requirement: that the award contain the reasons upon which it is based (unless the parties have agreed that no reasons are to be given). This particular requirement has given rise to debate in Australia concerning the standard of reasoning to be provided. This question is particularly important in the context of domestic arbitrations, where unsatisfactory or inadequate reasons may give rise to an error of law and thus constitute grounds for setting aside the award. **18.92**

The Victorian Court of Appeal considered this issue in the well-known domestic case *Oil Basins v BHP Billiton Ltd*. The Court concluded that the reasons put forth by an arbitral tribunal in its award must be of an equal standard to those of a judge in a well-reasoned judicial decision.[108] The New South Wales Court of Appeal, however, decided in *Gordian Runoff Ltd v Westport Insurance Corporation* that this level of detail was unnecessary to satisfy the requirements of the Uniform Acts.[109] Instead, the court in *Gordian Runoff* held that all that was required was a statement of the factual findings and legal or other reasons that lead them to their conclusions. Furthermore, the court concluded that arbitrators were not required to state the evidence on which they based their findings of fact, or the reasons for preferring certain evidence. Lastly, the decision reinforced that, unlike judges in court proceedings, arbitrators need not analyse in depth every individual argument put forth by the parties. **18.93**

The respondent in *Gordian Runoff* subsequently lodged an appeal to the High Court of Australia. In *Westport Insurance Corporation and ors v Gordian Runoff Ltd*,[110] the High Court followed the judgment of the English Court of Appeal in *Bremer Handelsgesellschaft mbH v Westzucker GmbH (No 2)*, which concluded that 'all that is necessary is that arbitrators should set out what, on their view of the evidence, did or did not happen, and should explain succinctly why, in the light of what happened, they have reached their decision and what their decision is'.[111] Since the High Court of Australia is the highest judicial authority in Australia and binds all state/territory jurisdictions, its decision in *Westport Insurance* applies to domestic arbitrations in New South Wales. **18.94**

This does not, however, currently apply to international arbitration in Sydney, as, unlike other Commonwealth jurisdictions, Australian courts have not yet considered the standard of a tribunal's reasons in international arbitration.[112] **18.95**

---

107 2010 Act, s 31(5); Model Law, Art 31(3).

108 *Oil Basins v BHP Billiton Ltd* [2007] 18 VR 346.

109 in *Gordian Runoff Ltd v Westport Insurance Corp* [2010] 267 ALR 74.

110 *Westport Insurance Corp and ors v Gordian Runoff Ltd* [2011] 244 CLR 239.

111 *Bremer Handelsgesellschaft mbH v Westzucker GmbH (No 2)* [1981] 2 Lloyd's Rep 130.

112 The Supreme Court of India has, for example, concluded that in an international arbitration, an award that states that an arbitral tribunal has taken into consideration the dispute, claims, and counterclaims and then merely declares the tribunal's findings on each disputed point, without any attempt at further explanation, is not a reasoned award, *Gora Lal v Union of India* [2003] 12 SCC 459. The issue of the standard of reasons required of a tribunal in relation to an award has also been addressed in Canada, where the Superior Court of

Time limit for making award

18.96 While there are no statutory time limits for making either a domestic or international arbitral award in Sydney, parties may choose to participate in expedited proceedings in which the award must be rendered within a specified time period. Rule 27 of the ACICA Expedited Arbitration Rules, for example, provides that the tribunal is to make a final award within four months of the appointment of the tribunal, subject to whether any counterclaim arises, in which case a period of five months is allowed.

18.97 Time limit problems may arise if the arbitration agreement between the parties fixes specific time constraints for the issuance of an award, which are then not adhered to by the arbitral tribunal. Under the Uniform Acts, there were provisions that allowed parties to apply to the courts to extend the time allowed for an arbitral tribunal to issue its award.[113] No such provisions exist in the 2010 Act, the Model Law, or the IAA. The most practical way to dispose of any potential timing issues is for the arbitral tribunal to write into its terms of reference a provision allowing it a reasonable extension of time to issue the award. Once the parties agree to and sign the Terms of Reference, their arbitration agreement is deemed amended and the problem avoided.

18.4.2 Mandatory rules as to substance

18.98 Arbitral awards in Sydney are not subject to stringent rules regarding their substance. There are currently no statutory limitations placed on arbitrators in relation to the remedies at their disposal. Any such limitations would require the agreement of the parties.

Remedies available to arbitral tribunals

18.99 A remedy explicitly provided for in domestic arbitration is specific performance of contract. Section 33A of the 2010 Act confers this power wherever a court would be empowered to do the same. While the Model Law and the IAA confer no equivalent express authority on international arbitral tribunals, the High Court of Australia has held that a term can be implied into an international arbitration agreement giving the tribunal authority 'to give the claimant such relief as would be available to it, in a court of law having jurisdiction with respect to the subject matter'.[114]

18.100 There are also no restrictions on the kind of damages that can be awarded, however, the permissibility of exemplary or punitive damages in Australia has not yet been tested.

Costs orders

18.101 Directions for costs are not mandatory in domestic or international arbitral awards, but are usually included for practical reasons. Section 33B(4) of the 2010 Act and section 27(2) of the IAA state that an arbitral tribunal *may*, in making an award, make orders for costs. Section 33B(4)(b) and (c) of the 2010 Act and section 27(b) and (c) of the IAA allow a tribunal to tax or settle the amount of costs to be paid, including any part of those costs, and to award costs to be taxed or settled in a party-party or lawyer-client arrangement. Section 33B(5) of the 2010 Act and section27(3) of the IAA provide for judicial review of the costs directed to be paid by an award. The criteria for judicial assessment, however, include that

Quebec found that expressing reasons in commercial terms as opposed to legal terms was sufficient, *Navigation Sonamar Inc v Algoma Steamships Ltd and ors* [1987] RJQ 1346.

[113] Commercial Arbitration Act 1984 (NSW), s 48.

[114] *Government Insurance Office of NSW v Atkinson-Leighton Joint Venture* [1981] 146 CLR 206.

that the costs have not already been assessed by the tribunal and are not the fees or expenses incurred by the arbitrators.

Both section 33B(1) of the 2010 Act and section 27(1) of the IAA provide that, in the absence of a contrary agreement between the parties, the costs of arbitration (including the fees and expenses of the arbitrators) are within the discretion of the arbitral tribunal. Similarly, parties to an international arbitration can opt out of section 27 of the IAA if both agree.[115] Under the old Uniform Acts, arbitrators had the express authority to outsource the calculation of costs to legal costs consultants.[116] While this has been omitted from the 2010 Act, it may still be possible, as the arbitral tribunal retains the general power to engage experts. **18.102**

It must, however, be noted that an arbitral tribunal may not simply direct in its award the payment of costs as determined by a consultant. To overcome this apparent hurdle, it is possible for an arbitral tribunal to appoint costs consultants for assessment purposes and then adopt their findings as their own. The amount of costs payable in both domestic and international arbitrations may also be limited by the tribunal. Both section 33B(2) of the 2010 Act and section 27(2)(d) of the IAA state that an arbitral tribunal may limit the amount of costs to a specified amount. **18.103**

Section 33B(6) of the 2010 Act and section 27(4) of the IAA provide for the situation where an award is issued that does not contain directions relating to costs. According to these provisions, a party is entitled, within 14 days of the issuance of the award, to apply to the tribunal for directions as to the payment of costs. Section 33B(7) of the 2010 Act and section 27(4) of the IAA compel the tribunal to hear the parties as to their cost queries and supplement the award issued with cost directions as it sees fit. **18.104**

Another situation where cost directions are not included in an award is the abortive arbitration: when an arbitration is commenced but fails to result in a final award. Interestingly, neither the IAA nor the Model Law addresses this situation. Section 33D(1) of the 2010 Act does deal with this in the context of domestic arbitrations, and provides that parties may apply to the tribunal within six months after the failure of an arbitration for an order on costs 'as it thinks just'. **18.105**

Directions relating to interest are not compulsory for arbitral awards in Sydney. An award for the payment of moneys does not automatically include interest. The application of an interest rate on sums payable under an arbitral award is at the discretion of the tribunal.[117] The imposition of interest on arbitral awards in Sydney is governed by a two-part mechanism; section 33E of the 2010 Act and section 25 of the IAA provide for interest up to the making of an award, while section 33F of the 2010 Act and section 26 of the IAA provide for interest on a debt under an award. **18.106**

Interest up to making of award

Both statutes confer discretionary power on an arbitral tribunal to order interest up to the making of an award. Section 25(1) of the IAA states that arbitrators *may* choose to make an award for interest on the entire or any portion of moneys payable under an award at a 'reasonable' rate as determined by the tribunal. Section 33E(1) of the 2010 Act provides for this **18.107**

[115] IAA 1974 (Cth), s 22(2)(h).
[116] Commercial Arbitration Act 1984 (NSW), s 34(1)(b).
[117] CAA 2010 (NSW), ss 33E and 33F; IAA 1974 (Cth), ss 25 and 26.

same power and again states that its provision is subject to any contrary agreement between the parties. Accordingly, the tribunal's discretion when awarding interest is curtailed when the contract out of which the arbitration arises, or the arbitration agreement itself, stipulates that interest should be applied to the sum payable under the award. In these circumstances, there is a well-recognized and enforceable right to interest, and if a particular rate is not contractually specified, the tribunal will be required to decide on a reasonable rate at which the interest will be levied. Tribunals are prevented from awarding compound interest in both domestic and international arbitrations by section 33E(2)(a) of the 2010 Act and section 25(2)(a) of the IAA.

Interest on debt under award

18.108 Section 33F(1) and (2) of the 2010 Act and section 26(1) and (2) of the IAA state that where the tribunal has made an award for the payment of an amount of money by a particular date, it *may* direct a party to pay interest on any unpaid portion of that amount that has not been paid on or before the due date. Again, section 33F(1) of the 2010 Act provides this power subject to contrary agreement by the parties, and section 22(2)(g) of the IAA restricts the tribunal's authority in section 26(1) in the same way. The tribunal may direct that the interest payable includes compound interest,[118] which is not allowed for interest up to the making of an award. In any case, the tribunal is allowed to determine a 'reasonable' rate of interest by section 33F(3) of the 2010 Act and secion 26(3) of the IAA. The period and amount on which interest on the debt under an award will be charged is clarified by section 33F(4) of the 2010 Act and section 26(4) of the IAA: interest is payable from the day immediately following the due date of the amount and on so much of the amount as remains unpaid. Finally, section 33F(5) of the 2010 Act and section 26(5) of the IAA indicate that any direction for additional interest on the debt under the award will form part of the award itself.

18.5 After the Award

18.5.1 Local standards and procedures for setting aside awards/appeals against awards

18.109 The major difference between recourse available against domestic awards and international awards in Sydney is the right to appeal: the legislation allows for the setting aside of both types of awards, however, only those of a domestic nature may have their substance reviewed. Unlike the 2010 Act, the Model Law as incorporated by the IAA contains no provision for substantive appeals and the IAA itself has not supplemented this exclusion with any provisions of its own.

18.110 A recent decision of the High Court of Australia affirmed the constitutional validity of the IAA's limited approach to the judicial review of arbitral awards, finding that the final and conclusive nature of an arbitral award is a consequence of the parties' agreement to have their dispute referred to arbitration.[119] The High Court therefore rejected an argument that the IAA undermined the institutional integrity of the Federal Court by not allowing the court to refuse to enforce an award on the basis of an error of law on the face of the award.

[118] CAA 2010 (NSW), s 26(2) and IAA 1974 (Cth), s 33F(2).
[119] *TCL Air Conditioner (Zhongshan) Co Ltd v The Judges of the Federal Court of Australia* [2013] HCA 5.

The High Court also rejected an argument that article 28(1) of the Model Law, in providing that 'the arbitral tribunal shall decide the dispute in accordance with such rules of law as are chosen by the parties', requires the tribunal to decide a dispute correctly, and that therefore an award containing an error of law was unenforceable. The Court held that such an interpretation of article 28(1) was not supported either by the text of the article itself, or by its drafting history. The High Court also rejected an argument that it is an implied term of every arbitration agreement that the tribunal's authority is limited to the correct application of the law. This decision highlights the importance of a supportive judiciary, particularly when it comes to the recognition and enforcement of awards. **18.111**

Sections 34 and 34A of the 2010 Act govern the setting aside of domestic awards and appeals against domestic awards respectively, while Article 34 of the Model Law applies only to the setting aside of international awards. **18.112**

Setting aside of awards in domestic and international arbitrations

Substantive criteria Pursuant to section 34(1) of the 2010 Act and article 34(1) of the Model Law, an application for setting aside an award will only be successful upon the establishment of the grounds set out in section 34(2) or (3) of the 2010 Act and Article 34(2) or (3) of the Model Law. Use of the words 'may' and 'only' in these provisions indicates discretion and limitations on the court's power to set aside an award; an application can *only* be made by satisfaction of the relevant criteria and even then the court *may* choose to set aside the award. **18.113**

Section 34(2)(a)(i)–(iv) of the 2010 Act and Article 34(2)(a)(i)–(iv) of the Model Law detail what must be proved by a party making an application to set aside an award, and reflect the grounds for refusing to enforce arbitral awards set out in Article V of the New York Convention. By these provisions, a party making an application must show that: **18.114**

(1) a party to the arbitration agreement was under some incapacity or the arbitration agreement is invalid under the law to which the parties have subjected it; or
(2) the party was not given proper notice of the appointment of an arbitral tribunal or of the arbitral proceedings or was otherwise not able to present its case; or
(3) the award relates to a dispute that is non-arbitrable under the arbitration agreement or makes decisions on matters beyond the scope of the dispute submitted to arbitration; or
(4) the procedure for the appointment of arbitrators or the arbitral procedure itself conflicted with a prior agreement between the parties.

Of interest also is the proviso in section 34(2)(a)(iii) that allows for the severance of decisions made in the award that are beyond the power of the arbitral tribunal. Where these decisions can be clearly distinguished from decisions that are legitimately made, they can be set aside by the court, while the remainder of the award stands. **18.115**

The grounds discussed here must be proved by the party applying to have the award set aside. In contrast, section 34(2)(b) of the 2010 Act and Article 34(2)(b) of the Model Law, together with section 36(1)(b) of the 2010 Act and Article 36(1)(b) of the Model Law, reserve to the court the discretion to set aside an award when either the matter was not capable of resolution by arbitration in the first place and/or the enforcement of the award would contravene public policy. **18.116**

There has been a trend in international arbitrations in Sydney to read the definition of public policy quite narrowly and to respect and recognize foreign laws. Foster J, in his decision in **18.117**

Traxys Europe SA v Balaji Coke Industry Pvt Ltd, followed the reasoning of the US Court of Appeals for the Second Circuit in *Parsons & Whittemore Overseas Co, Inc v Société Générale de l'Industrie du Papier (RAKTA)*,[120] and concluded that awards should be set aside only where their enforcement would 'violate the forum state's most basic notions of morality and justice'.[121] Further, the *Traxys* decision resolved that 'it is only those aspects of public policy that go to the fundamental, core questions of morality and justice' which may be considered in setting aside an award on grounds of contravention of public policy.[122] This is currently the approach taken to international arbitral awards in Sydney.

18.118 **Procedural requirements** Section 34(3) of the 2010 Act and Article 34(3) of the Model Law state that a party seeking to apply to have an award set aside must do so within three months from the date on which that party received the award.

18.119 Finally, section 34(4) of the 2010 Act and Article 34(4) of the Model Law permit a court faced with a request to set aside an award to suspend the setting aside proceedings for a period of time at its discretion in order to allow the arbitral tribunal to resume the arbitral proceedings or take other action aimed at eliminating the grounds for setting aside the award.

18.120 The length of time it will take to obtain judgment on an application to set an award aside, depends on the circumstances of the case and the complexity of the matters that the court must address. However, as a rough guide, an application to set aside would generally take about a year from the issuance of the award to judgment at first instance. If a party were to appeal, then it would be likely to take another six months to obtain a judgment from the Court of Appeal. Generally speaking, the unsuccessful party will be required to pay the successful party's costs, typically on a 'party-party' basis.[123] This will usually result in the recovery of around 40 per cent of the successful party's costs.

Appeals against awards

18.121 Under the IAA, there is no provision for substantive challenges to an award or by way of appeal for errors of law.

18.122 In contrast, section 34A of the 2010 Act allows for appeals on a question of law arising out of a domestic award. This provision is not based on the Model Law, but is adapted from section 38 of the Uniform Acts. Importantly, appeals will only be permitted when the parties have agreed to allow recourse to the court on questions of law and the court grants leave to appeal.

18.6 Conclusion

18.123 There are many factors to consider in choosing an arbitral seat. Different parties will have different priorities, but certain needs are universal. The need for a supportive judicial system, affordable and convenient facilities, and the availability of effective arbitral institutions are common to all arbitrations. Care must be taken when a decision is being made that due

---

120 *Parsons & Whittemore Overseas Co, Inc v Société Générale de l'Industrie du Papier (RAKTA)* 508 F 2d 969 (2d Cir 1974). The Court considered and interpreted the New York Convention's public policy ground for vacating an award in coming to its decision in this case.

121 *Traxys Europe SA v Balaji Coke Industry Pvt Ltd* [2012] FCA 276.

122 *Traxys* (n 121).

123 Party-party costs are the costs which one party recovers from another party in the arbitration, and are separate from, and in addition to, any award requiring the payment of money.

consideration be given to each of these factors, and that the importance of any one of these factors will not be unduly emphasized.

As can be seen from this chapter, Sydney has a robust legal framework that adheres to internationally accepted standards. Its judiciary is independent and supportive of arbitration, and Sydney offers affordable and convenient facilities for arbitration, as well as effective institutional support and the availability of specialized legal advice. Given its proximity to some of the world's economic hubs, Sydney is an ideal option for parties who are interested in an affordable, independent and supportive seat for international arbitrations. **18.124**

19

UNITED STATES (NEW YORK, MIAMI, HOUSTON)

*John Fellas and Hagit Elul**

19.1 Background

19.1.1 Overview of arbitration in the United States

19.01 The United States is favourable to international arbitration. In order to appreciate this, it is necessary to begin with the federal policy concerning arbitration, which is embodied in the Federal Arbitration Act (FAA).[1] The FAA, which applies to all arbitrations, whether domestic or international, was enacted in 1925 in response to widespread judicial hostility to arbitration agreements. State courts would often refuse to enforce agreements to arbitrate on the ground that such agreements ousted the jurisdiction of the courts.[2] The federal policy in

* The authors would like to thank Alex Patchen, Hughes Hubbard & Reed LLP, for his substantial contribution to this chapter.

[1] 9 USC §§ 1ff. Future references to the FAA will omit '9 USC'.

[2] See *Hall Street Associates, LLC v Mattel, Inc* 552 US 576, 581, 128 S Ct 1396 (2008): 'Congress enacted the FAA to replace judicial indisposition to arbitration with a "national policy favoring [it] and plac[ing] arbitration

favour of arbitration 'appli[es] in state as well as federal courts' and 'foreclose[s] state legislative attempts to undercut the enforceability of arbitration agreements'.[3]

In 1958, the United States became a signatory to the New York Convention[4] and, in 1975, to the Panama Convention.[5] Each Convention has been implemented in US law in the FAA.[6] The FAA is divided into three chapters. Thus, as noted, the first chapter was enacted in 1925 and governs cases involving interstate or foreign commerce. The second chapter contains legislation implementing the New York Convention, and applies only to agreements to arbitrate (and arbitral awards) that fall under the New York Convention. The third chapter contains legislation implementing the Panama Convention and applies only to agreements to arbitrate (and arbitral awards) that fall under the Panama Convention. **19.02**

The three chapters do not contain identical provisions, but Chapter 1 of the Federal Arbitration Act is incorporated into Chapter 2[7] and Chapter 3[8] to the extent it does not conflict with other provisions in those chapters or the conventions. Thus, for example, while Chapters 2 and 3 of the Federal Arbitration Act contain provisions governing a court's authority to compel arbitration pursuant to an agreement to arbitrate that falls under the New York Convention and the Panama Convention respectively, neither contains any provision regarding the authority of a court to stay litigation brought in contravention of an arbitration clause. For this, it is necessary for a party to an agreement that falls under the Conventions to rely on section 3 of Chapter 1 of the Federal Arbitration Act. Likewise, Chapter 3 incorporates certain provisions of Chapter 2.[9] **19.03**

As a result of the FAA, the New York Convention, and the Panama Convention, the federal policy in favour of arbitration is said to apply with special force when it comes to international contracts. As the Court of Appeals for the Second Circuit noted in *David L Threlkeld & Co, Inc v Metallgesellschaft Ltd (London)*: **19.04**

> As a point of departure, we note that federal policy strongly favors arbitration as an alternative dispute resolution process. While it is still the rule that parties may not be compelled to submit

agreements on equal footing with all other contracts." ', quoting *Buckeye Check Cashing, Inc v Cardegna* 546 US 440, 443, 126 S Ct 1204 (2006); *Gilmer v Interstate/Johnson Corp* 500 US 20, 24, 111 S Ct 1647 (1991).

[3] *Southland Corp v Keating* 465 US 1, 10, 16, 104 S Ct 852 (1984).

[4] Convention on the Recognition and Enforcement of Foreign Arbitral Awards of 1958 (New York, 10 June 1958, 21 UST 2517, 330 UNTS 38).

[5] Inter-American Convention on International Commercial Arbitration of 1975 (Panama City, 30 January 1975, OAS/SER A20 (SEPEF), 14 ILM 336 (1975)).

[6] The New York Convention is codified at Chapter 2 of the Federal Arbitration Act, 9 USC § 201ff. The Panama Convention is codified at Chapter 3 of the Federal Arbitration Act, 9 USC § 301ff.

[7] The Federal Arbitration Act, Ch 2, § 208 provides: 'Chapter 1 applies to actions and proceedings brought under this chapter to the extent that chapter is not in conflict with this chapter or the Convention as ratified by the United States.' See also *Yusuf Ahmed Alghnim & Sons WLL v Toys 'R' Us, Inc* 126 F 3d 15, 20 (US Ct of Apps (2nd Cir), 1997), cert denied, 522 US 1111, 118 S Ct 1042 (1998); *Oil Basins Ltd v Broken Hill Proprietary Co Ltd* 613 F Supp 483, 486 (US D Ct (SDNY), 1985).

[8] The Federal Arbitration Act, Ch 3, § 307 provides: 'Chapter 1 applies to actions and proceedings brought under this chapter to the extent Chapter 1 is not in conflict with this chapter or the Inter-American Convention as ratified by the United States.' See also *Siderurgica del Orinoco (Sidor) CA, v Linea Naviera de Cabotaje, CA* 1999 WL 632870 (US D Ct (SDNY), 1999); *Productos Mercantiles e Industriales, SA v Faberge USA* 23 F 3d 41, 45 (US Ct of Apps (2nd Cir), 1994): 'the legislative history of the Inter-American Convention's implementing statute... clearly demonstrates that Congress intended the Inter-American Convention to reach the same results as those reached under the New York Convention'.

[9] FAA, Ch 3, § 302 provides that: 'Sections 202, 203, 204, 205 and 207 of this title shall apply to this chapter as if specifically set forth herein, except that for the purposes of this chapter "the Convention" shall mean the Inter-American Convention.'

a commercial dispute to arbitration unless they have contracted to do so, federal arbitration policy requires that 'any doubts concerning the scope of arbitrable issues should be resolved in favor of arbitration'.[10]

19.05 The policy in favour of arbitration is even stronger in the context of international business transactions. Enforcement of international arbitral agreements promotes the smooth flow of international transactions by removing the threat and uncertainty of time-consuming and expensive litigation. The parties may agree in advance how their disputes will be expeditiously and inexpensively resolved should their business relationship sour. Stability in international trading was the engine behind the Convention on the Recognition and Enforcement of Foreign Arbitral Awards. This treaty—to which the United States is a signatory—makes it clear that the liberal federal arbitration policy applies with special force in the field of international commerce.

19.06 This federal policy in favour of arbitration does not require parties to arbitrate in the absence of an agreement,[11] but it does entail that when parties have agreed to arbitrate they are bound by that agreement.[12] This policy animates the manner in which courts approach the enforcement of agreements to arbitrate. Thus, courts have issued pro-arbitration decisions on such issues as the scope of an arbitration clause,[13] whether to issue an anti-suit injunction in order to enforce an agreement to arbitrate,[14] or whether to impose sanctions for an improper challenge to an arbitration award.[15]

19.1.2 Recent trends in arbitration jurisprudence

19.07 One of the striking aspects of US arbitration jurisprudence over recent years is the number of arbitration-related cases the United States Supreme Court has chosen to hear. Almost without exception, the decisions of the Supreme Court have been favourable to arbitration, limiting court interference in the process and typically resolving questions about the allocation of authority between courts and arbitrators in favour of arbitration.[16] In addition, having

[10] *David L Threlkeld & Co, Inc v Metallgesellschaft Ltd (London)* 923 F 2d 245, 248 (US Ct of Apps (2nd Cir), 1991) (internal citations omitted); See *Mitsubishi Motors Corp v Soler Chrysler-Plymouth, Inc* 473 US 614,629-31, 105 S Ct 3346 (1985); *Deloitte Noraudit v Deloitte Haskins & Sells* 9 F 3d 1060, 1063 (US Ct of Apps (2nd Cir), 1992): 'The federal policy favoring arbitration is even stronger in the context of international arbitrations.'

[11] See *Volt Information Sciences, Inc v Board of Trustees of Leland Stanford Junior Univ* 489 US 468, 109 S Ct 1248 (1989).

[12] *Genesco, Inc v T Kaiuchi & Co Ltd* 815 F 2d 840, 845 (US Ct of Apps (2nd Cir), 1987).

[13] *Moses H Cone Memorial Hospital v Mercury Construction Corp* 460 US 1, 24–25, 103 S Ct 927 (1983), 'any doubts concerning the scope of arbitral issues should be resolved in favor of arbitration', whether the issue concerns a construction of the language of the agreement itself, or a defence to arbitrability. See also *Mitshubishi Motors Corp v Soler Chrysler-Plymouth, Inc* 473 US 614, 105 S Ct 3346 (1985).

[14] *Paramedics Electromedicina Comercial Ltda v GE Medical Systems Information Technologies, Inc* 369 F 3d 645, 652 (US Ct of Apps (2nd Cir), 2004), affirming an anti-suit injunction; *Storm LLC v Telenor Mobile Communications AS*, 2006 WL 3735657 (US D Ct (SDNY), 2006), enjoining Ukrainian litigation brought in breach of an arbitration clause since such litigation frustrates the federal policy in favour of arbitration.

[15] *World Business Paradise, Inc v Suntrust Bank* 403 Fed Appx 468, 470 (US Ct of Apps (11th Cir), 2010) (unpublished), imposing sanctions for frivolous petition to vacate arbitral award; *DigiTelCom Ltd v Tele2 Sverige AB* 2012 WL 3065345 (US D Ct (SDNY), 2012), imposing sanctions on a party submitting a petition making a frivolous challenge to an arbitration award because 'where parties agree to arbitration as an efficient and lower-cost alternative to litigation, both the parties and the system itself have a strong interest in the finality of those arbitration awards... litigants must be discouraged from defeating the purpose of arbitration by bringing such petitions based on nothing more than dissatisfaction with the tribunal's conclusions'.

[16] See *Rent-A-Center, West v Jackson* 130 S Ct 2772, 177 L Ed 2d 403 (2010), when an agreement delegates the authority to determine the arbitrability of the agreement to the arbitrator, all challenges to that agreement are to be resolved by arbitration unless a party makes a specific challenge to the provision delegating such

opened the door to class arbitration in 2003,[17] in its more recent decisions, the Supreme Court has limited the ability of parties to bring cases as class arbitrations.[18] Similarly, lower courts have issued decisions favourable to arbitration, such as imposing sanctions for frivolous challenges to arbitration awards.[19]

There are several arbitral institutions sited in New York. These include the American Arbitration Association (AAA), and its international division, the International Center for Dispute Resolution (ICDR). The AAA administers all types of commercial dispute resolution. In addition to its general commercial rules, it has specialized rules for complex disputes, labour and employment disputes, construction disputes, election disputes, and commercial will and trust disputes. The ICDR was established in 1996 to administer international cases, and offers multilingual staff able to navigate the cultural and procedural differences typical to international disputes. The ICDR also has its own set of arbitration rules—the International Dispute Resolution Procedures. Other arbitral institutions with an established presence in the United States are the CPR International Center for Conflict Prevention and Resolution, which offers rules for administered and non-administered arbitrations, and JAMS. The ICC Court of Arbitration recently opened an office in New York to service North American disputes. **19.08**

For those interested in arbitrating in New York, the New York International Arbitration Center (NYIAC) was formed in 2012 with the support of over 30 law firms with offices in New York City. NYIAC is not an arbitral institution; it will not administer cases and has no arbitration rules. It is designed to provide hearing rooms, disseminate information on arbitrating in New York, and to promote the benefits of New York as a place for international arbitration. **19.09**

19.1.3 Comparison with other regional and national venues

This chapter will focus primarily on New York, because it is the most popular venue for international arbitration in the United States. It will also discuss key distinctions that are **19.10**

---

authority to the arbitrator; *Preston v Ferrer* 552 US 346, 128 S Ct 978 (2008), when parties agree to resolve all disputes arising under a contract, questions concerning the validity of the entire contract are to be resolved by an arbitrator, not by a court; *Buckeye Check Cashing v Cardegna* 546 US 440, 126 S Ct 1204 (2006), assertion that a contract was void on the ground of illegality was to be determined by the arbitrator rather than the court; *Pacificare Health Systems v Book* 538 US 401, 123 S Ct 1531 (2003), whether or not claims under the Racketeer Influenced and Corrupt Organizations Act (RICO) were arbitrable before an arbitrator, rather than the court, to consider at first instance; *Howsam v Dean Witter Reynolds, Inc* 537 US 79, 123 S Ct 588 (2002), holding that procedural questions, such as contractual time limits for asserting claims contained in arbitral rules, are presumptively for an arbitrator, not a court, to decide.

[17] *Green Tree Financial Corp v Bazzle* 539 US 444, 156 L Ed 2d 414 (2003), plurality opinion holding that arbitrators, rather than courts, should decide whether an arbitration agreement permits class action.

[18] See *AT&T Mobility v Concepcion* 131 S Ct 1740, 179 L Ed 2d 742 (2011), holding that state laws prohibiting contracts from disallowing class-wide arbitration are invalid on the ground that they are pre-empted by the FAA; *Stolt-Nielsen v AnimalFeeds Intl Corp* 559 US 662, 130 S Ct 1758 (2010), holding that where an arbitration clause is 'silent' as to class arbitration, the FAA pre-empts a finding that parties have consented to class arbitration because 'the differences between bilateral and class action arbitration are too great for arbitrators to presume, consistent with their limited powers under the FAA, that the parties' mere silence on the issue of class-action arbitration constitutes consent to resolve their disputes in class proceedings'.

[19] *Digitelcom Ltd v Tele2 Sverige AB* 2012 WL 3065345, *7 (US D Ct (SDNY), 2012): 'Thus, although courts should be careful not to chill parties' good-faith challenges to arbitration awards where there are serious questions of the tribunal's impartiality or authority, litigants must be discouraged from defeating the purpose of arbitration by bringing such petitions based on nothing more than dissatisfaction with the tribunal's conclusions.'

present in Miami, Florida and Houston, Texas, which, after New York, are also popular venues for international arbitration.

19.1.4 Underlying framework of the US legal system's treatment of international arbitration

19.11 It is important to understand the basic framework of the US legal system to fully comprehend the impact of selecting a location in the United States as a venue for international arbitration. First, the United States is a common law system. A common law system relies upon the concept of precedent, whereby the courts are bound to follow legal principles established by previous court decisions in the same jurisdiction. While US courts can be controlled by specific statutes and regulations, they look to precedential decisions[20] to determine the proper manner in which to interpret and apply them.

19.12 The US legal system is further distinguished among common law systems because it is a dual court system; one system—the federal system—run by the US government (the 'federal courts') and one run individually by each state. Based on the federalist principles, each state is free to operate its court system without regard for the operations of other states or the federal court as a whole. As will be discussed in more detail later, issues arising out of international arbitration are most often heard in federal courts as opposed to state courts. Therefore, this chapter will focus on federal court decisions, except where there is interplay between the federal courts and an individual state court.

19.13 The FAA sets forth the federal legislative framework governing arbitration. As a dual court system, the courts will look to the state law where the court is located to address key substantive issues. While federal law governs many procedural aspects of arbitration, federal courts also look to the precedent of the state court where the federal court is located to address underlying substantive issues. For example, when the court analyses the formation of the contract between the parties, it looks to the substantive law of the state with respect to that analysis.[21] Determining whether an issue is a procedural or substantive issue, as well as whether a federal law pre-empts state law, requires the courts to perform conflicts of laws analysis.

19.14 Since an arbitration agreement is a specialized form of a contractual agreement, the 'interpretation of an arbitration agreement is generally a matter of state law'.[22] The FAA places such agreements on an equal footing with other contracts and therefore requires courts to enforce them according to the contracts terms.[23] As such, just as a contract can be invalidated, so an arbitration agreement 'may be invalidated' by 'generally applicable contract defenses, such as fraud, duress, or unconscionability'.[24]

[20] In general, each court system has three levels: the trial court, the intermediate appellate court, and the highest level appellate court. The trial court is bound to follow the precedent of both the highest and intermediate appellate courts in its jurisdiction. It is not bound to follow judicial decisions from other jurisdictions, but often looks to such jurisdictions for guidance when rendering its own decisions. With respect to the three venues that are the focus of this chapter, New York lies within the Second Circuit, Houston lies in the Fifth Circuit, and Miami lies in the Eleventh Circuit. The Circuit Court is the intermediate appellate court for each circuit and the United States Supreme Court is the highest court in the US. The federal trial courts within the various circuits are referred to as District Courts.

[21] *Solymar Investments Ltd v Banco Santander SA* 672 F 3d 981, 991 (US Ct of Apps (11th Cir), 2012).

[22] *Stolt-Nielsen SA v AnimalFeeds Intl Corp* 559 US 662, 130 S Ct 1758, 1773 (2010).

[23] *Rent-A-Center, West, Inc v Jackson* 130 S Ct 2772, 2776, 177 L Ed 2d 403 (2010).

[24] *Rent-A-Center, West* (n 23) citing *Doctor's Associates, Inc v Casarotto* 517 US 681, 687, 116 S Ct 1652 (1996)).

The conflict of law analysis becomes much more complex with respect to issues that are related to, but distinct from, the validity of the arbitration agreement itself. Thus, although state law generally applies to issues concerning the validity of the arbitration agreement, federal law generally governs the scope of the arbitration agreement.[25] **19.15**

New York Convention

The New York Convention requires that signatory states recognize and enforce arbitration agreements and arbitral awards issued in other contracting states. There are a few limited exceptions to the enforcement of such international arbitration agreements and awards, which will be discussed later. **19.16**

Chapter 2 of the FAA sets forth the manner in which the courts shall enforce the New York Convention. Chapter 2 applies to any written arbitration agreement or arbitral award that relates to a commercial relationship between a US citizen and non-US citizen, or when a relationship between US citizens 'involves property located abroad, envisages performance or enforcement abroad, or has some other reasonable relation with one or more foreign states'.[26] Under this section, a corporation is deemed to be a US citizen 'if it is incorporated or has its principal place of business in the United States'.[27] **19.17**

Panama Convention

The United States is also a signatory to the Panama Convention.[28] The Panama Convention was negotiated among the members of the Organization of America States (OAS) and has been adopted by a number of states in South, Central, and North America. The Panama Convention is modelled after the New York Convention, with a few differences. One difference is that, unlike the New York Convention, the Panama Convention does not contain a provision requiring the courts to refer a dispute to arbitration.[29] However, the US legislation implementing the Panama Convention grants US courts this authority.[30] Another difference is that the Panama Convention provides that if the parties to the arbitration agreement do not expressly agree on the rules governing the arbitration, the arbitration will be governed by the Rules of Procedure of the Inter-American Commercial Arbitration Commission (IACAC).[31] **19.18**

The United States' implementation of the Panama Convention is substantively similar to that of the New York Convention, and is set forth in Chapter 3 of the FAA.[32] In fact, Section 302 incorporates by reference a number of the non-conflicting enabling statutes for the New York Convention.[33] If an application for judicial assistance falls under both the **19.19**

[25] See eg *Applied Energetics, Inc v NewOak Capital Markets, LLC* 645 F 3d 522, 526 (US Ct of Apps (2nd Cir), 2011), holding that it is appropriate to apply state law to determine whether the obligation to arbitrate exists; *Re Labatt Food Serv, LP* 279 SW 3d 640, 643 (Tex S Ct, 2009): 'Under the FAA, state law generally governs whether a litigant agreed to arbitrate, and federal law governs the scope of the arbitration clause.'; *Re Kellogg Brown & Root, Inc* 166 SW 3d 732, 738 (Tex S Ct, 2005); See *Re Labatt* 279 SW 3d, 643, noting that: 'It is not entirely clear, however, if state or federal substantive law governs whether nonsignatories are bound to arbitrate under an agreement subject to the FAA.'

[26] FAA § 202.

[27] FAA § 202.

[28] 14 ILM 336 (30 January 1975).

[29] cf New York Convention, Art II(3).

[30] FAA § 302(a).

[31] FAA § 302(b).

[32] FAA §§ 301–307.

[33] The FAA incorporates FAA §§ 202, 203, 204, 205, and 207 as if they were part of Ch 3.

New York and the Panama Convention, the Panama Convention is the governing agreement if the majority of parties to the arbitration agreement are citizens of Panama Convention signatories.[34]

Subject matter jurisdiction

19.20 In order for an action to be maintained in federal, rather than state court, there must be a basis for the federal court to exercise subject matter jurisdiction over the dispute.[35] Federal courts are granted subject matter jurisdiction over actions that involve international arbitration, ie disputes falling within the ambit of the New York or Panama Conventions.[36] In order to gain subject matter jurisdiction as a result of the New York or the Panama Convention, the arbitration agreement must meet a four part test: (1) there must be a written agreement; (2) that provides for an arbitration in the territory of a signatory of the applicable Convention; (3) the subject matter must be commercial; and (4) it cannot be entirely domestic in scope.[37] Except for actions arising under the New York or Panama Conventions, the FAA does not itself confer subject matter jurisdiction on a federal court.[38] Thus, for non-international cases arising under the FAA, a federal court must have an independent basis for exerting jurisdiction.[39] In cases that fall under the New York or Panama Conventions, the FAA allows a defendant to remove (ie transfer) a case from state court and place the dispute under the authority of the federal district court that encompasses the state court where the action was initiated.[40] The defendant's ability to remove an action is applicable only in actions to compel arbitration or to enforce an arbitral award. The FAA does not, however, provide federal subject matter jurisdiction for an application seeking to vacate an arbitral award because the New York and Panama Conventions do not deal with such proceedings.[41] Thus, an action

---

34 FAA § 305; *Banco de Seguros del Estado v Mutual Marine Offices, Inc* 230 F Supp 2d 362, 367, n 4 (US D Ct (SDNY), 2002), affd 344 F 3d 255 (US Ct of Apps (2nd Cir), 2003).

35 *Greenberg v Bear, Stearns & Co* 220 F 3d 22, 25 (US Ct of Apps (2nd Cir), 2000), federal courts only have jurisdiction over a matter where a federal law creates the cause of action, or there is a substantial question of federal law; see also 28 USC §§ 1330ff.

36 FAA § 203; FAA § 302 (incorporating FAA § 203 by reference so that it is applicable to arbitrations within the ambit of the Panama Convention).

37 See *Smith/Enron Cogeneration Ltd Partnership, Inc v Smith Cogeneration Intl, Inc* 198 F 3d 88, 92 (US Ct of Apps (2nd Cir), 1999). For a more detailed analysis of the application of the four part test, see JH Carter and J Fellas, *International Commercial Arbitration in New York* (OUP, 2010) 209–10.

38 *Scandinavian Reinsurance Co Ltd v St Paul Fire and Marine Ins Co* 668 F 3d 60, 71 (US Ct of Apps (2nd Cir), 2012); *Smith v Rush Retail Centers, Inc* 360 F 3d 504, 505 (US Ct of Apps (5th Cir), 2004), FAA § 4 'does not create an independent basis for federal jurisdiction'; *Baltin v Alaron Trading Corp* 128 F 3d 1466, 1469 (US Ct of Apps (11th Cir), 1997) (the same).

39 Such independent bases would include diversity jurisdiction or federal question jurisdiction. Diversity jurisdiction is available when the amount in dispute is over US$75,000 and the parties to the dispute are citizens of different states. See 28 USC § 1332. An action involving parties from two foreign, ie non-US, countries will not satisfy jurisdictional diversity requirements See *Intl Shipping Co, SA v Hydra Offshore, Inc* 875 F 2d 388, 391 (US Ct of Apps (2nd Cir), 1989): 'the presence of aliens on two sides of a case destroys diversity jurisdiction', quoting *Corporacion Venezolana de Fomento v Vintero Sales Corp* 629 F 2d 786, 790 (US Ct of Apps (2nd Cir), 1980).

Federal question jurisdiction is available where potential federal jurisdiction exists. *Vaden v Discover Bank* 556 US 49, 129 S Ct 1262, 1273–75 (2009), in any request to compel arbitration under FAA § 4, the district court can 'look through' the underlying dispute and seek to determine if there is any federal question jurisdiction; but see *Bittner v RBC Capital Markets* 331 Fed Appx 869, 871 (US Ct of Apps (2nd Cir), 2009) (unpublished), regarding a contract question that raises only state law questions that does not give rise to a federal question, so the district court does not have the authority to compel the parties to arbitration.

40 FAA § 205. The Panama Convention incorporates this by reference. FAA § 307.

41 See *Intl Shipping Co, SA v Hydra Offshore, Inc* 875 F 2d 388, 391 n 5 (US Ct of Apps (2nd Cir), 1989), holding that a district court cannot base jurisdiction on the Convention if the party invoking its provisions is

related to the vacatur of an award will not, by itself, be subject to the jurisdiction of the federal court. However, if the party resisting the vacatur of an arbitral award makes a cross application to enforce the arbitral award, the federal jurisdictional bases of the FAA would apply. An application to vacate an arbitral award may also be subject to federal court jurisdiction on diversity grounds, depending on the citizenship of the parties. It is important to note, however, that an action between two non-US parties does not create diversity subject matter jurisdiction.

Regardless of whether a proceeding is in a federal or state court, the FAA will govern, even in state court actions involving international arbitration.[42] **19.21**

Personal jurisdiction

In addition to subject matter jurisdiction, the court must also have personal jurisdiction to enforce an arbitration agreement or arbitral award. In general, if the parties agree to arbitrate a dispute in the United States, they have effectively consented to the jurisdiction of a court to compel the arbitration proceeding in that location. To confirm an arbitral award, a party must still establish that the court has personal jurisdiction over the other party.[43] **19.22**

Conflicts of laws—state versus federal arbitration statutes

While the FAA sets forth federal rules regarding arbitration that apply to both state and federal courts, many states have enacted their own statutes regarding arbitration. Both Texas and Florida have adopted the United Nations Commission on International Trade Law (UNCITRAL) Model Law on International Commercial Arbitration (1985). Texas adopted it in 1989.[44] In 2010, Florida adopted the Model Law, replacing the Florida International Arbitration Act with the Florida International Commercial Arbitration Act.[45] New York has not adopted the UNCITRAL Model law, but it has enacted its own set of statutes addressing arbitration.[46] **19.23**

A key consideration in a conflict of law analysis is the doctrine of pre-emption, which provides that under certain circumstance, a federal statute will pre-empt state law. In general, state law will be pre-empted if it is in direct conflict with federal law.[47] But if state law supplements rather than conflicts with federal law, it is possible that the state law would not be pre-empted, thereby making both federal and state law applicable. This can create complexity in situations where both the FAA and a state arbitration statute apply. This chapter will **19.24**

---

not seeking either to compel arbitration or to enforce an arbitral award; *Banco De Santander Central Hispano, SA v Consalvi Intl, Inc* 425 F Supp 2d 421, 425 n 2 (US D Ct (SDNY), 2006), noting that a district court does not have jurisdiction over an action to vacate an arbitral award under the Convention.

[42] *Vaden v Discover Bank* 556 US 49, 59, 129 S Ct 1262 (2009), the 'body of federal substantive law' generated by elaboration of FAA § 2 is equally binding on state and federal courts; *Moses H Cone Memorial Hospital v Mercury Construction Corp* 460 US 1, 103 S Ct 927 (1983): 'federal law in terms of the Arbitration Act governs that issue in either state or federal court'; *Re Kellogg Brown & Root, Inc* 166 SW 3d 732, 739 (Tex S Ct 2005), recognizing 'that it is important for federal and state law to be as consistent as possible in this area, because federal and state courts have concurrent jurisdiction to enforce the FAA'.

[43] See para 19.108.

[44] Tex Civ Prac & Rem Code Ann §§ 172.001ff.

[45] Fla Stat Ann §§ 684.0001ff.

[46] NY Civil Practice Law and Rules (CPLR) §§ 7501ff.

[47] See eg *AT&T Mobility LLC v Concepcion* 131 S Ct 1740, 1747–48, 179 L Ed 2d 742 (2011), holding that a state law that had the impact of revoking an agreement to arbitrate was pre-empted by the FAA since that law 'disfavor[ed] arbitration'.

indicate instances in which federal law differs from state law, or where one state's law differs from another state's law.

19.2 Commencing the Arbitration

19.2.1 Enforcing arbitration agreements

19.25 Court intervention is often sought when a party is resisting arbitration. Typical questions that arise in the context of a party seeking court intervention to enforce an arbitration agreement are (a) whether there is an agreement to arbitrate; (b) who decides these gateway jurisdictional issues—the court or the arbitrators; (c) what disputes fall within the scope of the agreement to arbitrate; and (d) who is a party to the agreement to arbitrate, or otherwise bound by the agreement.

Court's resolution of jurisdictional questions

19.26 The role of the courts in resolving jurisdictional questions has given rise to a significant amount of controversy and analysis. The underlying principle behind arbitration is that the parties have agreed to resolve their disputes outside the courtroom. Therefore, the first question that must be considered is whether the parties actually reached an agreement to arbitrate.[48] It is ultimately the court's responsibility to make this determination.[49]

19.27 For international disputes, the New York Convention and Panama Convention dictate that the agreement to arbitrate must be in writing.[50] The writing may be a clause in a contract signed by the parties or contained in an exchange of letters between them.[51] In the Second Circuit, a form purchase order containing an arbitration clause that was signed by only one party has been held not to be writing under the New York Convention.[52] In contrast, the Fifth Circuit has found that an arbitration clause in an unsigned contract meets the New York Convention's requirement for an 'agreement in writing'.[53]

19.28 **Court's application of doctrine of *competence-competence*** In the context of a petition to compel arbitration, once a court has concluded that there is an agreement to arbitrate, it then determines if the courts or the arbitrators should determine whether the dispute is properly

[48] *Volt Info Sciences, Inc v Board of Trustees* 489 US 468, 478, 109 S Ct 1248, 1255 (1989), parties cannot be forced to arbitrate a dispute which they have not agreed to arbitrate; eg *Wheat, First Securities, Inc v Green* 993 F 2d 814 (US Ct of Apps (11th Cir), 1993), it is for the courts to determine whether a contract containing a arbitration clause has been validly assigned before sending the dispute to arbitration).

[49] *Granite Rock Co v Intl Brotherhood of Teamsters* 130 S Ct 2847, 2850, 177 L Ed 2d 567 (2010), the court must first determine if the agreement was formed before it can determine the scope and enforceability of the arbitration clause; *Solymar Invs Ltd v Banco Santander SA* 672 F 3d 981, 989 (US Ct of Apps (11th Cir), 2012), a court must first review the formation of the agreement before it can determine if the arbitration agreement is valid; *Dedon GmbH v Janus et Cie* 411 Fed Appx 361, 363 (US Ct of Apps (2nd Cir), 2011), the court must confirm the existence of an agreement to arbitrate; *DK Joint Venture 1 v Weyand* 649 F 3d 310, 317 (US Ct of Apps (5th Cir), 2011), it is 'for the courts and not the arbitrator to decide in the first instance [...] a dispute over whether the parties entered into any arbitration agreement in the first place'.

[50] New York Convention, Art II(2), Panama Convention, Art I.

[51] New York Convention, Art II(2); *Glencore Ltd v Degussa Engineered Carbons LP* 848 F Supp 2d 410, 437 (US D Ct (SDNY), 2012), finding that the exchange of draft documents containing an undisputed arbitration clause was sufficient to be an 'exchange of letters' within the meaning of the New York Convention.

[52] *Kahn Lucas Lancaster, Inc v Lark Intl Ltd* 186 F 3d 210, 216–18 (US Ct of Apps (2nd Cir), 1999), partially abrogated on other grounds by *Sarhank Group v Oracle Corp* 404 F 3d 657, 660 n 2 (US Ct of Apps (2nd Cir), 2005); see also *Czarina, LLC v WF Poe Syndicate* 358 F 3d 1286, 1293 (US Ct of Apps (11th Cir), 2004), holding that the New York Convention did not apply where there was no signed agreement or exchange of letters.

[53] *Todd v SS Mut Underwriting Assn (Bermuda) Ltd* 601 F 3d 329, 335 n 11 (US Ct of Apps (5th Cir), 2010).

subject to the arbitration agreement.[54] In other words, the court must determine whether to apply the doctrine of *competence-competence*.

The doctrine of *competence-competence* is based on the principle that an international arbitral tribunal has the authority to determine disputes concerning its own jurisdiction. Under this doctrine, if a party claims that it did not consent to submit the dispute to arbitration, it is the arbitrators themselves who determine whether they have jurisdiction over the dispute. **19.29**

US courts have not adopted the doctrine of *competence-competence* wholesale. Instead, under US case law, there is a presumption that it is for the courts to determine questions of whether a dispute is subject to the jurisdiction of an arbitral tribunal. This presumption can be overcome only where there is 'clear and unmistakable' evidence that the parties intended to refer this threshold question to the arbitrators. The leading case is *First Options of Chicago, Inc v Kaplan*.[55] The United States Supreme Court addressed the question by analysing whether a 'court or arbitrator' has the authority to determine whether the parties have agreed to arbitrate. It concluded that ' "who has the primary power to decide arbitrability" turns upon what the parties agreed about that matter'.[56] The Court concluded that the general presumption in favour of arbitration does not necessarily result in a presumption that jurisdictional questions should be dealt with by the arbitral tribunal.[57] The basis for the presumption that a court should determine the scope of the tribunal's jurisdiction is that a party can only be forced to arbitrate issues that it has agreed to submit to arbitration. Without the presumption that a court determines jurisdiction, the general presumption in favour of arbitration 'might too often force unwilling parties to arbitrate a matter they reasonably would have thought a judge, not an arbitrator, would decide'.[58] **19.30**

The presumption in favour of judicial determination of the arbitrator's jurisdiction can be overcome if there is 'clea[r] and unmistakabl[e] evidence' that the parties intended the arbitrators to decide questions about the scope of their jurisdiction to arbitrate.[59] One way that **19.31**

---

54 *Webb v Investacorp, Inc* 89 F 3d 252, 258 (US Ct of Apps (5th Cir), 1996), after determining there is a valid agreement to arbitrate, the court then determines 'whether the dispute in question falls within the scope of that arbitration agreement'.

55 *First Options of Chicago, Inc v Kaplan* 514 US 938, 943, 115 S Ct 1920, 1923 (1995).

56 *First Options* (n 55) 943 (citations omitted). US courts use the term 'arbitrability' to refer broadly to whether a particular question is subject to arbitration. Thus, the term 'arbitrability' as used by US courts may refer to questions of whether there is an agreement to arbitrate, who is a proper party to the arbitration, what disputes fall within the scope of the arbitration agreement, and who decides questions of the scope of the tribunal's jurisdiction. This is in contrast to non-US jurisdictions which use the term 'arbitrability' to refer to categories of disputes, such as antitrust or consumer transactions, that are not capable of settlement by arbitration.

57 *First Options* (n 55) 944–5.

58 *First Options* (n 55) 944–5. See also *John Hancock Life Ins Co v Wilson* 254 F 3d 48, 53 (US Ct of Apps (2nd Cir), 2001): 'issues of "arbitrability" are presumptively for the court to decide', while 'issues other than "arbitrability" are presumptively for the arbitrator'; *Gen Motors Corp v Pamela Equities Corp* 146 F 3d 242, 248 (US Ct of Apps (5th Cir), 1998): 'the law creates a presumption that the parties did not agree to submit any question as to the arbitrator's own power to that very same arbitrator'; *Petrofac, Inc v DynMcDermott Petroleum Operations Co* 687 F 3d 671, 675 (US Ct of Apps (5th Cir), 2012), the court will not assume that the arbitrator can determine arbitrability without clear and unmistakable evidence of such selection; *Terminix International Co v Palmer Ranch LP* 432 F 3d 1327, 1332 (US Ct of Apps (11th Cir), 2005), without express authority to rule on the validity of the arbitration agreement, the arbitrator would lack authority to reach a determination on the agreement itself.

59 *First Options* 514 US at 944; *Rent-A-Center, West, Inc v Jackson*, 130 S Ct 2772, 2777, 177 L Ed 2d 403 (2010), recognizing 'that parties can agree to arbitrate "gateway" questions of "arbitrability," such as whether the parties have agreed to arbitrate or whether their agreement covers a particular controversy'; *Gen Motors Corp*, 146 F 3d at 248, recognizing that the parties can agree to arbitrate arbitrability only if there is 'clear and

the parties can establish clear and unmistakable evidence is to have the arbitration agreement explicitly state that the arbitrators shall have the authority to determine their own jurisdiction.[60] Even without an explicit provision that the arbitrators shall rule on questions of jurisdiction, the incorporation of arbitral rules that provide that the arbitrators shall decide their own jurisdiction or respond to jurisdictional objections also constitutes 'clear and unmistakable evidence'.[61] This will not, therefore, be an issue in international arbitrations conducted under the most popular arbitration rules, such as those of the ICC, AAA, ICDR, and UNCITRAL Arbitration Rules.

19.32 Having adopted the UNCITRAL Model Law, both Florida and Texas provide by statute that the arbitral tribunal can rule on its own jurisdiction, including objections to the validity or existence of the arbitration agreement itself.[62] If the tribunal concludes that it has jurisdiction, a party may, within 30 days, seek court intervention to review that determination.[63] The court's decision on this issue is not appealable and the tribunal may continue the arbitration proceeding while the court evaluates a party's request for review. A party's failure to seek immediate court review of the arbitrator's determination of jurisdiction will not constitute a waiver of the party's right under the FAA to later contest the tribunal's jurisdiction after an award is issued. This is because the FAA pre-empts the state law that provides deadlines for requesting intermediate review of the tribunal's jurisdictional determination.

19.33 **Court's application of separability doctrine** Another doctrine that is important when allocating authority between arbitrators and courts is the separability, or severability, doctrine. The separability doctrine serves to isolate the terms of the arbitration clause 'from the contract in which they are embedded'.[64] Based on this principle, a party's challenge to the validity of another provision in the contract, or even a challenge to the contract as a whole, will not affect the court's ability to enforce the agreement to arbitrate,[65] or the arbitral tribunal's power to determine the validity of the contract as a whole.[66]

---

unmistakable' evidence of such decision; *Merrill Lynch, Pierce, Fenner & Smith, Inc v Cohen* 62 F 3d 381, 384 (US Ct of Apps (11th Cir), 1995) (the same); *Schneider v Kingdom of Thailand* 688 F 3d 68, 71 (US Ct of Apps (2nd Cir), 2012), arbitrability is 'an issue for judicial determination [u]nless the parties clearly and unmistakably provide otherwise' (citations omitted).

[60] See *Re Checking Account Overdraft Litig* 674 F 3d 1252 (US Ct of Apps (11th Cir), 2012), enforcing a delegation provision that provides: 'Any issue regarding whether a particular dispute or controversy is . . . subject to arbitration will be decided by the arbitrator.'

[61] See *Petrofac, Inc v DynMcDermott Petroleum Operations Co* 687 F 3d 671, 675 (US Ct of Apps (5th Cir), 2012), the arbitration agreement's incorporation of AAA rules presented 'clear and unmistakable evidence that the parties agreed to arbitrate arbitrality'; *Republic of Ecuador v Chevron Corp* 638 F 3d 384, 394 (US Ct of Apps (2nd Cir), 2011), an arbitration agreement agreeing to resolve disputes under the UNCITRAL rules was clear and unmistakable evidence that the parties intended to have the arbitrators rule on questions of arbitrability; *Contec Corp v Remote Solution Co* 398 F 3d 205, 208 (US Ct of Apps (2nd Cir), 2005): 'We have held that when, as here, parties explicitly incorporate rules that empower an arbitrator to decide issues of arbitrability, the incorporation serves as clear and unmistakable evidence of the parties' intent to delegate such issues to an arbitrator.'; *Terminix Intl Co, LP v Palmer Ranch LP* 432 F 3d 1327, 1332 (US Ct of Apps (11th Cir), 2005): 'By incorporating the AAA Rules, including Rule 8, into their agreement, the parties clearly and unmistakably agreed that the arbitrator should decide whether the arbitration clause is valid.'

[62] Fla Stat Ann § 684.0017(1), Tex Civ Prac & Rem Code Ann § 172.082(a), respectively.

[63] Fla Stat Ann § 684.0017(3), Tex Civ Prac & Rem Code Ann § 172.082(g), respectively.

[64] *Prima Paint Corp v Flood & Conklin Mfg Co* 388 US 395, 403–4, 87 S Ct 1801 (1967).

[65] *Buckeye Check Cashing, Inc v Cardegna*, 546 US 440, 445, 126 S Ct 1204 (2006), holding that 'an arbitration provision is severable from the remainder of the contract'.

[66] See *Rent-A-Center, West, Inc v Jackson* 130 S Ct 2772, 2779, 177 L Ed 2d 403 (2010), since the defendant challenged the validity of the contract as a whole instead of the specific arbitration clause at issue, the Court must compel arbitration, 'leaving any challenge to the validity of the Agreement as a whole for the arbitrator';

Unless a party claims that the agreement to arbitrate is itself invalid, the arbitration clause is considered separate and insulated from challenges to the validity of the underlying contract.[67] However, if in the context of a court petition to compel arbitration a party challenges the validity of the arbitration clause—for example on grounds of fraud or misrepresentation—the court, and not the arbitrator, will consider that issue.[68] A party making such a challenge is required to show that there is 'some substantial relationship between the fraud or misrepresentation and the arbitration clause in particular'.[69] **19.34**

Scope of arbitration agreement In determining whether a particular dispute is within the scope of the arbitration agreement: 'Federal policy requires [courts] to construe arbitration clauses as broadly as possible.'[70] Accordingly, 'any doubts concerning the scope of arbitrable issues should be resolved in favor of arbitration'.[71] In performing the analysis, the court must first determine whether the arbitration clause is broad or narrow. The nature of the arbitration clause directs the court's analysis.[72] As a general rule, an arbitration clause is considered broad if it addresses all disputes that 'arise out of' or 'relate to' the contract.[73] If **19.35**

Jenkins v First Am Cash Adv of Georgia, LLC 400 F 3d 868, 882 (US Ct of Apps (11th Cir), 2005), a claim that the contract containing an arbitration clause was void *ab inito* was a matter for the arbitrators and not the court to examine. This principle is applicable to challenges brought in both state and federal courts. *See Buckeye Check Cashing, Inc v Cardegna* 546 US 440, 449, 126 S Ct 1204, 1210 (2006), 'regardless of whether the challenge is brought in federal or state court, a challenge to the validity of the contract as a whole, and not specifically to the arbitration clause, must go to the arbitrator'.

67 See *Chastain v Robinson-Humphrey Co* 957 F 2d 851 (US Ct of Apps (11th Cir), 1992), a claim that the entire agreement is itself invalid, so it is for the court to rule on before making a determination to send to arbitration.

68 See *Prima Paint*, 388 US at 403–4, 87 S Ct 1801, the Court would evaluate the claim if it was that there was 'fraud in the inducement of the arbitration clause itself'.

69 *Campaniello Imp Ltd v Saporiti Italia SpA* 117 F 3d 655, 667 (US Ct of Apps (2nd Cir), 1997); *Madura v Countrywide Home Loans, Inc* 344 Fed Appx 509, 515 (US Ct of Apps (11th Cir), 2009)(unpublished), a claim that a contract was void *ab initio* in its entirety as a result of a fraud in the inducement of the contract did not specifically challenge the arbitration agreement and was therefore for the arbitrators to hear and decide; *Garten v Kurth* 265 F 3d 136, 144 (US Ct of Apps (2nd Cir), 2001), posturing as to the benefit of arbitration was not sufficient to establish fraud in the creation of an arbitration clause itself and therefore the court ordered the dispute to be submitted to arbitration; *BDO Seidman, LLP v JA Green Dev Corp* 327 SW 3d 852, 859 (Tex Ct of Apps (Dallas), 2010), the party's claim that it entered into an arbitration agreement based on false representations thereby making the agreement unconscionable was a matter for the arbitrators to determine because the alleged bad acts focused on the formation of the agreement as a whole, not specifically the formation of the arbitration agreement (citing *Prima Paint*, 308 US at 402 and *Campaniello*, 117 F 3d at 667).

70 *Collins & Aikman Products Co v Building Systems, Inc* 58 F 3d 16, 19 (US Ct of Apps (2nd Cir), 1995) (internal quotation marks and citation omitted).

71 *Moses H Cone Memorial Hospital v Mercury Construction Corp* 460 US 1, 24–5, 103 S Ct 927 (1983); recognized by *Collins & Aikman* 58 F 3d at 19; *Jones v Halliburton Co* 583 F 3d 228, 235 (US Ct of Apps (5th Cir), 2009); *Ivax Corp v B Braun of Am, Inc* 286 F 3d 1309, 1320 n 23 (US Ct of Apps (11th Cir), 2002), because of the presumption of arbitrability, parties must clearly express any exclusions to the scope of the arbitration agreement.

72 *Collins & Aikman* (n 71) 20; *Pennzoil Exploration & Production Co v Ramco Energy Ltd* 139 F 3d 1061, 1067 (US Ct of Apps (5th Cir), 1998), a court must characterize the arbitration clause as 'broad' or 'narrow' to determine whether the dispute falls within its scope; but see *Ivax Corp v B Braun of Am, Inc* 286 F 3d 1309, 1320 (US Ct of Apps (11th Cir), 2002), the Eleventh Circuit finds there is a presumption of arbitrability under both narrow and broad arbitration clauses, and instead carefully examines the arbitration agreement itself.

73 *WorldCrisa Corp v Armstrong* 129 F 3d 71, 75 (US Ct of Apps (2nd Cir), 1997); *Genesco, Inc v T Kakiuchi & Co Ltd* 815 F 2d 840, 848 (US Ct of Apps (2nd Cir), 1987), the 'relating to' clause in an arbitration agreement was sufficiently broad to require the arbitration of fraudulent inducement and RICO claims). There is no bright line rule regarding the breadth of the clause and the decision can turn on the reading of the entire clause. cf *Pennzoil Exploration & Prod Co v Ramco Energy Ltd* 139 F 3d 1061, 1067 (US Ct of Apps (5th Cir), 1998), describing a 'narrow' interpretation of 'arising out of' language) *with Sedco v Petroleos Mexicanos Mexican National Oil* 767 F 2d 1140, 1145 (US Ct of Apps (5th Cir), 1985), 'arising out of' language was found to be 'broad' in context.

the arbitration clause is broad and the claims relate to the contractual relationship between the parties, 'then there is a presumption that the claims are arbitrable'.[74]

19.36 On the other hand, if an arbitration clause is 'narrowly worded and the dispute concerns a matter collateral to the contract calling for arbitration, "a court should test the presumption [in favour of arbitration] by reviewing the allegations underlying the dispute and by asking whether the claim alleged implicates issues of contract construction"'.[75] Courts often consider use of the words 'arising under' to be the 'magic' phrase in demonstrating that the parties agreed that the arbitration clause should be narrowly interpreted.[76] Thus, an agreement to arbitrate disputes 'arising under' a particular contract would be considered narrow and would not include matters that are collateral to the contract.[77] A matter is considered collateral if it is not fully related to the subject matter that gave rise to the arbitration agreement, and if so determined in connection with a narrow arbitration clause, that matter would be deemed beyond the purview of the arbitration clause.[78] Parties may also limit the scope of an arbitration agreement to specific disputes, or expressly exclude other disputes.[79]

19.37 **Waiver** It is possible for a party to waive its right to arbitration by actively participating in related litigation.[80] Again, the question arises of who determines—court or tribunal—whether there has been a waiver of arbitration. The Supreme Court has stated, in dicta, that

---

[74] *Collins & Aikman Products Co v Building Systems, Inc* 58 F 3d at 20; *Sunkyong Engineering & Construction Co Ltd v Born, Inc* 149 F 3d 1174 (US Ct of Apps (5th Cir), 1998), recognizing that there is a strong presumption in favour of arbitration unless it is clear that no interpretation of the arbitration clause would allow it to cover the dispute at issue; *Ivax Corp v B Braun of Am, Inc* 286 F 3d 1309, 1320 (US Ct of Apps (11th Cir), 2002), courts cannot twist the language of the contract to reach a determination that the parties agreed to arbitrate.

[75] *WorldCrisa Corp v Armstrong* 129 F3d 71, 74–5 (US Ct of Apps (2nd Cir), 1997), quoting *Collins & Aikman* 48 F 2d at 23).

[76] *IDEA Corp v WC & R Interests, Inc* 545 F Supp 2d 600, 606 (US D Ct (W D Tex), 2008), the arbitration clause was limited to disputes 'arising under' the agreement and was therefore narrowly construed, resulting in the court finding that the claimed dispute was not subject to arbitration because it did not directly relate to the contract; *Explo, Inc v Southern Natural Gas Co* 788 F 2d 1096, 1098–9 (US Ct of Apps (5th Cir), 1986) (citations omitted), recognizing that 'arises under' is a relatively narrow arbitration clause.

[77] eg *Buell Door Co v Architectural Systems, Inc* 2002 WL 1968223 (US D Ct (N D Tex), 2002), finding that 'arising hereunder' was a narrow arbitration clause and so the disputed issue did not fall within the scope of the arbitration clause and as a result the court refused to compel arbitration.

[78] *Louis Dreyfus Negoce SA v Blystad Shipping & Trading Inc* 252 F 3d 218, 224 (US Ct of Apps (2nd Cir), 2001): 'Where the arbitration clause is narrow, a collateral matter will generally be ruled beyond its purview'; *Jones v Halliburton Co* 583 F 3d 228, 241 (US Ct of Apps (5th Cir), 2009), holding that an attack on an employee while off-duty was not 'related to' her employment and therefore was not within the scope of the arbitration agreement with the employer.

[79] See eg *Negrin v Kalina* 2010 WL 2816809 (US D Ct (SDNY), 2010), narrow arbitration clause only covered certain disputes, such as disputes of profit distribution or compliance with by-laws; *World Rentals and Sales, LLC v Volvo Const Equip Rents, Inc* 517 F 3d 1240, 1246 (US Ct of Apps (11th Cir), 2008), an arbitration agreement expressly excluded affiliates from the agreement to arbitrate; *Becker v Davis* 491 F 3d 1292, 1301 (US Ct of Apps (11th Cir), 2007), arbitration cannot be compelled where the parties expressly excluded those claims from the agreement.

[80] *Republic Insurance Co v PAICO Receivables, LLC* 383 F 3d 341, 344 (US Ct of Apps (5th Cir), 2004), a party may waive its right to arbitration if it invokes the judicial machinery to 'the detriment or prejudice of the other party'; *Garcia v Wachovia Corp* 699 F 3d 1273, 1278 (US Ct of Apps (11th Cir), 2012), a party waived its right to arbitration where extensive pre-trial discovery resulted in significant expense and prejudice against the other party); *Opals on Ice Lingerie v Bodylines Inc* 320 F 3d 362, 368 (US Ct of Apps (2nd Cir), 2003): 'if a party participates in arbitration proceedings without making a timely objection to the submission of the dispute to arbitration, that party may be found to have waived its right to object to the arbitration'.

'the presumption is that the arbitrator should decide "allegation[s] of waiver"'.[81] However, courts often decide this issue themselves.[82] The party seeking to assert waiver by the other party has a heavy burden and must establish that the other party is not entitled to rely on the arbitration agreement because it 'engage[d] in protracted litigation that result[ed] in prejudice to the opposing party'.[83]

Jurisdiction over non-signatories to arbitration agreement Since an obligation to arbitrate a dispute arises under a contractual agreement, a non-signatory to the arbitration agreement can generally not be bound to arbitrate. However, there are certain limited circumstances in which a non-signatory may be bound to submit to an arbitration agreement, as long as there is some agreement to arbitrate. Again, in the context of a petition to compel arbitration that has been brought before a court, it is typically for the courts to determine whether a non-signatory can be bound to arbitrate.[84] In some circumstances, the party to the arbitration agreement seeks to avoid arbitration by filing suit against the other party (including its non-signatory officers and agents) as a way to avoid arbitration. In those circumstances, courts have granted the application of the non-signatory to compel the party to arbitrate under a related arbitration agreement.[85] Traditional state law principles of contract apply to whether a non-signatory may be bound to arbitrate.[86] These principles include: **19.38**

(1) *Incorporation by reference.* In some instances, a contract does not contain an arbitration clause, but instead incorporates by reference a document, such as a contract or other document, that does contain an arbitration clause.[87]

---

[81] *Howsam v Dean Witter Reynolds, Inc* 537 US 79, 84, 123 S Ct 588 (2002); quoting *Moses H Cone* (n 71) 24–5, 103 S Ct 927; *S & R Co of Kingston v Latona Trucking, Inc* 159 F 3d 80, 82–3 (US Ct of Apps (2nd Cir), 1998).

[82] *Keytrade USA, Inc v Ain Temouchent M/V* 404 F 3d 891, 897 (US Ct of Apps (5th Cir), 2005), denying a party's claim of waiver of arbitration and recognizing that the Fifth Circuit has a presumption against a finding of waiver of arbitration.

[83] *Brookridge Funding Corp v Northwestern Human Resources, Inc* 170 Fed Appx 170, 171 (US Ct of Apps (2nd Cir), 2006), finding waiver where a party had participated in the underlying litigation, including litigating the case to trial without claiming that the dispute was subject to arbitration; *Krinsk v SunTrust Banks, Inc* 654 F 3d 1194, 1200 (US Ct of Apps (11th Cir), 2011), the party seeking waiver has a heavy burden, but the court will look to the totality of the circumstances to see if the party 'has acted inconsistently with the arbitration right, and, second, [they] look to see whether, by doing so, that party has in some way prejudiced the other party' (internal quotations omitted); *Re Mirant Corp* 613 F 3d 584, 590–3 (US Ct of Apps (5th Cir), 2010), finding that a party waived its right to arbitration where it filed numerous pleadings and motions, despite the party's reservation of rights to compel arbitration contained in its papers.

[84] See *DK Joint Venture 1 v Weyand* 649 F 3d 310, 317 (US Ct of Apps (5th Cir), 2011): '[it] is for the courts and not the arbitrator to decide in the first instance[...] a dispute over whether the parties entered into any arbitration agreement in the first place.' *Arthur Andersen LLP v Carlisle* 556 US 624, 129 S Ct 1896, 1902 (2009); *Merrill Lynch Inv Managers v Optibase Ltd* 337 F 3d 125, 129 (US Ct of Apps (2nd Cir), 2003).

[85] *Grigson v Creative Artists Agency LLC* 210 F 3d 524, 526–8 (US Ct of Apps (5th Cir), 2000), a signatory plaintiff could not use the status of a defendant as a non-signatory to prevent defendants from compelling arbitration under the agreement; *Re Vesta Insurance Group, Inc* 192 SW 3d 759 (Tex S Ct, 2006), applying the FAA and compelling a party to arbitration with non-signatory officers and agents of the other parties to 'hold [...] the plaintiff to his agreement to arbitrate'; *Merrill Lynch Investment Managers v Optibase Ltd* 337 F 3d 125, 131 (US Ct of Apps (2nd Cir), 2003), recognizing greater scope for a non-signatory to compel a signatory to arbitrate than vice versa; *Thomson-CSF, SA v American Arbitration Assn* 64 F 3d 773, 779 (US Ct of Apps (2nd Cir), 1995), signatory was bound to arbitrate with a non-signatory at the non-signatory's insistence because of 'the close relationship between the entities involved'.

[86] *Arthur Andersen LLP v Carlisle* 556 US 624, 631, 129 S Ct 1896 (2009); *Bridas SAPIC v Govt of Turkmenistan* 345 F 3d 347, 356 (US Ct of Apps (5th Cir), 2003); *Employers Ins of Wausau v Bright Metal Specialties, Inc* 251 F 3d 1316, 1322 (US Ct of Apps (11th Cir), 2001); *Thomson-CSF, SA v American Arbitration Assn* 64 F 3d 773, 776 (US Ct of Apps (2nd Cir), 1995).

[87] *Progressive Cas Ins Co v CA Reaseguradora Nacional De Venezuela* 991 F 2d 42, 48 (US Ct of Apps (2nd Cir), 1993); *World Rentals and Sales, LLC v Volvo Construction Equipment Rents, Inc* 517 F 3d 1240, 1245 (US

(2) *Assumption by conduct.* A non-signatory 'may be bound by an arbitration clause if its subsequent conduct indicates that it is assuming the obligation to arbitrate'.[88] Thus, a non-signatory's participation in an arbitration, or the sending of a representative to participate in the arbitration, may bind the non-signatory to the arbitration agreement.[89]

(3) *Agency.* A non-signatory may be bound to arbitrate if its agent signed an arbitration agreement on behalf of their principal.[90]

(4) *Veil-piercing/alter ego.* Under the alter ego or piercing the corporate veil theory, a non-signatory can be bound to arbitrate if it is the alter ego of the actual signatory to the arbitration agreement. The standard for piercing the corporate veil is similar to the standard for piercing the corporate veil in contract liability and considers whether '(1) the owner exercised complete control over the corporation with respect to the transaction at issue and (2) such control was used to commit a fraud or wrong that injured the party seeking to pierce the veil'.[91]

(5) *Estoppel.* A court may compel a non-signatory to arbitrate a dispute pursuant to an arbitration agreement under the grounds of equitable estoppel—also known as 'intertwined claims' estoppel.[92] This theory applies where a signatory to a written agreement that contains an arbitration clause relies on the terms of the written agreement to assert claims against the non-signatory. Intertwined claims estoppel may also apply where a signatory makes clear allegations that the signatory and non-signatory's dispute relates to 'substantially interdependent and connected' conduct.[93]

Ct of Apps (11th Cir), 2008), finding that the agreement incorporated by reference the arbitration clause in another agreement, but since that agreement had a very limited arbitration clause, the court declined to compel arbitration; *The Rice Co (Suisse), SA v Precious Flowers Ltd* 523 F 3d 528, 538 (US Ct of Apps (5th Cir), 2008), the company would be subject to arbitration of a standard form contract incorporated by reference if the parties had not had explicit discussions regarding arbitrability; *Scott v Prudential Sec, Inc* 141 F.3d 1007, 1013 (US Ct of Apps (11th Cir), 1998), a party who registered as a member of broker consented to arbitrate as a result of incorporation by reference of member rules containing an arbitration provision.

[88] *Thomson-CSF, SA v American Arbitration Assn* 64 F 3d 773, 777 (US Ct of Apps (2nd Cir), 1995).

[89] See *Gvozdenovic v United Air Lines, Inc* 933 F 2d 1100, 1105 (US Ct of Apps (2nd Cir), 1991), flight attendants manifested a clear intention to arbitrate by sending a representative to act on their behalf in an arbitration process; *Interpool Ltd v Through Transport Mutual Insurance Assn Ltd* 635 F Supp 1503, 1504–5 (US D Ct (S D Fla), 1985), a party standing in the shoes of a prior entity to get the benefit of a contract is subject to the terms of the arbitration agreement in that contract.

[90] *DK Joint Venture 1 v Weyand* 649 F 3d 310, 314 (US Ct of Apps (5th Cir), 2011); *Board of Trustees of City of Delray Beach Police and Firefighters Ret System v Citigroup Global Markets, Inc* 622 F 3d 1335, 1342 (US Ct of Apps (11th Cir), 2010), it is for the court and not the arbitrator to determine whether a signatory had the authority to bind a non-signatory to the agreement. The converse is not true. An agent is not personally bound to arbitrate simply because it signed an arbitration agreement on behalf of a disclosed principal. See *Covington v Aban Offshore Ltd* 650 F 3d 556, 559 (US Ct of Apps (5th Cir), 2011), where the disclosed principal and third-party are parties to a contract, the agent who signed on behalf of the disclosed principal is not subject to the arbitration agreement.

[91] *Bridas SAPIC v Govt of Turkmenistan* 345 F 3d 347, 359 (US Ct of Apps (5th Cir), 2003), citing *American Fuel Corp v Utah Energy Dev Co, Inc* 122 F 3d 130, 134 (US Ct of Apps (2nd Cir), 1997); *Variable Annuity Life Ins Co (VALIC) v Dull* 2009 WL 3064750 (US D Ct (S D Fla), 2009): 'the relationship between the signatory and the alter ego must be one where the alter ego so dominates and controls the affairs of the signatory such that the signatory cannot be said to have any independent existence or will of its own'.

[92] *Choctaw Generation Ltd Partnership v American Home Assurance Co* 271 F 3d 403, 406 (US Ct of Apps (2nd Cir), 2001), a court can 'estop a signatory from avoiding arbitration with a nonsignatory when the issues the nonsignatory is seeking to resolve in arbitration are intertwined with the agreement that the estopped party has signed'.

[93] *Grigson v Creative Artists Agency LLC* 210 F 3d 524, 527 (US Ct of Apps (5th Cir), 2000), quoting *MS Dealer Service Corp v Franklin* 177 F 3d 942, 947 (US Ct of Apps (11th Cir), 1999); *Escobal v Celebration Cruise Operator, Inc* 482 Fed Appx 475, 476 (US Ct of Apps (11th Cir), 2012) (unpublished), finding that

(6) *Third-party beneficiary.* A non-signatory may enforce an arbitration agreement, or be bound by an arbitration agreement, as third-party beneficiary if '(1) the parties to the contract intended to secure a benefit to [the non-signatory] and (2) entered into the contract directly for [the non-signatory's] benefit'.[94]

19.2.2 Court assistance in compelling or dismissing arbitration

Petitions to compel arbitration

The FAA grants courts the authority to compel both domestic arbitrations, and international arbitrations arising under the New York or Panama Conventions.[95] With respect to domestic arbitrations, under section 4 of the FAA the court can only compel the arbitration to take place in the district in which the application was filed.[96] **19.39**

If the court has subject matter jurisdiction because the matter falls within the ambit of the New York or Panama Conventions,[97] the court is empowered to 'direct that arbitration be held in accordance with the agreement at any place therein provided for, whether that place is within or without the United States'.[98] If the arbitration agreement does not specify a venue, the court's authority to direct the location of the arbitration is derived from section 4 of the FAA, which only grants the court the power to compel arbitration in its own district.[99] **19.40**

---

a party's dispute against a cruise ship was intertwined with a suit against the cruise ship, therefore subjecting the non-signatory to arbitration; *Talk Fusion, Inc v Ulrich* 2011 WL 4102215 (US D Ct (M D Fla), 2011); *Thomson-CSF, SA v American Arbitration Assn* 64 F 3d 773, 779 (US Ct of Apps (2nd Cir), 1995). See also *Choctaw Generation Ltd Partnership v American Home Assurance Co* 271 F 3d 403, 406 (US Ct of Apps (2nd Cir), 2001), a finding of intertwined estoppel 'should only be made after careful review of the relationship between the parties, the contracts they signed, and the issues that arose between them'; *American Bureau of Shipping v Tencara Shipyard SPA* 170 F 3d 349, 353 (US Ct of Apps (2nd Cir), 1999), bound a non-signatory vessel owner to an arbitration clause based on a contract between the classification society and the shipyard.

94 *Re Palm Harbor Homes* 195 SW 3d 672, 677 (Tex S Ct, 2006), finding a third-party beneficiary who would be subject to the arbitration clause in the agreement; *ConocoPhillips Co v Graham* 2012 WL 1059084 (Tex Ct of Apps (1st Dist), 2012), a contract itself contained clear evidence that there was a second category of claims that could be arbitrable, which was placed in the contract for the purpose of providing a benefit to third-parties; *Fleetwood Enterprises, Inc v Gaskamp* 280 F 3d 1069, 1076 (US Ct of Apps (5th Cir), 2002), applying Texas Law to find that there was no third-party beneficiary agreement); *Peters v The Keyes Co* 402 Fed Appx 448, 451 (US Ct of Apps (11th Cir), 2010), a non-signatory can qualify as a third-party beneficiary only if the agreement was for the primary and direct benefit of that person; *McPheeters v McGinn, Smith and Co, Inc* 953 F 2d 771, 773 (US Ct of Apps (2nd Cir), 1992), a third-party beneficiary only exists if the parties to the contract intended to confer a benefit on the third party; but see *Spear, Leeds & Kellogg v C Life Assurance Co* 85 F 3d 21, 27 (US Ct of Apps (2nd Cir), 1996), an insurer of a stock exchange customer could invoke the arbitration provisions of the stock exchange as a third-party beneficiary of the agreement between the stock exchange member and the stock exchange.

95 FAA § 4; FAA § 206; FAA § 303, respectively; See also *Dean Witter Reynolds Inc v Byrd* 470 US 213, 217, 105 S Ct 1238 (1985), the court '*shall* direct the parties to proceed to arbitration on issues as to which an arbitration agreement has been signed'.

96 FAA § 4; *Oil Basins Ltd v Broken Hill Proprietary Co Ltd* 613 F Supp 483, 486 (US D Ct (SDNY), 1985); *Control Screening LLC v Technological Application and Prod Co (Tecapro), HCMC-Vietnam* 687 F 3d 163, 171 (US Ct of Apps (3rd Cir), 2012), a district court may compel arbitration only within its district; *Bauhinia Corp v China National Machinery & Equipment Import & Export Corp* 819 F 2d 247, 250 (US Ct of Apps (9th Cir), 1987).

97 See para 19.20.

98 FAA §§ 206, 303, respectively.

99 *Control Screening LLC v Technological Application and Prod Co (Tecapro), HCMC-Vietnam* 687 F 3d 163, 171 (US Ct of Apps (3rd Cir), 2012), a district court may compel arbitration under the New York Convention within its district because the venue specified in the contract was unclear; *Bauhinia Corp v China National Machinery & Equipment Import & Export Corp* 819 F 2d 247, 250 (US Ct of Apps (9th Cir), 1987) (the same).

19.41 A party is entitled to bring a petition to compel arbitration based on section 4 of the FAA only if there is 'failure, neglect or refusal of another to arbitrate'.[100] There is no comparable provision in Chapter 2 or 3, but courts have required this same showing to be made with respect to a petition to compel an international arbitration.[101]

19.42 In the event that the court concludes that certain claims fall under the arbitration agreement, while others do not, it will compel the parties to arbitrate the claims subject to the agreement, while retaining jurisdiction over the other claims. This can result in two separate proceedings in two distinct forums.[102]

19.43 State statutes also provide for compelling a party to arbitrate. Florida and Texas both distinguish between compelling arbitration in domestic or international arbitration. The law in both states is similar. If it is a domestic arbitration, on the petition of a party, the court shall order the parties to arbitrate upon the 'showing of (1) an agreement to arbitrate; and (2) the opposing party's refusal to arbitrate'.[103] This does not apply in international arbitration.[104] In international arbitration, a party can request the court to stay the proceeding and refer the matter to arbitration only in the context of a 'pending judicial proceeding'.[105] If the arbitration agreement applies to the pending matter, the court will stay the proceedings and refer the matter to arbitration.[106] Such request must be made prior to submitting the requesting party's first 'substantive' filing.[107]

19.44 While the judiciary has not yet ruled on this inherent gap in a party's ability to compel a party to arbitration without having first been subject to a pending action, it is likely that the FAA would pre-empt any such limitation on the ability to enforce arbitration agreements and would provide a means for a party to directly seek the enforcement of an arbitration agreement in state court.[108]

---

[100] FAA § 4.

[101] *Empresa Generadora De Electricidad Itabo v Corporacion Dominicana De Empresas Electricas Estatales ('CDEEE')* 2005 WL 1705080 (US D Ct (SDNY), 2005), refusing to compel an international arbitration where the parties were already in arbitration; *Hartford Acc & Indem Co v Equitas Reinsurance Ltd* 200 F Supp 2d 102, 110 n 9 (US D Ct (D Conn), 2002), holding that plaintiffs were not aggrieved under FAA § 4 because: 'It is not known at this time whether one or more of the arbitration defendants will actually refuse to arbitrate' and without such refusal, the court would not have a 'a justiciable case or controversy in the first instance'.

[102] *KPMG LLP v Cocchi* 132 S Ct 23, 26, L Ed 2d 323 (2011), remanding refusal to compel because two of four claims were not arbitrable did not mean that the other two claims should be separated and referred to arbitration.

[103] Tex Civ Prac & Rem Code Ann § 171.021; Fla Stat Ann § 682.03.

[104] Tex Civ Prac & Rem Code Ann § 172.001(d), the rules for international arbitration supersede the rule to compel arbitration; 1A Tex Jur Pl & Pr Forms § 30:51 (2nd edn). While Florida does not specifically state that its international arbitration law supersedes its general arbitration law, a Florida court's authority to compel arbitration is limited to arbitrations 'subject to' the general arbitration law. Fla Stat Ann § 682.03(1). Florida's predecessor statute for international arbitration did allow for a party to apply to the court to compel arbitration. See Fla Stat Ann § 684.22 (repealed 30 June 2010).

[105] Tex Civ Prac & Rem Code Ann § 172.174; Tex Civ Prac & Rem Code Ann § 172.171: 'A court may not intervene in a matter' governing the arbitration of international commercial disputes except as otherwise provided under statute or applicable federal law. Fla Stat Ann § 684.0009(1); Fla Stat Ann § 684.0007.

[106] Tex Civ Prac & Rem Code Ann § 172.174(a); Fla Stat Ann § 684.0009(1).

[107] Tex Civ Prac & Rem Code Ann § 172.174(b); Fla Stat Ann § 684.0009(1).

[108] FAA § 2; *Southland Corp v Keating* 465 US 1, 104 S Ct 852 (1984): 'In creating a substantive rule applicable in state as well as federal courts, Congress intended to foreclose state legislative attempts to undercut the enforceability of arbitration agreements.'; *OPE Intern LP v Chet Morrison Contractors, Inc* 258 F 3d 443, 447 (US Ct of Apps (5th Cir), 2001), Texas courts 'have held that the FAA pre-empts other state laws that preclude parties from enforcing arbitration agreements'.

New York does not have separate state statutory schemes for domestic and international arbitration. In New York, a party that is 'aggrieved by the failure of another to arbitrate may apply for an order compelling arbitration'.[109] The requirement that there must actually be a failure to arbitrate mirrors the provisions of the FAA. **19.45**

Demand for arbitration under New York CPLR § 7503(c)

New York state law contains a unique feature that shifts the burden of court action to the party resisting arbitration. New York law provides that a party may, but is not required to, serve a demand for arbitration or, a notice of intent to arbitrate that explicitly states that, unless the party served applies to the court to stay the arbitration within 20 days after service, that party will be 'precluded from objecting that a valid agreement was not made or has not been complied with and from asserting in court the bar of a limitation of time'.[110] This allows a party filing an arbitration to shift the burden to the adversary to promptly seek a judicial stay of arbitration on the grounds that (a) the arbitration agreement procedures have not been complied with, or (b) the arbitration is barred by the statute of limitations. A party receiving such notice must raise any such objection before the court within 20 days of receipt, or it waives the right to seek a stay of arbitration in court on these grounds. The 20 day limitation in section 7503(c) of the NY CPLR is limited to those specific objections, and does not apply to many situations, including those where the parties 'never agreed to arbitrate'.[111] Although the statute specifically refers to the objection 'that a valid agreement was not made', the New York Court of Appeals has reasoned that because arbitration is a creature of contract, it 'cannot impute to the Legislature an intent to bind persons to the arbitral process by their mere inaction for 20days where no agreement to arbitrate has ever been made'.[112] **19.46**

Neither the Second Circuit nor the New York Court of Appeals has addressed whether this NY provision might be pre-empted by the FAA, which does not contain such a provision. Certain lower courts have concluded that 'because the FAA does not address the mechanics of staying an arbitration . . . New York courts borrow CPLR § 7503(c) for limitation period purposes'.[113] In the light of its unsettled nature, a party served with notice under this provision would be wise to seek court intervention within the 20 day limitations period. **19.47**

Stay/dismissal of litigation brought in contravention of arbitration clause

The FAA allows a party to seek a stay of pending litigation filed in contravention of an arbitration clause.[114] The courts have the authority to issue a stay for actions brought in a US court. If the litigation was commenced in a court outside the United States, then appropriate remedy would be for an anti-suit injunction, discussed at paragraphs 19.55–19.62. While **19.48**

[109] NY CPLR § 7503. See also *Matter of Cullman Ventures, Inc* 252 AD 2d 222, 682 NY S 2d 391 (NY S Ct, Apps Div (1st Dept), 1998), denying motion to compel arbitration under CPLR § 7503 where a party was not refusing to participate in arbitration sited in New York and had commenced proceedings in Indiana.

[110] NY CPLR § 7503(c).

[111] *Matarasso v Cont Cas Co* 56 NY 2d 264, 267, 436 NE 2d 1305 (NY Ct of Apps, 1982).

[112] *Matarasso* (n 111). See also *Aetna Life & Cas Co v Stekardis* 34 NY 2d 182, 185, 313 NE 2d 53 (NY Ct of Apps, 1974); *Fiveco, Inc v Haber* 11 NY 3d 140, 145, 893 NE 2d 807, 810 (NY Ct of Apps, 2008), a petition to stay arbitration was time-barred since a party had never disputed the existence of an agreement to arbitrate.

[113] *Favara, Skahan, Tabaczyk Ltd v Ewing* 1992 WL 80659 (US D Ct (SDNY), 1992); but see *PMC, Inc v Atomergic Chemetals Corp* 844 F Supp 177, 182 (US D Ct (SDNY), 1994), NY CPLR § 7503 does not apply in cases under the FAA.

[114] FAA § 3, incorporated by reference based on the residual clauses in the FAA, chs 2 and 3; FAA §§ 208, 307.

the FAA provides for a stay of litigation during the pendency of arbitration, courts will often dismiss the lawsuit without prejudice instead.[115] The denial of a stay is subject to an immediate right to appeal.[116]

19.49 In evaluating a motion to stay a litigation pending arbitration, the court applies a four-part test:

> ... first, it must determine whether the parties agreed to arbitrate; second, it must determine the scope of that agreement; third, if federal statutory claims are asserted, it must consider whether Congress intended those claims to be nonarbitrable; and fourth, if the court concludes that some, but not all, of the claims in the case are arbitrable, it must then decide whether to stay the balance of the proceedings pending arbitration.[117]

19.50 A party can challenge the arbitrability of a claim based on a federal statute by arguing that Congress intended disputes subject to the statute to be non-arbitrable. The party making that challenge has the burden of demonstrating Congressional intent. The courts evaluate such challenge by applying the three-part 'McMahon test:' (a) the plain reading of the statute; (b) the statute's legislative history; or (c) identifying an inherent conflict between arbitration and the statute's underlying purposes.[118] In general, the courts are reluctant to conclude that Congress intended a matter to be non-arbitrable.[119]

19.51 The federal policy in favour of enforcing arbitration agreements can come into conflict with the US Bankruptcy Code, which is grounded on a policy of centralized dispute resolution. Congress has not offered any legislative guidance on how to reconcile these competing policies. As a result, the courts have been left to determine when arbitration clauses are enforceable in bankruptcy. In bankruptcy matters, courts have found that Congress intended certain aspects of bankruptcy law to be non-arbitrable, and have therefore refused to enforce arbitration agreements with respect to such claims. Whether a dispute is subject to arbitration in the bankruptcy context depends on whether the dispute is a 'core' or 'non-core' proceeding. A core proceeding relates entirely to the bankruptcy case, while a non-core proceeding does not arise under bankruptcy law.[120] The courts generally recognize that while the bankruptcy court has no discretion to stay non-core proceedings, or to refuse to refer

---

[115] *Rubin v Sona Intl Corp* 457 F Supp 2d 191, 198 (US D Ct (SDNY), 2006).

[116] *Arthur Andersen LLP v Carlisle* 556 US 624, 627, 129 S Ct 1896 (2009), applying FAA § 16(a)(1)(A).

[117] *Oldroyd v Elmira Savings Bank, FSB* 134 F 3d 72, 75–6 (US Ct of Apps (2nd Cir), 1998).

[118] *Shearson/American Express v McMahon, Inc* 482 US 220, 226–7, 107 S Ct 2332 (1987).

[119] *CompuCredit Corp v Greenwood* 132 S Ct 665, 673, 181 L Ed 2d 586 (2012), enforcing an arbitration agreement with respect to a Credit Repair Organizations Act claim; *Shearson/American Express v McMahon, Inc* 482 US 220, 226–7, 107 S Ct 2332 (1987), enforcing an arbitration agreement with respect to a Racketeer Influenced and Corrupts Organizations Act (RICO) claim; *Gilmer v Interstate/Johnson Lane Corp* 500 US 20, 29, 111 S Ct 1647 (1991), enforcing an arbitration agreement with respect to an Age Discrimination in Employment Act claim; *Mitsubishi Motors Corp v Soler Chrysler-Plymouth, Inc* 473 US 614, 637, 105 S Ct 3346 (1985), enforcing an arbitration agreement with respect to the Clayton Antitrust Act; *Guyden v Aetna, Inc* 544 F 3d 376, 384 (US Ct of Apps (2nd Cir), 2008), claims with respect to Sarbanes-Oxley whistleblower protection are arbitrable; but see *Arciniaga v General Motors Corp* 460 F 3d 231, 235–6 (US Ct of Apps (2nd Cir), 2006), recognizing that the explicit language in the Motor Vehicle Franchise Contract Arbitration Fairness Act of 2002 would prevent disputes relating to motor vehicle franchisee contracts from being arbitrated, but after a narrow reading of the statute concluding that related contracts did not fall under that restriction and could be arbitrated.

[120] A representative list of a core proceeding is set forth in the Bankruptcy Code, 28 USC § 157. The list includes matters relating to the administration of the estate, proceedings with respect to preferences, and determinations as to the dischargeability of specific debts.

them to arbitration, it does have this discretion with respect to core proceedings.[121] Even with core proceedings, the court still needs to determine whether arbitrating the claim would 'inherently conflict with the underlying purposes of the Bankruptcy Code'.[122] Only in that case can a court stay arbitration or decline to refer a matter to arbitration.

Unlike a federal statute that may declare a claim to be non-arbitrable, any state statute that purports to limit a party's ability to arbitrate a dispute would be pre-empted by the FAA.[123] **19.52**

If a court determines that only a portion of a party's claims are arbitrable, the proper procedure is for the court to sever the matter, referring the arbitrable claims to arbitration and retaining the remaining claims under its jurisdiction.[124] **19.53**

With respect to staying arbitration in the light of pending state court actions, New York, Texas, and Florida courts are explicitly granted this authority.[125] In all three jurisdictions, a request for such a stay must be made before the requesting party submits its first substantive statement regarding the dispute in the court proceedings.[126] **19.54**

Anti-suit injunctions

US courts have the power to issue an anti-suit injunction—ie an order enjoining a person subject to their jurisdiction from prosecuting a foreign lawsuit.[127] Though typically used in the context of parallel litigation, anti-suit injunctions have also been issued to enjoin foreign litigation brought in contravention of an arbitration clause. **19.55**

Although an anti-suit injunction is directed at a party to the foreign suit,[128] and not at a foreign court, the effect of an anti-suit injunction is to interfere with proceedings in a foreign court. The issuance of an anti-suit injunction thus, implicates international comity, ie the **19.56**

---

121 *Re Gandy* 299 F 3d 489, 495 (US Ct of Apps (5th Cir), 2002), declining to compel arbitration where the disputes related to core proceedings, and would defeat the purposes of the bankruptcy code; *Crysen/Montenay Energy Co v Shell Oil Co (Re Crysen/Montenay Energy Co)* 226 F 3d 160, 166 (US Ct of Apps (2nd Cir), 2000).

122 See n 121 (*Re Gandy* at 1069–70). See also *Re Electric Machinery Enterprises, Inc* 479 F 3d 791, 796 (US Ct of Apps (11th Cir), 2007); *Re National Gypsum Co* 118 F 3d 1056 (US Ct of Apps (5th Cir), 1997); *Re US Lines, Inc* 197 F 3d 631, 640 (US Ct of Apps (2nd Cir), 1999).

123 See *AT&T Mobility v Concepcion* 131 S Ct 1740, 179 L Ed 742 (2011), holding that state laws prohibiting contracts from disallowing class-wide arbitration are invalid on the ground that they are pre-empted by the FAA.

124 *KPMG LLP v Cocchi* 132 S Ct 23, 26, L Ed 2d 323 (2011), remanding refusal to compel because two of four claims were not arbitrable did not mean that the other two claims should be separated and referred to arbitration; *Doe v Princess Cruise Lines Ltd* 657 F 3d 1204, 1221 (US Ct of Apps (11th Cir), 2011), compelling arbitration on five claims that fall within the scope of the arbitration agreement, while retaining the remaining non-arbitral claims for further prosecution; *Collins & Aikman Products Co v Building Systems, Inc* 58 F 3d 16, 20 (US Ct of Apps (2nd Cir), 1995), if some claims are arbitral and others are not, then the court will 'sever those claims subject to arbitration from those adjudicable only in court'.

125 NY CPLR § 7503(b); Tex Civ Prac & Rem Code Ann § 172.174(a); Fla Stat Ann § 684.0009(1).

126 NY CPLR § 7503(b); Tex Civ Prac & Rem Code Ann § 172.174(b); Fla Stat Ann § 684.0009(1).

127 See eg *China Trade and Development Corp v MV Choong Yong* 837 F 2d 33, 35 (US Ct of Apps (2nd Cir), 1987); *United States v Davis* 767 F 2d 1025, 1038 (US Ct of Apps (2nd Cir), 1985); *Mutual Service Insurance Co v Frit Industries, Inc* 358 F 3d 1312, 1325 (US Ct of Apps (11th Cir), 2004); *Kaepa, Inc v Achilles Corp* 76 F 3d 624, 626 (US Ct of Apps (5th Cir), 1996). The remedy of an anti-suit injunction is not one found in either the Convention or in the FAA, but rather is a common law doctrine.

128 Failure to comply with an anti-suit injunction, therefore, is a contempt of court, and punishable as such. See *Paramedics Electromedicina Comercial Ltda v GE Medical Systems Information Technologies, Inc* 369 F 3d 645, 658 (US Ct of Apps (2nd Cir), 2004), affirming the imposition of daily contempt fines on a party that failed to abide by an anti-suit injunction, but remanding to district court to reconsider the amount of the daily fine.

'recognition which one nation extends within its own territory to the legislative, executive, or judicial acts of another'.[129]

19.57 Two threshold requirements must be met before a court will consider issuing an anti-suit injunction. First, the 'parties must be the same in both matters'.[130] An injunction may be granted even where the litigation involves a non-signatory to the arbitration clause, if the court finds that one of the grounds for binding a non-signatory to arbitration is satisfied.[131] Second, 'resolution of the case before the enjoining court must be dispositive of the action to be enjoined'.[132] Courts have found this second factor to be satisfied where the issue before the enjoining US court was whether the claims asserted in the foreign litigation were the subject of a valid arbitration agreement.[133] The focus is not on the merits of the underlying claims in the foreign litigation, but whether these claims properly belong in arbitration.

19.58 In the event that the two threshold requirements are satisfied, the circuit courts of appeals differ on how much weight should be accorded to considerations of international comity.[134] Some circuits place great weight on international comity, and grant anti-suit injunctions only rarely.[135] Others take a more liberal view of anti-suit injunctions.[136] Thus the Fifth Circuit, which includes Houston, has stated: 'We decline... to require a district court to genuflect before a vague and omnipotent notion of comity every time that it must decide whether to enjoin a foreign action.'[137] The Second Circuit falls between these two approaches. While

[129] *Somportex Ltd v Philadelphia Chewing Gum Corp* 453 F 2d 435, 440 (US Ct of Apps (3rd Cir), 1971), cert denied, 405 US 1017, 92 S Ct 1294 (1972). See also *China Trade* (n 127) 35: 'The fact that the injunction operates only against the parties, and not directly against the foreign court, does not eliminate the need for due regard to principles of international comity, because such an order effectively restricts the jurisdiction of the court of a foreign sovereign.'

[130] See *China Trade* (n 127) 35.

[131] *Paramedics Electromedicina Comercial Ltda v GE Medical Systems Information Technologies, Inc* 369 F 3d 645 (US Ct of Apps (2nd Cir), 2004), affirming an anti-suit injunction with respect to Brazilian litigation involving a non-signatory, based on the non-signatory's close identity with a signatory to an arbitration agreement.

[132] See n 131.

[133] 369 F 3d at 653.

[134] International comity is the recognition that one nation allows within its territory to the legislative, executive, or judicial acts of another nation. As applied to anti-suit injunctions, it is the deference a US court grants to proceedings taking place in another jurisdiction.

[135] Generally speaking, the Third, Sixth, and DC circuits adopt a 'conservative' approach. Under this approach, the courts attach great weight to comity considerations and grant anti-suit injunction rarely and typically only under two circumstances: (1) when the foreign action is a threat to the jurisdiction of the US court, or (2) on grounds of public policy. See eg *Answers in Genesis of Kentucky, Inc v Creation Ministries Intern Ltd* 556 F 3d 459, 471–2 (US Ct of Apps (6th Cir), 2009); *Gau Shan Co v Bankers Trust Co* 956 F 2d 1349, 1355–8 (US Ct of Apps (6th Cir), 1992); *Laker Airways Ltd v Sabena, Belgian World Airlines* 731 F 2d 909, 926–7 (US Ct of Apps (DC Cir), 1984); *Compagnie des Bauxites de Guinea v Ins Co of N America* 651 F 2d 877, 887 (US Ct of Apps (3rd Cir), 1981), cert denied, 457 US 1105, 102 S Ct 2902 (1982). The Eleventh Circuit (which embraces Florida) has not spoken directly on the issue, but has affirmed, without opinion, a decision by the Middle District of Alabama declining to enter an anti-suit injunction based on the restrictive approach. See *Mutual Service Casualty Insurance Co v Frit Industries, Inc* 805 F Supp 919 (US D Ct (MD Ala), 1992), affd, 3 F 3d 442 (US Ct of Apps (11th Cir), 1993). But see *Canon Latin America, Inc v Lantech (CR), SA* 453 F Supp 2d 1357 (US D Ct (S D Fla), 2006), following a liberal approach and granting an anti-suit injunction with respect to Costa Rican litigation in order to enforce the forum selection clause.

[136] The Fifth, Seventh, and Ninth Circuits attach less weight to considerations of international comity, and thus take a more liberal view of when an anti-suit injunction should be issued. See eg *Kaepa, Inc v Achilles Corp* 76 F 3d 624, 626–7 (US Ct of Apps (5th Cir), 1996); *Allendale Mutual Insurance Co v Bull Data Systems, Inc* 10 F 3d 425, 431–2 (US Ct of Apps (7th Cir), 1993); *Seattle Totems Hockey Club, Inc v National Hockey League* 652 F 2d 852, 855–6 (US Ct of Apps (9th Cir), 1981), cert denied, 457 US 1105, 102 S Ct 2902 (1982).

[137] *Kaepa, Inc v Achilles Corp* 76 F 3d 624, 626–7 (US Ct of Apps (5th Cir), 1996).

the Second Circuit places great weight on comity and counsels that injunctions restraining foreign litigation be 'used sparingly' and 'granted only with care and great restraint',[138] it also considers a variety of other factors. These factors include whether the foreign litigation would: (a) frustrate a public policy in the enjoining forum; (b) be vexatious; (c) threaten the issuing court's jurisdiction; (d) result in prejudice to other equitable considerations; or (e) result in delay, inconvenience, expense, inconsistency, or a race to judgment.[139] Two of these factors are accorded 'greater significance': whether the foreign action threatens the enjoining forum's jurisdiction or its 'strong public policies'.[140]

In granting anti-suit injunctions in aid of arbitration, courts tend to focus on the federal policy 'favoring the liberal enforcement of arbitration clauses' which 'applies with particular force in international disputes'.[141] As explained by one district court in *Storm, LLC v Telenor Mobile Comm AS*: 'Attempts to interfere with arbitration of international disputes are so powerfully disapproved... that "an attempt to sidestep arbitration" might be "sufficient to support a foreign anti-suit injunction." Where this factor is present, little else is required to authorize an injunction.'[142] **19.59**

Nonetheless, courts do exercise restraint in ensuring the injunction is no broader than necessary to protect the federal policy favouring arbitration. Thus, courts ensure, for example, that the injunction is aimed only at the parties who should properly be arbitrating and remains in effect only for the duration of the arbitration.[143] **19.60**

Despite the strong federal policy favouring the enforcement of arbitration agreements in international disputes, courts have under certain circumstances denied anti-suit injunctions where a party commenced litigation outside the United States in breach of an arbitration clause. While the courts' reasoning has varied, the courts found it relevant in each of these cases that the party commencing the foreign litigation was not refusing to participate in the **19.61**

---

138 See *China Trade* (n 127) at 35–6.

139 See *Ibeto Petrochem Indus Ltd v M/T Beffen* 475 F 3d 56, 64–5 (US Ct of Apps (2nd Cir), 2007). The First Circuit follows a similar approach, placing great weight on considerations of international comity, but also considering the 'totality of circumstances' generally. According to the First Circuit, there is a rebuttable presumption against an anti-suit injunction which 'may be counterbalanced by other facts and factors particular to a specific case'. See *Quaak v Klynveld Peat Marwick Goerdeler Bedrijfsrevisoren* 361 F 3d 11, 19 (US Ct of Apps (1st Cir), 2004).

140 *China Trade* (n 127) 36.

141 *Paramedics Electromedicina Comercial* 369 F 3d at 654. See also *Ibeto Petrochem Indus Ltd v M/T Beffen* 475 F 3d 56, 64–5 (US Ct of Apps (2nd Cir), 2007), anti-suit injunction warranted in an international maritime dispute, where a party to an arbitration agreement had brought suit in Nigeria, because of the strong federal policy favouring arbitration, and because of other 'equitable considerations such as deterring forum shopping' and avoiding 'inconvenience, inconsistency [in the application of law] and a possible race to judgment'; *Kahara Bodas Co v Perusahaan Pertambangan Minyak Dan Gas Bumi Negara* 500 F 3d 111 (US Ct of Apps (2nd Cir), 2007), affirming the granting of an anti-suit injunction where the dispute involved cross-jurisdiction attempts to enforce and vacate an arbitral award; *Storm, LLC v Telenor Mobile Comms AS* 2006 WL 3735657 (US D Ct (SDNY), 2006), enjoining parties to an arbitration agreement in a shareholder dispute from litigating in Ukraine, and finding sufficient similarity between non-identical parties in parallel proceedings based on the alter ego theory; *Suchodolski Associates, Inc v Cardell Finance Corp* 2006 WL 3327625 (US D Ct (SDNY), 2006), enjoining a party to an arbitration agreement from proceeding with litigation in Brazil, noting that to the extent Brazilian action asserted non-arbitrable claims, only those claims could proceed through litigation; *SG Avipro Finance Ltd v Cameroon Airlines* 2005 WL 1353955 (DFE), (US D Ct (SDNY), 2005), enjoining a party to an arbitration agreement from proceeding with litigation in Cameroon.

142 *Storm, LLC v Telenor Mobile Comm AS* 2006 WL 3735657, at *9.

143 *Ibeto Petrochem Indus Ltd v M/T Beffen* 475 F 3d at 65.

arbitration.[144] In such circumstances, courts have found that the party engaged in the foreign litigation is not attempting to sidestep the arbitration, but rather, may be raising a genuine challenge to the arbitration of the dispute.[145] Comity will also weigh against an injunction where the dispute has little connection to the United States, other than the presence of an arbitration located there, and where, in contrast, the foreign forum has a strong interest in the dispute.[146]

19.62 Courts may also be reluctant to grant an anti-suit injunction precluding a party from prosecuting an action to annul an arbitrator's award.[147] At the same time, courts would be amenable to confirming an arbitration award that required a party to terminate a related foreign litigation.[148]

Dismissal of arbitration on forum non conveniens grounds

19.63 According to case law, a court may dismiss an action to confirm or enforce a foreign arbitral award on the grounds that the forum is 'inconvenient' under the doctrine of *forum non conveniens*. This doctrine allows the court discretion to dismiss cases when a plaintiff's ability to bring the claim would not be fundamentally compromised, yet it would be fairer to the defendant or more efficient if the case were handled elsewhere.[149]

19.64 In considering dismissal for *forum non conveniens*, the courts consider whether (a) a foreign plaintiff's choice of a US forum should be granted deference; (b) an adequate alternative forum is available; and (c) the balance of private and public interest factors weigh in favour of proceeding in the alternative forum.[150]

19.65 Ordinarily, increased deference is given to a US litigant's choice of a US forum, whereas less deference is given to a foreign litigant's choice of a US forum. Where a foreign plaintiff brings suit in the United States, it is reasonable to assume that the selection was made for forum-shopping reasons, rather than genuine convenience and therefore less deference

---

[144] *LAIF X SPRL v Axtel SA de CV* 310 F Supp 2d 578 (US D Ct (SDNY), 2004), affd, 390 F 3d 194, 199 (US Ct of Apps (2nd Cir), 2004); *Comverse, Inc v American Telecom, Inc* 2006 WL 3016315 (US D Ct (SDNY), 2006), denying an anti-suit injunction aimed at litigation in Chile where the defendant was not refusing to participate in the New York arbitration, and where Chilean litigation was being prosecuted on the defendant's behalf by a Chilean government agency under Chilean anti-competition laws. See also *Empresa Generadora de Electricidad Itabo, SA v Corporacion Dominica de Empresas Electricas Estatales* 2005 WL 1705080 (US D Ct (SDNY), 2005), denying a motion to compel arbitration and request a preliminary anti-suit injunction directed at litigation in the Dominican Republic in a dispute between two Dominican Republic companies on the grounds that there was no irreparable harm where the respondent was participating in the arbitration and arguing before the tribunal that its Dominican Republic claims were not subject to arbitration.

[145] *LAIF X SPRL* 390 F 3d at 200, denying an anti-suit injunction where 'it cannot be said that Telinor's conduct [in commencing Mexican litigation] is an evasion of the arbitral forum or an "attempt to sidestep arbitration"'.

[146] *LAIF X SPRL* (n 145) 200: 'Comity militates strongly against an injunction' where a case before a Mexican court involved the status of a Mexican shareholder in a Mexican corporation under Mexican law; *Comverse, Inc v American Telecom, Inc* 2006 WL 3016315 (US D Ct (SDNY), 2006), comity weighed against an anti-suit injunction where the Chilean government had a strong interest in enforcing its anti-competition laws.

[147] *Karaha Bodas Co, LLC v Perusahaan Pertambangan Minyak Dan Gas Bumi Negara* 335 F 3d 357 (US Ct of Apps (5th Cir), 2003), refusing to grant an anti-suit injunction of an action to annul an arbitral award.

[148] *Rintin Corp, SA v Domar Ltd* 374 F Supp 2d 1165, 1170 (US D Ct (S D Fla), 2005) affd, 476 F 3d 1254 (US Ct of Apps (11th Cir), 2007), affirming the panel's award requiring termination of related litigation based on a court's issuance of anti-suit injunctions related to arbitral proceedings.

[149] *Piper Aircraft Co v Reyno* 454 US 235, 255–6, 102 S Ct 252 (1981); *Gulf Oil Corp v Gilbert* 330 US 501, 67 S Ct 839 (1947).

[150] *Pollux Holding Ltd v Chase Manhattan Bank* 329 F 3d 64, 74–5 (US Ct of Apps (2nd Cir), 2003); *Vasquez v Bridgestone/Firestone, Inc* 325 F 3d 665, 671 (US Ct of Apps (5th Cir), 2003); *Republic of Panama v BCCI Holdings (Luxembourg) SA* 119 F 3d 935, 951 (US Ct of Apps (11th Cir), 1997).

should be accorded to its choice of forum.[151] However, consideration must be made of the plaintiff's reasons for choosing a US forum in determining the amount of deference to be granted.

'An alternate forum is adequate if the defendants are amenable to service of process there, and if it permits litigation of the subject matter of the dispute.'[152] While each alternate forum must be independently evaluated, courts have tended to find that other countries that are signatories to the New York and Panama Conventions are adequate forums for proceedings related to enforcing arbitration awards and agreements.[153] **19.66**

The private interest factors pertain to the convenience of the litigants, including, for example, the location of party and non-party witnesses, or the location of documents. Where issues concerning the arbitrability of claims or the enforcement of an award turn on the testimony of witnesses located abroad, this factor may weigh in favour of dismissal.[154] **19.67**

The public interest factor requires consideration of which country has a greater interest in the dispute. This factor can be influenced by considerations of judicial economy, for example where there is already an action pending in the foreign country, or by the choice of law applicable to the underlying issues.[155] While the United States has an interest in enforcing international arbitration agreements, this interest will not necessarily weigh against dismissal on grounds of *forum non conveniens* if the underlying dispute strongly implicates the interests of the foreign country.[156] **19.68**

---

[151] *Iragorri v United Technologies Corp* 274 F 3d 65, 71–3 (US Ct of Apps (2nd Cir), 2001); *Re Vioxx Products Liab Litig* 2009 WL 1636244 (US D Ct (E D La), 2009) affd *sub nom Adams v Merck & Co Inc* 353 F Appx 960 (US Ct of Apps (5th Cir), 2009); *Exter Shipping Ltd v Kilakos* 310 F Supp 2d 1301, 1323 (US D Ct (N D Ga), 2004), citing *Sigalas v Lido Mar, Inc* 776 F 2d 1512, 1520 (US Ct of Apps (11th Cir), 1985).

[152] *Pollux Holding* (n 150) 75; *Tyco Fire & Security, LLC v Alcocer* 218 Fed Appx 860, 865 (US Ct of Apps (11th Cir), 2007); *Empresa Lineas Maritimas Argentinas, SA v Stork-Werkspoor Diesel, BV* 1991 US Dist LEXIS 1404 (US D Ct (E D La), 1991).

[153] See *Figueiredo Ferraz E Engenharia de Projeto Ltda v Republic of Peru* 665 F 3d 384 (US Ct of Apps (2nd Cir), 2011), dismissing on *forum non conveniens* grounds in favour of Peru as an alternative forum; *Re Arbitration between Monegasque De Reassurances SAM v Nak Naftogaz of Ukraine* 311 F 3d 488 (US Ct of Apps (2nd Cir), 2002), dismissing in favour of Ukraine as an alternative forum.

[154] *Pollux Holding* (n 150) 75, the location of party and non-party witnesses in England weighed in favour of dismissal; *Oil Basins Ltd v Broken Hill Proprietary Co Ltd* 613 F Supp 483 (US D Ct (SDNY), 1985), dismissing a motion to compel arbitration where witnesses were located in Australia; *Re Monegasque* (n 153), witnesses in Ukraine in an action to enforce an arbitral award; *DTEX, LLC v BBVA Bancomer, SA* 508 F 3d 785, 800 (US Ct of Apps (5th Cir), 2007). See also *E-One, Inc v R Cushman & Associates, Inc* 2006 WL 2599130 (US D Ct (M D Fla), 2006) report and recommendation adopted, 2006 WL 2598458 (US D Ct (M D Fla), 2006).

[155] See *PepsiCo Inc v Oficina Central de Aseroria y Ayuda Tecnica* 945 F Supp 69, 71 (US D Ct (SDNY), 1996), staying a motion to compel arbitration to permit a Venezuelan court to determine the threshold issue of the arbitrability of Venezuelan law claims; *Oil Basins Ltd* 613 F Supp at 491, dismissing a motion to compel arbitration where 'Australian law will necessarily play a major role in the resolution of the dispute'; *Iberian Tankers Co v Terminales Maracaibo*, C.A., 322 F Supp. 73, 74 (US D Ct (S D NY), 1971), dismissing a motion to compel arbitration where Venezuelan law bore on the arbitrability of claims. See also *DTEX* 508 F 3d at 802; *E-One, Inc* 2006 WL 2599130 at *12.

[156] See *Figueiredo Ferraz* 665 F 3d at 391–2, finding US interest in the enforcement of arbitration agreements must give way to the significant interest the alternative forum, Peru, had in enforcing its own statutes. cf *Louisiana Power & Light Co v City of Thibodaux* 360 US 25, 28–9, 79 S Ct 1070 (1959), observing that abstention in favour of foreign litigation is appropriate where the litigation is 'intimately involved with sovereign prerogative' and it is important to ascertain the meaning of another jurisdiction's law 'from the only tribunal empowered to speak definitively'. See also *DTEX* 508 F 3d at 802–3; *Aldana v Del Monte Fresh Produce NA, Inc* 578 F 3d 1283, 1298 (US Ct of Apps (11th Cir), 2009).

19.2.3 Appointment of arbitrators

19.69 In general, the court's role in selecting arbitrators is limited, and is one of secondary resort.[157] There are two instances in which a court may be called upon to provide for the appointment of an arbitral tribunal. The first is where an arbitration agreement calls for the appointment by a non-existent entity or one that has ceased to exist. In these cases, courts have used discretion to craft remedies such as court appointment of the arbitrator,[158] developing an ad hoc arbitrator selection system,[159] specifying the arbitration rules to be used,[160] and declaring the arbitration agreement unenforceable.[161] The second instance is where the arbitration agreement does not contain specific appointment procedures, or the parties do not follow the agreed upon procedures, or 'if for any other reason there shall be lapse in the naming of an arbitrator or arbitrators or umpire, or in filling a vacancy'.[162] The court's power to appoint an arbitrator arises only if one of these events has occurred.[163]

19.70 New York state law has a similar rule allowing a state court to appoint an arbitrator if the agreement does not contain a provision for selecting an arbitrator, if that provision is not followed, or if an arbitrator fails to act.[164] The state laws of both Florida and Texas have similar provisions.[165] The courts do not have a specific roster, and instead judges use their discretion in selecting arbitrators.

---

[157] FAA § 5 applies to the court's appointment of arbitrators. It states:

> If in the agreement provision be made for a method of naming or appointing an arbitrator or arbitrators or an umpire, such method shall be followed; but if no method be provided therein, or if a method be provided and any party thereto shall fail to avail himself of such method, or if for any other reason there shall be a lapse in the naming of an arbitrator or arbitrators or umpire, or in filling a vacancy, then upon the application of either party to the controversy the court shall designate and appoint an arbitrator or arbitrators or umpire, as the case may require, who shall act under the said agreement with the same force and effect as if he or they had been specifically named therein; and unless otherwise provided in the agreement the arbitration shall be by a single arbitrator.

[158] *Global v Lloyds* 465 F Supp 2d 308, 310–11 (US D Ct (SDNY), 2006), the Court appointed the arbitrators.

[159] *Magi XXI v Stato Della Citta Del Vaticano* 2008 WL 3895915, *4 (US D Ct (EDNY), 2008), where rules were instituted to comply with the generic 'College of Arbitrators' in the arbitration clause, which the Court held was a generic arbitration panel where the two arbitrators appointed by each party then selected a neutral arbitrator.

[160] *HZI Research Ctr v Sun Instruments Japan Co, Inc* 1995 WL 562181 (US D Ct (SDNY), 1995), the Court appointed AAA to administer the arbitration where the specific entity in the arbitration agreement did not exist.

[161] *Re Salomon* 68 F 3d 554 (US Ct of Apps (2nd Cir), 1995), *Lea Tai Textile* 411 F Supp 1404 (US D Ct (SDNY), 1975); but see *Peters Fabrics v Jantzen, Inc* 582 F Supp 1287 (US D Ct (SDNY), 1984), since rules between competing arbitration organizations were similar there was an agreement to arbitrate.

[162] FAA § 5, 206; *Brown v ITT Consumer Finance Corp* 211 F 3d 1217, 1222 (US Ct of Apps (11th Cir), 2000), the dissolution of a specified arbitral forum could be remedied by the court's appointment of an arbitrator under FAA § 5; *Re Service Corp Intl* 355 SW 3d 655, 659 (Tex S Ct, 2011), recognizing the right under FAA § 5 to appoint an arbitrator if the agreement does not contain the conditions or if the parties fail to follow the agreed upon procedures; *Ore & Chemical v Stinnes Interoil, Inc* 611 F Supp 237 (US D Ct (SDNY), 1985), the Court appointed the arbitrators.

For matters falling under the Panama Convention, if the agreement does not set forth the appointment of arbitrators, then they shall 'be appointed in accordance with Article 3 of the [Panama] Convention', FAA § 303.

[163] *Re Service Corp Intl* 355 SW 3d 655, 659–60 (Tex S Ct, 2011), vacating the appointment of a court-appointed arbitrator where the parties' agreement called for appointment by the AAA, where the time for the AAA to appoint an arbitrator had not yet lapsed.

[164] NY CPLR § 7504.

[165] Tex Civ Prac & Rem Code Ann § 172.054; Fla Stat Ann § 684.0012.

19.2.4 Interim relief in aid of arbitration

Interim relief or preliminary relief refers to the pre-award interim measures a court or tribunal may take to ensure the efficacy of the arbitral process. Interim relief could include, for example, an order preserving assets or property that is the subject of the dispute, or the preservation of evidence. Interim measures may be requested before or during arbitration, but are often requested before a tribunal is even constituted. Some arbitral institutions have addressed this by establishing special 'emergency arbitrator' procedures for applications for interim relief in the early stages of an arbitration.[166] **19.71**

Parties also may seek court intervention for interim relief in aid of arbitration. The FAA does not contain any provision concerning interim relief. The state arbitration statutes in New York, Florida, and Texas, on the other hand, do specifically address the issue of interim relief. Accordingly, both federal and state courts will look to the relevant state arbitration statute in considering applications for interim relief in aid of arbitration. **19.72**

New York

Parties seeking provisional relief from a New York court in aid of arbitration can rely on section 7502 of the New York Civil Practice Law and Rules (CPLR), which permits a party to apply to a court for an order of attachment or preliminary injunction in aid of an arbitration pending inside or outside the United States, whether it is subject to the Conventions or not.[167] The interim measures may be granted 'only upon the ground that the award to which the applicant may be entitled may be rendered ineffectual without such provisional relief'.[168] **19.73**

Section 7502(c) requires that the arbitration proceeding must either already be constituted or be commenced within 30 days from the order granting the provisional relief, or else the order will expire and be rendered null and void. However, this 30 day period is subject to judicial extension upon a showing of 'good cause'. Though the statute is silent on this issue, if the 30 day period expires, presumably a party may reapply for the provisional relief at a later time when the arbitration has commenced. Good cause includes, for example, ongoing settlement negotiations during which the party who obtained the provisional relief abstained from commencing arbitration proceedings. **19.74**

In order to be entitled to provisional relief under section 7502(c) the applicant must make a four-part showing. **19.75**

First, the applicant must show that the arbitration award 'may be rendered ineffectual without such provisional relief'. This language has been construed as requiring a showing that the specific 'res' or money which is the target of the provisional application should be regarded as the subject of the arbitration.[169] Thus, a lack of assets to cover the arbitral award would ordinarily be sufficient to render an arbitral award ineffectual. This is because section 7502(c) is not intended to create a mechanism for a guarantee for every potential arbitration **19.76**

---

166 ICDR International Dispute Resolution Procedures, Art 37; 2012 ICC Rules of Arbitration, Art 29 and App V.

167 CPLR § 7502(c). CPLR § 7502(c) was amended in 2005 in response to prior New York court rulings holding that it applied only to arbitrations within the state of New York and did not apply to arbitrations falling under the Conventions.

168 CPLR § 7502(c). See also *SG Cowen Securities Corp v Messih* 224 F 3d 79 (US Ct of Apps (2nd Cir), 2000); *Invar Intern, Inc v Zorlu Enerji Elektrik Uretim Anonim Sirketi* 86 AD 3d 404, 927 NY S 2d 330 (NY S Ct, Apps Div (1st Dept), 2011).

169 *Winter v Brown* 49 AD 3d 526, 853 NY S 2d 361 (NY S Ct, Apps Div (2nd Dept), 2008).

judgment.[170] An arbitration award will not be rendered ineffective where the resisting party has more than enough assets to pay any award and there is no evidence that the resisting party is attempting to hide assets.[171] In addition, the applicant must show (a) a likelihood of success on the merits of the dispute, (b) irreparable harm in the absence of the relief, and (favourable balance of the equities. (This three-part standard is the same as the showing required for a preliminary injunction in US litigation.) Because an attachment is considered a harsh remedy, it is sparingly granted, even where the statutory criteria of section 7502 are met.[172]

19.77 While on its face the scope of section 7502(c) is limited to the provisional remedies of 'attachment and preliminary injunction', a New York state appellate court has held that if the parties themselves have specifically agreed by contract that other forms of provisional relief may be sought, the court may grant such other relief. Thus, in *HSBC Bank USA v National Equity Corp*, the court granted an application for the seizure of certain collateral in connection with an arbitration concerning a default on the underlying contractual debt. In that case, the arbitration clause permitted the parties to provide for provisional relief 'including but not limited to injunctive or mandatory relief or the appointment of a receiver'.[173]

19.78 In New York, the availability of preliminary injunctions outside section 7502(c) is limited. The Second Circuit has held that a court has no power to issue a preliminary injunction preventing the disposal of assets in an action at law before an arbitration award has been reduced to a judgment of the court.[174] However, courts have distinguished this rule as permitting preliminary injunctions prior to a confirmed arbitral award where a party claims an equitable interest in the matter being enjoined, or where the action is being brought for a violation of a statute (such as trademark or copyright statutes) that permits such interim relief.[175]

19.79 An application for provisional relief in aid of arbitration may be made *ex parte* and the party seeking relief may be required to post an undertaking in an amount to be fixed by the court. The purpose of the undertaking is to cover damages to the other party if the provisional relief is later vacated as unwarranted. If an *ex parte* application for relief is later vacated by the court as unwarranted, the party subject to the injunction is entitled to all costs and damages, including the undertaking and attorneys' fees.[176]

---

170 *Erickson v Kidder Peabody & Co* 166 Misc 2d 1, 4–5, 630 NY S 2d 861 (NY S Ct (NY Cty), 1995).

171 See *Spiegel v DH Blair & Co, Inc* 289 AD 2d 22, 23, 733 NY S 2d 602 (NY S Ct, Apps Div (1st Dept), 2001), noting that despite the petitioner's allegation that the respondent would not be able to satisfy the arbitration award, 'where there is no evidence that respondents are hiding or dissipating assets, the article 75 court properly observed the limitations upon its discretionary authority in denying petitioner's application'; *Cheng v Worldco, LLC* 2003 WL 22964397, *4 (NY S Ct (NY Cty), 2003): 'petitioner would be required to show that [respondent] was more than in financial trouble, but had done, or was attempting to do, an act such as disposing of, or secreting property'.

172 *Spiegel* 289 AD 2d at 23: 'Although requests for provisional relief pursuant to CPLR 7502(c) are addressed to the discretion of the motion court, discretion to grant such relief is "limited".'. See also *Musket Corp v PDVSA Petroleo, SA* 512 F Supp 2d 155 (US D Ct (SDNY), 2007): 'Satisfaction of the statutory criteria, however, does not guarantee that a court will issue such relief. Such relief is discretionary, and since attachment is a harsh remedy, the court must exercise care in its application.' (citation omitted).

173 *HSBC Bank USA v National Equity Corp* 279 AD 2d 251, 719 NY S 2d 20 (NY S Ct, Apps Div (1st Dept), 2001).

174 See *ContiChem v Parsons Shipping Co Ltd* 229 F 3d 426 (US Ct of Apps (2nd Cir), 2000).

175 See *Motorola, Inc v Abeckaser* 2009 WL 1362833 (US D Ct (EDNY), 2009); *Trafalgar Power, Inc v Aetna Life Ins Co* 131 F Supp 2d 341, 349 (US D Ct (NDNY), 2001).

176 See CPLR § 6212(e), pertaining to attachment; § 6312(b), pertaining to preliminary injunction.

Texas

Texas also grants the courts the authority to grant interim relief in aid of arbitration that occurs in any location.[177] Such relief can include an injunction to preserve the status quo pending the arbitration.[178] In considering a request for interim relief, the courts give preclusive effect to findings of fact of the arbitration tribunal in the arbitration, including a finding of fact relating to the probable validity of the claim that is the subject of the order for interim relief.[179] **19.80**

The tribunal also has authority to issue interim measures.[180] An interim measures award is enforceable in court in the same manner as a final award.[181] **19.81**

Florida

Florida also provides the courts with the power to issue interim relief in relation to arbitration proceedings.[182] In fact, the courts are granted the same power of issuing an interim measure in relation to arbitration proceedings, irrespective of whether the arbitration proceedings are held in Florida, as it has in relation to court proceedings. The court is required to exercise this power 'in accordance with its own procedures and in consideration of the specific features of international arbitration'.[183] The court's authority to grant such relief can occur 'before or during arbitral proceedings' and can serve to aid an arbitration occurring in any location.[184] **19.82**

Under Florida's international arbitration statute, the tribunal has equal authority to grant interim relief as the courts.[185] The statute also permits parties to seek a preliminary order for interim measures on an *ex parte* basis.[186] Such preliminary order does not constitute an award and is not enforceable by a court.[187] However, once notice is given and an award of interim measures is made by the tribunal, it is entitled to recognition as an arbitral award and can be enforced in a court.[188] **19.83**

---

[177] Tex Civ Prac & Rem Code § 172.175, 'A party to an arbitration agreement may request an interim measure of protection from a district court before or during an arbitration.'; Tex Civ Prac & Rem Code § 172.001(b), section 172.175 applies to international arbitrations in any location; *Senter Investments, LLC v Veerjee* 358 SW 3d 841, 843 (Tex Ct of Apps (Dallas), 2012), finding that Tex Civ Prac & Rem Code § 171.086(a)(3)(A), (b)(1) provides similar relief with respect to general arbitrations. Prior to the adoption of the Texas International Arbitration Act, Texas courts would apply general provisional relief standards to applications for interim relief in aid of arbitration. See eg *RGI, Inc v Tucker & Associates, Inc* 858 F 2d 227, 230 (US Ct of Apps (5th Cir), 1988).

[178] *RGI, Inc v Tucker & Associates, Inc* 858 F 2d at 230, affirming a preliminary injunction preventing a party from terminating a contract pending resolution of the arbitration.

[179] Tex Civ Prac & Rem Code § 172.175.

[180] Tex Civ Prac & Rem Code § 172.143.

[181] Tex Civ Prac & Rem Code § 172.143.

[182] Fla Stat § 684.0028. The Florida International Arbitration Act was adopted in 2010. There are no cases to date applying the provisions of § 684.0028. Prior to 2010, Florida courts would not grant preliminary injunctive relief in the absence of language of the agreement to arbitrate authorizing such relief. See *Global Tel*Link Corp v Scott* 652 F Supp 2d 1240, 1248 (US D Ct (M D Fla), 2009), holding that the Court did not have the authority to grant interim relief since the agreement to arbitrate only addressed the court's jurisdiction over the final award and did not make any reference to interim relief); *Rath v Network Marketing, LC* 790 So 2d 461, 466 (Fla Ct of Apps (4th Dist), 2001) (the same).

[183] Fla Stat § 684.0028. Comparatively, see Fla Stat § 682, omitting mention of the availability of interim relief in general arbitrations.

[184] Fla Stat § 684.001. See also, Fla Stat § 684.0002(2), Sections 684.0028 and 684.001 apply to international arbitrations in any location.

[185] Fla Stat § 684.0018.

[186] Fla Stat § 684.002.

[187] Fla Stat § 684.0021.

[188] Fla Stat § 684.0026.

19.3 During the Arbitration

19.84 Once a matter has been referred to arbitration, a court's involvement during the arbitration itself is limited.[189] A 'court does not have the power to review an interlocutory ruling by an arbitration panel'.[190]

19.3.1 Role of court in deciding challenges to arbitrators

19.85 In general, it is the role of the institution administering the arbitration and the agreed-upon arbitral rules to specify the procedures for challenging and replacing an arbitrator. The FAA does not contain any provisions for addressing arbitrator challenges prior to the award. Federal courts have thus held that parties have limited ability to raise challenges to arbitrators in the course of the arbitration proceedings.[191] Nonetheless, it has been held that courts retain the 'inherent power' to consider a challenge to an arbitrator in a pre-award application.[192] The burden would be higher than the burden to vacate an award based on misconduct.[193] Even where courts have recognized their authority to take such action, they have been reluctant to do so.[194]

19.86 State arbitration statutes may also be used to raise challenges to arbitrators. New York state law permits a party to apply to a court for immediate assistance if the agreed method of appointment of arbitrators is not followed.[195] New York state courts have used this rule to

[189] *LaPrade v Kidder Peabody & Co, Inc* 146 F 3d 899, 903 (US Ct of Apps (DC Cir), 1998), the FAA 'contemplates that courts should not interfere with arbitrations by making interlocutory rulings'.

[190] *Michaels v Mariforum Ship, SA* 624 F 2d 411, 414 (US Ct of Apps (2nd Cir), 1980): 'The language of the Act is unambiguous: it is only after an award has been made by the arbitrators that a party can seek to attack any of the arbitrators' determinations in court.'; *Re Universal Service Fund Telephone Billing Practices Litigation* 370 F Supp 2d 1135, 1138 (US D Ct (D Kan), 2005), despite not condoning the manner in which the arbitration stated, 'the court is not authorized by the Federal Arbitration Act, 9 USC §§ 1-16(FAA), to interfere with the ongoing arbitration proceeding'; *Re Ihi* 324 SW 3d 891, 894 (Tex Ct of Apps (14th D, Houston), 2010), applying the FAA and holding that 'until an award has been made, a court is simply without authority to review the validity of arbitrators' interlocutory rulings'; *Loc 100, Transport Workers Union of Am, AFL-CIO v New York City Transit Auth* 237 AD 2d 606, 655 NY S 2d 602, 603 (NY S Ct, Apps Div (2nd Dept), 1997): 'Courts do not have jurisdiction to review interlocutory arbitration decisions…, and may only intervene after there has been a final determination at the conclusion of the arbitration proceeding.'

[191] *Gulf Guaranty Life Insurance Co v Connecticut Gen Life Insurance Co* 304 F 3d 476, 490 (US Ct of Apps (5th Cir), 2002): 'it is well established that prior to issuance of an award, a court may not make inquiry into an arbitrator's capacity to serve based on a challenge that a given arbitrator is biased'; *Aviall, Inc v Ryder System, Inc* 110 F 3d 892, 895 (US Ct of Apps (2nd Cir), 1997), the FAA does not provide for pre-award removal of an arbitrator.

[192] *Bronx-Lebanon Hospital Center v Signature Medical Management Group, LLC* 6 AD 3d 261, 775 NY S 2d 279 (NY S Ct, Apps Div (1st Dept), 2004), exercising inherent authority to consider a challenge to an arbitrator for bias; *Astoria Medical Group v Health Insurance Plan of Greater New York* 11 NY 2d 128, 132 (NY Ct of Apps, 1962): 'courts have an inherent power to disqualify an arbitrator before an award has been rendered'; *Metro Prop and Cas Ins Co v JC Penney Cas Ins Co* 780 F Supp 885, 894 (US D Ct (D Conn), 1991): 'it simply does not follow that the policy objective of an expeditious and just arbitration with minimal judicial interference is furthered by categorically prohibiting a court from disqualifying an arbitrator prior to arbitration'; but see *Corp Printing Co, Inc v New York Typographical Union No 6* 601 F Supp 323, 328 (US D Ct (SDNY), 1984), holding that the timing to challenge an arbitrator is after an award has been made.

[193] Regarding vacating an award based on arbitrator misconduct, see para 19.125.

[194] *Application of York Hannover Holding AG v American Arbitration Assn* 1993 WL 159961 (US D Ct (SDNY), 1993), holding that 'Under New York law, it is clear that a court has the equitable power to intervene before a final arbitration award is made', but finding that the high standard was not met in that case.

[195] CPLR § 7504: 'If the arbitration agreement does not provide for a method of appointment of an arbitrator, or if the agreed method fails or for any reason is not followed, or if an arbitrator fails to act and his successor has not been appointed, the court, on application of a party, shall appoint an arbitrator.'

entertain challenges to arbitrators and to reconsider institutional decisions on disqualifications of arbitrators.[196]

Texas and Florida have Model Law-based international arbitration statutes that expressly allow a party to seek immediate court intervention regarding the challenge of an arbitrator.[197] If the parties have agreed on a challenge procedure (either expressly or by reference to arbitration rules), then those procedures govern.[198] If there is no agreement, the parties must file a written challenge with the arbitral tribunal within 15 days of becoming aware of a circumstance giving rise to the challenge. If the challenged arbitrator does not withdraw, the arbitral tribunal shall rule on the challenge.[199] If the challenge is not successful, within 30 days of the decision rejecting the challenge, the party may file a request with the court seeking a determination on the challenge.[200] The court's determination is not appealable. While this proceeding is pending, the arbitral tribunal, including the challenged arbitrator, can continue with the arbitration proceedings.[201] **19.87**

19.3.2 Role of court in compelling testimony/evidence[202]

The term discovery is used in the United States to refer to the exchange of information and the taking of pre-hearing evidence. US litigation typically involves broad discovery, which can include document exchange and depositions (witness examination under oath). Discovery procedures are aimed at preventing surprises at trial. Discovery can generally be taken on any matter that is not subject to privilege and that is relevant to a party's claim or defence in a case.[203] Discovery is conducted by the parties themselves, through the exchange of document requests and the service of deposition notices. Court involvement in the discovery process arises only when there is a disagreement on the scope of discovery, for example when one party is abusing the discovery process or one party is resisting discovery. US-style discovery, while broad in the context of litigation, does not spill over into international arbitration. Courts recognize that discovery is limited in international arbitration. Thus, unless **19.88**

---

196 See eg *Shomron v Fuks* 286 AD 2d 587, 730 NY S 2d 90 (NY S Ct, Apps Div (1st Dept), 2001), relying on CPLR § 7504 in holding AAA improperly disqualified the arbitrator.

197 Tex Civ Prac & Rem Code Ann § 172.059; Fla Stat Ann § 684.0014. These provisions do not apply to arbitrations that are not 'international' arbitrations as described in their respective statutes. The statutory schemes for general arbitrations do not contemplate these procedures. See Tex Civ Prac & Rem Code Ann §§ 171.001ff; Fla Stat Ann §§ 682.01ff.

198 Tex Civ Prac & Rem Code Ann § 172.059(a); Fla Stat Ann § 684.0014(1). Note that neither of these statutes allows a party to waive their ability to file a challenge of the arbitrators with the appropriate court, as set forth in Tex Civ Prac & Rem Code Ann § 172.060 and Fla Stat Ann § 684.0014(3).

199 Tex Civ Prac & Rem Code Ann § 172.059(c); Fla Stat Ann § 684.0014(2).

200 Tex Civ Prac & Rem Code Ann § 172.060 and Fla Stat Ann § 684.0014(3).

201 Tex Civ Prac & Rem Code Ann § 172.060 and Fla Stat Ann § 684.0014(3).

202 For proceedings taking place outside the US, a federal district court 'may order' a person in that district to give testimony or produce documents 'for use in a proceeding in a foreign or international tribunal', 18 USC § 1782(a). The case law is divided on whether an arbitration is considered to be a 'tribunal'. cf *Re Consorcio Ecuatoriano de Telecomunicaciones SA v JAS Forwarding (USA), Inc* 685 F 3d 987, 994 (US Ct of Apps (11th Cir), 2012), finding that a private arbitration with its seat in Ecuador met the requirements for being a foreign or international proceeding and therefore this statute was applicable; with *Republic of Kazakhstan v Biedermann Intl* 168 F 3d 880, 883 (US Ct of Apps (5th Cir), 1999), concluding that 'the term "foreign and international tribunals" in § 1782 was not intended to authorize resort to United States federal courts to assist discovery in private international arbitrations'; *Natl Broad Co, Inc v Bear Stearns & Co, Inc* 165 F 3d 184, 191 (US Ct of Apps (2nd Cir), 1999), finding that a private international arbitration did not meet the requirements of a tribunal set forth in 18 USC § 1782); *Re Operadora DB Mexico, SA de CV* 2009 WL 2423138 (US D Ct (M D Fla), 2009), ICC arbitration is not a tribunal under the analysis required by § 1782.

203 See Fed R Civ P, r 26(b).

the parties have agreed otherwise, US-style discovery will not be used in the context of an international arbitration.[204]

19.89 The rules of the major arbitral institutions located in the United States reflect the international approach of minimal discovery in international arbitration. For example, the ICDR Guidelines For Arbitrators Concerning Exchanges of Information state that: 'The tribunal shall manage the exchange of information among the parties in advance of the hearings with a view to maintaining efficiency and economy.'[205] The Guidelines further note that depositions are generally not appropriate in international arbitration.[206] In international arbitration, the scope of discovery is typically defined by the tribunal. Discovery takes place by the service of document requests and the exchange of documents. As in US litigation, the involvement of the tribunal is not required unless there is a disagreement between the parties regarding the scope of proper discovery.

19.90 While discovery between parties can take place without court or tribunal intervention, pre-hearing discovery of third parties may lead to the involvement of a court. The FAA empowers arbitrators to issue subpoenas to third parties to appear before the tribunal 'as a witness and in a proper case to bring with him or them any book, record, document, or paper which may be deemed material as evidence in the case'.[207] If the party does not comply, 'upon petition the United States district court for the district in which such arbitrators . . . are sitting may compel the attendance . . .' of the party. Failure to comply with such court order may result in contempt by the court.[208] If a court holds a party in contempt, it can order that party to pay fines, and in severe instances can order that party to be arrested.

19.91 There is a split among jurisdictions about the court's ability to compel non-party, pre-hearing discovery.[209] Many courts, including the Second Circuit in the *Life Receivables* case, have concluded that an arbitrator's authority to subpoena third parties is restricted 'to situations in which the non-party has been called to appear in the physical presence of the arbitrator and to hand over the documents at that time'.[210] Neither the Fifth nor the Eleventh Circuits have issued decisions on this issue yet. However, district courts in both jurisdictions have followed the reasoning of the Second Circuit.[211]

---

[204] See eg *Oriental Commercial & Shipping Co Ltd v Rosseel, NV* 125 F R D 398, 400 (US D Ct (SDNY), 1989): 'As a general rule, the discovery provisions of the Federal Rules of Civil Procedure are not available as an incident to an arbitration proceeding.'; *Suarez Valdez v Shearson Lehman/American Exp, Inc* 858 F 2d 648, 649–50 (US Ct of Apps (11th Cir), 1988) (Tjoflat, J., concurring), agreement to arbitrate 'indicates the parties' preference for more informal, less expensive procedures', and allowing continued discovery in court 'would subject the parties to the very complexities, inconveniences and expenses of litigation that they determined to avoid'. cf *La Comision Ejecutiva Hidroelecctrica Del Rio Lempa v El Paso Corp* 617 F Supp 2d 481, 487 (US D Ct (S D Tex), 2008): 'the Court may find it determinative that "arbitration is intended as a speedy, economical, and effective means of dispute resolution," and, thus, that extensive discovery through federal courts would harm, rather than benefit, international comity'.

[205] ICDR Guidelines For Arbitrators Concerning Exchanges of Information, Guideline 1.

[206] ICDR Guidelines (n 205) Guideline 6. See also CPR Rules for Non-Administered Arbitration, Rule 11: 'The Tribunal may require and facilitate such discovery as it shall determine is appropriate in the circumstances, taking into account the needs of the parties and the desirability of making discovery expeditious and cost-effective.'

[207] FAA § 7.

[208] FAA § 7.

[209] See *Life Receivables Trust v Syndicate 102 at Lloyd's of London* 549 F 3d 210, 215 (US Ct of Apps (2nd Cir), 2008), acknowledging a circuit split, but finding that FAA § 7 does not compel pre-hearing discovery from a non-party.

[210] *Life Receivables* (n 209) 215.

[211] *Empire Fin Group, Inc v Penson Fin Services, Inc* 2010 WL 742579 (US D Ct (N D Tex), 2010), adopted the reasoning of the Second Circuit and held that the FAA cannot compel production from a non-party that

The court's ability to issue subpoenas for testimony or documents is subject to the limits of its subpoena power. Under Federal Rule of Civil Procedure 45(b)(2), a subpoena 'may be served at any place within the district of the court by which it is issued, or at any place without the district that is within 100 miles of the place of the deposition . . . specified in the subpoena'.[212] Many courts have ruled that this 100-mile territorial limit extends to arbitral subpoenas.[213] This means that a court located in the district of the place of arbitration, which would be the court of venue in an FAA section 7 proceeding, would not necessarily have subpoena authority over a witness located more than 100 miles away. However, the Eighth Circuit has held that, at least with respect to the production of documents, a subpoena in connection with an FAA arbitration did not require compliance with Rule 45(b)(2)'s territorial limit.[214] A New York state court has adopted a position different from that of the Second Circuit, and held that in an FAA arbitration, upon a showing of 'special need or hardship', the court can direct a non-party to provide pre-hearing discovery.[215] This decision came down before the Second Circuit's decision in *Life Receivables*, so it may not hold up to further scrutiny, but this may provide a workaround for obtaining pre-hearing discovery from non-parties if there is an exigent need to do so. **19.92**

A party can also seek to rely on an individual state's statutes relating to pre-hearing discovery as a way to work around the gap in the pre-hearing and territorial limitations of the Federal Rules. Texas and Florida both have statutes specifically tailored towards obtaining discovery in aid of arbitration.[216] New York does not have a specific statute with respect to discovery in aid of arbitration, but does have general procedures in place for obtaining such disclosure.[217] Using these procedures would allow pre-hearing discovery as well as potentially avoiding the territorial limit for federal subpoenas. It is unclear whether these statutes would be pre-empted by the FAA, but since these procedural rules would not negatively affect the federal policy of enforceability of arbitration agreements, it is questionable whether they would be pre-empted.[218] **19.93**

Separate from the potential workaround of using state statutes, there is another approach that would work on a global basis. The FAA's grant of authority to subpoena a non-party is limited to causing the person to appear before the tribunal itself. However, there does not appear to be any restriction against having the tribunal convene, in a location that addresses any geographical limitations, simply for the sake of a pre-hearing deposition or document **19.94**

is not in connection with the non-party's attendance at an arbitration hearing; *Kennedy v Am Express Travel Related Services Co, Inc* 646 F Supp 2d 1342, 1344 (US D Ct (S D Fla), 2009), holding that 'an arbitrator is not statutorily authorized under the FAA to issue summonses for pre-hearing depositions and document discovery from non-parties'.

212 Fed R Civ P, r 45(b)(2).

213 See eg *Dynergy Midstream Services LP v Trammochem* 451 F 3d 89, 90 (US Ct of Apps (2nd Cir), 2006), holding that the FAA 'does not authorize nationwide service of process'; *Legion Insurance Co v John Hancock Mutual Life Insurance Co* 33 F Appx 26, 27–8 (US Ct of Apps (3rd Cir), 2002): 'under the FAA, Rule 45 also governs the service of arbitration subpoenas'.

214 *Re Security Life Insurance Co of America* 228 F 3d 865, 872 (US Ct of Apps (8th Cir), 2000).

215 *ImClone Systems Inc v Waksal* 22 AD 3d 387, 802 NY S 2d 653 (NY S Ct, Apps Div (1st Dept), 2005).

216 Tex Civ Prac & Rem Code Ann § 172.172 and Fla Stat Ann § 684.0038.

217 NY CPLR § 3102.

218 *Re Houston Pipe Line Co* 311 SW 3d 449, 451 (Tex S Ct, 2009), applying Texas procedures to an FAA arbitration to determine that the Court would be authorized to order pre-hearing discovery if it had been appropriate in this case); but see *ImClone Systems Inc v Waksal* 802 NY S 2d 653 653 (NY S Ct, Apps Div (1st Dept), 2005), holding that NY CPLR § 3102 was pre-empted by the FAA.

production. Since many arbitrations occur on a piecemeal basis and take place over a number of months, this is an elegant, if not costly, approach. Courts have enforced discovery that takes place in this manner.[219]

19.3.3 Ability of foreign practitioners to appear in an arbitration as counsel or arbitrator

19.95 The appearance of foreign practitioners to serve as counsel or arbitrators in matters occurring within the United States can introduce complex issues centred on the unauthorized practice of law. In general, in the United States, an attorney is only authorized to appear before the courts in which he is admitted. Each state has its own registration requirements, and being admitted to practice in one state does not authorize an attorney to practice in another state. If someone is found to be practicing law in a state in which he is not admitted, that person could be subject to both civil and criminal penalties.

19.96 The threshold question to examine is if appearing before an arbitral tribunal constitutes engaging in the practice of law. There is no uniformity among jurisdictions on this issue.[220] New York and Texas have not issued any specific statutes or guidelines for the ability of a foreign attorney to represent a client in an arbitration in the United States.[221] The leading New York case on this issue held that because of the unique nature of arbitration, representing a party in arbitration is not the practice of law.[222] Texas has not addressed this situation through case law. However, legal commentary in Texas suggests that a tribunal may authorize a foreign lawyer's appearance in the arbitration.[223] Rule 1-3.11 of the Rules Regulating the Florida Bar permit an appearance by a foreign lawyer in an arbitration seated in Florida where the lawyer is admitted in a foreign jurisdiction, is appearing for a client who resides in, or has an office in the lawyer's home state, and where the appearance relates to the lawyer's practice in his home jurisdiction.[224] In practice, foreign lawyers routinely represent parties in arbitrations seated in New York, Texas, and Florida.

19.97 Other jurisdictions have taken different positions on this issue. In California, US attorneys not admitted in California require the approval of the arbitrators, in order to represent a

[219] See *Stolt-Nielsen SA v Celanese AG* 430 F 3d 567, 579 (US Ct of Apps (2nd Cir), 2005), enforcing a subpoena to require a non-party to appear before a preliminary hearing before the arbitration panel—even if it may have been done to aid testimony prior to the final merits hearing; *Hay Group, Inc v EBS Acquisition Corp* 360 F 3d 404, 413 (US Ct of Apps (3rd Cir), 2004).

[220] See generally KM Blankley et al, 'Multijurisdictional ADR Practice: Lessons for Litigators' (2009) 11 Cardozo J Conflict Resol 29, but note that limitations on attorneys not admitted in any court in the US may be even more restrictive than those detailed in this article.

[221] Solely with respect to international conciliation proceedings, Texas statute states that a party may 'be represented or assisted by a person of the party's choice'. Tex Civ Prac & Rem Code Ann § 172.204.

[222] *Williamson v John D Quinn Construction Corp* 537 F Supp 613, 626 (US D Ct (SDNY), 1982), a non-New York lawyer participating in New York arbitration did not constitute unauthorized practice of law; *Prudential Eq Group, LLC v Ajamie* 538 F Supp 2d 605, 608 (US D Ct (SDNY), 2008) (following *Williamson*); *but see Nisha, LLC v TriBuilt Const Group, LLC* 388 SW 3d 444, 451 (Ark S Ct, 2012), a nonlawyer's representation of a corporation in arbitration proceedings constitutes the unauthorized practice of law.

[223] 48A *Handbook of Texas Lawyer and Judicial Ethics*, Vol 48-48B (Texas Practice Series, 2013) § 10:5: 'Generally, a non-judicial tribunal, such as an arbitration panel, can bestow a similar "blessing" role, by authorizing the non-Texas lawyer's participation in the proceeding.', citing *Colmar Ltd v Fremantlemedia North America, Inc* 344 Ill App 3d 977, 938–93, 801 NE 2d 1017, 1021–9 (Ill Ct of Apps, 2003, app denied), the arbitrator did not exceed his authority in allowing an out-of-state lawyer to represent a party to arbitration proceeding, and the lawyer did not violate the state's unauthorized-practice restrictions by doing so.

[224] Florida Disciplinary Rule of Conduct 4-5.5 also allows representation by a foreign attorney in an arbitration seated in Florida.

client before a California-seated tribunal,[225] but foreign attorneys do not qualify for this approval regime.[226] In Connecticut, a similar restriction applies in domestic arbitrations.[227]

There are no restrictions as to the nationality of the arbitrator.[228] There is no requirement that an arbitrator must be an attorney. **19.98**

19.3.4 Local requirements for conduct of arbitration hearings

Because US law favours party autonomy in arbitration, as long as the parties follow the agreed upon arbitral procedure, there are few external procedures that govern international arbitration in the United States. The FAA contains no specific provisions that govern arbitration hearings. Typically, as is the case with international arbitration elsewhere, fact and expert witness testimony is submitted in advance in writing in lieu of direct testimony, and cross-examination takes place at the hearing. However, these typical procedures may be varied by the parties or the tribunal. The number of written submissions varies on a case-by-case basis. There are no specific laws or court decisions that dictate any limitations of language of testimony, nor are there laws concerning the swearing in of witnesses. **19.99**

The state arbitration statutes provide for limited procedures with respect to hearings. The New York CPLR provides that the arbitrator has the power to administer oaths.[229] Section 7506 of the CPLR also requires that in advance of the arbitrator being sworn to 'hear and decide the controversy faithfully and fairly', the CPLR gives each party the right to present and cross-examine witnesses, and to be represented by an attorney at any stage in the proceeding.[230] The CPLR further provides that all determinations of the tribunal must be made by the majority.[231] **19.100**

The Florida and Texas international arbitration statutes, which are based on the UNCITRAL Model Law, provide that the parties shall decide the procedure to be followed by the tribunal, and in the absence of such agreement, the tribunal shall set the procedures it deems appropriate.[232] Each party has a right to request a hearing, to fully present its case, and to examine arbitrator-appointed experts.[233] **19.101**

---

225 Cal Civ Proc Code § 1282.4, allowing an attorney admitted in another US jurisdiction to represent a party in an arbitration so long as the attorney receives permission from the arbitrator and notifies the California State Bar of his appearance.

226 DD Caron and LD Harhay, 'A Call to Action: Turning the Golden State into A Golden Opportunity for International Arbitration' (2010) 28 Berkeley J Intl L 497, 500. There is a limited exception for allowing a foreign attorney to represent a party participating in an international conciliation. Cal Civ Proc Code § 1297.351: 'A person assisting or representing a party need not be a member of the legal profession or licensed to practice law in California.'

227 Conn Gen Stat Ann § 51-88 (West), prohibiting the practice of law by non-Connecticut attorneys, but excluding parties acting as agents or representatives in international arbitration.

228 Tex Civ Prac & Rem Code Ann § 172.052; Fla Stat Ann § 684.0012(1). New York has not formally addressed this issue.

229 CPLR § 7505.

230 CPLR § 7506(c)–(d).

231 CPLR § 7506(e).

232 Fla Stat Ann § 684.003; Tex Civ Prac & Rem Code Ann § 172.103.

233 Fla Stat Ann §§ 684.0029, 684.0035, 684.0037; Tex Civ Prac & Rem Code Ann §§172.101, 172.111, 172.116.

19.4 The Award

19.4.1 Mandatory rules as to form

19.102 The FAA does not prescribe the form of the award. A written award signed by the arbitrators is required under the relevant arbitration laws of New York, Florida, and Texas.[234] Traditionally in US domestic practice, an arbitrator is not obliged to provide reasons for his decision.[235] This is not the case in international arbitration, in which reasoned awards are the norm. The Model Law-based international arbitration statutes of Florida and Texas require that unless the parties agree otherwise, the award 'must state the reasons on which it is based'.[236] While New York arbitration law does not expressly require the award to state the reasons on which it is based,[237] courts may vacate an award if the arbitrators do not provide an award in the form agreed by the parties.[238] As a reasoned award is required by all of the arbitration rules under which parties to an international arbitration are likely to arbitrate, it is only in truly ad hoc arbitration that the parties would need to include the requirement of a reasoned award in their arbitration agreement.

19.4.2 Mandatory rules as to substance

19.103 An arbitrator has broad discretion in fashioning a remedy appropriate to the case, subject only to limitations imposed by party agreement. Thus, the arbitrator can award damages, specific performance, equitable relief, declaratory relief, and interest.[239] Unless the parties expressly agree otherwise, arbitrators are authorized to award 'punitive damages'[240] The arbitrators do not exceed their authority so long as it is rationally relatable to the purpose of the original agreement.[241]

19.104 For parties to international arbitrations outside the United States, victory often includes an award of arbitration costs. These arbitration costs include not only the costs of the arbitrators and the arbitral institution, but also the costs of attorneys. The situation is different in the United States because of the general (but not universal) rule here that litigants bear their own

[234] CPLR § 7507; Fla Stat Ann § 684.0042; Tex Civ Prac & Rem Code Ann § 172.141.

[235] Rule 42 of the AAA Commercial Arbitration Rules (2009) provides that the 'arbitrator need not render a reasoned award unless the parties request such an award in writing prior to appointment of the arbitrator or unless the arbitrator determines that a reasoned award is appropriate'. See also, *Cat Charter, LLC v Schurtenberger* 646 F 3d 836, 844 (US Ct of Apps (11th Cir), 2011), quoting *United Steelworkers of America v Enterprise Wheel & Car Corp* 363 US 593, 598, 80 S Ct 1358 (1960): 'Arbitrators have no obligation to the court to give their reasons for an award.'; *Dawahare v Spencer* 210 F 3d 666, 670 (US Ct of Apps (6th Cir), 2000), the Sixth Circuit declined to adopt a requirement that an arbitrator provide reasons for the award.

[236] Tex Civ Prac & Rem Code Ann § 172.141; Fla Stat Ann § 684.0042.

[237] NY CPLR § 7508 only requires the award to be in writing, signed and affirmed by the arbitrators; *Wall St Associates, LP v Becker Paribas Inc* 27 F 3d 845, 849 (US Ct of Apps (2nd Cir), 1994): 'Arbitrators are not required to provide the rationale for their award.'

[238] *Cat Charter, LLC v Schurtenberger* 646 F 3d 836, 843 (US Ct of Apps (11th Cir), 2011): 'An arbitrator may also exceed her authority by failing to provide an award in the form required by an arbitration agreement.'; *American Centennial Insurance Co v Global Intl Reinsurance Co Ltd* 2012 WL 2821936 (US D Ct (SDNY), 2012) (the same).

[239] Tex Civ Prac & Rem Code § 172.144, permitting an award of interest.

[240] *Mastrobuono v Shearson Lehman Hutton, Inc* 514 US 52, 115 S Ct 1212 (1995).

[241] See *American Laser Vision, PA v The Laser Vision Institute, LLC* 487 F 3d 255, 258–9 (US Ct of Apps (5th Cir), 2007), abrogated on other grounds by *Hall Street Associates, LLC v Mattel, Inc* 552 US 576, 128 S Ct 1396 (2008); *Executone Info Systems, Inc v Davis* 26 F 3d 1314, 1320 (US Ct of Apps (5th Cir), 1994); *Anderman/Smith Operating Co v Tennessee Gas Pipeline Co* 918 F 2d 1215, 1219 (US Ct of Apps (5th Cir), 1990): 'arbitrators have traditionally enjoyed broad leeway to fashion remedies'.

legal fees. US domestic arbitration rules often reflect this approach.[242] However, the rule is not ironclad and there are grounds upon which a victor in an international arbitration with its venue in the United States can recover legal fees.

The FAA is silent on the recoverability of arbitration costs and attorney's fees. Courts have held that the FAA does not preclude an award of costs and attorney's fees where the arbitral tribunal otherwise has the authority to award such costs and fees.[243] **19.105**

The state arbitration acts of New York, Texas, and Florida also do not preclude an award of arbitration costs and attorney's fees. New York law provides that: 'Unless otherwise provided in the agreement to arbitrate, the arbitrators' expenses and fees, together with other expenses, not including attorney's fees, incurred in the conduct of the arbitration, shall be paid as provided in the award.'[244] Like the FAA, '[the CPLR] does not bar the award of attorney's fees; it merely does not grant authority to do so'.[245] There is no provision regarding the recovery of costs or fees in Florida's international arbitration statute. Florida's general arbitration statute provides for the recovery of expenses associated with the arbitration, but not for the recovery of attorney's fees.[246] With respect to international arbitrations, Texas grants the arbitral panel the discretion to award costs, including 'legal fees and expenses'.[247] **19.106**

It has also been held in these states that an arbitral tribunal has the authority to award legal fees if the parties' contract expressly provides for the recovery of attorney's fees.[248] Even in the absence of an express contract, an arbitral tribunal may award legal fees if the parties have evidenced the intent to permit such recovery. Essentially, the tribunal must find an implicit agreement between the parties to the arbitration that the successful party will recover its legal fees. Such an implicit agreement may be found where (a) the institutional arbitral rules chosen by the parties permit the recovery of attorney's fees[249] or (b) the **19.107**

---

[242] eg the AAA Commercial Rules, art R-43(d) permits an award for attorney's fees only if all parties have requested such an award or if it is authorized by law or the arbitration agreement.

[243] *Painewebber, Inc v Bybyk* 81 F 3d 1193, 1202 (US Ct of Apps (2nd Cir), 1996); *Turnberry Associates v Service Station Aid, Inc* 651 So 2d 1173, 1175 (Fla S Ct, 1995): 'Absent a clear directive from the legislature, we see no reason why the parties may not also voluntarily agree to allow the collateral issue of attorney's fees to be decided in the same forum as the main dispute.' See also *Stone & Webster, Inc v Triplefine Intl Corp* 118 Fed Appx 546, 550 (US Ct of Apps (2nd Cir), 2004); *IBK Enters, Inc v One Key, LLC* 19 Misc 3d 1131, *5, 866 NY S 2d 92 (NY S Ct (Kings Cnty), 2008); *Cassedy v Merrill Lynch, Pierce, Fenner & Smith, Inc* 751 So 2d 143, 145, 149 (Fla D Ct of Apps (1st Dist), 2000).

[244] NY CPLR § 7513.

[245] *Kamakazi Music Corp v Robbins Music Corp* 684 F 2d 228, 231 (US Ct of Apps (2d Cir), 1982).

[246] Fla Stat Ann § 682.11: 'Unless otherwise provided in the agreement or provision for arbitration, the arbitrators' and umpire's expenses and fees, together with other expenses, not including counsel fees, incurred in the conduct of the arbitration, shall be paid as provided in the award.'

[247] Tex Civ Prac & Rem Code Ann § 172.145(b). In an unpublished decision the Fifth Circuit has held that this statute authorizes an arbitrator to award costs and legal fees in an international arbitration seated in Texas. *Saipem America v Wellington Underwriting Agencies Ltd* 2009 WL 1616122 (US Ct of Apps (5th Cir), 2009).

[248] See eg *Dunhill Franchisees Trust v Dunhill Staffing Systems, Inc* 513 F Supp 2d 23 (US D Ct (SDNY), 2007).

[249] *Shaw Group, Inc v Triplefine Intl Corp* 2003 WL 22077332 (US D Ct (SDNY), 2003), affd 322 F 3d 115 (US Ct of Apps (2nd Cir), 2003), confirming an arbitrator's award of attorney's fees because the contract provided for arbitration under the ICC Rules of Arbitration which authorized the award of legal fees to the prevailing party); *IBK Enters, Inc v One Key, LLC* 19 Misc 3d 1131, *5, 866 NY S 2d 92 (NY S Ct (Kings Cnty), 2008), declining to vacate an award where the parties had incorporated the AAA Construction Arbitration Rules into their contract, and such rules expressly empowered the arbitrator to award attorney's fees; *Cassedy v Merrill Lynch, Pierce, Fenner & Smith, Inc* 751 So 2d 143, 145, 149 (Fla D Ct of Apps (1st Dist), 2000), directing the trial court to reinstate an arbitrator's award of attorney's fees on the ground that the arbitrator was authorized to award such fees by virtues of the parties' NASD submission agreement—which committed to

conduct of the parties during the course of the arbitration proceedings, evidences an agreement on the recovery of legal fees. The conduct found sufficient to support a legal fee award has included, for example, requests by both parties for attorney's fees in their pleadings, discussion of attorney's fees in correspondence, or at hearings with the arbitral tribunal, or even the parties' silence in response to the tribunal's statement that it intended to issue an award of attorney's fees.[250]

19.5 After the Award

19.5.1 Confirmation of award

19.108 The process by which an arbitral award is recognized and transformed into a judgment of the court is commonly referred to in US practice as 'confirmation' and 'entry of judgment'. To confirm a foreign or international arbitral award pursuant to the New York or Panama Convention, a court is required to have personal or *quasi in rem* jurisdiction over the parties.[251] Where a party agrees to arbitrate in New York, Florida, or Texas they are deemed to consent to personal jurisdiction in that particular state for the purpose of the enforcement of arbitral awards.[252] Where the arbitration is located outside the state, personal jurisdiction must be established through traditional analysis of the activities and contacts of the person or corporation.[253]

19.109 In addition to personal jurisdiction, there must also be subject matter jurisdiction. With respect to Convention awards, the FAA provides for direct subject matter jurisdiction to confirm an award and enter judgment.[254] A party can seek to confirm a Convention award within three years from the issuance of the award.[255] An action under section 207 of the FAA pre-empts section 9 of the FAA, which applies to—predominantly domestic—non-Convention awards.[256]

19.110 For the confirmation and entry of non-Convention awards, Chapter 1 of the FAA governs.[257] Its rules are more stringent than an application to confirm a Convention award.

---

arbitration 'the present matter in controversy, as set forth in the attached statement of claim, answers *and all related counterclaims and/or third party claims which may be asserted.*') (emphasis added).

[250] See eg *Synergy Gas Co v Sasso* 853 F 2d 59, 64 (US Ct of Apps (2nd Cir), 1988), *Spector v Torenberg* 852 F Supp 201, 210 (US D Ct (SDNY), 1994), *Clarendon Marketing, Inc v CT Chems* 1993 WL 300041 (US D Ct (SDNY), 1993).

[251] See *First Inv Corp of Marshall Islands v Fujian Mawei Shipbuilding Ltd* 703 F 3d 742 (US Ct of Apps (5th Cir), 2012); *Frontera Resources Azerbaijan Corp v State Oil Co of the Azerbaijan Republic* 582 F 3d 393, 397 (US Ct of Apps (2nd Cir), 2009); *S & Davis Intl, Inc v Republic of Yemen* 218 F 3d 1292, 1303–5 (US Ct of Apps (11th Cir), 2000).

[252] See *Insurance Corp of Ireland Ltd v Compagnie des Bauxites de Guinee* 456 US 694, 704, 102 S Ct 2099 (1982), noting that 'lower federal courts have found such consent [to personal jurisdiction] implicit in agreements to arbitrate'; *Reed & Martin, Inc v Westinghouse Electric Corp* 439 F 2d 1268 (US Ct of Apps (2nd Cir), 1971); *Harch Hyperbarics, Inc v Martinucci* 2010 US Dist LEXIS 98159, 13 (US D Ct (E D La), 2010); *Bozo v Bozo* 2012 US Dist LEXIS 175412, 2 (US D Ct (S D Fla), 2012).

[253] See generally CA Wright et al, *Federal Practice and Procedure* (3rd edn, West Publishing Co, 2002) Vol 4, Civil § 1069.

[254] FAA § 207, incorporated by FAA § 302 so as to apply to Panama Convention awards.

[255] FAA § 207.

[256] *Phoenix Aktiengesellschaft v Ecoplas, Inc* 391 F 3d 433, 437 (US Ct of Apps (2nd Cir), 2004), FAA § 207 pre-empts FAA § 9's requirement that the arbitration agreement contain a consent for confirmation as a precondition to confirming a Convention award in the courts; *McDermott Intl, Inc v Lloyds Underwriters of London* 120 F 3d 583, 588–9 and n 12 (US Ct of Apps (5th Cir), 1997).

[257] FAA § 9.

An application to confirm an award under this chapter must be made within one year[258] In addition, a party can seek confirmation and entry of the award, only if, in the arbitration agreement, the parties 'have agreed that a judgment of the court shall be entered upon the award made pursuant to the arbitration'.[259] The specific language that is required in the arbitration agreement is unclear.[260] However, as long as the arbitration agreement contains language that indicates that the decision of the arbitrators will be final, this constitutes, in the Second, Fifth and Eleventh Circuits, consent sufficient to allow confirmation under section 9 of the FAA.[261]

The procedures involved in enforcing an international arbitral award are straightforward. Parties seeking to confirm or to vacate an arbitral award in federal court proceed by filing a motion or petition to confirm, rather than a complaint.[262] Where a party is found within the district where the petition is to be heard, service can be made in the same manner as service of a motion pursuant to Federal Rule of Civil Procedure 5.[263] Where the adverse party is located outside of the United States or in a different district from that of the court where the petition is made, service must be made pursuant to rule 4 of the Federal Rules of Civil Procedure.[264] **19.111**

A party's petition to confirm the arbitration award must include the arbitration agreement and the arbitral award.[265] Failure to include such documents at the time of filing is a ground to deny confirmation.[266] If the award or arbitration agreement is in a language other than English, a certified translation of these documents must be supplied.[267] Parties may also submit in support of the motion or petition 'affidavits, legal briefs, and documentary evidence in support of the order sought'.[268] **19.112**

The 'basic thrust' of the Conventions was 'to liberalize procedures for enforcing foreign arbitral awards'.[269] Therefore, once a petition is made with a copy of the award and arbitration agreement and the jurisdictional requirements have been satisfied, the burden shifts to the adverse party to resist enforcement. **19.113**

In the context of an international arbitration: 'The party opposing enforcement of an arbitral award has the burden to prove that one of the seven defenses under the New York Convention **19.114**

---

258 FAA § 9.

259 FAA § 9.

260 See generally, E Van Ausdall, 'Confirmation of Arbitral Awards: The Confusion Surrounding Section 9 of the Federal Arbitration Act' (2000) 49 Drake L Rev 41, 50.

261 See *I/S Stavborg v National Metal Converters, Inc* 500 F 2d 424, 426–7 (US Ct of Apps (2nd Cir), 1974); *Place St Charles v JA Jones Const Co* 823 F 2d 120, 124 (US Ct of Apps (5th Cir), 1987); *Booth v Hume Publishing, Inc* 902 F 2d 925, 930 (US Ct of Apps (11th Cir), 1990); cf *PVI, Inc v Ratiopharm GmbH* 135 F 3d 1252, 1254 (US Ct of Apps (8th Cir), 1998), refusing to confirm an arbitration award where the arbitration agreement did not contain explicit consent to confirm.

262 FAA § 6 provides that 'any application [under the FAA] shall be made and heard in the manner provided by law for the making or hearings of motions'.

263 FAA § 9.

264 Fed R Civ P, r 4(h)(2).

265 FAA § 13.

266 See eg *Czarina, LLC v WF Poe Syndicate* 358 F 3d 1286, 1291 (US Ct of Apps (11th Cir), 2004), a party seeking to confirm a Convention award must provide the court with a copy of the written agreement; *Ameriprise Bank, FSB v PNC Bank, National Association* 2012 WL 5906400 (US D Ct (W D Pa), 2012), acknowledging that the requisite documents under FAA § 13 were filed with the motion to confirm an award.

267 New York Convention, Art IV.

268 *Moses H Cone Memorial Hospital v Mercury Construction Corp* 460 US 1, 22 n 26, 103 S Ct 927 (1983).

269 *Parsons & Whittemore Overseas Co v Société Générale de L'Industrie du Papier* 508 F 2d 969, 973 (US Ct of Apps (2nd Cir), 1974).

applies.'[270] 'The burden is a heavy one, as the showing required to avoid summary confirmance is high.'[271] There are only seven grounds authorized by the Convention. They are:

i. Under Article V(1) of the Convention:
   (a) The parties to the agreement... were... under some incapacity, or the said agreement is not valid under the law...; or
   (b) The party against whom the award is invoked was not given proper notice of the appointment of the arbitrator or of the arbitration proceedings...; or
   (c) The award deals with a difference not contemplated by or not falling within the terms of the submission to arbitration, or it contains decisions on matters beyond the scope of the submission to arbitration...; or
   (d) The composition of the arbitral authority or the arbitral procedure was not in accordance with the agreement of the parties...; or
   (e) The award has not yet become binding on the parties, or has been set aside or suspended by a competent authority of the country in which, or under the law of which, that award was made.
ii. Under Article V(2) of the Convention:
   (a) The subject matter of the difference is not capable of settlement by arbitration or
   (b) The recognition or enforcement of the award would be contrary to the public policy of the country in which enforcement or recognition is sought.[272]

19.115 While a primary jurisdiction has its full range of powers to set aside an arbitral award (discussed in the following paragraph), a court in a secondary jurisdiction may only refuse or stay enforcement of an award on the limited grounds specified in the Convention.[273]

19.116 Consistent with the aim of the New York Convention, parties seeking to enforce arbitral awards in the United States can expect efficient resolution of enforcement proceedings.

19.5.2 Recourse against an award under the FAA

Setting aside an award rendered in the United States

19.117 US Courts have recognized that the New York Convention 'mandates very different regimes for the review of arbitral awards (1) in the countries in which, or under the law of which, the award was made, and (2) in other countries where recognition and enforcement are sought'.[274] The location in which the award was made is the primary jurisdiction, with the other countries where recognition is sought being secondary jurisdictions. The primary jurisdiction for the confirmation of an award is the court where, or under the law of which, the award was made.

19.118 If the setting aside of the award is sought in a primary jurisdiction, local law applies regarding the setting aside. In the United States, that would be the FAA. Thus, for an arbitration award that is rendered in the United States (even if it falls under the New York/Panama

270 *Encyclopaedia Universalis SA v Encyclopaedia Britannica, Inc* 403 F 3d 85, 90 (US Ct of Apps (2nd Cir), 2005).

271 *Encyclopaedia Universalis* (n 270) (citations, ellipsis, and internal quotation marks omitted).

272 New York Convention, Art. V; *Yusuf Ahmed Alghanim & Sons v Toys 'R' Us, Inc* 126 F 3d 15, 19 (US Ct of Apps (2nd Cir), 1997).

273 *Gulf Petro Trading Co, Inc v Nigerian National Petroleum Corp* 512 F 3d 742, 747 (US Ct of Apps (5th Cir), 2008).

274 *Karaha Bodas Co v Perusahaan Pertambangan Minyak Dan Gas Bumi Negara* 335 F 3d 357, 364 (US Ct of Apps (5th Cir), 2003), quoting *Yusuf Ahmed Alghanim & Sons v Toys 'R' Us, Inc* 126 F 3d 15, 23 (US Ct of Apps (2nd Cir), 1997) (internal quotation marks and brackets omitted).

Convention), the domestic provisions of the FAA apply, with section 10 of the FAA applying in actions to vacate an arbitration award.[275]

Section 10(a) of the FAA sets forth specific grounds for setting aside (commonly referred to as 'vacating') or modifying an arbitration award:[276] 19.119

(1) where the award was procured by corruption, fraud, or undue means;
(2) where there was evident partiality or corruption in the arbitrators, or either of them;
(3) where the arbitrators were guilty of misconduct in refusing to postpone the hearing, upon sufficient cause shown, or in refusing to hear evidence pertinent and material to the controversy; or of any other misbehavior by which the rights of any party have been prejudiced; or
(4) where the arbitrators exceeded their powers, or so imperfectly executed them that a mutual, final, and definite award upon the subject matter submitted was not made.[277]

This section applies to any award rendered in the United States (even if it falls under the New York/Panama Convention), because the Conventions deal only with enforcement and not with setting aside. Section 10 of the FAA does not confer subject matter jurisdiction, so an action to vacate an award may only be maintained in federal court if there is an independent basis for jurisdiction.[278] 19.120

The party seeking to vacate an award has a very high burden.[279] The review of an arbitration award is guided by the 'national policy favoring arbitration with just the limited review needed to maintain arbitration's essential virtue of resolving disputes straightaway'.[280] Thus, under federal law, parties cannot expand the scope of judicial review so as to provide a Court with additional grounds for vacating or modifying an arbitration award.[281] 'A court's review of an arbitration award is instead severely limited.'[282] 19.121

Parties seeking to vacate an arbitral award proceed at their own risk. Courts show little tolerance for dilatory conduct in the context of set aside proceedings. When faced with frivolous challenges to arbitral awards, courts have been willing to sanction the party resisting enforcement and require them to compensate the prevailing party for their legal expenses.[283] 19.122

---

275 *Telenor Mobile Communications AS v Storm LLC* 524 F Supp 2d 332, 343 n 8 (US D Ct (SDNY), 2007): 'In fact, the only courts with authority to vacate an arbitral award are courts at the seat of the arbitration.'

276 FAA § 10 sets forth the grounds to vacate an award, and FAA § 11 sets forth the ground to modify or correct an award.

277 FAA § 10.

278 *Baltin v Alaron Trading Corp* 128 F 3d 1466, 1469 (US Ct of Apps (11th Cir), 1997); *Smith v Rush Retail Centers, Inc* 360 F 3d 504, 506 (US Ct of Apps (5th Cir), 2004); *Greenberg v Bear, Stearns & Co* 220 F 3d 22, 26 (US Ct of Apps (2nd Cir), 2000); *Yusuf Ahmed Alghanim & Sons v Toys 'R' Us, Inc* 126 F 3d 15 (US Ct of Apps (2nd Cir), 1997); *Intl Ship Co, SA v Hydra Offshore, Inc* 875 F 2d 388, 391, n 5 (US Ct of Apps (2nd Cir), 1989), affirming the district court's holding that a motion to vacate a Convention award did not have subject matter jurisdiction.

279 *DH Blair & Co v Gottdiener* 462 F 3d 95, 110 (US Ct of Apps (2nd Cir), 2006): 'A party moving to vacate an arbitration award has the burden of proof, and the showing required to avoid confirmation is very high.'

280 *Hall Street Associates, LLC v Mattel, Inc* 552 US 576, 584, 128 S Ct 1396 (2008) (citations and internal quotation marks omitted).

281 *Hall Street Associates, LLC v Mattel, Inc* 552 US 576, 578, 128 S Ct 1396 (2008).

282 *Scandinavian Reinsurance Co Ltd v Saint Paul Fire & Marine Insurance Co* 668 F 3d 60, 71 (US Ct of Apps (2nd Cir), 2012) (internal quotations omitted).

283 *DigiTelCom Ltd v Tele2 Sverige AB* 2012 WL 3065345 (US D Ct (SDNY), 2012), issuing sanctions against a law firm and requiring the reimbursement of attorneys' fees for a frivolous motion to vacate an arbitral

Award produced by corruption, fraud, or undue means

19.123 To vacate an award on the grounds of corruption, fraud, or undue means, there must be evidence of intentional malfeasance on the part of a party.[284] Accepting an adverse inference instead of agreeing to produce documents is not sufficient malfeasance to meet this standard.[285] However, if an award was the result of perjured testimony, that award may be vacated.[286]

Evident partiality or corruption in the arbitrators

19.124 Section 10(a)(2) of the FAA provides that the courts may vacate an award 'where there was evident partiality or corruption in the arbitrators, or either of them'. Evident partiality is more than an appearance of bias, and will be found where a 'reasonable person would have to conclude that an arbitrator was partial to one party to the arbitration'.[287] The party alleging arbitrator bias has the burden of proof.[288] To establish evident partiality, it is not necessary to prove actual bias.[289] An arbitrator's failure to disclose certain relationships or interests is strongly suggestive of bias, but a non-substantive failure to disclose a relationship does not warrant vacating an award.[290]

Arbitrators committed misconduct by refusing to postpone the hearing or hear relevant evidence

19.125 An arbitral award can be vacated under section 10(a)(3) of the FAA when an arbitrator has been 'guilty of misconduct in refusing to hear evidence pertinent and material to the controversy'.[291] The concern is to ensure the 'fundamental fairness' of the proceeding.[292] It is not to undertake evidentiary review of the arbitration proceedings.[293] It is hard to find instances in which this can be established, but a clear case of arbitrator misconduct involved holding hearings during the specific time that one party stated he was unavailable.[294] Refusing to grant an adjournment to accommodate a key witness whose wife just had a resurgence of cancer was also misconduct sufficient to require the vacating of the award.[295]

---

award; *Ingram v Glast, Phillips & Murray* 196 F Appx 232, 233 (US Ct of Apps (5th Cir), 2006), upholding sanctions of attorneys' fees, costs, and expenses against attorneys for their bad-faith conduct, which included the pursuit of post-arbitration litigation 'knowing that it was a "complete sham"'; *BL Harbert Intl, LLC v Hercules Steel Co* 441 F 3d 905 (US Ct of Apps (11th Cir), 2006), expressing a future intention to issue sanctions for frivolous petitions to vacate an arbitral award.

284 *National Casualty Co v First State Insurance Group* 430 F 3d 492, 499 (US Ct of Apps (1st Cir), 2005).

285 *National Casualty Co* (n 284).

286 *Red Apple Supermarkets/Supermarkets Acquisitions v Loc 338* 1999 WL 596273 (US D Ct (SDNY), 1999).

287 *Morelite Construction Corp v New York City District Council Carpenters Benevolent Funds* 748 F 2d 79, 84 (US Ct of Apps (2nd Cir), 1984).

288 *Morelite Construction* (n 287) 72.

289 *Scandinavian Reinsurance Co Ltd v Saint Paul Fire & Marine Insurance Co*, 668 F 3d 60, 72 (US Ct of Apps (2nd Cir), 2012).

290 *Scandinavian Reinsurance* (n 289) 72–3, 77: 'nondisclosure does not by itself constitute evident partiality'; *Positive Software Solutions, Inc v New Century Mortgage Corp* 476 F 3d 278, 285 (US Ct of Apps (5th Cir), 2007) (*en banc*), finding that there was no evident partiality where the arbitrator had failed to disclose he was previously a joint representative with counsel for one of the parties.

291 FAA § 10(a)(3).

292 *Tempo Shain Corp v Bertek, Inc* 120 F 3d 16, 20 (US Ct of Apps (2nd Cir), 1997); *Hoteles Condado Beach v Union De Tronquistas Local 901* 763 F 2d 34, 39 (US Ct of Apps (1st Cir), 1985), an arbitrator 'must give each of the parties to the dispute an adequate opportunity to present its evidence and argument'.

293 *Tempo Shain Corp* and *Hoteles Condado Beach* (n 292).

294 *Tube & Steel Corp of America v Chicago Carbon Steel Prods* 319 F Supp 1302, 1304 (US D Ct (SDNY), 1970).

295 *Tempo Shain Corp v Bertek, Inc* 120 F 3d 16, 20 (US Ct of Apps (2nd Cir), 1997).

Arbitrators exceeded their authority

The FAA permits a court to vacate the arbitral award where the arbitrators 'exceeded their powers'.[296] The Second Circuit has 'consistently accorded the narrowest of readings' to the FAA's authorization to vacate awards pursuant to section 10(a)(4).[297] They focus on determining 'whether the arbitrators had the power based on the parties' submissions or the arbitration agreement, to reach a certain issue, not whether the arbitrators correctly decided that issue'.[298] **19.126**

The Supreme Court recently stated, in the context of vacating an arbitration award under section 10(a)(4) of the FAA, that: 'It is only when [an] arbitrator strays from interpretation and application of the agreement and effectively dispense[s] his own brand of industrial justice that his decision may be unenforceable.'[299] **19.127**

Manifest disregard of the law

In 2008, the Supreme Court ruled that the four grounds in section 10 of the FAA were the exclusive ground to vacate an arbitration award.[300] Prior to that decision, courts regularly held that in addition to the four factors previously mentioned, an arbitral award that was in manifest disregard of the law could be vacated.[301] **19.128**

After *Hall Street*, the Second Circuit has taken the approach that manifest disregard of the law 'reconceptualized as a judicial gloss on the specific grounds for vacatur enumerated in section 10 of the FAA, remains a valid ground for vacating arbitration awards'.[302] Other circuits, including the Fifth and Eleventh, have held that after *Hall Street*, the doctrine of manifest disregard does not survive.[303] The Supreme Court itself has not yet decided this issue.[304] Despite the significant attention that has been given to the manifest disregard doctrine, it is of little practical use in challenging international arbitral awards. Since the Second Circuit began to apply the doctrine of manifest disregard in 1960, none of the arbitral awards vacated on that ground was an international or Convention arbitration.[305] **19.129**

---

296 9 USC § 10(a)(4).

297 *Westerbeke Corp v Daihatsu Motor Co Ltd* 304 F 3d 200, 220 (US Ct of Apps (2nd Cir), 2002) (citation omitted).

298 *Westerbeke Corp* (n 297) 220, quoting *DiRussa v Dean Witter Reynolds Inc* 121 F 3d 818, 824 (US Ct of Apps (2nd Cir), 1997).

299 *Stolt-Nielsen SA v AnimalFeeds Intl Corp* 559 US 662, 130 S Ct 1758, 1767 (2010).

300 *Hall Street Associates, LLC v Mattel, Inc* 552 US 576, 578, 128 S Ct 1396 (2008).

301 *Hall Street* (n 300) discussing the reliance on manifest disregard of the law in attempts to vacate an arbitration award.

302 *Stolt-Nielsen SA v AnimalFeeds Intl Corp* 548 F 3d 85, 94 (US Ct of Apps (2nd Cir), 2008) revd and remanded sub nom on other grounds *Stolt-Nielsen SA v AnimalFeeds Intl Corp* 559 US 662, 130 S Ct 1758 (2010); *T Co Metals, LLC v Dempsey Pipe & Supply, Inc* 592 F 3d 329, 339–40 (US Ct of Apps (2nd Cir), 2010) (internal quotation marks omitted): 'manifest disregard remains a valid ground for vacating arbitration awards'.

303 See *Frazier v CitiFinancial Corp, LLC* 604 F 3d 1313, 1324 (US Ct of Apps (11th Cir), 2010), judicially created grounds for vacatur, such as 'manifest disregard' are no longer valid reasons for vacating an arbitration award in the light of *Hall Street*; *Citigroup Global Markets, Inc v Bacon* 562 F 3d 349, 358 (US Ct of Apps (5th Cir), 2009): 'manifest disregard of the law as an independent, nonstatutory ground for setting aside an [arbitration] award must be abandoned and rejected . . . arbitration awards under the FAA may be vacated only for reasons provided in § 10'.

304 See *Stolt-Nielsen SA v AnimalFeeds Intl Corp* 559 US 662, 130 S Ct 1758, 1768, n 3 (2010): 'We do not decide whether "manifest disregard" survives our decision in *Hall Street* . . .'.

305 See 'The "Manifest Disregard of Law" Doctrine and International Arbitration in New York', Report by the Committee on International Commercial Disputes of the New York City Bar Association (August 2012) 6.

Local procedures for setting aside/annulment

19.130 Section 12 of the FAA sets forth the procedure by which a party may apply to vacate, modify, or correct an award. It provides:

> iii. Notice of a motion to vacate, modify, or correct an award must be served upon the adverse party or his attorney within three months after the award is filed or delivered. If the adverse party is a resident of the district within which the award was made, such service shall be made upon the adverse party or his attorney as prescribed by law for service of notice of motion in an action in the same court. If the adverse party shall be a nonresident then the notice of the application shall be served by the marshal of any district within which the adverse party may be found in like manner as other process of the court. For the purposes of the motion any judge who might make an order to stay the proceedings in an action brought in the same court may make an order, to be served with the notice of motion, staying the proceedings of the adverse party to enforce the award.

19.131 Thus, section 12 sets forth: (i) how a challenge is to be made to an arbitration award—motion; (ii) the time limit within which it should be made—three months after the award is 'filed or delivered'; and (iii) the mode of service on an adverse party. The latter provision requires some comment. As drafted, section 12 applies only to a party that is within the United States—either a resident of the district within which the award was made or a resident of another district in the United States.

19.132 When dealing with a party that is resident outside the United States, it would be possible to use rule 4 of the Federal Rules of Civil Procedure, which has rules regarding the service of process on non-US residents. Alternatively, some courts have held that service of a submission challenging an arbitration award rendered in New York would be proper if it 'provided the fair notice required by due process'.[306]

19.133 The resolution of a motion to set aside an arbitration award typically takes between three months and one year from the date of filing, with six months being a reasonable estimate in most cases.

19.6 Conclusion

19.134 The United States—and New York, Florida, and Texas in particular—offers a favourable venue for international arbitration. The Federal Arbitration Act offers a simple, yet effective, framework for the enforcement of arbitration agreements and arbitral awards. The jurisdictional provisions of Chapter 2 of the Federal Arbitration Act enable a party seeking to enforce an arbitration agreement or award to find relief in the federal courts, which are well accustomed to dealing with issues concerning international arbitration. Courts in the United States recognize that the hallmark of international arbitration is party autonomy and efficiency. Courts will act to further the strong federal policy in favour of arbitration by strictly enforcing arbitration agreements and awards, while at the same time, minimizing judicial interference with the arbitral process. That said, courts will offer support where needed, for example in the context of interim relief in aid of arbitration, or the enforcement of arbitral subpoenas. In addition to enjoying legislative and judicial support, parties to international arbitration can find the institutional support they need from experienced arbitral institutions that offer well-developed arbitral rules.

---

[306] *Lucent Techs, Inc v Tatung Co* 2003 WL 402539, *1 (US D Ct (SDNY), 2003).

20

VIENNA

Nikolaus Pitkowitz

20.1 Background

20.1.1 History and development

Austria's arbitration law dates back to 1781, when arbitration rules were first codified.[1] **20.01**
Subsequently, in the Austrian Code of Civil Procedure (*Zivilprozessordnung*, hereinafter 'ACCP') of 1895, a dedicated chapter on arbitration was introduced which remains the

[1] The General Court Procedures (*Allgemeine Gerichtsordnung*) of 1 May 1781, No 13 IGS contains, in §§ 270–274, general norms on the conduct of arbitration, including the writing requirement for arbitration agreements and the possibility for the parties to waive any recourse to arbitral awards, in which case the court may only be addressed in case of apparent fraud.

source of today's arbitration law. The most notable changes to the ACCP were made in 1983 and 2006, in order to adapt to international arbitration standards.[2]

20.02 The ACCP enshrines the statutory rules of Austrian arbitration law in its sections 577–618, which substantially implement the UNCITRAL Model Law on International Arbitration (the Model Law) and do not differentiate between domestic and international arbitration. In addition to the ACCP, the Austrian Enforcement Act (*Exekutionsordnung*) regulates the enforcement of foreign arbitral awards, in accordance with treaties such as the New York Convention.[3]

20.03 With close to 250 years of arbitration tradition, Austria has established a solid legal basis, which is further reinforced by the extensive arbitration case law of the Austrian Supreme Court. Looking at the legal framework, and in particular the case law, Austria must be considered an 'arbitration friendly' jurisdiction. Arbitration is given significant status in Austria's legal system; courts support arbitration and arbitral awards are very rarely set aside. These factors have certainly helped Vienna to become one of the best respected and busiest international arbitration venues.

20.04 In addition, a broad collection of commentaries, treatises and essays by academics and practitioners (many written in English) address almost every conceivable arbitral issue. Several Austrian universities have departments focusing on arbitration, the most renowned of which is the University of Vienna, with scholars dedicated to commercial arbitration as well as to investment arbitration.

20.05 With this legal toolbox readily available and few restrictions on services rendered by non-Austrians, international arbitrations pending in Austria attract practitioners as arbitrators, party-counsel, or consultants from all around the world. Practitioners are also attracted by the annual William C Vis International Commercial Arbitration Moot, the world's biggest arbitration event, attracting some 300 University teams and 900 arbitrators, which celebrated its twentieth anniversary in 2013, as well as by numerous arbitration conferences every year, including the Vienna Arbitration Days.

20.1.2 VIAC and the Vienna Rules

20.06 Vienna has a remarkable tradition of institutional arbitration. In 1949, arbitral institutions were formed by the Austrian Federal Chamber of Commerce, initially handling both domestic and international arbitration cases.[4] On 1 January 1975 the Austrian Federal Chamber of Commerce established the Vienna International Arbitral Centre (VIAC).[5] VIAC only

[2] Schiedsrechtsänderungsgesetz 2006 ('SchiedsRÄG 2006') BGBl I 2006/7. The 2006 changes generally apply to all arbitration proceedings initiated and arbitration agreements concluded after 1 July 2006. SchiedsRÄG 2006, art VII.

[3] See also ACCP, § 614 which expressly states that international treaties prevail over Austrian law.

[4] The establishment of arbitral institutions falls within the competence of the Austrian Regional Economic Chambers of Commerce (*Wirtschaftskammern*) following a model of arbitration rules used by the Board of Directors of the Austrian Federal Chamber of Commerce, Schieds- und Schlichtungsordnung für die ständigen Schiedsgerichte der Wirtschaftskammern, 17 March 1949.

[5] See W Melis, 'Schiedsgerichtsbarkeit der Österreichischen Handelskammern seit 1946' in *Völkerrecht, Recht der internationalen Organisationen, Weltwirtschaftsrecht : Festschrift für Ignaz Seidl-Hohenveldern* (1988) 367 with further references; W Melis, 'Austria' (1979) IV YB Commercial Arbitration 2.

handles international disputes.[6] There are also other arbitration centres in Austria dealing with both domestic and international disputes.[7] In addition, Vienna is often selected as a seat for ICC arbitrations and ad hoc arbitrations (particularly under the UNCITRAL Arbitration Rules). It is estimated that in 2012 in total of more than 200 arbitration cases were pending in Vienna.

The exceptional reputation of VIAC has made an important contribution to promoting Vienna as an arbitral venue. During the last ten years the VIAC caseload has more than doubled. The typical duration of VIAC proceedings is one year. As of the end of 2010 there were 70 international cases pending before the VIAC with an aggregate amount in dispute of €3.25 billion; as of the end of 2011 there were 83 cases pending with an aggregate amount in dispute of €683 million. At the end of 2012 there were 79 cases pending before VIAC with an aggregate amount in dispute of €826 million. By the end of April 2013, 80 international arbitral proceedings were pending at VIAC, with an aggregated amount in dispute of €1.4 billion.[8] These statistics cover only international cases fully administered by VIAC. In addition, VIAC also administers a substantial number of ad hoc cases pending in Austria, usually when it has been agreed upon or designated as an appointing authority under the UNCITRAL Arbitration Rules. **20.07**

The Vienna Rules, promulgated by VIAC, are aimed at providing a lean and flexible framework. In 2012 VIAC initiated a comprehensive review process aimed at modernizing, overhauling, and streamlining its rules. The process included a widely distributed user survey, a number of discussion rounds, and a road show. Given the overwhelming positive feedback on the existing rules, the reform commission decided to maintain the lean and flexible approach. The new rules were adopted in May 2013 and will apply to all proceedings commenced after 1 July 2013. The most important changes are: **20.08**

- *Joinder of third parties.* The arbitral tribunal has the authority to order joinder of third parties either at the request of one of the parties or at the request of that third party. The tribunal is thereby granted wide discretion, provided that it has heard all parties and the third party to be joined. When deciding on the joinder, the arbitral tribunal must also determine the manner of such joinder (ie with a full party status or as mere *amicus curiae*). The provision also recognizes the right of a third party included as a party to participate in the formation of the arbitral tribunal.[9]
- *Consolidation of proceedings.* The VIAC executive board has the power to consolidate proceedings upon request by the parties or when the same arbitral tribunal (or sole arbitrator) has been appointed.[10]

---

[6] A dispute qualifies as 'international' if either not all (at least one of) the parties have their place of business or their residence outside Austria at the time of the conclusion of the arbitration agreement. In addition the Vienna Rules can be explicitly agreed upon by domestic parties for disputes of an international character.

[7] Most notably the nine arbitral centres established and administered by the chambers of commerce of each Austrian province. In Vienna that is the Permanent Arbitral Centre of the Vienna Chamber of Commerce (*Ständiges Schiedsgericht der Wirtschaftskammer Wien*). Another Austrian arbitral centre handling international and domestic disputes is the Court of Arbitration of the Vienna Stock Exchange, dealing with disputes in its capacity as a securities and commodities exchange.

[8] Vienna International Arbitration Centre, 'VIAC STATISTICS 2012' (March 2013), avaialble at <http://www.viac.eu/en/service/statistics/89-service/statistiken/122-viac-statistics-2012>.

[9] Vienna Rules 2013, art 14.

[10] Vienna Rules 2013, art 15.

- *Multi-party proceedings.* In line with the established principles under the former rules, the principle of party autonomy in multi-party proceedings prevails under the new Vienna Rules. If one party or a group of parties fails to agree on a nominee to be confirmed as arbitrator, the failure to reach agreement will not automatically invalidate the nomination by the other side. Only in exceptional cases does the VIAC executive board have the authority to replace an arbitrator already appointed. In that respect the Vienna Rules deviate from the so-called *Dutco* approach.[11]
- *Costs.* The system of flat rate costs (as compared to hourly rates for arbitrators) has remained unchanged, since it means that parties have the opportunity to plan ahead and has proved to be an incentive for arbitrators to streamline the proceedings. The VIAC cost scale, which is internationally considered to be on the moderate side, has been slightly amended, to permit more flexibility, especially for arbitrators' fees.[12] This also permits the Secretary General to apply cost incentives to arbitrators effectively handling a dispute. The Vienna Rules 2013 also contain an explicit obligation of both parties to jointly fund the costs of the arbitration[13] and grant the arbitral tribunal the power to direct the defaulting party to pay its share of the cost advance.[14]
- *Expedited proceedings.* The Vienna Rules 2013 also contain specific fast-track regulations which are, however, only applicable if the parties explicitly agree to these under an opt-in mechanism. For expedited proceedings there is an obligation to render a final award within six months (unless extended).

20.1.3 Mandatory rules

20.09 Austrian arbitration law recognizes a very high degree of party autonomy. Nevertheless, there are certain provisions of Austrian arbitration law that are generally considered mandatory for all arbitrations seated in Austria, regardless of any agreement by the parties. Although most of these provisions are addressed in greater depth later, for ease of reference they are summarized here. Many of these mandatory rules (eg due process provisions) require that a party raises a timely objection.

20.10 The mandatory provisions concern:

- the writing requirement of the arbitration agreement;
- the need for an uneven number of arbitrators—for impartial and independent arbitrators—and the right to request court assistance for the appointment of arbitrators, the right to challenge arbitrators, and the right of an arbitrator to prematurely terminate his function;
- the obligation to conduct the proceedings so that the parties are treated fairly and equally, granted the right to be heard, and have the right to appoint counsel of their choice;
- the right to request support from state courts;
- the limitations on the arbitrability of disputes;
- the form and effects of an arbitral award, the rules governing correction, interpretation and amendment of the arbitral award, and the right to challenge an arbitral award;
- the limitations on arbitration for consumers and in employment matters.

---

11 See (n 63); Vienna Rules 2013, art 18(4).
12 Vienna Rules 2013, art 44(7).
13 Vienna Rules 2013, art 42(2).
14 Vienna Rules 2013, art 42(4).

20.1.4 Arbitration Amendment Act 2013

While there are no major changes expected in the Austrian arbitration landscape, one amendment aimed at further streamlining the arbitration process has been resolved lately. Under the Arbitration Amendment Act 2013,[15] legal actions aimed at setting aside arbitral awards no longer run through all three instances of the Austrian court system, but are directly filed with, and decided by, the Austrian Supreme Court.[16] The amendment was finally approved by Parliament in summer 2013. **20.11**

20.1.5 Comparison with other venues

Vienna has a very diverse and widespread base. In 2012, VIAC was administering proceedings with parties from 43 different countries.[17] The majority of these proceedings were seated in Vienna.[18] Vienna is traditionally the leading arbitration venue for Central and Eastern Europe (CEE) disputes but has in recent years increasingly become attractive also on a global level, particularly for North American and Asian matters. Foreign companies doing business with CEE partners often select Vienna. Vienna's leading role in the CEE region is based on a number of factors distinguishing it from other arbitral venues in Europe. Among these are the stability and predictability of the Austrian legal system, its arbitration friendly approach, Austria's status as a neutral country, its cultural diversity and its track record of bridging disputes between East and West. The accessibility of Vienna and convenience certainly also play an important role. Vienna, the capital of Austria, is located in the heart of Europe and considered the hub of Central and Eastern Europe. More than 420 million people can reach Vienna within two hours. Vienna features a large number of (reasonably priced) five star hotels and excellent arbitration facilities. **20.12**

Some eastern European venues are still struggling with legal and other problems.[19] To name a few, in Russia and Ukraine, the arbitrability of shareholder disputes is questioned.[20] In 2012, Hungary enacted legislation prohibiting arbitration affecting state-owned property.[21] Several jurisdictions limit the parties' right to freely nominate arbitrators,[22] or restrict the language of the arbitration proceedings.[23] **20.13**

---

[15] The new regime under the Arbitration Amendment Act 2013 (SchiedsRÄG 2013) will apply to proceedings commenced after 31 December 2013. (Note: at the time of finalizing this chapter, the Act had been politically approved but not yet ratified by the Austrian Parliament).

[16] ACCP, § 615.

[17] VIAC—Vienna International Arbitration Centre (n 8).

[18] Under the Vienna Rules the seat of arbitration can also be outside Austria.

[19] For some examples of 'misconduct' see V Khvalei, 'Guerilla Tactics in International Arbitration, Russian View' in C Klausegger et al (eds), *Austrian Yearbook on International Arbitration 2011* (Manz'sche Verlags- und Universitätsbuchhandlung, 2011) 335. The corruption of the legal system in a number of Eastern European countries is a frequent topic of debate.

[20] PJ Pettibone, 'The Nonarbitrability of Corporate Disputes in Russia' (2013) 29 Arb Intl 263.

[21] G Bárdosi, 'The Award and the Courts, Hungary: New Rules on Arbitration Related to National Assets' in C Klausegger et al (eds), *Austrian Yearbook on International Arbitration 2013* (Manz'sche Verlags- und Universitätsbuchhandlung 2013) 181.

[22] C Bán, 'Hungary' in G Wegen and S Wilske (eds), *Arbitration in 55 Jurisdictions Worldwide* (Getting the Deal Through, 2013) 235; O Filatov and P Byelousov, 'Ukraine' in Wegen and Wilske 479.

[23] ES Sherby and S Sabzerou, 'Israel' in G Wegen and S Wilske (eds), *Arbitration in 55 Jurisdictions Worldwide* (Getting the Deal Through, 2013) 262; M Rubino-Sammartano, 'Italy' in Wegen and Wilske, 270; J El Ahdab and M Eid, 'Qatar' in Wegen and Wilske, 366; CI Stoica, D Aragea, and A Buga, 'Romania' in Wegen and Wilske, 374.

20.14 Arbitrations in Austria follow an international standard. The legal framework in Austria can generally be compared with that of most other venues that have implemented the UNCITRAL Model Law, such as Germany. Because Austria is a civil law jurisdiction, courts generally take an inquisitorial rather than an adversarial approach. Also, the Austrian ACCP has few mechanisms for obtaining document production. Nevertheless, international arbitrations pending in Austria will typically follow international standards and Austrian courts recognize this.

20.15 On a European level, when parties cannot agree to Vienna as venue for the arbitration, they often opt for one of the other leading European venues, such as Switzerland, Paris, London, or Stockholm. In contrast to Vienna, none of these jurisdictions has adopted the UNCITRAL Model Law. Switzerland (like Austria) is praised for its neutrality. Switzerland is also the only leading European arbitration venue that is not an EU Member State. This may be seen as an advantage, protecting awards from annulment for violation of EU (competition) law, but may also lead to unexpected results, as, for example, in cases of insolvency.[24] Paris is well respected as venue of arbitration and seat of the ICC Court of Arbitration. However, the reduced scope of mandatory provisions under French arbitration law grants arbitrators significantly more flexibility but also makes proceedings less predictable.[25] London is usually only chosen when the parties agree on English law as the governing law. Since all continental European legal systems are based on civil law that is not often the case for intra-European commercial contracts. The main difference between London and Vienna (apart from the higher cost of arbitration proceedings in London) is the possibility to appeal against substantive errors in the arbitral award under English law.[26] Stockholm is sometimes chosen as an alternative to Vienna in Russia-related matters due to its historic role in US-Russian trade relations.

20.16 On a global level, Singapore and Hong Kong are often chosen as alternatives to Vienna when Asian parties are involved. For North American parties, New York is often selected as an alternative venue and the ICDR Rules are frequently selected.

20.2 The Arbitration Agreement

20.2.1 General

20.17 At the outset, it is important to discuss the Austrian legal position on the effectiveness and validity of an arbitration agreement. The existence of a valid arbitration agreement is a prerequisite for the jurisdiction of an arbitral tribunal. As a general rule, Austrian law thereby grants arbitral tribunals (and not state courts) the primary responsibility to determine that issue.

[24] See in this respect the 2009 *Elektrim* case (BGE 4A 428/2008), in which the Swiss Supreme Court (contrary to a court in an EU Member State in a parallel proceeding) found an arbitration clause to be invalidated by insolvency proceedings. G Nater-Bass and O Mosimann, 'Effects of Foreign Bankruptcy on International Arbitration' in C Klausegger et al (eds), *Austrian Yearbook on International Arbitration 2011* (Manz'sche Verlags- und Universitätsbuchhandlung, 2011) 163.

[25] See in that respect the much debated case in which French and UK courts arrived at contradicting decisions. A Malek and C Harris, 'A pilgrimage to Paris: Dallah v. Pakistan' in J El Ahdab (ed) (2010) 2(4) Intl J of Arab Arb 22; see also *Dallah Real Estate & Tourism Holding Co v Ministry of Religious Affairs, Government of Pakistan* [2010] UKSC 46; J Grierson and M Taok, 'Comment on Dallah v. Pakistan' (2009) 26(3) J Intl Arb 467; N Pengelley, 'Pyramids and Pilgrimages: An Arbitration Agreement with a State-Created Entity is Not an Arbitration Agreement with a State' (2009) 13(2) Vindobona J Intl Commercial Arb 293, 306.

[26] Arbitration Act 1996, s 69.

20.2.2 Interpretation of arbitration agreements (double nature)

The Austrian Supreme Court has ruled in a long-standing line of cases that an arbitration agreement has a double nature—that it has both a procedural and a contractual aspect. It must be primarily interpreted under procedural law and only secondarily under applicable contract law. Since Austrian procedural law does not contain any explicit interpretation rules, the 'primary' interpretation method in effect only mandates the primacy of the literal wording, which, as the case law emphasizes, must always constitute the limit for any interpretation. **20.18**

While the procedural interpretation will always follow Austrian law, for the secondary interpretation method, the contract law applicable to the arbitration agreement will need to be applied. This will be Austrian law if this is expressly or impliedly agreed. An implied agreement could, for example, exist if the parties have chosen Vienna as the seat of arbitration.[27] When applying Austrian law, general contract interpretation rules are, in principle, used as guidelines. These consider the intention of the parties and also attempt to fill any lacunae. In cases of doubt, the interpretation favouring arbitration will be applied. However, given the primacy of procedural interpretation, even an extensive interpretation must always be tested against the wording of the arbitration clause, in its widest possible meaning.[28] **20.19**

The Austrian Supreme Court generally takes a wide and thus arbitration-friendly approach to the scope of an arbitration clause. For example, the Supreme Court has confirmed that an arbitration clause includes tort claims, provided that the circumstance on which the tort claim is based would also constitute a breach of the contract (double qualification test).[29] Also, ancillary agreements may fall within the scope of an arbitration clause, if these are intrinsically connected to the main agreement.[30] **20.20**

Austrian law recognizes the separability doctrine[31] even though the ACCP does not expressly refer to it.[32] The Austrian Supreme Court has repeatedly held that the validity of an arbitration agreement must be examined independently of the underlying contract.[33] **20.21**

20.2.3 Substantive requirements of arbitration agreements

For the substantive validity of an arbitration agreement, both the parties and the relationship out of which the dispute may arise must be sufficiently defined and the agreement must **20.22**

---

27 As a consequence of the separability of the arbitration agreement, the law governing the arbitration agreement must be examined independently of the law of the underlying contract. While a choice of law for the main contract may imply also a choice of law for the arbitration agreement, this will generally not be the case if the parties have explicitly chosen a seat in another country; see also C Hausmaninger, '§§ 577 bis 618 ZPO' in H Fasching and A Konecny (eds), *Kommentar zu den Zivilprozessgesetzen* (2nd edn, Manzsche Verlags- und Universitätsbuchhandlung 2007) Vol 4, pt 2, § 581, para 276; G Zeiler, *Schiedsverfahren: ss 677-618 ZPO idf SchiedsRÄG 2006* (2nd edn, Neuer Wissenschaftlicher Verlag, 2006) § 581, paras 125ff; A Fremuth-Wolf, 'Section 581' in S Riegler et al (eds), *Arbitration Law of Austria: Practice and Procedure* (Juris Publishing, 2007) § 577, paras 67–68.

28 Hausmaninger, in Fasching and Konecny, *Kommentar* (n 27) § 581, para 225.

29 Hausmaninger, in Fasching and Konecny, *Kommentar* (n 27) § 581, para 230; J-P Lachmann, *Klippen für die Schiedsvereinbarung* (SchiedsVZ, 2003) 29; W Voit, in H-J Musielak, *Kommentar ZPO* § 1029, para 23.

30 Hausmaninger, in Fasching and Konecny, *Kommentar* (n 27) § 581, para 242.

31 Model Law, Art 16(1)

32 W Rechberger and W Melis, in W Rechberger (ed), *Kommentar zur ZPO* (3rd edn, Springer-Verlag, 2006) § 577, para 16.

33 OGH 17 April 1996, 7 Ob 2097/96 z; OGH 6 September 1990, 6 Ob 572/90; OGH 18 April 1985, 7 Ob 551/85; OGH 10 October 1962, 1 Ob 215/62; OGH June 16 1982, 1 Ob 628/82.

include a submission to arbitration.[34] Under Austrian law, non-specific or uncertain terms in arbitration agreements are considered void, whereas the agreement itself is void only if the entire agreement is non-specific or uncertain.[35] A general clause stating that 'all disputes that may arise between two parties for any reason shall be submitted to arbitration' is not sufficiently specific and would render the agreement void.[36]

20.23 In addition, Austrian arbitration law is not strictly limited to arbitration clauses in bilateral contracts, but also recognizes arbitration clauses in other legal instruments. Section 581(2) ACCP, for instance, confirms the validity of arbitration clauses in such documents as testamentary dispositions, documents establishing a private foundation, or articles of association.

20.24 Unlike in certain other jurisdictions, including Germany,[37] under Austrian law there is no need to enter into a specific arbitration agreement for shareholder disputes.[38] However, it is generally necessary to include all shareholders (a) in the arbitration agreement, and (b) in the proceedings if the award may have an effect on other shareholders. Such inclusion in the proceedings should comprise notification of the commencement of the arbitration proceedings, participation in the formation of the arbitral tribunal, and participation in the proceedings as a party.

20.2.4 Form requirements of arbitration agreements

20.25 Formal requirements, especially the 'in writing' requirement, must not be overlooked. While the Austrian Supreme Court is generally regarded as arbitration friendly, Austrian courts are more likely to set aside arbitral awards for violation of form requirements than for any other reason.[39]

20.26 Under the old ACCP, it was undisputed that Austrian law requirements of form would apply to all arbitration agreements—with no choice of law option for the parties—if the award was to be rendered in Austria. Presumably, this would include international arbitrations seated in Austria.[40] The 2006 amendment of the arbitration law brought no change[41] and unfortunately there is still controversy in international cases about whether ACCP provisions mandate the form requirements, or whether Article II of the New York Convention, which is also part of Austrian law, should apply instead.[42]

---

[34] H Fasching, *Schiedsgericht und Schiedsverfahren im österreichischen und im internationalen Recht* (Manz, 1973) 26.

[35] OGH 9 September 1987, 3 Ob 80/87.

[36] F Schwarz and C Konrad, *The Vienna Rules—A Commentary on International Arbitration in Austria* (Kluwer Law International, 2007) 20, para 1-049.

[37] See German Supreme Court 29 March 1996, II ZR 124/95—'Arbitrability I' and 6 April 2009, II ZR 255/08—'Arbitrability II'. As a consequence of these two decisions, the German Institute of Arbitration (DIS) had introduced supplementary rules for corporate disputes.

[38] OGH 11 November 2011, 3 Ob 191/11a.

[39] N Pitkowitz, *Die Aufhebung von Schiedssprüchen* (Manz, 2008) 152–82; Schwarz and Konrad (n 36) para 1-054.

[40] Hausmaninger, in Fasching and Konecny *Kommentar* (n 27) § 581, para 280: 'Under the old law it was undisputed that the formal validity is determined by the law in which the arbitral award is made, which is the seat of the tribunal'; referring to OGH 26 April 2006, 7 Ob 236/05i JBl 2006, 726; OGH 17 November 1971, 8 Ob 233/71 JBl 1974, 629.

[41] ACCP, § 577 explicitly calls for an application of ACCP, § 583 (the 'form requirement') not only in cases in which the seat of the tribunal is in Austria (ACCP, § 577(7)) but also in cases where the seat is outside Austria or not yet determined (ACCP, § 577(2)).

[42] OGH 17 November 1971, 8 Ob 233/71; OGH 26 April 2006, 7 Ob 236/05i. In the 1971 decision the Austrian Supreme Court had held that the formal requirements of an arbitration agreement in cases where the

The content of the writing requirement differs under the old and new ACCP. For arbitration agreements concluded before 1 July 2006, section 577(3) of the old ACCP required the arbitration agreement to be 'in writing or be contained in telegrams,[43] telexes or in electronic representations exchanged by parties'. Handwritten signatures were not required. The indication of the name of the party to the contract in an email was sufficient to satisfy the writing requirement.[44] **20.27**

In the new ACCP, the formal requirements for the conclusion of an arbitration agreement have been modified and are more liberal. Section 583(1) ACCP stipulates two alternatives for the valid conclusion of an arbitration agreement: that it be contained either in a 'document signed by the parties' or 'in letters, faxes, e-mails, or other forms of communication exchanged between them that provide proof of the existence of the agreement'.[45] **20.28**

Section 583(2) ACCP further clarifies that an agreement that fulfils the form requirements of section 583(1) and refers to a document containing an arbitration agreement is equally valid; physical attachment of the arbitration agreement to the signed document is therefore not necessary as long as the separate document is made 'part of the contract'. It must be stressed that section 583 does not establish an evidentiary rule and the 'in writing' requirement can be proven by any available legal means, including oral testimony.[46] **20.29**

It is generally held that the acceptance of an offer to conclude an arbitration agreement must also be made in writing and an oral acceptance is not sufficient.[47] Also, the invalidity of the arbitration agreement cannot be cured by reliance on principles of good faith, subsequent external facts (*Vertrauen auf den äußeren Tatbestand*) or 'implied power of attorney' (*Duldungs- und Anscheinsvollmacht*).[48] There are, however, several recognized exceptions for when an arbitration agreement may be concluded in a different form, or a defect in the formation of an agreement may be cured. These include assignment,[49] failure to challenge jurisdiction immediately at the commencement of the proceedings,[50] and *venire contra factum* **20.30**

recognition and enforcement of an Austrian arbitral award could become subject to the laws of another state, must be assessed according to the provisions of the New York Convention. Austrian scholars had disputed this decision. Walter Rechberger had argued that it was a singular judgment, and that the provisions of the New York Convention aimed at the recognition and enforcement of foreign awards (W Rechberger, in B Bachmann et al (eds), *Grenzüberschreitungen—Beiträge zum Internationalen Verfahrensrecht und zur Schiedsgerichtsbarkeit. Festschrift für Peter Schlosser* (Mohr Siebeck, 2005) 733). Paul Oberhammer had called it a landmark decision, since the Austrian Supreme Court had been one of the first courts worldwide to declare the provisions of Art II(2) New York Convention applicable even in proceedings that were based on the Austrian Code of Civil Procedure (P Oberhammer, in C Fischer-Czermak et al (eds), *Festschrift für Rudolf Welser* (Manz, 2004) 759ff). In its 2006 decision, the Supreme Court found its previous decision 'noteworthy' (*beachtenswert*), but fails to take an explicit position as to its future applicability. It finds this issue not to be relevant in the case at hand, since the formal requirements according to the ACCP had been met anyway.

43 See also OGH 12 November 1952, 2 Ob 723/52.

44 C Liebscher and A Schmid, 'Country Reports—Austria' in F-B Weigand (ed), *Practitioner's Handbook on International Arbitration* (CH Beck, 2002) 542.

45 Schwarz and Konrad (n 36) para 1-064.

46 Schwarz and Konrad (n 36) para 1-069.

47 A Reiner, *Das neue österreichische Schiedsrecht/The New Austrian Arbitration Law* (LexisNexis, 2006) § 583, para 42; EM Runesson and S Arvmyren, 'Sweden' in G Wegen and S Wilske (eds), *Arbitration in 55 Jurisdictions Worldwide* (Getting the Deal Through, 2013) 434; there is no written form requirement in Sweden.

48 OGH 29 March 2006, 7 Ob 64/06x.

49 A Fremuth-Wolf, *Die Schiedsvereinbarung im Zessionsfall* (Verlag Österreich, 2004).

50 ACCP, § 583(3).

proprium.[51] In view of the strict writing requirement, Austrian law does not recognize the 'group of companies' doctrine, jurisdictional veil piercing, or other legal theories to bind third parties to an arbitration agreement.[52]

20.31 For arbitration agreements with consumers and in labour matters, strict form (and substantive) requirements apply that practically exclude arbitration in most cases.[53] The arbitration agreement must be personally signed, contained in a separate agreement, and accompanied by written legal advice on the consequences of agreeing to arbitration. Most importantly, the arbitration agreement can be concluded only after the dispute has arisen. Whether a person should be deemed a consumer is to be determined in accordance with the Austrian Consumer Protection Act, which contains a very broad definition of 'consumer', which also includes shareholders in a corporation, unless they hold a controlling share.[54] Labour matters include labour related disputes between employers and employees and among employees, and pension related disputes.

20.2.5 Objections as to formal defects

20.32 An arbitration agreement lacking the formal requirements is considered to be without any legal effect[55] and this means that any arbitral tribunal constituted pursuant to it, lacks jurisdiction. However, under section 583(3) ACCP, 'a defect as to form of the arbitration agreement is cured in the arbitration proceedings by the making of submissions on the subject in dispute, if an objection to the defect is not raised, at the latest, at the same time as such submissions are made'. A party will thus be barred from raising an objection based on formal defects if it fails to do so upon 'the first entering of an appearance in the case'.[56]

20.3 Commencing Arbitration

20.33 On the one hand, section 578 ACCP limits the powers of state courts in connection with arbitrations to those matters explicitly stated in the law. On the other hand, a number of provisions in the ACCP oblige courts to support arbitrations. One important area of court support concerns the commencement of arbitration.

20.3.1 The role of courts in appointing arbitrators

20.34 According to section 587(1) ACCP, the parties are free to agree on the procedure to appoint the arbitrator or arbitrators. The role of the courts[57] in the selection process depends on

[51] See in particular ACCP, § 584(5): '*A party that invoked the existence of an arbitration agreement at an earlier stage in the proceedings may not, at a later stage, claim that such agreement does not exist unless the relevant circumstances have changed since.*' (emphasis added).

[52] Hausmaninger, in Fasching and Konecny, *Kommentar* (n 27) § 581, para 204.

[53] See ACCP, §§ 617ff.

[54] OGH 24 April 2012, 2 Ob 169/11h.

[55] Liebscher and Schmid (n 35) 543 with further references to OGH January 19 1996, 8 Ob 1211/95; OGH 28 February 1991, 6 Ob 507, 508/90; OGH 23 October 1928, 3 Ob 648/28 SZ X/303; OGH 7 February 1933, 3 Ob108/33 SZ XV/29; OGH 27 March 1935, 1Ob 249 ZBl 1935/367, 757; OGH 14 October 1982, 8 Ob 556/82; OGH 26 January 2000, 7Ob 368/98p; OGH 27 February 2001, 1 Ob 273/00d; OGH 17 May 2001, 7 Ob 67/01f; OGH 31 August 1984, 1 Ob 20/84—confirmed in OGH 21 June 2005, 5 Ob 127/05w; OGH 20 October 2005, 2 Ob 235/05f.

[56] Schwarz and Konrad (n 36) paras 1-082–1-083.

[57] According to ACCP, § 615 the Regional Court either designated in the arbitration agreement or designated under the rules of the Austrian Jurisdiction Act, § 104 is competent for this decision. Alternatively the competence is determined by the venue of the arbitral tribunal.

whether the parties have chosen a procedure. If they have done so, by agreeing that institutional rules should govern their proceedings, this procedure will take priority. For example, pursuant to article 20 of the Vienna Rules, the Board of the VIAC will make the appointment when the parties fail to nominate an arbitrator.[58] In the event the procedure fails (eg the institution does not make a timely appointment), section 587(3) ACCP will apply as a fallback provision. According to section 587(3), any party may apply to the court[59] for the appointment of arbitrators—unless the agreement on the appointment procedure provides another means for securing the appointment—if (a) a party fails to act as required under such procedure, or (b) the parties or the arbitrators are unable to reach an agreement in accordance with such procedure, or (c) a third party (eg an institution) fails to perform any function entrusted to it under such procedure within three months of receipt of a written notice.

In the event the parties have not chosen an appointment procedure, section 587 ACCP provides recourse to default rules and court support, unless agreement can be reached within four weeks: **20.35**

- In arbitrations in which the parties have agreed on a sole arbitrator, the arbitrator shall, at the request of a party, be appointed by the Regional Court, if the parties have been unable to agree on the arbitrator within four weeks of receipt of a written request to do so from one party to the other party.
- In arbitrations with three arbitrators, each party nominates one arbitrator.[60] These two appoint the third arbitrator, who acts as presiding arbitrator. If the tribunal consists of more than three arbitrators, each party nominates the same number of arbitrators, and the party-appointed arbitrators appoint an additional arbitrator, who acts as presiding arbitrator.[61] If a party has failed to appoint an arbitrator within four weeks of receipt of a written request from the other party to do so, or if the parties are not notified of the appointment of the arbitrator to be appointed by the party-appointed arbitrators within four weeks of their appointment, the appointment will, at the request of a party, be made by the Regional Court.
- In multi-party arbitrations, the parties on each side must agree on a common arbitrator within four weeks. If the parties fail to agree, the Regional Court will appoint the arbitrator. If one side fails to agree, the arbitrator already appointed by the other side will not be removed.[62] Austrian law thus does not follow the *Dutco* approach, which requires that the entire tribunal be newly appointed if one side has failed to appoint an arbitrator.[63] The Austrian solution is considered to be a compromise between the right of a party to appoint

---

58 VIAC usually hands down its decision in less than three weeks.

59 ACCP, § 615 (n 57).

60 Pursuant to ACCP, § 586(2) three arbitrators are the default rule unless the parties explicitly agree on another number of arbitrators.

61 Under ACCP, § 586(1), if the parties have agreed on an even number of arbitrators, these must appoint two presiding arbitrators in order to arrive at an uneven total number.

62 ACCP, § 577(2).

63 Decision of the French Cour de Cassation of 7 January 1992 in *BKMI Industrieanlagen GmbH et Siemens AG v Dutco Constructions* [1992] 21 Cass Civil Ire 75, para 470 which held that 'the principle of the equality of the parties in the designation of arbitrators is a matter of public policy'. As a direct response to *Dutco*, the ICC revised art 10 of its rules in 1998 to permit the court to appoint *all* arbitrators in cases where one side cannot agree on an arbitrator. The LCIA Rules (8.1) even went one step further and were revised to *mandate* the Court to *appoint* all arbitrators in cases where the alignment of interests has not been demonstrated. The Vienna Rules chose a different path. Under the Vienna Rules, if the respondents fail to jointly nominate an arbitrator, the

its arbitrator and the need for efficient proceedings. The Vienna Rules apply the same principle.[64]

- Under a catch-all provision, an arbitrator can also be appointed by the Regional Court upon the application of a party if the appointment procedure cannot be completed for other reasons within four weeks after receipt of the written notification of a party to the other party, or if the agreed procedure will not result in an appointment within a reasonable period of time.[65]

20.36 The request by a party to another party to appoint an arbitrator must specify the claim asserted in arbitration and the basis for the arbitration agreement.[66] Otherwise, it will not trigger the four-week deadline.[67] Austrian law has not implemented Article 11(1) of the UNCITRAL Model Law, according to which an arbitrator must not be excluded from the office solely on the grounds of his or her nationality, since this principle is already well established under Austrian law and needs no specific mention.[68] However, the court, when appointing an arbitrator, must give due regard to any qualifications required of the arbitrator by the agreement of the parties (which could include nationality) and to such considerations as are likely to secure the appointment of an independent and impartial arbitrator. Sitting Austrian judges are disqualified from serving as arbitrators.[69] There is no appeal permitted against the court decision. If the party appointment takes place prior to the first instance court decision, and one party furnishes evidence thereof, the party appointment prevails and the court application must be dismissed.[70]

20.3.2 The role of courts in resolving jurisdictional questions

20.37 The arbitral tribunal has the authority to decide on its own jurisdiction (*Kompetenz-Kompetenz* principle).[71] The tribunal's decision on jurisdiction must be rendered in the form of an arbitral award.[72] A jurisdictional award is subject to court review (regardless of whether jurisdiction is affirmed or denied) and can thus be challenged under section 611 ACCP, either because 'a valid arbitration agreement does not exist' or 'the arbitral tribunal denies its jurisdiction despite the existence of a valid arbitration agreement'.[73] It is within the discretion of

VIAC Board makes an appointment. The nomination of the claimant's side will, however, remain effective (multiple claimants must agree on an arbitrator before proceeding with the arbitration). This solution prevents multiple respondents from sabotaging the claimant's appointment by simply not nominating an arbitrator jointly. See also R Bevilacqua and T Ugarte: 'Ensuring Party Equality in the Process of Designating Arbitrators in Multi Party Arbitration. An Update on the Governing Provisions' (2010) 27 J Intl Arb 1, 9–49.

[64] According to the Vienna Rules 2013, arts 18 and 20(3) the VIAC Board is granted the option to remove already appointed arbitrators in an exceptional case or if the arbitrator fails to step back after he has been challenged.

[65] ACCP, § 587(6).

[66] ACCP, § 587(4).

[67] B Kloiber and H Haller, in B Kloiber, *Das neue Schiedsrecht: Schiedsrechts-Änderungsgesetz 2006* (ecolex Spezial, Manz, 2006) 26.

[68] P Oberhammer, *Entwurf eines neuen Schiedsverfahrensrechts* (Manz, 2002) 64; Hausmaninger, in Fasching and Konecny, *Kommentar* (n 27) § 587, paras 6ff.

[69] Law on the Service of the Judges, § 63(3)('*Richterdienstgesetz*').

[70] ACCP, § 587(7).

[71] ACCP, § 592; Vienna Rules, art 24(2) provides that the 'sole arbitrator (arbitral tribunal) shall rule on its own jurisdiction. The ruling can be made together with the ruling on the case or by separate arbitral award.'

[72] J Power, *The Austrian Arbitration Act—A Practitioner's Guide to Sections 577–618 of the Austrian Code of Civil Procedure* (Manz, 2006) § 592, para 4.

[73] GB Born, *International Commercial Arbitration—Commentary and Materials* (2nd edn, Kluwer Law International, 2001) 6; Schwarz and Konrad (n 36) para 19-027.

the arbitral tribunal to continue or stay the arbitration proceedings while the jurisdictional challenge is pending. In practice, the tribunal will generally continue in order to avoid delaying the arbitration. If the court then denies the jurisdiction of the tribunal, the proceedings will be considered terminated and any resulting award invalid and subject to challenge pursuant to section 611 ACCP.[74]

20.3.3 The arbitration agreement as a bar to court proceedings

Under section 584 ACCP the institution first seised (arbitral tribunal or court) will have the power to decide on its jurisdiction (*Kompetenz-Kompetenz*). This rule also applies if the seat of an arbitral tribunal is outside Austria or not yet determined.[75] **20.38**

Hence, if arbitral proceedings are commenced first, even if the arbitral tribunal has not decided on its jurisdiction, as a general rule the mere *lis pendens* will prevent the assertion of a parallel court claim. If a dispute that is subject to an arbitration agreement is brought before the court, the court may decline to hear the matter at the respondent's request or even *ex officio*.[76] When declining to hear the matter, the state court will dismiss the case on procedural grounds for lack of jurisdiction.[77] **20.39**

In certain cases the state court must nevertheless assume jurisdiction: **20.40**

- if a timely objection to the jurisdiction of the arbitral tribunal is raised and the arbitral tribunal is unable to decide on its jurisdiction within a reasonable time;[78]
- if the respondent participates in the litigation without objecting to the court's jurisdiction;[79]
- if the arbitral tribunal had denied jurisdiction—pursuant to section 584(2) ACCP, the court may not, in such a case, dismiss an action on the grounds that an arbitral tribunal would in fact be competent to hear the matter.

A state court may, however, even in the case of an objection, agree to hear a matter if it determines that the arbitration agreement is null and void, inoperative, or incapable of being performed.[80] An arbitration agreement has been held to be incapable of being performed in situations in which the arbitral tribunal itself declined jurisdiction, the institution had been dissolved without any replacement, the institution refused to administer the proceedings, an expressly agreed arbitrator was unable to perform the function, and when one of the parties had become poverty-stricken.[81] Generally, the Austrian Supreme Court has adopted an arbitration-friendly stance; holding in a recent case in which the arbitration institution provided for in an arbitration agreement entered into almost 125 years ago no longer existed, **20.41**

[74] Schwarz and Konrad (n 36) para 19-028 with further references.

[75] ACCP, § 577(5).

[76] A Von Saucken, *Die Reform des österreichischen Schiedsverfahrensrechts auf der Basis des UNCITRAL-Modellgesetzes über die internationale Handelsschiedsgerichtsbarkeit: ein Diskussionsbeitrag* (Paul Lang, 2004) 99.

[77] More precisely the court would be qualifying the existence of an arbitration agreement as an unwaivable lack of jurisdiction pursuant to the Austrian Jurisdiction Act (JN), § 104(3). See Oberhammer (n 68) 195.

[78] C Liebscher, *The Austrian Arbitration Act 2006: Text and Notes* (Kluwer Law International, 2006) annotated text to ACCP, § 584.

[79] According to ACCP, § 584(1) the court must not dismiss a claim brought before the court which is subject to the arbitration agreement between the parties or the proceeding if the respondent makes submissions on the substance of the dispute or orally pleads before the court without making an according objection. See also Schwarz and Konrad (n 36) para 1-087; Liebscher (n 68) annotated text to ACCP, § 584(1).

[80] Kloiber and Haller (n 67) 22.

[81] OGH 11 November 2011, 3 Ob 191/11a.

that the arbitration agreement will be considered incapable of being performed only if it was impossible to re-model a comparable institution.[82] The arbitration agreement was found to be inoperative in cases where arbitration would not have been able to provide an effective remedy. Other examples were cases in which a party relied in bad faith on an arbitration agreement, or in which effective legal protection could otherwise have been endangered (eg for lack of enforceability).[83]

20.42 When an action is dismissed by a court because of the jurisdiction of an arbitral tribunal, or an arbitral tribunal declines jurisdiction and defers to a court or another arbitral tribunal, or when an arbitral award is set aside on grounds of lack of jurisdiction of the arbitral tribunal, the other proceedings will be deemed to be properly continued if the action is brought without delay before the competent court or arbitral tribunal. A party, who has at an earlier stage in the proceedings, relied upon the existence of an arbitration agreement may not at a later stage claim that it does not exist unless the relevant circumstances have changed.

20.43 It is uncertain under Austrian law whether a declaratory claim to determine the existence or non-existence of an arbitration agreement may be asserted.[84]

20.3.4 The role of courts in enjoining arbitration

20.44 In Austria, anti-suit injunctions are generally not recognized. It is thus held to be inadmissible to request a court to enjoin a party from proceeding with an arbitration or litigation in a foreign jurisdiction. However, in general, Austrian law gives arbitration priority over court proceedings and thus requires that courts decline to hear a claim which is already pending before an arbitral tribunal (see the preceding section). Conversely, the *lis pendens* of previously commenced court proceedings will not prevent the institution of arbitral proceedings.

20.3.5 Interim measures

20.45 Austrian courts are explicitly authorized by law to issue interim or protective measures with respect to arbitration proceedings. Section 585 ACCP provides, in that respect, that the existence of an arbitration agreement neither prevents a party from seeking an interim or protective measure from a court, nor prevents a court from granting such relief. Article 33(5) of the Vienna Rules also expressly authorizes the parties to apply to a domestic court or any other competent authority for interim measures of protection.

20.46 A party may seek relief in all phases of the arbitration proceedings (ie before commencement, during the entire course of the proceedings, and even after the arbitral tribunal closes the proceedings), provided that it is not yet possible to seek enforcement of the arbitral award. Austrian law thereby recognizes the following general reasons: first, the likelihood that the enforcement of the final award will be endangered or significantly aggravated; second, the concern that satisfaction of the claim will be endangered or significantly aggravated; and third, the prevention of force or the avoidance of irreparable harm. The general principle that the preliminary measure must not anticipate the final decision does not apply for the third scenario. The reasons stipulated by law can be used to rely on a wide scope of categories under which preliminary relief may be sought, most importantly to protect the enforcement of the award, to preserve the status quo, to prevent irreparable harm, and to preserve evidence.

[82] OGH 11 November 2011, 3 Ob 191/11a.
[83] Hausmaninger, in Fasching and Konecny, *Kommentar* (n 27) § 583, para 56.
[84] Hausmaninger, in Fasching and Konecny, *Kommentar* (n 27) § 584, para 33.

The possibility of reversing the effects of an authorized provisional remedy has become a general rule. In principle, the court should only order measures that would permit a return to the original status quo if the claim ultimately fails on the merits. However, it can also be argued that measures that can be reversed by means of financial compensation should be permitted. Consequently, in cases where both parties may suffer irreparable harm, the court will need to weigh the interests and only grant a provisional remedy if the potential harm suffered by the party seeking the measure significantly outweighs the harm to the counterparty. In practice, Austrian courts have adopted such a weighing approach and, for example, approved preliminary injunctions enjoining a party from engaging in competitive activities, prohibiting shareholder voting, and provisionally permitting a team player to participate in a competition. **20.47**

Article 33(1) of the Vienna Rules generally echoes the situation under the ACCP. An interim measure may only be granted at the request of a party after hearing the opposing party. The arbitral tribunal must consider such measure necessary in respect of the subject matter of the dispute. A measure may be deemed necessary if the enforcement of the claim would be frustrated or considerably impeded, or there is a danger of irreparable harm. Measures are to be ordered in writing and a signed copy is to be served on each party. **20.48**

It should be noted that under section 394 Austrian Exekutionsordnung (Enforcement Act), EO, the respondent has the right to claim damages if the interim measure proves unjustified. However, section 593(5) ACCP states that the domestic court enforcing an order of an arbitral tribunal may not decide on the damage claim of section 394 EO. The ACCP does not specifically clarify whether the domestic court or the arbitral tribunal is competent to decide on the damage claims. This will need to be assessed under general rules, including the scope of the arbitration clause.[85] **20.49**

20.4 During the Arbitration

20.4.1 The role of courts in deciding challenges to arbitrators

The procedure for challenging arbitrators is regulated by section 589 ACCP, which follows a three-step procedure. **20.50**

- First, the challenge may be resolved if the challenged arbitrator resigns or is removed from office by mutual agreement of the parties.[86]
- Second, the parties are free to agree on a challenge procedure.[87] If the parties have not agreed on a specific procedure or if the applicable rules do not specify a different procedure, the challenge must be filed in writing with the arbitral tribunal within four weeks after composition of the arbitral tribunal, or when a party becomes aware of the grounds for a challenge. The arbitral tribunal will then decide on the challenge. The challenged arbitrator is entitled to participate in the decision, except when he himself has raised

[85] Hausmaninger, in Fasching and Konecny, *Kommentar* (n 27) § 593, para 47.

[86] Under ACCP, § 589(2) if the other side agrees to the challenge request, the arbitrator will thus be removed even against his will.

[87] The parties can, for example, delegate the task to a third party or an institution, agree certain time limits, majority requirements, etc., as long as the parties to the proceedings are treated in a fair way as mandated in ACCP, § 594(2).

concerns as to his impartiality and independence, and requested a decision on that issue.[88] This does not, of course, apply in the case of a sole arbitrator.[89]

- Third, if the challenge is rejected, the challenging party may request a court to decide on the challenge.[90] The challenge request to the court must be made within four weeks after notice of the decision rejecting the challenge. This period may not be modified by party agreement.[91] The decision of the court is not appealable.

20.51 The challenge decision is rendered by the Austrian Supreme Court and is not appealable.[92]

20.52 If the court decides that the challenge is not justified, the issue of the arbitrator's lack of impartiality and independence cannot be raised later as a basis to set aside the award.[93] Only if the grounds for challenge became apparent after the end of the arbitration proceedings can a party make a set-aside claim under section 611 ACCP.[94]

20.53 A lack of independence that a party learns about only after the conclusion of the arbitral proceeding can be challenged on the grounds of section 611 ACCP. However, it is not possible to set aside an award under this provision if the four-week period pursuant to section 589 ACCP has expired. The same applies if the tribunal has denied the challenge before and the parties did not refer the matter to the court according to section 589 ACCP.[95]

20.54 This can lead to three different situations for the domestic court: (a) the arbitral tribunal stays its proceedings and waits for the challenge to be decided by the domestic court; (b) the court renders its decision before the arbitral tribunal renders an award; or (c) the arbitral tribunal renders an award before the domestic court decides on the challenge. In any case, if the court does not grant the challenge, the existence of a ground for challenge may no longer be relied upon in a setting-aside proceeding pursuant to section 611 ACCP. If, however, the domestic court grants the challenge after an arbitral award has been rendered, this award can be attacked pursuant to section 611(2)(4) ACCP.

20.55 When deciding on a challenge, the requirements under section 588 ACCP need to be considered. Under that provision, an arbitrator is obliged to disclose all circumstances that may give rise to doubts as to his impartiality and independence or that contradict the parties' agreement. This disclosure obligation is ongoing and also arises if such circumstances only become apparent during the course of the proceedings. Unless otherwise agreed, a party may not challenge an arbitrator it has appointed, unless the challenge is based on circumstances the party became aware of only after the appointment.

---

[88] OGH 18 December 2002, 7 Ob 265/02f; H Fasching, *Aktuelle Probleme des Unternehmensrechts: Festschrift Gerhard Frotz zum 65. Geburtstag* (Manz, 1993) 775; Hausmaninger, in Fasching and Konecny, *Kommentar* (n 27) § 589, paras 72–74.

[89] P Binder, *International Commercial Arbitration And Conciliation In UNCITRAL Model Law Jurisdictions* (Sweet & Maxwell, 2005) para 3-064.

[90] ACCP, §§ 615 and 616 set out which court has jurisdiction in this matter.

[91] Power (n 72) § 589, para 6.

[92] ACCP, § 615. See n 15. For proceedings commenced before 1 January 2014, the court of first instance will decide.

[93] Rechberger and Melis, in Rechberger, *Kommentar zur ZPO* (n 32) § 590, para 4; Reiner (n 47) § 589, para 85; Power (n 72) § 589, para 7.

[94] Hausmaninger, in Fasching and Konecny, *Kommentar* (n 27) § 589, para 38.

[95] S Riegler, in S Riegler et al, (eds), *Arbitration Law of Austria: Practice and Procedure* (Juris Publishing, 2007) § 531.

There is extensive Austrian case law on the issue of impartiality and independence. Most of these cases are in connection with judges rather than arbitrators, and the situation is not necessarily comparable. The IBA Guidelines on Conflicts of Interest[96] are regularly cited in connection with challenge requests. Courts have considered these but seldom relied (solely) on the guidelines in their decisions.[97] 20.56

20.4.2 The role of courts in compelling testimony/evidence

In general, the parties to the arbitral proceeding are free to agree on how witness testimony should be presented. In the absence of such agreement, the arbitral tribunal has discretion to determine the procedure. Written witness statements and subsequent cross-examination are frequently used in this regard. Witnesses are usually questioned not only by counsel but also by the arbitrators. The parties may agree on a set of rules that regulate testimony and evidence. In practice, the IBA Rules on Evidence are often applied as guidelines.[98] 20.57

In order to ensure an effective arbitral process, the interference of state courts is reduced to a minimum. This principle is reflected in section 578 ACCP: 'The court may only act in matters governed by this chapter if so provided in this chapter.' Therefore, only in a few instances are the courts allowed to intervene in arbitral proceedings, and such cases must always be subject to a specific statutory basis in Austrian arbitration law.[99] One of these exceptions is contained in section 602 ACCP, according to which either an arbitral tribunal, or a party with the consent of the arbitral tribunal, may seek the assistance of courts for measures that fall outside the powers of the arbitral tribunal. 20.58

One such measure is the administration of an oath. This task is considered part of the sovereign powers attributed to the state.[100] Giving false testimony under oath before a state court is an independent criminal offence subject to six months' to five years' imprisonment.[101] Also, since the arbitral tribunal has no power to force a witness to testify, it may request assistance from a state court in that respect. The state court could then impose sanctions to force witness testimony.[102] When such a judicial examination is conducted, the arbitral tribunal (in full or represented by individual members of the tribunal) and the parties are entitled to be present and ask questions.[103] 20.59

The arbitral tribunal may also seek the assistance of Austrian and foreign authorities in connection with the taking of evidence, for example summoning witnesses or ordering document production. Likewise, Austrian courts are obliged under section 602 ACCP to assist foreign tribunals in these areas. If such a request comes via a foreign court, regardless of its 20.60

[96] IBA Guidelines on Conflicts of Interest in International Arbitration as approved on 22 May 2004 by the Council of the International Bar Association (the 'IBA Guidelines').

[97] Most challenge decisions by courts of first instance are unpublished. That statement is based on the author's personal experience in several challenge proceedings.

[98] IBA Rules on the Taking of Evidence in International Arbitration as adopted by a resolution of the IBA Council on 29 May 2010 by the International Bar Association.

[99] Schwarz and Konrad (n 36) para 20-251.

[100] NA Schoibl, in Bittner et al (eds), *Festschrift für Walter H Rechberger* (Springer, 2005) 513ff; Hausmaninger, in Fasching and Konecny, *Kommentar* (n 27) § 602, para 1.

[101] Austrian Penal Code, § 288.

[102] C Liebscher, 'Austria', in F-B Weigand, *Practitioner's Handbook on Commercial Arbitration* (OUP, 2009) para 2.127.

[103] ACCP, § 602(1).

location, section 38(2) (2) of the Austrian Jurisdiction Act obliges Austrian courts to provide support, except where the request is incompatible with principles of Austrian law.

20.61 It is generally held that an arbitral tribunal does not have the right to refer a specific issue to the European Court of Justice for a preliminary ruling.[104] This is unfortunate, since an incorrect application of European law by the arbitral tribunal could lead to the subsequent setting aside of its arbitral award.

20.4.3 Restrictions/requirements regarding the ability of foreign practitioners to appear in an arbitration as counsel or arbitrators

20.62 Austrian arbitration law does not contain any limitations on foreign practitioners appearing in arbitrations as representatives, advisers, or arbitrators. Section 594(3) ACCP specifically stipulates that: 'The parties may be represented or advised by persons of their choosing.' This right cannot be excluded or limited. Likewise, article 13 of the Vienna Rules provides that: 'The parties shall have the right to be represented or advised by persons of their choice in the proceedings before the sole arbitrator (arbitral tribunal).'

20.63 Consequently, there is no need for a party to use an attorney as its representative. It can also be represented or advised by any other person, for example, a civil law notary[105] or a non-lawyer.[106] In practice, foreign counsel regularly appear in international arbitrations conducted in Austria.

20.64 Likewise, there are no limitations under Austrian law as to the nationality of the arbitrators. Austrian law has not implemented Article 11(1) of the Model Law, according to which no arbitrator must be excluded from the office solely on the grounds of his or her nationality, because this principle is already established in Austrian law.

20.65 Of course, foreigners may need a visa to enter Austria; a visa to enter any EU Member State including Switzerland (Uniform Schengen Visa) will generally also permit entry to Austria.[107] Finally, foreign advisers may be subject to local rules, for example European attorneys acting in arbitrations in Austria will be subject to the Austrian Bar Rules.[108]

20.4.3 Confidentiality

20.66 Austrian arbitration law does not contain a general provision on the confidentiality obligations of arbitrators. However, under Austrian contract law, arbitrators are subject to a strict duty of confidentiality derived from the general contractual duty of care. According to article

[104] ECJ, 23 March 1998, RsC-102/82 *Nordsee*; ECJ 1 June 1999, RsC-126/97, *Eco Swiss v Benetton*; M Schwaiger, 'Preliminary Ruling According to Article 234 EC Treaty and Arbitral Tribunals' in C Klausegger et al (eds), *Austrian Arbitration Yearbook 2007* (CH Beck, Stampfli & Manz, 2007) 307.

[105] ErläuterungenRV SchiedsRÄG 2006, 17.

[106] J Lew, L Mistelis, and S Kröll, *Comparative International Commercial Arbitration* (Kluwer Law International, 2003) 541, para 21.67.

[107] For details, see Einreisevoraussetzungen für Österreicher im Ausland (General Information on Visas), available at <http://www.bmeia.gv.at/aussenministerium/buergerservice/pass-und-visum/visainformation-englisch.html>.

[108] According to the Austrian Act of EU Attorneys, §§ 4 and 7, foreign lawyers from EC Member States acting in Austria are subject to Austrian professional rules and are under the supervision of the Austrian Bar Association. These provisions provide for the implementation of the European Directive (EWG) 77/249 pursuant to which the provisions of the host country (Austria) are generally only binding to the extent that these do not contradict the rules of the Code of Conduct for European lawyers (CCEL). It is generally held that Austrian bar rules do not conflict with the CCEL.

16(2) of the Vienna Rules, the arbitrators are 'bound to secrecy in respect of all matters coming to their notice in the course of their duties'. In addition, article 2(4) of the Vienna Rules provides that the members of the Board of VIAC are 'bound to secrecy on all matters coming to their notice in the course of their duties'. The same applies to the Secretary General of VIAC (Vienna Rules, art 4(4)).

Pursuant to article 30(4) of the Vienna Rules: 'Hearings shall be private.' This is one of the very few cases where the Vienna Rules limit the wide discretion of the arbitrator(s) to conduct hearings. **20.67**

Neither Austrian law, nor the Vienna Rules, impose any express confidentiality obligations on the parties. It is generally understood that an implied confidentiality obligation is imposed.[109] However, there is no case law confirming that position. Therefore, if confidentiality of the parties is a concern, it should be specifically addressed in the arbitration agreement. **20.68**

Under section 616(2) ACCP at the request of a party demonstrating a legitimate interest, the public may be excluded from court proceedings connected to arbitrations. This unique provision of Austrian law grants the parties the opportunity to protect the confidentiality of the arbitration also in connected court proceedings. However, the mere fact that the matter relates to arbitration will not suffice to exclude the public. Instead, additional arguments such as an express confidentiality agreement or the concern of a detriment to one of the parties in case of a public hearing, must be advanced. Irrespective of the exclusion of the public, as a general rule under Austrian law, state court decisions will only be published in anonymous and redacted format. **20.69**

20.4.4 Local requirements for the conduct of arbitration hearings

Generally, the parties are free to agree on the rules of procedure, subject to a few mandatory provisions of Austrian Arbitration law. The following provisions are considered mandatory: (1) the principle of fair and equal treatment of the parties;[110] (2) the obligation to grant each party the right to be heard,[111] and (3) the right of each party to be represented and advised by counsel of its choice.[112] **20.70**

The ACCP does not provide for a default award if a party fails to participate in the proceedings. The ACCP does not impose a requirement for an oral hearing with or without the participation of all of the parties. By contrast, the Vienna Rules stipulate in article 28 the framework for an arbitral proceeding including an oral hearing. If one of the parties does not appear at a hearing, even though it has been summoned, the tribunal may not automatically accept the arguments of the party in attendance. Rather, article 29(2) of the Vienna Rules states that if a party fails to participate, the arbitral tribunal must nevertheless proceed with the arbitration.[113] **20.71**

---

[109] A Fremuth-Wolf, 'Confidentiality in Arbitration' in S Riegler et al, *Arbitration Law of Austria: Practice and Procedure* (Juris Publishing, 2007) 661, 670; V Oehlberger, 'How Confidential is Arbitration in Austria? A Comparative Analysis' in C Klausegger, et al (eds), *Austrian Yearbook on International Arbitration 2011* (Manzsche Verlags- und Universitätsbuchhandlung, 2011) 65.

[110] ACCP, § 594(2).

[111] ACCP, § 594(2).

[112] ACCP, § 594(3).

[113] Schwarz and Konrad (n 36) paras 20-148, and 20-259ff.

20.72 Austrian arbitration law does not contain any language regulations. While under article 5 of the Vienna Rules, the parties' correspondence with the Board and Secretary General must be in English or German, there are no limitations under the Vienna Rules on the language of the proceedings. Unless there is an explicit agreement, the arbitrators will determine the language under article 26 of the Vienna Rules, taking into consideration the languages of the parties and their counsel.[114]

20.5 The Award

20.5.1 Mandatory rules as to form

20.73 According to section 606(1) ACCP, the formal requirements for an award are that the award has to be made in written form and must be signed.[115] In principle, the arbitral award must be signed by all arbitrators. However, unless otherwise agreed by the parties, the signature of the majority of members of the arbitral tribunal is sufficient, where one or more arbitrators are unable or refuse to sign the award.[116] These two requirements may not be waived. An award that does not meet these requirements is called a 'non-award'[117] in Austria, and is subject to a set-aside claim under section 611 ACCP as it fails to satisfy the minimum standards of an award, or subject to a declaratory judgment qualifying it as a non-award under section 612 ACCP.

20.74 Unless otherwise agreed among the parties, the award must include the reasons upon which it is based.[118] However, the parties may also exclude this obligation implicitly and at any time, even after the award is rendered, without any specific formal requirement. As a consequence, the parties may also agree that failure to state reasons will not constitute grounds to have the award set aside.[119]

20.75 The award must indicate the date and place it was rendered.[120] This provision corresponds to Article 31(3) of the Model Law, which provides that the award is deemed to have been made at the place of arbitration. Section 606(3) ACCP extends this to the date of the arbitral award,[121] which is therefore deemed to have been issued on the date stated.[122] According to the Austrian Supreme Court, the lack of a date does not constitute a ground for setting aside an award, as it is not found in the exhaustive list of grounds set forth in section 611 ACCP. This clearly establishes that the date is not an essential element of the award.

20.76 The same standard applies to the indication of the seat. Thus, the specification of the seat has only declaratory effect, since the seat of the arbitral tribunal is determined in accordance

---

[114] Schwarz and Konrad (n 36) paras 20-148, 6-003.

[115] ACCP, § 606(1).

[116] S Riegler, in S Riegler et al (eds), *Arbitration Law of Austria: Practice and Procedure* (Juris Publishing, 2007) § 606, para 18.

[117] H Holtzmann and J Neuhaus, *A Guide to the UNICITRAL Model Law on International Commercial Arbitration* (Kluwer Law and Taxation, 1989) art 21, 837; M Roth, 'Country Report—Austria', in F-B Weigand (ed), *Practitioner's Handbook on International Arbitration* (CH Beck, 2002) art 31, para 3.

[118] ACCP, § 606(2).

[119] P Schlosser, in C Berger, F Stein, and M Jonas, *Kommentar zur Zivilprozessordnung* (22nd edn, Mohr Siebeck, 2002) § 1054, para 10.

[120] ACCP, § 606(3).

[121] Von Saucken (n 76) 283.

[122] Riegler (n 116) § 606, para 28.

with section 595 ACCP. The seat of an arbitral tribunal is a fiction and not necessarily the place where hearings or deliberations actually take place.[123] However, the seat is important in order to determine the law applicable to the arbitral proceedings and the 'nationality' of the award, which are relevant for determining where the award can be challenged and what requirements must be satisfied to enforce it.[124] If the parties have not agreed on the seat of the arbitration, the seat will be determined by the arbitral tribunal.

After the award is issued, an original signed by the arbitrator must be delivered to each party.[125] In domestic cases, this requirement is generally satisfied by using registered mail with a return receipt; in international cases by international courier service. An arbitral award may also be delivered via email, provided that the requirements for a secure electronic signature (section 2(3) of the Austrian Signature Act) are complied with. Nevertheless, it is certainly recommended and preferable to deliver to the parties, signed hard copies of the award, as this is also required in various jurisdictions for the purposes of recognition and enforcement of the award. The date of service of the arbitral award is significant for various time limits, particularly for a request for correction and interpretation of the award or for an additional award pursuant to section 610(1) ACCP, and for the challenge of an award according to section 611(4) ACCP. **20.77**

Section 606(5) ACCP states that the award and the documentation of service are 'joint documents' of the parties and the arbitrators. This provision must be seen within the context of proceedings before Austrian domestic courts in accordance with section 304(1) and (3) ACCP. This provision stipulates that a party holding a joint document cannot refuse a disclosure request to provide the court with this document if the other party requires it. Thus, in arbitral proceedings, a party may request the production of the arbitral award or documents regarding service from either the opposing party or the arbitrators.[126] The arbitral tribunal may discuss with the parties the safekeeping of the award and documentation of its services. Therefore, it is the parties' and the tribunal's responsibility to determine whether, and how, the original of the award and the documentation of its service will be stored. **20.78**

Under section 606(6) ACCP, the presiding arbitrator must confirm the legal effect and enforceability of the arbitral award in writing. This provision might seem unusual, since the Model Law does not provide for such a confirmation. The historic root of this Austrian peculiarity is that arbitral awards are directly enforceable. The failure to provide a confirmation does not constitute a ground for setting aside the award. In proceedings under the Vienna Rules, the confirmation is provided by VIAC. **20.79**

According to section 1(16) of the Austrian Enforcement Act, a domestic arbitral award constitutes an executory title in itself. Thus, if an arbitral award has been provided with a confirmation of legal effect and enforceability, it is enforceable per se in Austria, without the need of any further measures (*exequatur*).[127] However, section 606 ACCP is not applicable to a foreign award, which is defined as an award rendered by an arbitral tribunal with a seat outside Austria and must first be recognized in Austria. Article 36 of the Vienna Rules contains specific rules for awards that closely follow those of section 606 ACCP. **20.80**

[123] Holtzmann and Neuhaus (n 117) art 31 para 839; Reiner (n 47), § 606, para 157.
[124] Von Saucken (n 76) 282; Power (n 72) § 606, para 6; Roth (n 117) art 31, para 13.
[125] ACCP, § 606(4).
[126] Official Comments, § 606; Power (n 72) § 606, para 8.
[127] Power (n 72) § 606, para 10.

20.81 It is generally held that an arbitral award should follow certain basic rules for court judgments of state courts. These rules are set forth in section 417(1) ACCP and require at the minimum the names of the members of the arbitral tribunal, the names of the parties (and of any other interested parties involved in the case), and the operative part (decision on the claims).[128] Furthermore, an award must clearly state the specific obligations a party is ordered to perform.[129] While the failure to include these elements may not necessarily give rise to an annulment it could certainly affect the enforceability.

20.5.2 Mandatory rules as to substance

20.82 Generally, the arbitral tribunal will award interest in accordance with the law applicable to the substance of the dispute. Austrian law does not differentiate between pre-award and post-award interest. Unless otherwise agreed, a creditor may claim compound interest as of the date of filing a claim. Statutory interest in Austria is 4 per cent above the base rate. The statutory rate applies in the absence of a specific agreement between the parties.[130]

20.83 Which party must bear the costs of the arbitral proceedings is generally determined by the arbitral tribunal under applicable law. The arbitral tribunal must take into account the circumstances of the case, and particularly the outcome of the proceedings. The arbitral tribunal must also assess the amount of any compensation. In this regard, the possibility of any set-off between the parties is also taken into consideration.[131] Austrian law, if applicable, would generally use a 'loser pays' rule, whereby the relationship of the parties' respective prevailing and losing claims will be netted. For example, if a claimant makes a claim of 100 but the tribunal awards only 80, the claimant will obtain 60 per cent of its costs. If only 40 were awarded to the claimant, the respondent would be entitled to reimbursement of 20 per cent of its costs.[132]

20.6 After the Award

20.6.1 Available remedies

20.84 Austrian law has three distinct remedies after the issuance of an arbitral award:

- a request to the arbitral tribunal for correction, interpretation, or amendment of the award (section 610 ACCP);
- a claim for setting aside the award (section 611 ACCP); and
- a claim for a declaratory judgment determining the existence or non-existence of an arbitral award (section 612 ACCP)—which is an Austrian peculiarity.

20.85 Unless otherwise agreed between the parties, there are no further possibilities of seeking legal remedies in Austria such as appeals, appeals on points of law, declaratory actions[133] against

---

[128] KH Schwab and G Walter, *Schiedsgerichtbarkeit* (7th edn, Beck, 2005) para 19-9.

[129] OGH 18 November 1934, RZ 1935, 39.

[130] Austrian General Civil Code, § 1000.

[131] C Liebscher, 'Austria' in C Liebscher and A Fremuth-Wolf, *Arbitration Law and Practice in Central and Eastern Europe* (Juris Publishing 2006) AUS-60.

[132] The 'netting' calculation is as follows: in the first example, the claimant succeeded with a claim of 80 and the respondent with a defence of 20 which—after netting (80 minus 20)—results in a 60% cost reimbursement obligation from the respondent to the claimant. In the second example, the claimant succeeded with a claim of 40 and the respondent with a defence of 60 which—after netting (40 minus 60)—results in a 20% cost reimbursement obligation from the claimant to the respondent.

[133] OGH 6 February 1923, OB II/49.

arbitral awards,[134] or decisions on preliminary issues[135] by an arbitral tribunal that are rendered within the scope of the ACCP.

20.6.2 Request for correction, interpretation, or amendment

Section 610 ACCP provides that unless otherwise agreed, either party may, within four weeks of receipt of the award, request the arbitral tribunal (a) to correct any errors in computation, any clerical or typographical errors, or any errors of a similar nature; (b) to explain certain parts of the award;[136] or (c) to amend the award by rendering an additional award as to claims asserted in the arbitral proceedings but not disposed of in the award. Prior to making a decision upon such a request, the other party must have an opportunity to be heard.[137] **20.86**

This provision applies to interim, partial, and final awards even though they may not be separately challengeable under section 611 ACCP.[138] The question of whether the award contains any errors that can be corrected in the sense of section 610 ACCP depends on the extent to which such errors are apparently clerical (eg arithmetical or typographical errors or errors of a similar nature).[139] **20.87**

The arbitral award must be interpreted so as to clarify whether it actually contains an error that requires correction, or whether the arbitral award is inconsistent in itself, which would then reduce the effectiveness of the award or render it ineffective, and might even constitute a ground for annulment.[140] Austrian courts do not interpret decisions rendered by arbitral tribunals in the same (subjective) way as they would interpret contracts, but rather in the (objective) way statutes would be interpreted.[141] **20.88**

20.6.3 Austrian standards for setting aside/annulment

Under section 611 ACCP, the parties may file a court action aimed at setting aside an arbitral award within three months after receipt of the award. As a preliminary matter, a party may not bring a setting-aside action unless the arbitral award addresses the merits of the case and makes a final decision, at least in part.[142] Thus, in the event of bifurcation, an award dealing with the grounds of the claim (without determining the amount) will generally not be challengeable. Likewise, an award that only addresses costs will not be challengeable.[143] As an exception to this rule, jurisdictional decisions are challengeable.[144] While the right to challenge an award requires a final decision, the challenge itself can be directed against a part of the decision. **20.89**

---

[134] This also applies to cases in which it is doubtful whether or not the agreement on which the arbitral award is based actually constitutes an arbitration agreement. OGH 24 September 1981, 7 Ob 623/81.

[135] OGH 15 June 1967, 1 Ob 119/67.

[136] The Vienna Rules 2006 stated that explanation is only possible if both parties agree to it. This has been removed in the Vienna Rules 2013; Pitkowitz (n 39) paras 478–481.

[137] ACCP, § 610, implementing Model Law, art 33.

[138] Zeiler (n 27) 274ff.

[139] H Schumacher, 'Ein Schiedsspruch—und was nun?' (2006) *Zeitschrift für Schiedsverfahren* 70.

[140] W Rechberger, 'Die Widerspüchlichkeit eines Schiedsspruchs als Aufhebungsgrund nach österreichischem Recht' (2006) *Zeitschrift für Schiedsverfahren* 169.

[141] Walter Rechberger, 'Die Widerspüchlichkeit eines Schiedsspruchs als Aufhebungsgrund nach österreichischem Recht' (2006) *Zeitschrift für Schiedsverfahren* (2006) 169.

[142] OGH 8 March 2006, 7 Ob 252/05t; OGH 7 Ob 545/92 SZ 65/95; K Heller, 'Die Anfechtbarkeit von Teil- und Zwischenschiedssprüchen in Österreich' in *Praxis des Internationalen Privat- und Verfahrensrecht* (Gieseking Verlag, 1994) 142.

[143] OGH 8 March 2006, 7 Ob 252/05t.

[144] ACCP, § 611(1) second sentence.

20.90 Only awards made by tribunals seated in Austria are challengeable.[145] The venue stated in the award is deemed to be the seat of the arbitration.[146] Foreign arbitral awards are thus not subject to setting aside claims,[147] even if a foreign court has determined that Austrian courts have jurisdiction.[148] However, defects in foreign arbitral awards may be raised in the course of opposing recognition and enforcement of a foreign award in Austria.

20.91 Section 611(2) ACCP lists the grounds for setting aside an arbitral award. This list is considered exhaustive and mandatory. Therefore the parties cannot agree on other grounds. Moreover, no grounds may be waived by the parties in advance. Of the eight grounds for setting aside, six can be pursued only upon explicit application (which must be contained in the statement of claim requesting annulment). Two grounds (lack of arbitrability and violation of *ordre public*) may also be considered *ex officio*.[149] Procedural defects will generally not be challengeable unless they were raised immediately in the course of the proceedings.[150]

20.92 Since the introduction of the Arbitration Act in its (more or less) present form in 1895, the Austrian Supreme court has dealt with close to 200 setting aside cases and only very rarely set aside an arbitral award.[151]

20.93 The specific setting aside grounds closely follow the Model Law and the New York Convention (in the order of section 611 ACCP):

- *Defective arbitration agreement* This encompasses (a) the lack of a valid arbitration agreement, (b) the denial of jurisdiction by the arbitral tribunal despite a valid arbitration agreement, or (c) the incapacity of a party to conclude a valid arbitration agreement. On this ground both affirmative and negative jurisdictional decisions may be challenged.[152]
- *Lack of due process* This includes (a) cases in which the opportunity to freely appoint an arbitrator has been denied (eg if not all parties participated in the appointment process),[153] and (b) violation of the right to be heard, which also comprises the right to challenge an arbitrator, or (c) where an effective defence was impossible for other reasons.[154] Despite the broad language, the Austrian Supreme Court has been reluctant[155] to set aside awards based on due process arguments.[156] The Austrian Supreme Court has accepted challenges

---

[145] ACCP, § 577.
[146] ACCP, § 606(3).
[147] OGH 27 March 1929, 2 Ob 238/29; OGH 23 September 1913.
[148] OGH 5 March 1936, 3 Ob 171/36.
[149] ACCP, § 611(3).
[150] ACCP, § 579 ('*Rügepflicht*')—Preclusion is generally only possible if there are provisions which determine the underlying problem to have been relevant during the arbitral proceedings. This applies in particular to lack of arbitrability (ACCP, § 582), defects in the arbitration agreement (ACCP, § 583), defects in the composition of the arbitral tribunal (ACCP, §§ 586ff), and procedural errors (ACCP, §§ 594ff). In these cases, preclusion is only excluded if the party either (unsuccessfully) took timely action against one of the defects listed, or if it had no knowledge of the defect.
[151] N Pitkowitz, 'Digest of Austrian Case Law on Setting Aside Arbitral Awards' in C Klausegger et al, *Austrian Arbitration Yearbook 2008* (CH Beck, Stämpfli & Manz, 2008) 433ff.
[152] Pitkowitz (n 151) 237ff; Kloiber and Haller (n 67) 56; See also Pitkowitz (n 39) paras 135ff.
[153] Pitkowitz (n 151) 241ff.
[154] S Riegler, in S Riegler et al (eds), *Arbitration Law of Austria: Practice and Procedure* (Juris Publishing, 2007) § 611, para 35; see also Pitkowitz (n 39) paras 183ff.
[155] Basically, only the entire removal of the right to be heard has been accepted as grounds for setting aside, and only in very limited cases a partial removal. This has been criticized by A Reiner, '*Schiedsverfahren und rechtliches Gehör*' in *Zeitschrift für Rechtsvergleichung und Europarecht mit ZER* (Manz, 2003) 52ff; and Pitkowitz (n 39) paras 199–200; see also OGH 24 April 2013, 9Ob27/12d.
[156] OGH 20 November 1996, 3 Ob 2374/96f RZ 1997, 72.

on due process grounds in cases in which oral hearings were conducted and the arbitral tribunal did not itself hear the parties, but delegated this function to a third person;[157] in which a party was not permitted to respond to another party's request;[158] in which the arbitral tribunal refused to convene an oral hearing despite a party's request;[159] and in which a party could not be represented by its attorney through no fault of its own.[160]

- *Ultra petita*[161] This ground may be invoked if the arbitral tribunal exceeds its scope of jurisdiction by (a) deciding a dispute not covered by the arbitration agreement, (b) deciding matters that exceed the scope of the arbitration agreement, or (c) granting relief that was not sought by the parties.[162] Given the broad interpretation of arbitration agreements, this ground for challenge is rarely successful.
- *Defective composition of the arbitral tribunal* This ground may be invoked if the composition or constitution of the arbitral tribunal conflicts with mandatory rules or the agreement of the parties. The rule affirms the primacy of party autonomy by putting violations of composition rules stipulated in arbitration agreements on a par with violations of the legal requirements of the ACCP.[163] Lack of impartiality and independence may constitute such a ground,[164] which can, however, only be raised after termination of the arbitration, since otherwise an immediate challenge must be raised. The effect on the outcome of the arbitration due to an improperly composed arbitral tribunal is not taken into consideration. The right to challenge the award on this ground, however, lapses if a party who has knowledge of the defective composition does not immediately object.[165]
- *Violation of Austrian procedural ordre public* Under this ground, violations of the most basic and fundamental procedural protections enshrined in Austrian law can be challenged.[166] This provision was newly introduced in 2006 as a supplement and catch-all to the due process ground.[167] The precise scope of section 611(2)(2) ACCP is yet to be ascertained in court decisions. In the absence of such Supreme Court decisions, commentators suggest that it may apply to a broad range of potential procedural defects, including denial of the right to be heard;[168] incapacity of a party to the proceedings; absence of representation or arbitrator bias;[169] and failure to conduct evidentiary proceedings or sole reliance on the assertions of one party without any justification.[170]
- *Fraud* This can be asserted as an annulment ground if an arbitral award was obtained by criminal acts, such as fraud, false testimony (but only if the testimony was given in a state court),[171] or the forging of particular protected documents.[172] The discovery of new facts

[157] OGH 3 May 1899, GlUNF 603.
[158] Reiner (n 47) § 610, para 189; Power (n 72) § 610, para 6.
[159] OGH 30 June 2010, 7 Ob 111/10i.
[160] N Pitkowitz, 'Setting Aside Arbitral Awards Under the New Austrian Arbitration Act' in C Klausegger, et al (eds), *Austrian Yearbook on International Arbitration 2007* (CH Beck, Stämpfli Verlag, 2007) 241ff.
[161] See also Pitkowitz (n 39) paras 222ff.
[162] Pitkowitz (n 160) 243ff; Zeiler (n 27) 261, 264.
[163] Pitkowitz (n 160) 245ff; Zeiler (n 27) 261, 264; see also Pitkowitz (n 39) paras 265ff.
[164] Liebscher (n 78) annotated text to ACCP, § 611.
[165] ACCP, § 579; Schwarz and Konrad (n 36) para 27-053.
[166] Pitkowitz (n 160) 249ff; See also Pitkowitz (n 39) para 318ff.
[167] See Pitkowitz (n 160) 249ff.
[168] OGH 24 April 2013, 9Ob27/12d.
[169] Reiner (n 47) § 611, para 199.
[170] Oberhammer (n 68).
[171] Pitkowitz (n 160) paras 359–361; OGH 9 June 1937, 3 Ob 402/37.
[172] Riegler (n 154) § 611, para 73.

or evidence is not sufficient. The time period for filing an action to set aside an award on this ground is four weeks after a final criminal judgment confirming the incriminating offence, and in any event expires after ten years.[173]

- *Lack of objective arbitrability* Generally, the scope of arbitrability in Austria is very wide: (a) all pecuniary matters are arbitrable and (b) non-pecuniary matters are arbitrable to the extent the parties are capable of concluding a settlement.[174] The following three matters are explicitly not arbitrable: claims based on family law, claims based on tenancy protection laws,[175] and claims based on condominium ownership laws. Apart from these, matters infringing the sovereign powers of the state (eg in administrative matters) are not arbitrable.[176] The Austrian Supreme Court has held that shareholder disputes are arbitrable.[177]
- *Violation of Austrian substantive ordre public* The term 'ordre public' includes the basic principles of the Austrian Constitution and of criminal, private, and procedural as well as public law.[178] The Austrian Supreme Court has been reluctant to set aside arbitral awards for breach of *ordre public* and has also refused to fully review the underlying arbitral proceedings to assess this. Cases in which awards were set aside on this ground include violations of EU law[179] and excessive interest (107% per annum).[180]

20.6.4 Local procedures for setting aside/annulment

20.94 Under Austrian law, an arbitral award will have the same effect as a final and binding court judgment—independent of the pendency of setting aside proceedings.[181] If the setting aside proceedings are successful, of course, the award will lose its legal effect in Austria, though it might nevertheless still be recognized abroad.[182]

20.95 In the past, setting aside proceedings ran through all three instances of the Austrian court system. This has been criticized because it led to delays.[183] The 2013 Arbitration Amendment Act[184] now grants the Austrian Supreme Court exclusive jurisdiction to decide all setting aside claims as first and final instance.[185]

20.96 Austrian court proceedings trigger court fees, which must ultimately be paid by the loser of the proceedings. Court fees for revision by the Supreme Court are 5 per cent of the value in

---

173 Reiner (n 47) § 611, para 201.

174 ACCP, § 582.

175 Pitkowitz (n 39) para 374—these are generally matters under the Rent Act, § 37, such as increases in rent and incidentals, refurbishments, accounting, etc.

176 Pitkowitz (n 39) para 369.

177 Pitkowitz (n 39) paras 371 and 377–387.

178 Riegler, in S Riegler et al (n 154) § 611, para 86; N Pitkowitz, *Klimt Decision violating public policy?* (ecolex, 2007) 663.

179 OGH 5 May 1998, 3 Ob 2372/96m; OGH 23 February 1998, 3 Ob 115/95. See also Pitkowitz (n 39) paras 427–428.

180 OGH 26 January 2005, 3 Ob 221/04b.

181 ACCP, § 507.

182 See also Schwarz and Konrad (n 36) para 27-063.

183 C Liebscher, *Reform des österreichischen Schiedsrechts* (RdW, 1999) 328ff, who would have preferred the jurisdiction of the Supreme Court of Justice right from the beginning; A Reiner, *Anmerkung zum Entwurf eines Schiedsrechts-Änderungsgesetzes 2005* (ecolex, 2005) 523ff; K Neuteufel, *Art XXIX EGEO und das New-Yorker Übereinkomen über die Anerkennung und Vollstreckung ausländischer Schiedssprüche* (ÖJZ, 2006) 433ff, appreciates the uniformity of this system of several instances, in view of the large number of cases involving high amounts in dispute, but criticizes the time it takes.

184 SchiedsRÄG 2013 (n 15).

185 ACCP, § 615. See n 15. Applicable for proceedings commenced after 31 December 2013.

dispute.[186] The value of the dispute is generally the pecuniary amount in relation to which annulment is sought; if annulment of a non-pecuniary award is sought the evaluation by the arbitral tribunal will be taken as guideline.

The question of the admissibility of an action to set aside an award also raises the question of who is entitled to challenge an arbitral award. It is indisputable that the parties to the arbitration are entitled to request the setting aside of 'their' arbitral award.[187] Under Austrian law, the parties' place of origin or a connecting factor for the matter in dispute is insignificant, as long as the seat of the arbitration is in Austria.[188] If the arbitration proceedings involve a party joined to the dispute, that party must be included in the setting aside proceedings.[189] According to the Austrian Supreme Court, a party is entitled to point out defects in the arbitration proceedings only if that party has itself been affected by such a defect.[190] A party may thus not base its annulment request on procedural errors only affecting the opposing party. However, there is no need to demonstrate a particular interest in an action for a declaratory judgment. The existence of an arbitral award and the assertion of a reason for setting aside is sufficient to request a declaratory judgment according to section 612 ACCP.[191] **20.97**

As a consequence of the consensual nature of arbitration, without its approval it is impossible to extend the legal effect of an arbitral award to a third party. This applies also to interim measures concerning third parties ordered by an arbitral tribunal.[192] As a consequence, third parties, namely persons that were not recognized as parties in the arbitrations (or in respect to whom the arbitral tribunal denied jurisdiction), will generally not be entitled to challenge an arbitral award. A different view may be taken in exceptional circumstances, such as cases of legal succession or when that party may otherwise be affected by the award.[193] In addition, provisions such as compulsory joinder are unknown in arbitration proceedings. Also, Austrian law applies a dogmatically clear distinction between the parties to the dispute and other parties involved.[194] **20.98**

Even though in view of these considerations a third party does not appear to be entitled to contest an arbitral award issued between different parties, as a general rule, a third party affected by an arbitral award should be entitled to request set aside if the third party was joined as a party to the arbitration proceeding.[195] Consequently, recourse to the setting aside **20.99**

[186] Court Fee Act ('Gerichtsgebührengesetz') item (TP) 3.

[187] Zeiler (n 27) 274ff.

[188] OGH 1 February 1980, 2 Nd 502/80; see also E-M Bajons, 'Zur Nationalität internationaler Schiedssachen' in *Festschrift für Winfried Kralik* (Manz, 1986) paras 3 4ff with further references.

[189] OGH 24 March 1988, 6 Ob 1512/88.

[190] OGH 1 December 1954, 3 Ob 689, 690/54.

[191] OGH 6 February 1923, Ob II/49.

[192] B Kloiber, 'Vorläufige oder Sichernde Maßnahmen durch Schiedsgerichte' (2006) *Zivilrecht aktuell* 247 and G Zeiler, 'Erstmals einstweilige Maßnahmen im Schiedsverfahren' (2006) *Zeitschrift für Schiedsverfahren* 79ff.

[193] J-P Lachmann, *Handbuch für die Schiedsgerichtsbarkeit* (2nd edn, Schmidt, 2002) 462ff; K Massuras, *Dogmatische Strukturen der Mehrheitsparteienschiedsgerichtsbarkeit* (Lang,1998) 524; F von Schlabrendorff, 'Parallele Verfahren, Aufnahme von Dritten, Verbindung von Verfahren—Erfahrungen aus der Praxis der ICC' in KH Böckstiegel et al (eds), *Die Beteiligung Dritter im Schiedsverfahren* (Carl Heymanns Verlag, 2001) 69.

[194] Geimer, in Böckstiegel et al, *Die Beteiligung Dritter im Schiedsverfahren* 73; R Merkin, *Arbitration Law* (3rd edn, informa, 2004) 15-8/4ff.

[195] Controversial. This view is supported by Zeiler, who is of the opinion that third parties who have intervened in support of a party may bring an action to set aside the award, Zeiler (n 18) 274. However, this statement is only made with reference to cases in which the intervening third party has actually joined the dispute, which means that a consensus must have been reached by the parties to the arbitration.

provisions of section 611 ACCP (in contrast to section 610 ACCP governing the correction of clerical errors) is not expressly restricted to the parties to the arbitration proceedings.

20.100 Pursuant to section 611(4) ACCP the period for filing an action for setting aside is generally three months and begins on the date of receipt of the award by the party bringing the action, or of service of the award, as the case may be.[196] Service of an ineffective arbitral award is also capable of triggering the three month period.[197]

20.101 For grounds under section 611(2)(6) ACCP (fraud), the period is four weeks and commences on the date of actual knowledge of the circumstances giving rise to the challenge (section 534 ACCP).

20.7 Conclusion

20.102 Austria is an arbitration-friendly UNCITRAL Model Law jurisdiction with a long and stable history of supporting arbitration. A wealth of decisions by the Austrian Supreme Court and a wealth of legal commentaries offer clear guidelines to the arbitration practitioner and only very few surprises. The Vienna Rules are among the most streamlined sets of modern institutional arbitration rules, that provide substantial flexibility for arbitral proceedings.

[196] G Backhausen, *Schiedsgerichtsbarkeit unter besonderer Berücksichtigung des Schiedsvertragsrechts* (Manz, 1990) 163.

[197] OGH 17 June 1953, 2 Ob 378/53. See also OGH 24 July 1997, 6 Ob 186/97i, discussing the effects of the mere acknowledgement of receipt of an award.

INDEX